Also by John Cassidy

CAPITALISM AND ITS CRITICS

CAPITALISM AND ITS CRITICS

A History: From the
Industrial Revolution to AI

John Cassidy

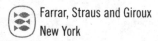
Farrar, Straus and Giroux
New York

Farrar, Straus and Giroux
120 Broadway, New York 10271

Grateful acknowledgment is made for permission to reprint the following material:
Global average GDP per capita graph (p. 15), from "Data Page: Global Average GDP per
Capita over the Long Run," from Max Roser, Pablo Arriagada, Joe Hasell, Hannah Ritchie,
and Esteban Ortiz-Ospina, "Economic Growth," 2023; data adapted from World Bank, Jutta
Bolt and Jan Luiten van Zanden, Angus Maddison. Retrieved from https://ourworldindata.org
/grapher/global-average-gdp-per-capita-over-the-long-run.
"Elephant Curve" graph (p. 493), from Christoph Lakner and Branko Milanovic, "Global
Income Distribution: From the Fall of the Berlin Wall to the Great Recession," Policy Research
Working Paper WPS6719, World Bank, December 2013, http://documents.worldbank.org
/curated/en/914431468162277879/Global-income-distribution-from-the-fall-of-the-Berlin
-Wall-to-the-great-recession.

Library of Congress Cataloging-in-Publication Data
Names: Cassidy, John, 1963– author.
Title: Capitalism and its critics : a history: from the industrial revolution to AI / John Cassidy.
Description: First edition. | New York : Farrar, Straus and Giroux, [2025] | Includes
    bibliographical references and index.
Identifiers: LCCN 2024039937 | ISBN 9780374601089 (hardcover)
Subjects: LCSH: Capitalism—History. | Economic history.
Classification: LCC HB501 .C293 2025 | DDC 330.12/209—dc23/eng/20241031
LC record available at https://lccn.loc.gov/2024039937

Designed by Patrice Sheridan

Our books may be purchased in bulk for promotional, educational, or business use. Please
contact your local bookseller or the Macmillan Corporate and Premium Sales Department at
1-800-221-7945, extension 5442, or by email at MacmillanSpecialMarkets@macmillan.com.

www.fsgbooks.com
Follow us on social media at @fsgbooks

To Lucinda, Beatrice, and Cornelia

Contents

CAPITALISM AND ITS CRITICS

Introduction

All history books are products of their own time, this one included. The original idea for it came to me in 2016, during the insurgent presidential campaign of Senator Bernie Sanders, and I made the final edits to the text shortly after Donald Trump was elected to a second term. Sanders, you may recall, claimed that the US economy was "rigged" and promised to make it work for "working families and not just for the billionaire class."[1] Trump was a billionaire himself, of course, but that didn't prevent him from positioning himself as the tribune of a forgotten working class and parlaying the grievances and discontents of many non-rich Americans all the way to the White House, twice.

The rising disaffection with American capitalism that Sanders (and, indeed, Trump) drew upon in 2016 proved to be a lasting phenomenon. In 2018 the polling firm Gallup found that fewer than half of Americans ages eighteen to twenty-nine had a positive view of capitalism, compared to slightly more than half who had a positive view of socialism.[2] Rising antipathy toward capitalism wasn't confined to the United States. In 2017 the British polling firm Populus asked people to list the traits that they associated with socialism, capitalism, and various other "isms." For capitalism, the most commonly chosen phrases were "innovative," "greedy," and "selfish." For socialism, the three most popular choices were "fair," "for the greater good," and "delivers most for most people." The survey was commissioned by the pro–free market Legatum Institute. "I believe that free enterprise policies are a key driver of prosperity," Matthew Elliott, a senior fellow at the institute, said when the poll was released. "Sadly though, it appears that a large proportion of British voters do not share this view."[3]

Originally, I conceived of the book as a shortish history of contemporary capitalism and the economic debates it has engendered, from the collapse of the Soviet Union to the present. However, I was quickly forced to confront the fact that many of the criticisms of modern capitalism—from complaints about rapacious platform monopolies and self-dealing bankers to laments about the impact of technology on working conditions and inequality—have roots in economic developments and debates that took place during the rise of industrial capitalism in Britain and even before that. Writing in the late eighteenth century, Adam Smith, no enemy of the profit motive, railed against colonial monopolies like the East India Company, whose privileged position and egregious self-dealing marked them out as preindustrial analogues of the too-big-to-fail banks that taxpayers bailed out during the Global Financial Crisis of 2007–2009. (Like the banks, the East India Company, which effectively ruled great swaths of the subcontinent, received a massive government bailout.)

As factory capitalism developed in northern England, some preindustrial craft workers broke into textile mills and smashed new machinery that was threatening their livelihoods. For a long time, the Luddites, as they came to be known, were dismissed as antediluvian enemies of modernity. In a world where artificial intelligence is now threatening to eliminate countless jobs, their concerns about new technology look more reasonable. Criticisms of the growing gap between rich and poor were another feature of early industrial capitalism. In 1829 the Romantic poet Robert Southey wrote: "Great capitalists become like pikes in a fishpond, who devour the weaker fish; and it is but too certain that the poverty of one part of the people seems to increase in the same ratio as the riches of another."[4]

Eventually I decided to expand the project into a broader history of capitalism and its critics. To be sure, I couldn't hope to cover everything, or nearly everything. Back in the 1950s, the English historian G. D. H. Cole wrote a history of socialist thought that took up seven volumes. The first volume alone, which was devoted to "The Forerunners," contained fifty principal characters.[5] In whittling things down, I was greatly helped by the fact that, over the centuries, the central indictment of capitalism has remained remarkably consistent: that it is soulless, exploitative, inequitable, unstable, and destructive, yet also all-conquering and overwhelming. "Our true monarch is not Victoria but Victor Mammon," John Ruskin, the English art critic and philosopher, wrote in 1866.[6] A hundred and fifty-five years later the NPR journalist and podcaster Rund Abdelfatah commented: "Capitalism is an economic system, but it's also so much more than that. It's become a sort of ideology, this all-encompassing force that rules over our lives and our minds."[7]

In tracing efforts to critique capitalism and resist its onward march, I have tried to explain the various iterations that the system has gone through, from the rise of factory production, to the switch from sole proprietors, to large corporations as the dominant form of capitalist enterprise, all the way up to the digital revolution and its latest offshoot, the commercialization of artificial intelligence. But this is not a standard economic history. Although it contains discussions of GDP figures and wage trends and technological developments, as well as some political history, it concentrates mainly on the lives and works of individual writers and critics. By engaging with the theories and commentaries of my subjects, I have sought to illuminate how the world appeared to them in their time and their environment. If there is a conceit to the book, it lies in trying to tell the history of capitalism through the eyes of its critics.

Many of my subjects are economists, but not all. Two of them are groups: the Luddites, and the dependency theorists of the 1950s and '60s who emphasized the barriers to economic development facing postcolonial nations. Of the individuals profiled, some led the conventional lives of academics, although their thinking was far from conventional. (Thorstein Veblen, John Maynard Keynes, Joan Robinson, and Stuart Hall are examples.) Others were gentlemen scholars (William Thompson and Thomas Carlyle); journalist-authors (Henry George, John Hobson, Paul Sweezy); socialist revolutionaries (Karl Marx, Rosa Luxemburg); and economists who worked for international organizations (Raúl Prebisch and Samir Amin). One of the subjects—Friedrich Engels—doubled as a revolutionary *and* a capitalist co-owner of a Manchester cotton mill. Another, Eric Williams, started out as a historian and ended up as the prime minister of his country, Trinidad and Tobago.

In addition to Luxemburg and Robinson, some more pioneering women feature in the book. The chapters on Anna Wheeler, an Irish feminist who was an associate of William Thompson, and Flora Tristan, a French writer who called for the establishment of a General Union consisting of all male and female workers, discuss the rise of female factory workers, who outnumbered male workers in many early textile factories. The chapter on Silvia Federici, an Italian expatriate who cofounded the New York branch of Wages for Housework, focuses on domestic work, which typically has been unpaid and carried out by women. As Federici and her colleagues emphasized, this unwaged labor is essential to the maintenance and reproduction of the capitalist workforce, without which the system couldn't operate.

The history of capitalism is usually told through accounts of depersonalized forces; competition, technology, colonialism, profit, and so on. While there are advantages to this methodology—it helps us see the broad trends that have shaped modern life—there is also a potential downside to it. Certain historical outcomes, such as the rise of fascism or the demise of communism, can appear to have been largely inevitable. Focusing on individual critics at definite points in time allows us to see the contingency that is also part of history, the avenues and ideas that were not pursued, and the enduring possibilities of imagining other economic arrangements.

During the first half of the nineteenth century, critics from the right as well as the left made a moral argument about how the factory system dehumanized workers and upended long-established social norms. The word *socialism* came into usage in Britain and France, but its meaning then was very different from its modern association with redistribution programs and state intervention more generally. Many early socialists had little faith in the government, which they regarded as a corrupt institution dominated by the upper orders. They believed the best way forward was to establish self-ruling cooperative communities in which both work and rewards would be shared on a more equitable basis. After some efforts to establish these new communities foundered, Marx and Engels, in their 1848 *Communist Manifesto*, dismissed the ideas that motivated them as "utopian socialism."[8] Marx, particularly in his early writings, emphasized that industrial capitalism alienated workers from their true selves, but his main goal was to discover and analyze the system's laws of motion. He focused on the system's inner contradictions and the emergence of the industrial working class, the proletariat, as a revolutionary force.

In the United States and other countries, the late nineteenth and early twentieth centuries saw the emergence of huge industrial combines and a spendthrift plutocracy, which Thorstein Veblen, for one, subjected to merciless inspection. This period also saw the rise of imperialism, which Vladimir Lenin famously described as the highest stage of capitalism. Rosa Luxemburg, a Polish associate of Lenin in the socialist Second International, but very much her own thinker, argued that the capitalist system could survive only by assimilating and destroying precapitalist societies. Lenin and Luxemburg viewed the outbreak of the First World War as confirmation of their theories, but their hopes that it would lead to wholesale revolutions in the imperialist countries were dashed. The only successful uprising took place in peasant-dominated Russia, where Lenin's Bolsheviks eventually seized power and were then confronted with the monumental task of building a socialist economy from scratch.

Capitalism survived the Great War, but it was about to meet its greatest test. During the Great Depression, economic output plunged, jobless rates skyrocketed, and political extremism flourished. Karl Polanyi, who witnessed the rise of authoritarianism in Austria firsthand, concluded that fascism and socialism were the only logical outcomes of unbridled capitalism. Would-be reformers looked for a less drastic alternative. Keynes, a defender of free market capitalism but not an uncritical one, provided the theoretical justification for a fix that in retrospect seems obvious: using tax and spending policy to drag the economy out of slumps. This approach, when it was combined with the expansion of social insurance promoted by Franklin Delano Roosevelt and William Beveridge, and the reforms of the international economic system introduced at the 1944 Bretton Woods conference, seemed to cure capitalism of some of its pathologies—only for them to turn up again in spades after the Keynesian system unraveled, the Soviet Union collapsed, and the neoliberal era dawned. The "end of history" lasted for but a couple of decades before it generated a fierce populist backlash.

Throughout the book, I emphasize the global nature of capitalism, which was evident even before it metamorphized into industrial capitalism. In the United States, the East India Company, the subject of my first chapter, is perhaps best known for the role its ships played in the Boston Tea Party. But the company's monopoly on the import of tea to the American colonies, which so infuriated the patriots, was only a small element of its trading operations, which extended across four continents. Another large-scale profit-driven enterprise that spanned the oceans during the era of colonial capitalism and features early in my narrative is the infamous triangular trade, in which millions of Africans were transported to the Americas as enslaved workers to labor on plantations that grew sugar, cotton, and tobacco. One of the first writers to point out that colonialism and the slave trade helped create the material basis for the rise of industrial capitalism was Eric Williams in his 1942 book, *Capitalism and Slavery*. I devote much of Chapter 20 to Williams and the heated debates his work has engendered. This follows a chapter about another critic of colonialism, the Indian economist J. C. Kumarappa, a longtime associate of Mahatma Gandhi who is increasingly recognized as a pioneer of ecological economics. Williams and Kumarappa were both deeply interested in the relationship between the core and the periphery of the global capitalist system, as were the postwar dependency theorists in Latin America, who are the subjects of Chapter 21. Another thinker who always thought in global terms was Samir Amin, a Marxist French Egyptian economist who spent much of his working life in sub-Saharan Africa and whose critique of globalization I discuss in Chapter 26.

Although my narrative ranges across the globe, most of my subjects are from Europe and the United States. To that extent, this is a Eurocentric book, or, equivalently, a book centered on the global capitalist core. The reasons for this focus are straightforward. The first three industrial nations were Britain, Germany, and the United States, and it was in these countries, and also France, that the new economic system was first subjected to systematic critical analysis. Given this focus, some readers may ask: Where is Max Weber? Or Emma Goldman? Or John Kenneth Galbraith? I didn't have space to include everybody. Some of my choices were dictated by a desire for subjects who capture an entire epoch, others by a wish to highlight lesser-known figures who made interesting contributions.

In other words, this is *a* history of the system and its critics, not *the* history. Of necessity, it covers a lot of ground. Capitalism by its very nature is a process of change, and over the centuries the critiques of it have moved with the times. One recurring theme, though, has been capitalism in crisis. From its earliest days, industrial capitalism has zigzagged between periods of prosperity, when it seems all-conquering, and episodes of panic and contraction. Indeed, it is barely hyperbole to say that capitalism is always in crisis, recovering from crisis, or heading toward the next crisis.

In the late summer of 1857, the New York branch of the Ohio Life Insurance and Trust Company, a chartered institution that held a banking license and was widely regarded as a model of midwestern stolidity, suddenly collapsed, sparking a financial panic on Wall Street.[9] As depositors rushed to get their money out of banks, the stampede spread to other cities, more financial firms failed, and the prices of financial securities and commodities plunged. The panic reached across the Atlantic to Paris and London, where interest rates increased sharply as credit dried up. From his regular seat in the reading room of the British Museum, in Bloomsbury, Karl Marx followed these developments with rising excitement. In October 1857 he wrote to Engels, who was staying in the Channel Islands for health reasons: "The American crisis—its outbreak in New York was forecast by us in the November 1850 *Revue*—is BEAUTIFUL and has had IMMEDIATE repercussions on French industry, since silk goods are now being sold in New York more cheaply than they are produced in Lyons."[10] On October 26 a bank in Liverpool collapsed. A couple of days later, two banks in Glasgow went under. "The AMERICAN CRASH is superb and not yet over by a long chalk," Engels wrote in his reply to Marx. He also noted that credit was starting to dry up on the European continent: "That means that, for the next 3 or 4 years, commerce will again be in a bad way. *Nous avons maintenant de la chance.*"[11]

But the hopes that Marx and Engels harbored for an imminent collapse of international capitalism were to be disappointed. As the financial crisis deepened, the authorities on both sides of the Atlantic intervened. In the United States, the Treasury Department announced it would use some of its gold stocks to recapitalize banks and keep money and credit flowing. In Britain, the government suspended the Bank Charter Act of 1844, a move that made it easier for the Bank of England to print money. These steps didn't prevent an economic slump from developing, but they did help avert a wholesale financial disintegration. Eventually the banking system stabilized, confidence revived, and the economy started growing again.

Over the past two centuries, variations of this story have played out many times, demonstrating capitalism's powers of recuperation and governments' ability to act as its crisis manager. Some economists have even argued that capitalism's recurrent crises are the way the system resolves some of its inner contradictions. Two adherents of this view appear in this book. Nikolai Kondratiev, a Russian economist who theorized that capitalism evolved in "long waves" of roughly fifty years' duration, is treated at length. The Austrian bon vivant Joseph Schumpeter, whose theory of "creative destruction" is beloved of Silicon Valley disrupters, makes several cameo appearances.

Many of my other subjects highlighted capitalism's inability to resolve some of its perennial challenges, such as generating sufficient demand for all the goods and services that it produces, and creating enough investment opportunities to soak up all the profits and savings it generates. Marx, Hobson, Luxemburg, Keynes, and Robinson all explored these tendencies. To four of the five (Keynes is the exception), the basic problem is the division of the economy into capitalists and workers, which creates one class of people who struggle to pay for everything they need to live a decent life, and another class who have so much money that they struggle to spend it all. Marx and his followers believed that this division would eventually generate so much inequality, and such huge social chasms, that the workers would rise up and overthrow the system.

So far, history has falsified this prediction, partly because of something that few foresaw in the nineteenth century: the rise of big government. The modern state's role as a constraining and a supportive force for industrial capitalism is another central theme in this narrative, beginning with the chapter on Keynes. The rise and fall of Keynesian social democracy, which I also refer to as "managed capitalism," occupies much of the second half of the book. When managed capitalism was in the ascendancy, during the decades after the Second World War, some of the most influential criticisms of the system came from the right. That is why Friedrich Hayek and Milton Friedman, the two patron saints of neoliberalism, find their way into a tome about critics of capitalism. In discussing the neoliberal counter-revolution, I trace its origins to the crisis of Keynesianism that two of my other subjects, Michał Kalecki and Paul Sweezy, intuited back in the 1940s.

By the first decades of the twenty-first century, the challenges facing global capitalism were proliferating, and, as mentioned above, the basic legitimacy of the system was being questioned. The accelerating impact of climate change spurred the rise of radical environmentalism and the "degrowth" movement, the origins of which can be traced to yet another of my subjects, the Romanian-American economist Nicholas Georgescu-Roegen, who argued in the 1970s that the earth had reached its economic carrying capacity. Other alarming developments included rising inequality, financial instability, the emergence of giant tech monopolies that seemed to operate by their own rules, and the threat of massive job displacements with AI. To some observers, these challenges portended an intensifying crisis, perhaps even a terminal one. To other commentators, they presented a historic opportunity to create a new economic paradigm, one that was more sustainable, egalitarian, and inclusive. In my final chapter, I discuss some of the arguments raised in this debate.

Finally, a few comments on terminology and sourcing. Although the word *capital* has been in use for hundreds of years to describe various forms of money and wealth, the term *capitalism* emerged only in the middle of the nineteenth century, when it was often used pejoratively. In 1850 the French socialist leader Louis Blanc described capitalism as "the appropriation of capital by some to the exclusion of others."[12] In writing about the "capitalist mode of production," Marx emphasized the appropriation of "surplus value" that workers had created, but the general idea was the same. Eventually the term "capitalism" was applied to any market-based economic system in which "the means of production were owned by private proprietors" who hired managers and workers.[13] Debates continue about when capitalism itself, rather than the moniker applied to it, came into existence. I follow the lead of the German historian Jürgen Kocka, the author of an invaluable short history of capitalism, in treating merchant capitalism, plantation economies, and industrial capitalism as variants of the same genus—one characterized by widespread mobilization of capital and production for profit in an environment of secure property rights.[14] Following convention, I date the birth of industrial capitalism to the 1770s in England.

My primary source is the writings of my subjects, which I have quoted from and paraphrased extensively. For biographical details and historical context, I consulted memoirs, interviews, and published letters. I also relied extensively on secondary works, such as biographies and histories of economic thought. Wherever possible, I have tried to credit these sources, either in the text or in the endnotes. In writing about broader economic history, I have drawn from official sources for data on things like unemployment rates, GDP growth, and the distribution of wealth. But I have also tried to synthesize a very large amount of information from secondary materials, including books, official or semiofficial reports, and academic studies. Here, too, I have tried wherever possible to make my sourcing clear.

Researching and writing this book was a mammoth task but also a very rewarding one: I learned a great deal. Still, I am reminded of Marx's famous remark: "The philosophers have hitherto only interpreted the world in various ways. The point, however, is to change it." Regardless of what view one takes of Marx's politics, it's easy to sympathize with these sentiments, but history demonstrates that the challenge of putting them into practice is formidable and enduring. If any readers of this book are inspired to come up with new ideas for reforming the economy and making it work better for everybody, including generations to come, writing it will have been doubly worthwhile.

1

William Bolts and the East India Company

On August 1, 1771, Richard Arkwright, an inventor who hailed from Preston, Lancashire, rented, along with four business partners, a piece of land in the Derbyshire village of Cromford. On a lease that the partners signed, they recorded their intention "to Erect and Build one or more Mill or Mills for Spinning, Winding, or throwing Silk Worsted Linen Cotton or other Materials."[1] Originally a wigmaker, Arkwright had, two years earlier, patented a spinning frame, a hefty contraption that used wooden and metal rollers to stretch and twist cotton threads into yarn. There is still controversy over whether Arkwright invented his frame or stole the design from others. In any case, after experimenting with horses to power his new machine, he decided that a waterwheel would be more effective. Running through the land he leased at Cromford, there was a river, Bonsall Brook, as well as an underground channel, or sough, that drained water from some nearby lead mines.

Arkwright and his partners built a five-story mill and a large waterwheel. In a local newspaper, they posted a job listing for skilled artisans—clockmakers, wood turners, a blacksmith—and unskilled workers. When Cromford Mill started production in 1772, it employed about two hundred people. Many of them were women and children, who were willing to work for lower wages than adult men.

Cromford Mill wasn't the world's first mechanized textile factory. The nearby Lombe's silk mill was also water-powered: it had been operating since 1721. Nonetheless, Arkwright and his partners were true pioneers of the factory system. Their mill set new standards for technology, productivity, and employee discipline. It operated around the clock, with two twelve-hour shifts, and its workers were required to keep strict time. If they were late or left their posts early, their pay was docked. As the business expanded, the mill owners constructed small housing units nearby, so their employees could walk to work. In 1776 they built a second mill on the same site.[2]

Today Cromford is part of a UNESCO World Heritage Site. It is commonly associated with the start of the industrial revolution, a term popularized by the English historian Arnold Toynbee in the late nineteenth century. During the decades after the mill opened, other British entrepreneurs would copy it, building dozens of spinning mills, particularly in the Lancashire city of Manchester and its surrounding towns. The factory system—based on mechanization, nonanimate power, and wage labor hired by capitalists— would gradually spread to other British industries, including woolen textiles, and to other countries, including the newly independent United States. Pointing to the vertiginous rise in output, productivity, and trade that this system unleashed, the historian Eric Hobsbawm described its emergence as "probably the most important event in world history, at any rate since the invention of agriculture and cities."[3]

Hobsbawm issued this judgment in 1962. Subsequent historical research has qualified it somewhat. Cotton-led industrialization didn't transform the rest of the British economy as rapidly as was once thought. Between 1780 and 1820, overall GDP growth remained relatively slow—less than 1.5 percent a year.[4] If we take a longer-term view, however, Hobsbawm's basic point surely stands, as the chart of world GDP over the past two millennia on the next page shows.[5] It looks like a hockey stick. For nearly eighteen hundred years, GDP was flat. In the early 1800s, it took off, slowly at first, then more steeply, eventually almost vertically. As output and productivity rose year by year, planet Earth was able to support many more people. The world's population rose from about 790 million in 1750 to roughly 8 billion in 2023.[6] Without sustained economic growth, this more than tenfold increase simply wouldn't have been possible.

The activities of Arkwright and his associates went largely unheralded by metropolitan writers and journalists. Derbyshire and Lancashire were remote from London, and few of the city's inhabitants took notice of what

GLOBAL AVERAGE GDP PER CAPITA IN INTERNATIONAL DOLLARS, YEARS 1–2022

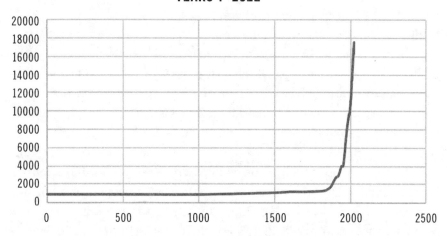

was happening there. Capitalism was already thriving in Britain, but it was mercantile capitalism rather than industrial capitalism. Britain had firmly established property rights, extensive trading links, and a stock market in London's financial district, which is known as the City. The British capital, with a population of about three-quarters of a million, had surpassed Paris as Europe's biggest metropolis.

The mercantile system revolved around the British Empire, which was largely a commercial enterprise, and its crown jewel was the lucrative trade with India. Many members of Britain's ruling class were involved, directly or indirectly, with the Indian trade, and they monitored it closely. Indeed, as Arkwright was busy getting Cromford Mill up and running, the metropolitan elites were consumed with a scandal involving the East India Company, a royally chartered trading monopoly that controlled key parts of the subcontinent.[7] The Company was criticized in Parliament and became the subject of a tell-all book by a longtime employee named William Bolts, who claimed it was impoverishing Indian producers by forcing the Indians to accept ultralow prices for their products. The British presence, far from benefiting Indians, as defenders of the Company claimed, had been "rendered hateful to the natives by oppressions, has occasioned desertions of many of the people, [and] is in general odious in India,"[8] Bolts wrote.

Bolts was an unlikely corporate whistleblower. Little is known about his early life except that he was born in 1735 in Amsterdam, moved to England when he was fourteen, and spent some time working in Lisbon. By early adulthood, then, he had lived in three countries that established great trading empires: Holland, Britain, and Portugal.[9] In 1759 Bolts obtained a job as a "factor," or junior manager, at the East India Company, and he moved to Bengal, a vast state in northeastern India that encompassed much of modern-day West Bengal, Bangladesh, Jharkhand, and Odisha. As a major producer of cotton fabrics and many agricultural products, Bengal was the Company's source of business and profits.

The East India Company was founded on December 31, 1600 under a charter issued by Queen Elizabeth I that granted it a monopoly on all British trade east of the Cape of Good Hope. Initially, it was an informal alliance of "merchant adventurers" who pooled their money to finance individual trading voyages. Nothing much distinguished it from other British trading ventures established in the same era, including the Muscovy Company, the Levant Company, and two enterprises that helped to establish Britain's American colonies: the Virginia Company and the Plymouth Company. For a long time, the British East India Company was dwarfed by its Dutch rival, the United East India Company, known as the VOC, which was established in 1602. The Dutch company was another state-chartered enterprise, and it was also the world's first publicly traded, joint-stock corporation: rather than being owned by a single proprietor or a group of partners, it issued shares that traded on the newly created Amsterdam Stock Exchange. Issuing stock was a revolutionary invention, because it allowed investors to diversify their risks. Rather than staking their money on a single trading voyage that might end in disaster, a wealthy individual could buy stock in the VOC and spread the bet across all its operations.

In 1619, the VOC established an Asian headquarters in what is now Jakarta, the capital of Indonesia. It cornered the trade in nutmeg, mace, cloves, and other spices that gave the Maluku Islands their European name, the Spice Islands, but its dominance didn't last. During the seventeenth and eighteenth centuries, Britain spent heavily on its military, particularly its navy, which enabled it to expand its commercial activities in areas previously controlled by the Dutch. In those days, there was no conception of commercial enterprise and state activity as strictly separate entities. The British state was effectively an arm of a landed oligarchy, many members of which invested in the Company and other imperial ventures. The Royal Navy protected the company's ships and enforced its trading monopolies by excluding foreign competitors and, where necessary, by going to war with them. The Company also had its own sizable military force made up largely of British officers and Indian soldiers. Together, the Company and the British state constituted a formidable military-commercial complex, which established a lucrative form of monopoly capitalism. Following the lead of the VOC, the Company evolved into a joint-stock business with an elaborate corporate structure. Its stockholders elected a Court of Directors that met weekly and served as the Company's ruling body. The directors chose a chairman, who ran the company. Under him there were ten executive committees, including treasury, accounts, legal, and shipping. From the company's headquarters on Leadenhall Street, its officials issued orders to its far-flung trading posts, telling them what goods to buy and keeping a sharp eye on costs.

During the early eighteenth century, the company shifted its focus from Indonesia to India, where it began buying cotton fabrics and other goods, then shipping them to Britain. At that time, Bengal was the world's biggest manufacturer of cotton. Its products ranged from inexpensive white calicoes to the finest soft muslins. These cloths proved enormously popular with Britons, who were happy to cast off the itchy woolen undergarments they had worn for centuries. By 1740, Bengal was producing about two-thirds of all the goods that the company shipped to Britain.[10] Some of these items were then reexported to non-British destinations, including slave-trading ports on the west coast of Africa.

As a trading enterprise, the Company looked to "buy cheap and sell dear." Until the middle of the eighteenth century, it operated from fortified coastal trading posts, known as "factories." Although its soldiers protected these forts, the Company operated under the sufferance of India's rulers, principally the Mughal monarchs, who hailed from central Asia. The Mughals made foreigners trade through Indian intermediaries, and they prohibited practices that would damage the interests of local producers, such as colluding to keep down prices.

The decline of the Mughal dynasty into internal feuding gave the company a chance to improve its position and seize power.[11] At the Battle of Plassey in 1757, two years before Bolts arrived in Bengal, the British forces, under the leadership of Robert Clive, a bookkeeper turned soldier who had joined the Company as a nineteen-year-old, defeated the forces of the nawab of Bengal, the provincial governor under the Mughal Monarchy. This victory enabled the company to drive out its French and Dutch rivals and trade in goods from which it had previously been excluded, such as salt. In 1765, after another big military victory, Clive persuaded Shah Allam II, the Delhi-based Mughal monarch, who was still the nominal ruler of Bengal, to grant the Company the diwani—the authority to set and collect taxes on his behalf in the states of Bengal, Bihar, and Orissa. This bestowal represented an extraordinary advance for the British. Under the Treaty of Allahabad, the Company was obliged to send the Mughal monarch a fixed sum of money every year. Clive was confident it could set the tax rates high enough to guarantee itself a hefty financial surplus.[12]

Clive left in place the formal trappings of Mughal rule in Bengal, installing a new and more pliant nawab. But real power now resided at the company's factory in Kolkata, which the British called Calcutta. In creating what was effectively a corporate state Clive and his colleagues transitioned from traditional merchant capitalism to full-scale corporate plunder. As a trading concern, the Company had shipped large quantities of silver bullion from London to India on a regular basis to pay for the goods it bought there. After obtaining the diwani, the company used Indian money to pay for the Indian goods it purchased. It was able to "carry out the whole trade of India for three years without sending out one ounce of bullion," one of Clive's associates later recalled.[13]

When William Bolts got to Bengal, he wasn't yet twenty-five, and his salary was modest. The attraction of a job with the Company had little to do with the formal pay. The real lure was the opportunity for Company men to trade commodities inside India on their own account, a practice the Company had long endorsed. These lucrative trades enabled many of its employees to build up a personal fortune, or "competence," which they eventually took back to England.[14] The richest of them became known in Britain as nabobs, which was probably an anglicization of the Hindi word *nawab*, which referred to a governor.

As a Dutch native, Bolts was an atypical Company employee, but he had an aptitude for languages that served him well. After arriving in Calcutta, he learned to speak Bengali. Although he was a fairly low-level employee, he quickly teamed up with two more senior colleagues, William Hay and John

Johnstone, to form a private trading company that dealt in many different goods, including diamonds, saltpeter—the raw material for dynamite—cotton, and opium. After the Battle of Plassey, the British traders largely ignored the old Mughal rules. Operating through Indian intermediaries known as *banyans* and *gomasthas*, they moved into new geographic regions and exploited the Company's role as the de facto government to force local producers to accept lower prices, which increased their profits when they resold the goods on the open market. Another lucrative line of business they entered was "tax-farming," which involved teaming up with local tax collectors, or *zamindars*, to skim off some of the levies that Indian farmers paid.[15]

Many of the Company's employees exploited this permissive environment. The abuses became so onerous and objectionable to the residents of Bengal that even the new nawab, Mir Qasim, whom the company had installed as a puppet ruler, complained. "Setting up their colours, and showing Company passes, [company employees] use their utmost endeavours to oppress the peasant farmers, merchants and other people of the country," Qasim wrote in a 1762 letter to Henry Vansittart, who was the Company's top official in Bengal from 1760 to 1764. "They forcibly take away the goods and commodities of the merchants for a fourth part of their value; and by way of violence and oppression they oblige the farmers to give five rupees for goods that are worth but one."[16]

In 1765 Clive returned to India from England as Vansittart's replacement. He had a brief to crack down on corruption, which was starting to become notorious in London. In *The Anarchy*, a sweeping 2019 history of the Company and its plunder, the author William Dalrymple points out that this was a case of appointing a poacher as a gamekeeper. After his victory at Plassey, Clive had gifted himself from the Moghul treasury roughly £234,000 (equivalent to more than £25 million in today's money). The nawab had also given Clive a landed estate, a *jagir*, that had an annual rental value of nearly £30,000. Insisting that these payments were legitimate rewards for his services to the company, Clive declared himself outraged at the finagling and self-dealing that greeted him on his return to Calcutta. In a letter to one his fellow directors, he wrote: "I shall only say that such a scene of anarchy, confusion, bribery, corruption, and extortion was never seen or heard of in any country but Bengal; nor such and so many fortunes acquired in so unjust and rapacious a manner."[17]

During the year 1756 alone, according to one estimate, the Company's employees in India sent home to England about £80,000 from their trading gains. In the decade after Plassey, these annual remittances jumped more than sixfold, to about £500,000[18] (in today's money, more than £60 million). Clive forced Company employees to sign contracts saying they would no longer accept corrupt payments, or "gifts," from local authorities. He cracked down on private trading by setting up a Company-run Society of Trade and granting it a monopoly on the internal trade of certain items, including salt, betel nuts, and tobacco.[19]

Clive also targeted individuals whom he regarded as particularly corrupt, including John Johnstone, Bolts's trading partner. Clive confiscated Johnstone's property in Bengal and asked the Company's directors to prosecute him for illegal trading. The Company ordered Bolts to return to Calcutta from Benares, another city on the Ganges, where he had extensive private trading interests. After he failed to obey this edict, the Company suspended him. Rather than submitting to the new policies, Bolts resigned in November 1766 and continued trading as a private individual. The following year, his bosses ordered his deportation to England and, after he departed, imprisoned three of his *gomasthas*. The Company's directors in London endorsed the decision to send Bolts home, saying it was justified by his "conspicuously oppressive" trading, his "repeated instances of disobedience to the orders of his superiors abroad—and above all by the basest ingratitude to the Company under whom he had acquired an ample fortune." Before long Bolts would exact his revenge.[20]

After his return to London, he launched a public campaign against the Company and the senior executives whom he claimed had wronged him, Clive included, claiming that they were the real crooks. His old partner Johnstone joined him in his crusade, which they took to the Company's headquarters on Leadenhall Street, to the press, and to the Houses of Parliament at Westminster, where two of Johnstone's brothers were MPs. Other Company men who resented its crackdown on private trading, and who considered Clive a hypocrite, joined in the attack.[21]

If Bolts's campaign against the Company had taken place in flush times, it might not have received much attention. Between 1769 and 1772, however, the Company suffered a series of financial calamities. After acquiring the diwani, it had raised its annual dividend to 12 percent, but the increase in revenues wasn't as big as Clive and others had hoped, and the dividend payments drained the Company's treasury. In May 1769 a Company ship arrived in London bearing news of renewed fighting in southern India, where, a couple of years earlier, Hyder Ali, the ruler of the Kingdom of Mysore, had reacted to British encroachments by attacking some of the company's trading outposts. Investors panicked, and the Company's stock plummeted. Many members of the British political establishment, including the writer Edmund Burke and his brother Richard, suffered big losses.[22]

Worse was to come. In the second half of 1769, a severe drought struck Bengal, and in 1770 a terrible famine began. The human cost was unfathomable: estimates of the death toll range from 1.2 million, an estimate cited by some modern historians, to 10 million, cited at the time by Warren Hastings, a senior Company official who would eventually become the first governor-general of Bengal.[23] Controversy still surrounds the Company's role in the famine. Obviously, it wasn't responsible for the annual monsoon rains failing to arrive, but its response to the resultant crop failures was heartless in the extreme. "As soon as the dryness of the season foretold the approaching dearness of rice, our Gentlemen in the Company's service were as early as possible in buying up all they could lay hold of," an anonymous correspondent wrote in *Gentleman's Magazine*, a London monthly.[24] When the price of rice jumped forty-fold, one junior employee made £60,000 (£9 million in today's money), according to one account.[25]

Profiteering wasn't the Company's only crime. Even as the drought decimated the incomes of Indian farmers, it continued to levy land taxes and enforce payment, sometimes to the point of executing Indians who wouldn't or couldn't pay. "Platoons of sepoys"—Indian soldiers serving under the British—"were marched out into the countryside to enforce payment, where they erected gibbets in prominent places to hang those who resisted the tax collections," Dalrymple wrote. "Even starving families were expected to pay up; there were no remissions authorized on humanitarian grounds."[26]

Not all of these details became known in Britain, but some newspapers and magazines did print stories about starving Indians selling their children for food. Public opinion swung against the Company, and questions were raised in Parliament. Bolts saw his chance. In early 1772 he published a two-volume book about the Company's role in India. Its title was anodyne—*Considerations on India Affairs; Particularly Respecting the Present State of Bengal and Its Dependencies*—but its contents were incendiary. After *London*

Magazine, a publication closely connected to the Whig Party, published some extracts, they circulated widely at Westminster and in the City of London.

Bolts asserted that when Clive and other senior executives of the Company clamped down on private trades, they hadn't been trying to eliminate corruption or protect the interest of Indians, but merely trying to enrich themselves. Clive alone had earned tens of thousands of pounds from the creation of the Society of Trade, Bolts claimed. Echoing the complaints of Mir Qasim, the puppet nawab, he also accused the Company of systematically exploiting Indian producers in the years since the Battle of Plassey. "The English, with their Banyans and black Gomastahs," he wrote, "arbitrarily decide what quantities of each goods each manufacturer shall deliver, and the *prices* he shall receive for them."[27] Bolts even argued that the ravages of the Bengal famine could be traced in part to Clive's campaign to suppress competition and create a lucrative monopoly for the Company and its most executives.

Much of Bolts's account was self-serving. He claimed that the private trading activities that he and others were engaged in benefited the Indian population because they were based on free competition and fair prices. Given all the finagling Company employees were involved in, and the fortunes that many of them earned, it's safe to discount these protestations of innocence. But Bolts's broader account of how the Company exploited Indian producers had more substance. He singled out its treatment of Bengal's cotton weavers, who had long taken pride in their independent status and relative prosperity. "The roguery practised in this department is beyond imagination, but all terminates in the defrauding of the poor weaver," Bolts wrote, "for the prices which the Company's gomastahs . . . fix upon the goods are in all places at least fifteen per cent, and in some even forty per cent less than the goods so manufactured would sell for in the public Bazár, or market, upon a free sale."[28]

How had this situation come about? Bolts provided a clear answer: the Company had turned into an out-of-control corporate leviathan. The representatives of the Company had "become the Sovereign of a rich and potent kingdom, and their government in Bengal a military as well as [a] civil government."[29] Inevitably, Bolts went on, the "interests of the Company as sovereigns of Bengal and at the same time as monopolizers of all the trade and commerce of those countries, operate in direct opposition and are mutually destructive of each other."[30] As custodian of the most valuable territory in the British Empire, the Company had a responsibility to take care of it and its people, which would benefit Britain over the long term. But as a monopolistic business, the Company was incentivized to squeeze out as much profit as it could, regardless of the broader consequences. Its tactics since Plessey, Bolts wrote, amounted to "the idiot-practice of killing the prolific hen to get her golden eggs all at once."[31] The only real solution to this problem, he went on, was for the British Crown to assert sovereignty over Bengal and the other British strongholds and leave the Company to concentrate on its traditional trading business. It had become "an absolute necessity for the British legislature to separate the Merchant from the Sovereign for the preservation of both."[32]

Bolts was pursuing a vendetta. He had been kicked out of India, some of his business partners had been arrested, and a few months before his book appeared, the British government, at the behest of the Company, had ordered him to pay a 30 percent tax on the profits he had garnered from his trading. (Unable to pay the bill, he was declared bankrupt in 1773.)[33] Historians have cast doubt on some of Bolts's assertions, including his claim that certain Indian winders of raw silk, who were known as *nagaads*, became so enraged at how the Company was treating them that they cut off their own thumbs to avoid being forced to work.[34] Bolt's allegation that the ravages of the famine could be traced to Clive's campaign to suppress competition was outlandish. In a March 1772 parliamentary debate, Clive himself remarked: "How a monopoly of salt, betel nut and tobacco in the years 1765 and 1766 could occasion a want of rain and scarcity of rice [years later] is past my comprehension."[35]

Still, for all of Bolts's unreliablity as a witness, many of the abuses that he identified were subsequently confirmed by other accounts, including an internal Company report that was prepared later in the 1770s for one of its top executives. In Bengal, the anonymous author of this report wrote, "the Company went to market as Sovereigns and Tyrants." Rather than gaining the cooperation of local producers and paying them market prices, its local representatives "forced the manufacturers to Work for them and to work at an under price, at the same time that they prohibited private merchants from dealing" with them. In this manner, "a general Monopoly was at once rigorously established."[36]

In modern terms, the Company report provided a textbook description of a particular type of monopoly known as a "monopsony"—a market in which a single large buyer can exploit its leverage over many small sellers who have no alternative to dealing with it. Once the Company had driven out its French and Dutch competitors, it had an enormous amount of market power, and as Bolts and the anonymous report noted, it didn't hesitate to exploit this position.

And yet for all these advantages, the Company had managed to get itself into financial difficulty by paying such high dividends. In the summer of 1772, shortly after Bolts's book was published, its directors, having seen the Indian business collapse during the famine, were forced to ask the British government for a bailout—a loan of at least a million pounds. The news that the mighty East India Company was virtually bankrupt prompted a financial panic in which a number of banks failed. And in a development that foreshadowed the Global Financial Crisis of 2007–2009, the news that it was asking Parliament for a rescue caused widespread outrage. In another precursor, the government of Lord North, the Tory grandee who would lead Britain through most of the American Revolutionary War, decided that the Company was too big and important to be allowed to fail. It accounted for roughly half of Britain's foreign trade, and it was by far the country's biggest taxpayer. Moreover, many members of Parliament were shareholders.

Negotiations dragged on through the first half of 1773. Eventually the government agreed to extend the Company a loan of £1.4 million. Simultaneously, Parliament asserted some control over its operations. In the Regulating Act of 1783 and the East India Act of 1784, Parliament created the post of governor-general of Bengal, the occupant of which would supposedly exercise ultimate authority over the Company's operations in Bengal, Madras, and Bombay. The legislation also created a new government-appointed executive council in Calcutta, and a Bengal Supreme Court, with four English judges, to resolve trading disputes.[37]

The government appointed Warren Hastings, an independent-minded Company veteran, as the first governor-general of Bengal. During his time in India, Hastings would overhaul the Company's business affairs and build some essential public infrastructure, including granaries and a postal service. Despite these improvements, the reforms failed to resolve the fundamental conflicts of interest that Bolts had identified. And many of the Company's onerous practices remained in place, including the hefty land taxes that impoverished many Indian farmers. In 1782 some farmers in Dinajpur and

Rangpur, two areas that are now in Bangladesh, rose up in revolt. The following year there was another violent uprising in neighboring Awadh. A new drought in Bengal and further military conflicts in the South added to the Company's difficulties. Despite having repaid its government loan, it found itself in renewed financial difficulties. In March 1783 its directors asked Parliament for another bailout, which caused more public outrage.

By this stage, Bolts had left England. After being declared bankrupt, he moved across the English Channel, where, with the backing of some Belgian financiers, he launched several new trading ventures to India and Africa. None of these schemes enjoyed enduring success, and by 1782 he was again bankrupt. Ever hopeful, he sought out more backers for a venture to ship goods from the northwestern coast of America to China and Japan. That plan didn't work out either, and Bolts subsequently struggled to find financial backers. He spent some time in Portugal, where his business career had started. When he died in 1808 at the age of seventy, he was forgotten and reportedly living in a Paris poorhouse.[38] But some of his criticisms of corporate capitalism would live on, even if they weren't widely associated with him.

2

Adam Smith on Colonial Capitalism and Slavery

On June 27, 1772, David Hume, the great Scottish philosopher, penned a letter from his home in Edinburgh to his friend Adam Smith, a former professor of moral philosophy at Glasgow University, who he knew was working on a book about the economy. "We are here in a very melancholy Situation: Continual Bankruptcies, universal Loss of Credit, and endless Suspicions," Hume wrote. "Do these Events any-wise affect your Theory? Or will it occasion the Revisal of any Chapters?"[1] A couple of weeks earlier a Scottish financial house known as the Ayr Bank had collapsed, setting off a financial panic that rattled the money centers in Edinburgh, London, and Amsterdam.[2] The financial troubles of the East India Company, and its request for a government bailout, were also in the news.

There is no record of what Smith replied to Hume. When he received the letter, he was living in his hometown of Kirkcaldy, Fife. Some years earlier, he had taken leave of his professorship for a better-paid post: tutoring the young Duke of Buccleuch. Approaching fifty, Smith had already published one highly acclaimed book, *The Theory of Moral Sentiments*, in which he examined the basis of morality. The new book he was working on addressed the question of why some countries got rich while others stayed poor. Despite his reputation as an absent-minded professor, Smith followed current events closely, and he was politically connected. During the previous decade, he had acted as an informal adviser to Charles Townshend, who had served as president of the Board of Trade and was then chancellor of the exchequer in the Whig government of William Pitt the Elder. It was Townshend who had imposed hefty import duties in the American colonies, including tariffs on tea that the East India Company transported from Asia, a policy that was causing great ruptures. Smith didn't have anything to do with the tariffs, but he remained close to the Whigs.

In 1776, the year the thirteen American colonies declared their independence, Smith finally published his book: *An Inquiry into the Nature and Causes of the Wealth of Nations.* Usually referred to by the last four words of its title, it was a landmark in economic thought. In the opening chapters, Smith argued that the key to rising productivity and economic growth is "the division of labor," in which production is split up into a number of different tasks, with each worker concentrating on an individual one. To illustrate his point, he described how a workshop that made metal pins divided production into "about eighteen distinct operations," including drawing out the wire, straightening it, cutting it, grinding it, and attaching the pin head to it. If ten workers carried out all these tasks themselves, they could each make at most twenty pins a day, Smith said. By having them concentrate on individual tasks, the workshop produced forty-eight thousand pins each day—a truly massive increase in productivity.[3]

Smith's famous description of a pin workshop is a reminder that manufacturing was common in Britain well before the opening of Cromford Mill, but it was mostly small-scale manufacturing. Foreshadowing a debate that continues to this day, Smith insisted that the fruits of increased production and higher productivity trickled down to everybody, including the poor. "It is the great multiplication of the productions of all the different arts," he wrote, "in consequence of the division of labour, which occasions, in a well-governed society, that universal opulence which extends itself to the lowest ranks of the people."[4] Smith said the key to achieving this outcome was to rely on a competitive market system, which coordinated production without any central control and prevented any individual, or group, from hogging all the gains. In a competitive market of this nature, he wrote, the pursuit of profit by a businessman or tradesman guides his actions and investments in a direction "which is most agreeable to the interest of the whole society,"[5] as if he were "led by an invisible hand to promote an end which was no part of his intention."[6]

Based upon Smith's exposition of the division of labor and the invisible hand, he is usually portrayed as an enthusiastic proponent of free market capitalism, or what he referred to as "commercial society." Broadly speaking, this characterization is accurate. Years before Smith published *The Wealth of Nations*, he wrote elsewhere: "Little else is requisite to carry a state to the highest degree of opulence from the lowest barbarism, but peace, easy taxes, and a tolerable administration of justice; all the rest being brought about by the natural course of things. All governments which thwart this natural course . . . are unnatural, and to support themselves are obliged to be oppressive and tyrannical."[7] In his 2023 book, *Visions of Inequality*, the economist Branko Milanović, a leading scholar of global income disparities, pointed out that Smith's faith in the free market was partly based on a conviction that it led to high incomes and wages, which Smith called "the very essence of public opulence."[8] As Milanović also emphasized, Smith's emphasis on raising wages and living standards marked a major break with prior economic doctrines, which regarded wealth and treasure, particularly gold and silver bullion, as the main measure of a country's strength and well-being.

But though Smith certainly believed in the power of free commerce and competitive markets to generate growth and prosperity, there was another side to him that often gets overlooked. Even as he defended the general principle of organizing society on the basis of private enterprise and profit-seeking, he was deeply suspicious of individual business owners and tradesmen because of their tendency to eliminate competition and stiff their customers whenever they could. "People of the same trade seldom meet together," he wrote, "even for merriment and diversion, but the conversation ends in a conspiracy against the public, or in some contrivance to raise prices."[9]

Smith was even more dubious about large-scale businesses, particularly merchant capitalist enterprises like the East India Company, which had been founded on the basis of royal monopoly grants. In trying to justify the privileged and protected status that these businesses enjoyed, their defenders argued it would enable Britain to run a positive trade balance and build up its wealth. Although the trade monopolies were privately owned and operated, they were viewed, effectively, as arms of the state. During the early seventeenth century, Thomas Munn, a merchant who became a director of the East India Company, had expressed these arguments in a pair of books. Smith referred to the economic philosophy Munn expounded as "mercantilism," and one of his goals in writing *The Wealth of Nations* was to challenge it. In a letter he wrote several years after the book's publication, he described it as a "very violent attack . . . upon the whole commercial system of Great Britain."[10] If mercantilism was a form of capitalism—and it surely was—Smith was a noted critic of capitalism as well as its greatest philosopher.

Smith's treatment of mercantilism and colonialism was largely confined to the second half of *The Wealth of Nations*, books four and five. Many readers don't get that far, which is a pity. Smith wasn't entirely opposed to colonialism. He admired the rapid economic progress of the North American colonies, which he attributed to "plenty of good land, and liberty to manage their own affairs their own way," which included encouraging free trade among themselves and with the British colonies in the Caribbean.[11] "All of them taken together," Smith wrote, "they make a great internal market for the produce of one another."[12] But all too often, he believed, colonialism had failed to adhere to liberal trading principles and descended into monopoly and plunder, which ended up imposing large costs on British consumers and taxpayers. Challenging the basic mercantilist claim that establishing colonies generated large economic benefits, Smith wrote, "no country has yet been able to engross itself anything but the expense of supporting in time of peace and of defending in time of war the oppressive authority which it gains over them. The inconveniences resulting from the possession of its colonies, every country has engrossed to itself completely."[13]

The main objects of Smith's criticism were the great colonial trading houses, particularly the East India Company. Before the creation of the company and its Dutch counterpart, the VOC, Smith pointed out, Portugal had "enjoyed almost the whole of [the East Indies trade] for more than a century together without any exclusive company."[14] By replacing competition with state-sponsored monopolies, Smith argued, the Dutch and British governments effectively granted these companies the power to raise the prices of the items that they sent back to their home countries. In the case of the East India Company, British consumers and taxpayers had been forced to pay "not only for all the extraordinary profits" that the company made at various times, but also "for all the extraordinary waste which the fraud and abuse, inseparable from the management of the affairs of so great a company, must necessarily have occasioned."[15]

There doesn't seem to be any evidence that Smith read William Bolts's exposé of the East India Company. But in describing the company's parasitic presence in India, he covered some of the same ground. In one passage, he focused on the company's exports of opium, which was largely produced in the eastern state of Bihar, then part of Bengal, to other Asian countries. "It has not been uncommon, I am well assured, for the chief, that is, the first clerk of a factory, to order a peasant to plough up a rich field of poppies, and sow it with rice or some other grain," Smith wrote. "The pretence was, to prevent a scarcity of provisions; but the real reason, to give the chief an opportunity of selling at a better price a large quantity of opium, which he happened then to have upon hand."[16] Far from being atypical, Smith said, these types of actions were inherent in the extractive business model that the East India Company and other chartered trading monopolies relied on. "In the spice islands," he wrote, "the Dutch are said to burn all the spiceries which a fertile season produces beyond what they expect to dispose of in Europe, with such a profit as they think sufficient." On some of the islands, he went on, the VOC's policies had virtually destroyed the local vegetation and led to depopulation. The English "have not yet had time to establish in Bengal so perfectly destructive a system," Smith added. "The plan of their government, however, has had exactly the same tendency."[17]

As well as criticizing the practices of the East India Company as a whole, Smith discussed the lucrative private trading that its employees engaged in, and he expressed skepticism about the ability of senior executives, particularly those based in London, to curtail it. Virtually all the Company men in India traded on their own account, he pointed out. Given the riches they could accumulate, "it is in vain to prohibit them from doing so," he argued. Nothing could be more foolish "than to expect that the clerks of a great counting-house at ten thousand miles distance, and consequently almost quite out of sight, should upon a simple order from their masters, give up at once doing any sort of business upon their own account, abandon for ever all hopes of making a fortune, of which they have the means in their hands."[18]

Smith's account of how the Company operated was at least partly based on personal knowledge. One of his cousins, Patrick Ross, served as chief engineer in its Madras factory. While Smith was writing *The Wealth of Nations*, his biographer Ian Simpson Ross reports, he offered to recommend a former student of his, an impecunious minor member of the Scottish gentry, to his cousin for employment.[19] (There is no record of whether the young man did join the Company.) In 1773, Smith's name was put forward for a parliamentary commission that had been set up to investigate how the company ended up needing a bailout. Rather than taking up this post, Smith expressed his thoughts in his book.

In another unconscious echo of Bolts, he argued that the fundamental issue with the Company wasn't the poor character of its employees, but the conflicts created by their accession to political power in Bengal. As effectively the rulers, their interests should be wholly aligned with the interests of the territory that they governed, Smith pointed out, but "as merchants their interest is directly opposite to that interest."[20] Their goal was to make as large a profit as they could in the shortest time possible. "It is a very singular government in which every member of the administration wishes to get out of the country . . . as soon as he can," Smith wrote scathingly, "and to whose interest, the day after he has left it and carried his whole fortune with him, it is perfectly indifferent though the whole country was swallowed up by an earthquake."[21]

Although Smith focused on the East India Company, he extended his criticisms to other chartered trading monopolies. "Such exclusive companies . . . are nuisances in every respect," he wrote, "always more or less inconvenient to the countries in which they are established, and destructive to those which have the misfortune to fall under their government."[22] Entrenched by fiat, the trading monopolies could expand at will, without fear of competition or effective oversight. In describing the consequences of this system, Smith used a medical metaphor: "Great Britain resembles one of those unwholesome bodies in which some of the vital parts are overgrown, and which, upon that account, are liable to many dangerous disorders."[23]

While Smith emphasized the economic costs of mercantilism, his critique went beyond dollars and cents. He also emphasized the link between mercantile capitalism and war. During the second half of the seventeenth century, Parliament had introduced the Navigation Acts, which limited imports to Britain from foreign suppliers, required almost all items involved in the colonial trade to be transported on British ships, and forced colonies like India to obtain almost all their supplies from Britain. To enforce this protectionist legislation, the government built up the Royal Navy, which engaged in a series of wars with Britain's trading rivals, particularly the Dutch. "Commerce, which ought naturally to be, among nations, as among individuals, a bond of union and friendship, has become the most fertile source of discord and animosity," Smith remarked. He also lamented the emergence of an early military-commerce complex, which dominated colonial policy and resisted efforts at reform. Representatives of colonial interests, he noted, had long served as the "principal advisers"[24] to the politicians and officials who set up and sustained the mercantile system. Consequently, government policy often reflected the "the mean rapacity, the monopolising spirit of merchants and manufacturers."[25]

For all his criticism of mercantilism, Smith was a big supporter of developing global commerce on the basis of free trade. He described Columbus's journey to the Americas and Magellan's journey around the Cape of Good Hope as "the two greatest and most important events ever recorded in the history of mankind." In opening up the possibility of trade between Europe and distant continents, these voyages created the potential for both sides to make huge gains "by enabling them to relieve one another's wants, to increase one another's enjoyments, and to encourage one another's industry." But the plunder carried out by the European colonizers, particularly the Spanish in Latin America, had squandered this historic opportunity and created disastrous results, especially for the Indigenous peoples. "At the particular time when discoveries were made," Smith wrote, "the superiority of force happened to be so great on the side of the Europeans that they were enabled to commit with impunity every sort of injustice in those remote countries."[26]

Another great injustice, of course, was the transatlantic slave trade. Between 1501 and 1866, according to the latest scholarly estimates, roughly 12.5 million Africans were forcefully transported to the Americas, about half of them to the Caribbean and roughly another 40 percent to Brazil.[27] The profit motive and demand for labor drove this dreadful phenomenon. In the fifteenth century, Portuguese colonists established sugar plantations in some islands they occupied off the west coast of Africa, including Madeira, Cape Verde, and São Tomé and Príncipe. By 1500, these plantations were exporting sugar to Holland, France, and Britain, where the population was rapidly developing a sweet tooth. Making sugar was very lucrative but also very labor intensive. Clearing fields, planting sugarcane, harvesting it, crushing it, and refining it into the finished product took many hours of arduous work. Cut off from the African mainland, the plantation owners faced an endemic shortage of workers. To relieve it, some of them started to import enslaved workers from Kongo (Congo) and Ndongo (Angola).

In the 1530s the Portuguese moved this business model across the Atlantic and established sugar plantations in coastal regions of Brazil. Initially, they forced local people to work the fields. But mortality rates among the Indigenous workers were very high, and before long the plantation owners began importing enslaved Africans. Between 1600 and 1625, according to the SlaveVoyages Database, Portuguese slave ships carried an estimated 180,000 Africans to Brazil, which became the world's largest sugar producer.[28] (By 1866, the cumulative number of Africans transported to Brazil would climb to an astonishing 5.5 million, of whom about 4.9 million disembarked alive.)[29]

Seeing the commercial successes that Portugal was enjoying, some of its European rivals sought to mimic them. Spain established sugar plantations on the island of Hispaniola, which today comprises the Dominican Republic and Haiti. France set up plantations on Martinique and Guadeloupe and in the western parts of Hispaniola, which it acquired from Spain in 1697. Britain established plantations in Barbados and Jamaica and also in the smaller Leeward Islands of Antigua, St. Kitts, Nevis, and Montserrat. Some of the British plantations were initially staffed by indentured British workers who, in return for their passage, were obliged to toil in the fields for seven years. But these workers struggled to adapt to the tropical conditions, and their mortality rates were high. The British planters started to import enslaved Africans in large numbers, and before very long British traders came to dominate the slave trade. According to one estimate, between 1640 and 1807, British ships transported some 3.1 million enslaved Africans across the Atlantic.[30]

When the survivors of this transshipment arrived in the Americas, they were sold at auction and transported to their final locations. In the mid-eighteenth century, the British plantations alone had hundreds of thousands of enslaved workers, including about seventy thousand in Barbados. Each year the plantations exported more than forty thousand tons of sugar to England and Wales.[31] By the standards of the time, sugar production was carried out on a very large scale. Some of the plantations owned and employed several hundred enslaved people; as the American historian Joyce Appleby commented in a 2010 book, they were "factories in the fields."[32]

Histories of capitalism that focus exclusively on the rise of the factory system in Britain and other Western countries tend to overlook this fact. While plantation agriculture wasn't directly comparable to industrial capitalism, which relied on wage labor and machinery, it certainly involved large-scale mobilization of capital and production of marketable commodities for profit.

Going by the definition that I gave in the introduction, it was a form of capitalism, and an innately global one at that. As the historian Richard Sheridan pointed out in his 1974 book *Sugar and Slavery: An Economic History of the West Indies, 1623–1775*, "The New World plantation represented a combination of African labour, European animal husbandry, and American soil and climate."[33]

Sugar plantations, in particular, generated high rates of profit. In the seventeenth century, economic historians have calculated, the rate of return on capital invested in the British plantations was as high as 30 percent. Even in the middle of the eighteenth century, when there was more competition, the rate of return was in the double digits, whereas the yield on British government bonds was only about 3 percent.[34] The British plantation owners repatriated much of the profit they made and built large country estates, many of which still exist. In Parliament, plantation owners were a powerful lobbying force. Like the wealthy retirees from the East India Company, they were known as "nabobs." Among the eminent English families that owed their fortunes, entirely or in large part, to Caribbean plantations worked by enslaved people were the Baylys, Beckfords, Codringtons, Fullers, Lascelles, Longs, and Pennants.[35] In 2013 researchers discovered that the Conservative politician David Cameron, who was then Britain's prime minister, had a distant relation who owned more than two hundred enslaved people.[36]

Smith acknowledged the immense profits that the Caribbean plantations generated, but he didn't dwell on the fact that they were produced by slave labor. Indeed, he suggested that they could have made even more money if they had relied on wage labor, writing: "The experience of all ages and nations, I believe, demonstrates that the work done by slaves, though it appears to cost only their maintenance, is in the end the dearest of any"—meaning the most expensive on a productivity-adjusted basis. Since wage workers could earn money and acquire property, they had an incentive to work hard and produce more, Smith argued. The enslaved worker had no rights, received no wages, and had no prospect of acquiring property. Work "can be squeezed out of him by violence only, and not by any interest of his own," Smith wrote.[37]

Versions of Smith's argument have found some modern adherents, particularly in debates about whether slavery in the United States held back or promoted the development of American capitalism. But the argument has a couple of obvious weaknesses. Smith didn't acknowledge the enormous difficulties plantation owners would have faced in finding enough willing wage workers—the very issue that gave rise to the slave trade in the first place. And he downplayed the role that slavery played in expanding global trade and developing the economies of slave-trading nations. When Smith published *The Wealth of Nations*, Liverpool was the world's biggest slave port. In 1776 alone, according to the SlaveVoyages Database, more than seventy slave ships left its docks destined for the Bight of Benin, the Bight of Bonny, Sierra Leone, and other African destinations.[38] These vessels were stocked with items that African slave traders valued highly: cotton and woolen textiles, guns, gunpowder, brass wares, earthenware, and alcohol. "Textiles came from Lancashire and Yorkshire, copper and brass goods from Warrington, North Cheshire and Staffordshire, guns and ammunition from Birmingham," Anthony Tibbles, the former keeper of slavery history at National Museums Liverpool, wrote in a 2000 article. "But the town's merchants also had to develop wider links to obtain some goods—there was a strong demand for East Indian cloth in West Africa . . . They, therefore, had to obtain such goods from London and sometimes Amsterdam."[39] Other British trading ships sailed directly from their home ports to the Americas carrying goods destined for the slave plantations. Among the goods that a typical sugar plantation imported were tools for its field hands, a steam engine to power its cane crushers, guns for its overseers, clothes for its laborers, and sugar sacks to hold its produce.

As this list indicates, the triangular trade was a major intercontinental enterprise, which gave a substantial boost to many ancillary industries, including shipbuilding, merchant shipping, banking, insurance (the slave ships were insured), textiles, armaments, and brass and iron works. The mercantilist writers whom Smith criticized emphasized the broad economic benefits that colonialism and slavery generated for Britain. In a 1745 book defending the triangular trade, Malachy Postlethwayt, an economist and lexicographer, described Britain's Atlantic empire as "a magnificent superstructure of American commerce and naval power on an African foundation."[40] If the African trade ceased to exist, he argued, "hundreds of thousands of Britons making goods for the triangular trade will lose their jobs and go a begging." Moreover, "we can have no sugar, tobacco, rum etc. Consequently the public revenue, arising from the importation of plantation produce, will be wiped out."[41]

In 1767 Sir James Steuart, a countryman of Smith, published *An Inquiry into the Principles of Political Economy,* in which he advocated the standard suite of mercantilist policies: protecting domestic industry, subsidizing exports, and engaging in state-sponsored colonialism. Steuart's analysis of slavery was more nuanced than Postlethwayt's. He said its usefulness depended on the conditions in which it was applied. Enslaving workers had the effect of "discouraging invention and ingenuity," he wrote, foreshadowing Smith. For this reason, Steuart recommended banning slavery from manufacturing industries. But he also argued that in conducting "laborious operations which are of a simple nature," such as plantation agriculture in tropical climates, slave labor was the only viable option. "Could the sugar islands be cultivated to any advantage by hired labour?" Steuart asked.[42]

Rather than addressing this question directly, Smith argued that colonialism and slavery were an unnecessary diversion from free commerce. He was much less concerned than many of his countrymen about the prospect of losing the American colonies, which he predicted would go on to become one of the world's "greatest and most formidable" empires. He also argued that colonial ventures had been "continually drawing capital from all other trades," and that, consequently, "many other branches of foreign trade, particularly of that to other parts of Europe, have been continually decaying."[43] Rather than directing so much effort and resources to protecting and expanding its long-distance colonial trade, Britain should focus on building up domestic markets and foreign ones closer to home, Smith said. "The industry of Great Britain, instead of being accommodated to a great number of small markets, has been principally suited to one great market," he wrote. "But the whole system of her industry and commerce has thereby been rendered less secure, the whole state of her body politic less healthful than it otherwise would have been."[44]

It's hard to say for sure whether Smith's favored development strategy—free trade focused on Europe—would have been viable for Britain. But his argument that colonialism and mercantilism had held back its economy is hard to sustain. In 1500, Britain was "little more than a sheep walk," the economic historian Robert Allen has noted."[45] By the time *The Wealth of Nations* was published, the percentage of Britain's population that lived in urban areas had tripled, and the proportion that worked in agriculture had fallen from three-quarters to less than half. Income per capita had risen by about 50 percent—slow growth in modern terms, but rapid by previous standards—and the adult literacy rate had risen more than eightfold, to 53 percent. The country had a far-flung empire and was the dominant maritime power.[46]

To be sure, colonialism and mercantilism weren't solely responsible for this metamorphosis. Revolutions in agriculture, science, and politics all played key roles. But the process of economic and political modernization took place in the context of government-sponsored globalization and imperialism. The "fiscal-military state"—a term coined by the historian John Brewer—was purposefully raising its capacity to wage wars, particularly naval wars, for commercial practices.[47] In Smith's eagerness to discredit mercantilism and extol the virtues of the invisible hand, he downplayed this transformation and underestimated its impact.

On the other hand, Smith's argument that letting the North American colonies go wouldn't impoverish Britain turned out to be prescient, and so did his endorsement of free trade. After establishing its independence, the United States quickly became a key trading partner of its former colonial overlord. And once Britain established itself as the world's leading industrial power and its lowest-cost producer, removing mercantile restrictions on its exports and imports made sense because it could successfully undercut its trading rivals. From a strategic perspective, Smith's analysis was well ahead of its time.

In 1784 he published a third edition of *The Wealth of Nations* that included a new section tracing the histories of the chartered trading monopolies, including the East India Company, which was back in the news because of its renewed financial problems.[48] Barely a decade after being bailed out in the early 1770s, Smith noted in the new edition, the Company had been "once more reduced to supplicate the assistance of government."[49] The source of the company's problems was another costly military conflict—this one in southern India, where the sultan of Mysore, Hyder Ali, had attacked company forces near Madras. The expense of confronting Ali's forces had brought the company back to the verge of bankruptcy, and Smith despaired about the prospects of it ever being "fit to govern, or even to share in the government of a great empire."[50]

In his new material, Smith adduced another reason why the chartered trading companies tended to get into financial trouble: they were joint-stock companies rather than traditional business partnerships. Many modern textbooks emphasize how investing in stocks enables investors to spread their risks and protect their capital. Smith expressed a very different view. In a partnership, he pointed out, the owners of the business put their entire wealth on the line, which imbues them with some caution. By contrast, the executives of a joint-stock company enjoy limited liability: their financial risk is limited to the value of the shares they own. Smith warned: "The directors of such companies . . . being the managers rather of other people's money than of their own, it cannot well be expected that they should watch over it with the same anxious vigilance with which the partners in a private copartnery frequently watch over their own." He went on: "Negligence and profusion, therefore, must always prevail, more or less, in the management of the affairs of such a company."[51]

Passages like this one further belie the common perception that Smith was an unqualified defender of capitalism. His endorsement of "commercial society" was predicated on the preservation of competition, free trade, and individual responsibility. Anything that threatened these virtues, he opposed. The publication of *The Wealth of Nations* turned him into a public figure. In 1778 the government in London gave him a well-paid official post as commissioner of Scottish customs (tariffs), and he moved to Edinburgh, where he lived with his mother. In 1883, William Pitt the Younger became Britain's prime minister. Pitt had read *The Wealth of Nations* and was determined to enact some of the principles it expounded. His government reduced the import duties on tea, wines, spirits, and tobacco. It sought to encourage trade with Europe and signed a trade treaty with France. Responding to public outrage about the renewed financial troubles of the East India Company, it created a new Board of Control to oversee its operations from London and strengthened the powers of the governor-general in Bengal.

Pitt's reforms weren't entirely successful, but they heralded an important shift from protection toward free trade, and from commercial colonialism toward formal empire. The mercantile capitalism that had provided the backdrop to *The Wealth of Nations* was about to be supplanted by industrial capitalism. In the years after Cromford Mill opened, Thomas Arkwright licensed his water frame technology to other entrepreneurs, and by 1788 well over a hundred Cromford-like mills were operating across northern England, Wales, and Scotland. Another important moment came in 1781, when the Scottish inventor James Watt patented his rotative steam engine. Four years later, a mill near Nottingham became the first cotton spinning factory to use Watt's engine. The cotton industry represented the future, but it was deeply integrated into the old colonial system that Smith had critiqued. Even before it started importing raw cotton produced on slave plantations in the American South, it sourced its key input from plantations in the West Indies and mainland South America, particularly Brazil. Some cloths that the industry produced were shipped in the opposite direction across the Atlantic, as well as to slave trading ports in Africa. These exports "flowed, in effect, within the same channels of the Atlantic economy that Britain had spent two hundred years and untold treasure building," the Harvard historian Sven Beckert noted in his 2014 opus, *Empire of Cotton*.[52]

Smith, for all his perspicacity, could have no inkling of the impact that cotton and industrialization would have on the economy, society, and policy-making. On July 17, 1790, at the age of sixty-seven, he died at his house in Edinburgh. That same year, an enterprise called Piccadilly Mill became the first cotton mill in Manchester to use a steam engine manufactured by Boulton and Watt, a firm that James Watt had established with his business partner Matthew Boulton. The fast-growing Lancashire city was on its way to replacing Bengal as the global leader in cotton manufacturing, and to giving its name to a school of economics based on Smith's ideas: the Manchester School.

3

The Logic of the Luddites

In the early hours of April 12, 1812, more than one hundred men approached Rawfolds Mill, a four-story building on the banks of the River Spen at Liversedge in West Yorkshire. This is Brontë country—a landscape of bleak moors, steep valleys, and small towns and hamlets. The members of the crowd, who had gathered on the moor hours earlier, were armed with muskets, sticks, hatchets, and heavy blacksmiths' hammers. When they reached the mill, the men at the front broke windows in an effort to gain entry. Some of them fired shots into the dark factory. Unbeknownst to the attackers, the mill's owner, William Cartwright, had been preparing for trouble.

During the previous twelve months, there had been a series of attacks on textile factories and workshops in central and northern England. The outbreak had begun in Nottinghamshire in early 1811, when some stocking knitters had stormed their employers' premises and disabled new machinery that they blamed for undercutting their wages and reducing them to penury. The attacks had spread to the neighboring county of Derbyshire; to Lancashire, the center of cotton manufacturing; and to the West Riding of Yorkshire, home to many woolen mills. Cartwright and other Yorkshire mill owners had been trying to mechanize the ancient art of "dressing" woven woolen cloth, which involved raising the nap and cutting it into finished pieces. For centuries, a tight-knit group of skilled workers, known as "shearers" or "croppers," had carried out this task manually using the spiked heads of teasel plants and handheld shears. Cartwright was trying to replace some of these workers with new machines: gig mills, which employed metal rollers to raise the nap, and shearing frames operated by a single millhand turning a crank. Weeks earlier a group of unidentified men had attacked a cart carrying some new machinery to Rawfolds Mill.

Since then Cartwright had been staying in the mill overnight with some of his other employees and armed reservists from the Cumberland Militia, one of many military units that the British authorities had dispatched to centers of unrest. According to one historian, more troops were deployed to put down the machine-breaking attacks than the Duke of Wellington had under his command in the Peninsular War against Napoleon Bonaparte.[1] The members of the Cumberland Militia had been ordered to repulse any assault on the Rawfolds Mill. When the attack began, they opened fire on the crowd. Some of Cartwright's men dropped rocks from the roof of the mill. The attackers, who hadn't been expecting much resistance, quickly scattered, leaving behind some of their weapons and two young men who had been seriously wounded. One of them had lost his job at the mill; the other was a saddler's apprentice from the nearby town of Huddersfield. Within forty-eight hours, both died from their wounds. At a subsequent inquest, a coroner issued a verdict of "justifiable homicide."[2]

For months the authorities searched for the organizers of the attack, employing paid informers. In January 1813, at York Castle, they put on trial fourteen croppers, who were charged with riot and machine breaking, which the Westminster Parliament, dominated by landowners and business interests, had the previous year deemed a capital offense in a special Frame-Breaking Act.[3] The court at York discharged some of the defendants, but five others were found guilty and sentenced to death.[4] In trials related to other incidents of violence and machine breaking in West Yorkshire, nine other men were also convicted.

On January 16, Yorkshire's official executioner, a former sheep stealer named William Wilkinson, swung the fourteen condemned men from a scaffold outside the castle. "I do not think any of them had a proper sense of the Crime they died for," one witness to the mass hangings, a Colonel Norton, recounted. "I mean any of the eight I call Luddites."[5]

It isn't clear where the term *Luddite* originated. Some accounts trace it back to Ned Ludd, a youthful textile worker from Leicestershire, a county just to the south of Nottinghamshire, who is said to have smashed a knitting frame in 1779 after being whipped for idleness. There's no documentary confirmation of Ludd's existence, however. The English historian Brian Bailey, whose book *The Luddite Rebellion* formed the basis of my account of the attack on Rawfolds Mill, suggests the term might go back to folk memories of King Ludeca, an Anglo-Saxon monarch who died in battle in AD 827.[6] Wherever the name came from, many of the machine-breakers identified "General Ludd" or "Captain Ludd" as their leader. A couple of weeks after the attack on Rawfolds Mill, in April 1812, the owner of a nearby woolen mill that had also introduced new machinery, a man named William Horsfall, was shot dead while riding home from a market. A public letter sent the day after Horsfall's assassination, which hailed "the avenging of the death of the two brav youths who fell at the sege of Rawfolds," began: "By Order of General Ludd."[7]

Watching the machine-breaking incidents from distant London, many members of the British government, which was still at war with Napoleon's France, regarded the participants as Jacobin insurrectionists. Brutal suppression was their response. As well as executing some Luddites, the British authorities deported others to penal colonies in Australia and elsewhere. But Luddism wasn't a revolutionary movement: it was a defensive reaction to a new economic system that, in places like Liversedge, was threatening the livelihoods of many skilled workers. Far from trying to overthrow the socio-economic system, the Luddites were trying to preserve their place within it.

If the Luddites weren't revolutionaries, they also weren't mindless opponents of modernity, as they have sometimes been portrayed. There was a clear logic to their actions, and it was essentially a conservative logic. With virtually no political representation or power—the voting franchise excluded the vast majority of the population—many of them concluded that violent protest was their only option. "The burning of Factorys or setting fire to the property of People we know is not right, but Starvation forces Nature to do that which he would not," one Yorkshire cropper wrote. "We have tried every Effort to live by Pawning our Cloaths and Chattles, so we are now on the brink for the last struggle."[8]

Industrialization involved the creation of new technologies, new jobs, new work norms, a new sexual division of labor, new patterns of geographical development, and new conglomerations of power and wealth. In the two decades since Adam Smith's death, the pace of development had accelerated, particularly in the cotton and woolen textile industries. By 1812, Manchester and the mill towns that surrounded it employed tens of thousands of people. The fastest-growing concentration of mills was in Ancoats, a Manchester neighborhood that was located next to the newly opened Rochdale Canal. Murrays' Mills, which was built by the Scottish brothers Adam and George Murray, consisted of two eight-story buildings, and its machinery was powered by steam engines built by Boulton and Watt.[9] The mills employed more than twelve hundred people and attracted visitors from near and far.

As the output of its mills rose, Lancashire began to replace India in many parts of the world as a supplier of cotton fabrics. Between 1780 and 1810, the value of its exports had increased from less than half a million pounds to more than £10 million.[10] The rise of the Lancashire industry was built on local endowments (including coal used to power the steam engines) and entrepreneurship but also on imported labor and raw materials, including immigrants from Ireland and raw cotton from the Caribbean islands and, increasingly, from the slave plantations of the American South. Much of this cotton came in through the port of Liverpool. Although Parliament had abolished the slave trade in 1807, following a lengthy campaign by William Wilberforce and his colleagues in the Evangelical movement, there was no prohibition on transporting products made by enslaved labor, and indeed, the rapid growth of the Lancashire cotton industry depended on these shipments continuing.

Although the advance of mechanization was most visible in cotton manufacturing, it was by no means confined to it. Across the Pennine Hills, in the West Riding of Yorkshire, the ancient woolen industry was also being transformed. In Leeds, on the banks of the River Aire, the merchant-manufacturer Benjamin Gott built the world's largest woolen mill, where, in 1793, he installed a steam engine from Boulton and Watt.[11] By 1800, Gott's factory employed more than a thousand people. Its organization was a testament to Smith's division of labor.[12] From the initial task of sorting and cleaning raw yarn to the final job of packing the finished cloth, there were twenty-nine separate production processes. Some of them quickly yielded to steam-powered mechanization. Other tasks, including the actual weaving of yarn, were carried out by hand. As Gott's business grew, his factories "dressed and blanketed a large part of the armies of England, Russia, Prussia, and Sweden," one historian recounted. "He served North American fur traders as well as Boston society; he sold cloth in South America and China, not to mention Germany and the Mediterranean countries."[13] A few miles from the Leeds city center, Gott bought a large estate and constructed a Greek Revival stone mansion. (Today it serves as the clubhouse of a municipal golf course that is named after him. As a teenager, the author of this book used to play there.)

Britain's technological leadership and growing economic power were abundantly evident to contemporaries. Shortly after the Napoleonic Wars ended, the French free market economist Jean-Baptiste Say traveled around the country. "It is not the military power of England, nor even that of her navy, which has given her a preponderating influence on the Continent, nor can it be said that it is her gold; for since 1797 she has had nothing but a paper money," Say wrote in an 1815 account of his trip. "But it is her wealth and her credit that have enabled her to exert this influence. And as these powerful weapons are the result of her whole economy, it is that which principally claims our attention."[14] Watt's steam engines, and the wide range of uses to which they had been put, particularly impressed the visiting Frenchman. "They spin and weave cotton and wool; they brew beer and they cut glass," he wrote. "I have seen some which embroider muslin and churn butter. At Newcastle and at Leeds, walking steam engines draw after them waggons of coal; and nothing more surprises a traveller, at first sight, than to meet in the country these long convoys, which proceed by themselves, and without the assistance of any living creature."[15]

The technological wonders that Say described were products of competition and the profit motive. Capitalist entrepreneurs like Cartwright and Gott were forever on the lookout for new machinery and new production methods. In a competitive environment, introducing new technology and reorganizing the workplace was a business imperative. The only limits to the process of mechanization were the pace at which science progressed and the resistance of workers whose living standards were threatened by the new Leviathan.

Among these embattled workers were the stocking knitters of the English Midlands, who in the early nineteenth century numbered in the tens of thousands. Under the "putting out" system that was common in the preindustrial era, many of them worked in their own cottages, where they knitted their products using hand-powered wooden frames. Others were employed in workshops owned by merchant-hosiers. Making stockings wasn't a factory industry, but the intensification of work that attended the rise of industrial capitalism increasingly affected it. During the late eighteenth century, a new breed of capitalist merchant emerged, who rented machinery to stockingers and purchased their output. There were widespread complaints that these intermediaries, sometimes referred as "bag hosiers," were exploiting the stockingers and undercutting the prices of their products.

A wartime slump in the textile industry intensified these tensions. Under Napoleon's Continental System, the French sought to bar British goods from Europe. In response, the British government issued a series of Orders in Council that blockaded French ports and sought to prevent neutral countries from trading with France. Demand for stockings and other goods fell sharply. Many of the merchant-hosiers responded by manufacturing cheaper new products, known as "cut-ups," which were made on wider frames from larger pieces of woven material that were stitched together in a seam. Compared to traditional stockings, cut-ups were of poor quality, but their low prices made them popular. As their sales grew, the stocking knitters saw their incomes decline sharply.[16] Between 1807 and 1812, their wages fell by about a third, according to one account.[17] Simultaneously, wartime pressures were causing the prices of corn and other foodstuffs to increase, making it increasingly hard for many knitters to feed their families.

Stocking knitters weren't a radical group. But as craft workers, they considered themselves to be entitled to protection by limits on competition that, in some cases, dated back hundreds of years. Many of these restrictions had statutory backing. In 1663 King Charles II granted a charter to the stockingers guild, which was called the Framework-Knitters Company, empowering it to inspect competing goods and destroy them if they had been manufactured shoddily or deceitfully. Although the royal charter had long fallen into disuse, the knitters invoked it in an 1812 declaration, claiming it gave them the right to "break and destroy" any frames that made cheap knock-offs or that belonged to hosiers who did "not pay the regular price heretofore agreed to by the Masters and Workmen."[18]

In March 1811 a crowd of knitters in the market town of Arnold broke into some workshops and smashed dozens of wide frames. Eight months later, in the town of Bulwell, knitters led by a fellow calling himself Ned Ludd attacked the house of a merchant-hosier named Edward Hollingsworth, who owned a large number of the loathed wide frames. Hollingsworth tried to defend his property. During the melee, a knitter named John Westley was shot dead, making him the first fatality of the Luddite protests.

Initially, some members of Britain's ruling class expressed sympathy for the protesters. "The high price of every thing necessary for their subsistence presses now still heavier upon these poor people," the Duke of Newcastle, who was serving as the lord lieutenant of Nottinghamshire, wrote to Richard Ryder, the home secretary. "I hope we may be able by some means to relieve them."[19] Other authority figures were much less sympathetic. George Coldham, the town clerk of Nottingham, who was also a leading figure in the Hosiers' Association, a local trade group, pleaded with Ryder to crush the protests with force before they spread further. "If the People are once taught that they can accomplish the objects of their wishes by a system of Terror," Coldham wrote, "I feel assured that they will proceed further than breaking Frames and it is Difficult to say who may be the next Objects of their Vengeance."[20]

In the woolen textile industry, the resistance to new methods of production was led by the croppers. Like the protesters at Liversedge, some of them worked in the mills. Others were employed in specialized workshops, which took in unfinished cloth and processed it for final sale. In both cases the croppers were well paid and highly independent. "The Cropper strictly speaking is not a servant," an 1803 article in the *Leeds Mercury* noted. "He does not feel, or call himself as such, but a cloth-worker, and partakes much more of the nature of a shoe-maker, joiner, taylor, &c. . . . Like them, he comes and goes, stops a longer, or a shorter time . . . according as he may chance to have work."[21]

During the 1790s, the merchant-manufacturers of Leeds had announced their intention to introduce new machines—shearing frames and gig mills— that automated some of the tasks carried out by the croppers, but the hostile reaction forced them to postpone their plans.[22] Still, the new technology represented an ongoing threat to the croppers. In trying to prevent the deployment of the new machines, they, like the stocking knitters, appealed to ancient precedent—a ban on early prototypes of gig mills, which King Edward VI had introduced in 1551. Some members of Parliament at Westminster were sympathetic to the knitters' plight, but the legislature ultimately took the side of the mill owners. In 1809 it repealed all prior legislation that had regulated the introduction of gig mills and shearing frames.[23]

Faced with a hostile state, the West Riding croppers took their resistance underground, creating secret societies and reciting oaths of loyalty. It wasn't until after machine-breaking attacks broke out in the Midlands that they engaged in violence. In January 1812, someone set on fire a Leeds finishing mill that was using gig mills. The disturbances quickly spread to Halifax and Huddersfield, two sizable towns, and to the Spen Valley, where the abortive assault on Rawfolds Mill was followed by further exercises in intimidation. One mill owner in Huddersfield received a letter from "General Ludd" that read: "Information has just been given in that you are a holder of those detestable Shearing Frames . . . If they are not taken down by the end of next Week, I will detach one of my Lieutenants with at least 300 Men to destroy them . . . and if you have [the] Impudence to fire upon any of my Men, they have orders to murder you, & burn all your Housing."[24] In Leeds, Benjamin Gott, whom the croppers fiercely disliked, received an anonymous note that said: "No doubt you are Informd as to the proceedins of the Ludites . . . Be Carful of your Self for a few Weeks—alter your usal walks to your Business."[25]

Threats like these were more often issued than carried out. But between 1811 and 1813, there was unrest in many parts of northern England. In Lancashire, it centered on the handloom weavers—men, women, and children who wove cotton yarn into cloth on wooden handlooms, often in their own homes. Ironically, the early stages of industrialization had been a boon to the weavers. The new spinning machines invented by Arkwright, James Hargreaves, and others greatly increased the British cotton industry's capacity to produce yarn. Because the intricate process of weaving yarn into cloth for decades proved too complicated to mechanize, the demand for the labor of handloom weavers increased sharply. Between 1780 and 1812, the number of handlooms more than quadrupled, from 37,000 to 208,000.[26]

Most weavers were paid piece rates, which rewarded them for producing more. Until about 1800, they appear to have enjoyed rising incomes. Many weavers lived in cottages that had workshops, and handlooms, on the second floor, where the light was best. One contemporary described these "dwellings and small gardens" as "clean and neat—all the family well clad—the men with each a watch in his pocket, and the women dressed to their own fancy."[27]

The weavers' reprieve from the rigors of industrial capitalism was only temporary. In 1785 Edmund Cartwright, an inventor from Nottinghamshire who was also a cleric, patented a crude weaving machine, or loom, that could be powered by water or steam. Cartwright worked to improve his invention, obtaining a final patent in 1792. The new machine didn't take off immediately—it wasn't easy to use and required more tinkering—but during the early nineteenth century, some Lancashire mill owners started to employ power looms in significant numbers. This development, together with a slump in the global demand for textiles during the Napoleonic Wars, caused weavers' incomes to fall sharply. According to one estimate, between 1804 and 1810 their wages fell by more than 40 percent.[28]

Initially, the weavers reacted to this hardship peacefully. Under the repressive Combination Acts of 1799 and 1800, forming labor unions, or other types of workers' associations, was illegal. Even without any formal organization, though, the weavers gathered about 130,000 signatures for a petition demanding the introduction of a minimum wage, which they submitted to the House of Commons. In May 1808 Parliament rejected the petition, provoking an immediate response. In cotton towns across Lancashire, there were strikes and riots. During one of these protests, the Rochdale jail was burned down. The weavers, like the croppers, took their resistance underground, forming clandestine committees and swearing secret oaths. There was sporadic violence, but nothing on a large scale until March 1812, a month before the attack on Rawfolds Mill, when, in Stockport, a town just east of Manchester, unknown attackers set alight a factory-cum-warehouse whose owner, William Radcliffe, had introduced power looms.[29]

The following month a crowd of thousands attacked a mill containing power looms at Middleton, just north of Manchester. "Vollies of stones were thrown, and the windows smashed to atoms; the internal part of the building being guarded, a musket was discharged in the hope of intimidating and dispersing the assailants," the *Manchester Gazette* reported.[30] "In a very short time the effects were too shockingly seen in the death of three, and it is said, about ten wounded." The following day a crowd of protesters returned to the Middleton mill. After failing to gain entry, they burned down the house of its owner, Daniel Burton. Military units confronted the rioters. In the ensuing violence, at least seven more people were killed.[31]

The Luddite protests fused with more generalized discontent about the depressed wartime economy and the rising cost of living, which was driving many workers to near starvation. During the spring and summer of 1812, food riots broke out in towns and cities across northern England, including Leeds, Sheffield, and Carlisle. In the middle of April, a Stockport mill that used power looms was burned down, and a second mill, which used new machines to dress the woven yarn, was threatened. Its owner, Thomas Garside, received an anonymous letter, signed "General Justice," that threatened to burn down his factory if he didn't remove the new machinery. "Remember We have given you fare Warning and if your factory is Burn, it is your own fault," the letter said. "It is Not our Desire to doo you the Least Injury But We are fully Determined to Destroy Both Dressing Machines and Steam Looms."[32]

Messages like this one confirm that the primary target of the Luddites was the industrial system rather than individual factory owners. The machine breakers may have lacked formal education, but they understood how industrial capitalism was affecting them and the fact that they couldn't rely on the government or any other powerful institutions to protect them. In some cases, the Luddites extended their threats to businesses that were helping to support the factory owners. In the town of Wigan, near Manchester, an anonymous correspondent calling himself Falstaff addressed a letter to a fire insurance company, in which he invoked the name of "General Ludds" and demanded that the firm cease insuring any business owner "who keeps winding machines or any other such like things in their Employment." The letter writer identified a number of other businesses whose premises "will be looked into in short time if they continue in said way of Robbing the Poor of their Bread."[33]

Lacking formal organization and confronted by a ruling elite that didn't hesitate to employ state violence, the Luddites were fighting for a cause that was largely, but not entirely, hopeless. For a time, the stocking knitters of Nottinghamshire and Derbyshire did manage to prevent the spread of cheap "cut-ups," and the price of stockings rose, although only temporarily. Elsewhere, the designation of machine breaking as a capital offense, followed by the trials and executions of 1813, had the deterrent effect that the authorities intended. The number of attacks on factories declined sharply, even as the trends that had given rise to them accelerated. Mechanization and the drive to cut costs continued to undermine the economic position of the stockingers and croppers; the weavers had it worst of all. Their wages, after rebounding for a few years between 1810 and 1815, went into another long, and this time irreversible, decline. By 1820, weekly wage levels were about 60 percent below their level of twenty years earlier, and by 1830 the decline had reached about 80 percent.[34] Parliamentary reports from the 1820s and '30s are replete with harrowing descriptions of weavers dressed in rags and struggling to feed themselves and their families.

One witness to a select committee recounted visiting a starving family in the small town of Westhoughton, northwest of Manchester: "We there found on one side of the fire a very old man, apparently dying, on the other side a young man about eighteen with a child on his knee, whose mother had just died and been buried."[35] This was immiseration before the term came into use. As the weavers saw demand for their services disappear and their incomes collapse, many of them were forced out of the industry or left of their own volition. Between 1820 and 1845, their numbers fell from 240,000 to 60,000.[36]

In history books, the Luddite movement is often portrayed as a struggle over mechanization and the social impact of technical progress. But as the historian E. P. Thompson pointed out many years ago in his classic work, *The Making of the English Working Class*, that was only part of the story. What was at stake, Thompson wrote, wasn't simply workers' opposition to new machinery but "the freedom of the capitalist to destroy the customs of the trade, whether by new machinery, by the factory-system, or by unrestricted competition, beating-down wages, undercutting his rivals, and undermining standards of craftsmanship." The most central issue was the morality, or immorality, of a new economic system that, in the minds of its victims, was violating a long-established set of social values and reciprocal obligations. The Luddites "saw *laissez-faire* not as freedom, but as 'foul Imposition,'" Thompson pointed out. "They could see no 'natural law' by which one man, or a few men, could engage in practices which brought manifest injury to their fellows."[37]

Even some members of the upper orders sympathized with these sentiments. One of them was the romantic poet Lord Byron, whose maiden speech in the House of Lords, delivered on February 27, 1812, amounted to a passionate defense of the Luddites. Byron, who was only twenty-four, had recently returned from a grand tour of Europe and the Levant to his mother's home in Nottinghamshire, where some stocking knitters were busy attacking workshops. "During the short time I recently passed in Nottinghamshire, not twelve hours elapsed without some fresh act of violence; and, on the day I left the county, I was informed that forty frames had been broken the preceding evening," the young poet told the assembled peers. "But whilst these outrages must be admitted to exist to an alarming extent, it cannot be denied that they have arisen from circumstances of the most unparalleled distress."[38]

Byron went on to describe how the domestic impact of the Napoleonic Wars and the introduction of new types of knitting frames had combined to decimate the knitters' incomes and throw many of them out of work. Only desperation could drive such an "honest and industrious body of the people"[39] to resort to violence, he said, and he criticized the government and its supporters in the Lords for sending in the military to put down the protests:

> You call these men a mob, desperate, dangerous and ignorant, and seem to think that the only way to quiet the 'Bellua multorum capitum,' is to lop off a few of its superfluous heads . . . Are we aware of our obligations to a mob? It is the mob that labour in your fields and serve in your houses— that man your navy, and recruit your army—that have enabled you to defy all the world, and can also defy you, when neglect and calamity have driven them to despair! You may call the people a mob; but do not forget that a mob too often speaks the sentiment of the people.[40]

Byron also criticized the Frame-Breaking Act, which Parliament was then debating, and the prospective capital punishments associated with it. "How will you carry the Bill into effect?" he asked. "Will you erect a gibbet in every field, and hang up men like scarecrows? or will you proceed (as you must to bring this measure into effect) by decimation? Place the country under martial law? depopulate and lay waste all around you?"[41] Even as Byron appealed for an understanding of the workers' cause, he must have known that his speech would have no impact on policy. The stocking knitters themselves, before resorting to machine breaking, had in vain appealed for a parliamentary intervention on their behalf. That precedent didn't put Byron off. In 1816 he returned to the defense of the machine breakers, this time in verse. In the first stanza of his poem "Song for the Luddites," he wrote:

> As the Liberty lads o'er the sea
> Bought their freedom, and cheaply, with blood,
> So we, boys, we
> Will die fighting, or live free,
> And down with all kings but King Ludd![42]

4

"It is time . . . to seek for a radical, a permanent cure of the evils that afflict society"

William Thompson's Utilitarian Socialism

The immiseration of handicraft workers wasn't the only downside of industrialization. Two years after Byron wrote his tribute poem to the Luddites, an underground journal based in London, *Black Dwarf*, published a firsthand account of conditions in the Manchester cotton mills, where a new class of industrial workers, many of them women and children, were working long hours for low wages. The anonymous author, who identified himself as a cotton spinner, invited his readers to "stand in an avenue leading to a factory a little before five o'clock in the morning, and observe the squalid appearance of the little infants and their parents taken from their beds at so early an hour in all kinds of weather."[1]

In the mills of Ancoats and other cotton-manufacturing districts, workers—some of them as young as eight or nine—were working twelve- or fourteen-hour days. To prevent the yarns from snapping, mill owners kept their factories hot and damp, which caused respiratory ailments. The owners also imposed strict discipline on their workers. "There they are (and if late a few minutes, a quarter of a day is stopped in wages) locked up until night locked up in rooms heated above the hottest days we have had this summer," the cotton spinner wrote, "and allowed no time, except three quarters of an hour at dinner, in the whole day." The mill owners in their domestic lives put on an "ostentatious display of elegant mansions, equipages, liveries, parks, hunters, hounds, &c," the writer noted. At work, their overriding goal was to "keep wages low for the purpose of keeping the spinners indigent and spirit-less . . . as for the purpose of taking the surplus to their own pockets."[2]

The use of the term *surplus* is instructive. From Byron and his fellow poet Robert Southey, to the Tory patricians Richard Oastler and Michael Sadler, a number of upper-class Englishmen inveighed against the depredations that industrial capitalism was bringing in its wake, echoing some of the Luddites' complaints. But whereas these critiques tended to be cast in moral terms, a group of critics from the left focused on the economics of the new system and the possibilities of replacing it with something fairer and more communal. These thinkers didn't have much, if any, influence on policymaking, which increasingly hewed toward laissez-faire. But they helped lay the intellectual foundations for a political countermovement to industrial capitalism: socialism.

William Thompson was born in 1775 in the Irish port of Cork. He hailed from a wealthy family, which was part of the Protestant ascendancy that ruled Ireland. His father, John Thompson, was a merchant who imported, among other things, sugar, rum, and tea, and exported Irish butter. (He also served as the mayor of Cork.) Some details of William Thompson's early life are lacking, but he appears to have been well educated and spent time in France and the Low Countries.[3] The Irish historian Fintan Lane says that he became a partner in the family firm in 1800 and took it over five years later, when his father retired. A successful businessman he wasn't. In 1808 a court declared him bankrupt, with £13,000 in debts outstanding. Fortunately for him, his father owned a large estate near the scenic coastal village of Glandore. When John Thompson died in 1814, William inherited this land, which was cultivated by tenant farmers. It gave him an annual income of roughly £600, which enabled him to concentrate on his real passion: reading and writing.[4]

Thompson became an active member, and benefactor, of the Royal Cork Institution, an educational center that maintained a library of scientific works and put on public lectures. His main interests were philosophy and political economy, but he also read widely about science, medicine, and agriculture. A confirmed atheist, he seems to have taken delight in outraging many of his social peers, particularly the churchgoing ones, Protestant and Roman Catholic. In Glandore, some of the local folk referred to him as "the philosopher" and considered him a magician. "It is said in the locality that he read the latest books on medicine, tested their theories on his sick neighbors, and when he effected a cure he would jokingly tell his patients not to thank God but his pills and the devil," Thompson's first biographer, Richard Pankhurst, wrote. "Such atheistic utterances were regarded indulgently by an unquestioning Catholic community because of his unfailing kindness and good humour."[5]

Unlike many Irish landlords of the time, Thompson cared about the welfare of his tenant farmers, who, like the vast majority of the Irish population under British rule, were poor and illiterate. To help raise them up, he advocated education reform. In 1818 he published a pamphlet that called for "a cheap and liberal system of education, adapted to active life, superior to what schools can teach."[6] Thompson was heavily influenced by the philosopher Jeremy Bentham and his doctrine of utilitarianism, which demanded that all institutions and policies be evaluated based on whether they contributed to the "greatest happiness of the greatest number."[7] Bentham was another fervent advocate of education reform, and Thompson sent the great man a series of letters. Evidently Bentham was impressed by his correspondent. In 1819 he invited Thompson to stay at his home in Queen's Square Place, Westminster, and share his regimented daily regime. "Hour of dinner, six," Bentham wrote to Thompson; "tea between nine and ten; bed, a quarter before eleven. Dinner and tea in society; breakfast my guests, whoever they are, have at their own hour, and by themselves."[8]

Despite his admiration for Bentham, Thompson didn't initially take up his invitation. Instead, he turned his attention to a book about the distribution of wealth and income. This project was inspired, he would later explain, by a public lecture he attended in Cork, where "a gentleman celebrated for his skill in the controversies of political economy thought proper to descant on the blessings of the *inequality* of wealth, as now established; on the dependence and consequent gratitude which the poor should feel to the rich; on the too-great freedom and too-great equality of wealth of the United States of America."[9] Outraged by these arguments, Thompson embarked on a study of political economy, initially with a view to preparing a brief public lecture about it. The project turned into a multiyear endeavor.

In the fall of 1822, Thompson did visit London. From October until February 1823, he stayed at Bentham's townhouse. Evidently, he was an entertaining guest. A young woman named Henrietta Wheeler, whose mother knew the Irishman, and who was in attendance while Bentham sat for a portrait recounted Thompson insisting that he could play the part of the Harlequin, a popular comic figure in the theater of the time. After gathering his cloak around him, Thompson "capered, kicked, and frisked and flung about for some time *à la* harlequin, whilst his enlightened and discerning audience were in strong convulsions on the floor," Wheeler wrote to her sister.[10]

Bentham advised Thompson to visit Hazelwood School, near Birmingham, a Utilitarian institution that the pupils ran themselves using a Benthamite rulebook. Among the public figures that Thompson met through Bentham were Joseph Hume, a radical member of Parliament; John Black, the editor of *The Morning Chronicle*, a Whig newspaper; and the Scottish intellectual James Mill, whose textbook *Elements of Political Economy* had recently appeared.[11] Mill was also the author of a multivolume history of India, which portrayed the East India Company as a civilizing influence in a backward and morally degraded society. A couple of years after it was published, the Company gave Mill a lucrative sinecure as an advocate and "examiner of Indian correspondence."[12] (In subsequent years, Mill's brilliant son, John Stuart Mill, would also work for the Company.)

There is no record of whether Thompson met David Ricardo, the economic theorist who was another member of Bentham's circle. But his writings indicate that he studied Ricardo's work closely, including his 1817 book *On the Principles of Political Economy and Taxation*, which argued that the economy, like the rest of nature, was subject to inviolable natural laws. In Ricardo's model of the economy, there are three inputs to the production process—labor, capital, and land—but it is only labor that creates value. (Raw materials, machinery, and buildings contribute merely their own value.) It is therefore the quantity of labor inputs that determines a commodity's value in the marketplace. If a certain item takes one hour of labor to make and another item takes two hours, the second item will sell for double the price of the first. This labor theory of value, as it came to be known, can be traced back to Adam Smith and even to John Locke, the Enlightenment philosopher. Ricardo expressed it most clearly, however.

Thompson also studied the works of two radical continental thinkers: Henri de Saint-Simon and Jean Charles Léonard de Sismondi.[13] Saint-Simon was a French aristocrat who fought alongside Lafayette in the American Revolution, went into land speculation, and in his forties started publishing books about economics. He divided society into two groups: the productive industrial class (*les industriels*), which consisted of entrepreneurs, engineers, and manual workers; and the idle class (*les oisifs*), which included landlords, rentiers, and assorted loafers. In Saint-Simon's technocratic vision of the future, enlightened businessmen (*les grandes industriels*) would replace the landed elite as the ruling class, but unlike the old aristocracy, they would rule benevolently, exploiting advances in science and technology to organize production for the benefit of all, including the poor. Saint-Simon's ideas didn't have much immediate impact on policy, but they attracted a group of followers, the Saint-Simonians, who continued to expound various versions of them after his death in 1825.

Sismondi, a Swiss scholar who started out as a disciple of Adam Smith, is best known for his 1819 book, *New Principles of Political Economy*, in which he reversed course and critiqued the laissez-faire ideas associated with Smith and Jean-Baptiste Say, which posited that a market economy was self-organizing and stable. Reacting to the deep slump that afflicted France and other countries after the Napoleonic Wars, Sismondi took the Latin term *proletarii*, which referred to propertyless Roman citizens, and applied it to the industrial working class, which was experiencing joblessness and severe hardship.[14] He called for extensive public welfare programs, including unemployment and sickness benefits, financed by progressive taxes.

Sismondi also warned that the very productiveness of the new system made it potentially unstable. He argued that as technical progress raised the economy's capacity, the supply of goods could well exceed overall demand, which was limited by the level of wages. This imbalance could lead to lengthy gluts, in which businesses would be forced to lay off workers, resulting in widespread joblessness and hunger. "Let us beware of this dangerous theory of equilibrium which is supposed to be automatically established," Sismondi wrote, referring to the reassuring doctrine of laissez-faire. "A certain kind of equilibrium, it is true, is reestablished in the long run, but it is after a frightful amount of suffering."[15]

Thompson never did deliver the brief lecture on political economy that he had planned to give. But in 1824, he published a lengthy book titled *An Inquiry into the Principles of the Distribution of Wealth Most Conducive to Human Happiness*. For readers who persevered with this hefty tome, it contained an original and broad-ranging analysis that began with Thompson highlighting what he viewed as the central paradox presented by British industrialization: rapid technological progress and unprecedented levels of production accompanied by widespread poverty and destitution. "How comes it," he asked, "that a nation abounding more than any other in the rude materials of wealth, in machinery, dwellings, and food, in intelligent and industrious producers, with all the apparent means of happiness . . . should still pine in privation?"[16] The answer, Thompson went on, was to be found in the basic structure of the new economy: the rigid dividing line between propertyless "producers" of wealth—i.e., the workers—and the property-owning elite of "capitalists," who owned the factories and machinery used in the production process. "The tendency of the existing arrangement of things as to wealth is to enrich a few at the expense of the mass of the producers," Thompson stated bluntly.[17]

Having defined the nature of the problem as he saw it, Thompson shifted into prescriptive mode, setting down fifteen "natural laws" on which "all just distribution of wealth ought to be founded." The first two laws amounted to restatements of Ricardo's labor theory of value and Bentham's admonition to promote the greatest happiness of the greatest number. The third law was more novel, and it was key to Thompson's egalitarian philosophy: "All members of society . . . being similarly constituted in their physical organisation, are capable, by similar treatment, of enjoying equal portions of happiness."[18] In other words, all people are equally effective happiness machines.

These three principles, in themselves, were sufficient to justify an egalitarian outlook. Thompson further developed the argument by invoking another principle that he borrowed from Bentham, which can be summarized in the statement that an extra hundred pounds is worth a lot more to a poor person than to a rich one because the poor person's need is far greater. This idea, which economists today refer to as the diminishing marginal utility of income, Thompson stated thus: "Of 1,000 portions of the matter of wealth, the first 100, suppose are necessary to repel hunger and thirst and support life. The use of this first portion is as life to death . . . The effect of these second 100 in intensity of enjoyment is so infinitely beneath that produced by the first 100 as to be incapable of any comparison." He continued: "Every hundred added is less and less productive of absolute increase of happiness to the possessor."[19]

After establishing this key point, Thompson went on to argue that it was impossible to justify, on logical grounds, the diversion of income from poor workers to rich capitalists, because the "*evil* of the loss and *its consequences* to the productive laborer exceed in a degree very great, though not being capable of being put down in numbers, the advantages of the gain to the rapacious." This is the classic utilitarian argument for equality of income and wealth. It can be shown mathematically that if people are equally effective happiness machines and the marginal utility of income is uniformly diminishing, the wealth distribution that maximizes total happiness is an equal one, with everybody enjoying the same level of riches. Thompson didn't develop the argument formally, but in laying out its basic elements he was arguably the first economist to make a rigorous argument for socialism.

Unlike some of his socialist successors, Thompson didn't demand perfect equality: he accepted that some inequity could be justified if it raised overall output and wealth. But he also insisted that the gaping chasms between rich and poor that were arising in the new industrial economy couldn't be defended on this basis. They arose not from the greater productivity of the capitalist class but from its monopoly on the ownership of capital and the neediness of its workers, which enabled it to pay low wages and generate high profits. "What accumulated wealth there is in such a community, is gathered into the hands of the few; and as well from its bulk as from its contrast with the surrounding poverty, it strikes every eye," Thompson wrote. "The productive laborers, stript of all capital, of tools, houses, and materials to make their labour productive toil from want, from the necessity of existence, their remuneration being kept at the lowest compatible with the existence of industrious habits . . . The extremes of luxury and magnificence prevail. The evils of inequality are pushed to the utmost."[20]

This passage relied on the idea that wages would stay at or close to subsistence levels, which was a common theme of classical economics. Where Thompson departed from orthodoxy was in combining it with the labor theory of value to generate a general theory of exploitation. He pointed out that if workers' wages were held at subsistence levels but the prices of the goods they produced reflected the amount of labor embodied in them, workers would get paid less than the value they created. Thompson referred to value that workers created but failed to receive in wages as "surplus value"—he seems to have been the first writer to use this term—and he identified it as the fundamental driver of economic inequality.[21]

In making this argument, Thompson zeroed in on a key issue in any economy. How should an individual capitalist, an investor, or a government be rewarded for supplying the funds that a business uses to buy the equipment and raw materials its workers require to produce goods (or services) that people want to buy? In Thompson's time (and still today), orthodox economists glossed over this question by assuming that any revenues in excess of a business's costs would naturally accrue to the supplier of capital as profit. Thompson pointed out that this wasn't the only possible way to organize, or think about, an industrial economy. He suggested looking at things from the perspective of producers—i.e., workers—who have the ability to create value but lack the inputs and machinery they need to make marketable commodities. In an ideal world, how should they reward owners of capital for supplying them with these things? One option, Thompson said, would be to give the capitalist a sum sufficient to "replace the waste and value of the capital" he supplied, and also to provide him with the means to "support him in equal comfort with the more actively employed productive laborers."[22]

The difference between this arrangement and the existing one was "immense," Thompson noted.[23] If it were ever adopted, he pointed out, it would enable workers to receive more of the value they created and raise their living standards. The capitalist mogul wouldn't lose everything—his capital would still yield a steady return—but he would "be but reduced to a situation intermediate in point of *wealth* between his present situation and that of the present degraded labourer."[24] In a ringing passage, Thompson made it very clear which of the two arrangements he preferred. As "the idle possessor of these inanimate instruments of production," he thundered, the capitalist "procures ten times, a hundred times, a thousand times, as much of the articles of wealth . . . as the utmost labour of such [an] efficient [worker] can procure for them."[25]

Thompson didn't base his argument for radical changes solely on moral grounds. He also insisted that rewarding workers in the same manner as capitalists would generate higher levels of output and productivity. When workers' wages were stuck at or near subsistence levels, they had little incentive to exert themselves or learn new skills, he pointed out. By contrast, in an economy where "the whole of the products of labour [are] ensured to the producer, the utmost energy would be employed in production, and necessarily in the acquisition and retaining of those means or instruments indispensable to render labor productive."[26] Switching to this type of compensation system would have a dramatic impact, Thompson argued: "Four times, or, perhaps, ten times the quantity of production, on the whole, would be obtained."[27]

These numbers were outlandish: even a twofold increase in production would have been remarkable. But the novelty of Thompson's analysis was striking. Combining an incentives argument that harked back to Smith and a labor theory of value derived from Ricardo, he made the case that it was feasible to simultaneously expand the economy and reduce inequality, which in turn would fulfill the utilitarian goal of raising human happiness. "The mass of national wealth would be immensely greater than at present, though no person might possess ten times more accumulated capital than his neighbour," he wrote. "All the increase of happiness proved to arise from equality of distribution would prevail; and men would produce for the sake of the *absolute* comforts to be derived from wealth, not for the sake of mere *relative* comforts, of a comparison of their superiority with the wretchedness of their fellow-creatures."[28]

After this extended theoretical discussion of inequality and exploitation, Thompson moved on to the practical question of how to implement his egalitarian ideas, and the answer he provided was to organize the economy around self-governing cooperative communities. He said that establishing communal entities of this nature was the best way to create a more equal society and maximize human happiness. In arguing in this direction, he was following in the footsteps of two visionaries from either side of the English Channel.

The lesser-known one, at least in Britain and Ireland, was the Frenchman Charles Fourier. Born in Besançon, near the Swiss border, in 1772, Fourier, the son of a small businessman, spent the first half of his life in obscurity as a merchant and traveling salesman. In his thirties, he started to write and turned out to have a lively imagination. In a book published in 1808, he argued that human societies ascend and then descend through thirty-two periods, the highest of which was Harmony. To create this idyll, he proposed arranging the world on the basis of self-contained communities that he called "phalanxes," each consisting of about sixteen hundred people. Members of a phalanx would live together in a large building, a phalanstery, which would have communal dining rooms and educational facilities, as well as individual apartments. Each community would be largely self-supporting, and work would be divided equally, with tasks rotated to avoid boredom.[29]

Fourier's ambitious vision initially attracted little interest outside France. Thompson was more heavily influenced by Robert Owen, a Welsh industrialist and philanthropist who was a major figure in early nineteenth-century Britain. In 1817, during the economic slump after the Napoleonic Wars, when large numbers of unemployed workers were roaming the country, Owen had called for the creation of "Villages of Co-operation," where jobless workers could live and grow their own food without being a burden on the state. Owen quickly came to view his proposed communities in much broader terms—as the basis for a society based on cooperation rather than competition, where technology would be exploited for the benefit of all rather than the few. "New scientific power will soon render human labor of little avail in the creation of wealth," he declared during a speaking tour of Europe. "Wealth can be created in such abundance as to satisfy the desires of all."[30] The task was to spread it out effectively.

Owen had risen to fortune and fame as a philanthropic cotton manufacturer. He was born in 1771, in the small market town of Newtown, Montgomeryshire, where his father was the local postmaster and ironmonger. After leaving school at ten, he took a job as a lowly draper's apprentice, but his career progressed rapidly. When he was nineteen, he got a job managing a cotton mill in Manchester and was soon promoted to part owner. The callous treatment of workers that he saw in the new cotton factories appalled him. In 1799, together with some associates, he bought a complex of water-powered cotton mills at New Lanark, a village south of Glasgow, in Scotland, where he set out to demonstrate that workers could be more productive if they were treated as humans.[31]

The New Lanark mills didn't pay particularly high wages, but Owen shortened the workday, built sturdy cottages for his employees, and provided them with cheap goods from a company store. He refused to employ children below the age of ten or eleven, which, by the standards of the day, was a progressive stance. Visitors from far and wide flocked to New Lanark, and Owen became a public figure. After the Napoleonic Wars, he launched a campaign to restrict child labor, which culminated in the passage of the Cotton Mill and Factories Act of 1819, which prohibited the employment of anyone under the age of nine and limited to twelve hours the workday of children ages nine to sixteen. Although the legislation lacked an effective enforcement mechanism, its passage helped establish the principle that factory capitalism should be regulated.

In *Report to the County of Lanark*, a pamphlet published in 1820,[32] Owen expanded upon his vision of communal living, which shared some things with Fourier's vision. Owen said the inhabitants of his new communities would live in purposefully constructed buildings arranged around a square. Each family would have a private apartment with its own bedrooms, but the sitting areas and kitchens would be communal. Owen was a believer in early education for children of both sexes. "Men are, and ever will be, what they are, and shall be made, in infancy and childhood," he wrote. In each of his proposed communities, schooling would be mandatory. There would be two purpose-built schoolhouses: one for children ages two to six, the other for those ages six to twelve.

Owen's proposals attracted the attention of some workers' groups. In 1821 a meeting in London of printers and other tradesmen established a Cooperative and Economical Society. In its constitution, the new organization said its ultimate goal was to "establish a village of unity and mutual co-operation, combining agriculture, manufactures, and trades, upon the plan projected by Robert Owen of New Lanark."[33] This venture didn't make much immediate progress, however, and Owen got frustrated. In 1825, the year after Thompson published the *Inquiry*, Owen and his son William sailed to the United States with the goal of establishing a new cooperative community in Harmony Township, Indiana, where land was cheaper than it was in Britain. The Rappites, a German community of farmers and artisans, had put their settlement on the banks of the Wabash River up for sale. In January 1825, Owen purchased the Rappites' land, some twenty thousand acres. Weeks later, he went to Washington and addressed the House of Representatives about his ambitious experiment in communal living. By the summer of 1856, it had been renamed New Harmony and attracted hundreds of eager participants.

In the *Inquiry*, Thompson hailed Owen as a bold visionary and said his proposals for independent cooperative communities were "the result of a rare union of profound thought and unequalled practical knowledge."[34] He also endorsed some of the details of Owen's plans, such as constructing housing in squares, or quadrangles, and providing schools and exercise grounds. But even as Thompson praised some of Owen's practical ideas, he developed his own ideas for enacting them. While the two shared the same goals, they had different political and philosophical outlooks.

Although Owen was a radical, he believed in the possibility of reform within the existing political system. He held out hopes for the state endorsing his new communities and helping to finance their establishment. Thompson was far less hopeful about the prospects for peaceful reform. He wasn't a revolutionary; he abhorred violence. "[T]he employment of such an instrument would annihilate production" and undermine any notion of economic security, he wrote.[35] But he also believed that the British political system was utterly corrupted and that the state, far from being an agency of progress, served mainly to secure the property rights of the wealthy.

More orthodox scholars had recognized this function, of course, but they had viewed it in a positive light. In *The Wealth of Nations*, Adam Smith portrayed the securing of property rights as the mark of human progress from the "Age of Hunters" to the "Age of Commerce." The framers of the US Constitution held a similar view. By contrast, Thompson wrote: "What has been hitherto worshipped under the false name of security, has been the security of a few at the expense of the plunder, the degradation of the many, particularly of the whole mass of the operatives, the real producers of wealth."[36] Further on in the book, he added:

> As long as two hostile masses of interest are suffered to exist in society, the owners of labour on one side and the owners of the means of labouring on the other, as long as this unnatural distribution is forcibly maintained—for without force, wielded by ignorance, it could not be maintained—so long will, perhaps as much as nine-tenths of attainable human happiness never be brought into existence, and so long will ninety-nine one hundred parts of attainable human happiness be sacrificed.[37]

Unlike Marx and Engels, Thompson didn't go quite so far as to call the state the executive committee of the bourgeoisie. He did write that excessive wealth inequality "necessarily leads to the usurpation of the powers of legislation, as well as of the executive and judicial authority, by those unqualified by education to exercise them aright, and with interests hostile to the general, or national interest."[38] As an example of this corruption, Thompson cited the British government's repeated coddling of the East India Company despite its repeated abuses and financial problems. "Legally plundering the people with whom they trade, to make up for the balance of losses caused by every species of waste and abuse!" he wrote. "Why, then, does this Company continue to exist? Private sinister interest and political considerations support it."[39]

To Thompson, government and "the whole system of human regulations"—by which he meant things like monopoly charters—were "little more than a tissue of restraints and usurpations of one class over another."[40] To someone with these beliefs, it was an illusion to believe that the state, at least in its current form, could play much of a productive role. Thompson was skeptical of all forms of authority. His socialism had an anarchistic streak that emphasized decentralization, individual initiative, and self-governance. In the second half of the *Inquiry*, he set out his proposals for a "System of Voluntary Equality" based on these principles and on "Mutual Co-operation."[41]

The central idea was similar to Robert Owen's: establish new communities in which most of the property would be commonly owned, production would be organized on a communal basis, and income would be divided equitably, if not necessarily equally. In Thompson's version, each community would consist of between five hundred and two thousand people; it would grow its own food and operate its own manufacturing workshops. Since each individual "co-operator" would be both a productive worker and a part owner of the community's land and capital, class divisions would be eliminated. "There would be no other interest in the community, but that of producers; there would be no capitalists," Thompson wrote.[42] The members of the community would "be alternately employed in agricultural and manufacturing industry," and the variety of work would make their lives "more productive, more healthful, and more pleasant."[43]

Despite the clear echoes of Fourier and Owen, Thompson also had some distinctive ideas of his own about how to organize these new cooperative communities. To obtain items that they couldn't grow or manufacture themselves, they would engage in trade with other communities. Exchange values would be set on the basis of how much labor each good embodied. In all transactions, "the greater interests, that of the labourer, would preponderate."[44] Inside each community, the communal principle would extend to domestic life. Everybody would be "fed and clad out of the common store," and children and young people would sleep in "common dormitories for the different sexes and ages." Single adults and married couples would have private apartments, but there would be "public rooms for dining, reading, lectures, amusements, &c."[45] Reflecting Thompson's commitment to atheism and popular representation, the new communities would guarantee "entire freedom as to thought and worship," and they would be run by committees "appointed by election, or rotation, or seniority, or any other manner that may be proposed to such community and by them agreed on."[46]

Thompson envisaged the establishment of his new communities as a gradual process, with the early ones serving as models for later ones, but his ultimate objective was to replace the existing organization of society, not merely build a cooperative alternative alongside it. In keeping with his passion for local self-government and his skepticism about existing political institutions, he wanted to radically downsize the state. Once the principles of cooperation and self-governance had been established, they would have eliminated not just the "passion for individual accumulation and display of wealth," Thompson wrote, but also the need for "almost all . . . of the ordinary functions of government."[47] The central government would still provide for national defense and other public goods, but the individual communities would pay for it on a voluntary basis, and these financial contributions would be "inconceivably small."

Although Thompson was little known to the British public, his ideas about cooperative communities attracted some attention in metropolitan circles. In 1825 he and others engaged in a public debate at Chancery Lane with John Stuart Mill, who was then a teenage prodigy and a defender of economic orthodoxy. "The principal champion on their side was a very estimable man, with whom I was well acquainted, Mr. William Thomson, of Cork," Mill recounted in his autobiography, without revealing the outcome of the debate. Some accounts say Thompson had the better of the exchanges.[48]

Thompson also engaged with Thomas Hodgskin, a former officer in the Royal Navy, whose 1825 book, *Labour Defended Against the Claims of Capital*, paralleled the *Inquiry* in some ways. Like Thompson, Hodgskin invoked the labor theory of value and argued that workers were being exploited by being deprived of their full product. He described the capitalist as an "oppressive middleman who eats up the produce of labor," and he portrayed the state as an instrument of the ruling classes, averring that "no laws for the protection of capital are thought too severe."[49]

Despite these similarities, Hodgskin's approach differed from Thompson's in important respects. He believed that the root of exploitation was the monopoly power employers exercised over their workers. In many cases, he pointed out, they refused to employ people who had quit other jobs in search of higher wages. In a truly competitive labor market, Hodgskin argued, workers would be able to obtain much higher wages. Thompson disagreed. In 1827, writing under the nom de plume "One of the Idle Classes," he published *Labor Rewarded*, a book-length response to Hodgskin, in which he insisted that the only way to guarantee workers the full fruit of their labors was to abandon competition—i.e., capitalism—and move to cooperative production. "It is time to cast aside the little expedients of the day," he wrote, "and the year, and to seek for a *radical, a permanent* cure of the evils that afflict society."[50]

Although cooperative ideas were making some progress, the cooperative movement itself was running into difficulties. In 1828, Owen left New Harmony, where his new community had already dissolved. From the beginning, it had been plagued by practical problems, including a lack of detailed plans for production and a surfeit of dreamers and adventurers over industrious tradesmen and cultivators. After the community degenerated into splinter groups, and Owen fell out with his American partner, William Maclure, he decided to quit the venture and return to England. Once he got back, he resumed a leading role in the British cooperative movement, which in his absence had experienced mixed fortunes.[51]

On the positive side, following the founding of the London Co-operative Society, in 1824, similar organizations were being established in other cities and towns. They were often associated with labor groups. Initially, the new cooperative societies focused on establishing community-operated stores, where workers could buy cheap, unadulterated goods, and on setting up labor exchanges, where people could find work. Some of these ventures showed great promise, but Thompson's goal of setting up independent cooperative communities proved elusive.

The immediate challenge was money. Where would the funding come from to buy land and to build housing and workshops? In an article for *Co-operative Magazine*, published by the London Co-operative Society, Thompson claimed that a start could be made if workers saved as little as sixpence a week and deposited the money in a bank. "Resolve; make a beginning," he wrote. "Your own happiness and that of your descendent will be secured; the selfish principle of competition will soon everywhere give way to the benign principle of universal Co-operation."[52] Thompson insisted that as few as two hundred people could create a viable new community, and that the minimum sum required, at least in Ireland, was only about twenty pounds per head. But despite his encouraging words, he couldn't raise the money to get one of these ventures going. Neither could anybody else.

Evidently, Thompson wasn't too disheartened. In 1830, he published a lengthy guidebook for organizers of cooperative communities, which included tips for cultivation and crop rotation, dietary suggestions, recommendations on what machinery to purchase, and much else besides.[53] He continued to insist that communities as small as two hundred people would be viable, although he said the ideal number would be about two thousand. His guidebook said that the new communities would eliminate the "master evil" of the competitive system: enforced joblessness and the poverty that accompanied it.[54] Once cooperation replaced profit-making as the fundamental organizing force, employment would be guaranteed for everybody, and poverty would be eliminated. This was "the simple basis of Co-operative Political Economy."[55]

Thompson's enthusiasm for forming small communities created a rift between himself and Owen, whose failure in Indiana had convinced him that the only practical way to establish a cooperative economy was through large-scale mobilization of people and capital, with extensive government support.[56] In a March 1830 letter to Owen, Thompson tried to keep relations cordial: "While you are boldly operating on the whole mass, I am endeavoring to arrange a little part of the social machine, not forgetting its connections with the whole."[57] The differences between the two men couldn't be papered over, though. In April 1832, at a national Co-operative Congress held in London, Owen refused to associate himself with any new community that hadn't raised at least £240,000 in seed capital. The dispute between the two leaders of the movement dragged on. At a second congress in the autumn of 1832, Owen again opposed Thompson's plans. In a speech cited by the biographer Richard Pankhurst, he expressed "the greatest possible esteem for Mr. Thompson," but he also "begged leave to assure him that he knew little of this matter."[58]

Despite Owen's opposition, the Co-operative Congress approved a motion to press ahead with plans to establish a modest-size new community somewhere in Britain. In theory, that was a big victory for Thompson. In practice, the local cooperative societies couldn't raise enough money to make his ideas a reality.[59] Owen's goal for a government-led initiative to establish larger cooperative communities was frustrated, too. Once the members of the traditional British ruling class realized that he and his fellow cooperators were intent on replacing the existing economic system rather than merely reforming it, they turned against the cooperative movement. Naturally, the new industrial elites weren't in favor of supplanting industrial capitalism either, and they were rapidly gaining political strength. In passing the Great Reform Act of 1832, Lord Grey's Whig government expanded the voting franchise to include many male members of the propertied middle class, but continued to exclude virtually all the working class. Between 1832 and 1867, when the Second Reform Act was passed, the House of Commons represented an alliance of landed, financial, and industrial capital, to which the socialistic schemes of Owen, Thompson, and their followers were anathema.

In believing that the economy and the class system could be transformed by voluntarism and appeals to reason rather than by mass political action, Owen and Thompson were naive. And yet, despite the demise of the New Harmony experiment and the failure to establish similar ventures in Britain, the "co-operators" left an impressive legacy. Even today, Britain's Co-op (formally known as the Co-operative Group Limited) operates more than two thousand retail stores, an insurance company, a legal services provider, and a funeral company. Elsewhere, in many parts of the world, there are cooperative consumer unions, retailers, banks, farms, energy companies, and manufacturers. (The largest such entity is the Mondragon Corporation, a federation of local cooperatives based in the Basque region of Spain.) But Thompson's legacy was also an intellectual one. In combining the labor theory of value with a subsistence theory of wages, he created an analytical framework that Marx and his disciples would adopt and develop. And in formulating a utilitarian case for equality and wealth distribution, he created a template that socially minded liberals, Fabian socialists, and social democrats could use to their advantage. Not many figures in the history of socialism would manage to straddle the divide between revolutionism and social democracy: Thompson did. And that wasn't his only contribution. In the context of his time, he was also an early feminist.

5

Anna Wheeler and the Forgotten Half of Humanity

At some point during the early 1820s, when Thompson was working on his first book, he met Anna Wheeler, a learned and well-connected Irish widow. It's not clear how the meeting came about. Wheeler, whose husband, a dissolute Irish aristocrat, had died several years earlier, lived in Paris, where she maintained a literary salon that was frequented by followers of Saint-Simon and Fourier. She was a frequent visitor to London, where she mixed in Owenite circles and was acquainted with Jeremy Bentham. The philosopher's papers indicate Wheeler dined at his home twice in May 1824. He sent her several of his books, including one on prison reform, *Panopticon*. It seems likely that Wheeler and Thompson met through Bentham. In any case, the two forged a deep and enduring friendship, which was based on their shared interest in progressive politics, the cooperative movement, and women's rights.

In early nineteenth-century Britain and Ireland, even upper-class women like Wheeler couldn't escape systematic discrimination. Family property was passed down to male heirs, and girls of all backgrounds rarely received any advanced education. Once a woman got married, which usually happened early in her life, she effectively became a dependent of her husband. If she earned any money, it belonged to him. Although a mother was expected to keep house and bring up children, the legal power to determine her children's future rested with the father. A woman couldn't file a court case, sign a legal contract, demand a divorce, or even make a will on her own account. And she couldn't vote to change this oppressive system because the suffrage was restricted to men.

In 1825, just a year after the appearance of Thompson's *Inquiry*, he published a second book, which addressed gender inequality and discrimination. Like its predecessor, it had a long title, but this one was more pointed: *Appeal of One Half the Human Race, Women, Against the Pretensions of the Other Half, Men, to Retain Them in Political, and Thence in Civil and Domestic, Slavery.*[1] In searing prose, Thompson lambasted the patriarchy for keeping women down for thousands of years and demanded fundamental changes, including the abolition of "that disgrace of civilization, the present marriage code."[2] Thompson was the sole author of the *Appeal*, but in an "Introductory Letter to Mrs. Wheeler," which appeared at the beginning of the text, he informed his readers that its contents reflected his conversations with Wheeler and made clear that he regarded it as a joint work. Addressing Wheeler directly, he said he had "endeavored to arrange the expressions of those feelings, sentiments, and reasonings, which have emanated from your mind."[3]

Wheeler was born Anna Doyle in 1785 in Clonbeg Parish, County Tipperary, which is about fifty miles northeast of Thompson's Cork. Her mother, Anna Dunbar, was a homemaker. Her father, Nicholas Doyle, was a senior cleric in the Protestant Church of Ireland, but he died when Anna was two years old. She grew up with her mother and two siblings, Bessie and John. An uncle, John Doyle, who had served as a British Army officer in the Peninsular Wars, became a surrogate father to the family. Although the Doyles weren't particularly rich, they were socially prominent and well educated. Anna's godfather, Henry Grattan, was an Irish patriot and statesman who opposed the 1800 Acts of Union, which made Ireland officially part of the United Kingdom.[4]

Despite the social privilege that Anna's family enjoyed, she was still a female in a deeply patriarchal and conservative society. "Anna's early role models for worldly success, freedom and mobility, were predictably men," Dolores Dooley, a lecturer in philosophy at the University of Cork, wrote in her deeply researched 1996 book *Equality in Community*, which examined the writings of Wheeler and Thompson. "Early on she learned how to collaborate with men even if, later on, the project would be the emancipation of women!"[5]

When Anna was fifteen, a young heir named Francis Massy-Wheeler, whose family owned an estate in the neighboring county of Limerick, spotted her at the horse races and took a shine to her. According to Dooley's account, Anna's mother regarded Massy-Wheeler as spoiled, rich, and irresponsible. Despite her protests, Anna agreed to marry him and take his name. The union, which began in 1800, turned out as Anna's mother had feared. Massy-Wheeler was a gambler, an idler, and a heavy drinker. He was also abusive. The couple had six children, four of whom died in infancy. The two survivors were both girls, Henrietta and Rosina.[6]

Despite her domestic troubles, Anna was a dedicated autodidact with a passion for serious books. Her daughter Rosina would later recount her "stretched on a sofa, deep in the perusal of some French or German philosophical work that had reached her via London."[7] Rosina said that Anna's views were "strongly tainted" by the works of the English author Mary Wollstonecraft, the early English feminist, whose 1792 book, *A Vindication of the Rights of Woman*, argued that women were the intellectual equals of men and should be afforded the opportunity to contribute equally to society.[8] Wheeler also read the French rationalists Baron d'Holbach and Denis Diderot, which may have contributed to her growing skepticism about organized religion.[9]

In 1812 Anna left Massy-Wheeler and took her daughters to Guernsey, a British dependency off the coast of Normandy, where her uncle John—who by then had risen to the title of Sir John Doyle—was serving as the lieutenant governor. The move to Guernsey's Government House, a grand eighteenth-century building overlooking the sea, opened a new world to Anna. She socialized with eminent visitors from Paris and London, and traveled to the French capital. After Sir John's term as governor ended, she moved to the nearby French city of Caen, in Normandy, where, according to one of her grandsons, "she became the *bel esprit* of a little group of socialists and freethinkers."[10]

In 1820 Massy-Wheeler died, leaving his wife and daughters practically nothing. Evidently, he had gambled and drunk his way through the family estate. Thereafter, Anna, who kept the surname Wheeler, seems to have relied on the financial support of her uncle and on her own efforts to earn money. For a period, she lived in London. One job she took on was translating the works of progressive French writers, including Fourier. It may have been from her reading of Fourier that she became interested in the idea of setting up new cooperative communities that would redefine the role of women. Like Thompson, Fourier described women as the slaves of men. In his phalanxes, the sexual division of labor was to be largely abolished. Cooking and childrearing were to be communal activities, women were to engage in work tasks that agreed with them, and the institution of monogamous marriage was to be gradually replaced with more open-ended relationships.

Given Wheeler's experience of marriage, it is easy to see why Fourier's ideas appealed to her. In his "Introductory Letter to Mrs. Wheeler," Thompson provided a fairly detailed description of her commitment to female liberation and wholesale social change. "You look forward, as I do, to a state of society very different from that which now exists," he wrote.

> You look forward to a better aspect of society, where the principle of benevolence shall supersede that of fear, where restless and anxious individual competition shall give place to mutual co-operation and joint possession; where individuals in large numbers, male and female, forming voluntary associations, shall become a mutual guarantee to each other for the supply of all useful wants . . . where perfect freedom of opinion and perfect equality will reign amongst the co-operators; and where the children of all will be equally educated and provided for by the whole.[11]

Thompson also noted that he had encouraged Wheeler to write about sexual politics herself—to "take up the cause of your proscribed sex . . . in your own name." The "leisure and resolution to undertake the drudgery of the task were lacking," he added.[12] This statement doesn't entirely clear up the question of why Wheeler didn't write her own book. Sexism may well have played a role. Despite the pioneering efforts of Wollstonecraft, it was still extremely difficult for female authors to find a publisher or get taken seriously. When, some years later, Wheeler did compose some essays, she published them under a pseudonym. Another thing that may have weighed on Wheeler was that, unlike Thompson, she didn't have a generous family inheritance that would enable her to pursue a literary career. It seems likely that these factors were at least as inhibiting to her as an aversion to the "drudgery" of writing.

The *Appeal* originated, and was structured, as a response to an article opposing woman suffrage that the philosopher and historian James Mill published in 1820 as a supplement to *Encyclopaedia Britannica*. Writing on the subject of government, Mill made the argument that representative democracy and broad suffrage were the best guarantees of good governance. But in defining broad suffrage, Mill excluded women, citing as his justification a legal doctrine known as "coverture," which claimed that men were best situated to represent the interests of their wives and families. The spectacle of an eminent scholar associated with the Philosophical Radicals making this antediluvian argument outraged Thompson and Wheeler, who waited for someone to issue a rebuttal. After Bentham and other leaders of the utilitarian movement failed to rise to the challenge, Thompson decided to compose something himself.[13]

Thompson began the *Appeal* by turning Mill's argument about coverture against him. How, he asked, could the interests of all women be adequately represented in Parliament by men, when about one in six women had neither a father nor a husband?[14] Based on Mill's logic, Thompson pointed out, all fatherless and single women, at least, should be enfranchised, whereas many adult men—those who still lived at home and had a father to look out for them—didn't need a vote. This was an effective debating point and typical of Thompson's didactic style. He followed it up by going beyond logic chopping to insist that the male monopoly of the suffrage wasn't based on any high-minded theories at all: it was simply "an engine of ulterior oppression" designed to help men maintain their power and privileges.[15] Far from using their votes to better the lives of the female members of their families, men had reduced their wives to "involuntary breeding machine[s] and household slave[s]"[16] and raised their daughters within "artificial cages of restraint and imbecility."[17]

The *Appeal* was particularly scathing about the idea that women freely entered marriages. "Each man yokes a woman to his establishment, and calls it a *contract*," it said. "Audacious falsehood! A contract! Where are any of the attributes of contracts, of equal and just contracts, to be found in this transaction? A contract implies the voluntary assent of both the contracting parties."[18] The reality was that women, lacking any prospect of making a living of their own or establishing any financial independence, were forced to marry "on whatever terms their masters have willed, or starve: or if not absolutely starve, they must renounce at least all the means of enjoyment monopolized by the males."[19] With men holding all power, including the power of the purse, the family home became the "eternal prison-house of the wife."[20]

The patriarchy wasn't a new topic for Thompson. In the *Inquiry*, he had lamented the "domestic slavery of one half of the human race" and demanded: "Give men and women equal civil and political rights . . . Let property on the death of the parents be equally divided between all the children male and female."[21] In writing the *Appeal*, he expanded his arguments in many directions. Since no correspondence between Wheeler and Thompson appears to have survived, it's hard to single out specific areas in which she shaped his views, but Thompson himself suggested that Wheeler's influence was pervasive, writing in his introductory letter to her: "To separate your thoughts from mine were now to me impossible, so amalgamated are they with my own."[22]

Thompson's blistering criticisms of marriage likely reflected Wheeler's views and experience. One area where her voice came through particularly clearly was in Thompson's argument that legal and institutional reforms, although urgent, must be accompanied by drastic changes in how men thought about women and behaved toward them. "But I hear you indignantly reject the boon of equality with such creatures as men now are," with their "ignorance and vanity" and "animal appetite," Thompson wrote, referring to Wheeler. "With you I would equally elevate both sexes."[23] Writing in his own voice, Thompson also addressed his fellow men, saying:

> Three or four thousand years have worn threadbare your vile cloak of hypocrisy. Cast aside this tattered cloak before it leaves you naked and exposed. Clothe yourself with the new garments of sincerity. Be rational human beings, not mere male sexual creatures. Cast aside the ferocious brute of your nature; give up the pleasures of the brute, those of mere lust and command, for the pleasures of the rational being.[24]

Having originated as a response to James Mill's article on government, the *Appeal* largely focused on legal and political questions. But Thompson and Wheeler were also acutely aware of economic changes that were drastically changing women's role in society. In preindustrial times, many women had been wage earners, to be sure. Domestic service—working for rich people as servants and housekeepers—was a major employer of female labor. So was preindustrial manufacturing. Under the "putting out" system, women had worked in their homes as spinners, weavers, knitters, and sewers. Usually a merchant supplied them with raw materials and paid them on a piecework basis: the more they produced, the more they earned.

With the rise of the factory system, out-work became in-work, and women entered the textile mills in large numbers. According to estimates provided to the British Parliament in 1834, 58 percent of the workforce in the cotton industry was female. In the silk industry, the figure was even higher: 78 percent. In the wool industry, it was 41 percent.[25] The majority of these female factory workers were young. The same 1834 report indicated that 16 percent of them were under the age of thirteen, and 51 percent were between thirteen and twenty. Indeed, the story of the early industrial revolution is largely a story of young female workers, although that is not how some histories have presented it. In the mills of Manchester and other cotton-producing areas, women worked day and night shifts, and if they were over sixteen, there was no legal limit to the length of their workday. (It wasn't until 1844 that Parliament finally imposed a limit of twelve hours for adult women.)

There were similar developments in the United States. In the Massachusetts textile town of Lowell in the 1820s, mill owners recruited teenage girls and young women from farms and villages throughout New England. Many "mill girls," as they came to be known, lived in large dormitory-style boardinghouses owned by the mill owners.[26] They worked twelve to fourteen hours a day, five days a week, and half a day on Saturday. The work was arduous, the discipline strict, and the work conditions crowded and unregulated. But for many young New England women, working in the new factories was more remunerative than staying on their families' farms.

On both sides of the Atlantic, factory owners valued female and child workers for their dexterity, sobriety, and acceptance of lower wages. Historians still debate the extent to which they were exploited financially. After analyzing figures presented to the 1834 parliamentary commission, Joyce Burnette, an economic historian at Wabash College, reported that women working in Lancashire cotton factories were paid 8.60 shillings a week, compared to men's wages of 19.12 shillings a week—a huge gap.[27] But Burnette also pointed out that women tended to carry out less productive tasks, and she argued that they usually received market rate wages for the jobs they did. Other historians have challenged this conclusion, noting that women were often assigned jobs and paid according to customs that reflected sexist norms. In some cases, they were actively excluded from high-paying skilled trades.

From the early days of the industrial revolution, many men who worked in textile mills regarded female labor as a threat to their jobs and wages. This attitude was particularly prevalent among male mule spinners, who minded machines that were used to spin cotton. In Glasgow, some women who entered the trade were subjected to violent attacks. As late as 1829, a national meeting of mule spinners passed a resolution to restrict the job to "the son, brother, or orphan nephew of spinners, and the poor relations of the proprietors of the mills."[28]

Low wages and employment restrictions weren't the only challenges that female factory operatives faced. Even as they went out to work, they remained largely responsible for raising children and unpaid household labor. In scholarly papers and a 2010 book, *Childhood and Child Labour in the British Industrial Revolution*, the historian Jane Humphries has provided a compelling portrait of family life in a time of roiling change.[29] Childcare was expensive if it was available at all. Working mothers often had to rely on one of their older children to look after the youngest. To boost the family budget, other siblings were often sent out to work. Many fathers, whether they were at work or at the local tavern, were largely absent from the home.[30]

As upper-class intellectuals who mixed in metropolitan circles, Wheeler and Thompson didn't have much firsthand experience of women in the new industrial economy. The *Appeal* didn't directly discuss their situation, but it did insist that women should enjoy equal opportunities in the workplace. To make this possible, the first necessary step was to "abolish all prohibitory and exclusive laws," particularly the marriage code. "Women then might exert in a free career with men their faculties of mind and body, to whatever degree developed, in pursuit of happiness by means of exertion, as men do."[31]

These statements came from a passage at the end of Thompson's introductory letter to Wheeler, in which he summed up their message of gender equality and tied it to the overall utilitarian project of creating a fairer, more rational society, "a more comprehensive system, founded on equal benevolence, on the true development of the principle of Utility." Simply leveling the legal playing field for women and men wouldn't be sufficient to achieve this goal, Thompson explained, because it would leave in place other inegalitarian aspects of "competition"—i.e., capitalism. Orthodox economists, he went on, were guilty of ignoring this reality and "leaving the great bulk of human beings to eternal ignorance and toil." The passage ended with an invocation: "To a new science, the *social science*, or the science of promoting human happiness, that of political economy, or the mere science of producing wealth by individual competition, must give way."[32]

Wheeler was fully committed to both parts of the grand project, liberating women and reorganizing society on a more equitable basis. During the 1820s, she came into contact with Robert Owen and Charles Fourier. Some correspondence from these relationships has survived, and it suggests that Wheeler was just as forthright in expressing her views with them as she was with Thompson. In one letter to Owen, she lamented that humans had "hitherto been taught nothing but the most pernicious errors," then went on to criticize organized religion, patriotism, and the pursuit of "bit by bit reforms."[33] Wheeler lived for some time in Paris with her two adult daughters and sought to replicate the political and intellectual networks she had developed in Caen. She came across Fourier, whose proposals for independent cooperative communities were beginning to gain a following, and she began to act as his translator from French to English and vice versa.

Wheeler also tried to get the "co-operators" on both sides of the English Channel to cooperate with each other, but these efforts weren't very successful. In 1826 she introduced Fourier to some members of the London Co-operative Society, only to have him complain to her: "They are not very sharp and they were bloated with dogmatism. The Owenite school is extremely weak."[34]

One point of commonality between Fourier and the British cooperators was a struggle to find investors willing to finance their ambitious plans. (Only after Fourier's death, in 1837, would some of his disciples, in the United States and elsewhere, establish versions of his phalanxes.) Like many visionaries, Fourier believed his insight wasn't being fully recognized. At times, Wheeler tried to buck him up. "You feel some disappointment when you see how little society appreciates your generous efforts," she wrote in an 1830 letter, "but I think this must necessarily be the fate of the small number of wise philanthropists who commit themselves to such a hopeless struggle."[35]

By this time, Wheeler had returned to London following the early death of her elder daughter, Henrietta—the one who had described Thompson doing his harlequin dance at Bentham's house. Wheeler's other daughter, Rosina, married Edward Bulwer-Lytton, an English novelist and aristocrat. Anna was now in her early forties, but the approach of middle age hadn't dulled her spirit or moderated her views. At a family dinner with Rosina and Bulwer-Lytton, she met Benjamin Disraeli, a future British prime minister who was then an ambitious young novelist. In a letter to his sister, Disraeli described Wheeler as a combination of Jeremy Bentham and Meg Merrilies, a figure from an eponymous Keats poem who was "a gypsy, and lived upon the moors." Disraeli went on to say that Wheeler was "very clever but awfully revolutionary. She poured forth all her systems upon my novitiate ear, and while she advocated the rights of women, Bulwer abused system-mongers and the fairer sex, and Rosina played with her dog."[36]

If Wheeler had once harbored reservations about expressing her views publicly in her own voice, she had overcome them. In 1829 she spoke at a public meeting in a chapel near Finsbury Square, in central London, on the "Social Condition of Women." She began her speech by noting that poor health and "deep domestic sorrow"—the death of Henrietta—had robbed her mind of "much of its energy and elasticity." Also, she went on:

> I feel the difficulty of employing a moderate language, in speaking of the degraded position of my sex . . . But what appears to me the most cheerless part of my task—I would almost say the "forlorn hope of my enterprise"—is that I am doubtful, whether any material good can be effected by this and similar lectures, seeing as I do, the rottenness of our institutions, and those especially which smell of rank injustice, in the disabilities set up against half the human race: WOMAN!

Addressing arguments often made at the time to justify the subjugation of women, Wheeler dismissed the notion that they were weaker than men in mind and body. "All the researches of anatomy, have not yet been able to prove a difference in the brain of either," she said. "Both receive the same impressions, arrange and preserve ideas, for memory and imagination; judge, compare, and analyze; nor can indeed any difference be pointed out, but, that the organs of women are generally smaller, but equally fitted to the purposes for which they are intended." The real source of women's diminished status wasn't biology but discrimination, Wheeler insisted.

Like Mary Wollstonecraft before her, she singled out the failure to provide proper schooling for girls as a particularly pernicious practice, which deprived women of the opportunity to fulfill their potential and also ended up hurting men. She told her audience: "'*Knowledge is power,*' says men, to keep women our slaves, we must keep them ignorant. Strange that men should calculate so badly! Who has not discovered even in the most ordinary actions of life, that ignorance makes a bad servant and a vexatious companion?" Wheeler went on: "Let a woman receive a rational education, and the only insuperable barrier is removed, to a state of social happiness, hitherto unknown to our wretched species . . . Wisdom dictates such a course, necessity requires it!"[37]

At the end of her speech, Wheeler brought up Frances Wright, a Scottish-born freethinker and feminist dynamo who, in 1825, settled in the United States. Wright formed a cooperative community in Nashoba, Tennessee, and later moved to New Harmony, Indiana, where she edited a newspaper and associated with Robert Owen's son, Robert Dale Owen, who had stayed in America after his father left. Wright was known for espousing a variety of progressive causes, including the abolition of slavery, birth control, sexual freedom, liberal divorce laws, and universal education for both sexes. These were all causes dear to Wheeler, who declared of Wright: "May she find an echo in every instructed woman, and an active ally in every man!"

Wheeler's address was reprinted in an Owenite magazine, *The British Co-operator*. She was also associated with another progressive publication, *The Crisis*, for which she translated articles from French and contributed some pieces of her own using a pseudonym. In Paris, some young female writers were trying to combine the precepts of feminism with the cooperative doctrines of Saint-Simon and Fourier. One article that Wheeler translated, in 1833, came from Jeanne Victoire, a working-class Parisian who was associated with the Saint-Simonians. Declaring that "the time is arrived when woman shall find *her place*," it went on to argue that this could be achieved only "on condition of forming ourselves into *one solid union*" comprising "women of the privileged class" and working-class women standing together. Only by uniting could women gain the power to tell men that "the social edifice must be re-built."[38] As a renegade member of the privileged class herself, Wheeler doubtless agreed with these sentiments.

It's not clear how much contact Wheeler and Thompson had as they got older and Thompson's health gradually failed him. On March 28, 1833, at the age of fifty-seven, he died at his home in Cork from complications of a respiratory illness. Later in the year, Wheeler wrote a lengthy letter eulogizing him that was read out at a literary salon hosted by Lord and Lady Hampden. The letter announced the passing of Thompson and called him "the devoted friend of humanity, the uncompromising supporter of systems of equal interest." It went on: "Society has lost a man, and humanity a friend, a great man in a very humble citizen—an ambitious man in one who lived and died in obscurity!" Wheeler also praised Thompson's unremitting commitment to improving the welfare of the masses, noting that "the greatest happiness principle was that which not only guided the pen but governed the minutest action of Mr. Thompson's useful and laborious life."[39] As the historian Dooley noted in her book about Thompson and Wheeler, this letter illustrated the "intimacy of affection" that had developed between the two.[40]

In Thompson's will, he left Wheeler an annual annuity of £100. He asked for his estate to be bequeathed to the cooperative movement and his body to be donated for anatomical examination "to aid in conquering the foolish and frequently most mischievous prejudice against the public examination of corpses."[41] By the time the will was read, Thompson's body had already been buried in a local graveyard on the orders of a nephew. In a final outrage to respectable Cork society, a local physician, Dr. Donovan, exhumed the corpse and preserved it for medical research. According to Thompson's biographer Pankhurst, the medic later said that the body had actually been bequeathed to him on the condition of his "stringing up the bones" and sending them to Wheeler "as a memento of love."[42] Whether that was a final joke or a provocation from the provocateur of Glandore isn't clear. In any case, that wasn't the end of things. Thompson's relatives challenged his will, and the case dragged through the Irish courts for decades. Eventually the family won, and the cooperative movement never got Thompson's land.

In the years following his death, Wheeler remained a supporter of the movement even as its grand ambitions were frustrated. Thompson's effort to establish a prototype community in Cork had come to naught. So had similar efforts in England and France. In 1836, a year before Fourier died, Wheeler wrote to him: "Now, I grieve that there is no Phalanstaire which would enable me to return to die in France."[43] But Wheeler also tried to assure the philosopher that his life hadn't been in vain. She told him he had the "satisfaction of knowing that you have nobly performed your part to suffering and stupid humanity too perverted and corrupted now by a long course of error to lend their aid to your redeeming projects."[44]

During the 1830s, Wheeler also became friends with two Parisian feminists, Desirée Veret and Flora Tristan. Veret, a Parisian seamstress and Saint-Simonian, was a cofounder of *Tribune des Femmes*, a pioneering journal written and managed by women. Tristan was a French-Peruvian writer who initially made a name for herself by writing about her trip to find her family in Peru. In 1839 Tristan visited London to take stock of the great metropolis. Wheeler showed her around Bethlem Royal Hospital, a pioneering psychiatric hospital that included a wing for the criminally insane. In a book that Tristan subsequently wrote about her time in England, she recounted that Wheeler "gave me detailed information on every inmate whose case was in any way remarkable."[45]

Wheeler's interest in social causes stayed with her to the end. As she aged, she suffered from poor health, but it isn't clear when she died. Dooley says it was sometime between 1848 and 1851. Like Thompson, Wheeler had devoted much of her time on earth to the project of creating a more egalitarian society and eliminating divisions based on class and gender. In her lifetime, she never received much acclaim or recognition. Yet as Dooley noted, her journey from rural Ireland to the salons of London and Paris "offers a major challenge and counter-position to any society governed by a philosophy of competitive individualism."[46]

6

Flora Tristan and the Universal Workers' Union

When Flora Tristan visited London and toured Bethlem Royal Hospital with Anna Wheeler, she was a thirty-five-year-old writer living in Paris. Months earlier, she had suffered serious gunshot wounds during an attempted murder by her estranged husband. The attack, which was carried out in broad daylight on Rue du Bac, had been widely reported in the newspapers, and Tristan's name had become well-known. In England, however, she was anonymous. As she and Wheeler were walking around the psychiatric wards at Bethlem, they encountered, among all the British patients, a Frenchman, a Monsieur Chabrier, who was being held at the hospital on the grounds that he believed he was God. The patient talked politely to Tristan and said he had been wrongly confined. "His observations were so just and his reflections so profound that I did not think it possible that he could be insane," Tristan recounted.[1]

A bit further on in her tour of the hospital, Tristan encountered Chabrier again. This time he was agitated, and his body was trembling. "Listen!" he said. "Know you, my sister, that I am sent from your God, I am the Messiah announced by Jesus Christ. I come to accomplish his work; I come to make an end of every kind of servitude, to deliver woman from man, the poor from the rich, and the soul from sin."[2] The Frenchman pushed a homemade crucifix at Tristan and, throwing himself crying at her feet, declared that she looked like the Holy Virgin. At the urging of the warders, the visitors broke away.

Tristan herself was a Christian believer with a strong sense of personal mission, and Chabrier's outburst didn't change her opinion of him. In fact, she strongly agreed with the leveling sentiments that he had expressed. "As I saw it, these were not the words of a madman: Jesus, Saint-Simon, and Fourier had all spoken thus," she recalled in her book. Before leaving the hospital, she spotted Chabrier for a third time. He was kneeling on the same spot where he had accosted her, praying. "In this attitude, he looked so beautiful that I thought of him as a new St. John," she wrote. "Can this man be mad? . . . His soul is in revolt against every sign of baseness, corruption and hypocrisy and he cannot restrain his holy indignation. I saw in him all the signs of exaltation but none of madness."[3]

Flora Célestine Thérèse Henriette Tristán y Moscoso was born on April 7, 1803, in Paris. Her mother, Anne-Pierre Laisnay, was a middle-class Frenchwoman whose family fled the country during the revolution and settled in Spain, where she met and married Don Mariano de Tristán y Moscoso, a Spanish Peruvian military officer who was serving as head of a Peruvian division of the Spanish army. Don Mariano's family had moved from Spain to the South American colony in the seventeenth century and grown rich and powerful. In 1802, he and Anne moved to the outskirts of Paris and settled in the upscale Vaugirard neighborhood, which would later be assimilated into the fifteenth arrondissement. The couple had two children: Flora and a younger brother.[4]

Several years later Don Mariano died suddenly, leaving no will and no French marriage certificate to prove that Anne-Pierre was his wife. It seems that the marriage had been officiated by a refugee priest who hadn't registered it with the authorities. Technically a single mother, Anne-Pierre was deprived of her inheritance rights. She and her children were forced to give up their family home and move to the countryside. In 1818, when Flora was fifteen, they moved back to the city and took a garret apartment near Place Maubert, on the Left Bank, then a gritty area inhabited by artisans, shopkeepers, and students.

Flora took a job as an assistant for a young printmaker, André Chazal, whose brother Antoine was a well-known artist. In 1821, when Flora was seventeen, the pair married. Flora later claimed her mother forced her into a union with a man she never loved. The marriage produced two children, but it quickly degenerated into fighting and bickering. In early 1825, after discovering that she was pregnant for a third time, Flora left Chazal and moved back in with her mother. Since the government of Louis XVIII, the restored Bourbon monarch, had voided a divorce law introduced during the revolution, legal separation wasn't an option. In 1828 Flora's elder son died, leaving her with a daughter, Aline, and a younger son, Ernest.

As an illegitimate daughter and impecunious mother who had abandoned her spouse, Tristan came to view herself as an outcast from respectable society, a pariah. For lengthy periods, according to some accounts, she left her children with her mother and went to England to work as a lady's maid.[5] Having been deprived of a higher education, she educated herself by reading widely. Living on the Left Bank, she encountered some followers of Henri de Saint-Simon, who had died in 1825, and attended some of their meetings. According to one of her biographers, Dominique Desanti, the speakers that she heard included Barthélemy-Prosper Enfantin, a charismatic figure who had taken Saint-Simon's technocratic ideas in a more spiritual direction.[6] An early supporter of women's rights, Enfantin demanded the legalization of divorce and the replacement of "the tyranny of marriage" with a system of "free love." (In 1832 the authorities sentenced Enfantin to a year in jail for endangering public morality.)

Such encounters exposed the Roman Catholic Tristan to more radical and secular dogmas. Although she retained her religion, she would eventually incorporate some of these progressive ideas into an early form of Christian socialism, which combined belief in God with a profound concern for the masses. In what turned out to be a life-changing meeting, she also ran into a Peruvian man who knew her father's family in South America.[7] Afterward, she wrote to her uncle, Don Pío de Tristán y Moscoso, who had once been provisionally appointed as the Spanish viceroy to Peru. In her letter, she identified herself as Don Pío's niece, included a copy of her birth certificate, and described her straitened circumstances. Don Pío wrote back acknowledging Tristan as "my brother's natural daughter." He said he would send her silver from his mother's fortune, which she could invest to provide a modest income for her family, and that he was sending her 2,500 francs to tide her over in the meantime. But he refused to recognize the marriage of Flora's parents as legitimate.[8]

Eventually Tristan decided to travel to Peru. Leaving Aline in the care of a friend (Ernest was living with Chazal at the time), she set sail from

Bordeaux on April 7, 1833, her thirtieth birthday, and didn't return to Europe until early 1835.[9] On the outward journey, which took several months, she was the only female on board the ship. According to her subsequent account, the captain fell in love with her and asked her to marry him. When she reached Arequipa, her uncle invited her to stay with the family. Don Pío still wouldn't recognize the legitimacy of Flora's parents' marriage despite her protests, but he reminded her of the silver he had already secured for her, worth 15,000 francs—a considerable sum. Although Tristan didn't come away with the full inheritance to which she felt entitled, the journey to Peru exposed her to her upper-class heritage and spurred her development as a writer. Throughout her travels, she kept detailed notebooks, which formed the basis of her first full-length book, the travelogue *Peregrinations of a Pariah*, which was published in 1838.[10]

The Peru that Tristan wrote about had recently gained its independence from the Spanish Empire, but its society reflected the country's brutal history under the rule of the conquistadors and their descendants. Independence hadn't removed the rigid divide between the colonial elite and the impoverished Indigenous population. Peru was predominantly an agricultural country. However, its mountains contained vast deposits of silver, which were dug up by Indigenous laborers who were forced to leave their homes and work in the mines. In a brief foreword dedicated "To the Peruvians," Tristan noted that she had been greeted with great warmth, but addressing the Peruvian elites directly, she also indicated that her portrait would be an unsparing one. "The upper class is profoundly corrupted," she wrote, and "from cupidity, love of power, and other passions, its egotism leads it into the most antisocial endeavors."[11]

Tristan went on to highlight the poverty and "degradation" of ordinary Peruvians, and she called on rich Peruvians to help the poor to advance themselves, rather than oppressing them and fearing their potential political power. "When all individuals will have learned to read and write," she wrote, "when the public press will have penetrated to the very huts of the Indians, then, upon encountering in the people judges whose censure you will fear and whose votes you will seek, you will acquire the virtues that you now lack."[12]

The body of *Peregrinations* combined detailed accounts of Tristan's adventures, which included witnessing a short civil war, with broader analysis. She attributed the pathologies of Peruvian society to the exploitative nature of Spanish colonialism, which had left the elite disdainful of productive work. Before independence, many of them had made their fortunes "in government offices, in illegal commerce, and, finally, through exploitation of the mines; very few of these fortunes had as their origins the cultivation of the land," she wrote. She contrasted this colonial heritage to "English America," where "wealth . . . was acquired only by agriculture or regular commerce, [and as a result] there was considerable equality in its distribution."[13] Doubtless, this analysis was a bit oversimplified, but in 2001 the Harvard scholars Daron Acemoglu, Simon Johnson, and James A. Robinson would make a similar argument about the economic impact of colonialism, distinguishing between extractive institutions of the sort that the Spanish created in Latin America and more inclusive institutions, including an independent legal system, that the British established in North America and Australasia.[14] Tristan was an autodidact rather than an academic, but she had a very sharp eye. (In 2024, Acemoglu, Johnson, and Robinson were awarded an economics Nobel.)

To an even greater extent than the British in India, the conquistadors in Peru and other Latin countries had been primarily interested in extracting wealth as quickly as possible and shipping it back to Spain, rather than developing the territories they occupied for the long term. The Spanish Crown granted monopolies to favored interests, imposed trade restrictions to keep out competitors, and—under the notorious encomienda system—forced the Indigenous people to pay tributes to their colonial overlords, often in the form of forced labor. Outright slavery was never as prevalent in Peru as it was in some other South American colonies, particularly Brazil. Nonetheless, many thousands of Africans had been transported there to work in silver mines and on agricultural plantations. In 1821 General José de San Martín, whose army liberated Peru, had outlawed the slave trade, but he hadn't freed people who were already enslaved.

Tristan described visiting a sugar plantation owned by a "Monsieur Lavalle," which had nine hundred enslaved workers: four hundred men, three hundred women, and two hundred children. Since the ban on purchasing enslaved workers had gone into effect, Lavalle told Tristan, his workforce had been reduced from fifteen hundred, and he was having difficulty restocking it. Lavalle also defended the violence that was routinely inflicted on enslaved workers: "It is unfortunately too true that one can drive them only with the whip."[15] As Tristan left the plantation, she stopped at a hut, where she encountered two young Black women who had recently given birth to babies that died. "One was eating raw corn," Tristan recounted, "the other, young, and very beautiful, looked at me with her large eyes; her look seemed to say: 'I let my baby die because I knew he would not be free like you; I preferred him dead to being a slave.'"[16]

When Tristan visited Lavalle's plantation, the United Kingdom Parliament was in the process of abolishing slavery in the British Empire. On August 1, 1834, the Slavery Abolition Act went into effect, outlawing the owning, buying, and selling of enslaved workers. The British law didn't apply to Peru, of course, but Tristan described how she tried to persuade Lavalle that emancipating his workers and providing them with an education would turn them into more productive employees—the same argument that Adam Smith had made. "All these beautiful dreams are superb as poetry," Lavalle replied. "But for an old planter like me, I am sorry to tell you, not one of your fine ideas can be realized."[17]

Tristan's positive descriptions of Peruvian society were largely confined to its female citizens, whom she described as "much superior to [Peruvian men] in intelligence and moral force."[18] Although most Peruvian women were in traditional marriages, they retained their own names and their autonomy, Tristan noted, going out by themselves to the theater, public meetings, and even bullfights. She credited some of this individual initiative to the traditional clothing that many Peruvian women wore: a saya, which wrapped around the hips and midriff, and a long scarf, or *manto*, that covered most of the upper body, including parts of the face. European women "from childhood are slaves to laws, values, customs, prejudices, styles, and everything else," Tristan wrote. "Under the *saya*, the Lima woman is *free* [and] enjoys her independence . . . never is she subject to constraint."[19]

After Tristan returned to Paris, she used her newfound financial independence to find more comfortable living quarters for herself and her children. Eventually they settled on Rue du Bac, in the seventh arrondissement, where Tristan worked on her writing and renewed her acquaintance with some of the freethinking groups that had grown up in the French capital. As well as Enfantin and his band of devotees, these included the followers of the aging Charles Fourier, who had their own charismatic leader, Victor Prosper

Considérant, a young ex-military officer who had resigned his commission to devote his life to activism. Considérant was the founder and editor of a political journal, *The Phalanx*, as well as the author of a three-volume exposition of Fourierist ideas.[20]

Tristan also met some feminist writers, including the novelist George Sand. Tristan was sympathetic to the causes of emancipating women and reorganizing society on a cooperative basis, but as yet she didn't have much of a platform for her views. In August 1835 she took matters into her own hands and paid a visit to Fourier, who was then in his early sixties, at his home in Montmartre. She presented the philosopher with a draft of a pamphlet she had written that called for the establishment of public hostels where women visiting from foreign countries could stay for a time. (The idea had come to Tristan during her own travels.) The following month Tristan sent Fourier a follow-up note enclosing a finished copy of her pamphlet, the printing of which she had paid for, and offering her services in the cooperative cause. The note said: "I can assure you that you will find in me a strength uncommon to my sex, a *need* to do good, and a deep gratitude to all those who procure for me the means to be *useful*."[21]

Tristan was ambitious and practical-minded. Although she followed the debates between Fourier's followers and the Saint-Simonians, her primary concern was translating progressive ideas into concrete action. In October 1835 she sent Fourier another note, in which she asked him to introduce her to Considérant "and to two or three other ladies who share our ideas."[22] A meeting took place,[23] and on September 1, 1836, *The Phalanx* published a lengthy letter from Tristan, in which she expressed some reservations about the Fourierist movement and its highfalutin language: "I tell you, sir, that many people, amongst whom I count myself, find the science of Mr Fourier very obscure," she said. And she went on to argue that the key challenge facing progressives was institutional rather than intellectual. They needed to build a mass organization—"an organization that allows man, in satisfying all the demands of his nature . . . to find happiness."[24]

Robert Owen was a man with experience in trying to build a popular movement. During a trip Owen made to Paris, Tristan invited him to her apartment, where they discussed his ideas on setting up new schools for working-class children.[25] Like Owen, Tristan believed that broadening access to education was key to eliminating social and sexual disparities. But even as she endorsed some of the ideas that Owen and other founding figures of the socialist movement had put forward, she held back from committing herself to one group or creed. "I am neither a Saint-Simonian, nor a Fourierist, nor an Owenian," she would later write.[26]

At the start of 1838, *Peregrinations of a Pariah*, which Tristan had been working on for years, was finally published and established her reputation as a writer. But its impact on her financial fortunes was catastrophic. The allowance that Don Pío sent her each year had enabled her to enjoy a bourgeois lifestyle: she had a spacious apartment, she hosted soirées, and she even had her portrait painted by fashionable young artists. But when Don Pío learned about his niece's searing descriptions of himself, his family, and his country, he cut off the payments and had a copy of *Peregrinations* burned in a local square. The pariah was back on her own.[27]

And her relationship with her estranged husband had gone from bad to worse. For years, the couple battled in the courts over custody of their children. In 1837 Tristan had Chazal arrested for allegedly sexually assaulting their daughter, Aline. The authorities kept him in jail for a month or so, but didn't end up charging him.[28]

Chazal was furious at his imprisonment, and the publication of *Peregrinations* may have unbalanced him further. In the summer of 1838, he purchased a pair of pistols and started stalking Tristan. On the afternoon of September 10, he walked up to her outside a wine merchant's shop on Rue du Bac and shot her at close range. Staggering into a nearby store, Tristan said to the shopkeeper, "Arrest that man. He's the one who's murdered me. He's my husband." Chazal was arrested and taken into custody. Somehow, despite the bullet lodged in her chest, Tristan survived. Newspaper reports of the shooting turned her into something of a celebrity, and her book sales increased. Chazal was convicted of attempted murder and sentenced to twenty years of hard labor. After the verdict was issued, the courts finally annulled the marriage.[29]

As Tristan was recovering from her wounds, she finished a novel: *Méphis*, a love story about a Spanish singer, Marequita, who bore at least some resemblance to the author (some of Tristan's friends referred to her as "the Andalusian"), and a mysterious Italian, Méphis, who represented the working classes. In May 1839 Tristan traveled to England and stayed there for a number of weeks, mostly in its sprawling capital. *Promenades dans Londres*, her second travelogue, was published in 1840. It recorded her impressions and incorporated some materials she had accumulated during previous visits.

The book, which would eventually be published in English under the title *The London Journal of Flora Tristan*, began: "What an enormous city London is! Its huge size, out of all proportion to the area and population of the British Isles, simultaneously calls to mind the commercial supremacy of England and her oppression of India!"[30] Anna Wheeler wasn't the only local whom Tristan recruited to show her around. Dressed up as a Turkish man, she attended a night session at the House of Commons, where women weren't allowed. The Irish nationalist Daniel O'Connell, who had created the Catholic Association, which united the impoverished Irish masses behind a successful campaign to allow Catholics to hold public office, impressed her greatly.[31] She also went to the horse races at Ascot[32] and visited one of the West End "finishes"—late-night drinking clubs where upper-class men consorted with lower-class prostitutes, getting them drunk and then forcing them to drink vinegar and mustard.[33] "This drink almost always gives her horrible convulsions, and the jerkings and contortions of the unfortunate thing provoke laughter and intimately amuse the honorable society," Tristan wrote. "It is horrible! But this life, repeated every night, is the prostitutes' only hope of fortune, for they have no hold on a sober Englishman. The sober Englishman is so chaste as to be a prude."[34]

Tristan was determined to see all London had to offer, including its teeming working-class districts. In St. Giles, an impoverished Irish neighborhood, she saw "old men huddled in a little straw that had become a dung heap, young men covered in rags," and "hovels" that "rarely have paved floors," where "father, mother, sons, daughters, and friends sleep pell mell."[35] On Horseferry Road, Westminster, Tristan visited the world's first public gas works, which supplied the fuel for streetlights. The gas was produced from coke—specially treated coal—burned in vast furnaces. Tristan described how the "stokers . . . armed with long pokers, opened the ovens and took out the flaming coke, which fell in torrents." With no protections from the heat or the dust, many of these workers developed chest ailments and died of "consumption"—tuberculosis—Tristan reported, citing a foreman as her source.[36]

She also ventured outside London. "Unless you have visited the factory towns," she wrote, "and seen the workers of Birmingham, Manchester, Glasgow, Sheffield, Staffordshire, etc., you cannot appreciate the physical sufferings and moral debasement of this class of the population."[37] She reported that the workers were poorly paid and "shut up twelve to fourteen hours a day in mean rooms where they breathe in, along with foul air, cotton, wool, and linen fibers, particles of copper, lead, iron, etc., and frequently go from insufficient nourishment to excessive drinking."[38] They looked "pale, rickety, and sickly," Tristan wrote, adding, "I do not know whether the painful expression that is so general among [them] should be attributed to permanent fatigue or to their utter despair."[39]

The regimentation and discipline of the British factories struck Tristan as dehumanizing. "In English factories you don't hear, as in ours, singing, chatter, and laughter," she wrote. "The master doesn't want a memory of outside existence to distract the workers from their task for one minute: he requires silence, and deathlike silence reigns, the worker's hunger gives such power to the master's word." If the factory owner has no work to offer, "the worker dies of hunger; if he is sick, he succumbs on the straw of his pallet, unless, near death, he is received in a hospital; for it is a favor to be admitted there."[40]

Even as Tristan lamented how English factory owners treated their workers, she acknowledged the stupendous power of the new machinery they were employing. Echoing Jean-Baptiste Say a generation earlier, she wrote: "I have seen a steam engine with the power of 500 horses! Nothing is more awe-inspiring than the sight of motion imparted to these masses of iron whose colossal forms frighten the imagination and seem to go beyond the power of man . . . Upon recovering from your stupor and fright, you look for man. He can hardly be seen, reduced by the proportions of everything else around him to the size of an ant."[41]

As a disciple of the free market, Say had an unrestrained admiration for the productive power of industrialization. Tristan also recognized the enormous potential of mechanization, but she couldn't bring herself to believe that an economic system based on the pursuit of profit was capable of exploiting new technology for the good of all. "If at first I felt humiliation at seeing man annihilated, no longer functioning except like a machine," she wrote, "I soon saw the immense improvement that would one day come from these discoveries of science; brute force wiped out, physical work executed in less times, and more leisure to man for cultivating his intelligence." Instead of stopping there, she added: "But if these great benefits are to be achieved, there must be a social revolution; and that revolution will come, for God has not revealed such admirable inventions to men only to have them remain the slaves of a handful of manufacturers and landed proprietors."[42]

Despite the language that she used sometimes, Tristan wasn't a revolutionary. In Paris, of course, there were some genuine insurrectionists. One group of them was associated with the tradition of Gracchus Babeuf, the proto-communist who was executed in 1797 for conspiring to overthrow the Directory. ("We aspire to live and die equal, the way we were born: we want *real* equality or death," Babeuf and his comrades declared in their "Manifesto of Equals.")[43] In May 1839 hundreds of members of the Société des Saisons, a Babeufist entity, tried to storm the National Assembly, the Hôtel de Ville, and the Palace of Justice. Their goal was to overthrow the July Monarchy of Louis Philippe, which had taken power in 1830 and boasted the wealthy bourgeoisie as its primary social base. The French authorities easily put down the attempted rising. Then they sentenced to death two of its leaders, Louis-Auguste Blanqui, a journalist of Italian descent, and Armand Barbès, a lawyer. (The sentences were later commuted to life in prison.) Tristan had little sympathy for the conspirators. As a Christian, she opposed violence. She also thought that the Blanquist coup attempt and earlier violent protests in Lyon had provided cover for the French government to clamp down on legitimate protest groups.

Tristan believed in peacefully organizing workers of both sexes en masse. She took inspiration from the British Isles, where there had been two large-scale efforts to mobilize ordinary people: in Ireland, O'Connell's Catholic Association; and on the British mainland, Chartism, the mass movement that, during her visit to England in 1839, had been preparing to petition Parliament for enactment of its Six Points, which included universal male suffrage and a secret ballot. At Dr. Johnson's Tavern, off Fleet Street, Tristan attended a National Convention of Chartists. Among the attendees were Feargus O'Connor, a former Irish MP who edited the *Northern Star* newspaper; James Bronterre O'Brien, another radical journalist who hailed from the Emerald Isle; and William Lovett, a cofounder of the London Working Men's Association. "O'Connor is a vigorous, fiery orator whose brilliance is inspiring," Tristan wrote in her book on London. "O'Brien is remarkable for his sound reasoning, his lucidity, his calm manner and his profound knowledge of history."[44]

France had nothing to compare to Chartism, but Tristan wasn't discouraged. She visited artisanal workshops and corresponded with labor activists who were trying to organize workers on a smaller scale.[45] Her interlocutors included Jacques Gosset, a Parisian blacksmith; Pierre Moreau, a locksmith from Auxerre; and Agricol Perdiguier, a carpenter from Avignon. Although Tristan's roots were far from working class, her effort to reach across class and gender lines was sincere. She believed that workers had great potential and were merely lacking knowledge of their own collective strength. And she was convinced that it was her mission—a religiously ordained one—to be their guide and instructor.

To this end, Tristan started working on a short book, *The Workers' Union*, which was eventually published in 1843. Despite the success of *Promenades of London*, which French critics hailed as an important work of social criticism, she had difficulty finding a publisher for a book aimed at workers. Eventually she decided to finance its publication herself and asked her friends and associates to contribute. Among those who agreed to make donations were Considérant, Sand, and Adolphe Blanqui, a brother of the jailed revolutionary.[46] After raising more than fifteen hundred francs, Tristan personally carried her manuscript, which ran to about 125 pages, to the printer.

The book began: "TO ALL WORKERS, MEN AND WOMEN, Hear me!" During the past twenty-five years, Tristan noted, some of the most "intelligent and devoted men" in the country had carried out studies showing that "the working class is materially and morally in an intolerable condition of poverty and grief."[47] Despite these warnings, the government had refused to acknowledge this crisis or take any steps to alleviate it, so responsibility had fallen on the workers themselves. "Now the time has come to *act*, and it's for *you* and *you alone* to do so in the interest of your own cause," Tristan wrote. "For you, it's a case of life . . . or death! . . . that horrible death that kills bit by bit: *poverty and hunger!*"[48]

But what were the workers to do? Tristan ruled out violence. "The action for you to take is not armed revolt, uprisings in the public square, burnings and pillage," she said. "No because destruction instead of bettering your situation will make things worse. The uprisings in Lyon and Paris are good proofs." She went on: "As for action on your part there is only one that is legal, legitimate, and avowable to God and mankind; it is the Universal Union of Men and Women Workers."[49] Alone, workers were weak, but together they had power, Tristan noted. "Well, then! Abandon your isolation: unite with each other! *Union makes for strength.* You have numbers on your side, and numbers are everything."[50]

In 1840s France, unlike in Britain, labor unions were illegal. Workers didn't even have full freedom of movement: they were required to carry an internal passport (*livret d'ouvriers*) that stated their place of employment and certified they were free of debts. Despite this hostile environment to labor, there had been efforts during the 1830s to create workers' associations, particularly in craft industries like printing and textiles, where cheap labor and new technology represented threats. But these initiatives were localized and largely confined to artisans. They didn't advance the labor movement very far beyond the craft guilds that dated back to medieval times.

Tristan's proposal was designed to overcome the historic divisions between workers of different trades and skill levels. Her union would be open to any worker, she explained, with each member contributing annual dues of two francs. In workplaces, the union would press for higher wages and better conditions. In the political realm, it would demand representation for workers in the French parliament. And in each community, it would establish a "Workers' Union Palace"—a superhostel providing healthcare for injured workers, education for children, and shelter for the elderly and infirm.

A key element of Tristan's proposal was its explicit class basis. If the workers overcame their internal divisions, she argued, they could organize themselves as a class, just as the bourgeoisie had done in 1789 when its members had "recognized equality of rights for everyone," but "seized for themselves alone all the gains and advantages of this conquest." The Universal Workers' Union would redress this imbalance by organizing the working class and demanding a "RIGHT TO WORK," Tristan said. The only property that the workers possessed was their arms, and "the *free use* and guarantee of that property must be recognized *in principle* (and also in reality)."[51]

This proposal for job guarantees wasn't entirely novel. Other socialist writers had recognized the precariousness of employment as a central problem in an economy based on the profit motive. In 1840, the writer and future politician Louis Blanc had published a pamphlet, *The Organization of Labor*, in which he called on the French government to supplant the competitive private-enterprise economy, which he regarded as ruinous, with a nationwide system of workshops, "Ateliers Sociaux," where workers would be guaranteed jobs and get to choose their own bosses. In Blanc's vision, these publicly owned workshops would compete with capitalist firms—and eventually outcompete them because their employees would work harder in enterprises they controlled. Tristan's full employment proposal was different. Rather than bringing in the government to create new worker-run firms, it relied on workers at existing businesses organizing themselves into a general union, and employers recognizing their right to work.

"But, someone is going to say again, what you demand for the working class is *impossible*," Tristan acknowledged. Business owners would "simply not listen," and "since those who manage the governmental machine are the owners of land and capital, it is evident that they will never consent to grant such rights to the working class."[52] This was where organizing the workers into a single class came in. "Notice what force a body united by the same interests can have," Tristan wrote, again referencing the French bourgeoisie after the revolution. "Once this class IS CONSTITUTED it becomes so strong that it can appropriate every power in the land."[53]

The universalism of Tristan's proposal distinguished it from other efforts to organize and unite the working class. Even in Britain, where Owen and his associates had tried to set up a national labor organization, the goal had been to create an umbrella group for different unions rather than to combine them into one. Tristan envisaged a single organization with a physical presence—the workers' palaces—in every district of France. Another thing that made her proposal transformative was that her Universal Workers' Union would admit female workers alongside males and recognize "the *legal equality* of men and women as being the only means of constituting the UNITY OF HUMANITY."[54]

In a chapter titled "Why I Mention Women," Tristan argued that organizing female workers was necessary to unite all workers and remedy past injustices. "Up to the present time, woman has counted for nothing in human societies," she wrote. "What has been the result? That the priest, the legislator, and the philosopher have treated her as a *real pariah*. Women (half of humanity) have been *left outside of the church*, outside of the *law*, outside of *humanity*."[55] This was Tristan writing in the spirit of Mary Wollstonecraft and Anna Wheeler. And like those feminist pioneers, she supplemented her moral arguments with an appeal to the self-interest of male workers.

Lower-class women, Tristan wrote, had "so many irritations"—haughty husbands, greedy employers, unruly children—that they tended to be "brutal, mean, sometimes harsh," which prompted their spouses to seek refuge in the local tavern.[56] Addressing male workers directly, she said that the best way to remedy this situation was for them to ensure their wives and daughters received a "rational, solid education, suitable for developing all their good, natural bents."[57] If women were treated as equals and encouraged to fulfill their talents, "you would have for sisters, for lovers, for wives, for friends, educated women well brought up and whose everyday dealings could not be more agreeable for you."[58]

This passage clearly reflected an acknowledgment on Tristan's part that her proposals wouldn't get anywhere without the support of male workers. But her main appeal to men was based on economics and the harsh logic of capitalism in the raw. In many trades, she pointed out, women were doing the same jobs as men but were getting paid half as much. Male workers tried to justify these pay differentials on the grounds that they were more productive, Tristan said, but this wasn't true: in jobs demanding nimbleness and dexterity, such as spinning, women often produced more output than men. "What is happening?" she wrote. "The manufacturers, seeing the women laborers work *more quickly* and at *half price*, day by day dismiss men from their workshops and replace them with women. Consequently the man crosses his arms and dies of hunger on the pavement! That is what the heads of factories in England have done."[59]

Right now, men were suffering the consequences of unrestricted competition, Tristan went on, but things wouldn't end there. "Once started in this direction, women will be dismissed in order to replace them with *twelve-year-old children*. A saving of *half the wages!* Finally one gets to the point of using only *seven- and eight-year-old children*. Overlook one injustice and you are sure to get thousands more."[60] Tristan insisted that the only lasting solution to this problem was to create a union strong enough to protect all workers, male and female, guaranteeing full employment at livable wages for everybody. "It is on behalf of *your own interest, men*," she declared; "it is *for your betterment, you men*; finally, it is *for the universal well-being of all men and women* that I enlist you to demand rights for women, and, while waiting, to acknowledge them at least *in principle*."[61] If workers heeded her call, then in twenty-five years, Tristan predicted, "ABSOLUTE EQUALITY for men and women" would be inscribed in the laws of France. "Sons of '89," she concluded, "that is the work that your fathers have bequeathed to you!"[62]

The reaction to *The Workers' Union* was mixed. Some labor activists resented being preached to by an upper-class woman. Other readers were more receptive but objected to Flora's descriptions of some workers as drunkards. Perdiguier, the Avignon carpenter, accused her of claiming credit for an idea—a universal workers' union—that others, himself included, had also put forward.[63] An anonymous reviewer in *The Workshop*, a progressive publication, mocked Tristan in blatantly sexist terms: "O'Connell in skirts, who knows? . . . The Free Woman, the Woman-Messiah whose coming Enfantin the revealer announced to us."[64] From the far left, Étienne Cabet, a disciple of Blanqui, dismissed as naive Tristan's notion of uniting the working class and attaining power peacefully.[65]

In other quarters, the reaction was more positive. In *The Phalanx*, Enfantin published an extract of *The Workers' Union* and wrote a favorable notice.[66] After Tristan distributed copies of her book to workshops throughout Paris, some workers and activists embraced it. They included the German exile Arnold Ruge, an associate of the young Karl Marx. Ruge attended a weekly get-together that Tristan held at her apartment on the Rue du Bac. He was surprised to meet ordinary workers who had read *The Workers' Union*, and he was stirred by its author, noting that her "tall stature and the nobility of her features animated by the fire in her black eyes made her speech twice as impressive."[67]

The uneven reception for *The Workers' Union* wasn't surprising. Tristan was a woman; she lacked the support of any political organization; and some of her ideas seemed impractical to many. The proposal to set up workers' palaces nationwide wasn't backed up with any proper cost estimates, and it was surely fanciful to suppose that individual contributions would provide enough money to finance them. At one of Tristan's meetings, the labor activist André Saive, who had created a mutual aid society for hatmakers, pointed out that most workers were too poor to pay an annual subscription of two francs. "You still don't know the workers very well, Madame," Saive said. "The worker earns just what he is forced to spend to go on living."[68]

Tristan wasn't put off by these criticisms. In *The Workers' Union*, she had acknowledged that her vision of mobilizing working-class men and women in a single organization was a genuinely grand one, and she had described it as divinely sanctioned. But merely "to write a book for the people is to throw a drop of water into the sea," she wrote. She also said she had always known that once the book was published she would have "another duty to perform": to go "from town to town, from one end of France to the other," and speak to the workers directly. "I have decided that the moment has come to act, and that for whoever loves the workers and wishes to devote body and soul to their cause, there is a fine mission to fulfill," she wrote. "One must follow the example set by the first apostles of Christ . . . God tells me that it will succeed. That is why I enter this new way with confidence."[69]

Tristan was as good as her word. On April 12, 1844, she set off from Paris. Traveling by riverboats and horse-drawn carriages, she went southeast to Burgundy and Dijon, then on to Lyon and Provence, before moving northwest, through Languedoc, to Toulouse and Bordeaux. As she had during her trip to Peru, she traveled alone. At some stops, friends or distant associates put her up, but in many places she stayed in modest hotels. On arriving in a new town, she would speak with virtually anyone who would listen: workers' groups, labor activists, local politicians, even factory owners and bishops.[70]

In a diary that Tristan kept during her trip, she described the challenges she faced. In some towns, she struggled to find anybody interested in what she was saying. In other places, she attracted large crowds. She was subjected to harassment by local policemen and judicial authorities who regarded her as a dangerous radical. She also suffered from exhaustion and illness. Her indomitable character and irreverent spirit kept her going. Toward the end of September, she set off from Toulouse to Bordeaux. In the town of Agen, she wrote ironically: "At last I have what I have long desired—The apparatus of the police and army—thirty men to break up one of our meetings!"[71]

That was Tristan's final diary entry. By the time she reached Bordeaux, the city from which she had departed for Peru eleven years earlier, she was seriously ill, stricken by an ailment that might well have been typhoid. A well-meaning pair of teachers took her into their home, and a few of her friends managed to come and see her on her sickbed. On November 14, 1844, Tristan died at the age of forty-one. Her body, rather than being transported back to Paris, was buried locally in a Carthusian cemetery, with some local workers serving as pallbearers.

Posthumously, Tristan was hailed as a tribune of the women's movement and the workers' movement. In 1846 one of her admirers, the writer Alphonse Constant, who later used the pen name Éliphas Lévi, published a book of her writings titled *Woman's Emancipation; or, The Pariah's Testament*. A couple of years later, in the Bordeaux graveyard, a white marble column was erected, bearing the inscription: "TO THE MEMORY OF MADAME FLORA TRISTAN, AUTHOR OF THE WORKERS' UNION. THE GRATEFUL WORKERS."[72]

7

Thomas Carlyle on Mammon and the Cash Nexus

William Thompson and Flora Tristan believed in progress. Even as they criticized a system that divided society into rival camps and denied workers the full product of their labors, they worked to create new forms of social organization that would allow humanity to take advantage of modern science and technology in order to build a more just world. But from the Lowlands of Scotland came a darker and more withering voice; a voice that portrayed industrial capitalism as a moral wasteland and excoriated laissez-faire economics but also expressed little faith in democratic or socialistic remedies; a voice that was deeply skeptical of mechanization, science, and many other aspects of modernity; a voice that venerated strongman autocrats and would be hailed as a forerunner of fascism. Yet this was also a voice that, in its own time, was hailed by Charles Dickens, Ralph Waldo Emerson, and many other prominent figures.

Thomas Carlyle was born in Ecclefechan, a village about twenty miles from the town of Dumfries, on December 4, 1795. His parents, a stonemason and a homemaker, were pious and God-fearing Presbyterians who read the Bible to their nine children daily and hoped that Thomas, their eldest son, would become a minister. Roaming the rolling countryside around Ecclefechan, Carlyle developed a love of nature that would stay with him for life. After attending a fee-paying local high school, he studied mathematics and moral philosophy at Edinburgh University, and spent a couple of years as a schoolteacher. At some point, he realized there was a problem with his parents' plans for him: although he still believed in God, he had lost his faith in the Christian church.[1] He returned to Edinburgh, where he studied German and became enamored with German literature, especially Goethe, who was another nature lover. He decided to become a writer. To make ends meet, he translated German books and wrote explanatory entries for an encyclopedia. In 1827—by which time he had married a fellow Scot, Jane Baillie Welsh—he published his first piece in the prestigious *Edinburgh Review*. Its subject was Johann Paul Friedrich Richter, a German romantic novelist.

A nervous bookworm who suffered from chronic indigestion and other disorders, including impotence, Carlyle didn't have much firsthand knowledge of the industrial revolution, or of the world outside Scotland. He did have opinions, which he wasn't shy about expressing. When, in 1829, *The Edinburgh Review* asked him to review three books about the current and future state of society, he handed in a piece that declared: "Were we required to characterise this age of ours by any single epithet, we should be tempted to call it, not an Heroical, Devotional, Philosophical, or Moral Age, but, above all others, the Mechanical Age."[2] Headlined "Signs of the Times," the article went on:

> On every hand, the living artisan is driven from his workshop, to make room for a speedier, inanimate one. The shuttle drops from the fingers of the weaver, and falls into iron fingers that ply it faster. The sailor furls his sail, and lays down his oar; and bids a strong, unwearied servant, on vaporous wings, bear him through the waters. Men have crossed oceans by steam; the Birmingham Fire-king has visited the fabulous East . . . There is no end to machinery. Even the horse is stripped of his harness, and finds a fleet fire-horse invoked in his stead. Nay, we have an artist that hatches chickens by steam; the very brood-hen is to be superseded! . . . We war with rude Nature; and, by our resistless engines, come off always victorious, and loaded with spoils.[3]

Of course, Carlyle wasn't the first to remark on the wonders of steam and other technological advances. But he brought a fresh perspective to his observations. For now, he remarked, he would leave to the "Political Economists" the question of "how wealth has more and more increased, and at the same time gathered itself more and more into masses." He would concentrate on how the "mechanical genius of our time" had diffused itself into the realms of the "internal and spiritual." At the individual and collective level, he wrote, the mechanical pursuit of measurable progress and monetary gain had vanquished higher values. "Men are grown mechanical in head and in heart as well as in hand. They have lost faith in individual endeavor, and in natural force of any kind." In education, politics, and science these trends were entrenched. Even religion had been affected. "This is not a Religious age," Carlyle remarked. "Only the material, the immediately practical, not the divine and spiritual, is important to us. The infinite, absolute character of Virtue has passed into a finite, conditional one; it is no longer a worship of the Beautiful and Good; but a calculation of the Profitable."[4]

The abandonment of society's traditional moorings, the substitution of the practical for the transcendental, explained the widespread unease about the future, Carlyle said. He placed much of the blame on utilitarian thinkers of the mechanical age, the followers of Bentham and Mill, whose equation of happiness with material progress he lumped alongside the promises of deluded chiliasts down the ages. "At such a period, it was to be expected that the rage of prophecy should be more than usually excited," he wrote. "Accordingly, the Millennarians have come forth on the right hand, and the Millites on the left. The Fifth-monarchy men prophesy from the Bible, and the Utilitarians from Bentham. The one announces that the last of the seals is to be opened, positively, in the year 1860; and the other assures us that 'the greatest-happiness principle' is to make a heaven of earth, in a still shorter time."[5]

The teachings of the Millenarians and the Utilitarians were so unrealistic that they might simply "dissipate, and die away in space," Carlyle commented in this essay.[6] But as the 1830s proceeded, it became clear to him that industrial capitalism and utilitarianism were making further advances. The Great Reform Act of 1832 extended the franchise to many members of the emerging industrialist class. The Poor Law Amendment Act of 1834 applied the harsh precepts of political economy to the labor market, presenting many impecunious members of the lower orders with a choice between starving and entering the loathed workhouses that Dickens would immortalize in *Oliver Twist*. As the decade went on, many members of the working class coalesced behind the Chartist movement and demanded political rights that the Reform Act had denied to them, including universal male suffrage.

As these events unfolded, Carlyle became a major literary figure, hailed at home and abroad. In the summer of 1830, a package arrived from Paris. Sent by a member of the Saint-Simonian Society, it contained a copy of Henri de Saint-Simon's *Nouveau Christianisme*, in which the French philosopher called for a new Christian brotherhood of man. After reading "Signs of the Times," some followers of Saint-Simon "thought they had found a kindred soul in England, and, to some extent, they were right," the American scholar Fred Kaplan, the author of a deeply researched biography of Carlyle, notes.[7] Like the French utopian socialists, Carlyle rejected materialism, criticized the ruling class, and called for spiritual renewal. Unlike Saint-Simon, however, he had no faith in technology as a redeeming force. Still, Carlyle was sympathetic enough to the French cause to translate Saint-Simon's work into English.

Carlyle's early writings also reached the United States, where the rise of modern science and industrialization had generated a counterreaction that took the form of a religious revival and Romanticism. This was the era of the Second Great Awakening, when Adventism and Mormonism sprang up. In New England intellectual circles, members of the Transcendentalist movement rejected the mechanical and the rote. They celebrated the glories of the natural world, the unity between humankind and nature, and the potential for individual spiritual revelation.

Ralph Waldo Emerson, the Transcendentalist poet and philosopher, read and admired Carlyle's early essays on German literature. Like the Scot, Emerson came from a religious background: he had served for years as a Unitarian minister. During a visit to Europe in 1833, Emerson met John Stuart Mill, who advised him to look up Carlyle. Emerson traveled to Scotland and showed up uninvited at the door of the remote farmhouse that the writer and his wife shared. The man who answered it was "tall and gaunt, with a cliff-like brow," Emerson later recalled, but also "full of lively anecdote, and with a streaming humour which floated everything he looked upon."[8] This wasn't the maudlin fellow that Carlyle's wife and family were familiar with. Grateful to the American for making the journey to Scotland, the Scot struck up a lasting friendship with his visitor.

Like the Saint-Simonians in France, Emerson and his associates in the United States viewed Carlyle as a soulmate who venerated nature, individualism, and spirituality. How far Carlyle actually shared the views of the American Transcendentalists can be debated, but he kept up a long correspondence with Emerson. In 1831 Carlyle published the novel that made his literary reputation, *Sartor Resartus*, an elaborate satire that purported to tell the story of a German philosopher named Diogenes Teufelsdröckh. A few years later Emerson arranged for the book to be published in the United States. He did the same thing for Carlyle's three-volume history of the French Revolution, which appeared in 1837. After reading that work, Emerson commented that Carlyle possessed "an imagination such as never rejoiced before the face of God, since Shakespeare."[9]

By the time Carlyle's history appeared, he and Jane had moved from Scotland to London, where they leased a house on Cheyne Row, Chelsea. They became fixtures of the capital's literary scene, meeting Dickens, Coleridge, Tennyson, and others. Although Carlyle also associated with J. S. Mill and other Philosophical Radicals who constituted a progressive faction of the ruling Whigs, he remained a party of one. Unlike most of the Radicals, he was deeply skeptical of laissez-faire economics, utilitarianism, and any dogma of social improvement. He also placed little stock in the many official and unofficial inquiries that were delving into many aspects of British life—including marriage laws, the finances of the Church of England, and the material conditions of the working classes—and publishing voluminous reports packed with statistics. "A witty statesman said you might prove anything by figures," he wrote in *Chartism*, a lengthy pamphlet he wrote in 1839 and published the same year. "We have looked into various statistic works, Statistic-Society Reports, Poor-Law Reports, Reports and Pamphlets not a few . . . with as good as no result whatever . . . Conclusive facts are inseparable from inconclusive except by a head that already understands and knows."[10]

The political movement that gave Carlyle the title of his pamphlet arose from a feeling of betrayal on behalf of the politically active elements of the working class. After the passage of the Great Reform Act and the Poor Law Amendment Act, their leaders organized a great extraparliamentary movement to turn Britain's oligarchical political system into a democracy. The 1838 People's Charter, which listed the movement's demands, was written by the leaders of the London Working Men's Association, which was founded in 1836. But the great strength of Chartism was that its support was drawn from many different sources all across Britain: labor unions; local friendly societies, which were often based at public houses; radical newspapers, such as Feargus O'Connor's *Northern Star*; and countless individuals.

In June 1839 the Chartists presented a petition containing 1.3 million signatures to the House of Commons, which summarily rejected it. Large demonstrations followed, a few of which turned violent. In Wales, thousands of Chartists marched through the center of Newport and demanded the release of some of their brethren who had been imprisoned. They were met by hundreds of special constables and soldiers from a British Army regiment that was stationed nearby. In the ensuing confrontation, both sides fired shots, and more than twenty Chartists were killed. The leaders of the Newport Rising, as it came to be called, were tried for high treason, convicted, and sentenced to death. After a national outcry, the sentences were commuted to exile in Australia.[11]

Rather than dwelling on the violence in Newport or the events that had led up to it, Carlyle took a broader approach. In his opening chapter, which he titled "Condition-of-England question," he described Chartism as the product of "bitter discontent grown fierce and mad."[12] According to the newspapers, "a Reform Ministry has 'put down the chimera of Chartism' in the most felicitous effectual," he noted. But in reality, "the living essence of Chartism has not been put down . . . The matter of Chartism is weighty, deep-rooted, far-extending; did not begin yesterday; will by no means end this day or tomorrow."

Official efforts to downplay the economic deprivations of the working class were unconvincing, Carlyle said. Figures on wages were scant, and even where they were available they didn't say anything about the variability of income and employment, which was "perhaps even more important than . . . quantity."[13] Then there was the mental strain of working in the industrial economy. "The labourer's feelings, his notion of being justly dealt with or unjustly; his wholesome composure, frugality, prosperity in the one case, his acrid unrest, recklessness, gin-drinking, and gradual ruin in the other—how shall figures of arithmetic represent all this?" Carlyle asked.[14] Despite all these questions, the authorities had gone ahead and passed a draconian reform to the Poor Law. Perhaps that measure was intended as an experiment to answer the question of whether a worker who was willing to work could find employment at a living wage, Carlyle suggested, before adding: "Chartism is an answer, seemingly not in the affirmative."[15]

Carlyle insisted that the real root of popular discontent was misrule on the part of the governing class, which had violated its duty to protect the social norms and mutual bonds that were an essential part of civilization. He referred to this new mode of governance as "*laissez-faire*," which "having passed its New Poor-Law, has reached the suicidal point." The Scot was interpreting the famous French phrase not only in its economic sense but also in its literal meaning of doing nothing and letting things, including bad things, happen. In preindustrial times, he noted, the aristocracy had engaged with the lower orders not just as employers or landowners but "in many senses still as soldier and captain, as clansman and head, as loyal subject and guiding king." But when this paternalistic system had been in place, "Cash Payment had not then grown to be the universal sole nexus of man to man," Carlyle said. Now, "with the triumph of Cash, a changed time has entered."[16]

Here, for the first time, was Carlyle's famous invocation of the "cash nexus" as the basis of social relations in a modern industrial society. "O reader," he wrote, "to what shifts is poor Society reduced, struggling to give still some account of herself, in epochs when Cash Payment has become the sole nexus of man to men!"[17] Carlyle wasn't blind to the wealth and new consumer products that industrial capitalism was producing, but he insisted that money and materialism couldn't fulfill the spiritual needs of the rich or the poor. "Cash is a great miracle; yet it has not all power in Heaven, nor even on Earth," he wrote. "'Supply and demand' we will honour also; and yet how many 'demands' are there, entirely indispensable, which have to go elsewhere than to the shops, and produce quite other than cash, before they can get their supply!"[18]

If people needed more from life than capitalism and utilitarianism had to offer, where could they find it? Not from their rulers, who had effectively admitted "that they are henceforth incompetent to govern, that they are not there to govern at all, but to do—one knows not what!" It was this abdication of governance, Carlyle said, that had created the vacuum into which Chartism and other popular political movements had stepped:

> What are all popular commotions and maddest bellowings, from Peterloo to the Place-de-Grève itself? Bellowings, *in*articulate cries as of a dumb creature in rage and pain; to the ear of wisdom they are inarticulate prayers: "Guide me, govern me! I am mad, and miserable, and cannot guide myself!" Surely of all "rights of man," this right of the ignorant man

to be guided by the wiser, to be, gently or forcibly, held in the true course by him, is the indisputablest. Nature herself ordains it from the first.[19]

This was one dark side of Carlyle's political philosophy—an unvarnished contempt for ordinary people, whom he referred to as "the multitude." In his estimation, popular demands for political representation were merely a sublimated appeal for more effective aristocratic rule. Democracy was ultimately self-negating, he wrote: it "is, by the nature of it, a self-cancelling business; and gives in the long-run a net-result of *zero*."[20] At most, it could provide a temporary stopping point on the road to a more durable and more autocratic form of government: "Not towards the impossibility, 'self-government' of a multitude by a multitude; but towards some possibility, government by the wisest, does bewildered Europe struggle."[21]

The reactionary nature of these passages was surely evident. But lest any readers might have misinterpreted it, or perhaps assumed that their author had been carried away by his own rhetoric, Carlyle reiterated his central message:

> Cannot one discern too, across all democratic turbulence, clattering of ballot boxes and infinite sorrowful jangle, needful or not, that this at bottom is the wish and prayer of all human hearts, everywhere and at all times: "Give me a leader; a true leader, not a false sham-leader; a true leader, that he may guide me on the true way, that I may be loyal to him, that I may swear fealty to him and follow him, and feel that it is well with me!" The relation of the taught to their teacher, of the loyal subject to his guiding king, is, under one shape or another, the vital element of human Society; indispensable to it, perennial in it; without which, as a body reft of its soul, it falls down into death, and with horrid noisome dissolution passes away and disappears.[22]

As well as being a disbeliever in democracy, Carlyle was a racist and an antisemite. In *Chartism*, he referred to a "sooty African."[23] Elsewhere, he wrote of "crowds of miserable Irish" in their "rags and laughing savagery"[24] and "usurious insatiable Jews."[25] That such a prominent writer would so openly express his racial and ethnic prejudices reveals much about Victorian Britain.

Far from being ostracized for his bigotry, Carlyle was hailed as "the sage of Chelsea."

In 1839 the British economy went into a slump, which created widespread joblessness and swelled the ranks of the Chartists. The following two years saw poor harvests, which kept food prices high and prompted workers to demand higher pay. Sporadic political unrest continued. In 1842 the Chartist leaders prepared a second petition of Parliament, which reiterated their political demands and called attention to the "wretched and unparalleled condition of the people." During the summer of 1842, tens of thousands of textile workers in Lancashire and Yorkshire went on strike. To ensure that production stopped, some of the mill workers removed boiler plugs from steam engines. In August, striking mill workers held a series of mass demonstrations in Manchester that, although largely peaceful, became known as the Plug Riots. The striking workers demanded higher wages, shorter working hours, and the enactment of the Charter. The authorities responded with mass arrests. Subsequently, hundreds of demonstrators were put on trial, and their leaders, including O'Connor, the newspaper editor, were charged with inciting riots.[26]

In this unsettled atmosphere, the "Condition of England" question that Carlyle had raised continued to dominate political and policy debates. He didn't return to it immediately. After he completed the *Chartism* pamphlet, he prepared a series of public lectures that he subsequently published under the title *On Heroes, Hero-Worship, and the Heroic in History*. At the start of his first lecture, Carlyle expostulated a theory of history as the work of great men: "For, as I take it, Universal History, the history of what man has accomplished in this world, is at bottom the History of the Great Men who have worked here."[27] The lectures were organized on this basis. In one entitled "The Hero as Prophet," he singled out Mohammed, the founder of Islam. Dante and Shakespeare featured in a lecture on "The Hero as Poet," and Oliver Cromwell and Napoleon in "The Hero as King."

Given Carlyle's upbringing in a family of Calvinists and his veneration of autocrats, it was perhaps inevitable that he would write a book about Cromwell, the Puritan soldier who served as the dictatorial Lord Protector of Britain after the English Civil War. In late 1842 he took a break from this project, which never came to fruition, to write another book on the state of Britain. His biographer Kaplan suggests that this idea might have been prompted by the publication of a parliamentary "Report on the Sanitary

Condition of the Labouring Population of Great Britain," which showed, among other things, that workers in industrial Manchester lived considerably shorter lives than workers in rural Rutland. In a letter to Edwin Chadwick, the Utilitarian social reformer who had prepared the report, Carlyle called this gap in life expectancies "one of the most hideous facts . . . in the history of *Mammon-Worship* and *Laissez-Faire*."[28]

Rather than writing another journalistic essay in the vein of *Chartism*, Carlyle concocted an elaborate history lesson, which he told through a number of real and imagined characters and a godlike narrator. He titled the book *Past and Present*. Combining dazzling wordplay with characteristic overstatement, it began by pointing out that of England's 15 million productive workers, "some two millions it is now counted, sit in Workhouses, Poor-law Prisons; or have 'out-door relief' flung over the wall to them."[29] This economic distress was a ringing indictment of the political system, Carlyle said. The Great Reform Act and Benthamite radicalism had failed, and Chartism had risen up. "All England stands wringing its hands, asking itself, nigh desperate, What farther?"[30]

The crisis wasn't merely, or mainly, economic, Carlyle insisted. Above all, it was moral. In adopting the religion of money, the country had abandoned the path of virtue, with consequences that were always going to be disastrous. "Money is miraculous . . . but also what never-imagined confusions, obscurations has it brought in; down almost to total extinction of the moral-sense in large masses of mankind!" Carlyle wrote. Adopting the biblical voice of God, he went on: "Behold, ye shall grow wiser, or ye shall die! Truer to Nature's Fact, or inane Chimera will swallow you; in whirlwinds of fire, you and your Mammonisms, Dilettantisms, your Midas-eared philosophies, double-barrelled Aristocracies, shall disappear!"[31]

Having set the scene, Carlyle shifted back in history to a more settled society: the twelfth-century Benedictine monks at Bury St. Edmund's Abbey in East Anglia. Drawing on a recently republished chronicle written by a monk who lived at the abbey, one Jocelinus de Brakelonda, he portrayed its inhabitants as devout, if primitive, believers who were in communication with a higher spiritual power. The abbot, one Samson of Tottington, Carlyle described as a heroic figure who had displayed the sort of leadership found in all great historical figures. Before he took over, Carlyle explained, the monastery had fallen into debt and dilapidation, with rain running in and the monks often drunk. Samson, an austere, abstemious figure, a man of few words but decisive action, had rapidly turned the abbey around. Roofs were repaired, debts were repaid. The monks returned to their prayers and found new moral purpose.

Carlyle's premise was absurd but clear. In this remote twelfth-century monastery there could be found an antidote to the anarchic, Godless industrial society that had arisen in nineteenth-century Britain—a society in which the cash nexus dictated social relations and capitalists like his fictitious Bobus Higgins, a sausage maker from Houndsditch who fed adulterated meal to his swine, held sway. "In brief, all this Mammon-Gospel of Supply-and-Demand, Competition, Laissez-faire, and Devil take the hindmost, begins to be one of the shabbiest Gospels ever preached," Carlyle remarked.[32] Raising himself onto his tallest soapbox, he went on:

> We have profoundly forgotten everywhere that *Cash-payment* is not the sole relation of human beings; we think, nothing doubting, that *it* absolves and liquidates all engagements of man. "My starving workers?" answers the rich mill-owner: "Did not I hire them fairly in the market? Did I not pay them, to the last sixpence, the sum covenanted for? What have I to do with them more?"—Verily Mammon-worship is a melancholy creed.[33]

Carlyle's call to lift up the poor had persuaded the Saint-Simonians that he was one of them, and his invocations of "Nature" had attracted the attention of the American Transcendentalists. *Past and Present* convinced a new generation of radicals and socialists that his intent was benign. But it wasn't. He despaired of ordinary people, of politicians (such as "Sir Jabesh Windbag," one of his fictional creations), and of the prospects for democratic reform. If change were to come, Carlyle insisted, it would have to be imposed from above by an authoritarian hero-figure, a modern-day Cromwell or Frederick the Great. "Oliver Cromwell," he wrote, "whose body they hung on their Tyburn gallows because he had found the Christian Religion inexecutable in this country, remains to me by far the remarkablest Governor we have had here for the last five centuries or so."[34] Of Frederick the Great, the enlightened absolutist who ruled Prussia for much of the eighteenth century, Carlyle remarked, "I reckon that this one Duke of Weimar did more for the Culture of his Nation than all the English Dukes and *Duces* now extant, or that were extant since Henry the Eighth gave them the Church Lands to eat, have done for theirs!"[35]

Carlyle didn't flat-out call for an autocracy—he may have thought that would be a provocation too far—but he didn't shy away from raising the prospect of it, or from warning of what else may lay ahead if the ruling class didn't mend its ways. Addressing directly the "Captains of Industry," Bobus Higgins and his ilk, he warned them that their workers "will not march farther for you, on the sixpence a day and supply-and-demand principle: they will not; nor ought they, nor can they." The way things were going, Carlyle wrote, "it is becoming inevitable that we dwindle in horrid suicidal convulsion . . . Will not one French Revolution and Reign of Terror suffice us, but must there be two? There will be two if needed; there will be twenty if needed; there will be precisely as many as are needed. The Laws of Nature will have themselves fulfilled. That is a thing certain to me."[36]

In closing his narrative, Carlyle returned to the theme of crisis and dissolution. In a country where "millions of men can get no corn to eat," he wrote, the people would rise up and shoot for food the "Last Partridge of England"— a reference to the game bird that British aristocrats loved to hunt.[37] The only way to avoid this outcome was for the country to abandon Mammon and return to virtue under the leadership of a great man. Before ending with some lines from Goethe's "The Mason Lodge," Carlyle made another reference to Frederick the Great, whom he would later make the subject of a mammoth and admiring biography: "In hope of the Last Partridge, and some Duke of Weimar among our English Dukes, we will be patient yet a while."[38]

In progressive and literary circles, the reaction to *Past and Present* was generally positive. Ignoring or misinterpreting its reactionary political message, reviewers focused on its indictment of industrial capitalism and laissez-faire economics. George Owen, editor of the Owenite journal *The New Moral World*, recorded his gratification in finding "the true philosophy of Socialism . . . arrayed in the gorgeous and striking drapery of Carlyle*ism*."[39] J. S. Mill, in his 1845 article "The Claims of Labour," credited Carlyle and his "indignant remonstrance with the higher classes on their sins of omission against the lower," for having to brought to the center of debate the plight of the working classes.[40]

The influence of *Past and Present* would be a lasting one. John Ruskin, the Victorian art critic and polymath, for decades kept an annotated copy. Finally he gave it away, remarking that he no longer needed it "because it has become a part of myself."[41] When, in 1860, Ruskin published *Unto This Last*, his own searing examination of wealth, materialism, and political economy, Carlyle's influence was readily evident. In another of Ruskin's essays, on the nature of value and wealth, he cited Carlyle's writings explicitly and remarked of them, "All has been said that needs to be said, and far better than I shall ever say it again."[42] Dickens, who addressed the condition of England in his own inimitable fashion, was also a fan of Carlyle. He dedicated to him his 1854 novel, *Hard Times*, which was set in a fictional mill town.[43]

In the United States, too, *Past and Present* was highly praised. "Since Burke, since Milton, we have had nothing to compare with it," Emerson wrote in *The Dial*, the in-house journal of the Transcendentalists.[44] He praised Carlyle as a writer who "in an age of Mammon and of criticism . . . never suffers the eye of his wonder to close . . . He cannot keep his eye off from that gracious Infinite which embosoms us."[45] Emerson did express some reservations about Carlyle's overbearing writing style, noting "the habitual exaggeration of the tone wearies whilst it stimulates." But he went on to remark that Carlyle, in his "strange half mad way," had entered the realm of literary greatness and was "the indubitable champion of England."[46] Emerson's close friend Henry David Thoreau agreed with this assessment. In an essay on Carlyle and his works, which appeared in 1847, Thoreau wrote: "For fluency and skill in the use of the English tongue, he is a master unrivaled." Thoreau even forgave the Scot his exaggerations, saying: "He who cannot exaggerate is not qualified to utter truth."[47]

The Transcendentalists weren't the only Americans to draw inspiration from Carlyle. In the South, some defenders of slavery hailed a writer who shared their argument that industrial capitalism, based on free wage labor and the profit motive, represented an unwarranted incursion on the natural order of society. In 1848 *The Southern Quarterly Review*, a journal based in Charleston, published a piece on Carlyle's works that claimed, "The spirit of Thomas Carlyle is abroad in the land."[48] The following year, the Scot published an unsigned article in *Fraser's Magazine* titled "Occasional Discourse on the Negro Question." Ostensibly, this piece consisted of a public address lamenting the economic decline of the British West Indies since slavery had been abolished. The speaker wasn't identified, but Carlyle's anonymous narrator informed readers that his words were written down by a disreputable reporter, "Dr. Phelin M'Quirk," and were left behind when M'Quirk skipped his digs without paying the rent. "As the colonial and negro question is still alive, and likely to grow livelier for some time," the narrator went on, "we have accepted the article, at a cheap market rate; and give it publicity, without, in the least, committing ourselves to the strange doctrines and notions shadowed forth in it."[49]

Perhaps Carlyle included this qualification as an insurance policy lest he be identified as the article's author, which was virtually inevitable given his unique writing style. His anonymous speaker described the Black plantation workers who had been freed on the West Indian islands as "sitting yonder, with their beautiful muzzles up to the ears in pumpkins, imbibing sweet pulps and juices; the grinder and incisor teeth ready for every new work, and the pumpkins cheap as grass in those rich climates; while the sugar crops rot round them, uncut, because labor cannot be hired, so cheap are the pumpkins."[50] The speaker went on: "Quashee, if he will not help in bringing out the spices, will get himself made a slave again (which state will be a little less ugly than his present one), and with beneficent whip, since other methods avail not, will be compelled to work."[51]

Although the article clearly reflected Carlyle's racist views, its main purpose was to criticize the British abolitionists, whom he termed "Exeter Hall," and free market economists, such as Smith, who had argued that wage labor would be more efficient and profitable than slave labor. Carlyle's anonymous speaker claimed that in the Caribbean, but not just there, the ending of slavery had proved economically disastrous. "Alas, in many other provinces, beside the West Indian," he said, "that unhappy wedlock of Philanthropic Liberalism and the Dismal Science, has engendered such all-enveloping delusions, of the moon-calf sort—and wrought huge woe for us, and for the poor, civilized world, in these days!"[52]

The description of economics as "the dismal science" is another of Carlyle's famous aphorisms. He was correct that production on British sugar plantations did fall sharply after the abolition law was passed. But he conveniently ignored the fact that this was largely because the planters refused to pay the wages that the formerly enslaved workers demanded and opted to import indentured labor instead, largely from India. Faced with competition from plantations in Cuba and Brazil, which had maintained slavery, the British planters believed they had been unfairly treated. It seems likely that Carlyle picked up his account of the situation in the West Indies from some of them. His anonymous speechifier, at the end of his address, called for the establishment of new working arrangements on the plantations that would have been tantamount to a restoration of slavery. Addressing the freed Blacks, the speaker said:

> You are not "slaves" now; nor do I wish, if it can be avoided, to see you slaves again: but decidedly you will have to be servants to those that are born *wiser* than you, that are born lords of you—servants to the whites, if they *are* (as what mortal can doubt they are?) born wiser than you . . . And if "slave" mean essentially "servant hired for life," or by a contract of long continuance, and not easily dissoluble—I ask, Whether in all human things, the "contract of long continuance" is not precisely the contract to be desired, were the right terms once found for it?[53]

It didn't take long for Carlyle to be outed as the author of the article. Subsequently, Mill, a strong supporter of abolition, said in a letter to the editor of *Fraser's Magazine* that the "doctrines and spirit" of the piece "ought not to pass without remonstrances."[54] In the American South, pro-slavery interests saw more to like in the article. In 1850, *DeBow's Review*, a monthly business magazine based in New Orleans, reprinted it under the headline "Carlyle on West India Emancipation." An editor's note said "When British writers can so speak, it is time for Northern fanaticism to pause and reflect."[55] Whatever Carlyle's intentions had been in writing "Occasional Discourse on the Negro Question," he was hailed in the South as a fellow defender of slavery. If he had wanted to distance himself from the article, he could have done so. He didn't. Instead, in 1853, he approved its republication in England with an even more incendiary title, which included a racial epithet.

In the twentieth century, Carlyle's racist views and his love of autocrats would make him a favorite of right-wing extremists, including Nazi leaders. In the *Führerbunker*, according to some accounts, Goebbels read Hitler extracts from Carlyle's biography of Frederick the Great.[56] During Carlyle's lifetime, however, it was his critiques of capitalism and materialism that attracted the most attention. In January 1844 *Deutsch-Französische Jahrbücher*, a Paris newspaper published by leftist German exiles, printed a review of *Past and Present* that began: "Of all the fat books and thin pamphlets which have appeared in England in the past year for the entertainment or edification

of 'educated society,' the above work is the only one which is worth reading." The article quoted long extracts from Carlyle's book and noted: "If we
discount a few expressions that have derived from Carlyle's particular standpoint, we must allow the truth of all he says." The shortcoming of *Past and
Present*, the reviewer wrote, was not in analysis but in prescription: Carlyle
was "vague and hazy about the future." He spoke about creating a spiritual
renewal and recognizing the true value of work, but he didn't mention the
English socialists at all, and his analysis was shot through with dubious religious arguments. "As I have said," the review went on, "we too are concerned
with combating the lack of principle, the inner emptiness, the spiritual deadness, the untruthfulness of the age; we are waging a war to the death against
all these things, just as Carlyle is, and there is a much greater probability that
we shall succeed than that he will, because we know what we want."[57]

The author of these words was Friedrich Engels, a young German socialist who had just returned home to Barmen after spending a couple of years
in Manchester. At the time when he wrote the review of *Past and Present*, he
was working on a book of his own.

8

Friedrich Engels and
The Communist Manifesto

By the early 1840s, Manchester was Britain's second largest city.[1] Together with the adjoining town of Salford, it had a population of more than a quarter of a million. Its skyline was dominated by the tall chimneys of steam-powered cotton mills that belched black smoke into the Lancashire sky. Tens of thousands of men, women, and children worked in these factories, and the city had many other manufacturing facilities: tanneries, foundries, glass-works, and metalworking shops. As the center of the global cotton industry, it was also a thriving commercial center, with countless warehouses and a grand exchange building, where merchants and traders dealt in yarns of all kinds. In an age when the railroad was about to become king, Manchester already boasted lines to Liverpool (the world's first intercity link) and Leeds. A line to London, via Birmingham, was under construction.[2]

In late 1842 Friedrich Engels, who was just twenty-two, arrived in Salford to work at a cotton thread factory that his father co-owned. He hailed from Barmen, an industrial town in the Rhineland, which was then part of Prussia. His family of pious Lutherans owned a successful linen bleaching business, but during the 1830s Engels's father, Friedrich Sr., had quarreled with his siblings and entered a partnership with two Dutch brothers, Godfrey and Peter Ermen. By the early 1840s, the firm of Ermen and Engels had opened its factory in Salford, which, in honor of the new British monarch, it named Victoria Mill.[3]

Engels was a reluctant capitalist. When he was seventeen, his father had forced him to start a business apprenticeship, first in Barmen, then in the port city of Bremen. To the horror of Friedrich Sr., his son had progressive views and wanted to become a writer. In an 1839 newspaper article that he wrote under the pseudonym Friedrich Oswald, he described the factories in his native Wuppertal Valley as "low rooms where people breathe in more coal fumes and dust than oxygen."[4] In 1841 young Friedrich went to Berlin to do his military service. Away from the parade ground, he attended philosophy lectures at the University of Berlin and socialized with a group of radicals known as the Young Hegelians, who criticized organized religion and the Hohenzollern monarchy that ruled Prussia. The idealism of Georg Wilhelm Friedrich Hegel, who had died in 1831, provided the intellectual framework for the Young Hegelians' intellectual sallies, but the battlegrounds they fought on were rationality, freedom, and modernity. Although they differed on some key philosophical issues, they were united in viewing themselves as enemies of religious superstition and old ways in general. Engels fit right in. He chose private lodgings over the military barracks, acquired a dog, and drank heavily with his associates. The philosopher Bruno Bauer, one of the more prominent Young Hegelians, referred to the group as the "beer literati."[5]

Despairing at his son's behavior, the elder Engels decided to send him to England to work alongside Peter Ermen, who managed the Victoria Mill. Friedrich obeyed his father's order, but in November 1842, on his way to England, he stopped in Cologne to meet some editors from *Rheinische Zeitung* (Rhenish Newspaper), a left-leaning newspaper that had already published some anonymous freelance articles he had written. The top editor, recently appointed, was an intense young fellow from Trier, another city in the Rhineland, named Karl Marx. Evidently, the two didn't hit it off. Decades later, Engels would describe this initial encounter as "distinctly chilly."[6]

Engels worked in the Victoria Mill's office, handling orders and accounts. Despite his disdain for business, which he referred to as "a dog's life," he had a good head for figures.[7] On evenings and weekends, he attended talks at the Manchester Hall of Science, an Owenite institution dedicated to adult education, self-improvement, and cooperative socialism. Among the lecturers at the Hall of Science was John Watts, a former weaver turned schoolmaster who had published a book entitled *The Facts and Fictions of Political Economists*, which railed against the regimentation of factory life and described how an economic system based purely on pecuniary values was responsible for "depravity."[8] According to Tristram Hunt, the author of a highly informative 2009 biography, *Marx's General*, another working-class writer who influenced Engels was James Leach, a Chartist activist and former handloom weaver, who had written an anonymous polemic about life in the mills.

A third critic of early industrial capitalism who made a big impression on Engels was Carlyle. Although Engels didn't share Carlyle's conservative views on religion and politics, he admired him for puncturing hypocrisies and addressing what he described as "the lack of principle, the inner emptiness, the spiritual deadness, the untruthfulness of the age."[9]

Outside of work and the Hall of Science, Engels started a relationship with Mary Burns, a young Irish immigrant who may have been employed at Victoria Mill. (Some accounts say she was; others suggest she was in domestic service.)[10] Engels and Burns would be involved for about twenty years. (After Mary died, in 1863, Engels went on to marry her sister Lizzy.) Having a knowledgeable local chaperone must have been a great help to Engels, especially when, for journalistic purposes, he started visiting some of the city's poorest areas. Eventually he decided to write a book, *The Condition of the Working Class in England*, which was first published in Leipzig in 1845. Today, it is widely regarded as a classic account of early industrialization.

The book opens with the industrial revolution in England and the rise of the "industrial proletariat." Then it describes various parts of Manchester, including the Old Town, a cramped neighborhood on the banks of the River Irk, where many Irish immigrants lived. The Irish were among the city's most hard-up residents, and Engels wrote that the narrow courtyards that led down to the Irk "contain unqualifiedly the most horrible dwellings which I have yet beheld."[11] He described, at the end of one covered passage, "a privy without a door, so dirty that the inhabitants can pass into and out of the court only by passing through foul pools of stagnant urine and excrement."[12] The river itself was "a narrow, coal-black, foul-smelling stream, full of debris and refuse" from the local factories and residential buildings.[13] In one spot that Engels happened across, the residences consisted of "small one-storeyed, one-roomed huts, in most of which there is no artificial floor; kitchen, living-and sleeping-room all in one." The description goes on: "In such a hole, scarcely 5 feet long by 6 broad, I found two beds—and such bed-steads and beds!—which, with a staircase and chimney-place, exactly filled the room. In several others, I found absolutely nothing, while the door stood open, and the inhabitants leaned against it."[14]

Areas like the Old Town had no running water or proper sewage systems. Engels noted that cholera outbreaks were common. He also described some slightly more salubrious neighborhoods, including Ancoats, where "stand the largest mills of Manchester lining the canals, colossal six- and seven-storeyed buildings towering with their slender chimneys far above the low cottages of the workers."[15] This neighborhood had proper pavements and drains, and its residents were better off than the inhabitants of the Old Town, many of whom were casual workers rather than factory operatives. In a December 1842 article for *Rheinische Zeitung*, Engels acknowledged that full-time male factory workers in Manchester were paid higher wages than their counter-parts in Germany. "The worker there earns just enough to allow him to live on bread and potatoes; he is lucky if he can buy meat once a week," Engels wrote. "Here he eats beef every day and gets a more nourishing joint for his money than the richest man in Germany. He drinks twice a day and still has enough money left over to be able to drink a glass of porter at midday and brandy and water in the evening. This is how most of the Manchester workers live who work a twelve-hour day."[16]

Engels didn't include this passage in his book, which he described, while he was writing it, as an "indictment"[17] of the British bourgeoisie rather than an even-handed treatment. But it was an indictment packed with vivid de-tail. One thing lacking in Ancoats and other working-class districts, Engels noted, was any middle-class or upper-class residents. Manchester's property owners, himself included, lived in new housing developments on the city's outskirts—"in free, wholesome country air, in fine, comfortable homes, passed once every half or quarter hour by omnibuses going into the center of the city."[18] Engels said the contrast in living conditions between the two Manches-ters was reflected in the physical appearance of its residents. Echoing Flora Tristan and the anonymous *Black Dwarf* author, he wrote: "If one roams the streets a little in the early morning, when the multitudes are on their way to their work, one is amazed at the number of persons who look wholly or half-consumptive . . . These pale, lank, narrow-chested, hollow-eyed ghosts, whom one passes at every step, these languid, flabby faces, incapable of the slightest energetic expression."[19]

For whatever reason, Engels didn't describe the working conditions at the Victoria Mill, which he must have known well. (In Barmen, the Engels family was known as a benevolent employer.) But he did back up some of his assertions with materials drawn from official reports and parliamentary debates about industrialization, both of which proliferated during the 1830s and '40s. Drawing on a speech by Lord Ashley, a campaigner for a shorter workday, he wrote: "Of 419,560 factory operatives of the British Empire in 1839, 192,887, or nearly half, were under 18 years of age, and 242,296 of the female sex, of whom 112,192 were less than 18 years old."[20] Citing parliamentary testimony from doctors, Engels highlighted a "pretty list of diseases engendered purely by the hateful money-greed of the manufacturers!" He cited children with curved spines; workers with chronic chest ailments; pregnant women forced to work virtually until childbirth.[21] In another passage, he recalled traveling into the city with a local businessman and regaling him about the dilapidated condition of the workers' quarters: "The man listened quietly to the end, and said at the corner where we parted: 'And yet there is a great deal of money made here; good morning, sir.'"[22]

Best known for its vivid descriptions of Manchester and its inhabitants, *The Condition of the Working Class in England* also features a good deal of economic analysis. Indeed, it contains, at least in embryonic form, some of the key arguments that would subsequently be subsumed in "Marxist" economics. They were largely drawn, or developed, from the English socialists and socialist literature that Engels encountered at the Hall of Science, but they also reflected his own experiences. In an 1860s letter, he recalled that his stay in Lancashire "forcibly brought to my notice that economic factors, hitherto ignored or at least underestimated by historians, play a decisive role in the development of the modern world." The letter went on:

> I learnt that economic factors were the basic cause of the clash between different classes in society. And I realized that in a highly industrialized country like England the clash of social classes lay at the very root of the rivalry between parties and was of fundamental significance in tracing the course of modern history.[23]

For a German educated in the Hegelian tradition, which emphasized the power of ideas, recognizing the centrality of material factors represented a major shift. In writing his book, Engels fully embraced it. Sixty or eighty years ago England had been largely agricultural, he wrote. Now it was "a country like *no* other . . . with vast manufacturing cities; with an industry that supplies the world, and produces almost everything by means of the most complex machinery."[24] In 1834, England exported "556,000,000 yards of woven cotton goods, 76,500,000 pounds of cotton yarn."[25] But even as scientific progress and industrialization had given a huge boost to England's economic development, it had divided its society into two antagonistic groups: the bourgeoisie, which owned the means of production, and the propertyless proletariat. "The history of the proletariat in England begins with the second-half of the last century, with the invention of the steam engine and of machinery for working cotton,"[26] Engels stated flatly. In order to survive, the factory worker had no option but to sell his labor. "Left to himself he cannot survive a single day. The bourgeoisie has gained a monopoly of all means of existence in the broadest sense of the word."[27]

None of this would have come as news to William Thompson or other early socialists, of course. Like some of them, Engels went on to compare factory work to slavery. The main difference, he said, was that "the worker of today seems to be free because he is not sold once for all, but piecemeal by the day, the week, the year, and because no one owner sells him to another, but he is forced to sell himself in this way instead, being the slave of no particular person, but of the whole property-holding class."[28] To the modern reader, this comparison may well seem overwrought. But Engels was making an important point: in a capitalist system, the element of compulsion in the employer-worker relationship is disguised by a seemingly voluntary market transaction. Engels sought to remove the mask, declaring:

> The proletarian is, therefore, in law and in fact, the slave of the bourgeoisie, which can decree his life or death. It offers him the means of living, but only for an "equivalent" for his work. It even lets him have the appearance of acting from a free choice, of making a contract with free unconstrained consent, as a responsible agent who has attained his majority.
>
> Fine freedom, where the proletarian has no other choice than that of either accepting the conditions which the bourgeoisie offers him, or of starving, of freezing to death, of sleeping naked among the beasts of the forests![29]

Engels was a proud class traitor. Describing his book, he wrote in an 1844 letter: "I accuse the English bourgeoisie before the entire world of murder, robbery and other crimes on a massive scale."[30] But even as he adopted the framework of class conflict and exploitation, he also emphasized another important element of industrial capitalism: competition within each class. Capitalists were forced to compete for profits; workers had to compete for jobs. "Competition is the completest expression of the battle of all against all which rules in modern civil society," he wrote.[31] In theory, he went on, the workers in each trade could join together and demand higher wages. In practice, however, "the power-loom weaver is in competition with the hand-loom weaver" and the "unemployed or ill-paid hand-loom weaver [competes] with him who has work or is better paid, each trying to supplant the other."

This reference to the jobless was far from incidental. In a chapter on the workings of "competition," Engels noted the presence, even when the economy wasn't in a slump, of "an unemployed reserve army of workers"—workers who had lost their jobs, Irish immigrants, beggars, street sweepers, and the like.[32] These members of the "surplus" population ensured that "the competition among the workers is constantly greater than the competition to secure workers."[33] Engels described how this constant jostling for jobs held wages at or near subsistence levels. In boom times, when workers were hard to find, employers might bid up wages for a while, but this was a temporary phenomenon. Once the boom ended, employers regained the whip hand, and wages fell back.

Engels also provided a short but acute explanation of business cycles, which were a regular feature of early industrial capitalism. During the early stages of an upswing, he pointed out, the prices of goods tend to rise, which encourages manufacturers to churn out more of them in anticipation of further hikes. As production rises, "speculation forces prices still higher, by inspiring others to purchase."[34] Then comes the frenzied peak, when "daring speculators working with fictitious capital . . . hurl themselves into this universal, disorderly race for profits, multiply the disorder and haste by their unbridled passion."[35] Eventually the inevitable happens. Prices fall, "the market is disordered, credit shaken, one house after another stops payments, bankruptcy follows bankruptcy, and the discovery is made that three times more goods are on hand or under way than can be consumed."[36] This is the crisis stage of the cycle. Production slumps, workers are thrown out of jobs, and there is great hardship until the glut of goods is eliminated, prices stabilize, and the cycle starts over. "So it goes on perpetually—prosperity, crisis, prosperity, crisis, and this perennial round in which English industry moves is . . . usually completed once in five or six years."[37]

On the face of things, Engels's account of economic ups and downs—today we would call it a "model"—seemed to imply that capitalism could go on forever, endlessly repeating itself. He didn't accept this conclusion, however. In his final chapter, he argued that the system had an underlying weakness that would eventually prove fatal: rising inequality and class conflict. If Britain retained its "monopoly of manufactures," he wrote, the "proletariat would increase in geometrical proportion, in consequence of the progressive ruin of the lower middle class and the giant strides with which capital is concentrating itself in the hands of the few."[38] Eventually the proletariat would "embrace the whole nation with the exception of a few millionaires. But in this development, there comes a stage at which the proletariat perceives how easily the existing power may be overthrown, and then follows a revolution."[39]

Engels even provided a provisional timetable for this narrative. Based on a five- or six-year economic cycle, the next slump was due in 1846 or 1847. The political pressures produced by this downturn would lead to the enactment of the People's Charter, he predicted, but the real reckoning wouldn't come until the recession after that—the one due to begin in 1852 or 1853. By then, "the English people will have had enough of being plundered by the capitalists and left to starve when the capitalists no longer require their services . . . The war of the poor against the rich will be the bloodiest ever waged."[40]

In the summer of 1844, Engels left Manchester and returned home to Germany. He traveled there via Paris, where he met up with Marx, who had moved to the French capital the previous year after the Prussian authorities suppressed *Rheinische Zeitung*. Marx was now associated with another radical journal, *Deutsch-Französische Jahrbücher*, which he and another German émigré had founded. Despite the frostiness of their initial meeting in Cologne, Engels and Marx had much to discuss. From England, Engels had sent Marx an essay of his that expanded on some of the arguments he had made in his book.[41] Titled "Outlines of a Critique of Political Economy," it began with a discussion of Adam Smith's effort to overthrow the restrictive practices of mercantilism, which Engels described as historically necessary "so that the true consequences of private property could come to light . . . so that the struggle of our time could become a universal human struggle."[42] As industrialization proceeded, larger manufacturers and merchants tended to swallow up their smaller competitors. This "law of the centralisation of private property" meant that the "middle classes must increasingly disappear until the world is divided into millionaires and paupers."[43]

The essay impressed Marx, who agreed to publish it in *Deutsch-Französische Jahrbücher*. (In later years, he would describe it as "a brilliant sketch" and quote from it repeatedly.)[44] The two Germans met at Café de la Régence, near the Palais-Royale. According to legend, they talked and drank for ten days straight. Certainly, they had many common points of reference. Like Engels, Marx came from a prosperous family. He was born in Trier on May 5, 1818. His father, Heinrich, was a Jewish lawyer who had converted to Christianity and changed his name from Herschel. His mother, Henriette, hailed from a family of Dutch Jewish merchants. After Marx finished high school, he attended the University of Bonn for a year, then transferred to the University of Berlin, where, like Engels years after him, he associated with the Young Hegelians and drank heavily. But Marx was a much more serious student than Engels. At his father's behest, he studied law, but his real passion was philosophy. He devoured the works of Ludwig Feuerbach, whose 1841 *Essence of Christianity* described the Christian conception of God as an illusion. After completing his undergraduate studies, he wrote a doctoral thesis on the ancient Greek thinkers Democritus and Epicurus.

In other circumstances, Marx would probably have become a philosophy professor. The Young Hegelians' criticisms of the church and the state had prompted a government clampdown on universities, which blocked his path. In 1842 Marx moved to Cologne, where he began editing at *Rheinische Zeitung*. By the time he met up with Engels in Paris, he had married Jenny von Westphalen, a German woman four years his senior whose father was a civil servant and minor member of the Prussian nobility. He had also broken with some of the Young Hegelians over what he had come to perceive as their excessive focus on anticlericalism. In addition, he had developed a strong interest in political economy, which had prompted him to study Adam Smith, James Mill, and Jean-Baptiste Say, as well as some of the French and English socialists. In a set of notebooks that he kept between April and August 1844, he started to develop his own economic analysis, beginning from what he called "a contemporary fact of political economy": the alienation and immiseration of workers.[45] Bourgeois economists, in purporting to analyze how a competitive economy worked, had assumed what needed to be interrogated,

Marx wrote: "Political economy starts with the fact of private property, it does not explain it to us." Never short of intellectual confidence, he said his analysis would go deeper, seeking to "understand the essential connection of private property, selfishness, the separation of labor, capital and landed property, of exchange and competition, of the value and degradation of man, of monopoly and competition, etc."[46]

Marx couldn't know it, but this intellectual project would go through many iterations and take up most of the rest of his life. In his notebook, which would be published nearly a century later as *Economic and Philosophic Manuscripts of 1844*, he focused on how carrying out wage labor affected workers. Building on the Hegelian notion of alienation, in which human consciousness fails to understand its own true nature, he identified several ways in which the industrial system robbed people of their individuality and humanity. Factory workers, unlike farmers and artisans, had no control over the production process, so the goods they helped to produce meant nothing to them. ("The worker relates to the product of its labor as an alien object.") Also, their regimented working environment ran contrary to nature and violated their "species-being." Finally, the monolithic nature of the factory system isolated them from other people. In all these forms of alienation, Marx said, the central issue was that the worker had no control over his or her environment, and thus "sinks to the level of a commodity and becomes indeed the most wretched of commodities." The only enduring answer to this problem, he argued, was "the positive transcendence of private property as human self-estrangement, and therefore as the real appropriation of the human essence by and for man."[47]

This apparent call for the abolition of property seemed to echo Pierre-Joseph Proudhon, an anarcho-socialist French philosopher whose 1840 book *What Is Property?* contained the famous slogan "Property is theft!" Marx had studied the older French socialists, including Fourier, and he knew Proudhon personally: he claimed to have explained German idealism to him.[48] But even as he repeated Proudhon's call to transcend private property, he rejected the Frenchman's preferred alternative: worker cooperatives in which capital would be communally owned but workers would still work for wages. Marx dismissed this idea as "crude communism." Precisely what variant Marx favored, he didn't make clear; arguably, he never would. Nonetheless, he described communism in the abstract as "the true resolution of the struggle between existence and essence, between objectification and self-affirmation, between freedom and necessity, between individuals and species. It is the solution to the riddle of history and knows itself to be this solution."[49]

After their meeting at Café de la Régence, Engels and Marx were on the same wavelength. "Our complete agreement in all theoretical fields became evident and our joint work dates from that time," Engels would later recall.[50] After returning to his family home in Barmen, where he completed *The Condition of the Working Class in England*, he delivered a series of public speeches that attracted the attention of the Prussian authorities, who were monitoring democratic activists and other potential subversives. "Friedrich Engels of Barmen is a quite reliable man, but he has a son who is a rabid communist and wanders about as a man of letters," a police report noted.[51] The Prussian government also kept close tabs on German exiles in Paris. At its instigation in early 1845, the French authorities expelled a number of journalists associated with the radical German-language newspaper *Vorwärts*. One of those targeted was Marx, who moved to Brussels.[52]

After Engels had finished editing his book, he, too, moved to the Belgian capital. It was there that his writing partnership with Marx got going in earnest. So did the pair's political machinations. "The Germans . . . especially Marx, are plotting their usual mischief here," Michael Bakunin, the anarchist-leaning Russian socialist, who had also turned up in the Belgian capital, noted in a letter to an associate. "Vanity, malice, squabbles, theoretical intolerance and practical cowardice . . . The single word *bourgeois* has become an epithet which they repeat *ad nauseam*, though they themselves are ingrained bourgeois from head to foot."[53]

Fleeing domestic repression, German leftists had scattered across western Europe. Marx and Engels got the idea of creating an umbrella organization to unite them. During a study trip to London and Manchester in 1845, they met with members of an underground group called the League of the Just, which had been expelled from France after participating in the 1839 Blanquist rising. The London-based comrades, who had set up an organization called the German Workers Educational Association, welcomed the idea of coordinating with revolutionary groups in other countries. After Marx and Engels returned to Brussels, they established a Communist Correspondence Committee to facilitate this endeavor. During a visit to London in June 1847, they persuaded the London group to change its name to the Communist League.[54] As a small group of exiles, this fledgling organization didn't represent much of a threat to anyone, but Marx and Engels believed it merited a manifesto. At another meeting, in November 1847, they put forward a statement of "Principles of Communism," which Engels had drafted. Structured like a newspaper explainer, it consisted of twenty-five questions and answers. The first question was "What is Communism?" The answer was "Communism is the doctrine of the conditions of the liberation of the proletariat."[55]

The members of the Communist League differed on how to bring about this liberation. Wilhelm Weitling, a charismatic tailor who had a small but devoted following, was calling for an immediate uprising that would employ an army of ex-convicts to seize power and establish a new society based on common ownership of property. Engels and Marx shared the same ultimate goal as Weitling, which (in Engels's words) was to "institute a system in which all these branches of production are operated by society as a whole— that is, for the common account, according to a common plan, and with the participation of all members of society."[56]

This was the first, and perhaps clearest, statement that Marx and Engels produced about the nature of a future communist society. In 1847, however, they believed that communism wouldn't be feasible until capitalism had developed sufficiently to provide the material basis for a more equitable system. "In all probability," Engels wrote in his Q&A, "the proletarian revolution will transform existing society gradually and will be able to abolish private property only when the means of production are available in sufficient quantity." That meant different countries would proceed at their own paces depending on their level of development: "slowest and will meet most obstacles in Germany, most rapidly and with the fewest difficulties in England." In predominantly rural Germany, the first goal was to "establish a democratic constitution, and through this, the direct or indirect dominance of the proletariat." A democratic government could then introduce progressive taxation, inheritance taxes, a national education program for all children, and the "gradual expropriation of landowners, industrialists, railroad magnates and shipowners, partly through competition by state industry, partly directly through compensation in the form of bonds."[57]

Some members of the Communist League didn't like this gradualist approach. Nonetheless, in November 1847 the league approved Engels's statement of principles and agreed to change its title to *The Communist Manifesto*. The comrades also authorized Engels and Marx to draw up a version for publication. Marx took on the task of writing a final draft. In characteristic fashion, he had trouble finishing on time. After an urgent appeal from the league's executive, he completed the job in January 1848. A month later the twenty-three-page *Manifesto* was printed in London, although only in German. From its famous opening—"A specter is haunting Europe—the specter of Communism"[58]—to its ringing sign-off—"WORKING MEN OF ALL COUNTRIES, UNITE!"—it was all that a political call to arms should be: direct, impassioned, and substantive.

The heart of the *Manifesto* is contained in its first section, "Bourgeois and Proletarians," which begins: "The history of all hitherto existing society is the history of class struggles."[59] In tracing how the "bourgeois mode of production"—the term Marx and Engels used for industrial capitalism—emerged from feudalism, the opening passages emphasize the impact of European colonialism, which "gave to commerce, to navigation, to industry, an impulse never before known, and thereby, to the revolutionary element in the tottering feudal society, a rapid development."[60] As the market grew for goods of all kinds, the feudal workshop economy, with its closed labor guilds, couldn't keep up, and small-scale manufacturing took its place. But this system couldn't keep up, either: "Thereupon, steam and machinery revolutionised industrial production. The place of the manufacture was taken by the giant, Modern Industry, the place of the industrial middle class, by industrial millionaires, the leaders of whole industrial armies, the modern bourgeois."[61]

Here, writ large, is the materialist theory of history that Engels had embraced in Manchester. Grand economic forces drive societal evolution, and the bourgeoisie is their latest embodiment, speeding up the historical clock and sweeping all before it. The *Manifesto* goes on:

> The bourgeoisie, wherever it has got the upper hand, has put an end to all feudal, patriarchal, idyllic relations . . . and has left remaining no other nexus between man and man than naked self-interest, than callous "cash payment." It has drowned the most heavenly ecstasies of religious fervor, of chivalrous enthusiasm, of philistine sentimentalism in the icy water of egotistical calculation. It has resolved personal worth into exchange value,

and in place of the numberless indefeasible chartered freedoms, has set up that single, unconscionable freedom—Free Trade. In one word, for exploitation veiled by religious and political illusions, it has substituted naked, shameless, direct, brutal exploitation.[62]

And further:

> The bourgeoisie cannot exist without constantly revolutionizing the instruments of production, and thereby the relations of production, and with them the whole relations of society . . . Constant revolutionising of production, uninterrupted disturbance of all social conditions, everlasting uncertainty and agitation distinguish the bourgeois epoch from all earlier ones . . . All that is solid melts into air, all that is holy is profaned, and man is at last compelled to face with sober senses his real conditions of life, and his relations with his kind.[63]

This was language to fire up the members of the Communist League. But even as the *Manifesto* highlights the ungodly nature of the bourgeois epoch, it also acknowledges its unprecedented productivity. After noting that it "has accomplished wonders far surpassing Egyptian pyramids, Roman aqueducts, and Gothic cathedrals,"[64] the pamphlet lists some more of its achievements: "Subjection of nature's forces to man, machinery, application of chemistry to industry and agriculture, steam-navigation, railroads, electric telegraphs, clearing of whole continents for cultivation, canalization of rivers, whole populations conjured out of the ground—what earlier century had even a presentiment that such productive forces slumbered in the lap of social labour?"[65]

In his earlier Q&A, Engels had emphasized the global nature of the bourgeois epoch and suggested that the communist revolution would also have to be a worldwide phenomenon. The *Manifesto* takes up this theme of globalization, expanding upon its economic basis:

> The need of a constantly expanding market for its products chases the bourgeoisie over the entire surface of the globe. It must nestle everywhere, settle everywhere, establish connections everywhere.
>
> The bourgeoisie has through its exploitation of the world market given

a cosmopolitan character to production and consumption in every country. To the great chagrin of reactionists, it has drawn from under the feet
of industry the national ground on which it stood. All old-established
national industries have been destroyed or are daily being destroyed. They
are dislodged by new industries, whose introduction becomes a life and
death question for all civilized nations.[66]

These passages were written at a moment when Britain had established
itself as an industrial superpower, the United States was starting to catch up,
and France and (still divided) Germany were stirring. Britain, as the low-cost
producer of manufactured products, had adopted the self-interested stance
of promoting free trade. Many of its economic rivals, including the United
States, were erecting tariff walls to protect their developing industries. Marx
and Engels didn't dwell on the details of these economic strategies, but they
highlighted the social and cultural consequences of capitalism's onward
global march:

In place of the old wants, satisfied by the production of the country, we
find new wants, requiring for their satisfaction the products of distant
lands and climes. In place of the old local and national seclusion and
self-sufficiency, we have intercourse in every direction, universal inter-
dependence of nations. And as in material, so also in intellectual production. The intellectual creations of individual nations become common
property. National one-sidedness and narrow-mindedness become more
and more impossible, and from the numerous national and local litera-
tures, there arises a world literature.[67]

How far could this process of globalization and homogenization go? The
Manifesto is unequivocal:

The bourgeoisie, by the rapid improvement of all instruments of production, by the immensely facilitated means of communication, draws all,
even the most barbarian, nations into civilization. The cheap prices of
commodities are the heavy artillery with which it batters down all Chinese walls, with which it forces the barbarians' intensely obstinate hatred
of foreigners to capitulate. It compels all nations, on pain of extinction,

to adopt the bourgeois mode of production; it compels them to introduce what it calls civilization into their midst, i.e., to become bourgeois themselves. In one word, it creates a world after its own image.[68]

A member of the Communist League, on reading these descriptions of the capitalist economy and its wonders, could surely have been forgiven for wondering how such a mighty edifice would ever be toppled. In answering this question, the *Manifesto* invokes Goethe's ballad "The Sorcerer's Apprentice," in which the lazy trainee bestows magic powers upon a broom, with unintended and disastrous results.[69] The bourgeoisie plays the role of the sorcerer, and capitalism plays the role of the broom.

One of the unintended consequences of capitalism's immense productiveness, the *Manifesto* points out, is the emergence, at regular intervals, of "commercial crises": unsold goods pile up, workers are thrown out of their jobs, and "it appears as if a famine, a universal war of devastation, had cut off the supply of every means of subsistence."[70] Through the "enforced destruction of a mass of productive forces . . . the conquest of new markets, and by the more thorough exploitation of the old ones," the system has demonstrated a capacity to rebound from these slumps. However, each recovery is merely "paving the way for more extensive and more destructive crises" in the future.[71]

This passage closely follows Engels's analysis of economic cycles in *The Condition of the English Working Class*. The *Manifesto* goes on to identify the underlying problem as one of overproduction, which it describes as a creation of the bourgeoisie that is potentially fatal to it: "But not only has the bourgeoisie forged the weapons that bring death to itself; it has also called into existence the men who are to wield those weapons—the modern working class—the proletarians."[72] Again, this argument follows Engels's earlier work, but the *Manifesto* lays out in greater detail how the proletariat develops into a revolutionary class. Initially, its members are an "incoherent mass," broken up "by their mutual competition." Powerless to resist mechanization, they "destroy imported wares that compete with their labour, they smash to pieces machinery, they set factories ablaze, they seek to restore by force the vanished status of the workman of the Middle Ages." (Marx and Engels had studied the Luddites.) But as industrialization proceeds, it gradually "obliterates all distinctions of labour." The proletariat "not only increases in number; it becomes concentrated in greater masses, its strength grows, and it feels that strength more . . . The collisions between individual workmen and individual bourgeois take more and more the character of collisions between two classes."[73]

To boost their wages and defend their work conditions, workers organize and form labor unions. They may even secure some political advances: the *Manifesto* singles out the British Factory Act of 1847, which limited the workday to ten hours for women and for children under eighteen. Ultimately, though, this progress is illusory. The worker, "instead of rising with the progress of industry, sinks deeper and deeper . . . He becomes a pauper, and pauperism develops more rapidly than population and wealth. And here it becomes evident that the bourgeoisie is unfit any longer to be the ruling class in society . . . It is unfit to rule because it is incompetent to assure an existence to its slave within his slavery."[74]

This is the famous immiseration thesis. Whereas Engels, in *The Condition of the Working Class in England*, had qualified it with an acknowledgment that some factory workers earn more than others, and that wages can rise at least for a time, the *Manifesto* contains no such nuances. It presents the impoverishment of the workers as a remorseless process that ultimately destroys the system that generates it, because the oppressed proletariat, having no alternative, turns into a revolutionary class: "What the bourgeoisie therefore produces, above all, are its own grave-diggers. Its fall and the victory of the proletariat are equally inevitable."[75]

The *Manifesto* is a remarkable polemic. Even today the vividness and prescience of its language leap from the page, especially in its descriptions of globalization and the "world market." And yet it was written at a time when modern transport and communications technologies were at their dawn. The railways were largely confined to Britain and the United States. Although Samuel Morse had recently developed his telegraph, it was still a novelty. As Isambard Brunel's Great Western Steamship Company was transporting passengers between Bristol and New York, mariners in much of the world were relying on windsails. Industrial capitalism itself was far from ubiquitous. In his introduction to a 150th anniversary edition of the *Manifesto* published in 1998, the historian Eric Hobsbawm pointed out that in 1848 economies of continental Europe and North America were still primarily agricultural. Hobsbawm was surely correct when he said that the *Manifesto*'s descriptions of industrialization and globalization should be read as statements about "the necessary *long-term* historical tendencies of capitalist development" rather than as descriptions of mid-nineteenth century reality.[76]

Could the same be said about the *Manifesto*'s binary taxonomy of bourgeoisie and proletariat? Up to a point. In industrial cities like Manchester, the working class consisted of many different occupations—from factory workers to construction laborers to domestic workers to skilled artisans. Even in the cotton mills, there were many different jobs, each with its own skill set, pay scale, and social standing. Among the ranks of the propertied, striking divisions existed between the lower middle class, such as shopkeepers and small business owners; the professional middle class, which encompassed lawyers and merchants; and the nouveau riche factory owners. Marx and Engels insisted that capitalism was rapidly eliminating these internal class distinctions. In reality, this process was slow and uneven.

In explaining why the *Manifesto*'s confident prediction of a class war has so far turned out to be wishful thinking, it is vital to take account of these complications. A similar point applies to the immiseration thesis that Marx and Engels promulgated. Economic historians have long debated what happened to working-class living standards during the industrial revolution, but they generally agree that, starting in the mid-1840s or thereabouts, the wages of English workers rose steadily. According to Bank of England data,[77] between 1845 and 1865, average inflation-adjusted weekly wages increased by 30 percent. By 1900, wages were about 50 percent higher than they had been in 1850. In other parts of western Europe, the pattern was broadly similar. A 2014 study by researchers at the Paris-based Organisation for Economic Co-operation and Development (OECD) compared workers' wages in six countries to the cost of a basic "subsistence basket" of food goods necessary for human survival. On this basis, the researchers concluded that between the decades of the 1850s and the 1900s wages increased by more than 70 percent.[78]

Marx himself would eventually be forced to contend with the evidence that many British workers were seeing their wages rise. When he and Engels were writing the *Manifesto*, however, they were basing their analysis on the experiences of the early industrialization period, which provided more support for their immiseration thesis. Adam Smith argued that, as capitalist development progressed, wages would steadily increase, and the population would be elevated into a state of "opulence." But during the half-century from 1790 to 1840, according to calculations by Charles Feinstein, an English economic historian, the inflation-adjusted wages of British workers rose by just 12 percent—a barely perceptible increase year by year—despite much larger increases in output and output-per-worker.[79] In a 2009 paper titled "Engels' Pause," another economic historian, Robert Allen, pointed out that profits rose sharply during the same period, and the share of overall income accruing to owners of capital rose by about 5 percentage points while the labor share fell by the same amount. Workers didn't share the fruits of capital investment and productivity growth: wages stagnated while capitalists got richer. "Engels' description of the industrial revolution was, in many respects, an insightful one," Allen concluded.[80]

It should be noted that Feinstein's figures are disputed: other scholars have produced considerably higher estimates of British wage growth over the period. All estimates of economy-wide real wages are acutely sensitive to which workers are included in them and the cost-of-living indices used to deflate nominal wages. Still, if Feinstein's figures are even roughly accurate, industrialization and technological progress didn't translate into appreciably higher worker living standards for a considerable period.

But the immiseration thesis didn't age well. From the 1840s onward, the wages of British workers rose along with productivity, and in some periods, they grew even faster. Between 1860 and 1900, according to Allen's estimates, output-per-worker rose at an annual rate of 1 percent and real wages rose at a rate of 1.6 percent.[81] Consequently, the share of total income accruing to labor increased by 10 percentage points, and the share accruing to capital fell by the same amount.[82] The basic economic assumption underlying the *Manifesto* was that workers don't share the rewards of technological progress and productivity growth. After about 1850, this assumption no longer held—a point that Alfred Marshall, the leading orthodox economist of his day, would emphasize in his 1879 book *The Economics of Industry*.[83] If wages had continued to lag behind productivity growth, as they had done in the first half of the nineteenth century (and would again in the late twentieth century), subsequent history could well have followed the *Manifesto*'s predictions more closely.

When Marx and Engels were writing the *Manifesto*, they had no way of knowing that they were living through a historical inflection point for workers' living standards. The hardship and financial instability that characterized early industrial capitalism were continuing. In 1847 a speculative railroad boom had ended in a banking crisis that gripped the City of London and relented only after the British government suspended the Bank Charter Act of 1844 to enable the Bank of England to print more money. In Ireland, the Great Famine was raging. In France, following a poor harvest in 1846, the economy had entered a slump that led to rebellions in the countryside and bread riots in Paris and Lyon. Throughout France and Germany, representatives of the rising middle class were demanding more political rights, including, in some cases, universal suffrage.

In many parts of Europe, this febrile conjuncture created a potential alliance of convenience between middle-class radicals and alienated members of the working class. During the last week of February 1848, even before the Communist League could distribute copies of its newly printed *Manifesto*, a violent uprising began in Paris. Crowds packed the streets and erected barricades. On February 24, King Louis Philippe abdicated. The next day a provisional government declared a republic. Within weeks, the revolutionary impulse had spread to Berlin, Vienna, and many other European cities. But despite the hopes of Marx and Engels, it didn't spread to Britain. The Great Reform Act had already enfranchised large elements of the British middle class, which made the situation very different from that in other parts of Europe. And the British working-class movement, despite the repressive measures inflicted on it during the Chartist protests, remained largely committed to nonviolence.

The two German exiles, having no such compunctions, traveled from Brussels to Paris, and eventually moved home to Germany to catch up with the action there. Although they regarded the initial uprising as a bourgeois revolution, they were hopeful it would presage a continent-wide workers' insurrection. In Cologne, they created a new version of the newspaper they had worked on years earlier: *Neue Rheinische Zeitung* (New Rhenish Newspaper). Shaken by events, the absolutist rulers of Germany's various kingdoms had agreed to elections for a Constituent National Assembly. When it met in Frankfurt in May, most of its members were middle-class notables who were content to work alongside the ruling monarchs.

In Paris, more dramatic events were in train. The provisional government abolished slavery throughout the French Empire. On the domestic front, it took up a version of Louis Blanc's proposal for "national workshops," where jobless workers could obtain work or receive unemployment benefits. This policy drew a lot of impecunious people to the French capital. But a Constituent Assembly, which was elected on the basis of universal suffrage, turned out to be dominated by moderates and conservatives from outside Paris. On June 22 the government, responding to demands by members of the new Assembly, issued a decree closing the Paris workshops and requiring workers who were claiming relief to enlist in the army or leave for the provinces.

In the crowded eastern part of the city, workers and leftists took to the streets carrying banners emblazoned with the slogan "Work or Death." Barricades went up, and protesters clashed with members of the National Guard.[84] When news of the rising reached Germany, Marx and Engels were excited. In a June 27 editors' note in *Neue Rheinische Zeitung*, they proclaimed: "Paris bathed in blood; the insurrection growing into the greatest revolution that has ever taken place, into a revolution of proletariat versus the bourgeoisie."[85] The French government, acting as if it agreed with this analysis, empowered General Louis-Eugène Cavaignac, who had served for years in colonial Algeria, to crush the rebellion. Employing cannonfire to break through the barricades, Cavaignac's forces routed the insurgents, killing or wounding thousands of them.[86] By the end of June, Engels's "greatest revolution" had met a premature end. In the rest of Europe, further setbacks were to follow.

9

Karl Marx's Capitalist Laws of Motion

On August 24, 1849, the thirty-one-year-old Karl Marx traveled from Paris to London, where he was to live for the rest of his life.[1] The hopes that he and Engels had harbored for the revolutions of 1848 had been dashed. From Paris to Berlin to Vienna, the forces of reaction were back in the ascendancy. After the Prussian government shut down his newspaper, *Neue Rheinische Zeitung*, Marx had moved to France, where Louis Napoleon, the former emperor's nephew, had been elected as president, and rightist forces were consolidating power in the National Assembly. The French authorities quickly ordered Marx to leave Paris. He decided to move to London, where many of his associates in the Communist League now resided. A few weeks later, his wife, Jenny, who was pregnant, joined him. On November 5, 1849, their fourth child, a son called Guido, was born.

Life in London was tough on Marx and his family, who were perennially short of money. After initially living in Chelsea, they moved into a squalid two-room apartment at 64 Dean Street in Soho, then a poor, immigrant neighborhood. Subsequently, they moved down the block to another grotty flat at number 28. "In the whole apartment there is not one clean and solid piece of furniture. Everything is broken down, tattered and torn, with a half inch of dust over everything and the greatest disorder everywhere," a Prussian police spy reported in 1853.[2] During the seven-plus years that the Marx family lived in Soho, Karl and Jenny both suffered frequent illnesses. Three of their seven children died in infancy, Guido included. In June 1851, the couple's housekeeper, a German woman named Helene "Lenchen" Demuth, who had once worked for Jenny's parents, had a baby. According to an 1898 letter from a friend of Demuth, Engels said on his deathbed that Marx was the father. Other evidence also points to this conclusion, including a July 1851 letter from Marx to Engels, in which he said his home life was "in a state of siege," with "floods of tears," presumably Jenny's.[3] After putting the child up for adoption, Demuth stayed with the family.

Assuming Marx was the father, this obviously raises questions about his attitude toward women and domestic workers, neither of whom feature prominently in his economic analysis. In June 1850, he had obtained a ticket to the reading room of the British Museum, in nearby Bloomsbury, which would become his study. With colleagues from the German Workers Educational Association, he worked on the launch of another German-language journal, *Neue Rheinische Zeitung—Politisch-ökonomische Revue* (New Rhenish Newspaper—Political-Economic Review), which first appeared in early 1850. In a series of articles for the new publication, Marx examined the failure of the 1848 revolution in France. He claimed that the bloody putdown of the June rising had "created all the conditions under which France can seize the *initiative* of the European revolution."[4] He also hadn't given up hope of a revolution in Britain. In an article published in February 1850, he predicted that another great commercial crisis would arrive "as early as the end of spring, at the latest in July or August," and that it would "bear fruit of a very different type from all preceding crises."[5]

Marx's analysis of the class conflicts that gave rise to the 1848 revolutions was acute, but his prognostications were dubious. In Paris and other European cities, the left had been vanquished. Louis Napoleon remained firmly ensconced in power. (In December 1851 he would stage a military coup and later declare himself Emperor Napoleon III.) In Britain, the "hungry forties" had been left behind, and a great mid-Victorian boom was beginning. British capitalism was entering a new era in which heavy industries like railroads, steel, and steamships would play the leading role. In 1850 Britain's rail network already extended to six thousand miles, and by 1870 it would nearly triple in size.[6] During the same twenty-year period, as iron steamships took over the oceans, the annual output of British shipyards rose from 13,000 tons to more than 250,000 tons.[7] British exports of railway machinery, including steam locomotives, rose almost tenfold.[8] As Marx scanned old editions of *The*

Economist in the British Museum reading room, the country was preparing to celebrate its status as the "workshop of the world"—a phrase Benjamin Disraeli coined—by hosting a vast expo in London's Hyde Park, "The Great Exhibition of the Works of Industry of all Nations," which would have thirteen thousand exhibits. They included James Naysmyth's steam hammer, Cyrus McCormick's mechanical reaper, and Goodyear's vulcanized rubber. Although it wasn't technically an exhibit, the event also featured the world's first public pay toilet.

Continental Europe was still well behind Britain in industrializing, but it was moving in the same direction. In the United States, capitalist enterprise was rapidly spreading across the continent. The recent accession to the Union of Texas and California, together with the creation of the New Mexico Territory, meant that a single goods market now stretched from the Atlantic to the Pacific. Following the discovery of gold in 1848 at Sutter's Mill, east of Sacramento, the great California gold rush had begun. With slavery having been abolished in the British Empire, the French Empire, and much of Latin America, the continued use of enslaved labor in the American South looked increasingly like an aberration. Even outside the US, forced labor hadn't disappeared, of course. To meet their labor needs, European colonies in the Caribbean, Latin America, and South Africa imported large numbers of indentured workers, often from Asia, who worked long hours in oppressive conditions. Overall, though, plantation capitalism was giving way to industrial capitalism as the principal form of economic organization.

Marx and Engels recognized the significance of these developments. Writing about the Great Exhibition in the *Political-Economic Review*, they noted jointly that "the bourgeoisie of the world has erected in the modern Rome its Pantheon, where, with self-satisfied pride, it exhibits the gods which it has made for itself."[9] In another article, Marx wrote: "Thanks to the gold of California and to the tireless energy of the Yankees, both coasts of the Pacific will soon be as thickly populated, as industrialized and as open to trade as the coast from Boston to New Orleans is now."[10] Toward the end of 1850, Marx and Engels acknowledged the nonarrival of the economic crisis they had been expecting, writing: "Given this general prosperity, wherein the productive forces of bourgeois society are developing as luxuriantly as it is possible for them to do within bourgeois relationships, a real revolution is out of the question." The article went on to say a new revolution could come about only "as a result of a new crisis," before adding, as if to reassure their readers, "but it will come, just as surely as the revolution itself."[11]

Meanwhile, from his seat, G7, in the British Museum reading room, Marx intensified his study of the "productive forces." Initially, he considered writing a multivolume book on political economy, but he didn't end up publishing anything until 1859, when a Berlin publisher put out *A Contribution to the Critique of Political Economy*, a dense and uncompleted work that Marx regarded as merely a preliminary investigation. Eight years later he published his magnum opus, *Capital: A Critique of Political Economy*. After his death, in 1883, it emerged that he had written a great deal besides these two books. In 1885 and 1894 Engels published two more volumes of *Capital* based on notes that Marx had compiled in the 1860s. In 1905 Karl Kautsky, a German socialist theoretician, published *Theories of Surplus Value*, a mammoth manuscript that Marx had worked on in 1862–63, which is sometimes regarded as volume IV of *Capital*. In 1939 and 1941, a Soviet press released the *Grundrisse*, another long manuscript drawn from notebooks that Marx kept in the late 1850s. Much of this mountain of material went over the same ground repeatedly. Marx was forever reworking and rethinking his theories.

The fact it took him eight years to publish two books—the *Critique* and *Capital*—can be attributed to several factors: his perfectionism, his intermittent poor health, and a lack of money that forced him to spend a lot of time writing journalism. Between 1852 and 1862, he was a European correspondent of the *New-York Daily Tribune*, a liberal newspaper founded by the journalist and social reformer Horace Greeley and edited by Charles Dana, a former resident of the Fourierist community at Brook Farm in West Roxbury, Massachusetts. Dana met Marx in Cologne in 1848. He was so impressed by him that he invited him to write for the *Tribune*, which supported the abolition of slavery and was anti–free trade. The paper published more than four hundred articles from Marx, some of which he coauthored with Engels. According to Dana, Marx became one of the best-paid contributors to the *Tribune*, which suggests that his claims of poverty may have been somewhat overstated.[12]

Marx came to resent having to write journalism because it distracted him from his studies. "The continual newspaper muck annoys me," he wrote to a friend in 1853.[13] "It takes a lot of time, disperses my efforts, and in the final analysis is nothing." That was a harsh judgment on a considerable body of work, which covered everything from British politics to Louis Napoleon to the Indian Rebellion of 1857. Marx's first articles about India were published in 1853, when the East India Company's charter was coming up for renewal by the British Parliament. Decades earlier, the firm's trading monopoly with the subcontinent had finally been revoked after protests by other British exporters and importers, but it still controlled great expanses of the subcontinent, including some of its biggest cities.

Marx wrote scathingly about British motivations in India. "The aristocracy wanted to conquer it, the moneyocracy to plunder it, and the millocracy to undersell it," he said in an August 1853 article.[14] Echoing William Bolts, Adam Smith, and other critics of the East India Company, he said it had furnished the areas it ruled with "no supply at all of public works, an abominable system of taxation, and a no less abominable state of justice and law."[15] But even as Marx criticized the greed and hypocrisy of the British colonialists, he argued that their presence was ultimately a progressive force. "England has to fulfill a double mission in India: one destructive, the other regenerating," he commented, "the annihilation of old Asiatic society, and the laying [of] the material foundations of Western society in Asia."[16]

In his engrossing 2016 biography of Marx, the English historian Gareth Stedman-Jones pointed out that he inherited from other Eurocentric thinkers, including Hegel and James Mill, a misleading "image of Asia as stationary, and without a history."[17] Indeed, Marx went further than his predecessors and identified an "Asiatic" mode of production based on "Oriental despotism" and isolated village communities that "restrained the human mind within the smallest possible compass, making it the unresisting tool of superstition."[18] From his perspective, which was ultimately that of the European Enlightenment, countries like India and China wouldn't make any progress until they were exposed to Western science and production methods. Marx acknowledged that the rise of British industry had had "devastating effects" on India's producers, including its hand weavers and hand spinners. But he also said the railroads that the British were starting to construct would become "truly the forerunner of modern industry." As other examples of modernizing developments, he pointed to the creation of a large internal market, the establishment of a professional army, and the emergence of a new class of Indians "imbued with European science."[19]

None of this should be taken to mean that Marx was a defender of British colonialism. Even as he pointed out its modernizing aspects, he made clear that the exploitation and wealth extraction on which it rested were preventing ordinary Indians from enjoying the benefits of economic and technological progress. "The Indians will not reap the fruits of the new elements of society scattered among them by the British bourgeoisie," he wrote, "till in Great Britain itself the now ruling classes shall have been supplanted by the industrial proletariat, or till the Hindoos themselves shall have grown strong enough to throw off the English yoke altogether." But in any case, he added, "we may safely expect to see, at a more or less remote period, the regeneration of that great and interesting country."[20]

When Marx wasn't writing for the *Tribune* or incapacitated by his ailments, he concentrated on his critique of economic orthodoxy. As I discussed in the Introduction, in 1857 a financial panic started in New York with the failure of the Ohio Life Insurance and Trust Company and quickly spread to the United Kingdom. It spurred Marx on. In a frenetic burst of activity between October 1857 and March 1858, he compiled the seven notebooks that make up the *Grundrisse*.[21] Many of the subjects they covered Marx would take up again in *Capital*, but they also contained a good deal of material that can't be found elsewhere, including a succinct characterization of industrial capitalism as a "permanently revolutionary" system that is constantly "tearing down all obstacles that impede the development of productive forces."[22]

Some of the most striking passages concerned automation. Marx distinguished between mechanization in a system based on wage labor and the profit motive, where science "appears, in the machine, as something alien and exterior to the worker," and mechanization in a future society where the machines are "the property of associated workers" and where a reduction in working hours, as productivity rises, would mean that "all members of society can develop their artistic, scientific, etc, education, thanks to the free time now available to all."[23] The enemy wasn't technology itself but the capitalist system in which it was embedded.

In terms of economic theory, the biggest innovation in the *Grundrisse* was Marx's claim to have discovered a "law" of declining profitability that held the key to the long-term dynamics of capitalism. In January 1858 he wrote to Engels, "I have overthrown the whole doctrine of profits as it previously existed."[24]

Fragmented, discursive, and running to more than eight hundred pages, the *Grundrisse* wasn't intended for publication. By early 1859, Marx had completed the shorter manuscript that was published in Berlin as *A Contribution to the Critique of Political Economy*. These days, it is remembered principally for its preface, in which Marx said that the basic "relations of production" are what "constitutes the economic structure of society, the real foundation, on which arises a legal and political superstructure and to which correspond definite forms of social consciousness."[25] This was the famous taxonomy of base and superstructure, with the former shaping the latter. "The mode of production of material life conditions the general process of social, political and intellectual life," Marx wrote. "It is not the consciousness of men that determines their existence, but their social existence that determines their consciousness."[26]

Some of the other material in the *Critique*, which included lengthy discussions of the nature of commodities and money, was rather dense. Even Engels complained that the book was "very abstract."[27] To Marx's disappointment, leftist publications in Germany virtually ignored it. He immediately set to work on a second volume, but it was never to appear. For more than a year, he became engrossed in a bitter dispute with Karl Vogt, a leader of the left in the Frankfurt Assembly, whom he accused of being in the pay of Louis Napoleon. He considered moving back to Germany, where Ferdinand Lassalle, one of his old comrades from the 1848 revolution, wanted him to coedit a new workers' newspaper. That idea came to nothing, and Marx eventually returned to his original idea of a multivolume work on economics.[28]

In pursuing this project, which generated no income, Marx had to rely heavily on the charity of Engels because his journalistic work was drying up. In 1862 the *Tribune*, which was by then primarily concerned with the American Civil War, ended its association with him. Fortunately for Marx and his family, Engels was prospering. In 1850, when the disappointments of the failed revolutions were fresh, he had returned to Manchester and rejoined Ermen and Engels. With the Victorian boom continuing, the firm bought a second mill. As a junior partner, Engels received a generous salary plus a share of the firm's profits. He kept two houses—one for himself and one for Lizzy—and regularly mailed cash to Marx. (For security reasons, he would cut the notes in half and send each half separately.) According to the biographer Tristram Hunt, he was at times "allocating over half his annual income to the Marx family." Over the years, Hunt says, the total remittances came to somewhere between £3,000 and £4000 (or $450,000 and $600,000 in today's terms).[29]

If Marx had quibbles about subsisting on the profits generated by Lancashire cotton workers, he didn't mention them in his letters to Engels. In January 1857, shortly after Jenny received an inheritance that enabled the family to move from its cramped Soho flat to a house in Kentish Town, he complained: "So here I am without any prospects and with growing domestic liabilities, completely stranded in a house into which I have put what little cash I possessed and where it is impossible to scrape along from day to day as we did in Dean Street . . . I thought I had tasted the bitterest dregs in life. Mais non!"[30] With help from Engels and a bequest from his own side of the family, Marx and Jenny eventually moved to a bigger house in a new development off Haverstock Hill. Marx had a study overlooking a park, but the move didn't cure his money worries or his ailments, which included painful boils on the nether regions of his anatomy. "Of all types of work, the purely theoretical is the most unsuitable when you have this devilish mess in your body," he complained to Engels.[31] In another letter, he declared: "At all events, I hope the bourgeoisie will remember my carbuncles until their dying day."[32]

Slowly but surely, he did make progress on his mammoth economics project, which had now been reconceived as a work of four volumes, three theoretical and one historical. In March 1865 he signed a contract with a Hamburg publisher, Meissner and Behre. "There are still three chapters to write to complete the theoretical part," he wrote to Engels a few months later.[33] In February of the following year, he told Engels that the manuscript was "ready" but added that it was "gigantic" and "not fit for publishing for anyone but myself, not even for you."[34] By November 1866, he had done enough cutting to send off a manuscript containing most of the first volume, which was devoted to economic production and value. In April 1867, after Engels mailed him thirty-five pounds to make the trip, he sailed to Hamburg and dropped off the rest of the manuscript. Five months later, the first print run of the first volume of *Capital* appeared in German.[35]

In a preface, Marx said his goal was "to reveal the economic law of motion of modern society."[36] To illustrate his analysis, he said, he would focus on Britain, the "locus classicus" of the "capitalist mode of production."[37] If German readers thought things weren't so bad in their kingdoms since industrial capitalism hadn't developed very far there, they should think again, he noted. The key issue wasn't whether the "social antagonisms that spring from the natural laws of capitalist production" had reached a higher or lower stage of development. "It is a question of these laws themselves, of these tendencies winning their way through and working themselves out with iron necessity. The country that is more developed industrially only shows to the less developed the image of its own future."[38]

The first (and arguably most fundamental) regularity that Marx identified was what I will refer to as his Law of Surplus Value: the only source of new economic value is workers' labor, and capitalists exploit workers by paying them less than the value they produce. Marx inherited this claim from Hodgskin, Thompson, and other British socialists, but he presented its genesis as a conundrum. Under slavery and feudalism, the exploitative nature of the employer-worker relationship was out in the open, but in a capitalist system, workers agree to sell their capacity to work—their "labor power." Moreover, competition ensures that all commodities, including labor power itself, are sold at their true market value. Marx regarded these two elements— wage labor and competition—as defining features of the capitalist mode of production. But how, then, does exploitation arise? Marx summed up the puzzle this way: "Our friend, Moneybags, who is as yet only an embryo capitalist, must buy his commodities at their value, must sell them at their value, and yet at the end of the process must withdraw more value from circulation than he threw into it at starting . . . These are the conditions of the problem."[39]

In writing about exploitation in the 1840s, Engels had adopted the same approach that Thompson and Hodgskin had taken, pointing to an asymmetry in bargaining power. If capitalists fail to reach a wage agreement with their employees, they can survive for a time on their accumulated profits. But if workers can't find employment, they quickly become destitute. Employers' leverage enables them to pay workers low wages and keep for themselves some of the revenues they produce. Marx wasn't content with this explanation, and he devoted much of the first half of *Capital* to expanding it.

His account of capitalist exploitation rested on two pillars: the labor theory of value, which he inherited from Smith and Ricardo; and the ability of employers to determine the length of the workday. Since labor power is a marketable commodity, its exchange value—i.e., the wage rate—will be determined, "as in the case of every other commodity, by the labour-time necessary for the production, and consequently also the reproduction, of this specific article," Marx wrote.[40] In plain language, workers are paid just enough money to provide them with a basic diet and shelter, so they can turn up for work the next day. If the cost of daily subsistence for an adult male worker was three shillings, he will be paid three shillings a day. Taking this example further, Marx assumed that the worker created market value at a rate of half a shilling an hour, so it would take him six hours to create enough value to cover the cost of his subsistence.[41] In most factories the actual workday for adult male workers lasted about twelve hours, which meant that workers spent about half their day creating value that accrued entirely to their employers. Marx called this part of the workday "surplus labor" and the value that the workers created during those hours "surplus value."

Here was the solution to the conundrum facing Moneybags. Even if he had to lay out an additional two shillings per worker each day for raw materials and wear and tear on his machinery, he would reap a daily profit of a shilling on each worker he employed, assuming the workday was twelve hours. "The trick has at last worked: money has been transformed into capital," Marx wrote. "Every condition of the problem is satisfied, while the laws governing the exchange of commodities have not been violated in any way."[42] Echoing Voltaire's Dr. Pangloss, Marx quipped: "Everything is for the best in the best of all possible worlds."[43]

To illustrate his Law of Surplus Value, Marx created an algebraic framework that was far ahead of its time. Nearly seventy years before John Maynard Keynes invented modern macroeconomics in his book *The General Theory of Employment, Interest, and Money*, Marx provided a coherent way to analyze economic aggregates, such as profits and wages and output. After explaining how value is created, he divided it into three separate components: C, which he called "constant capital," stood for the cost of raw materials and wear and tear to machinery; V, which Marx referred to as "variable capital," stood for the cost of labor power; and S represented surplus value.[44] Armed with data on these quantities, it is possible to track the total output that an economy produces ($C + V + S$); as well as the rate of profit ($S / (C + V)$); the rate of surplus value (S / V), which Marx referred to as the "rate of exploitation"; and the labor share in income ($V / (C + S + V)$). These days, virtually all governments rely on the Keynesian system of national accounting, and so the Marxian aggregates aren't used much, but they, too, provide an overall picture of the economy. As the Japanese economist Shigeto Tsuru pointed out in 1942, it is a relatively simple matter, in algebraic terms, to show how they relate to their Keynesian counterparts.[45]

Marx's second regularity was his Law of Accumulation, which he expounded in chapter 25 of *Capital: Volume I*. It may be more accurate to call it the Laws of Accumulation, because it contains several different elements. The basic idea is that competition forces capitalists to keep reinvesting the profits they generate in new plants and equipment: they can never rest. "Accumulate, accumulate! That is Moses and the prophets,"[46] Marx declared. If a business owner disobeys the Law of Accumulation, his firm will fall behind its competitors and may be forced out of business. To avoid this fate, capitalists constantly accumulate more capital, which generates more output and profit, which finances further investments, and so on.

But what happens to workers' living standards as the scale and capital intensity of production rises? In *The Communist Manifesto*, Marx and Engels insisted that the living standards and misery of the proletariat only get worse. In modern terminology, this can be regarded as a law of absolute immiseration. By the mid-1860s, however, Marx was obliged to acknowledge that in Britain, the most-advanced capitalist country, workers' wages were rising. In a growing capitalist economy, he pointed out, where businesses and markets are expanding, the workers' "surplus product"—the output they produce over and above that necessary to ensure them a subsistence standard of living—is generally increasing, and so is the demand for labor. In these circumstances, Marx conceded, "the requirements of accumulating capital may exceed the growth in labour power or in the number of workers; the demand for workers may outstrip the supply, and thus wages may rise."[47] When this happens, workers "can extend the circle of their enjoyments, make additions to their consumption fund of clothes, furniture, etc., and lay by a small reserve fund of money."[48]

Contrary to popular perception, then, Marx didn't hold that increases in workers' living standards were incompatible with capitalism. He did hold that wage increases never got "so far as to threaten the system itself."[49] If rising wages start to eat into profits, capitalists will rethink their expansion plans and shift to retrenchment. In these circumstances, Marx explained, demand for labor drops back, and the "price of labour falls again to a level corresponding with capital's requirements . . . whether this level is below, the same as, or above that which was normal before the rise of wages took place."[50]

Marx also highlighted another important factor that kept wage growth in check: the existence of an "industrial reserve army" of jobless workers. Marx, following Engels, regarded the constant presence of workers who are desperate for employment as another fundamental feature of industrial capitalism. Indeed, he described the tendency for pauperism to rise when unemployment was high and the ranks of the reserve army had been swelled as "the absolute general law of capitalist accumulation."[51] But the reserve army's disciplinary role wasn't confined to economic slumps, Marx insisted. It played a vital role throughout the economic cycle. "During the periods of stagnation and average prosperity, it weighs down the active army of workers; during the periods of over-production and feverish activity, it puts a curb on their pretensions" The presence of the reserve army "is therefore the background against which the law of the demand and supply of labour does its work. It confines the field of action of this law to the limits absolutely convenient to capital's drive to exploit and dominate the workers."[52]

Where does the reserve army come from? In *The Condition of the Working Class in England*, Engels had written, "every improvement in machinery throws workers out of employment, and the greater the advance, the more numerous the unemployed."[53] Marx developed this argument. He noted that job destruction wasn't confined to artisans. As factory owners invested in labor-saving machinery, they displaced many factory workers, too. "Capital acts on both sides at once," Marx wrote. "If its accumulation on the one hand increases the demand for labour, it increases on the other the supply of workers by 'setting them free' . . . The movement of the law of supply and demand of labour on this basis completes the despotism of capital."[54]

This discussion of the impact of technical progress inevitably evokes the Luddites and foreshadows contemporary fears about AI. In a long chapter titled "Machinery and Modern Industry," Marx referred to Ludditism explicitly, noting the "large-scale destruction of machinery which occurred in the English manufacturing districts during the first fifteen years of the nineteenth century."[55] He also wrote: "World history offers no spectacle more frightful than the gradual extinction of the English hand-loom weavers."[56] Like many observers, Marx portrayed the Luddites as protesters lacking an overarching ideology and critique of the new economic system responsible for their woes, which wasn't entirely accurate. "It took both time and experience," he wrote, "before the workers learnt to distinguish between machinery and its employment by capital, and therefore to transfer their attacks from the material instruments of production to the form of society which utilises those instruments."[57]

To Marx, who had long recognized the immense productive power of industrial capitalism, there was a vital distinction between the science of mechanization and its economic manifestation. He had no desire to halt technical progress. He wanted to change how it was used and how the wealth it generated was distributed. In his view, capitalism, even as it created the technological basis for material abundance, prevented the great majority of people from sharing in its fruits. Modest increases in workers' wages, and modest expansions in their ability to purchase consumer goods, "in no way alter the fundamental character of capitalist production," he wrote.[58] "[These] things no more abolish the exploitation of the wage-labourer, and his situation of dependence, than do better clothing, food and treatment, and a larger *peculium*, in the case of the slave."[59]

In many ways, Marx insisted, capitalism was becoming even more exploitative. Capitalists were speeding up production, introducing labor-saving machinery, and subjecting their employees to tougher discipline. This intensification of the work process ensured that workers' productivity rose faster than their wages did, which created new surplus value for the capitalists to appropriate. (The surplus value that was produced in this manner Marx referred to as "Relative Surplus Value.") But the process of exploitation went beyond the value extraction at the heart of the cash nexus. Evoking his earlier writings on alienation, Marx also emphasized the social and psychological impact of employers' never-ceasing efforts to raise productivity and profits. He said that these efforts:

> distort the worker into a fragment of a man, they degrade him to the level of an appendage of a machine, they destroy the actual content of his labour by turning it into a torment; they alienate from him the intellectual potentialities of the labour process in the same proportion as science is incorporated in it as an independent power; they deform the conditions under which he works, subject him during the labour process to a despotism the more hateful for its meanness; they transform his life-time

into working-time, and drag his wife and child beneath the wheels of the juggernaut of capital.[60]

This was Marx the thunderer. Since these harms were inseparable from the process of creating surplus value, he went on, "it follows therefore that in proportion as capital accumulates, the situation of the worker, be his payment high or low, must grow worse . . ."[61] "Accumulation of wealth at one pole is . . . at the same time accumulation of misery, the torment of labour, slavery, ignorance, brutalization and moral degradation at the opposite pole."[62]

Actually, in highlighting the chasm between the two ends of capitalist society and the increasing degradation of the workers, Marx was making a more nuanced argument than the one he and Engels had put forward in *The Communist Manifesto*. Indeed, one interpretation of volume I of *Capital* is that it replaced the *Manifesto*'s theory of absolute immiseration with a theory of relative immiseration that focused on rising inequality. In the second half of chapter 25 of *Capital*, which often gets ignored, he examined the path of wages, profits, and poverty in Britain from 1846 to 1866. At the end of this period, unskilled laborers in London earned about £1 a week and artisans earned about £1.75, or about £90 a year.[63] As a counterpoint, Marx reproduced some figures from the Inland Revenue, the British tax agency, which showed how, in 1865, 107 of the country's richest business owners made, on average, £103,526 in annual profits (equivalent to about £10.7 million in today's money).[64]

After he had laid out the huge income gaps that characterized Victorian England, Marx quoted the liberal politician William Gladstone, who had recently remarked: "While the rich have been growing richer, the poor have been growing less poor." "How lame an anti-climax!" Marx continued. "If the working class has remained 'poor,' only 'less poor' in proportion as it produces for the wealthy class 'an intoxicating augmentation of wealth and power,' then it has remained relatively just as poor. If the extremes of poverty have not lessened, they have increased because the extremes of wealth have."[65] In other words, relative immiseration has increased.

Another empirical tendency that Marx highlighted was the rise of big businesses and large-scale production. During the railroad mania of the 1840s, George Hudson, "the Railway King," had united many of the tracks linking London to the north of England into a single company. (Hudson's dubious financial practices eventually led him into bankruptcy.) In 1856 the industrialist John Brown had consolidated his Sheffield steelworks into a site that covered thirty acres and produced many different heavy goods, including railroad tracks, steel springs, and armored plate for warships. "The battle of competition is fought by the cheapening of commodities," Marx wrote. "The cheapness of commodities depends . . . on the productivity of labour, and this depends in turn on the scale of production. Therefore, the larger capitals beat the smaller."[66] To expand in size, businesses could build larger production plants—a phenomenon Marx referred to as "concentration" of capital—or take over weaker rivals and their factories, which Marx called "centralization" of capital. Both tactics led to the same outcome: the emergence of large capitalist enterprises organized along increasingly technocratic lines.

In Marx's day, most British companies were self-financed; they used their own profits to pay for investments. But another notable new development, particularly prevalent in France and Germany, was the emergence of banks, such as Crédit Mobilier and the Darmstadter Bank, that provided long-term financing to growing businesses. Marx commented that this new credit system has the effect of "drawing into the hands of individual or associated capitalists by invisible threads, the money resources which lie scattered in larger or smaller amounts over the surface of society; but it soon becomes a new and terrible weapon in the battle of competition and is finally transformed into an enormous social mechanism for the centralization of capitals."[67] How far could this process go? "In any given branch of industry centralization would reach its extreme limit if all the individual capitals invested there were fused into a single capital," Marx commented. "In a given society this limit would be reached only when the entire social capital was united in the hands of either a single capitalist or a single capitalist company."[68]

Since Marx claimed that rising inequality, concentration of capital, and financialization were all endemic features of industrial capitalism, each of them can be regarded as one of his laws of motion. In his presentation, however, they appeared within his lengthy exposition of the general law of accumulation. But for all the acute insights that these passages contained, they didn't explain why industrial capitalism was doomed. Some of them seemed to highlight its ability to evolve and adapt. In his penultimate chapter, "The Historical Tendency of Capitalist Accumulation," Marx sought to resolve this tension by introducing the same deus ex machina that he and Engels had relied on in the *Manifesto*. As the centralization of capital proceeds along with the "entanglement of all peoples in the net of the world market," an ever-smaller group of "capitalist magnates" come to "usurp and monopolize all the advantages of this process of transformation," he wrote. "The mass of misery, oppression, slavery, degradation and exploitation grows; but with this there also grows the revolt of the working class, a class constantly increasing in numbers, and trained, united, and organized by the very mechanism of the capitalist process of production."[69] This arrival on the scene of a revolutionary proletariat signals that the end is nigh:

> The monopoly of capital becomes a fetter upon the mode of production which has flourished alongside and under it. The centralization of the means of production and the socialization of labor reach a point at which they become incompatible with their capitalist integument. This integument is burst asunder. The knell of capitalist private property sounds. The expropriators are expropriated.[70]

When *Capital* was published, some readers noticed that Marx's prediction of capitalism's demise didn't include a timeline. Others raised theoretical objections. Engels, on seeing the page proofs, inquired of Marx why, if the application of labor power was the only source of surplus value, and fixed capital didn't generate any surplus value, capitalists would continue to invest in labor-saving machinery.[71] Marx replied that this was merely an initial volume and he had deliberately kept the analysis simple. In a follow-up volume, he would clear up any ambiguities, he said.

But in fact, Marx didn't publish any further economics books during his lifetime. In working on *Capital* in the early 1860s, he had prepared extensive notes for a second volume devoted to how capital circulates in the economy, and a third volume about the level and distribution of profits. However, apart from reworking some of this material in the 1870s, he made little concerted effort to turn it into book form. Shortly before his death, which came in 1883 as a result of bronchitis, he told his youngest daughter, Eleanor, that it would be Engels's responsibility to "make something of it."[72] As Marx's executor, Engels edited his notebooks for publication as *Capital: Volume II* and *Volume III*. But these volumes didn't resolve all the issues that the first volume had raised. In some instances, they further complicated them.

Volume II, *The Process of Circulation of Capital*, which was published in 1885, presented a mathematical model of an economy divided into two sectors. One of them—"Department I"—produces capital goods, such as machinery; the other sector—"Department II"—produces consumer goods, such as clothes and toys. Using this bare-bones framework, Marx analyzed whether a capitalist economy could reproduce itself from year to year ("simple reproduction") and grow ("expanded reproduction") in a stable manner. In intellectual terms, this toy economy represented a significant advance and is still of interest to economic theorists. But it didn't explain how capitalism would come to an end. In fact, it seemed to raise the prospect, under certain conditions, of the capital stock and economic output continuing to rise indefinitely in a process of eternal growth.

Volume III of *Capital, The Process of Capitalist Production as a Whole*, wasn't published until 1894. Unlike the previous two volumes, it did provide an economic explanation for an eventual capitalist breakdown: "the Law of the Tendency of the Rate of Profit to Fall."[73] This was the same law that Marx had written about in the *Grundrisse* but hadn't found space for in the first volume of *Capital*. Like the labor theory of value, it was another idea that Marx inherited from the classical economists and developed in his own way. Adam Smith had said the profit rate would eventually decline because businesses would run out of rewarding investment projects. David Ricardo's explanation was based on the notion that population growth would eventually lead to a shortage of land, which would drive up farmers' rents. Rising rents would then lead to higher food prices and higher subsistence wages, which, in turn, would crimp profits.

Marx's explanation rested on the labor theory of value and the fact that the capital intensity of production increases as capital accumulation proceeds. In layman's language, machinery takes the place of labor. But since labor power is the only source of value, the amount of surplus value falls relative to the amount of capital that businesses use, which is another way of saying that the profit rate declines. To illustrate this argument, Marx ran through an arithmetical example involving two countries at different stages of capitalist development: a less developed one with a low capital-to-labor ratio, and a more developed one with a high capital-to-labor ratio. His arithmetic showed that the profit rate in the first country would be 66⅔ percent, compared to a rate of just 20 percent in the second country.[74]

Marx was at pains to point out that a falling *rate* of profit didn't necessarily translate into a decline in the total *amount* of profits. He acknowledged that as productivity and capital intensity rose, the absolute level of profits would continue to rise as well. The progress of capitalism would result "on the one hand in a progressive tendency for the rate of profit to fall and on the other in a constant growth in the absolute mass of the surplus-value or profit appropriated."[75] The law of falling profits was therefore "doubled-edged."[76] It also applied over the long term. Marx devoted an entire chapter to "Counteracting Factors" that could slow or arrest the decline. They included more intense exploitation of labor, wage cuts, a bigger reserve army, and foreign trade.

Ultimately, however, Marx believed that the tendency of the profit rate to fall would prevail. In the *Grundrisse*, he had described this as "in every respect the most important law of modern political economy."[77] In the third volume of *Capital*, he didn't repeat this claim explicitly, but he portrayed falling profit rates as one of the central contradictions of capitalism. As capitalists sought to raise their profits by accumulating more and more capital, their efforts ended up having the opposite effect. Marx concluded: "The *true barrier* to capitalist production is *capital itself*."[78]

During the decade and a half following the publication of volume I of *Capital*, Marx spent much of his time engaging in politics and political commentary. After the establishment, in 1864, of the First International, a federation of leftist workers' groups from Britain, France, Germany, and other countries, he served on its central committee and as its chief theoretician—roles that enmeshed him in factional discord. At the start of the 1870s, the Franco-Prussian War and the establishment of the Paris Commune consumed Marx's attention. In June 1871 he published *The Civil War in France*, a short but biting polemic that was his most widely read work during his lifetime.

For Marx and other revolutionaries, the crushing of the Commune was a bitter blow. In Britain, meanwhile, there was still no sign of a workers' uprising. The Trades Union Congress, which was founded in 1868, focused on demands for higher wages and a shorter workday. In Germany, which Otto von Bismarck had unified in 1871, the Social Democratic Workers' Party (SAPD), a socialist body founded by two associates of Marx, William Liebknecht and August Bebel, met in the town of Gotha, in 1875. It adopted a political program that demanded universal suffrage and labor rights but stopped short of calling for a workers' revolution. An outraged Marx dismissed the Gotha Program as "the old familiar democratic litany."[79] Its promulgation raised anew the question of where and how the ultimate crisis of capitalism would arise.

The onus of answering this question shifted to Engels, who, following his retirement from Ermen and Engels, had moved to London and bought a house near Marx. Unlike his old friend, he was still in good health. In 1878, Eugen Dühring, a University of Berlin philosophy lecturer, published a book that criticized *Capital* and described Marx as a "scientific figure of fun."[80] Engels wrote a response that, in leftist circles, became known simply as *Anti-Dühring*. It glossed over many of the nuances in *Capital* and presented capitalism's coming demise as the inevitable consequence of a progressively more intense series of economic slumps. "Most people are too lazy to read stout tomes such as *Das Kapital* and hence a slim little pamphlet like this has a much more rapid effect," Engels remarked.[81] That judgment turned out to be correct. In 1880, a version of Engels's essay was republished under the title *Socialism: Utopian and Scientific*. For many Marxists around the world, it became the catechism.

Outside the socialist movement, Marx's analysis, and the classical economics on which he based it, eventually came to be seen as an anachronism. After 1890, when Alfred Marshall, a professor at Cambridge, published his *Principles of Economics*, most economists used supply and demand curves, rather than the labor theory of value, to explain how market prices get determined. In 1925, John Maynard Keynes dismissed *Capital* as an "obsolete economic textbook."[82] It would be more accurate to describe it as a mixed bag.

Marx certainly got some things wrong. Arguably, his biggest error was a failure to grasp that as capital accumulation proceeded and workers were equipped with more and more machinery, their wages would gradually increase along with their productivity. In Marx's economic model, wages are determined by the cost of reproducing labor power. Since that doesn't increase very much over time, neither do earnings. Capitalists appropriate virtually all of the economic surplus. Obviously, it's hard to reconcile this theory with the upward trend in wages since 1870. History suggests that productivity growth sets an upper bound for wage and profit growth, and the actual distribution of the surplus depends on a range of factors, including the strength of labor unions, the level of unemployment, and the extent of competition in product markets. Marx wrote about all these things, but his subsistence theory of wages, which he shared with other classical economists, ultimately led him astray.

Despite his errors, though, his overall conception of capitalism as a system of incessant expansion and change roiled by class conflict and technological advances was a powerful one. And he certainly highlighted some important features of the system that persist to this day. The role that the reserve army of jobless workers plays in disciplining the wage demands of the employed is one example. Others include the tendency for capital to become more concentrated and the gaping chasms in income and wealth that have endured despite a steady rise in overall living standards. The labor theory of value, too, can't be entirely dismissed. Although the volume of labor inputs provides a poor guide to day-to-day price movements, but over the long term—which is what Marx was primarily interested in—competition tends to keep prices close to the average costs of production. And since wages are the largest single cost that many firms have, the prices of many goods do, in fact, gravitate toward labor costs. Anwar Shaikh, an economist at the New School for Social Research, first documented this tendency in the 1980s.[83] A more recent paper from two of Shaikh's former students confirmed it. In 2021, Baki Güney Işıkara, of New York University, and Patrick Mokre, an economist at the Austrian Federal Chamber of Labor, published a paper showing that prices tended to follow labor costs in a dataset covering forty-two countries over the period from 2000 to 2017.[84]

Marx was mistaken in portraying the exploitation of labor as the only enduring source of profit. History has demonstrated that technological innovations, when backed with government patents, can bestow upon businesses sufficient market power to generate monopoly profits for long periods. But exploitation of workers is also an all-too-common reality. In the absence of strong labor laws, businesses can often exploit their market power over their employees to pay low wages. In some labor-intensive industries, paying poverty-level wages and mistreating workers remains a central feature of the capitalist business model, which is, of course, consistent with the Law of Surplus Value.

That said, considering the earnings of all workers in capitalist countries, the theory of absolute immiseration didn't hold up to history. In the century and a half from 1867 to 2015, according to recent research, average weekly wages in Britain rose almost tenfold on an inflation-adjusted basis.[85] But the theory of relative immiseration—large agglomerations of income and wealth piling up at one pole of the system as many workers and their families still struggle to get by—proved much more durable.

And even Marx's biggest detractors can't deny the basic assertion in his Law of Accumulation: a continual rise in capital stock, and the amount of capital per worker, is now regarded as a basic datum of capitalist economies. During the period 1867 to 1913, Britain's gross fixed capital stock, which includes machinery, buildings, ships, and vehicles, more than doubled in size.[86]

Finally, the Law of the Tendency of the Profit Rate to Fall, which has also generated a great deal of debate. In theoretical terms, Marx's demonstration of how this tendency arises from the labor-saving investments in machinery and other forms of fixed capital that capitalists make was far from watertight. Using algebra, it's straightforward to show that the relationship he highlighted is an equivocal one. Under some circumstances, rising capital intensity can be associated with a decline in the profit rate, but in others it can be associated with a rise. The outcome can go either way. As the German scholar Michael Heinrich put it in his useful introduction to the three volumes of *Capital*: "A long-lasting *tendency* for the rate of profit to fall cannot be substantiated at the general level of argumentation by Marx in *Capital*."[87]

The empirical evidence is also ambiguous. In his book *Marx 200*, Michael Roberts, a British economist, included a chart that shows the rate of profit in the United Kingdom falling from about 14 percent in the 1860s to about 8 percent in 2009.[88] In a 2014 paper, Esteban Maito, an economist at the University of Buenos Aires, found a similar downward trend for fourteen countries.[89] There have been contradictory findings, however. Ivan Trofimov, an economist at KYS Business School in Malaysia, examined data from twenty-one advanced countries for the period from the early 1960s to the early 2000s. In some places, including the United States, Trofimov identified a negative trend; in others, including Greece and Norway, there was a positive trend. In a third group of countries, including Australia and Sweden, there was no clear trend. "Overall, the behavior of profit rates was proven to be rather diverse, therefore it is unlikely that universal profit rates' laws hold, or that only one hypothesis is correct," Trofimov concluded in his 2017 paper.[90] That wasn't the final word, though. In a 2022 working paper, a group of economists associated with the University of Massachusetts at Amherst and St. Francis College constructed a world profit rate based on data from dozens of countries and found that it "displays a strong negative linear trend for the period 1960–1980 and a weaker negative linear trend from 1980 to 2019."[91]

While these studies provide some support for Marx's claim that rates of profit tend to decline over the long term, they also show numerous violations of the supposed "law." Taken overall, the historical record suggests that Marx underestimated the ability of capitalist economies to head off a falling profit rate with technological innovations, corporate consolidation, and assaults on the labor movement. During the decades after 1870, these counteracting factors would become more and more prevalent, particularly in a country that had always presented something of problem for his theories: the United States of America.

10

"We must make land common property"

Henry George's Moral Crusade

From Promontory Summit, Utah, about seventy miles northwest of Salt Lake City, the vast expanses of the American West stretch in every direction. Here, on May 10, 1869, Leland Stanford, a cofounder of the Central Pacific Railroad, tapped a symbolic golden spike into a final piece of track that linked his firm's line running east from Sacramento to the Union Pacific Railroad's line running west from Omaha. After Stanford, who was also a former governor of California, completed his allotted task, a crowd of railroad workers and dignitaries cheered. Then a four-character telegraph message was sent to New York and San Francisco: "D-O-N-E."[1]

The completion of the transcontinental rail link marked another victory over geography and topography for the rapidly expanding American republic. It also signaled a fresh triumph for American industrial capitalism, which just four years earlier had prevailed over Southern plantation capitalism in the Civil War. From distant London, Karl Marx saw this clearly. As long as slavery survived in North America, Marx believed, it would restrict industrial development and slowed the rise of a revolutionary class of wage workers. "Labour in a white skin cannot emancipate itself where it is branded in a black skin," Marx wrote in the first volume of *Capital*.[2] But "a new life immediately arose from the death of slavery. The first fruit of the American Civil War was the eight hours' agitation, which ran from the Atlantic to the Pacific, from New England to California, with the seven-league boots of the locomotive."[3] In August 1866, labor activists meeting in Baltimore had announced the creation of the National Labor Union and demanded an eight-hour workday. The new organization didn't get very far and folded in 1873, but Marx's point was a broader one about the transformation of the United States from a republic of farmers and small businessmen into a class-ridden industrial economy.

For decades, he had struggled to fit the United States into his materialist theory of history. Here was a young country with a fast-growing capitalist economy, modern technology, and a highly advanced political system that guaranteed the sanctity of private property. But it lacked the rigid class divisions of Europe. Marx identified the primary reason for American exceptionalism as the open frontier, the ready availability of cheap land, and the scarcity of free labor. He believed that as these factors were eliminated, the United States would increasingly become subject to industrial capitalism's normal laws of motion, and he was convinced that the Civil War had accelerated this process. The issuance of colossal war debts helped to create a "finance aristocracy of the vilest type," he noted, and the granting of immense tracts of public land to railroads and speculators had "brought a very rapid centralization of capital. The great republic has therefore ceased to be the promised land for emigrating workers."[4]

The extent to which slavery hindered or promoted the rise of industrial capitalism remains a subject of intense debate among historians. Members of the New History of Capitalism school emphasize that the Southern plantation economy was, in some ways, intensely capitalistic even as it didn't meet Marx's definition of capitalism. In her 2018 book *Accounting for Slavery: Masters and Management*, Caitlin Rosenthal, a historian at the University of California, Berkeley, pointed out that plantation owners used modern management techniques, such as maintaining detailed ledgers recording their captive workers' output and moving individuals around to maximize overall productivity.[5] They also used enslaved workers as collateral for bank loans, and in some cases, they took out life insurance contracts on them to protect themselves against loss.[6]

But even as this new research has deepened our understanding of the plantation economy, Marx and others were surely correct to identify its demise as a transformative moment in US history. After the Southern aristocracy was defeated, the Republican Party—the party of Lincoln—championed the interests of Northern industrialists, and the financial and physical capital that these interests wielded had a transformative impact on the country. "The age of the pony express, overland coach, and wagon train had closed," the historians Charles and Mary Beard commented in their classic two-volume *The Rise of American Civilization.* "Steam and steel were to master a continent."[7]

Issued in 1927, this assessment stands. Within a few decades of the end of the Civil War and the ceremony at Promontory Summit, much of the territory west of the Mississippi had been occupied and developed by European settlers. Part federally sponsored homesteading program, part ethnic cleansing, and part real estate play, this pell-mell rush to the Pacific had by 1900 driven the remaining Indigenous peoples from all but slivers of the land they had lived on. It had added to the Union nine new states: Colorado, Idaho, Montana, Nebraska, North Dakota, South Dakota, Utah, Washington, and Wyoming. In fulfilling its "manifest destiny"—a phrase coined in the 1840s—to expand from coast to coast, the United States created a market economy of continental proportions that supported a rapidly rising number of Americans. In 1870 the US population was nearly 40 million and had already surpassed the population of the United Kingdom. By 1915, it would reach 100 million.[8]

As the Beards noted, industry thrived. Between 1865 and 1900, US industrial production rose more than sixfold on a volume basis, according to an index developed by the economist Joseph H. Davis.[9] Steel production shot up from 380,000 tons in 1870 to 28.4 million tons in 1913.[10] By the eve of World War I, the United States produced about a third of global industrial output, eclipsing Britain's share at its nineteenth-century peak.[11] Rapid industrialization turned cities like Chicago and New York into teeming metropolises that demanded more and more farm goods. The development of labor-saving agricultural technology, such as threshing machines, raised productivity, and the completion of the rail network greatly reduced the cost of transporting grains and other foodstuffs, which enabled farmers in the Great Plains and Midwest to supply markets on both coasts and as far afield as Europe. Between 1860 and 1880, US exports of wheat and flour rose from 16 million bushels to 175 million.[12] Even in the South, agricultural output increased sharply, as the rise of sharecropping, small owner-occupied farms, and plantations that employed wage workers demonstrated that staples like cotton could be grown and harvested without slave labor. By 1890, US cotton production had nearly doubled from its antebellum peak.[13]

Everywhere, it seemed, history was speeding up. In 1870, of the 12.2 million employed Americans ages sixteen and over, 6.3 million of them—a majority—still worked in agriculture, with 5.9 million in other professions.

By 1880, the number of non-agricultural workers had tripled, and people working on the land—farmers, sharecroppers, farm laborers—were in the minority.[14] The post–Civil War decades saw the emergence of the consumer society, corporate America, and the modern banking system. Aaron Montgomery Ward, the founder of the eponymous mail-order catalogue, opened his business in 1872. Heinz, the food-processing company, was founded in 1869. The following year John D. Rockefeller founded Standard Oil of Ohio. In 1872 Andrew Carnegie began building his first steel mill, in Braddock, Pennsylvania. In 1876, Alexander Graham Bell, a Scottish-Canadian scientist who taught at Boston University, patented the telephone; the following year he created the Bell Telephone Company, which would later become AT&T. In 1876, Thomas Edison opened an industrial research laboratory in Menlo Park, New Jersey, using the proceeds from the sale of his quadruplex telegraph. During the Civil War, Congress had passed legislation that created a national currency and a system of nationally chartered banks. National City Bank of New York, the precursor to Citibank, received a charter in 1865. Chase National Bank, a precursor to JPMorgan Chase, was established in 1877.

With rapid industrialization came many of the challenges that Marx and other critics had pointed to in Britain and other European countries: financial instability, urban poverty, rising inequality, and class conflicts. In September 1873, Jay Cooke and Company—a Philadelphia finance house that had speculated heavily in railroad bonds—collapsed, setting off a wave of bank failures that prompted the New York Stock Exchange to close for ten days. Dozens of railroads also went bankrupt, and the broader US economy entered a period of deflation that didn't relent until 1879, prompting some scholars to refer to the period as "the long depression." In 1882–1885, 1887–1888, and 1890–1891, there were further economic downturns.[15] Regardless of the state of the business cycle, in places like New York and Chicago many people lived and worked in conditions reminiscent of those in 1840s Manchester: poverty and disease were rampant. Simultaneously, there emerged a class of industrial and financial magnates whose unimaginable riches and ostentatious style of living seemed more suited to a European aristocracy than a hardscrabble republic. Glaring economic divisions brought rising social tensions. In the middle of the 1870s, miners in Pennsylvania went on strike to protest wage cuts. In 1877, railroad workers across the eastern half of the United States halted rail traffic in disputes about wages and working conditions. The strikes led to violence and harsh crackdowns by the authorities. Throughout the South, meanwhile, rich and poor whites did all they could to negate the impact of the Thirteenth Amendment.

New economic conditions demanded new methods of analysis, but the American economics profession hadn't moved much beyond Adam Smith. In his widely used textbook, *Elements of Political Economy*, which first appeared in 1865, Arthur Latham Perry, an economist at Williams College, expounded the traditional virtues of competition, free trade, and the division of labor. Like many American economists of his era, Perry had a religious background; his father was a pastor. He infused his presentation of economic "science" with moral certitude and uplifting bromides. In a competitive economic system, he wrote, every individual "is naturally able to become a capitalist; economical laws present no obstacles to all men becoming rich."[16] Conscious efforts to improve the position of workers were usually counterproductive, Perry said. Laws to limit the workday represented an infringement on freedom of commerce. Strikes were "false in theory" because they violated the norms of free exchange, and they were "pernicious in practice" because they depleted the revenues from which labor and capital drew their recompense.[17] "Political economy is able to show that there is no natural opposition of interests between capitalists and laborers," Perry wrote, "that capital is just as dependent on labor as labor is dependent on capital; that each is equally interested in the prosperity of the other, and that thus a deep and admirable harmony subsists in this part, as in every other part, of the social organism."[18]

A more penetrating analysis was badly needed, and it emerged, in the first instance, from an unlikely source: an obscure Californian newspaper journalist who had dropped out of high school. Henry George was born in Philadelphia on September 2, 1839. His father, Richard George, was a devout evangelical Episcopalian who published religious books and sent his son to the local Episcopalian academy. In February 1853, George started at Philadelphia High School, but he was more interested in adventure books than in his lessons. A few months short of his fourteenth birthday, he quit school and got a job as a trainee clerk. He didn't like that, either. At fifteen, he went to sea and spent fifteen months as a "foremast boy" on a cargo ship whose captain was a member of his father's church. In 1857, the year he turned eighteen, he left home again, enrolling in the Lighthouse Bureau, the precursor agency to the US Coast Guard. He was supposed to be based in San Francisco, but shortly after reaching northern California, he resigned his government post and headed up to British Columbia, where a gold rush was under way. The idea was to open a store for miners with a cousin who lived in San Francisco, but it didn't work out. A few months later George returned south and eventually got a job as a printer at the *California Home Journal*, a weekly newspaper focused on the arts.[19]

In 1861 George married a young woman named Annie Corsina Fox. The couple's first child, Henry George Jr., was born the following year. George stayed in northern California and worked a series of jobs as a printer. By 1864, his wife was pregnant with their second child. At this stage, there was no indication that his life would amount to much. The family was often short of money, and George wasn't content as a printer. In his spare time, he wrote long entries in his diary and submitted short stories and nonfiction articles to newspaper editors. In April 1865, following the assassination of Lincoln, *Alta California*, San Francisco's oldest paper, published two tributes to the dead president that he had written. "Let us thank God for him . . . Let us place him in the Pantheon which no statue of a tyrant ever sullied—the hearts of a free people," one of the pieces said.[20] The following year George landed a job writing editorials for the *Daily Times*, a new newspaper founded by James McClatchy, a radical Republican who had previously edited the *Sacramento Bee* in California's capital. Within a year, he had been promoted to managing editor, overseeing the paper's editorials.

As an opinion editor, George was obliged to write about economics. The *Times*'s editorial line was pro-enterprise but anti-monopoly, which meant being anti-railroad and anti-land speculation. In the western states, the disposal and management of land was a highly charged political issue. Under the Homestead Act of 1862, any American citizen (or applicant for American citizenship) of twenty-one years or older who hadn't taken up arms against the Union could theoretically apply for a plot of land—160 acres, usually—to settle on and farm. Hundreds of thousands of people availed themselves of this opportunity, but, as Marx noted, individuals weren't the only ones who were given land. In a series of Pacific Railway Acts passed in the 1860s, Congress gifted vast tracts to the Union Pacific and the Central Pacific. Many Californians, George included, believed the railroads were colluding with rich land speculators to abuse these programs and enrich themselves at the expense of ordinary citizens. The freshman editorial writer wrote numerous articles criticizing the corrupt wealthy interests. In a piece published on July 4, 1868, under the headline "To What Are We Drifting," he wrote: "Capital is piled on capital, to the exclusion of men of lesser means, and the utter prostration of personal independence and enterprise on the part of the less successful masses."[21]

Later in 1868, George left the *Daily Times* and started writing again under his own byline. The article that first brought him widespread attention was titled "What the Railroad Will Bring Us." Appearing in a new journal, *The Overland Monthly*, it posited that San Francisco was about to become a big and prosperous city like New York, with its own Astors and Vanderbilts but also large numbers of impoverished residents. "The truth is, that the completion of the railroad and the consequent great increase of business and population, will not be a benefit to all of us, but only to a portion," the piece said. As California becomes rich, "let us not forget that the character of a people counts for more than their numbers; that the distribution of wealth is even a more important matter than its production."[22]

Some historians have traced George's populist politics to the low church evangelicalism of his upbringing. George himself would attribute his radicalism, and his focus on land, to his own experience. Later in life, he often spoke of an incident that took place one day when he was riding a horse in the foothills of Oakland, which was then a small settlement across the bay from San Francisco. Stopping for a rest, he encountered a passerby, who informed him that someone was selling nearby plots for the princely sum of a thousand dollars per acre. "Like a flash it came upon me that there was the reason of advancing poverty with advancing wealth," George recalled. "With the growth of population land grows in value, and the men who work it must pay for the privilege. I turned back amidst quiet thought, to the perception that then came to me and has been with me ever since."[23]

In 1871 George published his first lengthy piece of economic analysis, a pamphlet titled *Our Land and Land Policy*, which analyzed the history of land regulation at the federal and state levels. In "all the new States of the Union land monopolisation has gone on at an alarming rate," he stated, "but in none of them so fast as in California, and in none of them perhaps, are its evil effects so manifest."[24] In a country as vast as the United States, the danger wasn't that land would run out but that its price would rise so high "that the poor man cannot buy it."[25] The ongoing land grab by speculators and corporate interests wasn't merely wrong, the essay concluded, it was anti-American: "To say that the land of a country shall be owned by a small class is to say that that class shall rule it; to say—which is the same thing—that the people of a country shall consist of the very rich and the very poor, is to say that republicanism is impossible."[26]

Opposing the monopolization of land wasn't George's only cause. He also wrote articles criticizing the inflow to California of Chinese migrants, who worked on the railroads, mines, and other construction projects. Echoing a popular sentiment among working-class Californians, George claimed the Chinese arrivals were undercutting the wages of American workers. He also made some unsavory claims about the "Chinamen" having an alien culture and being unable to assimilate. In 1869, he published a lengthy letter in the *New-York Tribune* about Chinese immigration, in which he made these arguments, and called for an end to Chinese immigration.[27] He even wrote to J. S. Mill, the prominent English economist, eliciting a reply in which Mill agreed that "Chinese immigration, if it attains great dimensions, must be economically injurious to the mass of the present population." But Mill also noted that California had ample space to share with immigrants, and he said that at least some Chinese who came of their own volition should be admitted on the grounds that it would be beneficial to them.[28]

In December 1871, George, together with some business partners, launched a new evening newspaper, the San Francisco *Daily Evening Post*, which was aimed at the city's working classes and was priced at just a penny. It was a big hit, and its success encouraged George and his partners to overexpand. In early 1875 they launched a weekly edition—which quickly became the bestselling paper in California—then a new morning paper, the *Morning Ledger*. When the economic slump that had begun with the collapse of Jay Cooke's Philadelphia bank reached the West Coast, the *Daily Post* suffered big losses. Eventually it was forced to close down.[29]

George looked around for other work. Through the political connections he had established in Sacramento, he obtained a comfortable and well-paid state post as inspector of gas meters. With more time on his hands, he read more economics but was put off by what he regarded as the neglect of the moral dimension. Eventually he decided to write a book of his own that would remedy this failure and address the land question in depth. Working mainly at his family home in the Rincon Hill neighborhood of San Francisco, he wrote and rewrote. By early 1879 he had completed a manuscript that ran to more than five hundred pages. After originally trying out the clunky title *Political Economy of the Social Problem*, he settled on something more reader-friendly: *Progress and Poverty*. Three New York publishers rejected the manuscript, but George refused to accept failure. Drawing on his background in publishing, he decided to pay for an "Author's Edition," with a run of five hundred copies.[30]

In the summer of 1879, George's book was printed, and he sent copies to some famous people, including the British politician W. E. Gladstone. His display of initiative paid off. On learning of the self-published version, one of the New York publishers who had initially rejected the book, William H. Appleton, changed his mind. "It appears to me that it will create some sort of sensation anyway, and I don't think we shall lose anything by publishing it," he told a friend of George.[31] In January 1880, Appleton and Co. put out the first commercial edition of *Progress and Poverty*. The book went on to become one of the bestselling nonfiction books of the nineteenth century and was translated into many foreign languages.[32] Its astonishing success made George famous and inspired a new political movement, the Single Tax campaign, which has adherents to this day.

In his introduction to the book, George, like many commentators before him, acknowledged the wonders of the industrial economy:

> The forest tree transformed into finished lumber—into doors, sashes, blinds, boxes or barrels, with hardly the touch of a human hand; the great workshops where boots and shoes are turned out by the case with less labor than the old-fashioned cobbler could have put on a sole . . . the diamond drill cutting through the heart of the rocks, and coal oil sparing the whale . . . sheep killed in Australia eaten fresh in England, and the order given by the London banker in the afternoon executed in San Francisco in the morning of the same day.[33]

The great economic puzzle, George said, was that in "the countries where material progress has reached later stages . . . widespread destitution is found in the midst of the greatest abundance."[34] He went on: "The 'tramp' comes with the locomotive, and almshouses and prisons are as surely the marks of 'material progress' as are costly dwellings, rich warehouses, and magnificent churches."[35] It was in the older and richer sections of the Union, such as New York City, that "pauperism and distress among the working classes" was "becoming most painfully apparent."[36] George's goal, he said, was to find "the law which associates poverty with progress."[37]

Having defined the problem of poverty amidst plenty, George dismissed two explanations that orthodox economists had provided: the fixed wage fund theory and overpopulation. "Wages do not come from capital, but are the direct produce of labor," he wrote. "Each productive laborer, as he works, creates his wages, and with every additional laborer there is an addition to the true wages fund—an addition to the common stock of wealth."[38] As for the threat of overpopulation, which the English economist and cleric Thomas Malthus had warned about at the start of the nineteenth century, George dismissed it as a canard that the rich used to rule out any effort to raise working-class living standards. "I assert that the injustice of society, not the niggardliness of nature, is the cause of the want and misery which the current theory attributes to over-population," George wrote. "I assert that the new mouths which an increasing population calls into existence require no more food than the old ones, while the hands they bring with them can in the natural order of things produce more."[39]

What could explain the persistence of poverty and need in a growing economy? George's answer was the one that had come to him years earlier near Oakland: rising land prices and soaring land rents. As industrial and commercial development proceeded, it steadily raised the demand for land on which to build factories, housing, and offices, pushing up land prices. This price appreciation, in turn, pushed up rents, which crushed workers who needed accommodations and businesses that needed buildable land. But the rising cost of land greatly benefited one group of people who contributed nothing to production and merely exploited their good fortune in possessing some well-situated tracts of nature's bounty: landlords. This, George argued, was the fundamental division in society. "The antagonism of interests is not between labor and capital, as is popularly believed," he wrote, "but is in reality between labor and capital on the one side, and land ownership on the other."[40]

In carrying out their analysis, economists "should start from land," George argued.[41] As modern societies expanded, landlords were able to extract an ever-increasing share of the "total produce"—i.e., total income—in the form of higher rents.[42] In using the term *rent*, George was careful to point out that his meaning was somewhat different from the colloquial usage: monthly rents paid not merely for the occupation of land but for the use of buildings constructed on that land and other improvements that have been made to it, such as landscaping and drainage. These components of "rent" were more accurately described as interest on the capital that landlords had expended on their property, George said. But another part of rent payments simply reflected the location and scarcity value of the underlying land. This component was the true "land rent," and it rose inexorably with the progress of economic development.

To help his readers understand his meaning, George presented a simple equation showing how the total produce (or income) gets divided:

As Produce = Rent + Wages + Interest
Therefore, Produce − Rent = Wages + Interest[43]

This equation showed that "wages and interest do not depend upon the produce of labor and capital, but on what is left after rent is taken out," George wrote. "And hence, no matter what be the increase in productive power, if the increase in rent keeps pace with it, neither wages nor interest can increase."[44] To George, this was the fundamental law of political economy, and it explained how progress and poverty could coexist. Even as the economy's total produce steadily increased, much, if not all, of the increment was taken up by payments to landowners. Workers and businesses suffered. "The moment this simple relation is recognized, a flood of light streams in upon what was before inexplicable, and seemingly discordant facts range themselves under an obvious law," George wrote. "The increase of rent which goes on in progressive countries is at once seen to be the key which explains why wages and interest fail to increase with increase of productive power."[45]

George certainly wasn't the first writer to identify rising land values and increasing rents as a serious economic problem. In Britain, David Ricardo had focused attention on the financial windfall that landlords received as the population increased. The privileged position of the landed interest had featured strongly in the great political struggle over repealing the Corn Laws, a protectionist measure that raised prices and benefited landowners. J. S. Mill, George's onetime correspondent, had proposed taxing the "unearned increment" that landlords received from rising land values through no effort of their own. As he got older, Mill also supported various types of land reform, but he stopped short of endorsing the land nationalization that some radical British groups, including the Land and Labour League, were demanding.[46]

In *Progress and Poverty*, George cited Mill numerous times and laid out his own solution to the land issue, which on its face seemed to align him with the British radicals. In a chapter titled "The True Remedy," he wrote: "There is but one way to remove an evil—and that is to remove its cause. To extirpate poverty, to make wages what justice commands they should be, the full earnings of the laborer, we must therefore substitute for the individual ownership of land a common ownership. Nothing else will go to the cause of the evil—in nothing else is there the slightest hope. *We must make land common property*."[47]

Fighting words, but George didn't mean them literally. After raising the idea of converting all land to public ownership, he backed away from it: "To do that would involve a needless extension of governmental machinery—which is to be avoided."[48] A much better option, he argued, was to tax land heavily, while leaving in place private landowners. "Let them continue to call it *their* land," he wrote. "Let them buy and sell, and bequeath, and devise it. We may safely leave them the shell if we take the kernel. *It is not necessary to confiscate land; it is only necessary to confiscate rent.* We already take some rent in taxation. We have only to make some changes in our modes of taxation to take it all."[49]

This was the proposal that was to make George a household name and create a political movement. It became known as the Single Tax, because George argued that his new tax could replace existing taxes, which were mainly commodity and excise levies. (It wasn't until 1913 that American state legislatures ratified the Sixteenth Amendment to the Constitution and legalized a federal income tax.) In modern terms, George was proposing a land value tax, the revenues of which would increase in proportion to rising prices of land. George didn't say what rate the new tax would be set at, but the entire thrust of his argument was that it would be a hefty levy that prevented landlords from reaping the rewards of appreciation in land prices. The benefits of this proposal, George wrote, would "appear more and more important the more they are considered."[50]

Although his argument for the Single Tax was primarily a moral one,

George also claimed that shifting the tax burden to landlords would stimulate economic growth. The "needle of the seamstress and the great manufactory; the cart-horse and the locomotive; the fishing boat and the steamship; the farmer's plough and the merchant's stock, would be alike untaxed," he wrote. And with "all the burdens removed which now oppress industry and hamper exchange, the production of wealth would go on at a rapidity now undreamed of." Switching the burden of taxation from workers and businesses to landlords and landowners would be "like removing an immense weight from a powerful spring."[51] In some ways, George's language foreshadowed the incentive argument that his fellow Californian Ronald Reagan would use to promote tax cuts a century later. But of course, George, unlike Reagan, was proposing to raise taxes on at least one form of capital, and the wealthy interests who owned it.

Still, passages like this one show that George wasn't opposed in principle to capitalism and private enterprise. Although he sometimes gets labeled a socialist, he viewed himself as a Jeffersonian individualist railing against the corruption of the competitive free market system by land engrossment and other monopolistic abuses. His basic argument was reminiscent of the one that British radicals had made half a century earlier: workers were not receiving the full product of their labor. But whereas the likes of William Thompson and Thomas Hodgskin had blamed capitalists for taking more than their fair share, George blamed landlords. Introducing the Single Tax would rectify the problem, he insisted: "A new equilibrium would be established, at which the common rate of wages and interest would be much higher than now."[52] Wealth "would be distributed in accordance with the degree in which the industry, skill, knowledge, or prudence of each contributed to the common stock. The great cause which concentrates wealth in the hands of those who do not produce, and takes it from the hands of those who do, would be gone."[53]

The benefits of the Single Tax didn't end there, George argued. The revenue it generated "could be applied to the common benefit, as were the revenues of Sparta."[54] He listed some of the things that the money could be spent on: public baths, public gardens, museums, libraries, music and dancing halls, theaters, universities, technical schools, playgrounds, gymnasiums, and the establishment of public utilities: "Heat, light, and motive power, as well as water, might be conducted through our streets at public expense; our roads be lined with fruit trees; discoverers and inventors rewarded, scientific investigations supported; and in a thousand ways the public revenues made to foster efforts for the public benefit." In George's vision, these policies would be enacted at the local level, and the officials who implemented them would be accountable to the local electorate. The former inspector of gas meters was effectively proposing a program of municipal socialism to complement a competitive private sector. "We should reach the idea of the socialist, but not through governmental repression," he wrote. "Government would change its character, and would become the administration of a great co-operative society. It would become . . . the agency by which the common property was administered for the common benefit."[55]

To promote *Progress and Poverty*, George left his family in San Francisco and moved to New York, where he took a cheap apartment in a run-down neighborhood. The book's appearance didn't garner much immediate attention, and George was lonely and discouraged. Things began to change when the New York *Sun* hailed his work as a serious one that demanded attention. *The Nation* subsequently ran a lengthy review, and *The Atlantic Monthly* assigned it to two different reviewers, whose articles took up eight pages. As George's arguments began to gain traction, the defenders of economic orthodoxy felt obliged to respond. In the highbrow journal *Scribner's*, an eminent Yale economist, William Graham Sumner, wrote a scathing review. George wrote delightedly to a friend: "The thing begins to draw fire."[56]

Interest in *Progress and Poverty* wasn't restricted to intellectuals. One of its first champions was *The Irish World*, the leading Irish newspaper in America, which was highly critical of English landlords in the home country. The editor of *The Irish World* republished an article George had written, "The Irish Land Question." George met with Michael Davitt, the firebrand leader of the Irish National Land League, who was visiting New York. Davitt agreed to promote his book in Ireland. George's call for workers to receive the full fruits of their labor also drew the attention of New York's labor unions, which grew rapidly during the decades after the Civil War. His progressive spending program appealed to many reform-minded members of the middle class. And his proposal for a hefty land tax gained support from some industrialists, including A. B. Du Pont, a Cleveland-based scion of the prominent family, and Joseph Fels, a Philadelphia soap manufacturer.

Toward the end of 1880, Appleton, sensing it had a hit on its hands, put out a popular edition of *Progress and Poverty* priced at one dollar instead of two. Publishers in Britain and Germany eagerly purchased foreign rights. George was invited to give paid speeches, and a reformist Democratic congressman, Abram S. Hewitt, engaged him as a research assistant. The improvement in George's personal finances enabled him to move his family to New York, into a comfortable house on Kingsbridge Road in the Bronx. George was becoming a public figure.

In late 1881, *The Irish World* paid for him to go to Ireland, where the British authorities had imprisoned some nationalist leaders, including Davitt and Charles Stuart Parnell. From their prison cells, the Irish leaders issued a "No Rent Manifesto," in which they told the Irish tenant farmers not to pay their landlords. George was squarely on the side of Irish rebels. "This is the most damnable government that exists today outside Russia," he wrote to a friend shortly after arriving in Ireland.[57]

George also visited London, where the publisher Kegan Paul had put out a British edition of *Progress and Poverty*. He was invited to the Marylebone townhouse of Henry Mayers Hyndman, a wealthy businessman who had converted to socialism and founded Britain's first avowedly left-wing political party, the Social Democratic Federation. Hyndman was also the author of *England for All*, an 1881 book that translated into English the basic ideas of Marx and Engels. Although he and George both supported the Irish resistance, they didn't see eye to eye on economics. Hyndman subsequently said his visitor was "as exasperating as Kropotkin," the Russian anarchist. For his part, George complained that Hyndman had surrendered completely to the "mental influence" of Marxian dogma.[58]

Marx himself happened to be traveling in Germany during George's visit. A meeting between the two probably wouldn't have gone well. In a letter dated June 20, 1881, to Friedrich Adolph Sorge, a German communist who had moved to America, Marx said he had received three copies of *Progress and Poverty*, two of which he had given away. "Theoretically the man is utterly backward!" he wrote of George. "He understands nothing about the nature of surplus value and so wanders about in speculations which follow the English model but have now been superseded even among the English."[59] Marx dismissed George's proposal for a tax on land values as a "transitional measure" that would "leave wage labour and therefore capitalist production in existence." He went on: "The whole thing is therefore simply an attempt, decked out with socialism, to save capitalist domination and indeed to establish it afresh on an even wider basis than its present one." Marx did allow that George was a "talented writer," albeit one who displayed "the repulsive presumption and arrogance which is displayed by all panacea-mongers without exception."[60]

When George got back to the United States, in October 1882, New York's Central Labor Union feted him with a dinner at Cooper Union, a no-fee college that the philanthropist Peter Cooper established. The Central Labor Union had been founded as an umbrella group during his absence, and had adopted as one of its founding principles the Georgian statement "The land of every country is the common inheritance of the people."[61] The unions had also created a new political party, the United Labor Party, but in elections held in 1882 and 1883, the ruling Tammany Hall Democratic machine swept aside its candidates. Labor activism revived in 1886, when workers demanding an eight-hour day took part in strikes and demonstrations across the country.

In Chicago, the protests turned violent. On May 3 police shot and killed two strikers outside a plant owned by the McCormick Harvesting Machine Company. The next day, when police tried to break up a protest by workers and anarchists at Haymarket Square, someone tossed a homemade bomb in their path. At the end of the ensuing melee, seven policemen and at least four protesters were dead. The authorities put on trial eight anarchists—six of German heritage and one British immigrant—on charges of conspiracy. Despite the fact that some of the defendants hadn't been present at Haymarket Square, they were all convicted. Four of them were hanged, and one committed suicide.[62]

New York witnessed no violence or retributions on this scale. But during the first half of 1886, there were a number of boycotts and strikes, including one by streetcar drivers who were forced to work fourteen- or sixteen-hour days with no breaks. Faced with opposition from the owners of the streetcar lines, the police, the courts, and corrupt Tammany Hall politicians, the strike ended in an inevitable defeat, but it energized the labor movement.[63] The Central Labor Union revived the United Labor Party and resolved to challenge Tammany in the upcoming November 1886 elections. As its candidate for mayor, it settled on George.[64]

Initially, he was reluctant to accept the challenge. But after a Tammany official tried to warn him off, telling him he couldn't win but could only raise hell, he changed his mind, saying: "I do not want the responsibility and work of the office of the Mayor of New York, but I do want to raise hell!"[65] After being formally nominated at a United Labor Party conference in September 1886, George gained the support of a coalition of workers, middle-class reformers, and do-gooders. As his opponent, the Democrats selected Abram Hewitt, the congressman for whom George had worked years earlier. Hewitt campaigned in the manner befitting a Tammany candidate: barely at all. George barnstormed across the city, appearing at union meetings, reform clubs, and ethnic associations. He spoke at street corners from the back of a horse-drawn wagon. The labor unions provided campaign workers and donations; they even launched a daily pro-George newspaper, the *Leader*.

Although he was backed by organized labor, George promised to govern for all New Yorkers and rid the city of its corrupt leadership. As he had in *Progress and Poverty*, he also attacked the city's economic elite, particularly landlords, for leeching off the populace. The campaign platform of the United Labor Party had Georgian elements: it demanded the abolition of all taxes except a tax on land, which would be assessed at its full market value. Tammany and its allies, which included the local hierarchy of the Roman Catholic church, sought to portray George as a dangerous class warrior. In his acceptance speech for the nomination, George gave his response: "If this is a class movement, then it is a movement of the working class against the beggar-men and thieves . . . It is a movement of the masses against robbery by the classes."[66]

Ultimately, George's energetic campaigning and populist platform weren't enough to carry him to victory. On the Sunday before the election, the vicar-general of the New York archdiocese, which had strong ties to Tammany Hall, warned Catholic churchgoers that George's proposals were "unsound and unsafe, and contrary to the teachings of the church."[67] As the ruling party, Tammany also had election inspectors and vote counters on its side. When the votes were tallied on election night, November 2, they showed Hewitt with 90,552 votes, George with 68,110, and the Republican candidate, a young Teddy Roosevelt, with 60,435. George had officially finished in second place, but he would go to his grave convinced he had been cheated out of victory. A couple of months after the election, he wrote to a friend: "On a square vote I would undoubtedly have been elected."[68]

After the excitement of the New York mayoral run, George's political career fizzled. The following year he participated in a failed effort to launch a national United Labor Party. Thereafter he largely retreated to writing and promoting his policy agenda, which had now expanded beyond the Single Tax to include proposals to tackle monopolistic abuses by big businesses throughout the economy, not just landowners. In a collection of essays published in 1883 under the title *Social Problems*, George had written: "The big mill crushes out the little mill. The big store undersells the little store till it gets rid of its competition."[69] Passages like this one echoed Marx's warnings about the rising concentration of capital, but George still coupled them with a defense of competitive private enterprise: "Capital is a good; the capitalist a helper, if he is not also a monopolist."

The "truth in socialism," George went on, was that to make the economy work for everyone, the state would have to play a bigger role.[70] Expanding the arguments he had made in *Progress and Poverty*, he called for the public ownership of essential utilities, including water companies, electricity suppliers, and telegraph communications. Many of the services that these utilities provided should be free of charge, he argued. In an 1885 article, he suggested that some of the revenues from his Single Tax could be used to finance public pensions and disability insurance, and perhaps even "the payment of a fixed sum to every citizen when he comes of a certain age."[71] Some modern Georgists have seized upon this scheme as an early proposal for a universal basic income, although it actually resembled more closely the idea of a universal basic capital grant.

In any case, some of George's ideas were well ahead of their time. By calling for a land value tax, he was effectively proposing an annual tax on unrealized capital gains, an idea that would come back into vogue in the early twenty-first century. George's tax would have been restricted to land rather than applied to wealth in general, but in the context of his time this made some sense. In 1880, according to modern estimates, federal, state, and local government spending combined came to only about 3 percent of GDP.[72] Shifting the tax burden to land would have been far more viable then than it would be today, when government spending in advanced countries—including national and local spending—typically accounts for more than a third of GDP. Even punitive taxes on land and rents wouldn't come close to raising that amount. (In 2020, according to the US national income accounts, total rental income came to about $750 billion, or 3.5 percent of GDP.)[73]

If George's basic principle of taxing unearned wealth still resonates strongly, so does his broader critique of monopolization and rent extraction by powerful economic interests. Even outside of the monopolistic tech sector, many major US industries, such as energy, airlines, and electronic payments, are dominated by a handful of big companies. And even in parts of the economy that used to be competitive, private equity companies are busy "rolling up" small businesses and consolidating control. The late Georgist Andrew Mazzone, an economist and businessman, reworked the 2016 national income accounts to "encompass the broader instances of monopoly that are found in today's economy." He concluded that "together they amount to approximately 22 percent of GDP."[74] Economists with no affiliation to George have also warned about the decline of competition. During the Obama administration, a study by the White House Council of Economic Advisers concluded that "many industries may be becoming more concentrated . . . new firm entry is declining, and . . . some firms are generating returns that are greatly in excess of historical standards."[75]

Findings like these confirm the enduring pertinence of George's message, although reducing it to statistical tabulations arguably misses some of its essence. "Moral insight is the bedrock of George's economics," the New School economist Edward Nell, another Georgist, pointed out in his 2018 book *Progress and Poverty in Economics*. "He favored initial equality: everyone has an equal right to share in what the earth has to offer."[76] In George's worldview, rising monopoly power violated this basic moral principle, and the great agglomerations of wealth that it produced had pernicious effects not only on the economy but on democracy itself. In the final sections of *Progress and Poverty*, George issued this timeless warning:

> In theory we are intense democrats . . . But is there not growing up among us a class who have all the power without any of the virtues of aristocracy? We have simple citizens who control thousands of miles of railroad, millions of acres of land, the means of livelihood of great numbers of men; who name the Governors of sovereign states as they name their clerks, choose Senators as they choose attorneys, and whose will is as supreme with Legislatures as that of a French King sitting in bed of justice.[77]

If liberty and democracy were to be preserved, George went on, every single person "must have liberty to avail themselves of the opportunities and means of life; they must stand on equal terms with reference to the bounty of nature."[78] Citing the example of ancient Rome, he pointed to "the tendency to the unequal distribution of wealth and power" as the thing that had destroyed every previous civilization.[79] This was "the universal law," he concluded. "This is the lesson of the centuries. Unless its foundations be laid in justice the social structure cannot stand."[80]

11

Thorstein Veblen and the Captains of Industry

It was Mark Twain and his coauthor Charles Dudley Warner, in their 1873 novel *The Gilded Age*, who gave a label to an American era characterized by political corruption and vulgar displays of wealth.[1] And it was the economist Thorstein Veblen, in his 1899 book *The Theory of the Leisure Class*, who coined some of the most memorable terms to describe the sociology of that era, including "conspicuous consumption" and "the leisure class" itself. Although Veblen and the early Twain wrote more than a quarter of a century apart, their subject was the same: the corruption of values in a society increasingly based on the manic pursuit of wealth and the desire to show it off publicly.

By the time Veblen published his most famous works, the acceleration in capitalist development Henry George witnessed during the post–Civil War years had generated some of the largest agglomerations of private riches the world had ever seen, as entrepreneurs like Cornelius Vanderbilt, John D. Rockefeller, and Andrew Carnegie created huge industrial combines. Vanderbilt, also known as "the Commodore," was one of the original US railroad barons who fought with one another and consolidated their industry. When Vanderbilt died, in 1877, he left a fortune of some $100 million (nearly $3 billion in 2024 dollars). Rockefeller, through the Standard Oil Trust Agreement of 1882, combined forty companies involved in the production, refining, and marketing of oil under a single board of trustees. Although this arrangement fell short of full-scale merger, it enabled Standard Oil to eliminate price wars and other competitive threats. Seeing the success of the Rockefeller trust, other industrialists sought to replicate it. In 1887 Henry Osborne Havemeyer put together the Sugar Refineries Company, or Sugar Trust, which soon produced 98 percent of the sugar in the United States. In 1890 J. B. Duke created the American Tobacco Company, the constituent businesses of which controlled about 90 percent of the cigarette market.[2]

The creators of these behemoths claimed that their size and hierarchical organization enabled them to coordinate production, exploit economies of scale, and provide goods and services more cheaply. Some modern scholars, including the late Harvard business historian Alfred Chandler, have expressed sympathy with this argument. In his influential 1977 book, *The Visible Hand: The Managerial Revolution in American Business*, Chandler argued that small firms didn't have the capacity or know-how to organize, say, a nationwide oil distribution network or a factory assembly line. "Modern business enterprise became a viable institution only after the visible hand of management proved to be more efficient than the invisible hand of market forces in co-ordinating the flow of materials through the economy," Chandler wrote.[3]

More recently, the Berkeley economic historian Brad DeLong has emphasized the role that large corporations on both sides of the Atlantic played in fostering innovation. "What changed after 1870 was that the most advanced North Atlantic economies had invented invention," DeLong wrote in his 2022 book *Slouching Towards Utopia*, a sweeping economic history of the modern world. "They had invented not just textile machinery and railroads, but also the industrial research lab and the forms of bureaucracy that gave rise to the large corporation. Thereafter, what was invented in the industrial research labs could be deployed at national or continental scale."[4] DeLong wasn't mounting a defense of the trusts and their monopolization. His emphasis was on corporations operating in competitive markets that invested in science and product development as competitive weapons. Over the long term, he pointed out, this practice would become commonplace in many different industries, and the systematizing of innovation would have a transformative impact on economic growth and living standards.

To many contemporaries of Carnegie and Rockefeller, the organizational and scientific advances that came with the rise of big business weren't immediately obvious. They saw the great combinations squeezing out smaller competitors, monopolizing the market, and raising their profits. Reacting to public pressure, Congress in 1890 passed the Sherman Anti-Trust Act, which outlawed efforts to create monopolies, including any business combination "in the form of a trust or otherwise, or conspiracy, in restraint of trade or commerce among the several states."[5] The new law seemed strict on paper, but the industrial giants quickly found ways to get around it. Some followed the example of Standard Oil, which jettisoned its trust status and reorganized itself as a holding company. The Sugar Trust fought the federal government, and in 1895 the Supreme Court struck down a federal challenge to its monopoly. After this ruling, there were more consolidations, culminating, in March 1901, with J. P. Morgan's creation of US Steel, which combined Carnegie Steel and a number of its erstwhile competitors. At its inception, US Steel controlled two-thirds of the American steel market and was capitalized at $1.4 billion, making it the world's first billion-dollar corporation.[6]

As the robber barons—a term first applied to Vanderbilt—saw their fortunes grow to previously unimagined sizes, their spending became ever more showy. Cornelius II, the eldest grandson of Cornelius, constructed an Italian palazzo overlooking the Atlantic Ocean in Newport, Rhode Island. It boasted forty-eight bedrooms and an ornate Great Hall with a fifty-foot ceiling. This was merely a summer house. On Manhattan's Fifth Avenue, William H. Vanderbilt, Cornelius's eldest son and the father of Cornelius II, built mammoth adjoining brownstone townhouses—one for himself and his wife, and one for his two daughters—that stretched for an entire city block between 51st and 52nd Streets. Vanderbilt's "Triple Palace" featured Numidian marble colonnades, stained glass skylights, ornate bronze doors, and oak wainscoting taken from French châteaus. For decoration, there were Italian tapestries, Japanese embroidery, and art treasures transported from Europe. On the evening of March 26, 1883, the Vanderbilts hosted a fancy dress ball, at which Mrs. William K. Vanderbilt outfitted herself as a Venetian princess. Other guests came as Louis XVI, King Lear, and Joan of Arc.[7]

The rise of a plutocracy, and the transformation of the US economy on which it was based, cried out for serious economic analysis. Some younger American economists recognized that their profession wasn't rising to the challenge. In September 1885, they met at Saratoga Springs, New York, and founded the American Economic Association. In a manifesto for the new organization, Richard T. Ely, an economist at Johns Hopkins University who had studied in Germany and was skeptical of free market Anglo-American theories, declared, "We regard the state as an educational and ethical agency whose positive aid is an indispensable condition of human progress. While we recognize the necessity of individual initiative in industrial life, we hold that the doctrine of laissez-faire is unsafe in politics and unsound in morals."[8] Ely's colleagues watered down his language but retained part of it in a statement of principles.

As the commercial success of George's *Progress and Poverty* challenged the moribund US economics profession from without, the initiative of Ely and others breathed some life into it from within. Ely would eventually move to the University of Wisconsin, where he helped to create an institutionalist school of economics that emphasized history and structure over abstract theory. But the young economist who was to emerge as the most original challenger to the ruling orthodoxy wasn't to be found at Saratoga Springs.

In the summer of 1885, Veblen was a twenty-nine-year-old slacker lolling around the attic of his family's farmhouse in Nerstrand, Minnesota, which is about an hour south of Minneapolis. The sixth of twelve children in a family of Norwegian immigrants who spoke a Norwegian dialect at home, Veblen was far from a typical American farm boy. A year earlier, he had obtained a doctorate in philosophy from Yale. Despite a letter of recommendation from the university's president, the philosopher Noah Porter, who had supervised his thesis on Kant, Veblen had failed to land an academic post and returned home to Nerstrand, where he seemed content to spend his days reading.[9] "He read and loafed, and the next day, he loafed and read," one of his brothers subsequently recalled.[10]

There are suggestions that Veblen had contracted a debilitating disease—he would later say he had malaria. In 1888, he roused himself sufficiently to marry Ellen Rolfe, the niece of the president of Carleton College, whom he had met during their time there as undergraduates. The couple moved to the Rolfe family farm in Stacyville, Iowa. Some of Veblen's family members were keen for him to find gainful employment, but an effort to get the Santa Fe Railroad to hire him failed. Eventually Veblen decided to get a second doctorate, this time in economics, which was a more thriving field than philosophy. At the start of 1891, he enrolled at Cornell University, in Ithaca, New York.

Despite his long hiatus from academia, he was well prepared. At Carleton, in Northfield, Minnesota, where he had been an undergraduate, he had studied economics under a rising young scholar, John Bates Clark, who later described Veblen as a brilliant "misfit." (One talk he delivered at Carleton was titled "A Plea for Cannibalism.")[11] At Johns Hopkins, Veblen had taken classes with Ely. And at Yale, his minor subject had been economics.

The head of Cornell's economics department, James Laurence Laughlin, was an orthodox economist: he had prepared an abridged version of Mill's textbook, *Principles of Political Economy*, and was an expert on money and banking. Under Laughlin's tutelage, Veblen quickly cranked out three academic articles that were anything but radical. In "The Overproduction Fallacy," published in 1892, he dismissed the possibility of "general" overproduction as "palpably absurd."[12] In "Some Neglected Points in the Theory of Socialism," published the year before, he said that recent capitalist development had brought about "the most rapid advance in average wealth and industrial efficiency that the world has seen," along with a substantial "amelioration of the lot of the less favored." Although Veblen did acknowledge the growing attraction to socialism in some quarters, he attributed it to "envy" and "jealousy" driven by a desire for "economic emulation."[13]

In the fall of 1892, Laughlin left Cornell for the recently founded University of Chicago, which had hired him to create a department of political economy. The new university was located on a plot of land in the residential suburb of Hyde Park that the department store entrepreneur Marshall Field had donated. J. D. Rockefeller provided most of the money to build the new school, which he wanted to rival Harvard, Yale, and Princeton. He hired as Chicago's president a young Yale professor, William Rainey Harper, and gave him broad license to bring in academic stars. It was Rainey who offered Laughlin a job.

As a condition of acceptance, Laughlin insisted on bringing along three junior colleagues, one of whom was Veblen.[14] Shortly after arriving in Chicago, Laughlin established a new economics journal, the *Journal of Political Economy*, which he deputized Veblen to run on a day-to-day basis. As well as carrying out his editing duties, Veblen contributed articles of his own. He also taught classes and translated into English a book on public finance by the German scholar Gustav Cohn. Having arrived in Chicago as a "senior fellow," he was quickly promoted to the position of "reader," which carried an annual stipend of $600. Although this position wasn't tenured, it guaranteed Veblen at least some financial security.[15]

Outside the cloistered environs of Hyde Park, the US economy was entering another deep slump. On February 20, 1893, the heavily indebted

Philadelphia and Reading Railroad, one of the nation's biggest, declared bankruptcy, sending shudders through the financial markets. In early May these tremors turned to panic selling as the New Jersey–based National Cordage Company, the country's biggest manufacturer of rope, suddenly went into receivership. In a reprise of the Great Panic of 1873, several banks failed, and the fallout spread to the rest of the economy. "Never before has there been such a sudden and striking cessation of industrial activity," *The Commercial and Financial Chronicle* noted in September 1893. "Nor was any sector of the county exempt from the paralysis; mills, factories, furnaces, mines nearly everywhere shut down in large numbers . . . and hundreds of thousands of men [were] thrown out of employment."[16]

With no unemployment insurance or federal emergency relief in place, many of the jobless suffered great hardship. In the spring of 1894, Jacob Coxey, a populist Ohio businessman, assembled about five hundred unemployed workers to march on Washington and call for the establishment of a federal public works program financed by the issuance of currency. Since the 1870s, the United States had adhered to the gold standard, which tied the amount of money in circulation to the stock of gold. For years, the farmers of the West had been demanding a new currency backed by silver, which they hoped would raise the depressed prices of agricultural commodities. "Coxey's Army" went further than the proponents of "free silver": it demanded the printing of fiat currency backed only by the word of its issuer, the US government.[17]

Veblen wasn't very sympathetic to these demands. In a June 1894 commentary in the *Journal of Political Economy*, he dismissed the proposals for a fiat currency and a nationwide public works program as an "articulate hallucination" that assumed "the feasibility of paternalism, or socialism, on a scale that is not borne out by the experience of the past." Still, the emergence of the protests was a "new departure," Veblen went on, one that reflected a rejection of the American individualist creed and a growing acknowledgment that "the entire community is a single industrial organism, whose integration is advancing day by day, regardless of any traditional or conventional boundary lines or demarcations, whether between classes or between localities."[18]

The reference to society as a living organism reflected Veblen's fascination with evolution and anthropology, which strongly influenced virtually all his work. In embracing Charles Darwin's intellectual legacy, he was hardly alone, of course. "Evolutionism, organicism, adulation of science: these were familiar points of view, and often accepted ones, on the American intellectual landscape in the last quarter of the nineteenth century," Charles Camic, a sociologist at Northwestern University, wrote in his admirable 2020 biography of Veblen.[19] As they adopted an evolutionary perspective, some of Veblen's progressive peers veered down some very ugly byways, where they embraced eugenicist concerns that the proliferation of "unfit" elements of the population was undermining US economic prospects. In an 1894 article on immigration, Ely said Americans should "ponder well the effects which a large admixture of baser foreign elements is likely to have upon American nationality."[20] In a 1901 address, the sociologist Edward A. Ross, who had studied under Ely at Johns Hopkins, suggested that low birth rates among white Anglo-Saxon Americans could mean that "the higher race quietly and unmurmuringly eliminates itself," a phenomenon he referred to as "race suicide."[21]

Veblen had an enduring fascination with ethnology and race, but he didn't embrace this thesis. He was skeptical of any simplistic argument, including the effort by some Social Darwinists to equate the rise of capitalism with the survival of the fittest. The "competitive system" would not "by any means uniformly result in working out of favorable results by a process of natural selection," he wrote in an 1896 review of Italian criminologist Enrico Ferri's *Socialism and Positive Science*, which had recently been published in French.[22] (In addition to Norwegian and English, Veblen could read French, German, and Latin.)

Even as Veblen rejected reductionist evolutionary justifications of capitalism, however, he hailed Darwin and his disciple Herbert Spencer for breathing new life into the physical, biological, and psychological sciences. Referring to his own discipline, he quoted Ferri's judgment that the evolutionary approach had "barely rippled the surface of the still waters of that pool of orthodoxy in social science, Political Economy."[23] Veblen was determined to change this. In his classes, which included History of Political Economy, Economic Factors in Civilization, and Socialism,[24] he adopted an evolutionary approach, referring his students to monographs on ancient societies. "Economics is to be brought into line with modern evolutionary science, which it has not been hitherto," he wrote in a January 1896 letter to one of his graduate students, Sarah Hardy. "The point of departure for this rehabilitation, or rather the basis of it, will be the modern anthropological and psychological sciences, perhaps most immediately . . . folk psychology."[25]

Veblen was thinking about writing a multivolume book applying evolutionary ideas to economics. In a November 1895 letter to Hardy, he said he had composed part of an introductory chapter to the first volume, which would be titled *The Theory of the Leisure Class*. A month later, in yet another letter to Hardy, with whom he was becoming besotted, he said he hadn't yet reached "the doctrine of conspicuous waste," which would "constitute the substantial nucleus of this writing."[26] By conspicuous waste, Veblen meant spending that wasn't directed at meeting actual physical needs.

His intellectual interests reflected the times. As incomes rose, a culture of consumerism was rapidly developing in the United States. Across the country, new department stores were showcasing all sorts of products, from clothes to household goods: Wanamaker's in Philadelphia; Marshall Field's in Chicago; and Filene's in Boston. In the great interior, farmers and townsfolk were perusing the annual Sears, Roebuck and Co. catalogue for novelties and bargains. The 1897 edition ran to seven hundred pages and described itself as "AN ARTIFACT TO MAKE THE MOUTH WATER."[27] In response to heavy demand from its customers, Sears built a Gilded Age version of an Amazon distribution center on the West Side of Chicago. As catalogue houses catered to the mass market, upscale New York retailers, including the jeweler Tiffany's, the department store B. Altman, and the home furnishings store W&J Sloane, were serving the nouveau riche.

These developments fascinated Veblen. In 1894 he had published an article in *Popular Science Monthly* titled "The Economic Theory of Woman's Dress." For many high-end consumers, the piece pointed out, clothes were no longer worn merely for work and comfort; they had turned into "an index of wealth." For clothing to be an effective signaling device, Veblen explained, it must satisfy three cardinal principles: "expensiveness," "novelty," and "ineptitude." It must be perfectly clear to everybody that the wearer of the dress was "manifestly incapable of doing anything that is of any use," and that the monies that had been expended upon it represented pure "waste," or "conspicuously unproductive expenditures."[28]

This argument didn't mesh with the labor theory of value, which Marx and other classical economists had relied on, or with the new mathematical economic theories of the Englishman William Stanley Jevons and the Frenchman Leon Walras, which traced the value of goods to the incremental utility (or satisfaction) they yielded. Breaking with all orthodoxies was Veblen's intention. Unlike most American economists, he took Marx seriously and sympathized with some of the goals of socialism despite his skepticism, at this stage of his life, about its practicality. In the end, though, he regarded the materialist theory of history as teleological and "unfit . . . for the purposes of modern science."[29] As for the orthodox theory, he regarded its foundations as fundamentally unsound. He believed it was ahistorical and psychologically unrealistic to treat people as atomistic and entirely rational decision-makers.

Veblen developed this idea in a journal article titled "Why Is Economics Not an Evolutionary Science?"[30] "The hedonistic conception of man," he wrote, "is that of a lightning calculator of pleasures and pains, who oscillates like a homogeneous globule of desire of happiness under the impulse of stimuli that shift him about the area but leave him intact." But humans weren't "simply a bundle of desires," Veblen insisted. Their behavior emerged from "a coherent structure of propensities and habits," each one shaped by their hereditary traits, past experience, and current material circumstances. The proper goal of economics, he argued, was to analyze these factors and the institutions that they gave rise to in a process of cumulative "cultural growth."

Veblen intended to develop these themes in his book, but his writing was interrupted by a marital crisis, the first of many. It was prompted by his relationship with Hardy. In a February 1896 letter, he wrote to her: "I love you beyond recall."[31] Not only was Veblen still married, but Hardy was engaged to someone else. In March, Veblen confessed to his wife, Ellen, that he was in love with another woman and asked for a divorce. After Ellen refused and Hardy went ahead with her marriage, Veblen went into a decline. "Mr. Veblen's health is entirely broken down," Ellen wrote to Hardy in April 1897. "He says often that he will not live through the year."[32] Despite his heartache, Veblen eventually managed to finish his manuscript. In September 1898, he sent a final version to the publisher Macmillan, which had agreed to put it out on condition that he covered half of the production costs. Five months later *The Theory of the Leisure Class* appeared.[33]

In its opening chapters, Veblen developed his evolutionary approach. Like Smith, Marx, and many other European scholars, he divided human history into separate epochs, in his case "savage," "barbarian," and "civilized." In the savage epoch, when people lived as roving bands of hunters, there was "no hierarchy of economic classes"; everyone participated in the communal activity and shared the spoils.[34] The rise of a leisure class that did no productive work coincided with the emergence of barbarian societies, in which a privileged upper tier lived off the economic surplus that it appropriated from the people who produced it. Veblen divided these societies into lower and higher barbarism. As examples of the latter, he cited feudal Europe and Japan. In these sorts of societies, "a struggle between men for the possession of goods" develops.[35] Gradually "accumulated property . . . more and more replaces trophies of predatory exploit as the conventional exponent of prepotence and success."[36]

Veblen's stadial theory of history was essentially technological. His use of the term "civilized" didn't represent an endorsement of the modern era, which, in his view, shared some key economic attributes with the "barbarian" epoch. In his narrative, the rise of settled agriculture created societies that were productive enough to support an idle elite of chieftains and high priests. Eventually, humanity transitioned into the era of handicrafts and, finally, the age of machinery, in which the economic surplus was big enough to support a sizable leisure class, who were direct descendants of the ancient high priests and the feudal nobility. They largely lived off the work of others.

Rather than singling out the predations and excesses of the Vanderbilts and other individual members of this new elite, as other critics of the Gilded Age had done, Veblen focused on the group as a whole and identified two of its key features. Since the goal of the members of the leisure class in accumulating wealth was "to rank high in the comparison with the rest of the community in point of pecuniary strength," there was no level of absolute wealth, however large, that could satisfy the desire for more.[37] As Veblen put it: "Since the struggle is substantially a race for reputability on the basis of an invidious comparison, no approach to a definitive attainment is possible."[38] Moreover, the private possession of great riches didn't guarantee a high social standing. Because "esteem is awarded only on evidence," everybody must be made aware of the existence of this wealth.[39]

One way for the upper classes to advertise their wealth was by refraining from productive work and engaging in "conspicuous leisure." From ancient Greece onward, Veblen noted, "the life of leisure is beautiful and ennobling in all civilized men's eyes."[40] Reprising the argument he had made in his article on women's dress, he identified another signaling device: making wasteful purchases and engaging in "conspicuous consumption." Either of these tactics could be effective. "In the one case it is a waste of time and effort, in the other it is a waste of goods. Both are methods of demonstrating the possession of wealth, and the two are conventionally accepted as equivalents."[41] Veblen pointed out that many members of the leisure class adopted them simultaneously. He referenced the "quasi-peaceable gentleman of leisure" who "consumes freely and of the best, in food, drink, narcotics, shelter, services, ornaments, apparel, weapons and accoutrements, amusements, amulets, and idols or divinities."[42] Such a fellow is no longer "simply the successful, aggressive male . . . In order to avoid stultification he must also cultivate his tastes, for it now becomes incumbent on him to discriminate with some nicety between the noble and the ignoble in consumable goods."[43]

At a time when the robber barons and their families were rifling the châteaus of Burgundy and Provence to furnish and decorate their mansions, Veblen's barbs reached the bone. But his arguments about status seeking and conspicuous consumption weren't restricted to the ultrarich. Although this sort of behavior was most prevalent among the elite, it had extended down the social scale, because the "leisure class stands at the head of the social structure . . . and its manner of life and its standards of worth therefore afford the norm of reputability for the community."[44] Obviously, the middle and lower classes didn't have the means to shop at Tiffany's or import rugs from Asia, but they, too, felt obliged to keep up appearances and impress their peers. The "members of each stratum accept as their ideal of decency the scheme of life in vogue in the next higher stratum, and bend their energies to live up to that ideal," Veblen wrote. "On pain of forfeiting their good name and their self-respect in case of failure, they must conform to the accepted code, at least in appearance."[45] Even people on the lowest social rungs weren't immune to the urge for wasteful display: "No class of society, not even the most abjectly poor, forgoes all customary conspicuous consumption . . . Very much of squalor and discomfort will be endured before the last trinket or the last pretense of pecuniary decency is put away."[46]

Of all Veblen's contributions, the theory of conspicuous consumption is the one he is most famous for, and with good reason. As time goes by in any capitalist society and incomes rise, spending that Veblen would have classed as wasteful makes up an ever-larger proportion of overall consumer spending. But Veblen's discussion of conspicuous consumption represented only part of the critique that he presented in *The Theory of the Leisure Class*. He also focused on production.

Looking at the United States of the 1890s, with its monopolistic trusts and increasingly powerful financial sector, personified in the form of the Wall Street banker J. P. Morgan, Veblen divided the economy into two different sectors: "industry" and "business." The leaders of the first sector, the industrial class, were engaged in the task of making things and developing innovative new products and manufacturing processes. By contrast, the business class, or "pecuniary class," was composed of absentee factory owners, passive shareholders, financiers, and other owners of capital who were engaged merely in making money, or rather, in appropriating it from the productive classes. "Their office is of a parasitic character, and their interest is to divert what substance they may to their own use, and to retain whatever is under their hand," Veblen wrote. "The conventions of the business world have grown up under the selective surveillance of this principle of predation or parasitism. They are conventions of ownership; derivatives, more or less remote, of the ancient predatory culture."[47]

The distinction between productive and nonproductive work that Veblen drew wasn't exactly new. The French social theorist Henri de Saint-Simon, who was discussed previously, had envisioned an ideal society led by *les industriels*—the productive class of workers and industrialists. Veblen's taxonomy was in the tradition of Saint-Simon, but he emphasized how the pecuniary class had arranged things so it could make as much money, with as little effort, as possible. He cited a series of reforms that benefited its members, including "changes affecting bankruptcy and receiverships, limited liability, banking and currency, coalitions of labourers or employers, trusts and pools." The "institutional furniture of this kind is of immediate consequence only to the propertied classes, and in proportion as they are propertied," he wrote. "But indirectly these conventions of business life are of the gravest consequence for the industrial process and for the life of the community."[48]

Why so? Veblen argued that they undermined the efficiency gains on which economic and social progress ultimately rested. "The collective interests of any modern community centre in industrial efficiency," and this efficiency was "best served by honesty, diligence, peacefulness, good-will, an absence of self-seeking."[49] But these productive traits, Veblen said, were "present in a markedly less degree in the man of the predatory type than is useful for the purposes of the modern collective life."[50] Therefore, the very existence of the pecuniary class "acts to lower the industrial efficiency of the community and retard the adaptation of human nature to the exigencies of modern industrial life."[51]

Here again Veblen didn't single out individuals by name. He did make clear that the "captains of industry"—a term that was sometimes applied to entrepreneurs like Carnegie and Rockefeller—were members of the parasitic pecuniary class because they operated at many removes from the shop floor. "The captain of industry is an astute man rather than an ingenious one, and his captaincy is a pecuniary rather than an industrial captaincy," Veblen wrote. "Such administration of industry as he exercises is commonly of a permissive kind. The mechanically effective details of production and of industrial organisation are delegated to subordinates of a less 'practical' turn of mind—men who are possessed of a gift for workmanship rather than administrative ability."[52]

In presenting this caustic portrait of the new plutocrats, Veblen gave no hint as to whether it was to be taken as gospel or satire or something in between. Throughout *The Theory of the Leisure Class*, he affected the manner of a lab-coated entomologist looking through his magnifying glass and dutifully noting down what he saw. In a chapter titled "The Conservation of Archaic Traits," he said that the "tendency of the pecuniary life is, in a general way, to conserve the barbarian temperament, but with the substitution of fraud and prudence, or administrative ability, in place of that predilection for physical damage that characterises the early barbarian."[53] Yet even as modern society chiefly preserved "the quasi-peaceable, or bourgeois variant," of the barbarian mindset, it also preserved "in some measure of the predatory variant."[54] Veblen held that this "substitution of chicane in place of devastation takes place only in an uncertain degree."[55] But he also identified some character traits that the members of the pecuniary class shared with the ne'er-do-wells and delinquents who eked out a living on the bottom rungs of society: "The ideal pecuniary man is like the ideal delinquent in his unscrupulous conversion of goods and persons to his own ends, and in a callous disregard of the feelings and wishes of others and of the remoter effects of his actions."[56] In other words, he was a monster.

The Theory of the Leisure Class received mixed reviews. One orthodox economist said it was "vicious"; others described it as a valuable social study. The left-leaning sociologist Charles Henderson hailed its author as a closet socialist, which annoyed Veblen. The two most important reviews came from William Dean Howells, an eminent novelist and literary critic, and the Harvard economist John Cummings. Writing in the journal *Literature*, Howells praised Veblen's "cold, scientific" approach and said his subject matter would make for a good novel.[57] This review brought Veblen, hitherto an obscure academic, to the attention of many noneconomists. But it was Cummings's critical article, which appeared in Veblen's own *Journal of Political Economy*, that the author took most seriously. Cummings described *The Theory of the Leisure Class* as a "highly original" contribution "to the general theory of sociology."[58] But he also called its author "a master of sophistical dialectic," and he took to task, on economic grounds, the book's two most substantive contributions: the theory of conspicuous consumption and the theory of the nonproductive businessman.

Cummings didn't deny that members of the plutocracy were making showy purchases of incredibly expensive items. How could he? But the Harvard man did question Veblen's suggestion that these items were intrinsically worthless and their desirability resided solely in their trophy value. He pointed out that many costly goods required a great deal of labor to manufacture, which helped explain their high prices: "From the fact that things of lasting worth are commonly costly may have developed by association the notion that things costly are of lasting worth, without the entrance of the invidious element into our aesthetic judgment at all."[59] Turning to Veblen's "captains of industry," Cummings claimed that their high incomes reflected the value of the productive services they provided to the economy—services that benefited everybody, including their workers. "The rise in wages during the last quarter century," he wrote, "is to a very considerable extent, if not altogether, due to the confiscation by the community in general of the increment to production and labor efficiency which has resulted from improvements, inventions, and the industrial genius of a few." Far from providing evidence of parasitism and predation, the possession of great wealth "has become an evidence of economic efficiency and facility in apprehension and adoption of more productive exploitation of labor and environment."[60]

This defense of the pecuniary class struck at the heart of Veblen's critiques of capitalism and economic orthodoxy. As Charles Camic emphasized in his 2020 biography, one of Veblen's principal goals in writing *The Theory of the Leisure Class* was to challenge the claim that the earnings of the rich reflected their high productivity.[61] In the same year that Veblen's work appeared, John Bates Clark, his teacher from Carleton College, published a book titled *The Distribution of Wealth*, in which he argued that competition ensured that the level of profits and interest in the economy were equated to the "marginal productivity" of capital, just as wages were equated to the "marginal productivity" of labor. This theory amounted to a rationalization of inequality, and many American economists, including Cummings, adopted it wholesale. "Wealth is the product of industry," he wrote, "apportioned among the agents of its production as nearly as may be in proportion to the value of services by them severally executed." The strict line that Veblen had drawn between a productive industrial class and a nonproductive business class was "a distinction which cannot be maintained in fact."[62]

Veblen felt obliged to respond to Cummings's review. His initial salvo came in a piece published in the next issue of the *Journal of Political Economy*, where he defended his distinction between industrial and pecuniary employment, saying Cummings's "failure to apprehend the distinction does not affect its reality."[63] He expanded this argument in a paper he wrote for a conference at Harvard, which he then tried to turn into a short book, provisionally titled *The Captain of Industry and His Work*. By the summer of 1901, he had completed a manuscript, but his publisher Macmillan turned it down. Forced to rethink the project, Veblen spent two years revising it. He also came up with a new title, *The Theory of Business Enterprise*, and a different publisher, C. Scribner's Sons, which put out the book in September 1904.[64]

Although it lacked some of the sparkle of *The Theory of the Leisure Class*, *The Theory of Business Enterprise* was more focused, and its arguments were backed up by case studies. Veblen drew extensively from a multivolume report from the Industrial Commission, an official body that President William McKinley had set up in 1898 to examine railroad pricing, the broader issue of monopoly, and the impact of immigration on wages. He mentioned consumption, conspicuous or otherwise, only briefly. Perhaps for this reason, *The Theory of Business Enterprise* received much less attention than *The Theory of the Leisure Class*, but it remains essential reading.

During the early stages of industrial capitalism, Veblen wrote, the individual proprietor remained close to the shop floor and "kept an immediate oversight of the mechanical processes as well as the pecuniary transactions in which his enterprise was engaged."[65] He had an instinct for "workmanship" and took pride in the quality of his products. But as time went on, businesses got larger, production processes became more complicated, and the focus of attention of the "business man" shifted "to an alert redistribution of investments from less to more gainful ventures, and to a strategic control of the conjunctures of business through shrewd investments and coalitions with other business men."[66] Veblen argued that this financialization of the economy changed the moral code under which businesses operated: making a quick score became the main goal. Although the individual businessman perhaps still retained "a sense of equity, fair dealing, and workmanlike integrity," these values acted as "a conventional restraint upon pecuniary advantage, not in abrogation of it." Veblen went on acidly: "The code of business ethics consists, after all, of mitigations of the maxim Caveat emptor."[67]

To illustrate his point, Veblen cited the consolidation of the railroads, which he described as "a game, in which the end sought by the players is their own pecuniary gain and to which the industrial serviceability of the outcome is incidental only."[68] But he also insisted that the practices of eliminating competition, establishing monopoly power, and raising prices had extended far beyond the railroads: "It is very doubtful if there are any successful business ventures within the range of the modern industries from which the monopoly element is wholly absent," he wrote. "There are, at any rate, few and not of great magnitude. And the endeavor of all such enterprises that look to a permanent continuance of their business is to establish as much of a monopoly as may be."[69]

These comments about monopolization were timely, if not exactly pathbreaking. By 1904, the journalist Ida Tarbell's famous multipart exposé of Standard Oil had appeared in *McClure's* magazine, and Theodore Roosevelt was in the White House. He had created a Department of Commerce, and within it a Bureau of Corporations tasked with investigating the trusts. Roosevelt's Justice Department had filed a lawsuit to break up Northern Securities, a holding company that J. P. Morgan and several railroad barons had set up to consolidate three large railroad companies. In March 1904 the Supreme

Court ruled for the Justice Department, describing the creation of Northern Securities as "an illegal combination in restraint of interstate commerce."[70]

The novelty of Veblen's treatment of monopolization was that he framed it as a natural evolution of industrial capitalism rather than an aberration. The creation of trusts and the formal elimination of competition was but one aspect of this evolution, he argued. Others included the rise of advertising and the creation of brands that enjoyed a "monopoly of custom and prestige" and were able, therefore, to command premium price.[71] The money that firms spent on advertising "does not add to the serviceability of the output, except it be incidentally and unintentionally," Veblen wrote. It is part of the sales effort, "which is useful to the seller, but has no utility to the last buyer."[72] Money spent on advertising is therefore "wasteful" spending, and advertising is a "parasitic" industry.[73]

Finance was another sector of the economy that Veblen regarded with a great deal of skepticism. In the days of Adam Smith, he reminded his readers, the term *capital* referred to the stock of machinery, equipment, and raw materials that were used in production. But in an age of far-flung partnerships, joint-stock corporations, and holding companies that owned many different businesses, members of the business class conceived of capital as financial capital issued by businesses—stocks, bonds, debentures, and so on—the value of which was determined in financial markets. Whereas the sole proprietor's aim was to make the most productive use of his physical capital, Veblen said, the primary goal of the corporate or pecuniary capitalist was to maximize the value of his firm's financial capital.

Events had borne out this analysis. In February 1901, when J. P. Morgan merged Andrew Carnegie's eponymous steel company, which was based in Pittsburgh, with Elbert H. Gary's National Steel Company, which was based in Chicago, and several other metals businesses, he created in US Steel a giant that had 168,000 employees and operations in more than a dozen states. The new combine established its headquarters on lower Broadway in Manhattan, just off Wall Street. On its founding, the company issued $508 million in common stock, $510 million in preferred stock, and $391 million in bonds, giving it a total value of $1.4 billion. The accounting value of its underlying assets—its steel mills, rolling equipment, and so on—was only about half that amount. On April 1, 1901, US Steel's stock began trading on the New York Stock Exchange.

Veblen cited the formation of US Steel as an example of how businesses could be combined to raise their market capitalization well above the real economic value of their underlying assets. This excess value was known as "good will." "On this higher level of business enterprise," Veblen commented tartly, it "has a certain character of inexhaustibility, so that its use and capitalization in one corporation need not, and indeed does not, hinder or diminish the extent to which it may be used and capitalized in any other corporation."[74] He also highlighted another financial ruse that corporate insiders used to enrich themselves: a corporate recapitalization, in which a business issued or retired large blocks of stocks or bonds, sometimes in connection with a merger, but often just for the sake of it. This "traffic in vendible capital is the pivotal and dominant factor in the modern situation of business and industry," Veblen wrote.[75]

His portrait of the new financialized, trustified US economy, and the men who ran it, could hardly have been darker. Where economists like Cummings pointed to the economies of scale and other efficiencies afforded by industrial giants and joint-stock corporations, Veblen portrayed their creators as rent seekers who extracted great wealth from the economy without making any matching contribution to productivity. Like Adam Smith before him, he highlighted how the joint-stock corporate structure created the potential for conflicts of interest and outright abuses. Since the managers of businesses knew far more about their operations than outside shareholders did, they could easily "induce a discrepancy between the putative and the actual earning-capacity" of their firms "by expedients well known and approved for the purpose," Veblen wrote.[76] "Partial information, as well as misinformation, sagaciously given out at a critical juncture, will go far toward producing a favorable temporary discrepancy of this kind, and so enabling the managers to buy or sell the securities of the concern with advantage to themselves." Given the potential to make a quick financial killing, Veblen argued, business leaders even had an interest in creating industrial disturbances and dislocations, which they could then profit from—for instance, by picking up the assets of rival businesses on the cheap.

In 1921, when Veblen was old and famous and living in New York, he would describe the activities of the pecuniary class as "sabotage" in his book *The Engineers and the Price System*. In *The Theory of Business Enterprise*, his language was less loaded but he leveled essentially the same charge. Once capital was conceived of as financial capital, he wrote, it was "unavoidable" that "the business men in whose hands lies the conduct of affairs should play at cross-purposes and endeavor to derange industry."[77] Indeed, "this class of businessmen . . . have an interest in making the disturbances of the system large and frequent, since it is in the conjunctures of change that their gain emerges."[78] Problems of this nature were inevitable, Veblen said, in a system where "the material processes of industry are under the control of men whose interest centres on an increased value of the immaterial assets."[79]

When *The Theory of Business Enterprise* was published, Veblen was forty-six years old and still a lowly assistant professor. The success of his first two books had brought him some public attention, but in the world of economics he remained a maverick and, in some quarters, a suspected socialist. His personal life remained complicated. In 1906 he left Chicago for Stanford, which had offered him a promotion, but his reputation as a philanderer followed him west. In Palo Alto, Veblen's extramarital affairs continued, and in 1909 Stanford forced him to resign. (Two years later his wife, Ellen, finally divorced him.) After struggling to find another academic post, he took a job as a lecturer at the less vaunted University of Missouri, in the city of Columbia.

He stayed in Missouri for seven years and continued to write prolifically, elucidating themes new and old. There was truth to the critic H. L. Mencken's claim that Veblen often repeated himself, but his themes were timeless. The final chapter of *The Theory of Business Enterprise* was devoted to "The Natural Decay of Business Enterprise," which he linked to its expansionist and warlike tendencies. "Business interests urge an aggressive national policy and business men direct it," he wrote.[80]

Since the Spanish-American War of 1898, the United States had openly fashioned itself as an imperial power with territorial ambitions in the Caribbean, Latin America, and the Pacific. The business class supported these policies on the grounds that they reflected "an enthusiasm for the commercial aggrandizement of the nation's business men"[81] and diverted popular attention to "less hazardous matters than the unequal distribution of wealth or of creature comforts," Veblen wrote. In taking this stance, business leaders were making a Faustian pact with the forces of militarism and absolutism, he argued. Even when the "policy of warlike enterprise has been entered upon for business ends," the initiative tends to "shift from the business interests to the warlike and dynastic interests, as witness the history of imperialism in Germany and England." And this process "may easily be carried so far as to sacrifice the profits of the business men to the exigencies of the higher politics,"[82] ultimately leading to a "decline of business enterprise itself."[83] Veblen didn't claim that this calamitous outcome was inevitable. He remarked that there were powerful countervailing forces, and he described the final outcome as "something of a blind guess."[84] Despite these qualifications, however, the thrust of Veblen's argument was that the triumph of pecuniary values could well herald a return to barbarism. A decade after he issued this warning, the Western capitalist countries plunged into the hellscape of World War I.

12

John Hobson's Theory of Imperialism

During the summer and autumn of 1899, John Atkinson Hobson, a forty-year-old English economist and writer, visited South Africa on assignment for *The Manchester Guardian*, a liberal newspaper that was edited by the legendary C. P. Scott. Although Hobson had written several books on economics and a biography of John Ruskin, the Victorian art critic and polymath, he was little known to the British public. In 1898, however, he had published an essay in *The Contemporary Review*, a highbrow journal, in which he challenged the arguments of imperialists like Joseph Chamberlain, Britain's colonial secretary, and Cecil Rhodes, the British-born South African politician and mining magnate, who claimed that expanding Britain's already-vast empire was the best way to create markets for British products and jobs for British workers.[1] "The Empire, as I have always said, is a bread-and-butter question," Rhodes had declared a few years earlier, after attending a meeting of unemployed workers in London's East End. "If you want to avoid civil war, you must become imperialists."[2] In his article, Hobson dismissed this argument as a canard. He said that territorial conquests were unnecessary to promote trade, and he insisted that the root cause of deficient demand for British products was a domestic one: an inequitable distribution of income, which limited the purchasing power of the masses.[3]

Hobson's economic critiques of imperialism came to the attention of L. T. Hobhouse, a noted liberal philosopher who was also an editorial writer at *The Manchester Guardian*. It was Hobhouse who urged Scott to send Hobson to South Africa, which appeared to be on the brink of a war between rival colonial territories: Britain's Cape Colony, where Rhodes had served as prime minister from 1890 to 1896, and two small republics—the Orange Free State and the Transvaal—which Dutch settlers, known as Boers (or Afrikaners), had established earlier in the nineteenth century, after fleeing British rule in the Cape. For decades, there had been tensions between the British and the Dutch territories, but the root cause of the war scare was gold, which had been discovered in large quantities in the Witwatersrand region of the Transvaal. Rhodes and his fellow mining magnates and financiers, collectively known as the Randlords, were determined to gain control of the gold-mining regions. The Dutch colonists, led by Paul Kruger, president of the Transvaal, had vigorously resisted their demands.

To Hobson's delight, Scott, the *Guardian* editor, agreed to Hobhouse's idea of enlisting him as a correspondent. "Though I had no experience in newspaper work, except as an occasional reviewer, I seized the opportunity to see the working of imperialism at close quarters," Hobson would write years later.[4] When he reached Cape Town, British troops were gathering on the northern border with the Boer republics; fighting seemed imminent. Shortly after his arrival, Hobson made his way to the historic Groote Schuur estate, which the Dutch East India Company had built in the seventeenth century, when it relied on the Cape as a transshipment point on its Asia trade routes. Rhodes had leased the estate, and he used it to entertain visitors. Since arriving in South Africa in 1870 as the sickly seventeen-year-old son of a lowly Church of England minister, he had created a vast fortune for himself. After entering the diamond trade in the northern Cape, where the precious minerals were discovered in 1868, he had created, with the assistance of the Rothschild banking house, the world's largest diamond company, De Beers. Then he had entered politics as an unabashed imperialist who had ambitions of extending British rule from Cape Town to Cairo.[5]

As prime minister, Rhodes introduced racist laws that drove more native Africans from their lands and excluded them from the voting franchise. In tribal territories that are now in Zimbabwe, he obtained invaluable mining concessions for his British South Africa Company. The Boers had resisted his efforts to gain control of their land. In 1895, under the guise of defending the rights of foreign workers living in the Boer republics, who were known as Uitlanders, Rhodes dispatched hundreds of armed police to the Transvaal in an effort to spark an uprising. The Jameson Raid, as it came to be known, ended in ignominious failure and cost Rhodes his premiership. But he and his fellow Randlords hadn't given up on their ambitions to defeat the Boers and annex their territories. Moreover, they retained the enthusiastic support of senior British officials, including Sir Alfred Milner, the governor of Cape Colony, and Chamberlain, the colonial secretary.

As a visiting journalist, Hobson was able to speak with many of the major players in the Cape, including Milner, who told him that military action might be necessary to "break the dominion of Africanderdom."[6] He also spent several weeks in the Boer republics, where he found that that the threats to the Uitlanders had been "wildly exaggerated."[7] During his visit to Groote Schuur, Rhodes had expressed doubts that the outnumbered Boers would actively resist a British invasion.[8] This prediction turned out to be utterly mistaken.

The war that began in October 1899 lasted two and a half years and resulted in more than fifty thousand deaths—Dutch, African, and British. After the Dutch fighters adopted the methods of guerrilla warfare, the British Army confined their families and many members of the native Black population to shoddily constructed internment camps, where tens of thousands died from disease and malnutrition. Shortly after the shooting began, Hobson returned safely to England, where he published a series of articles blaming the war on the Randlords, imperialist British officials, and a jingoistic media. "The lesson I learned from this experience was the dominant power of a particularly crude form of capitalism operating in a mixed political field," he subsequently wrote. "It became evident that, while the politicians were hesitant and divided, the capitalists of the Rand were planning straight for war and were using the British Press of South Africa as their instrument for rousing the war-spirit in England."[9] He went on: "War came from the joint drive of capitalism in South Africa and the new imperialism in England."[10]

As the history of Groote Schuur illustrated, commercially driven European colonialism was nothing new to Africa and Asia. In a letter to Lord Rothschild, his principal financier, Rhodes himself referred to De Beers as "another East India Company."[11] What was different about late nineteenth-century imperialism was its scale and rapidity and the unabashed racism that was used to justify it. ("I contend that we are the finest race in the world and that the more of the world we inhabit the better it is for the human race," Rhodes wrote in 1877.)[12] In 1870 roughly 10 percent of the African continent was under European occupation. Thirty years later, after the monumental land grab that historians call the "Scramble for Africa," only about 10 percent of Africa was *unoccupied*. In rapid succession, the four major European powers—Britain, France, Germany, and Italy—greatly expanded their possessions on the continent, establishing territories with names like Anglo Egyptian Sudan, French West Africa, German South West Africa, Italian Somaliland, and the Belgian Congo. The surge of imperialism extended to Asia and the Americas. Exploiting the power of their battleships and the new Maxim machine gun, Britain expanded its possessions on the Malay Peninsula and in the Pacific. France colonized much of Indo-China. Germany occupied part of New Guinea and dozens of nearby islands in the Pacific. Russia and Japan made advances on parts of China. After the Spanish-American War of 1898, the United States annexed the Philippines, Guam, and Puerto Rico, and it temporarily occupied Cuba.

Of all the liberal thinkers who grappled with these developments, Hobson was arguably the most important. He was born in 1858 in Derby, an ancient market town in the English Midlands, which, since the industrial revolution, had developed into a manufacturing center for cotton textiles and other goods. His father was the churchgoing proprietor of a local newspaper who believed in peace, prosperity, and progress, and his son didn't start out as any kind of radical. "Born and bred in the middle stratum of the middle class of a middle-sized industrial town of the Midlands, I was favorably situated for a complacent acceptance of the existing social order," he recalled in his autobiography. "There was not stagnation anywhere, but a gradual orderly improvement in the standard of living, the working conditions, and the behaviour of most classes."[13] The high school that Hobson attended didn't offer economics, but he took a beginner's course through the Cambridge University Extension Movement, where the readings included Adam Smith and J. S. Mill. After leaving school, Hobson went to Lincoln College, Oxford. He did a degree in classics—the study of Greek and Latin—and occasionally attended political debates at the Oxford Union, where, in his words, "I heard nothing to disturb my complacent acceptance of the beneficent and equitable operation of laws of supply and demand in their *laisser-faire* environment."[14]

Hobson's thinking began to evolve after he left Oxford and became a schoolteacher in Exeter, a city in southwestern England. There, he met his future wife, an American writer named Florence Edgar. He also had a chance encounter with Alfred Mummery, a well-known mountaineer who had found a new way to scale the Matterhorn. Mummery was also a business-man interested in economics, endowed with what Hobson described as "a sublime disregard of intellectual authority."[15] One of the orthodoxies Mum-mery questioned was the claim that saving—or deferred consumption—was the key to prosperity. In Mummery's view, excessive saving was at the root of the long deflation and malaise that had afflicted Britain and other Western countries since the great financial panic of 1873. It was in this same economic environment that Henry George's *Progress and Poverty* had become a pub-lishing phenomenon in England, but Hobson was unimpressed by George's argument. In "concentrating upon a single form of unearned wealth"—land rents—"it enables its adherents to evade and arrest the wider claims of Social-ism," he wrote.[16]

Hobson thought a different explanation was needed for the problems that attended industrialization, including widespread unemployment and poverty, which were receiving a good deal of attention in Britain thanks to the social researcher Charles Booth and others. Mummery blamed these blights on oversaving by the rich. "For a long time I sought to counter his arguments by the use of the orthodox economic weapons," Hobson later re-called. "But at length he convinced me and I went in with him to elaborate the over-saving argument in a book entitled *The Physiology of Industry*, which was published in 1889."[17]

The book, which had a joint byline, argued that orthodox economists had made a mistake by focusing mainly on the productive capacity of the economy. From this perspective, the authors conceded, a high level of sav-ing seemed essential because it provided the funds that businesses needed to invest in factories, machinery, and other forms of capital. But saving and capital, they argued, were useful only insomuch that they facilitated the pro-duction of goods that people wanted to buy and had the financial resources to buy. If these conditions weren't satisfied, a high level of saving could "cause an accumulation of Capital in excess of that which is required for use, and this excess will exist in the form of general over-production,"[18] which in turn "throws labourers out of work, drives down wages, and spreads that gloom and prostration through the commercial world which is known as Depression in Trade; that, in short, the effective love of money is the root of all economic evil."[19]

In identifying oversaving as a chronic failure of capitalism, Mummery and Hobson were effectively making the same argument that John Maynard Keynes would popularize forty years later, when he wrote, "It should be obvious that mere abstinence is not enough by itself to build cities or drain fens."[20] Now known as "the paradox of thrift," this theory is a basic element of Keynesian economics and features in many textbooks. In 1889, though, concerns about generalized overproduction and oversaving were largely confined to Marxists and a few devotees of Sismondi, the early nineteenth-century Swiss dissident, and his British counterpart Thomas Malthus. Most economists stoutly believed in Say's Law, which said that an extended glut of goods was impossible because, if supply did exceed demand, prices would fall until the gap was eliminated. Thus, supply would create its own demand, and oversaving wouldn't be a problem. Hobson and Mummery reversed this logic, writing: "In the normal state of modern industrial Communities, consumption limits production and not production consumption."[21]

The Physiology of Industry didn't attract a big readership. It did succeed in getting Hobson effectively drummed out of the economics profession. By the time it was published, he had moved to London, where he applied for a job teaching university extension courses that catered to working adults. On the recommendation of an economics professor who had read the book and, in the words of Hobson, "considered it as equivalent in rationality to an attempt to prove the flatness of the earth," the program turned down his application.[22] Although he would go on to teach classes at the Oxford University extension program, he would never be offered a regular academic post.

Not to be put off, he quickly published a second book, *Problems of Poverty: An Inquiry into the Industrial Condition of the Poor*, which drew on government reports and Charles Booth's painstaking survey of working-class life in London. It was a shortish work with a fairly narrow focus. By contrast, Hobson's third book, *The Evolution of Modern Capitalism: A Study of Machine Production*, which appeared in 1894, was a grand tome in the tradition of Marx's *Capital*. Like Marx, Hobson emphasized the role technical progress played in capitalist development. He also drew attention to the monotony of factory work, and he said the goal of a progressive society should be "not the abolition of machinery, but the diminution of machine-tending, which attends the growing perfection of machinery, in order that the arts may be able to absorb a larger share of human exertion."[23]

By this stage, Hobson was starting to make a name for himself in London's intellectual circles. He mixed with socialists of the Fabian, Christian, and Marxian variety but professed to be a member of none of these groups.[24] When he read the first British edition of *Capital*, which was published in 1887, he was put off by the labor theory of value and a "Hegelian dialectic which used an empty intellectual paradox to impart an air of mysticism into quite intelligible historic processes."[25] Like many other liberal intellectuals at the time, Hobson was searching for a middle way between socialism and the old individualist doctrines. From 1896 to 1898, he was associated with *The Progressive Review*, a journal that published articles by writers ranging from the Liberal politician Herbert Samuel to the independent socialist (and future founder of the Labour Party) Keir Hardie. Despite his religious upbringing, Hobson was also an active member of the London Ethical Society, a British offshoot of the New York Society for Ethical Culture, which was dedicated to secular humanism and ameliorating the condition of the poor.[26]

Hobson regarded his primary intellectual goal as humanizing economic thinking and moving it beyond arid abstractions. Like George and Veblen, he stressed the importance of institutions and state capture. As the machinations of Rhodes and his colleagues made a war in South Africa seem inevitable, he got caught up in the political debates about imperialism that had split the Liberal Party into two warring camps, with the old Gladstonian wing on the anti-imperialist side, and Joseph Chamberlain's Liberal Unionists on the other. In 1895 Chamberlain had joined a coalition government with Lord Salisbury's Conservatives and obtained the post of colonial secretary, from which he promoted the idea of turning the far-flung British Empire into a formal federation and jettisoning free trade in favor of imperial protection. Aligning himself with Rhodes, Chamberlain supported the Jameson Raid; subsequently, he directed the British participation in the Boer War.

Hobson was aghast at these policies. After returning from South Africa and turning his series of articles for *The Guardian* into a short book on the background to the war, he started work on a broader study of imperialism and its economic roots.

Imperialism: A Study of the History, Politics and Economics of the Colonial Powers in Europe and America was published in London in 1902, just months after the war in South Africa ended. "Those readers who hold that a well-balanced judgment consists in always finding as much in favour of any political course as against it will be discontented with the treatment given here," Hobson wrote in a preface. "For the study is distinctively one of social pathology, and no endeavor is made to disguise the malignity of the disease."[27] With that disclaimer out of the way, he reexamined the claims from Rhodes and other imperialists that newly acquired colonial markets in Africa and other parts of the globe were of vital importance to the British economy. The reality, Hobson said, was that "the smallest, least valuable, and most uncertain trade is that done with our tropical possessions, and in particular with those which have come under imperial control since 1870."[28] (Here, Hobson was referring to places like Nigeria, Ashanti [Ghana], Egypt, and Kenya.) During the same period, he pointed out, Britain had expanded its trade most rapidly with other developed countries, particularly France, Germany, and the United States, and with its long-established and self-ruling colonies in Australasia and Canada. Thus, Hobson concluded, "the Imperialism of the last three decades is clearly condemned as a business policy, in that at enormous expense it has procured a small, bad, unsafe increase of markets, and has jeopardised the entire wealth of the nation in rousing the strong resentment of other nations."[29]

This passage echoed Adam Smith's critique of colonialism in *The Wealth of Nations*. It also raised anew the question of how the British government had been persuaded to embark on so many imperialist ventures. "The only possible answer is that the business interests of the nation as a whole are subordinated to those of certain sectional interests that usurp control of the national resources and use them for their private gain," Hobson wrote. "This is no strange or monstrous charge to bring; it is the commonest disease of all forms of government. The famous words of Sir Thomas More are as true now as when he wrote them: 'Everywhere do I perceive a certain conspiracy of rich men seeking their own advantage under the name and pretext of the commonwealth.'"[30]

Among the obvious beneficiaries of imperialism, Hobson identified armaments makers, shipbuilders, shipping companies, and members of the military. "These men are Imperialists by conviction; a pushful policy is good for them," he wrote.[31] To his list, he added "the great manufacturers for export trade," noting that, even though the new colonial markets were small, "Manchester, Sheffield, Birmingham, to name three representative cases, are full of firms which compete in pushing textiles, and hardware, engines, tools, machinery, spirits, guns."[32] Together these commercial interests constituted a sizable imperialism lobby, Hobson said. But he insisted that its influence on government policy was greatly exceeded by that of another big interest group: the financial capitalists in the City of London and beyond. "By far the most important economic factor in Imperialism is the influence relating to investments," he wrote. "The growing cosmopolitanism of capital is the greatest economic change of this generation. Every advanced industrial nation is tending to place a larger share of its capital outside the limits of its own political area, in foreign countries, or in colonies, and to draw a growing income from this source."[33]

Citing income tax data and estimates from the Irish journalist and statistician Michael George Mulhall, Hobson pointed out that between 1862 and 1893, the total volume of Britain's foreign investment had risen more than tenfold.[34] And between 1884 and 1900, the annual income it received from foreign investments had virtually doubled.[35] These developments hadn't merely altered the nature of British capitalism, Hobson argued: they had also transformed its foreign policy. "It is not too much to say that the modern foreign policy of Great Britain is primarily a struggle for profitable markets of investment," he wrote. "To a larger extent every year Great Britain is becoming a nation living upon tribute from abroad, and the classes who enjoy this tribute have an ever-increasing incentive to employ the public policy, the public purse, and the public force to extend the field of their private investments, and to safeguard and improve their existing investments. This is perhaps the most important fact in modern politics, and the obscurity in which it is wrapped constitutes the gravest danger to our State.[36]

Again, there were echoes here of Smith's critique of the East India Company and other state-chartered monopolies. But Hobson took the state capture argument further and generalized it, writing: "What is true of Great Britain is true likewise of France, Germany, the United States, and of all countries in which modern capitalism has placed large surplus savings in the hands of a plutocracy or a thrifty middle class."[37] The inclusion of the United States on Hobson's list of imperialist countries was no accident. He viewed the rapid expansion of American industry and finance during the post–Civil War era as the essential precursor to the imperialist thrust that had found its political champion in Theodore Roosevelt. "The adventurous enthusiasm of President Roosevelt and his 'manifest destiny' and 'mission of civilization' party must not deceive us," Hobson wrote. And he added:

> It is Messrs. Rockefeller, Pierpont Morgan, Hanna, Schwab, and their as-sociates who need Imperialism and who are fastening it upon the shoul-ders of the great Republic of the West. They need Imperialism because they desire to use the public resources of their country to find profitable employment for the capital which otherwise would be superfluous . . . American Imperialism is the natural product of the economic pressure of a sudden advance of capitalism which cannot find occupation at home and needs foreign markets for goods and for investments.[38]

Having laid out this economic theory of imperialism, Hobson went on to examine its underpinnings, further developing some of the arguments he had made in his earlier books about underconsumption and oversaving. "It is admitted by all business men that the growth of the powers of production in their country exceeds the growth in consumption, that more goods can be produced than can be sold at a profit, and that more capital exists than can find remunerative investment," he wrote. "It is this economic condition of affairs that forms the taproot of Imperialism."[39] Hobson also insisted that this state of affairs wasn't inevitable, and that the solution was in plain sight: raising the spending power of the masses. "If the consuming public in this country raised its standard of consumption to keep pace with every rise of productive powers, there could be no excess of goods or capital clamorous to use Imperialism in order to find markets," he wrote.[40] Some foreign trade would still take place, he added, but the home market would be able to absorb most of the products that the country's businesses produced.

Hobson had now reached the crux of his argument: the fundamental factor driving imperialism was a chronically lopsided distribution of income and wealth. If income were distributed according to needs, "consumption would rise with every rise of producing power, for human needs are illimit-able, and there could be no excess of saving," he wrote. "But it is quite other-wise in a state of economic society where distribution has no fixed relation to needs, but is determined by other conditions which assign to some people a consuming power vastly in excess of needs or possible uses, while others are destitute of consuming power enough to satisfy even the full demands of physical efficiency."[41] Citing the work of the social researcher and industrialist Seebohm Rowntree, who had recently published a detailed study of poverty in the English city of York, Hobson pointed out that "more than one-fourth of the population of our towns is living at a standard which is below bare physical efficiency."[42] He continued: "If, by some economic readjustment, the products which flow from the surplus saving of the rich . . . could be diverted so as to raise the incomes and the standard of consumption of this inefficient fourth, there would be no need for pushful Imperialism, and the cause of social reform would have won its greatest victory."[43]

Returning to the US experience, Hobson argued that oversaving and deficient demand constituted a particularly grave problem in a society "where multi-millionaires rise quickly and find themselves in possession of incomes far exceeding the demands of any craving that is known to them."[44] But Hobson also emphasized that the oversaving problem wasn't confined to one country: it afflicted all capitalist countries once their economies reached a certain level of development, inequality, and rent-seeking. "It is not industrial progress that demands the opening up of new markets and areas of investment, but mal-distribution of consuming power which prevents the absorption of commodities and capital within the country," he wrote. "The over-saving which is the economic root of Imperialism is found by analysis to consist of rents, monopoly profits, and other unearned or excessive elements of income, which not being earned by labour of head or hand, have no legitimate *raison d'être*."[45]

Until this point in his analysis, Hobson had refrained from offering any detailed prescriptions. Now, he called for an aggressive program of income and wealth redistribution, justifying it on practical as well as moral grounds. An economy in which so much of the consuming power is restricted to a tiny minority is "a suicidal economy even from the exclusive standpoint of capital, for consumption alone vitalises capital and makes it capable of yielding profits," he wrote. "An economy that assigns to the 'possessing' classes an excess of consuming power which they cannot use, and cannot convert into really serviceable capital, is a dog-in-the-manger policy."[46]

Given this imbalance, which Marx and some of his followers had also identified as one of capitalism's self-contradictions, moving to "deprive the possessing classes of their surplus will not . . . inflict upon them the real injury they dread," Hobson insisted.[47] To the contrary, it would raise domestic demand for the products businesses manufactured and undermine the economic arguments for imperialism, which he described, with an eye to the rising military tensions between the imperialist powers, as "a wrecking policy" for all concerned. "The only safety of nations," he concluded, "lies in removing the unearned increments of income from the possessing classes, and adding them to the wage-income of the working classes or to the public income in order that they may be spent in raising the standard of consumption."[48]

Particularly on the left, Hobson's theory of imperialism was to prove enormously influential. In bringing together inequality, poverty, unemployment, oversaving, and state capture, it seemed to supply a unified field theory of capitalist pathologies. It also provided an economic explanation for the shift from the trade-based colonialism that had been exercised by the East India Company and other similar ventures to the out-and-out imperialist land grabs of the late nineteenth century: this formal imperialism, as it came to be known, was an outgrowth of industrial capitalism and the huge surpluses of capital that it generated.

Like many grand theories, this one oversimplified some things and failed to account for others. Hobson was correct when he pointed to the massive outflows of financial capital from late nineteenth-century and early twentieth-century Britain. However, modern economic historians emphasize that most of these investments didn't go to the country's new colonies in Africa and Asia: they went to North America and South America. But even though this criticism of Hobson has some force, it doesn't negate his argument that finance capital played an important role in the scramble for Africa and parts of Asia. Hobson was well aware that most of Britain's foreign investments were directed toward the United States and other independent countries rather than its colonies. In his 1902 book, he cited contemporary estimates showing that in the 1890s, the majority of the income that Britain derived from its foreign investments came from these sources. But he also emphasized the growth in income derived from recently acquired colonies. "The investing and speculative classes in general also desire that Great Britain should take other foreign areas under her flag in order to secure new areas for profitable investment and speculation," he wrote.[49]

A more penetrating criticism of Hobson is that his analysis of finance capital was tarnished with antisemitism. In *The War in South Africa*, his 1900 collection of journalistic articles, he described the conflict as a "Jew-Imperialist design that is in the course of execution."[50] In *Imperialism: A Study*, he referred to international banking houses that form the "central ganglion of international capitalism . . . controlled, so far as Europe is concerned, chiefly by men of a single and peculiar race, who have behind them many centuries of financial experience, they are in a unique position to control the policy of nations."[51] It is a matter of record that Rhodes founded De Beers with backing from the British branch of the Rothschild banking concern, and that some prominent Randlords, such as Alfred Beit and Sigismund Neumann, were Jewish. But many of the mining magnates were gentiles. They included Rhodes himself; his partner Charles Rudd; Sir Julius Wernher, a partner of Beit; and Sir Joseph Robinson, the founder of Randfontein Estates. To the extent that Hobson's statements implied imperialist politicians like Joseph Chamberlain, Jules Ferry, and Teddy Roosevelt were controlled by Jewish banking interests, they were equally ahistorical. In singling out Jewish financiers and claiming that they exercised sweeping power over global capitalism, Hobson was peddling a trope that Hitler and other antisemitic rabble-rousers would later seize upon.

Offputting as these passages were, though, they weren't essential to Hobson's analysis. His economic theory of imperialism hinged on the search for profitable investment opportunities by financial capital in general, not by the subset controlled by Jewish banking houses. Nothing in his theory depended on the religion or ethnicity of the individuals who supplied the capital. Indeed, Hobson, by singling out one specific group, weakened his argument and made it appear less general than it was.

Viewed in broad terms, Hobson's theory of imperialism and his other writings on oversaving and industrial capitalism were a response to what late Victorians referred to as the "social question": the rise of the industrial working class and the attendant problems of poverty, inequality, and social strife. Marx's followers insisted that it was folly to believe these issues could be resolved within the existing economic system. Hobson and other progressive liberals, even as they jettisoned some elements of the liberal creed, retained an underlying faith in reform and progress. This British "New Liberalism," which also encompassed the writings of Hobhouse and the philosopher T. H. Green, aspired to transcend the old individualism while not entirely abandoning it. The New Liberals adopted an organic view of society, in which the social organism couldn't be reduced entirely to its constituent parts. In practical terms, they endorsed vigorous efforts to raise the living standards (and consuming power) of the working class, through labor union activities and new government programs, such as expanded schooling, public housing, and old-age pensions. They said that social reforms should be financed by taxing some of the "unearned elements" of income, which in their view constituted a significant part of all great fortunes.[52] Hobson argued that imperialism, and the costly military expenditures it entailed, blocked this progressive spending agenda, because it "visibly drains the public purse of the money which might be put to such purposes."[53]

The imperialists dismissed these arguments and continued to claim that expanding the colonial trade would safeguard British jobs. Chamberlain, who had made his name as a radical mayor of Birmingham, argued that introducing a system of imperial tariffs would provide the revenues to finance the sorts of social programs that Hobson and others were demanding. But popular revulsion at the atrocities of the Boer War turned the political climate against the imperial lobby. In the general election of 1906, the Liberal Party, which had campaigned on a platform of social reform and anti-imperialism, recorded a landslide victory. The recently founded Labour Party also won twenty-nine seats in the House of Commons.

In 1908 Herbert Henry Asquith, the Liberal leader who had recently been elevated from the post of chancellor of the exchequer to prime minister, replacing an ailing Henry Campbell-Bannerman, introduced an Old Age Pensions Act, which provided weekly benefits to people over seventy. After Asquith's promotion, David Lloyd George, a fiery Welsh orator who had staunchly opposed the Boer War, took over at the Treasury. In his famous "People's Budget" of 1909, Lloyd George proposed a series of tax increases to pay for new old-age pensions and other programs, including health and sickness benefits. He proposed raising the tax rate on high incomes from 3.75 percent to 5 percent, and the rate on very high incomes to 7.5 percent.[54] With an implicit hat tip to Henry George and Mill, he also proposed a 20 percent tax on increases in land value whenever a property was sold. The House of Lords, which was stuffed with landed aristocrats, voted the budget down, creating a constitutional crisis. The government called an election that produced a hung Parliament and left the Liberals to rely on support from the Labour Party and Irish nationalists. Lloyd George pressed ahead. In April 1910, amidst a grave constitutional crisis, the House of Lords finally relented and voted through the budget measures.

The Liberal reforms, which were extended in the National Insurance Act of 1911, had shortcomings, including the fact that they didn't cover everybody. In historical terms, however, they marked the foundation of the British welfare state, albeit in a fledgling form. Intellectually, they marked a transition from the individualistic liberalism of Smith and Mill to the social liberalism of Hobson and Hobhouse—a development that Hobson remarked on in his 1909 book *The Crisis of Liberalism*, in which he declared: "The old *laissez-faire* Liberalism is dead."[55]

It should be noted that not all the revenue Lloyd George raised in the People's Budget went to social reforms. Some of it was allocated to building new battleships, which the British defense establishment deemed essential to meet the rising threat from Kaiser Wilhelm II's Germany. Since succeeding his father in 1888, the Kaiser had pursued an aggressive foreign policy known as *Weltpolitik*, which aimed at making Germany a great global power and challenging Britain's naval supremacy. On March 31, 1905, Wilhelm docked his yacht in the Moroccan port of Tangier and went ashore to express his support for the country's independence, thereby violating a long-standing agreement between the European powers that, as they carved up the African continent, each would stick to its "sphere of influence." Morocco was in France's sphere of influence. The subsequent uproar relented only when Britain, Russia, Italy, and the United States took France's side and forced Germany to back down.

From a dynastic viewpoint, the rising frictions between Britain and Germany were an absurdity. King Edward VII, who had succeeded his mother, Queen Victoria, at the start of the new century, was Kaiser Wilhelm's uncle. In 1908 the two monarchs held a convivial meeting in the ancient German town of Kronberg. But family ties couldn't disguise the fact that the remarkable growth of German industry, and the strength of its scientific base, had turned the young nation into an economic power that was now the equal, or even the superior, of Britain. In 1870 Britain's GDP had been nearly 40 percent larger than Germany's, and in 1880 its share of global manufacturing production had been nearly three times as large. By 1913, Germany's economy was slightly bigger than Britain's, and it had also caught up with its manufacturing share.[56] In some heavy industries, particularly steel and chemicals, Germany had already left Britain far behind.

Like most of his fellow liberals, Hobson couldn't fully conceive of where the Anglo-German rivalry was heading. Imperialist conflicts in Africa were one thing. But an all-out conflict between the great powers would be so catastrophic that it would be totally contrary to reason, and also to the profit motive: therefore, it was out of the question. As the arms race continued, and more potential flash points arose, Hobson and many of his friends took up the cause of pacifism without fully realizing how perilous the situation was. "There was no real belief in the possibility of any early large-scale war, or in such a collapse of democracy as followed," he would later recount. "The long period of peace in Western Europe, the steady progress of popular self-government in all civilized countries, had fastened these achievements upon our minds as permanent testimonials to rationalism and ethics in the field of politics."[57]

This reassuring picture was an illusion that didn't make much of an impression on the far left, which interpreted rising tensions between the imperialist countries as a sign that the long-predicted implosion of capitalism was at hand and that it would be a violent one. Across continental Europe, various versions of this argument were being put forward. The most innovative one emerged from the central party school of the Social Democratic Party of Germany (SPD), Germany's workers' party, in Berlin, which employed a brilliant instructor and activist. Her name was Rosa Luxemburg.

13

Rosa Luxemburg on Capitalism, Colonialism, and War

Rosa Luxemburg was born in 1871, in the Polish city of Zamość, the fifth child of an educated Jewish family that was prosperous enough to keep domestic servants. Her grandfather had established a timber business, and he sent his children, including Rosa's father, to be educated in Germany. The eastern half of Poland, including Zamość, which is located about 150 miles southeast of Warsaw, was then part of the Russian Empire. When Rosa was still a toddler, her parents moved the family to Warsaw, where the schools were better than in Zamość. Around the age of three, she developed a hip disease that confined her to bed for a year and left her with a permanent limp. The ailment didn't dampen her spirits or hamper her intellectual development. According to her first biographer, Paul Frölich, she could read and write by the age of five, and not long after that, she was teaching the family servants to read.[1] Writing was an early passion. She submitted at least one piece of writing to a children's magazine. In 1884, when she was thirteen, Kaiser Wilhelm I visited Warsaw, and she wrote a poem to mark the occasion. It ended:

> Just one thing I want to say to you, dear William
> Tell your wily fox Bismarck
> For the sake of Europe, Emperor of the West,
> Tell him not to disgrace the pants of peace.[2]

After finishing elementary school, Luxemburg was admitted to an all-girls high school favored by the Russian administrative elite, where all lessons and conversations were conducted in Russian, and Polish was forbidden. She routinely aced her tests, and in her final year, she finished top of the class. For some reason, the school didn't award her the annual gold medal for academic achievement. Perhaps this was an example of discrimination, which even well-to-do Jews were forced to navigate. But Frölich suggests that it could also have been "on account of her rebellious attitude towards the authorities."[3] Details are scant, but either in her final years of high school or immediately after she graduated in 1887, Luxemburg began to mix with a group of young radicals who were associated with a banned group, the International Revolutionary Party Proletariat, often referred to as just the "Proletariat." The group fused an anti-tsarist position with pro-worker sentiments and a willingness to engage in violence. In some ways, it resembled Narodnaya Volya, the Russian revolutionary group that, in March 1881, had assassinated Tsar Alexander II.

What role Luxemburg played in Proletariat's activities isn't exactly clear: she seems to have agitated mainly in student circles. It is known that she was in regular contact with the group's leader, a working man named Martin Kasprzak, and that her activities drew the attention of the authorities. In 1889, facing the threat of arrest, she decided to leave Poland and cross into Germany. According to Frölich, Kasprzak organized her exit. When the two reached the area of the border, he told a local Catholic priest that "a Jewish girl had a burning desire to become a Christian, but could only do so abroad because of the vehement resistance of her relatives." The priest agreed to help, and "hidden under straw in a peasant's cart, Rosa Luxemburg crossed the border to freedom."[4]

Germany was only an interim destination for Luxemburg. Eventually she made her way to Zurich, which was a noted gathering place for Jewish refugees and socialists. In 1890 she enrolled at Zurich University, a progressive institution that admitted female students. After initially studying the natural sciences, she switched to the law department, which encompassed economics and other social sciences. After she completed her bachelor's degree, she started a doctoral dissertation on the industrialization of Poland. One of her advisers was Julius Wolf, a noted orthodox economist, who quickly recognized her talent despite disagreeing with her political views. "She came to me from Poland already as a thorough Marxist," Wolf would recall in his autobiography. But he also described Luxemburg as "the ablest of my pupils."[5]

In her dissertation, Luxemburg adopted a Marxian framework to explain that Poland, like the rest of the Russian Empire, was entering the industrial age. Successive tsarist administrations, seeing how far Russia was falling behind other European powers, had tried to stimulate industrial development. They eliminated internal tariffs to create a national market, introduced external tariff walls to keep out foreign competitors, and built railroads to reduce the isolation of many areas of the country. The 1861 emancipation of the serfs had already provided a ready source of wage labor. "Thus, after all the main conditions of industrial development—a domestic market, means of transport, an industrial reserve army—had been called to life in the years 1860–77," Luxemburg wrote, "the supervening tariff policy created a hot-house atmosphere of monopoly prices that placed Russian and Polish industry in an absolute El Dorado of primitive capitalist accumulation."[6] She cited statistics showing that between 1870 and 1890, industrial production in Poland virtually quadrupled, with wool and cotton textiles leading the way. The central city of Łódź turned into a "Polish Manchester"; near the western border with Prussia, "a whole new industrial area sprang up as though charmed out of the ground," while in Warsaw the "trade of the whole country was concentrated from now on in the Stock Exchange and in countless banking and commission firms."[7]

Soon after arriving in Zurich, Luxemburg met Leo Jogiches, another young radical, who had fled the tsar's police in Vilnius. Jogiches also hailed from a wealthy Jewish background. In high school, he "began to make revolutionary propaganda," Frölich relates, and subsequently founded a small revolutionary group, which led to his arrest and imprisonment.[8] Four years older than Luxemburg, Jogiches arrived in Zurich in 1890, where he associated with a group of Russian Marxists that included the noted theoretician Georgi Plekhanov, who was an associate of Engels. Jogiches was a self-confident and strident figure, but according to Luxemburg's longtime friend Clara Zetkin, he was also "one of those very masculine personalities—an extremely rare phenomenon these days—who can tolerate a great female personality in loyal and happy comradeship, without feeling her growth and development to be fetters on his own ego."[9] He and Luxemburg would be comrades and lovers for a decade and a half.

Jogiches used some family money to launch a Polish-language socialist magazine, *Sprawa Robotnicza*. Luxemburg wrote for the new journal and eventually edited it. In the Polish exile community, she quickly became a controversial figure, because she rejected the argument that the Polish Socialist Party, which was founded in 1892, should support national self-determination. Given the dependence of Polish industry on the Russian market, independence wasn't economically viable, she argued. And in any case, nationalism represented a diversion from the essential task of building up the working-class movement. In August 1893, when the Second International, the successor to Marx's First International, held a congress in Zurich, there was an attempt to remove Luxemburg and her associates from the Polish delegation.[10] Rising to oppose this effort, Luxemburg, who was then twenty-three, insisted that *Sprawa Robotnicza* "expresses the view of the Polish proletariat." According to one onlooker, "she advocated her cause with such magnetism in her eyes and with such fiery words that she enthralled and won over the great majority of the congress."[11]

On the national question, however, Luxemburg didn't prevail. Shortly after the conference, she and Jogiches and some of their allies quit the Polish Socialist Party and founded their own avowedly internationalist party: Social Democracy of the Kingdom of Poland (SDKP). Although it remained a splinter group, Luxemburg's disputes with the nationalists brought her to the attention of senior figures in the international socialist movement, including Karl Kautsky, a leading theorist in Germany's SPD, who published some of her articles on the political situation in Poland in his journal *Die Neue Zeit*. After completing her doctorate in early 1897, Luxemburg decided to move to Berlin. Jogiches tried to persuade her to stay in Zurich, but failed. To live in Prussia, she needed a residency permit. Resourceful as ever, she persuaded an older Polish friend who had a German husband to ask their son to marry her. The wedding ceremony took place in Basel in April 1897, and Luxemburg became Frau Gustav Lübeck. The following year she moved to the Prussian capital, never to associate with her husband again. Initially, at least, she didn't have a positive impression of her new home. "Berlin is the most repulsive place," she wrote to a friend, "cold, ugly, massive—a real barracks, and the charming Prussians with their arrogance as if each one of them had been made to swallow the very stick with which he had got his daily beating."[12]

Luxemburg arrived in Berlin just as a bitter ideological debate was beginning in the SPD. On one side was Eduard Bernstein, a socialist theoretician who had lived in exile in Britain for many years, and on the other side was Kautsky and much of the SPD's intellectual leadership. Bernstein was a long-time associate of Engels (who died in 1895) but had come to believe it was high time for socialists to accept the reality that many of the claims in *The Communist Manifesto* and *Capital* had been falsified, including the notion that capitalism was on the verge of a breakdown. Between 1896 and 1898, Bernstein wrote a series of articles on "Problems of Socialism" for *Die Neue Zeit*. In early 1899, he published his arguments in a book, *The Prerequisites of Socialism*, which was translated into English under the title *Evolutionary Socialism*.[13]

Since Marx's death in 1883 some of his followers had queried aspects of his work, but Bernstein's contribution amounted to a frontal assault. Challenging the basic Marxist claim that capitalism divided society into two classes—the bourgeoisie and the proletariat—squeezing out the property-owning middle class, he wrote: "The number of members of the possessing classes is to-day not smaller but larger." The record showed that as capitalism developed, "the middle classes change their character but they do not disappear from the social scale," Bernstein added.[14] He also criticized Marx's claim that the centralization of capital and the emergence of large monopolistic combines led to the demise of small businesses. "Trade statistics show an extraordinarily elaborated graduation of enterprises in regard to size," Bernstein wrote. "No rung of the ladder is disappearing from it."[15]

Bernstein's heresies didn't end there. He also questioned the notion that the cyclical crises endemic to capitalism were intensifying, and that one of them would eventually bring about a collapse. The emergence of cartels and monopolies was taming some of the anarchy of the market, he argued, and the expanded availability of credit was another stabilizing factor. Turning to politics, he pointed out that in many countries, the voting franchise was being extended to working people, labor unions were being legalized, and labor cooperatives were making progress. In some places, governments were introducing policies designed to improve the living standards of the masses. Bismarck's Germany had led the way. During the 1880s, it had introduced a national system of social insurance for illness, accidents, and old age. Given all these developments, Bernstein said, the key question was whether gradualist reform or a commitment to violent revolution during an economic crisis was the best strategy to secure working-class control of the state. "In my judgment," he wrote, "a greater security for lasting success lies in a steady advance than in the possibilities offered by a catastrophic crash."[16]

Although Kautsky agreed to publish Bernstein's essays in *Die Neue Zeit*, he was aghast at their content. "Your Marxism has collapsed," he wrote to his old comrade. "You have not developed it to a higher form but capitulated before its critics."[17] In public, Kautsky and other SPD leaders initially held off attacking Bernstein, who was a respected party veteran. Their reluctance to engage presented Luxemburg with an opportunity to make her mark in Berlin. In the summer of 1898, which she spent organizing voters in Silesia at the behest of the SPD, she began composing a lengthy response to Bernstein's arguments. Timing was key. A party congress was coming up in September, and she wanted to publish something before the gathering. "I am ready to give half my life for that article, so much am I absorbed in it," she wrote to Jogiches.[18]

In September 1898, a left-leaning newspaper in Leipzig published a series of pieces by Luxemburg that contested the claims Bernstein had made in his articles for *Die Neue Zeit*. When Bernstein's book appeared early the next year, the same newspaper published more critical pieces by Luxemburg. Subsequently, she combined her essays into a pamphlet, *Reform or Revolution?* The crux of her argument was that the developments highlighted by Bernstein hadn't changed the exploitative nature of capitalism, which was based on capitalists' owning the means of production. Even if labor unions and cooperatives could attenuate the "depressing tendency of economic development" on workers' living standards, she wrote, they were "totally incapable of transforming the *capitalist mode of production*."[19]

Luxemburg also pointed out that expansions of credit could destabilize the system, rather than stabilize it, and she dismissed as naive Bernstein's critique of the theory of the centralization of capital. While many small businesses still existed, she wrote, they merely played the role of "pioneers," creating new methods of production before larger companies swallowed them up. The development of rival capitals wasn't a onetime battle in which the "troops of the weaker party continue to melt away directly and quantitatively. It should rather be regarded as a periodic mowing down of the small enterprises, which rapidly grow up again only to be mowed down once more by large industry."[20] There was some evidence to back up Luxemburg's argument. As the German economy had grown at a breakneck pace, industrial consolidation had proceeded rapidly. In the steel industry, the vertically integrated Krupp and Thyssen corporations had emerged as dominant players. In the chemicals industry, BASF, Bayer, and Hoechst were already operating on a global scale and exporting most of their products.

Luxemburg reserved her most cutting criticisms for Bernstein's gradualist political strategy, which she described as turning "the sea of capitalist bitterness into a sea of socialist sweetness, by progressively pouring into it bottles of social-reformist lemonade."[21] In focusing on the narrow material advances that workers had made, his "theory tends to counsel us to renounce the social transformation, the final goal of Social-Democracy, and, inversely, to make of social reforms, the means of the class struggle, its aim," she wrote.[22] A revolutionary commitment to replacing capitalism with socialism was "the only decisive factor distinguishing the Social-Democratic movement from bourgeois democracy and from bourgeois radicalism."[23]

The publication of *Reform or Revolution?* burnished Luxemburg's reputation as a rising left-wing theoretician. Eventually, Kautsky and other senior figures in the SPD published their own criticisms of Bernstein's arguments, confirming a split in the party between "radicals" and "revisionists." Luxemburg had got in early. In 1900, Jogiches joined her in Berlin. By that time, the SDKP, the Polish socialist party they had founded, had become the SDKPiL: the Social Democracy of the Kingdom of Poland and Lithuania, and it still took up a good deal of their time. In 1903 Jogiches created a party magazine modeled on Kautsky's *Die Neue Zeit*, and Luxemburg wrote for the new publication. She also continued to publish in the German media. For a time, she served as the editor of the Leipzig newspaper that had published her critiques of Bernstein. But the appointment of such a firebrand led to an outcry from other publications, and the job lasted only a few months.[24] In 1905, Luxemburg was appointed to the board of *Vorwärts*, the SPD party newspaper, with which she'd previously had a fractious relationship.[25]

The energy and commitment that Luxemburg and Jogiches devoted to the socialist cause was boundless. Later in 1905, after a revolution broke out in Russia, they traveled under fake identities to Warsaw, where they were liable to be arrested and imprisoned at any moment. In March 1906 the authorities detained her. Initially, at least, Luxemburg kept her spirits up. "Here I am sitting in the Town Hall where 'politicals,' ordinary criminals and lunatics are all crowded together," she wrote in a letter to Kautsky and his wife, Luise. "My cell is a veritable jewel; with its present ornaments . . . it now contains 14 guests, fortunately all of them political cases."[26] She was transferred to a regular prison, then to a harsh high-security facility, the Warsaw Citadel, which was used to house long-term political inmates. Her health started to deteriorate, partly because, for a time, she engaged in a hunger strike. She ended up being held for four months. Finally her friends and family managed, through bribery, to get her released on medical grounds.[27]

Rather than returning directly to Berlin, Luxemburg went to Kuokkala in Finland, where Vladimir Lenin, the leader of the Russian Bolshevik Party, and some of his followers were based. Originally Luxemburg had supported the Bolsheviks' political rivals on the Russian left, the Mensheviks. But during the revolution of 1905, the bold efforts that Lenin and his colleagues had taken to instigate a full-scale workers' rising had impressed her, even though they failed. In Kuokkala, she spent a lot of time talking with the Bolshevik leader, and they established a political relationship that would endure for some years.[28] Meanwhile, Jogiches was still being held in Warsaw. At his trial, in January 1907, he refused to participate and was sentenced to eight years of hard labor in Siberia. The outlook for him seemed bleak, but somehow, aided by an associate who bribed a policeman, he managed to escape before being transported.[29]

By the time Luxemburg and Jogiches returned to Berlin and resumed their regular political activities, their imprisonment in Warsaw had added to their reputation on the German left. But their personal relationship had come to an end. The Austrian-British historian J. P. Nettl, in his monumental two-volume biography of Luxemburg, which was originally published in 1966, suggests that Jogiches betrayed Luxemburg with another woman in Poland, and that she immediately cut off relations with him. After the breakup, Nettl recounts, Luxemburg took a younger lover, Konstantin Zetkin, the son of her friend Clara Zetkin. When Jogiches heard about this match, he was so furious that he threatened to kill Luxemberg and Zetkin, prompting her to buy a revolver for self-protection.[30]

In 1907, the SPD's Central Party School, which provided instruction for political candidates and party workers, invited Luxemburg to join its teaching staff. Kautsky helped her secure the post by assuring the head of the school, "In Rosa Luxemburg you will be getting one of the best brains in Germany."[31] The return to academia sat well with Luxemburg. As part of her duties, she taught courses in political economy and economic history. Outside class, she began working on an introduction to Marxian theory, covering the history of capitalism and some basic economic concepts, such as commodity production and wage labor.

With the tensions between Germany and other European countries intensifying, Luxemburg also turned her attention to the economic roots of imperialism, which wasn't a new subject to her. In an 1899 letter to Jogiches, she had warned of the danger of wars of territorial acquisition carried out by "capitalist and state interests," adding: "It's clear that the dismemberment of Asia and Africa is the final limit beyond which European politics no longer has room to unfold."[32] In 1907, at the seventh congress of the Second International, she had joined Lenin in pushing through an anti-imperialist resolution that proclaimed: "Wars between capitalist states are as a rule the result of their rivalry for world markets."[33]

Toward the end of 1911, the year of the Agadir Crisis, Luxemburg decided to break off her textbook and focus her energies on a book about imperialism. "I want to find the *cause* of imperialism," she wrote to Konstantin Zetkin. "I am following up the economic aspects of this concept . . . It will be a strictly scientific explanation of imperialism and its contradictions."[34] Researching and writing the book, which Luxemburg titled *The Accumulation of Capital: A Contribution to the Economic Theory of Imperialism*, took more than a year of intense work, but she found the endeavor highly fulfilling. "The period while I was writing *Accumulation* belongs to the happiest of my life," she would later recount. "I lived really as if in a state of intoxication, day and night seeing nothing but this one problem that was unfolding itself so beautifully in front of me, and I don't know which afforded me greater pleasure: the thinking process, whereby I pondered a complicated question while walking slowly up and down the room . . . or the shaping of results into literary form on paper. Do you know that I wrote the entire 30 galleys in one go within four months—something unheard-of!"[35]

In the foreword to the book, which was published in 1913, Luxemburg said she hoped it would have "some implications for our practical struggle against imperialism."[36] She also emphasized that it was primarily a theoretical work that had arisen out of some problems she had encountered with Marx's treatment of "the reproduction of total social capital,"[37] or what we would call economic growth. Two aspects of *The Accumulation of Capital* were immediately obvious to anybody who opened it. It was a work of deep scholarship. As well as closely analyzing *Capital*, it discussed the work of many other economists, from the Ukrainian Mikhail Tugan-Baranovsky back to Sismondi, Malthus, and Ricardo. Secondly, even for readers familiar with the Marxist idiom, it was a dense read.

In the Marxist world, providing a "scientific explanation" of imperialism necessarily involved analyzing how it fit into the economic framework Marx had created in *Capital*. The heart of Luxemburg's argument related to the famous "reproduction schemes" in the final chapters of volume II. Marx had used these analytical devices, which divided the economy into two sectors— a capital goods sector ("Department I") and a consumer goods sector ("Department II")—to examine whether it was possible for a capitalist system to grow in a consistent manner, with saving and capital accumulation balancing each other. Tugan-Baranovsky, among others, had pointed out that Marx's analysis seemed to raise the possibility of perpetual balanced growth rather than catastrophic breakdown.

Luxemburg dismissed this possibility, saying it treated the capitalist economy as a "never-ending merry-go-around in mid air."[38] She asked who would buy all the new machinery—lathes, blast furnaces, stamping plants, and the like—that Department I churned out year after year. The natural answer was the capitalists in Department II, who would need the new equipment to expand their output of consumer goods. But this raised another question, Luxemburg pointed out: Who would buy all the additional consumer goods? Relying on the workers surely wasn't an option: they earned less than they produced, and their purchasing power was strictly limited. Another possibility was that the capitalists in Department I and Department II could continually expand their consumption. Although this was mathematically possible, it ran counter to the empirical reality that capitalists reinvested or saved much of the surplus value they expropriated. Luxemburg argued that it also ignored "the profound and fundamental antagonism between the respective capacities for production and consumption of capitalist society—an antagonism that is precisely the consequence of the accumulation of capital, that periodically erupts in crisis, and that drives capital constantly to expand its markets."[39]

Like Sismondi and Hobson before her, Luxemburg was zeroing in on the problem of overproduction and a shortfall of demand. But she addressed it from within the Marxian framework, and she argued that the only way for capitalism to survive and expand over the long term was for it to find an external source of demand. "The decisive fact," she wrote, "is that the surplus value cannot be realised by sale either to workers or to capitalists, but only if it is sold to such social organisations or strata whose own mode of production is not capitalistic." That was where imperialism came into the picture. By turning previously undeveloped areas into new markets and their inhabitants into new consumers, colonialism effectively acted as a Department III, which absorbed some of the additional output produced in the other two sectors and helped to keep them in balance. "Historically speaking, the accumulation of capital is a process of metabolism occurring between capitalist and precapitalist modes of production," Luxemburg explained. "The accumulation of capital cannot proceed without these precapitalist modes of production, and yet accumulation consists in this regard precisely in the latter being gradually swallowed up and assimilated by capital." She went on: "Accordingly, capital accumulation can no more exist without noncapitalist formations, than these are able to exist alongside it. It is only in the constant and progressive erosion of these noncapitalist formations that the very conditions of the existence of capital accumulation are given."[40] And again: "Accumulation is not merely an internal relation between the branches of the capitalist economy—it is above all a relation between capital and its non-capitalist milieu."[41]

The Communist Manifesto had described how the desire for new markets "chases the bourgeoisie over the entire surface of the globe."[42] In *Capital*, however, Marx had largely confined his theoretical analysis to a closed economy. Luxemburg was arguing that this approach couldn't explain the long-run dynamics of capitalism, including the lurch to imperialism.

Another distinctive feature of *The Accumulation of Capital* was the emphasis it placed on the damage that capitalism and imperialism did to Indigenous peoples and societies. In volume I of *Capital*, Marx had described the "extirpation, enslavement and entombment in mines" of the Indigenous peoples of the Americas, the "turning of Africa into a warren for the commercial hunting of blackskins," and the great starvation in Bengal, where "the English manufactured a famine by buying up all the rice and refusing to sell it again, except at fabulous prices." [43] Luxemburg acknowledged some of these passages, but she went on: "It should be noted, however, that all this is merely treated from the point of view of so-called 'primitive accumulation.' In Marx's account, the processes specified here merely illustrate the genesis of capital, the moment that it comes into the world—they constitute the birth pangs as the capitalist mode of production emerges from the womb of feudal society."[44]

Whether this was an accurate description of Marx's views can be debated. What is beyond question is that Luxemburg insisted imperialism and the violent exploitation of Indigenous peoples were a permanent and necessary feature of capitalist development. This wasn't just an issue of expanding the markets for goods, she argued. Echoing Hobson, she pointed out that colonies and underdeveloped countries generally also provided an invaluable outlet for surplus capital. Gaining access to raw materials and potential workers was also vital: "Capital cannot do without the means of production and labor-power of the entire planet—it requires the natural resources and labor-power of all territories for its movement of accumulation to proceed unimpeded. Since these are in actual fact overwhelmingly bound by the pre-capitalist forms of production . . . capital is characterized by a powerful drive to conquer these territories and societies."[45]

Given the needs of capital, Luxemburg argued, the violent subjugation of native peoples was inevitable. Wherever Western colonialists went, they encountered an ancient "natural economy" with socialistic features, such as commonly owned property, powerful village associations, and communal agriculture. Because these institutions and customs represented a barrier to capitalist development, the colonialists were obliged to destroy them. "Each new colonial expansion is accompanied by capital's relentless war on the social and economic interrelations of the indigenous inhabitants and by the violent looting of their means of production and their labor-power," Luxemburg wrote. "Capital knows no other solution to the problem than violence, which has been a constant method of capital accumulation as a historical process, not merely during its emergence, but also to the present day."[46]

In three chapters near the end of her book, Luxemburg described how this process had played out around the world. During the great westward expansion of the United States, the Indigenous people who stood in its path had been subjected to the "carnage of forty wars waged on them," and the survivors were "swept away like bothersome detritus, like herds of buffalo, and penned like wild game into 'reservations.'"[47] Turning to China, she detailed how, during the Opium Wars, Britain and France had forced the weakened Qing dynasty to provide access to European drug traders, noting: "Each of the more than forty Chinese Treaty Ports was paid for with streams of blood, carnage, and destruction."[48]

Where Marx had pointed to some incidental economic benefits of British rule in India, such as the import of scientific knowledge, Luxemburg described it as an unmitigated disaster for the Native population. "The British were the first conquerors of India to show a gross indifference toward the works of civilization that formed its public utilities and economic infrastructure," she wrote. "Arabs, Afghans and Mongols alike had initiated and maintained magnificent works of canalization, they had provided the country with a network of roads, built bridges across its rivers, and sunk wells."[49] For the British, by contrast, "it was not a question of ensuring the survival of the Indian community or supporting it economically, but rather of destroying it in order to seize its productive forces."[50] Luxemburg was equally critical of the French colonists in Algeria. Their "systematic and deliberate elimination and parcelization of communal property" had two goals, she insisted: to "shatter the power of the Arab clans as forms of social organization and thus to break their stubborn resistance to the French yoke"; and "to seize the land held by the Arabs for a millennium and to transfer it into the hands of French capitalists."[51]

After analyzing the causes and consequences of imperialism, Luxemburg argued that it was leading the industrial powers into confrontation, conflict, and ultimately, self-destruction. "As much as imperialism is a historical method to prolong the existence of capital, objectively it is at the same time the surest way to bring this existence to the swiftest conclusion,"[52] she wrote. The more forcefully the system uses militarism "to assimilate the means of production and labor-power of non-capitalist countries and societies," the more "the day-to-day history of capital accumulation on the world stage is transformed into a continuous series of political and social catastrophes and convulsions, which together with the periodic economic cataclysms in the form of crises, will make it impossible for capital accumulation to continue, and will turn the rebellion of the international working class against the rule of capital into a necessity, even before the latter has come up against its natural, self-created economic constraints."[53]

In making this catastrophist argument, Luxemburg was again challenging the socialist revisionists. But given her other divergences from Marxist orthodoxy, this wasn't sufficient to produce a positive reception for *The Accu-*

mulation of Capital. In *Vorwärts*, Gustav Eckstein, an Austrian associate of Kautsky, said Luxemburg had misinterpreted Marx and presented contradictory arguments. In *Die Neue Zeit*, Otto Bauer, another Austrian theorist, made a similar argument. Lenin, who had been living in the Polish city of Kraków, which was then part of the Austro-Hungarian Empire, was also highly critical. He described Luxemburg's argument that sustained accumulation and growth was impossible within a closed economy as "a fundamental error."[54] He was similarly unimpressed by her chapters on how imperialism impacted undeveloped societies. "The description of the torture of negroes in South Africa is noisy, colourful and meaningless," he wrote. "Above all it is non-Marxist."[55]

At the moment when Lenin read *The Accumulation of Capital*, he was having one of his periodic disputes with Luxemburg about revolutionary tactics. She believed that spontaneous mass action was the key to success; Lenin insisted that the workers needed a disciplined party to lead and guide them. This argument may well have colored his attitude to Luxemburg's book. Still, the question of whether her theoretical arguments held together was to be an enduring one. In his 1942 monograph *The Theory of Capitalist Development*, Paul Sweezy, a Harvard-trained Marxist economist, argued that Luxemburg had made a basic error. In criticizing Marx's reproduction schemes, she had assumed that as the economy expanded, the overall level of demand remained constant. In fact, Sweezy pointed out, when capitalists invest in more capital goods and add extra capacity to their factories, they typically hire more workers, who spend their incomes, and this raises the level of demand throughout the economy. Once this is recognized, he argued, Luxemburg's entire theory "collapses like a house of cards."[56]

But Luxemburg's argument would also find some prominent defenders. In 1951 Joan Robinson, a former student of Keynes at Cambridge University and a major theoretician in her own right, composed a foreword to a new edition of *The Accumulation of Capital*. Robinson conceded that Luxemburg had gotten some theoretical details mixed up, but she insisted that errors were easily outweighed by her recognition that Western industrial capitalism needed an external outlet for the surplus capital and goods it produced. "Few would deny," she wrote, "that the extension of capitalism into new territories was the mainspring of what an academic economist has called the 'vast secular boom' of the last two hundred years."[57] She conceded that Luxemburg had got some theoretical details mixed up, but she insisted that these errors were outweighed by the importance of the recognition that Western capitalism needed an external outlet for the surplus capital and goods it produced. "For all its confusions and exaggerations, this book shows more prescience than any orthodox contemporary could claim," Robinson concluded.[58]

Almost immediately after the publication of *The Accumulation of Capital*, Luxemburg started work on a rebuttal of her critics. The outbreak of World War I in July 1914 interrupted her work. On August 4, a week after the ruinous conflict between the Allies and Central Powers began, SPD deputies in the Reichstag voted unanimously to approve war credits—a boost in military spending authority—for the imperial government of Chancellor Theobald von Bethmann Hollweg. Luxemburg was devastated. Together with Clara Zetkin and Karl Liebknecht, an antiwar deputy who had reluctantly acceded to the SPD's policy of voting unanimously in the Reichstag, she formed the International Group within the party to oppose further war financing. They worked feverishly to recruit more deputies to publicly oppose the war, but when a big military funding bill came up for a vote in December 1914, Liebknecht was the only SPD deputy to vote against it.

As the German political class lined up behind the war effort, the government cracked down on antiwar activists; Liebknecht was conscripted into the military. From February 1915 to February 1916 (and again from July 1916 to November 1918), Luxemburg was held in prison, where she continued to write. "After two weeks I got my books and permission to work—they didn't have to tell me twice," she wrote to a friend from Barnimstrasse, a women's prison in Berlin.[59] In a pamphlet entitled *The Crisis of German Social Democracy*, which she wrote in 1915 under the pseudonym Junius, a reference to a Republican hero of ancient Rome, Luxemburg lambasted the SPD's leadership for supporting the war. She noted that the popular enthusiasm that greeted the war's outbreak had already been replaced by fretful faces, "shrapnel, drills, ammunition bags, marriage bureaus for war widows."[60]

Some antiwar activists blamed the elite Prussian Junker class or the perfidious British for leading Europe to disaster, but Luxemburg placed the responsibility squarely on capitalism and imperialism. "The events that bore the present war did not begin in July 1914 but reach back for decades," she wrote. "Thread by thread they have been woven together on the loom of an inexorable natural development, until the firm net of imperialist world politics has encircled five continents."[61] The war represented the apotheosis of this process: "Here capitalism reveals its death's-head, here it betrays that it has sacrificed its historic right of existence, that its rule is no longer compatible with the progress of humanity."[62] In such a disastrous conflict, Luxemburg insisted, there was nothing to be gained by a victory for either side: the only hope was for the workers of all the participant countries to come to their senses, reject the war, and overthrow the system that had produced it. "This madness will not stop," she declared, "until the workers of Germany, of France, of Russia and of England will wake up out of their drunken sleep; will clasp each other's hands in brotherhood and will drown the bestial chorus of war agitators and the hoarse cry of capitalist hyenas with the mighty cry of labor, 'Proletarians of all countries unite!'"[63]

The *Junius Pamphlet*, as it came to be known, was arguably Luxemburg's most powerful piece of writing. With the Great War dragging on, she wasn't the only leftist thinker who tried to make sense of the carnage. In Zurich, where he was living in exile with his wife, Nadezhda Krupskaya, Lenin was researching a book about the economics of imperialism. He read John Hobson's 1902 volume on the subject and also studied the work of Rudolf Hilferding, an Austrian Marxist economist whose 1910 book *Das Finanzkapital* (Finance Capital) emphasized two distinguishing characteristics of modern capitalism: the melding of industrial and financial capital through the banking system, and the emergence of monopolies and cartels. Hilferding argued that this new monopolistic capitalism was even more exploitative than the old competitive version, but he also pointed out a potential upside for socialists who wanted to transcend the system: "Once finance capital has brought the most important branches of production under its control, it is enough for society, through its conscious executive organ—the state conquered by the working class—to seize finance capital in order to gain immediate control of these branches of production."[64]

Hobson and Hilferding provided the intellectual foundations for Lenin's treatment of imperialism. Despite having read and criticized Luxemburg's *The Accumulation of Capital*, he didn't refer to it. His intellectual foil was Kautsky, who in 1914 had enraged him by refusing to break with the SPD leadership. More recently, Kautsky had also contested the argument— subscribed to by Lenin, Luxemburg, and many other Marxists—that the war heralded the death throes of the imperialist order. Writing in *Die Neue Zeit*, the socialist journal he had founded thirty years earlier, Kautsky suggested that after the conflict ended, a new system of "ultra-imperialism" could emerge—one in which a "holy alliance of imperialists," rather than fighting with each other, would peacefully divide up world markets, much as trusts and cartels divided up national markets.[65] "The longer the War lasts, the more it exhausts all the participants and makes them recoil from an early repetition of armed conflict, the nearer we come to this last solution, however unlikely it may seem at the moment," Kautsky concluded. To Lenin, this was heresy piled on top of betrayal.

Lenin wrote his tract in the spring of 1916. (It was published a year later in St. Petersburg.) Its basic thesis was contained in its title: *Imperialism, the Highest Stage of Capitalism*. Lenin started out by acknowledging his debts to the non-Marxist Hobson, whose book he described as "a very good and comprehensive description of the principal political and economic features of imperialism."[66] After also acknowledging the influence of Hilferding, he argued that this ultimate form of capitalism encompassed five basic elements:

1. The concentration of production and capital developed to such a high stage that it created monopolies that play a decisive role in economic life.
2. The merging of bank capital with industrial capital, and the creation, on the basis of this "finance capital," of a financial oligarchy.
3. The export of capital, which becomes extremely important, as distinguished from the export of commodities.
4. The formation of international capitalist monopolies that share the world among themselves.
5. The territorial division of the whole world among the greatest capitalist powers is completed.[67]

As examples of monopolization, Lenin pointed to cartels in Germany and trusts in the United States. He singled out the Tobacco Trust; Rockefeller's Standard Oil, which the US Supreme Court had ordered broken up several years earlier; and US Steel, which J. P. Morgan had assembled in 1901. These were all monopolies in the textbook sense of a single business that controls an entire market and dictates prices. But when Lenin used the term *monopoly*, he was also referring to what economists now call an "oligopoly"—a market dominated by a few huge firms. He cited the German chemical industry, on which BASF, Bayer, and Hoechst had a firm grip. In monopolistic markets, he wrote, an "approximate estimate of the capacity of markets is also made, and the combines divide them up amongst themselves by agreement." Also, "skilled labor is monopolized, the best engineers are engaged; the means of transport are captured; railways in America, shipping companies in Europe and America. Capitalism in its imperialist stage arrives at the threshold of the most complete socialization of production."[68]

As monopolization proceeded within capitalist countries, Lenin argued, competition intensified at the international level for natural resources and new markets: "The more feverishly the hunt for raw materials proceeds throughout the whole world, the more desperate becomes the struggle for the acquisition of colonies."[69] After citing Cecil Rhodes's claim that empire was "a bread-and-butter question," he mocked Kautsky's suggestion that capitalist enterprises could obtain raw materials in the free market, remarking that such a thing was "becoming more and more a thing of the past: monopolist syndicates and trusts are restricting it with every single day."[70] Following Hobson (and Luxemburg), Lenin also identified colonies as a necessary outlet for surplus capital. In some leading countries, he noted, "capitalism has become 'overripe' and (owing to the backward state of agriculture and the poverty of the masses) capital cannot find a field for 'profitable' investment."[71]

If Lenin's description of imperialism followed Hobson pretty closely, his analysis of "finance capital" owed more to Hilferding, whom he cited extensively. In Germany, he pointed out, six big banks had representatives on the board of directors of 344 industrial companies and 407 other companies, which operated in industries ranging from insurance to transport to hospitality. As finance capital tightened its grip on the economy, it "exacts enormous and ever-increasing profits from the floating of companies, issue of stock, state loans, etc., tightens the grip of financial oligarchies and levies tribute upon the whole of society for the benefit of monopolists."[72] He also emphasized the growing importance of joint-stock companies, in which the ownership and management of capital were distinct, with professional managers running companies on behalf of their stockholders: "Imperialism, or the domination of finance capital, is that highest stage of capitalism in which this separation reaches vast proportions."[73]

Turning to the political foundations of imperialism, Lenin challenged the consensus on the left that it was entirely an elite-driven phenomenon, with the working classes being passive observers or dupes for a jingoistic media. Underlying this analysis was an assumption that imperialism didn't deliver anything of value to the masses. Lenin rejected this claim. Some members of the working class had shared the spoils of imperialist ventures, he insisted, and this explained their support for imperialist politicians. "The receipt of high monopoly profits by the capitalists," he wrote, ". . . makes it economically possible for them to bribe certain sections of the workers, and for a time a fairly considerable minority of them, and win them to the side of the bourgeoisie of a given industry or given nation against all others."[74] He pointed to Britain as a country where this had been happening for decades. Ultimately, however, even the "opportunism" of parts of the labor movement couldn't prevent the inevitable conflicts between rival national capitals. Kautsky's vision of a peaceful "ultra-imperialism" was permeated with a spirit "absolutely irreconcilable with Marxism."[75] And "one will find nothing in it except reaction and bourgeois reformism."[76]

In presenting his arguments about how capitalism had developed since Marx's time, Lenin backed them up with statistics drawn from official reports and academic studies. With an eye for the tsarist censors, perhaps, he rationed his revolutionary rhetoric, saving most of his vitriol for Kautsky and other "opportunists" in the labor movement. Ironically, however, while some of Lenin's economic analysis would stand the test of time, history would also confirm parts of Kautsky's thesis. It would take another ruinous world war and the defeat of fascism to bring the major capitalist countries together. Eventually, though, they would conclude that international agreements that kept world markets open to their corporate exporters and investors were preferable to military warfare. From a leftist perspective, Kautsky's "holy alliance of imperialists" would come to fruition.

On the perfidy of Kautsky and other leaders of the SPD, Luxemburg agreed with Lenin. At the start of 1916, the antiwar International Group that she and Liebknecht and Zetkin had created renamed itself the Spartacus League. (The name came from the Thracian gladiator who led a slave revolt in 73–71 BC.) In April 1917 the Spartacus League merged with another antiwar group that had broken off from the SPD, the Independent Social Democratic Party. By this time, the February 1917 revolution in Russia had given Luxemburg hope that the war might finally be coming to an end. Later in the year, she welcomed the Bolsheviks' seizure of power. Although she and Lenin had had their differences over theory and tactics, she admired the speed and ruthlessness with which he and his colleagues acted. "All the revolutionary honor and capacity which western Social-Democracy lacked was represented by the Bolsheviks," she commented in a pamphlet she wrote in 1918.[77]

In watching events in Russia unfold, however, Luxemburg didn't suspend her critical faculties. Although she was a socialist revolutionary, she was also a democrat. She strongly disagreed with the Bolsheviks' decision, in January 1918, to dissolve the popularly elected Constituent Assembly. "Without general elections, without unrestricted freedom of press and assembly, without a free struggle of opinion, life dies out in every public institution, becomes a mere semblance of life, in which only the bureaucracy remains as the active element," she wrote. "Public life gradually falls asleep, a few dozen party leaders of inexhaustible energy and boundless experience direct and rule."[78]

This prophetic analysis wasn't published immediately. Luxemburg spent much of 1918 in prison. In the late summer, when an allied counteroffensive broke through the German lines, the troop morale was shattered, and the regime in Berlin crumbled from within. On November 9 the chancellor, Prince Maximilian of Baden, who himself had been in office barely a month, announced that Kaiser Wilhelm II had abdicated. The prince handed power to the parliamentary leaders of the SPD, Friedrich Ebert and Philipp Scheidemann, and Scheidemann declared Germany a republic. On that same day, the authorities released Luxemburg from prison in Breslau, and she hastened to Berlin. On November 11, an armistice went into effect.

The war was over, but Germany was in turmoil. Disgruntled military veterans were streaming back from the front. In many cities, workers' councils were demanding power. Rushing to keep up with events and seize the initiative, Leibknecht, Luxemburg, and some other Spartacists began publishing a new daily newspaper, *Red Flag.* "The abolition of capitalist rule and the realisation of a socialist order of society—this and nothing less is the historical theme of the present revolution," Luxemburg wrote in her first article after being released from prison.[79] She listed some immediate demands, which included the disarmament of the police; the establishment of a workers' militia (a "Red Guard"); a transfer of power to workers' and soldiers' councils; and the seizure of all large capitalist enterprises. The provisional government led by Ebert and Scheidemann had no intention of doing any of these things. It was intent on maintaining order. To this end, Ebert had reached a secret agreement with General Karl Groener, the Deputy Chief of Staff of the German army, in which the new president agreed to respect the army's independence and Groener agreed that his forces would support the government.

Inside the Spartacist groups, some radicals were calling for an immediate rising. Luxemburg, aware that the military was supporting Ebert's government, was skeptical about the chances of a successful revolution. In the last two days of 1918, the Spartacus League combined with other revolutionary groups to form the Communist Party of Germany (KPD) under the leadership of her and Liebknecht. In a speech to the party's founding congress, she suggested that the revolutionary timetable could be a lengthy one: "I shall not venture to prophesy how long the whole process will take."[80] Many of the younger Spartacists were in no mood to wait. On January 5, 1919, they instigated an armed uprising in Berlin. The government ordered the Freikorps, a nationalist militia largely made up of combat veterans, to enter the city and put down the insurrection.

Once the fighting began, Luxemburg joined the rising. At great danger to herself, she moved around the city supporting the Spartacist fighters. She also wrote supportive articles in *Red Flag*. But the Spartacists numbered only a few thousand, and they received no support from local police or army units. As the Freikorps rounded up Spartacist leaders, Luxemburg and Liebknecht went into hiding. From the Berlin suburb of Wilmersdorf, Luxemburg wrote another article for *Red Flag*, some copies of which were still being printed. Dated January 14, 1919, it ran under an ironic headline, "Order Reigns in Berlin," and it ended with a defiant declaration: "You stupid lackeys! Your order is built on sand. Tomorrow the revolution will rear ahead once more and announce to your horror amid the brass trumpets: 'I was, I am, I always will be!'"[81]

These were Luxemburg's last published words. On January 15 a unit of the Freikorps captured her and Liebknecht.[82] The unit's commanding officer interrogated them at an upscale hotel in the center of Berlin, then handed them over to some of his men, supposedly for transport to prison. Rather than taking Luxemburg there, one of the paramilitaries knocked her unconscious, shot her in the head, and tossed her body into the Landwehr Canal. Liebknecht was taken out of the hotel separately. After being beaten, he was shot in the back.

The killings sparked unrest in a number of German cities. As some leftists in these locales tried to launch uprisings, the army and the Freikorps crushed them, too. Back in Berlin, Jogiches, Luxemburg's former partner, who was also active in Spartacus League, tried to identify those ultimately responsible for the killing of her and Liebknecht, but he didn't get very far. In early March, he was arrested and murdered while in police custody.[83] Jogiches was fifty-one. Rosa Luxemburg was forty-seven. Her life had been cut short in brutal fashion. But in death her legend would only grow.

14

Nikolai Kondratiev and the Dynamics of Capitalist Development

A week after demonstrators took to the streets of Petrograd (St. Petersburg) on February 23, 1917 (by the old Julian calendar), Tsar Nicholas II abdicated, and a provisional government took power. It was made up of moderates from the Constitutional Democratic Party and some representatives from more radical groups, including the Party of Socialist Revolutionaries. The SRs, as they were known, were agrarian socialists whose support was based in the peasantry. Whereas Lenin's Bolshevik Party was committed to state control of agriculture and industry, the SRs' economic vision of the future was based on expanding Russia's self-governing village communities of peasant households, known as *mirs*. In May 1917 Viktor Chernov, a veteran SR, became minister of agriculture in the provisional government, which coexisted uneasily with new workers' councils (*soviets*) that had sprung up in Petrograd and other cities. One of Chernov's advisers was a young economist named Nikolai Dmitrievich Kondratiev.

The task facing Chernov, Kondratiev, and their colleagues was a forbidding one. In large parts of the country, acute food shortages that had contributed to the collapse of the tsarist regime were continuing. One of the provisional government's first acts was to introduce bread rationing and establish a state monopoly on the procurement and distribution of grain. The question of what to do about the land was another pressing issue. Many peasants were demanding a breakup of the great feudal estates. In some places, they were taking matters into their own hands, seizing the land and dividing it among themselves.

Kondratiev had firsthand experience of Russia's rural economy. He was born on March 17, 1892, near the town of Vichuga, about two hundred miles northeast of Moscow. The eldest of ten children in a poor peasant family, he attended school in the village of Khrenovo, where he developed radical views: at the age of fourteen, he was elected to a local SR party committee. According to an invaluable book about Kondratiev's life and works by the English historian Vincent Barnett, his political activism got him expelled from high school and jailed for seven months. In 1908 he moved to St. Petersburg, where, a few years later, he was admitted to the law school at St. Petersburg University. He studied political economy, and in 1915 he graduated with a first-class diploma. The same year he published a treatise on the economic impact of the *zemstvos*, the popularly elected local and regional councils that Tsar Alexander II had created in 1864, after he emancipated the serfs. Kondratiev emphasized the *zemstvos'* role in providing public services, such as education and healthcare. He said their activities constituted a "public law" economy that responded to public needs rather than market incentives.[1]

Scholarly and hardworking, Kondratiev seemed destined for a quiet life as an academic. The February revolution and its aftermath changed all that. As well as advising SR officials on food policy, he wrote pieces for an SR newspaper, *The People's Will*. At this stage, Kondratiev supported the idea of breaking up large estates and socializing the land, which he regarded as nature's dowry. In a pamphlet entitled *The Agrarian Question: Land and the Land Order*, he proposed allotting the peasants plots of communally owned land that were big enough for them to feed themselves and their families. When he entered the government, he had to subordinate his views on land reform to the immediate task of ensuring an adequate food supply and preventing mass starvation. To this end, he supported the introduction of rationing and central procurement of grain. But he was also concerned that the government's interventions, if they went too far, would have a negative impact on food production. "We see that under pressure from the developing crisis, there is a successive shift . . . to fixed prices and state purchasing of food," he wrote. "We are thus sliding on a downward slope towards extending the scope of government regulation of economic life towards wartime state socialism."[2]

In June 1917 Kondratiev was elected to the executive committee of the All-Russian Council of Peasant Deputies. A month later Alexander Kerensky, the charismatic leader of the moderate SRs, who was also vice-chairman of the Petrograd Soviet, became leader of a new coalition government composed of SRs, liberals, and Mensheviks, the left-wing rivals to the Bolsheviks. Kondratiev's stock rose. In the early fall, he was promoted to minister of food supply, a hefty responsibility for a twenty-five-year-old.

He couldn't know it, but his political career had already peaked. With Kerensky insisting on continuing the war, the provisional government's popularity had collapsed. As popular anger rose, it was outflanked by Lenin and the Bolsheviks, who were promising to deliver "peace, land, and bread." In a crucial development, the workers associated with the Petrograd Soviet turned against the government and embraced the Bolsheviks, electing Leon Trotsky, the veteran Bolshevik, as the soviet's chairman.

During the last week of October, the Bolsheviks seized power, with Trotsky playing a leading role in the takeover. Although Lenin had proclaimed "All Power to the Soviets!" it soon became clear that the Bolsheviks' immediate goal was to consolidate control for themselves. The new regime established a new body, the People's Commissariat of Food Supply. When Kondratiev and some colleagues at the Ministry of Agriculture refused to quit their offices, they were arrested and forced to leave. In December 1917, Kondratiev was elected a deputy from his home province to the national constituent assembly, which the provisional government had created to fashion a democratic constitution. But when the new assembly met, in January 1918, the Bolsheviks dissolved it after the first day, thereby ending Russia's short flirtation with parliamentary democracy.[3]

As Lenin and his colleagues cemented their control, Kondratiev returned to his studies. In 1918 he moved from St. Petersburg to Moscow, where he joined the Petrov Agricultural Academy, which had been set up in the 1860s to foster rural development. From his new perch in academia, Kondratiev continued to engage in policy debates. Although the Bolshevik Party controlled the government, it wasn't yet a monolithic dictatorship that quashed dissident views. In 1920 Kondratiev established a research center within the Petrov Agricultural Academy that he called the Conjuncture Institute.

The new institute started out tracking Russia's vast agricultural sector but soon expanded its coverage to other industries. It put out a monthly bulletin of economic statistics and analysis that was widely read by economists and government officials alike.

In 1920 Kondratiev resigned from the SR party, some members of which had called for the overthrow of the Bolsheviks and the reestablishment of parliamentary democracy. For a time, he joined another dissident political group, the Union for the Regeneration of Russia, but it had little impact. Despite his history as a former SR, his Conjuncture Institute was able to forge close ties to several government agencies, including the People's Commissariat of Finance (NKFin) and the People's Commissariat of Agriculture. From 1922, the year in which the Soviet Union was officially founded, NKFin was headed by Grigory Sokolnikov, a veteran Bolshevik who had been an early associate of Nikolai Bukharin, a Marxist theorist who was a prominent party figure. Sokolnikov had a doctorate in economics from a French university, and he valued the reports produced by Kondratiev's institute. In 1922 it became an official research arm of the NKFin, a status it retained until Stalin's regime closed it down at the end of the 1920s. The institute's staff swelled to more than fifty.[4] Among them were some brilliant young economists, including Eugen Slutsky, who had already developed the Slutsky equation that is still used in the formal theory of consumer demand.

Economic debates raged inside and outside the Bolshevik Party. As an orthodox Marxist, Lenin originally believed that Russia would need to undergo a lengthy stage of capitalist industrialization before it would be ready for the transition to socialism. After the revolution, he quickly departed from this idea. In *The State and Revolution*, a pamphlet he wrote in August and September 1917, he proposed the Paris Commune of 1870 as an economic model, demanding an immediate state takeover of heavy industries and the expropriation of the capitalists who owned them. After this change in ownership, workers' committees would take responsibility for organizing production, which Lenin portrayed as a trivial matter. "*All* citizens become employees and workers of a *single* countrywide state 'syndicate,'" he wrote. "All that is required is that they should work equally, do their proper share of work, and get equal pay; the accounting and control necessary for this have been *simplified* by capitalism to the utmost and reduced to the extraordinarily simple operations—which any literate person can perform—of supervising and recording, knowledge of the four rules of arithmetic, and issuing appropriate receipts."[5]

After taking power, Lenin and his colleagues quickly discovered that things weren't so simple. World War I was still raging, and the Russian economy was in chaos. In March 1918, Lenin ended Russia's involvement in the war by accepting a punitive peace settlement with the Central Powers in the Treaty of Brest-Litovsk. The respite from war proved temporary. Within months, counterrevolutionary White Armies invaded Russia on several fronts. In response to this new crisis, the Bolsheviks raised a Red Army under the leadership of Trotsky and adopted a draconian program of centrally directed economic production, which became known as War Communism. The regime requisitioned grain directly from peasant farmers and empowered its security police, the Cheka, to enforce this policy. In urban areas, it seized control of heavy industries, including coal and steel, and it amalgamated banks into a single state-controlled institution. It also banned private trade and workers' strikes.

The Red Army eventually drove back the White Armies, but the Bolsheviks' harsh economic policies proved counterproductive. Grain production declined further, and food prices continued to rise on the black market. Paper money lost its value, and many Russians resorted to bartering physical goods. Many urban workers abandoned the cities and returned to their villages: by the end of 1920, Moscow and Petrograd had lost more than 40 percent of their populations.[6] In 1920 industrial production was running at about a seventh of its 1913 level,[7] and the grain harvest was barely half of the prewar average.[8] After visiting the country that same year, the British novelist H. G. Wells wrote: "Our dominant impression of things Russian is an impression of vast irreparable breakdown."[9]

Kondratiev was scornful of what he regarded as a lack of economic expertise among the Bolshevik leaders; he believed they were improvising without any larger plan. "They issue slogans 'to seize' this or that part of the economic structure, absolutely ignoring how this is to be done or its consequences," he wrote in 1918.[10] As the economic situation deteriorated, popular unrest increased. At the beginning of March 1921, sailors, soldiers, and civilians in the port city of Kronstadt launched a rebellion, demanding free elections, a free press, the liberation of political prisoners, and a relaxation of controls on peasant farmers. Deploying the Red Army, the Bolsheviks crushed the rebellion using ground and air power. But Lenin realized that a drastic change of course was essential.

At the Tenth Party Congress, which took place as the uprising was being snuffed out, the Bolsheviks adopted a New Economic Policy (NEP) that met some of the rebels' demands. The government abandoned the wholesale requisitioning of grain, replacing it with a tax in-kind, and legalized private trade. Once the peasants had met the new tax and fed their families, they would be allowed to sell any surplus product on the open market. The government also reversed the nationalization of small businesses and converted some large firms it had taken over into independent trusts. Completing the U-turn, it introduced a new currency backed by gold.

The policy reversal quickly had the desired effect. Factory and farm production rebounded, inflation fell, and traders of all kinds reappeared. Some disgruntled Bolsheviks bemoaned the rise of *kulaks* (peasant proprietors) and "NEP men" (private traders), but they couldn't dispute the fact that the economy was recovering. By 1925, grain output had risen by more than half compared to 1920; industrial production had more than quintupled.[11]

Kondratiev supported the NEP. He continued to participate in official debates, particularly within Zemplan, the planning arm of the People's Commissariat of Agriculture. Like virtually all Russian economists in the 1920s, he believed planning was essential: the long-term development of the economy couldn't be left entirely to the anarchy of the market. Unlike many Bolshevik economists, however, Kondratiev didn't equate planning with centralized control of production and prices. He warned that this approach depended on a level of knowledge and forecasting ability that economists and government officials didn't possess. In his view, the proper role of planning was to coordinate the independent growth of different sectors, using policy tools such as taxes, subsidies, and public works, but also taking account of the objective tendencies of the economy, which included its natural resources, endowments of labor, and prior development.[12]

In 1924 Kondratiev started working on a broad economic plan for the farming sector, which Zemplan had commissioned. He argued that the main thing holding back Russian agriculture wasn't an obdurate peasantry but a series of structural problems: a lack of modern equipment, poor transport links, an overvalued exchange rate, and a dearth of scientific expertise. To help remedy these problems, Kondratiev called for extensive government interventions and regional specialization, with different parts of the Soviet Union producing farm products that were most suitable for their soil, climate, and workforces.[13] An obvious challenge to all economic development plans during this period was a lack of financial resources: the country was still recovering from a decade of war and chaos. To get around this problem, Kondratiev advocated the import of foreign capital to invest in Soviet agriculture, a proposal that wasn't as outlandish as it may sound. Before his death, Lenin supported granting concessions to foreign capitalists in some parts of the economy. Even the agricultural section of Gosplan, the state planning agency established in 1921, had said the Soviet Union should seek capital from a number of foreign countries.[14]

Kondratiev's proposals were part of a larger vision. Many Bolsheviks were determined to pursue a policy of rapid industrialization, which they believed would enable the Soviet Union to catch up with the capitalist West. Kondratiev argued that, at least initially, the country should concentrate on exploiting its vast stocks of land and natural resources to expand agriculture. By exporting farm products and other primary commodities, it could raise rural incomes, which would create a market for domestic industry. He drew up a list of the most promising exports: it included rye, wheat, pigs, butter, and poultry.

In 1924–25 Kondratiev made a fact-finding trip to Great Britain, Germany, and the United States under the auspices of the People's Commissar of Agriculture. During his trip, he took the opportunity to meet with some prominent Western economists. In Britain, he met John Maynard Keynes, the Cambridge economist whose criticisms of the punitive postwar Treaty of Versailles had made him famous. In New York, he discussed the work of the Conjuncture Institute with Wesley Mitchell, a Columbia professor who was an expert on business cycles. During his time in America, Kondratiev also visited farms, agronomy institutes, and the Department of Agriculture, in Washington, DC. After returning to Russia, he wrote a report about the extensive assistance that the US government provided to its farmers, which included supporting scientific research, providing subsidized credit, and operating local education programs. He cited a study that indicated that more than 80 percent of US farms had changed the techniques they used based on these programs.[15] His message was clear: Russia had a lot to learn from the United States and other Western countries.

Regardless of its economic merits, Kondratiev's economic development plan was politically explosive because it relied on privately operated farms. By this stage, he had moved beyond the SR vision of small, village-based communities operating cooperatively. In order to raise agricultural productivity and encourage the spread of the latest scientific techniques, he argued that the peasant farmers should be allowed to hire additional labor and lease additional land. In a 1926 article, he said it was a grave error to formulate economic policy based on disdain for kulaks and commercial agriculture, an attitude that was deeply ingrained in parts of the Bolshevik Party. "If this mistaken path is followed," he wrote, "it is necessary to see all its consequences, and to be reconciled to the dominance of the family-consumer order in peasant farms, with its low marketability, low accumulation, and slow growth of productive forces."[16]

Many Bolsheviks regarded the liberalization that came with the NEP as an emergency measure that needed to be reversed as soon as possible. Lenin, while he was alive, straddled the various factions. Although he had described the NEP as a retreat from socialist ambitions, he resisted calls for a policy reversal. Lenin's death in January 1924 left the fate of the NEP up in the air. Inside the party leadership, Bukharin, who had started out as a leftist hardliner, emerged as its most prominent defender. At a party conference in April 1925, he declared, "To the peasants, to all the peasants, we must say: Enrich yourselves, develop your farms, and do not fear that constraint will be put on you."[17] On the opposite side of the debate were Trotsky and Yevgeni Preobrazhensky, another veteran Bolshevik, who in 1919 had cowritten with Bukharin a book entitled *The ABC of Communism*. Trotsky and Preobrazhensky insisted that sticking with the NEP would condemn Russia to slow growth and render it hostage to the kulaks. Preobrazhensky cited Marx's analysis of how early capitalist accumulation had required the dispossession of the peasantry through the enclosure movement: primitive accumulation. He argued that socialist accumulation similarly "cannot do . . . without the expropriation of part of the surplus product of the countryside"—i.e., dispossession of the kulaks.[18]

As the heated debates about the NEP were going on, Kondratiev was pursuing a second line of research, which further alienated him from the authorities. In 1922, he published, through his research institute, a lengthy study entitled *The World Economy and Its Conjuncture During and After the War.*[19] The book addressed the acute global downturn that had impacted many industrial countries, including Germany and Britain, following the armistice. Some leftist observers had hailed this slump as the onset of a terminal decline for global capitalism. Kondratiev portrayed it as a cyclical phenomenon that the system would recover from, just as it had many times before. Drawing on examples going back to the dawn of the industrial revolution, he detailed the many economic ups and downs that had taken place in Britain and other capitalist countries.

In taking this line, Kondratiev was following Mikhail Tugan-Baranovsky, his onetime teacher in St. Petersburg, whose work included a history of business cycles in Britain. Tugan-Baranovsky believed that production crises were an inevitable part of capitalism, but he expressed skepticism that they heralded an overall breakdown in the system.[20] Kondratiev's study of the postwar economic crisis was squarely in this tradition. However, it also had a novel element. As well as discussing the short-term cycle, or "minor cycle," that characterized capitalist economies, and which Kondratiev said typically lasted for about ten years, it identified a "major cycle" that lasted for about half a century.

Since the onset of the capitalist era in the late eighteenth century, there had been three major cycles, each comprising a "rising wave" and a "falling wave," Kondratiev argued. The first major cycle had extended from 1789 to 1849, with a turning point in 1809. The second major cycle had lasted from 1849 to 1896, with a turning point in 1873. The third major cycle had begun in 1896 and had reached its peak in 1913, just before the start of the Great War. This major cycle was now entering its down wave, Kondratiev said, and he suggested that this descent would have major repercussions for economic development and social relations.[21]

In the early 1920s, there were no GDP statistics, and data on the industrial output of individual industries didn't go back very far. Kondratiev conceded that the evidence to support his theory of major cycles, which subsequently became known as "long cycles" or "long waves," was provisional. It consisted largely of an analysis of interest rates in western European countries going back to 1800 or thereabouts. But although Kondratiev's evidence was tentative, the larger implication of his theory was clear: while capitalism goes through extended ups and downs, it has no predetermined end date. At least in theory, the long cycles could continue indefinitely.

If Kondratiev's study had been published in London or New York, it would have been regarded as an interesting academic contribution. In Bolshevik Russia, it was greeted in some quarters as a challenge to the party dogma that an irretrievable capitalist collapse was inevitable. One of the first Bolshevik officials to attack Kondratiev's work was Trotsky, who had long taken an interest in economics. At a 1921 conference of the newly formed Communist International (Comintern), he had criticized the argument that global capitalism would rebound from its postwar slump as a "trait of opportunism."[22] Trotsky's experience commanding the Red Army during the civil war hadn't dimmed his appetite for intellectual disputation. In a long 1923 letter to the editors of a socialist academic journal, he described Kondratiev's theory that long cycles existed and evolved with the same "rigidly lawful rhythm" as minor cycles as "an obviously false generalization from a formal analogy."[23] Whereas short cycles were generated by the internal dynamics of the capitalist economy, Trotsky wrote, the long-term evolution of the system was largely determined by "external conditions," such as colonialist land grabs, conflicts between the imperialist nations, and political insurrections. "The acquisition by capitalism of new countries and continents," Trotsky wrote, "the discovery of new natural resources, and, in the wake of these, such major facts of 'superstructural' order as wars and revolutions, determine the character and replacement of ascending, stagnating, or declining epochs of capitalist development."[24]

Any effort to supplant this broad historical approach with "the methods of formalism," as Kondratiev had done, amounted to "splitting empty abstractions," Trotsky's letter went on. Rather than searching for major cycles in the data, the real intellectual challenge was to identify a single curve that traced capitalism's long-term path, "in both its non-periodic (basic) and its periodic (secondary elements) phases." To illustrate this idea, Trotsky presented a chart of his own that showed a single line rising slowly, then more rapidly, reaching a peak, and then gradually falling back. Trotsky said the line represented "twenty years of very gradual capitalist development (segment A-B); forty years of energetic upswing (segment B-C); and thirty years of protracted crisis and decline (segment C-D)." He acknowledged that this chart wasn't derived from any actual data, but he went on to suggest that it could provide "invaluable starting points for historical materialist investigations."[25]

Kondratiev didn't back down. In 1925 he published a new paper, "The Long Waves in Economic Life," in which he presented fresh data to support his theory and, without mentioning Trotsky directly, sought to refute the criticisms of his prior work. This paper, which appeared in the theoretical journal of the Business Research Institute of Moscow, received a great deal of attention from other Russian economists, and it was translated into German and English, although that process took some time. The new evidence it contained consisted of historical data on commodity prices, wages, coal production, and foreign trade from England, France, Germany, and the United States. After using a least squares regression to eliminate the long-term secular upward trend from this data, Kondratiev also converted his figures to nine-year moving averages to eliminate the effects of short cycles.[26] Having filtered the data in this manner, he presented it in charts, which showed distinctive up waves and down waves, each lasting roughly a quarter of a century. Based on these patterns, Kondratiev identified the same three "major cycles" he had written about previously. The only significant change from his 1922 study was that he moved the peak of the first long cycle from 1809 to 1814.[27]

One immediate criticism that Kondratiev's paper was met with was that it didn't contain a convincing explanation of what drove the major cycles he identified. But in his 1925 paper, and in a follow-up study he completed early in 1926, he did identify some of their recurring characteristics.[28] One of these regularities was that fundamental changes in the economic structure, such as the invention of powerful new technologies, tended to take place during the down wave of the major cycle. By contrast, social upheavals, such as wars and revolutions, tended to happen during the upswing. Kondratiev also discussed the mechanics of the long cycles, stressing the role played by capital investment. "The material basis of the long cycles is the wear and tear, the replacement and the increase of the fund of basic capital goods, the production of which requires tremendous investment and is a long process," he wrote.[29] Among the basic capital goods Kondratiev pointed to were "big plants, important railways, canals, large land improvement projects, etc."[30]

Based on these regularities, Kondratiev challenged the claim that capitalism's long-term path was "conditioned by causal, extra-economic circumstance and events." (Perhaps wisely, he didn't mention Trotsky by name.) He argued that the causation went in the other direction—from economics to external developments. "Wars and revolutions . . . influence the course of economic development very strongly," he wrote. "But wars and revolutions do not come out of a clear sky, and they are not caused by arbitrary acts of individual personalities. They originate from real, especially economic circumstances."[31] Along the same lines, Kondratiev argued that the acquisition of new territories and the opening of new markets "does not provoke the upswing of a long wave." Rather, "a new upswing makes the exploitation of new countries, new markets, and new sources of raw materials necessary and possible, in that it accelerates the pace of capitalist development."[32]

Even major technological innovations weren't entirely detached from the economic environment, Kondratiev insisted. Improvements in production techniques "have without a doubt a very potent influence on the course of capitalistic development," he wrote. "But nobody has proved them to have an accidental and external origin."[33] Scientific discoveries and inventions usually emerged from previous research and the "necessities of real life."[34] However, they were deployed throughout the economy only when conditions were favorable to big investments—during the up wave, that is. Therefore, Kondratiev concluded, "the development of technique itself is part of the rhythm of the long waves."[35]

In modern terms, Kondratiev was arguing that, in a capitalist system, long-term growth is self-sustaining, or endogenous. The system alternates between lengthy periods of above-trend and below-trend growth, but the overall pattern is one of continued expansion. During the long upswing, growth is driven by capital investment on major projects, such as new factories, land improvement schemes, and transport links. During the downswing, capital investment drops back and economic growth declines. Superimposed on this long cycle are short cycles, which last about a decade. But contrary to what had become the orthodox Marxist doctrine, there is no underlying tendency for the system to head toward a permanent breakdown.

On February 6, 1926, some of the Soviet Union's leading economists gathered at the Conjuncture Institute, where Kondratiev presented his theory and some fresh data to support it. After his presentation, a number of his colleagues from the institute, as well as some economists from other organizations, lit into his arguments. The attacks didn't end there. A week later one of Kondratiev's critics,

Dmitry Oparin, an economist who was associated with the Institute and served as an adviser to Gosplan, presented a longer and more detailed critique.

In his engaging 2015 book, *Postcapitalism: A Guide to Our Future*, the English writer Paul Mason noted that the verbatim record of the February 6 meeting "contains none of the fear and irrationality that Stalin's purges would soon inject into Soviet academic life."[36] But even though the debate was an open one, Kondratiev found few defenders. Oparin claimed the method he used to smooth over the short cycles—least squares analysis—had distorted his data on major cycles. Even if these cycles did exist, Oparin pointed out, there had been only two and a half of them since the dawn of capitalism, which wasn't enough to identify their turning points or other key characteristics.

V. E. Bogdanov, a professor of economics at Moscow University, criticized Kondratiev's methodology, too, claiming his long waves were statistical artifacts.[37] Bogdanov also challenged Kondratiev's economic analysis, saying investments in capital projects, even major ones like railroads and steel factories, couldn't determine the trajectory of the entire world economy over a period as long as fifty years. Effectively repeating Trotsky's point, Bogdanov argued that external factors, such as the decline of the Ottoman Empire and major scientific innovations, played a bigger role in driving long-term growth. Even if long waves did exist, he said, they were the result of the "random intersection of two essentially causal series"—the paths of historical events and the progress of scientific development.[38]

Also echoing Trotsky, some participants at the conference voiced ideological objections to the long wave theory. "We are dealing with an essentially perpetual movement of capitalism, first upwards and then downwards, and that it is not appropriate to dream of social revolution yet," Miron Nachimson, an agricultural economist, complained.[39]

Kondratiev took some of these criticisms seriously, others less so. From the beginning of his research, he had readily conceded that his limited datasets didn't allow him to prove definitively that long waves existed. Writing in the journal *Socialist Economy* in 1923, he commented: "We see the long cycle of capitalist conjuncture only as probable."[40] In his responses to his critics, Kondratiev reiterated these points. But he also insisted that it was highly probable long waves did exist.

As the debates about Kondratiev's long waves continued, the political environment was shifting. Two months before the February 1926 meeting at the Conjuncture Institute, the Fourteenth Party Congress had reaffirmed the party's support for industrialization as the central plank of economic development. Joseph Stalin, in his role as the general secretary, issued a report criticizing the argument that the Soviet Union "must for a long time yet remain an agrarian country, must export agricultural produce and import equipment." To adopt this stance "would mean that our country would never be able, or almost never be able, to become really industrialised," Stalin's report said.[41] It amounted to an explicit repudiation of the development strategy that Kondratiev was recommending.

To Stalin, who was maneuvering to become Lenin's undisputed successor, and many other Bolsheviks, Kondratiev's approach was too dependent on the global capitalist trading system and too gradualist. Many party members, led by Trotsky, were staunchly committed to launching a worldwide revolution, which they saw as the only way to supplant global capitalism. Stalin was beginning to espouse a more inward-looking strategy that became known as "socialism in one country" and was based on the notion that the Soviet Union could build a self-sufficient socialist society regardless of what happened elsewhere. In April 1926, the party's central committee called for "the reinforcement of the planning principle," which many Bolsheviks viewed as synonymous with rapid industrialization.[42] Later in the same year the regime reduced the procurement prices it paid farmers and issued a new tax on "super-profits" aimed at the NEP men.[43] The change in policy was accompanied by a change in personnel. At the Fourteenth Party Congress, Grigory Sokolnikov was demoted from the Politburo, the highest body of the party. With the star of Kondratiev's chief political sponsor in decline, he found his economic proposals subjected to public criticism. In a 1926 article, P. I. Popov, a senior Gosplan official, described the idea of allowing peasant farmers to hire labor and expand their operations by leasing more land as capitalist in spirit.[44]

The policy reversal gradually picked up steam. In June 1927 the Council of People's Commissars demanded a "united all-union plan" to promote industrialization.[45] Until about this point, Stalin had positioned himself as a centrist on economics, occupying the middle ground between Trotsky and Preobrazhensky on one side and Bukharin and supporters of the NEP on the other. A disappointing 1927 harvest proved to be a turning point. Stalin accused the kulaks of hoarding grain and railed against them. His political machinations gave him more flexibility. Weeks before the Fifteenth Party Congress, in December 1927, Trotsky and Grigory Zinoviev, a veteran Bolshevik and former associate of Lenin, were removed from the party's central committee. Subsequently, Trotsky was deported to Alma-Ata, a city in central Asia. Having exiled his main rival, Stalin moved ahead with an economic policy U-turn. In 1928 he presided over the launch of Gosplan's First Five-Year Plan, which set a goal of increasing industrial production by 180 percent.[46]

As Kondratiev's political isolation increased, he continued to do research. In 1928 he published another paper on long waves, which included new data on the prices of agricultural commodities and industrial goods.[47] Unlike his previous work, this study didn't prompt much discussion inside Russia. As Stalin's rule was becoming more dictatorial, the window for open discussions was fast closing. On May 2, 1928, the government dismissed Kondratiev from his post as head of the Conjuncture Institute "for introducing ideology alien to Soviet policy into his work."[48] For a time, he stayed on at the Institute as deputy director, but in official circles he was rapidly becoming a nonperson. Early in the following year, the *Soviet Russian Encyclopedia* dismissed his theory of long waves in six words: "This theory is wrong and reactionary."[49]

In January 1928 Stalin personally led a group of police and party officials to the Urals–West Siberia region, where they forcefully requisitioned grain from the peasants, shut down private markets, and imprisoned anyone who resisted. This return to the methods of War Communism was a precursor to a broader attack on the peasantry. In January 1930 the party's central committee formally approved a policy of setting up huge state-owned farms. To ensure that the peasants would join these new collectives, the regime used carrots and sticks. The sticks included punitive taxes and exile in Siberia for those who resisted.

The NEP era was over, and Kondratiev's middle way had been definitively abandoned. With Stalin intent on eliminating all real or perceived enemies, it didn't take the internal security apparatus long to get around to him. In June 1930 the authorities arrested him and accused him of being a member of a fictitious counterrevolutionary organization, the Labouring Peasants Party. The security apparatus detained him at the Butyrka prison in Moscow, which housed many political prisoners. According to Vincent Barnett, who examined KGB archives released in 1993, Kondratiev was interrogated at length by Yakov Agranov, a notorious henchman in the NKVD, the state security agency. Agranov extracted a fake confession from Kondratiev in which he admitted that the Labouring Peasants Party existed and was intent on reintroducing capitalist elements to the Soviet economy.[50]

There is written evidence that Stalin himself was personally involved in Kondratiev's detention and asked for harsh measures to be taken against him and other economists who weren't sufficiently supportive of his policies. "Run Messrs Kondratiev, Yurovskii, Chayanov etc through the mill," the Soviet leader wrote in an October 1930 note to the head of the OGPU, the Soviet secret police.[51] In another letter, to his longtime acolyte and number two, V. M. Molotov, Stalin wrote: "Kondratiev, Groman and another couple of scoundrels must certainly be executed."[52]

For a time, Kondratiev and Vladimir Groman, a former Menshevik who worked at Gosplan, escaped this fate. But in March 1931 Groman was convicted at the Menshevik show trial and sentenced to ten years in prison. The following January, Kondratiev, who was then thirty-nine years old, was tried and convicted of "kulak-professor" crimes.[53] After being sentenced to eight years of detention, he was sent to a political prison in Suzdal, a town located about 120 miles northeast of Moscow. In captivity, Kondratiev kept working as best he could. "I read the books they let me have; I've taken to mathematics, and I keep writing the book on trends," he wrote in a letter to his wife dated March 7, 1934.[54] In some of his prison correspondence, Kondratiev seemed reasonably upbeat, but the awful reality of his circumstances came through clearly. "It is four years since they had set me in this atmosphere of a monotonous dull stupor impairing both physical and mental health," he wrote on April 11, 1934. "And strictly speaking, I think I am lost for a further work in science. All those new and perhaps not disadvantageous ideas that occurred to me here are doomed to a gradual obliteration. The most devaluated value of today is human life and human thought."[55]

As for so many of Stalin's victims, there was no hope for Kondratiev. By 1938 he had served his eight-year sentence, but the dictator's Great Purge was then at its lunatic height. Instead of being released, Kondratiev was subjected to a second trial before a military tribunal. This proceeding took place on September 17, 1938, and it ended with the issuance of a death sentence. Later the same day the forty-six-year-old was taken to the Kommunarka shooting ground southwest of Moscow, a spot that Stalin's Interior Ministry used for many executions. A firing squad shot him to death.

During the ensuing decades, Kondratiev was largely written out of Soviet textbooks, which presented Stalin's policy of forced collectivization and industrialization as essential and highly successful. Although the precise figures are still disputed, there is general agreement that Soviet GDP and industrial output grew rapidly between 1928 and 1940. "There were impressive gains in heavy industries, mining and construction," the British historian Orlando Figes, no defender of the Bolshevik regime, notes. "The Soviet Union became the world's leading producer of oil, coal, iron ore, and cement, and it became a major world producer of manganese, gold, natural gas and other minerals."[56] But as Figes and other historians have also emphasized, the human cost of Stalin's policies, especially the forced collectivization of agriculture, was unfathomable. In many areas, peasant farmers resisted the state seizure of their property and slaughtered their livestock. In 1932–33, there was a terrible famine. In Ukraine alone, it killed more than 3 million people, according to modern estimates. "For the whole of the Soviet Union, the figure can be nearly doubled," Ian Kershaw wrote in his 2015 book, *To Hell and Back: Europe 1914–1949*.[57]

Despite the tragedy of collectivization, many Western economists came to regard Soviet industrialization as a successful, if brutal, example of a government giving a backward economy a "big push" toward modernization by making massive capital investments that were financed by squeezing the peasantry and the working class. More recently, however, some scholars have revived Kondratiev's argument that other viable development strategies were available to the early Soviet Union. "The collectivization of agriculture was not necessary for rapid growth," the economic historian Robert Allen wrote in a 2005 paper. "Industrial development would have been almost as fast had the five year plans been carried out within the framework of the NEP."[58] Questions have also been raised about the long-term economic impact of Stalin's policies. In 2017 Sergei Guriev, a prominent Russian economist, and three colleagues published a paper in the *Review of Economic Studies* in which they argued, in Guriev's words, "that while Stalin's industrialization was brutally effective in moving labor from farm to factory, it greatly undermined productivity growth in both agriculture and industry, so on balance it only slightly outperformed the Tsarist trend."[59]

These revisionist arguments aren't conclusive: there can be no guarantee that Kondratiev's export-based development strategy would have worked. In the late 1920s, many Western countries were reluctant to trade with the Soviet Union for political reasons. Even if this reluctance could have been overcome, the Great Depression of the 1930s, which saw global trade collapse, would have presented another huge challenge. Still, the idea that Soviet-style industrialization was the only option for a backward country like Russia—a notion that became widely accepted in many parts of the developing world—was built on erasing the proposals of Kondratiev to develop the agricultural sector and integrate the Soviet Union into the global economy, at least partially.

Even as Kondratiev's work was suppressed in the Soviet Union, his theory of long cycles continued to attract attention in the West, especially after Joseph Schumpeter, an eminent Austrian economist who taught at Harvard, featured it prominently in a 1939 book about business cycles. Schumpeter coined the term *Kondratiev cycle*,[60] which is often converted to *Kondratiev wave*. Fascination with Kondratiev's theory persisted even as some of Schumpeter's colleagues in US academia echoed some of the methodological criticisms that Soviet economists had put forward in the 1920s. In a 1943 article in *The Review of Economics and Statistics*, the same journal that earlier had published a translation of Kondratiev's article on long waves, George Garvy, an American economist at the National Bureau of Economic Research, went through Kondratiev's data in detail and concluded that "he did not succeed in showing the existence" of long cycles.[61]

These criticisms live on. Even relying on the most modern statistical methods, it is difficult to differentiate underlying trends from short-term movements in economic time series, and it's easy to identify spurious trends. Despite these difficulties, though, some contemporary economists have produced findings in the spirit of Kondratiev. After examining long-term data on GDP and intellectual patents for France, Germany, Great Britain, and the United States, three Greek economists wrote in *The Journal of Applied Economics* in 2018: "Our results confirm that long waves are present, explaining a significant share of overall variability of the actual data, both for economic activity as well as for the possibly underlying cause of applied technological evolution."[62]

In economics, statistical findings are rarely definitive. The main reason

Kondratiev's theory continues to fascinate is that, in broad terms, it seems to match our intuitive grasp of economic history. The first half of the twentieth century was so racked with wars and economic catastrophes that it's hard to interpret. After 1945, though, many Western economies expanded strongly for about thirty years, then entered a period of weaker growth that lasted for about a quarter of a century. Was this the fourth Kondratiev wave? Some economic observers think so, and they have identified a fifth wave that began in the mid-1990s, with major investments in the commercial development of the internet and online commerce. Unlike some of his latter-day followers, Kondratiev wasn't a technological determinist, but he did believe that industrial capitalism had strong powers of recuperation. Somewhat ironically, he made this argument just as the system's ability to rebound from periods of crisis was about to be tested to the brink. During the eight years that Kondratiev languished in prison, the major capitalist economies experienced a slump so severe and extended it persuaded some Western commentators and scholars that capitalism was a lost cause. Even those Western economists and policymakers who thought the system was salvageable agreed that its survival depended on making it more stable and equitable. This quest would center on the ideas and policy recommendations of the economist whom Kondratiev had met in England: John Maynard Keynes.

15

"The more troublous the times, the worse does a laissez-faire system work"

John Maynard Keynes's Blueprint for Managed Capitalism

In the summer of 1922 Roy Harrod, a young Englishman who had recently graduated from Oxford University with high honors, knocked on the door of 46 Gordon Square, a handsome Georgian row house in London's Bloomsbury neighborhood, where he had been invited to lunch. The economist John Maynard Keynes warmly greeted his visitor, who was there to seek career advice. Two other guests were also present, one of whom was a French economist. "The talk began without any pause; it was quick and animated," Harrod recalled many years later. "Keynes was discussing with the Frenchman the latest gossip about Continental statesmen, their mistresses, their neuroses, as well as their political manoeuvers . . . There was financial talk of the latest movements in the exchanges, budgetary positions, the international movement of money. This was still far beyond my ken."[1]

Keynes had shot to international fame with his 1919 polemic *The Economic Consequences of the Peace*. The book savaged the postwar Treaty of Versailles, in which the victors in the Great War, at the behest of France and Belgium, imposed heavy reparations on Germany. In his role as an economic adviser to the British Treasury, Keynes had been part of the British delegation at Versailles, but he left the conference early in protest at the punitive nature of the treaty. If the allies deliberately aimed to impoverish Germany and the rest of central Europe, "vengeance, I dare predict, will not limp," Keynes wrote. "Nothing can then delay for long that final civil war between the forces of Reaction and the despairing convulsions of Revolution, before which the horrors of the late German war will fade into nothing, and which will destroy, whoever is victor, the civilization and the progress of our generation."[2] Keynes's criticisms were well-founded. By 1922, the straitened government of the Weimar Republic had resorted to printing money, and a period of hyperinflation had begun. By the fall of 1923, prices would rise a trillion-fold relative to the prewar level, paper currency would be rendered virtually worthless, and many middle-class Germans would see their savings wiped out. Prices also rose sharply in other European countries, including Austria-Hungary, Czechoslovakia, and Greece, causing widespread hardship and undermining political stability.

Britain and France were in better shape than Germany, but they were still burdened with the enormous costs they had incurred in fighting the Great War. After entering the conflict as the world's largest international creditor, with vast overseas investments, Britain exited it heavily dependent on loans from the United States, which had been the principal economic beneficiary of the cataclysm. As America's bankers arranged credit for the allies, its manufacturers supplied them with armaments and other goods that Europe's war-torn economies couldn't supply. During the war years, US exports more than doubled, and US manufacturing production rose by 160 percent.[3] This performance would continue during the 1920s, a boom period for the United States. In 1914 the US economy was already the world's largest, but the combined production of the four major European economies— Britain, France, Germany, and Belgium—was larger. By the late 1920s, the US economy was nearly 50 percent bigger than the other four.[4]

In the developing world, too, the Great War unsettled the existing order. In India, Ireland, and Algeria, many people had joined allied armies during the conflict, and increasingly the citizenry demanded political rights from their colonial rulers. Nationalist movements also attracted support in Egypt, Iraq, and Vietnam. Acting through the Third International, or Comintern, which was founded in 1919, the Soviet Union encouraged these developments. The Comintern's second congress, which took place in 1920, passed a resolution that said every leftist party affiliated with the organization had "the obligation of . . . supporting every liberation movement in the colonies not only in words but in deeds."[5] In the United States and the Caribbean, meanwhile, some Black activists were expressing support for the independence of African nations. In an August 1921 speech to a meeting in New York of the Universal Negro Improvement Association, an organization that he had founded in 1914, the Jamaican Marcus Garvey Jr. declared: "This convention believes in the right of Europe for the Europeans, Asia for the Asiatics, and Africa for the Africans, those at home and those abroad."[6]

In Egypt and southern Ireland during the early 1920s, these stirrings led to independence. Elsewhere, the nationalist movements were as yet too weak to overthrow colonialist regimes, but the war and its aftermath had gravely weakened the imperial order and the trading relations it supported. Between 1914 and 1921, the volume of global trade fell by about a fifth. Many countries, including the United States and even Britain, moved to protect their own industries and partially or fully suspended participation in the gold standard, an international currency regime that tied the levels of exchange rates to the precious metal. Postwar efforts to reconstitute the pre-1914 economic system quickly faltered. As long as the Democrat Woodrow Wilson remained in the White House, it had seemed possible that the United States would take over Britain's role as the principal promoter of free trade and international economic coordination. But the United States was a reluctant hegemon. In November 1919 the Senate rejected the Versailles Treaty, principally because of opposition to US membership in the new League of Nations. After the 1920 elections, the protectionist Republican Party controlled the White House and both houses of Congress. It quickly raised tariffs on industrial and agricultural imports well above their prewar levels.

As a liberal internationalist, Keynes supported free trade and global economic integration. The son of another Cambridge economist, John Neville Keynes, he was born on June 5, 1883, and educated at Eton College, the traditional stomping ground of the British elite, and King's College, Cambridge. To all outward appearances, he was a typical upper-middle-class Englishman: tall, plum voiced, conservatively attired, and patriotic. After graduating from King's in 1905 with a first-class degree in mathematics, he joined the British civil service and worked for a couple of years in the India Office. There is no record of him raising any objections to British rule. "He believed the regime protected the poor against the rapacious money-lender, brought justice and material progress, and gave the country a sound monetary system: in short, introduced good government to places which could not develop it on their own," the historian Robert Skidelsky commented in his magisterial three-volume biography of Keynes.[7]

When Harrod visited him in Gordon Square, Keynes was splitting his time between King's College, where he held a teaching post, and London, where he was a prolific journalist, an economic adviser to the Liberal Party, and a member of the close-knit community of artists and writers known as the Bloomsbury Group. The Post-Impressionist painter Vanessa Bell, who was the sister of Virginia Woolf, occupied the upper floors of 46 Gordon Square with her husband, Clive Bell, an art critic. The author Lytton Strachey, another Bloomsbury member, kept a residence a few doors away at number 51. Adrian Stephen, a psychoanalyst who was the younger brother of Vanessa and Virginia, was at number 50. Woolf herself lived in a distant suburb with her husband, Leonard. She compared Gordon Square to the lions' house at the zoo. "One goes from cage to cage," she wrote to a friend. "All the animals are dangerous, rather suspicious of each other, and full of fascination and mystery."[8]

Keynes was a liberal progressive, but a very British one. He had no time for continental doctrines, including Marxism, which he regarded as muddled and outdated, or for the uneducated proletariat. ("The *Class* war will find me on the side of the educated *bourgeoisie*," he remarked in a 1925 address.)[9] Throughout his life, his basic attitude to capitalism didn't change much. It mirrored Winston Churchill's famous aphorism that democracy was the worst form of government except for all the others. Keynes believed that a properly run system of global commerce based on private enterprise would deliver rising living standards, promote civilization (which to his mind meant higher learning and the fine arts), and preserve individual liberty (which he held sacrosanct) more effectively than any other economic system. The phrase "properly run" is a vital qualifier. Keynes's faith in the market system didn't extend to supporting laissez-faire, which he viewed as another outdated dogma. Unlike his intellectual sparring partner (and fellow collector of antiquarian books), the Austrian economist Friedrich Hayek, he didn't invest the profit motive with any higher morality or free markets with magical powers of self-organization. To him, capitalism was defensible only insofar as it delivered material goods and preserved liberty.

In a famous 1930 essay, "Economic Possibilities for Our Grandchildren," Keynes looked ahead a century to a world in which, assuming capital accumulation and productivity growth continued to rise steadily, "we are all of us, on the average, eight times better off in the economic sense than we are today."

In this world of plenty, the basic economic problem of providing everyone with a decent standard of living would have been solved, Keynes said. People would work much shorter hours—say, fifteen hours a week—and spend the rest of their time as they wished. "The love of money as a possession—as distinguished from the love of money as a means to the enjoyments and realities of life—will be recognised for what it is, a somewhat disgusting morbidity, one of those semicriminal, semi-pathological propensities which one hands over with a shudder to the specialists in mental disease," Keynes wrote. And he went on: "All kinds of social customs and economic practices, affecting the distribution of wealth and of economic rewards and penalties, which we now maintain at all costs, however distasteful and unjust they may be in themselves, because they are tremendously useful in promoting the accumulation of capital, we shall then be free, at last, to discard."[10] Keynes was careful to point out, however, that this vision of a world moving beyond capitalist values was strictly a long-term one: "But beware! The time for all this is not yet . . . Avarice and usury and precaution must be our gods for a little longer still. For only they can lead us out of the tunnel of economic necessity into daylight."[11]

The immediate challenge was to harness capitalism's productive powers while containing its darker aspects. When Keynes greeted Harrod, he was already thinking hard about how to accomplish this task. By the time of his death, in 1946, his name would be attached to an economic policy framework that ushered in Western capitalism's most successful epoch and prompted even some of its most ardent antagonists to recalibrate their views.

The construction of this framework process took place in three stages. During the 1920s, Keynes intuited the basic monetary and fiscal apparatus that governments could use to guide capitalist economies. In the 1930s he elaborated on this framework and provided it with a theoretical justification that is now known as "Keynesian economics." And in the 1940s, as World War II wound down, he played an important role, as a British government official, in extending the Keynesian framework to the international sphere, where it operated under the global leadership of the United States.

Keynes began his great project with an attack on the gold standard. In Britain and other countries, many policymakers, bankers, and economists believed that a sustainable return to prosperity would be possible only if the old currency system was restored. Once a country joined the gold standard, its money supply was limited by its stocks of gold, which ruled out inflationary money printing of the sort witnessed in Weimar Germany. Keynes didn't deny that the system had been a linchpin of financial stability in the prewar era, but he argued that it was too rigid and outdated for the postwar world. In Britain, prices had more than doubled since 1914, which had put downward pressure on the value of sterling. The only way to restore the prewar parity with gold would be for the government to keep interest rates high enough to produce price deflation. With the unemployment rate still elevated from a postwar economic downturn, this policy would involve a great deal of additional economic pain, which Keynes believed was unnecessary and even dangerous.

In December 1923 he published *A Tract on Monetary Reform*, in which he described the gold standard as a "barbarous relic."[12] He called on the government to hand over responsibility for fighting inflation to the Bank of England, which could set interest rates considering the state of the domestic economy as well as the need to maintain price stability. If the economy was stuttering, it could reduce interest rates to give it a boost. If the economy was overheating, it could raise interest rates to cool it down and head off inflation. In modern terms, Keynes was calling for Britain to establish an independent monetary policy.

Another problem with the gold standard, he argued, was that so much gold had accumulated in the United States during and after the war that it had effectively become a "dollar standard." If Britain reentered the system, it would "surrender the regulation of our price level and the handling of the credit cycle" to the Federal Reserve System, which had been created in 1913 and primarily concerned itself with economic conditions in the United States.[13] Far better to delegate responsibility to the "Governors and Court of the Bank of England," Keynes insisted. The golden straitjacket no longer worked to Britain's advantage: it was time to create "a discretionary authority in the State to revise what has become intolerable."[14]

Keynes's attack on the gold standard was part of a larger argument about the need to move beyond nineteenth-century individualism and laissez-faire. Two days after the publication of the *Tract*, he delivered a lecture to the National Liberal Club in which he said, "It is obvious that an individualist society left to itself does not work well or even tolerably. The more troublous the times, the worse does a *laissez-faire* system work."[15] What was needed wasn't "out of date" socialism, Keynes went on, but well-thought-out interventions targeted at specific problems. His plan to replace the gold standard fell into this category, he insisted, and he issued a warning to "the Gentlemen of the City [of London] and High Finance": unless they embraced the need for change, "the system upon which they live will work so very ill they will be overwhelmed by irresistible things which they will hate much more than the mild and limited remedies offered them now."[16]

This warning was ignored. In April 1925 Churchill, who held the post of chancellor of the exchequer despite a shocking ignorance of economics, announced that Britain was rejoining the gold standard and setting the value of the pound at its prewar level of $4.86. Keynes wrote a withering pamphlet, *The Economic Consequences of Mr. Churchill*, in which he argued that this decision would condemn the British economy to many more years of stagnation and deflation. If the government insisted on rejoining the gold standard, Keynes added, it should have rejoined at a much lower parity to reflect the fact that the competitiveness of the UK economy had declined since 1914.

With an active monetary policy no longer a policy option, Keynes was already moving on to develop the second weapon in his armory: fiscal policy. In April 1924 David Lloyd George, the former Liberal prime minister, wrote a letter to *The Nation and Athenaeum*, a magazine that Keynes now co-owned, in which he called on the government to employ the jobless on worthwhile projects such as building public utilities. Lloyd George's letter sparked a lively debate, which Keynes entered, on May 24, with an article entitled: "Does Unemployment Need a Drastic Remedy?" His answer was that it most certainly did. The UK Treasury, Keynes wrote, should spend "up to (say) Sterling 100,000,000 per year on the construction of capital works," such as affordable housing, new roads, and electricity transmission lines.[17] To raise this money, the government could issue bonds and soak up some of the financial capital that was being invested abroad. "By conducting the national wealth into capital developments at home, we may restore the balance of our economy," he argued. "Let us experiment with boldness on such lines—even though some of the schemes may turn out to be failures, which is very likely."[18]

In making this proposal, Keynes was challenging two tenets of nineteenth-century liberalism: fiscal retrenchment and the freedom for capital to seek its highest return wherever that might be found. After some critics upbraided Keynes on the latter point, he wrote a second piece in which he said sticking by old principles was secondary to the imperative of reducing joblessness and employing idle resources. "In considering how to do this, we are brought to my heresy—if it is a heresy," he wrote. "I bring in the State; I abandon *laissez-faire*—not enthusiastically, not from contempt of that good old doctrine, but because, whether we like it or not, the conditions for its success have disappeared."[19] In making this argument, Keynes was more prescient than many of his peers, who believed that the key to restoring prosperity was to re-create the pre-1914 environment. Keynes recognized that this was impractical, at least from Britain's point of view. The war had shattered the country's finances, undermined its international leadership, and upended its social system. In a changed world, new thinking and new measures were essential to ensure economic stability and buttress the essential elements of capitalist liberal democracy.

Keynes developed this argument in a public lecture that he subsequently turned into a pamphlet, *The End of Laissez-Faire*. In it, he said: "The important thing for Government is not to do things which individuals are doing already, and to do them a little better or a little worse; but to do those things which at present are not done at all."[20] Among the actions that Keynes included in this category were collecting and distributing economic data, controlling excessive population growth, and allocating savings "along the most nationally productive channels." Still sensitive to classical liberal concerns about expanding the size of the state, he said that many of these activities could be carried out by semiautonomous bodies such as the Bank of England and the Port of London Authority. He also insisted that nothing he was promoting was "incompatible with what seems to me to be the essential characteristic of Capitalism, namely the dependence upon an intense appeal to the money-making and money-loving instincts of individuals as the main motive force of the economic machine."[21]

By the late 1920s, Keynes had settled into respectable middle age. In 1925 he shocked his friends by marrying Lydia Lopokova, a Russian ballerina who had danced with Nijinsky, consorted with Stravinsky, and been directed by Diaghilev. Despite the skepticism of the Bloomsbury set, the match turned out to be a long and happy one. At an old farmhouse that Keynes leased in Tilton, East Sussex, Lydia did her dance exercises while he worked on a second book on monetary theory, which would be published in 1930 under the title *A Treatise on Money*. He also remained politically active. Ahead of the May 1929 general election, he helped Lloyd George with his book *We Can Conquer Unemployment*, in which the former prime minister expanded upon his demand for an extensive program of public works financed by public debt issuance. Together with Hubert Henderson, a former colleague from Cambridge, Keynes also published a pamphlet, *Can Lloyd George Do It?*," which defended the Liberal leader's proposals. On election day, however, the Liberal Party won only 59 of the 615 seats in the House of Commons. The Labour Party, under Ramsay MacDonald, formed a minority government, which depended on Liberal support.

Within months, this government, like many others around the world, was engulfed by the Great Crash of October 1929 and its calamitous aftermath. Keynes initially underestimated the significance of the Wall Street break. In an article for *The New York Evening Post*, he predicted that it would usher in lower interest rates around the world, which would soon revive business investment.[22] This analysis proved far too optimistic. On both sides of the Atlantic, industrial production turned down sharply, and employers laid off workers in large numbers. Commodity prices, which had already been declining for some time, cratered, ushering in an agricultural depression. The price of wheat fell from $1.50 a bushel in the summer of 1929 to $0.49 a bushel in late 1932.[23] By May 1930, Keynes had changed his economic prognosis. "We are now in the depths of a very severe international slump, a slump which will take its place in history amongst the most acute ever experienced," he wrote in *The Nation*. "It will require not merely passive movements of bank rates to lift us out of a depression of this order, but a very active and determined policy."[24] Subsequent developments confirmed this diagnosis. By the end of 1930, the British unemployment rate had reached about 20 percent; the German rate was even higher. In the United States by the end of 1931, 16 percent of people were out of work, and the number was still rising.[25]

As prices, income, and employment all declined precipitously, many debtors—households, businesses, and farmers—defaulted on their bank loans. Pressures increased on banks, which, with no protections in place for depositors, were highly vulnerable to runs by nervous customers. In the final months of 1930, hundreds of American banks failed, including the Bank of United States, the fourth-biggest commercial bank in New York.[26] In May 1931 the banking crisis shifted to Europe. Creditanstalt, the biggest bank in Austria, collapsed under the weight of bad debts. The shock waves quickly spread to Hungary, then Germany. Central banks tried and failed to stabilize the situation. In July the German government took drastic action and suspended the convertibility of its currency for gold. It seemed to some observers that global capitalism was imploding.

Keynes viewed these developments with growing alarm. In November 1929 the Labour government appointed an independent Committee on Finance and Industry under the chairmanship of Lord Macmillan, an eminent lawyer, to examine how to revive the economy. Keynes was one of the economists appointed to the Macmillan Committee. During the first half of 1930, it held a series of private hearings, at which Keynes and other members questioned expert witnesses, including Montagu Norman, the governor of the Bank of England, and Sir Richard Hopkins, a senior Treasury official. Hopkins told the committee that the fundamental economic problem was a crisis of confidence, which would relent only if the government cut spending and restored the budget to balance. As the public finances improved, optimism would return, and business activity would pick up.

Keynes regarded the notion that business investment and hiring would rebound of their own accord if austerity policies were imposed as wrongheaded. In his *Treatise*, he had identified the gap between saving and investment (by which he meant capital investment) as the key to economic downturns. If investment fell short of saving, a downturn was inevitable. The key to reviving the economy, therefore, was to encourage businesses to expand their capacity. But they would do this only if they could be assured of selling their products and making a profit, which was very difficult in an economic downturn. "For the engine which drives Enterprise is not Thrift, but Profit," Keynes concluded.[27] His argument wasn't yet fully articulated, but the *Treatise* contained the germ of the Keynesian bargain between the state and the business sector, in which the government would employ its policy levers to maintain the conditions for profitable accumulation, and firms would go out and make capital investments and hire workers. After the Second World War, a version of this bargain would be struck in many advanced countries, including Britain and the United States. In the early 1930s, however, Western governments were still tied to old economic doctrines, and they were wary of expanding state intervention in the economy.

In Britain, it took a full-blown financial crisis to break the policy paralysis. In the summer of 1931, after Germany had left the gold standard, international investors started to sell sterling for gold, which depleted the Bank of England's stock of the precious metal. The bank raised interest rates to make sterling assets more attractive, but the selling continued. In late July a committee of experts chaired by Sir George May of the Prudential insurance company advised the Labour government to introduce a range of austerity measures that included cutting roadbuilding programs and slashing unemployment benefits by a fifth. The prime minister himself wrote to Keynes and asked him for advice. In his reply, Keynes described the committee's proposals as "a most gross perversion of social justice" and said they were pointless because "it is now nearly *certain* that we shall go off the existing gold parity at no distant date."[28] With the trade union movement and many Labour MPs strongly opposed to austerity measures, MacDonald and his cabinet couldn't agree on what to do. On August 24, 1931, MacDonald offered his resignation to King George V, who urged him to stay on and form a National Government with the support of Conservatives and Liberals. To the outrage of many Labour Party members, MacDonald agreed. In early September, the House of Commons approved a package of spending cuts, but investors and speculators continued to offload sterling regardless. Finally, over the weekend of September 19–20, after another week of heavy gold losses, the Bank of England and Downing Street gave up the fight. On Monday the 21st, the Chancellor of the Exchequer announced that Britain was suspending the convertibility of sterling to gold. Keynes, who had stayed in Tilton as the crisis unfolded, was vindicated. In a note to her mother-in-law, Lydia wrote: "M. is very pleased and says it is 'new chapter.'"[29]

Keynes was right: the demise of the gold standard was a historic moment. In the short run, however, the Great Depression only intensified on both sides of the Atlantic. Some of the images from its depths are still familiar: "Hoovervilles"—shantytowns of homeless people—springing up in many American cities; cloth-capped British workers walking hundreds of miles to London in the National Hunger March of September–October 1932; President Von Hindenburg, the World War I veteran, swearing in Adolf Hitler as chancellor of Germany on January 30, 1933. The nineteenth century had seen some major financial blowups, and the economic slump after World War I had been long and punishing, but industrial capitalism was now facing its greatest crisis. So were its defenders and would-be reformers.

Five weeks after Hitler's swearing-in, Franklin Delano Roosevelt, the newly elected Democratic president of the United States, delivered his inaugural address, in which he proclaimed, "The only thing we have to fear is fear itself." Roosevelt's predecessor, the Republican Herbert Hoover, after initially dithering, had taken a number of steps to stabilize the stricken US economy, including setting up the Reconstruction Finance Corporation to lend to stricken banks and support public works projects. But these initiatives had come too late. Roosevelt and his kitchen cabinet, which included a number of progressive academics, knew that more drastic actions were necessary. The day after the inauguration, Roosevelt declared a national banking holiday. On March 9, 1933, Congress passed an Emergency Banking Act that effectively introduced a system of federal deposit insurance, which ensured depositors couldn't lose their money. This measure restored public confidence in the banking system and put an end to the runs that had plagued the Hoover administration. Later in March, Roosevelt announced the creation of a Civilian Conservation Corps, which would provide work relief programs for unemployed young men across the country. And in April, he issued an executive order suspending US participation in the gold standard—a decision that Keynes hailed as "Magnificently Right."[30]

Although Keynes admired FDR's activism, his links to and influence on the Roosevelt administration were somewhat tenuous. Although the president was determined to tackle mass joblessness, he was hardly a proto "Keynesian." He had campaigned for office on a platform of reducing the federal deficit, and one of the first measures he introduced was a cut in federal salaries. Many of FDR's advisers believed that the quickest way to revive the economy was to stabilize prices, which had fallen sharply, by preventing cutthroat competition among firms and raising wages. This was the thinking behind the National Industrial Recovery Act, which Congress passed in June 1933. In May 1934, during a trip to the United States, Keynes met with Roosevelt at the White House. The president told Felix Frankfurter, his friend and legal adviser, that he had "a grand talk with Keynes and liked him immensely," but not much came of it.[31] Keynes pressed Roosevelt's advisers to raise the level of federal relief spending if they could. A year later the US administration did go down this route. In April 1935 Congress appropriated $4.9 billion dollars for a nationwide program of emergency relief and public works projects—schools, hospitals, highways, and the like, about $1.4 billion of which went to the new Works Progress Administration (WPA), which Roosevelt soon created by executive order.[32] The level of spending was unprecedented, but the creators of the WPA viewed it primarily as a public relief program designed to employ jobless workers, rather than as a measure designed to prop up overall demand.

The first conscious application of what came to be known as Keynesian stimulus policies occurred in Sweden, which, like Britain, was forced off the gold standard in September 1931. Two years later, the Swedish Social Democratic Party, which occupied roughly the same political space as Germany's SPD and Britain's Labour Party, formed a ruling coalition with the Agrarian Party. To tackle sky-high unemployment, the new government launched an ambitious program of public works, which it financed by issuing debt and running budget deficits. The political champion of this expansionist policy was the finance minister Ernst Wigforss, who had been influenced by Keynes's 1929 pamphlet, *Can Lloyd George Do It?* Several young Swedish economists, particularly Gunnar Myrdal and Bertil Ohlin, also provided an intellectual justification for this policy. Indeed, they antedated Keynes in arguing that the government should balance the budget over the full economic cycle, with surpluses in the years of strong growth offsetting deficits built up during recessions.[33] The Swedish medicine seemed to work. Between 1932 and 1937, the country's unemployment rate, as was reported at the time, declined from 22.4 percent to 10.8 percent.[34]

Keynes, meanwhile, was working on providing a more comprehensive theoretical justification for countercyclical public spending. His previous book, *A Treatise on Money*, hadn't explained what factors determined the overall level of output and employment. Since Keynes was calling on the government to use monetary and fiscal policy to achieve full employment, this was a big gap. The process of filling it began in 1932 and would take him nearly four years. It involved extensive discussions with his colleagues and students in Cambridge, and several iterations of writing and editing. By early 1935, he had completed a draft of a new book that was generally to his satisfaction. He had also settled on a title: *The General Theory of Employment, Interest and Money*. In a letter to George Bernard Shaw, the playwright and socialist, he wrote: "To understand my state of mind . . . you have to know that I believe myself to be writing a book on economic theory, which will largely revolutionise—not, I suppose, at once but in the course of the next ten years—the way the world thinks about economic problems." Immodest as it was, this prediction proved accurate.[35]

The General Theory, as it came to be known, was published in February 1936. Although it contained some vivid passages and brilliant insights, such as a comparison of stock market investing to picking the winner in newspaper beauty contests, it wasn't an easy read, even for professional economists. In fact, parts of the book were so dense that even today there are vigorous debates about what they really mean. Keynes had one interpretation; some of his younger and more radical colleagues had another; the bulk of the economics profession had a third. As Keynes indicated to Shaw, he believed he had invented a new theoretical framework that subsumed "the classical theory" as a special case. This new framework consisted of four basic features: the principle of effective demand, the Keynesian multiplier, the theory of the liquidity preference, and the notion of the marginal efficiency of capital. The first two concepts were the most important, because they underpinned Keynes's convictions that capitalism could be successfully managed and that the Great Depression had resulted from grave policy errors rather than an incurable flaw in the system.

The principle of effective demand states that the overall levels of output and employment are determined by "aggregate demand"—the sum of all individual demands for goods and services. Today this principle is widely regarded as a truism, but in 1936 it represented a departure from economic orthodoxy, which emphasized factors on the supply side of the economy, such as the level of wages, the state of technology, and rates of profitability. Contrary to some accounts, Keynes didn't ignore the supply side. In chapter 2 of *The General Theory*, he stated explicitly that the economy would come to rest where "the aggregate demand function" was "intersected by the aggregate supply function."[36] Supply factors determined the economy's potential output. However, Keynes rejected the classical claim that supply created its own demand, otherwise known as Say's Law. In his new framework, the aggregate demand curve determined where the economy came to rest, and its position was determined by the levels of consumer spending, business investment, government spending, and net exports.

In casting his analysis in terms of supply and demand curves, Keynes employed a method that had been familiar to economists since 1890, when Alfred Marshall published the first edition of his *Principles of Economics*. Marshall's supply-and-demand schedules represented the operation of a single product market—say, the market for concrete cinder blocks in Cleveland. Keynes's curves represented the entire economy—hence the term *macroeco-*

nomics. Depending on the relative positions of the aggregate demand and aggregate supply curves, the point where they intersected could occur at a high, low, or intermediate level of employment. "There is no reason in general for expecting it to be *equal* to full employment," Keynes wrote. "The effective demand associated with full employment is a special case, only realised when the propensity to consume and the inducement to invest stand in a particular relationship to one another."[37] What was worse, if the economy came to rest at a position where employment was below its full-employment level, it could easily get stuck there. Even if wages fell—the traditional remedy for hard times—that wouldn't restore full employment because firms, facing weak demand for their products, would still see no reason to hire more workers. In fact, falling wages could lead to a higher level of unemployment if they produced a further drop in aggregate demand.

In this setup, the level of aggregate demand is obviously vital, but what determines it? The multiplier provided the answer. Keynes picked up this concept from one of his brightest students, Richard Kahn, who in 1930 was elected to a fellowship at King's. In 1931 Kahn published an article in *The Economic Journal* entitled "The Relation of Home Investment to Unemployment," which explained how, in a country suffering from unemployment and excess capacity, a dollar's worth of new investment spending (by the public or private sector) can circulate through the economy and produce more than a dollar's worth of extra output and employment. Say a local government allocates $10 million to rebuild an old bridge across a river. When work starts on the repair project, it creates income for individuals who get hired to do the job. They will then spend some of their wages on goods and services produced by other people, who in turn will do the same thing. And so on. In this manner, the initial boost to capital investment leads to successive rounds of spending: it has a "multiplier" effect.

Keynes said that the size of the multiplier depended on how much slack there was in the economy. If there was full employment and most industries were operating at full capacity, additional spending would lead to higher prices: the multiplier would fall toward zero. But in 1936, Britain and most other advanced countries were far from full employment. Relying on figures from the Russian American economist Simon Kuznets, Keynes estimated that the US multiplier had been about 2.5 during the late 1920s, and he said it was likely even higher now that the economy was in a slump, with lots of resources lying idle.[38] Turning to Great Britain, Keynes argued that there was so much joblessness and spare capacity that it didn't matter exactly how the government increased its spending: the important thing was to raise aggregate demand in one way or another. "If the Treasury were to fill old bottles with banknotes," he wrote, "bury them at suitable depths in disused coalmines which are then filled up to the surface with town rubbish, and leave it to private enterprise on well-tried principles of laissez-faire to dig the notes up again . . . there need be no more unemployment . . . It would, indeed, be more sensible to build houses and the like; but if there are political and practical difficulties in the way of this, the above would be better than nothing."[39]

Not surprisingly, Keynes is often referred to as a prophet of the economic middle way. At least in theory, his policy framework provided a center path between laissez-faire and the state diktat associated with communism and fascism. In the final chapter of *The General Theory*, he discussed some of its political implications. Given the imperative of encouraging capital investment, the government would need to keep interest rates at very low levels, he explained, much lower than previously. "Now, though this state of affairs would be quite compatible with some measure of individualism," he went on, "it would mean the euthanasia of the rentier"—who lived on interest payments—"and, consequently, the euthanasia of the cumulative oppressive power of the capitalist to exploit the scarcity-value of capital."[40] It was this scarcity that kept interest rates high, but there was no reason why it had to continue, Keynes argued. If private savings were too small to finance the level of investment needed to maintain full employment, "communal saving through the agency of the State" could make up the shortfall.[41] The key point was that in order to keep up the level of aggregate demand, the government would need to use all the tools at its disposal, including low interest rates, tax and spending policies, and even a "somewhat comprehensive socialisation of investment."[42]

This passage was to cause a good deal of confusion. Despite some of the language it contained, Keynes hadn't changed his stripes and embraced wholesale state direction of the economy. The government's expanded role in bolstering capital investment "need not exclude all manner of compromises and of devices by which public authority will cooperate with private initiative," he hastened to add. "Moreover, the necessary measures of socialization can be introduced gradually and without a break in the general traditions of society."[43] Keynes also said that the policy approach he advocated was, in some respects, "moderately conservative in its applications."[44] Once the government had created a level of demand adequate to ensure full employment, it could largely rely on market forces to determine exactly what items were produced and consumed. The consequences for efficiency of decentralization were "even greater, perhaps, than the nineteenth century supposed," Keynes continued. "But, above all, individualism, if it can be purged of its defects and its abuses, is the best safeguard of personal liberty in the sense that, compared with any other system, it greatly widens the field for the exercise of personal choice."[45]

In interpreting these passages, it's important to remember the context in which Keynes was writing. By 1936 the fascist states of Germany and Italy had abandoned laissez-faire for central direction and free trade for autarky. In the Soviet Union, Stalin's regime had completed the brutal collectivization of agriculture and was investing massively in heavy industry. Some of Keynes's colleagues and students at Cambridge were embracing communism. The only way to save capitalism and democracy, he believed, was to rid the capitalist system of mass joblessness, even if that meant a significant expansion of state intervention. "It is certain that the world will not much longer tolerate the unemployment which, apart from brief intervals of excitement, is associated—and, in my opinion, inevitably associated—with present-day capitalistic individualism," he wrote. "But it may be possible by a right analysis of the problem to cure the disease whilst preserving efficiency and freedom."[46]

The argument that Western capitalism, left to its own devices, would eventually succumb to stagnation and high unemployment echoed some left-wing arguments, but Keynes remained the furthest thing from a Marxist. He portrayed capitalism not as an oppressive system that was doomed to collapse but as a trusty old vehicle that had developed a problem with its starter—"magneto trouble," as he put it in one of his journalistic essays about the great slump.[47] To his mind, the problem lay not with the vehicle but with the repair shop's failure to recognize what was ailing it and its refusal to apply new thinking about how to fix it. In his famous closing passage of *The General Theory*, he wrote:

> The ideas of economists and political philosophers, both when they are right and when they are wrong, are more powerful than is commonly understood. Indeed the world is ruled by little else. Practical men, who

believe themselves to be quite exempt from any intellectual influences, are usually the slave of some defunct economist. Madmen in authority, who hear voices in the air, are distilling their frenzy from some academic scribbler of a few years back.[48]

Over the long run, *The General Theory* was to prove enormously influential. In immediate terms, however, it didn't have much impact on policy. By 1936 the unemployment rate was finally falling on both sides of the Atlantic, and political pressure for additional relief spending was relenting. In Britain, Stanley Baldwin's National Government, which had taken office in 1935, concentrated largely on foreign policy and the threats presented by Hitler and Mussolini. In Washington and on Wall Street, concerns were rising over the budget deficit, which had exceeded 4 percent of GDP for most of FDR's first term.[49] In 1936–37 these concerns prompted the Roosevelt administration to reduce federal spending. Following this negative shock to aggregate demand, the US economy fell back into recession, just as Keynesian theory predicted.

On both sides of the Atlantic, what finally brought the Great Depression to a permanent end was the enormous expenditure on armaments before and during the Second World War. This was a Keynesian stimulus on a huge scale, but at the time it wasn't thought of, or labeled, as such. Keynesian methods weren't officially adopted until World War II and its aftermath. In 1944 Winston Churchill's government published a white paper on employment policy that began: "The government accept as one of their primary aims and responsibilities the maintenance of a high and stable level of employment after the war . . . A country will not suffer from mass unemployment so long as the total demand for its goods and services is maintained at a high level."[50] This passage could have been taken from *The General Theory*.

In the United States, there were parallel developments. In 1944 Alvin Hansen, a Harvard economist who had written an influential primer on *The General Theory* for an American audience, prepared a memorandum for policymakers in the Roosevelt administration, in which he called on the federal government to "ensure and underwrite an adequate volume of purchasing power and effective demand" by greatly expanding public investment and social spending.[51] This Keynesian thinking was subsequently reflected in the Employment Act of 1946, which said "it is the continuing policy and responsibility of the Federal Government . . . to coordinate and utilize all its plans, functions, and resources . . . to promote maximum employment, production, and purchasing power."[52]

Keynes spent much of the Second World War working on international questions and ways to avoid a repeat of the interwar period, when many countries had resorted to economic nationalism, introducing tariffs and engaging in competitive currency devaluations. The result had been financial chaos and a collapse in global trade. To prevent this from happening again, Keynes came up with an ambitious plan for a new international currency, which countries that ran into financial difficulties would be able to borrow at will from a new international lending agency. However, he knew that with Britain virtually bankrupt from financing the war, and with the United States emerging as an economic superpower, making any new international framework a reality depended on gaining the support of Washington.

The Roosevelt administration also wanted an open trading system, which would benefit US exporters. But with the dollar now in the ascendancy, it was wary of plans for a new international currency. Keynes engaged in a series of negotiations with Harry Dexter White, a senior US Treasury official. At an international conference in Bretton Woods, New Hampshire, in July 1944, where Keynes and White led the British and US delegations, representatives from more than forty countries agreed to create a system of fixed but adjustable exchange rates. To help make this system work, the Bretton Woods agreement provided for the establishment of an International Monetary Fund, which would have the power (but not the obligation) to help countries that ran into difficulties maintain a fixed exchange rate; an International Bank for Reconstruction and Development (later called the World Bank), which would help countries rebuild from the war; and an International Trade Organization, which would work to reduce tariffs and other barriers to trade. The proposal for a formal trade body ran aground in the US Senate, which still contained many protectionists. But in October 1947, twenty-three nations, including the United States, reached a General Agreement on Tariffs and Trade (GATT), which committed them to opening up markets. It would subsequently be expanded in long-running rounds of negotiation.

The Bretton Woods agreement didn't fulfill all of Keynes's hopes, and he bitterly resented that some American officials seemed intent on undermining what remained of Britain's international leadership role. But the new international framework did meet his basic goal of reestablishing an open trading order and addressing some of the pathologies of international capitalism that had blighted the interwar years, such as unrestricted speculative flows of financial capital. Although the Bretton Woods agreement contained a long-term commitment to the free movement of financial capital across borders, it allowed countries to maintain capital controls for the foreseeable future. "What used to be heresy is now endorsed as orthodoxy," Keynes commented approvingly.[53]

Although Keynes was referring here to the relatively narrow issue of controlling flows of hot money, his statement had application to economic policymaking generally. After the disasters of the interwar era, policymakers in many countries were open to the idea of fashioning a new economic order that stabilized global capitalism, eliminated some of its more offensive and self-destructive features, and allowed more countries to share its bounties. Critics on the left and right expressed skepticism about whether this order would be sustainable, but Keynes believed in it until the last breath he took, which was on April 21, 1946, at his Tilton farmhouse. He died of a heart attack. During the three decades after his passing, an age often referred to as the Keynesian Era, history appeared to prove him right: Western countries enjoyed unprecedented growth and prosperity. But some skeptics remained, including a then-little-known Austro-Hungarian writer and scholar who, during the interwar years, had witnessed the lurch toward fascism firsthand.

16

Karl Polanyi's Warnings About Capitalism and Democracy

If Keynes's belief in the salvageability of industrial capitalism and liberal democracy reflected his background in England, Edwardian liberalism, and the mandarin class of a global empire, Karl Polanyi's much darker view emerged from the tumult and extremism that his native central Europe experienced in the years after the Great War. He was born in 1886 in Vienna, which was then one of the capitals of the sprawling Austro-Hungarian Empire. Like Keynes, he was a product of the educated upper middle class. His father, Mihály Pollascek, was a Hungarian-born Jewish entrepreneur, whose engineering firm built railroads. When Polanyi was young, the family moved to Budapest, where it settled in an affluent neighborhood largely populated by assimilated Jews. The Hungarian capital had a lively arts scene, and Polanyi's mother, Cecilia Wohl, was an enthusiastic participant. A feminist and a free spirit, she founded a private women's college, hosted a literary salon, and created an Academy of Eurhythmics.

The Polanyi family, which adopted the Magyar form of its name after Mihály died, emphasized education. Karl and his three siblings were home-tutored in English, Latin, and Greek. (One of his brothers, Michael, would become an eminent scientist and philosopher.) After attending the exclusive Minta Gymnasium on a scholarship, Polanyi went to the University of Budapest, where he majored in law and cofounded a student's club called the Galileo Circle, which was dedicated to the "defence and propagation of unprejudiced science."[1] Hungary afforded Judaism the same legal status as Christianity, but antisemitism was still widespread, especially among the old Magyar elite. On one occasion, some conservative students tried to disrupt a meeting of Polanyi's student society, and he got into a brawl with them. The university expelled him, forcing him to finish his degree at the University of Kolozsvár, a city in Transylvania that was then under Hungarian rule.

As a young man, Polanyi leaned left. However, like Eduard Bernstein, the German revisionist socialist, he was skeptical of predictions of capitalism's imminent demise. In a 1910 essay entitled "The Crisis of Our Ideologies," he wrote: "The next period of the capitalist age will produce largely stable conditions of material existence."[2] Polanyi's mentor was Oszkár Jászi, a charismatic Hungarian sociologist who founded a progressive journal and espoused universal suffrage. In June 1914, Polanyi helped Jászi establish the National Citizens' Radical Party, which supported voting rights, state control of education, and distributing land from large estates to the peasantry. Just weeks after the new party was created, the First World War began. The period of capitalist stability ended a lot more quickly than Polanyi (and many others) had expected.

Viewing himself as a Hungarian patriot, he enlisted in the army. For almost three years, he served as a cavalry officer. Assigned to the Russian Front, he was part of a unit that built horse-drawn railways to move military supplies. The carnage and banality of the war appalled him. "Humanity is a Golem which stares with horror at its own frozen mask, the tortured soul at the terrible machine," he wrote to his aunt Irma.[3] In 1917 Polanyi became gravely ill with typhus and was sent home to recover. He survived the life-threatening illness, but its after-effects continued to bedevil him. In November 1918, after the war finally ended, Hungary severed its long-standing ties with Austria and proclaimed itself a republic led by Count Mihály Károlyi, a wealthy aristocrat.

Polanyi was still ailing during these events, but from his sickbed he supported Károlyi's coalition government, which included representatives of the Social Democratic Party of Hungary, the Hungarian equivalent of the German SPD, and Jászi's Radical Party. The new regime was subjected to withering attacks by the Party of Communists, which Béla Kun, a former journalist who had strong ties to the Russian Bolsheviks, had recently founded. Sufficiently recovered to deliver a lecture at the University of Budapest, Polanyi spoke out against the "rising Communist tide."[4]

With workers' councils springing up in Vienna and other cities, and with much of the country still occupied by foreign troops that had fought on the side of the allies against the Central Powers, Károlyi's coalition struggled to govern effectively and lasted only a few months. In March 1919 the Social Democrats joined with the Communists to take power and form a Hungarian Soviet Republic. Given the dire situation, Polanyi recognized the need for a government supported by the urban masses, and he accepted a post in the new People's Commissariat of Social Production.[5]

The new leftist regime introduced a range of progressive policies, including a right to work, a liberalization of the divorce laws, and free medical examinations and school meals for children. It also organized a military counteroffensive, which, for a time, pushed back the foreign soldiers, who included Romanians, Serbs, and Czech-Slovaks. Polanyi, by this time, was sick in the hospital again, but he seems to have been enthused. On May 2, 1919, he wrote to an associate: "I am joining the [Communist] Party."[6] That didn't happen. In his deeply researched 2016 biography of Polanyi, which I have relied on for many biographical details, the British political scientist Gareth Dale cited evidence that Polanyi regarded the Kun regime's economic policies, which included nationalizing thousands of businesses, as counterproductive.[7]

In June 1919, Polanyi traveled to Vienna for additional medical treatment, which meant he wasn't in Budapest to witness the demise of the Hungarian Soviet Republic. Its leaders had been hoping that the Allies would intervene to save the republic, but that didn't happen. In rural areas, many peasants and landowners turned against the Kun government, and the country spiraled into violence and terror. In August, with Romanian troops at the gates of Budapest, Kun and other high-ranking Communists fled to Austria.

After the Romanians occupied the capital, conservative paramilitaries, local police, and their political allies instigated a campaign of violence in which many supporters of the prior government were executed without trial. In early 1920, the National Assembly established a Kingdom of Hungary, in which Miklós Horthy, an ultraconservative navy admiral who had raised a "National Army" of anti-Communists to fight Kun's government, served as regent. The new regime was avowedly nationalist, Christian, and anti-socialist. It continued the so-called White Terror, in which thousands of people were killed and many others were imprisoned. Forces associated with the new regime also carried out anti-Jewish pogroms. Hungary was heading down a path that would see it ally with Mussolini's Italy and, eventually, with Hitler's Germany.

Polanyi wanted no part of this present or future. He settled in Vienna, and to support himself, he became a journalist. Initially, he worked on a Hungarian exile magazine edited by Jászi, who had also moved to Austria. Eventually he got a job with a Viennese current affairs magazine, *Der Österreichische Volkswirt* (The Austrian Economist). After starting out as a freelance book reviewer, in 1925 he became part of the publication's editing staff, which improved his financial position. By then, he was a married father. His spouse, Ilona Duczyńska, was an irrepressible Polish Hungarian who had trained in mathematics and engineering but quickly turned her energies to revolutionary activity. In Budapest, she had been an official in the Kun regime, and she had also spent a brief period in Moscow working for the Comintern. Subsequently, she had been expelled from the Hungarian Communist Party for criticizing some of its practices. In 1923 Polanyi and Duczyńska got married and had a daughter, Kari.

Like Weimar Germany, Austria had emerged from World War I as a democratic republic riven by class conflict, high rates of inflation, and right-wing paramilitary groups; the Austrian equivalent of Germany's Freikorps was the Heimwehr. During the 1920s, a series of center-right governments held office at the national level, but in Vienna the Social Democratic Workers' Party (SDWP), the Austrian sister party to the German SPD, oversaw a unique experiment in municipal socialism. "Red Vienna," as it came to be known, introduced an eight-hour workday, unemployment benefits, and an extensive system of public services. It built public health centers, kindergartens, bathhouses, and large municipal housing complexes, including the famous Karl Marx Hof. Polanyi spent more than a decade in Red Vienna and came to view it as a moral and intellectual inspiration. Although Ilona's politics were to the left of his, they both joined the SDWP. He would later say that Vienna and its socialist administration "achieved one of the most spectacular cultural triumphs of Western history."[8]

Interwar Vienna was also a maelstrom of intellectual activity, particularly in the social sciences, and Polanyi actively participated in some ongoing debates. During his recovery from typhoid at the end of the Great War, he had converted from Judaism to Christianity. When he moved to Vienna, he became friendly with several British Christian Socialists who had settled in the city. He was particularly influenced by the works of G. D. H. Cole, the English historian and guild socialist, whose vision of an ideal society combined political democracy with workers' control of their places of employment. In a 1921 letter to his brother Michael, Polanyi said that the "English socialist practice confirmed the direction of my work. To discuss social problems from a Christian viewpoint—this is my socialism."[9] In an article he wrote for the Hungarian exile magazine, Polanyi praised guild socialism for its pluralism and encouragement of independent groups such as trade unions, cooperatives, church associations, and municipal councils.[10] He envisaged a society where class conflict would be superseded by negotiations between groups representing producers (workers) and consumers.[11] He even set up a guild socialism study group. According to Gareth Dale, its members included a young philosopher, Karl Popper, and Peter Drucker, a fellow journalist who would go on to be a well-known writer on management.[12]

From across Europe, progressives flocked to Vienna to witness the latest innovations of the socialist administration. Austria as a whole remained deeply divided. It was a conservative rural country with a cosmopolitan urban capital ruled by leftists. Throughout the 1920s, there were occasional clashes between right and left. As in Germany, the onset of the Great Depression accentuated political tensions and eventually led to a breakdown. After the country's largest bank, Creditanstalt, collapsed in May 1931, the economic slump deepened, and the unemployment rate eventually rose to 25 percent. In May 1932 Engelbert Dollfuss, a thirty-nine-year-old former army officer and businessman, became chancellor of a new right-wing coalition, which consisted of his Christian Social Party, the Landbund, a right-wing peasants' party, and the Heimatblock, the political arm of the Heimwehr. Dollfuss had eyes on establishing an authoritarian government. His role model was Benito Mussolini, the leader of Italy, rather than Hitler, but events in Germany were to hasten his efforts.

On January 30, 1933, Germany's president, Paul von Hindenburg, a former field marshal who had led the Imperial Army during World War I, invited Hitler to serve as chancellor atop a coalition government. Hindenburg was acting on the advice of Franz von Papen, a conservative aristocrat who had recently served as chancellor. Von Papen argued that bringing Hitler and his National

Socialist party into the government in this manner would keep him "boxed in" and prevent the left from taking power. Alarmed by the rise of the Comintern-aligned Communist Party of Germany, which gained about 13 percent of the vote in a federal election held in July 1932, some business leaders supported this strategy, which proved disastrous. Within two months of becoming chancellor, Hitler had established a dictatorship that would last until he committed suicide in his Führerbunker on April 30, 1945.

On March 4, 1933, as Hitler's brownshirts were moving to eliminate their opponents in the Reichstag and elsewhere, Dollfuss staged a coup of his own. After the parliament in Vienna deadlocked on how to respond to a strike by railroad workers, he declared a state of emergency. With the police, the army, and many business interests supporting him, he claimed the power to rule without parliamentary approval and moved to ban three groups that he considered a threat: the Austrian Communist Party; the paramilitary arm of the SDWP (the Repubikanischer Schutzbund); and the Austrian Nazi Party, which had been emboldened by Hitler's seizure of power. As an Austrian nationalist, Dollfuss wanted no part of the Anschluss (unification with Germany) that the Nazis were demanding. In August 1933 he reached a mutual defense pact with Mussolini's Italy, and the following month, he merged the parties that made up his coalition in a new Fatherland Front—an Austrian version of Il Duce's National Fascist Party.

Although Dollfuss's government initially left in place the leftist administration in Vienna, it was an unabashedly authoritarian regime that censored the press and harried independent-minded journalists. Polanyi, who had risen to a senior editing post at *Der Österreichische Volkswirt*, could see where things were heading. He decided to move to London and create a new life for himself and his family. He left Vienna in January 1934, leaving behind, for the moment, his wife and daughter. Within weeks of his departure, violence broke out in the Austrian capital and other cities after elements of the Heimwehr tried to arrest some socialist politicians. Members of the banned Schutzbund barricaded themselves into Vienna's housing projects, including Karl Marx Hof, and squared off against the police and the Heimwehr. Dollfuss ordered the Austrian army to attack the socialists, which it did with gusto. After putting down the uprising, Dollfuss banned the SDWP, leaving his Fatherland Front as the only legitimate political organization in the country. He also introduced a new constitution that replaced parliamentary democracy with authoritarian corporatism on the Italian model. Austrofascism was born.

Polanyi had now seen two democratic leftist governments overthrown from the right in fifteen years. With fascism firmly established in much of western Europe, including its biggest country, he was determined to write about the phenomenon, but first he needed to get a job in his new home, London. He didn't find it easy, but through his contacts in the Christian Socialist community, he was eventually invited to coedit a collection of essays for a book entitled *Christianity and the Social Revolution*. The job gave him the opportunity to contribute an essay of his own.

At the time, there was a good deal of confusion about the relationship between fascism, Christianity, and capitalism. In 1929, Mussolini and the Vatican had signed the Lateran Treaty, in which the Italian dictator recognized papal sovereignty over the Vatican City and Italy's bishops agreed to take an oath of loyalty to the Italian state. In Germany, the Catholic Church originally opposed Hitler and the Nazis. Shortly after he took power, however, the Vatican negotiated a treaty with his regime—the *Reichskonkordat*—in which the German church agreed to stay out of politics in return for its followers being allowed to practice their religion freely. Polanyi regarded these accommodations with fascism as abominations. At the start of his essay, which was published in 1935 under the title "The Essence of Fascism," he wrote: "Victorious Fascism is not only the downfall of the Socialist Movement; it is the end of Christianity in all but its most debased forms."[13]

His argument wasn't based simply on the evil designs of Hitler, Mussolini, and their followers: it rested on philosophical foundations. Polanyi argued that in prioritizing individual development and natural rights, Christianity and socialism—his version of socialism, at least—were both based on individualism, whereas fascism represented the negation of individualism. Citing the works of Othmar Spann, a conservative Austrian philosopher who was popular at the time, he pointed out that many intellectuals sympathetic to fascism traced the rise of socialism to the emergence of individualism and democracy and believed that, in order to remove the socialist threat, it was necessary to eliminate the phenomena that gave rise to it. "Thus, if Socialism is not to be, democracy must go," Polanyi wrote. "This is the *raison d'être* of the Fascist movements in Europe."[14]

The essay also discussed fascism's relationship with capitalism. The fascists' propaganda, Polanyi pointed out, often coupled individual capitalists with socialists as enemies of the patriotic common people, but they largely spared big corporations from criticism. "The popular resentment against Liberal Capitalism is thus turned most effectively against Socialism without any reflection on Capitalism in its non-Liberal, i.e., corporative, forms," Polanyi wrote. "Though unconsciously performed, the trick is highly ingenious. First Liberalism is identified with Capitalism; then Liberalism is made to walk the plank; but Capitalism is no worse for the dip, and continues its existence unscathed under a new alias"—fascism, that is.[15] In the early days of capitalism, Polanyi noted, it had been taken for granted that capitalism and democracy were compatible, partly because they had emerged around the same time. This comforting assumption had now been challenged.

"The mutual incompatibility of Democracy and Capitalism," Polanyi wrote, "is almost generally accepted to-day as the background of the social crisis of our time."[16] The left widely assumed that democracy would lead to some form of socialism. On the right, too, many argued that democracy threatened capitalism because workers' parties gradually undermined the sanctity of property rights. Polanyi referred to a statement from Mussolini that democracy was an anachronism because "only an authoritative State can deal with the contradictions inherent in Capitalism."[17] In other essays that Polanyi wrote in the mid-1930s, he pointed out some of these contradictions, including a tendency for democratic parties to interfere with the market mechanism and undermine corporate profitability. In one of these pieces, he said that democracy and capitalism "have reached a deadlock, because they have become the instruments of two different classes of opposing interests."[18]

In "The Essence of Fascism," Polanyi emphasized the agreement on the left and the right that there were only two solutions to this problem: "The extension of the democratic principle from politics to economics, or the abolition of the Democratic 'political sphere' altogether."[19] In the first option, private ownership of the means of production would be ended, and the economy would no longer exist as an autonomous entity separate from politics. "This, essentially is Socialism," Polanyi remarked. The second option involved the abolition of the "democratic political sphere," thus creating a situation in which "only economic life remains; Capitalism as organized in the different branches of industry becomes the whole of society. This is the Fascist solution."[20]

Although Polanyi didn't, at this stage, explicitly endorse the catastrophist analysis that liberal capitalist democracy was doomed, his essay certainly suggested that history was moving in this direction. So far, he noted, neither the democracy/socialism nor fascism/capitalism options had been fully realized. In Russia, Polanyi wrote, socialism was "still in the dictatorial phase, although the tendency toward Democracy has become clearly discernible." (Like many on the European left, he initially was reluctant to recognize the reality of Stalinism.) In Germany and Italy, meanwhile, Hitler and Mussolini were moving "reluctantly towards the setting up of the Corporative State," seemingly mindful of the fact that "a generation which has known Democracy cannot be trusted to be ripe for corporative citizenship."[21]

Among Polanyi's English friends and associates, his article was well received, but it didn't bring him the full-time academic post that he had been hoping for. After Ilona and Kari moved to England in 1936, the family found life to be a financial struggle. Eventually Polanyi got a job teaching British social and economic history at the Workers' Educational Association, which provided evening instruction for people who hadn't had a higher education. He taught classes in Sussex and in Kent. The obligations of the job were taxing and the pay modest, but Polanyi used his lectures to develop his ideas about the historical roots of fascism, which he planned to turn into a book at some point.

In the meantime, he cited some of the historical material he was teaching in another essay, "The Fascist Virus," which he completed at the end of the 1930s. Mentioning, among other things, the rise and fall of Chartism in Britain, Polanyi noted that the tensions between democracy and capitalism went back to the early industrial era. During the rapid economic growth of the late nineteenth century, it had seemed possible that the two phenomena could coexist peacefully. "During this short period of time, capitalism and democracy seemed to flourish side by side," he wrote. "The illusion of harmony was the result of transitory factors, such as the enormous expansion of [the] market, the sharing of trade unions and labour parties in the benefits of the advance, as well as the false impression created by the American scene. The worldwide mass unemployment of the 1930s has caused a re-emergence of the dilemma of capitalism vs democracy."[22]

Although Polanyi, his wife and daughter, and his brother Michael were now living safely in England, the expansion of fascism's most pathological variant,

German National Socialism, presented a deadly threat to some of his family members who had stayed in Vienna, particularly his younger sister, Sophie, her husband, Egon, and their son Karl, who had developmental issues. By 1939, Austrofascism had succumbed to the Nazis and Hitler. In March 1938, German troops marched across the border to enforce an Anschluss. Soon after that, Gareth Dale recounts,[23] Egon was arrested in a random raid and sent to the Dachau concentration camp, near Munich. Shortly before the Second World War began, the Nazi regime agreed to grant passports to Sophie and Egon, despite his captivity, but it refused to release Egon unless they left young Karl behind or secured a visa for him. Refusing to abandon her son, Sophie stayed in Vienna.

Polanyi, meanwhile, was about to move again. His continued failure to obtain a full-time academic job in Britain had frustrated him, and in 1940, the year Hitler's forces invaded the Low Countries and France, Bennington College, in Vermont, offered him a post as a visiting lecturer. His old mentor, Oszkár Jászi, had been teaching in America for many years, at Oberlin College in Ohio. Polanyi accepted the job. Once more leaving behind Ilona, who didn't have a US visa, he sailed for the United States. After he had settled in the verdant foothills of the Green Mountains, he began working in earnest on his book, in which he intended to trace the clash between capitalism and democracy back to nineteenth-century Britain, and the creation of a society organized according to the precepts of laissez-faire. The "present world crisis is ultimately due to *market-economy*, as the first phase of industrial civilization," he wrote in a November 1940 letter to Ilona. "The past quarter century was a result of the dissolution of the international economic system based on that economy."[24]

The following year Polanyi obtained a fellowship from the Rockefeller Foundation that enabled him to stay at Bennington and concentrate on his book. To his delight, the college offered Ilona a lectureship in mathematics and physics, and she arrived in Vermont in December 1941. Other aspects of Polanyi's personal life were much less happy. In March 1941, as the Nazis' onslaught on the Jews of Germany and Austria intensified, his sister Sophie and her young son were transported to Poland. A month later Sophie's husband, Egon, was killed at Dachau. According to Dale, Sophie's last known location was a Jewish ghetto in the city of Kielce. Polanyi later wrote: "My dearest little sister was murdered by the madmen."[25]

Physically and psychologically, Bennington was a long way from the horrors taking place in central Europe. Polanyi continued to work on his manuscript, which he had provisionally titled *Origins of the Cataclysm: A Political and Economic Inquiry*. By the time it was ready for publication, in 1944, his publisher, Farrar and Rhinehart, had changed its title to *The Great Transformation: The Political and Economic Origins of Our Time*. "Nineteenth century civilization has collapsed," the first chapter began. "This book is concerned with the political and economic origins of this event, as well as with the great transformation which it ushered in."[26]

Polanyi quickly got to the heart of his argument, which was that the vanished civilization, which he largely equated with industrial Britain, had been built on an unstable foundation: laissez-faire economics. "Our thesis is that the idea of a self-adjusting market implied a stark utopia," he wrote. "Such an institution could not exist for any length of time without annihilating the human and natural substance of society; it would have physically destroyed man and transformed his surroundings into a wilderness."[27] Confronted with the ravages inflicted by the free market, society inevitably took steps to protect itself in the form of social reforms and other measures, Polanyi continued. "But whatever measures it took impaired the self-regulation of the market, disorganized industrial life, and thus endangered society in yet another way. It was this dilemma which forced the development of the market system into a definite groove and finally disrupted the social organization based upon it."[28]

This argument, which Polanyi developed at length throughout the book, actually consisted of two separate claims, and both of them concerned the role of the state. Going back to Adam Smith, orthodox economists had presented a narrative in which the rise of the free market economy represented a retreat of an overweening mercantile state and the spontaneous emergence of a decentralized, self-sustaining order based on individual self-interest. Polanyi insisted that this story was a myth, and that the free market had been imposed on society by a strong state. "There was nothing natural about *laissez-faire*: free markets could never have come into being merely by allowing things to take their course," he wrote. "Just as cotton manufactures—the leading free trade industry—were created by the help of protective tariffs, export bounties, and indirect wage subsidies, *laissez-faire* itself was enforced by the state."[29] Polanyi went on: "The road to the free market was opened and kept open by an enormous increase in continuous, centrally organized and controlled interventionism. To make Adam Smith's 'simple and natural liberty' compatible with the needs of a human society was a most complicated affair."[30]

Elaborating this point, Polanyi pointed out that in the period from the Napoleonic Wars to the abolition of the Corn Laws and the defeat of Chartism—1800 to 1848, roughly—the British state introduced three essential features of the laissez-faire system: a free labor market, free trade, and a stable currency. Polanyi laid particular emphasis on the Poor Law Amendment Act of 1834 that swept away the last vestiges of the old Speenhamland social welfare system, which had provided "outdoor relief" for workers in distress. As a disincentive to idlers, jobless workers were given the choice of fending for themselves or entering one of the spartan workhouses that featured in Dickens's *Oliver Twist*, where they were separated from their families and obliged to work in return for shelter and a daily crust. "The critical stage was reached with the establishment of a labor market in England, in which workers were put under the risk of starvation if they failed to comply with the rules of wage labor," Polanyi wrote. "As soon as this drastic step was taken, the mechanisms of the self-regulating market sprang into gear."[31] Workers were "physically dehumanized," and "the owning classes were morally degraded. The traditional unity of a Christian society was giving place to a denial of responsibility on the part of the well-to-do for the conditions of their fellows."[32]

By the 1830s, Polanyi said, "*laissez-faire* had been catalyzed into a drive of uncompromising ferocity."[33] He pointed out that the passage of the Poor Law Amendment Act, and other measures that enshrined the principles of laissez-faire, were possible only because Britain wasn't yet a proper democracy. Although the Great Reform Act of 1832 had broadened the franchise a little, it still excluded the majority of the population. In subsequent years, when the Chartists demanded universal suffrage (for men), Polanyi noted, their "leaders were jailed; their adherents, numbered in millions, were derided by a legislature representing a bare fraction of the population, and the mere demand for the ballot was often treated as a criminal act by the authorities."[34] This repressive stance was inevitable because it "would have been an act of lunacy to hand over the administration of the New Poor Law with its scientific methods of mental torture to the representatives of the selfsame people for whom that treatment was designed."[35] It was only later in the nineteenth century, after industrial capitalism had been given time to develop and wages had risen, that the voting franchise was extended to British workers. And even then, Polanyi pointed out, many ardent free marketeers were distinctly unenthusiastic about this development: "Inside and outside

England, from Macaulay to Mises, from Spencer to Sumner, there was not a militant liberal who did not express his conviction that popular democracy was a danger to capitalism."[36]

Polanyi's other major claim was that laissez-faire wasn't ultimately sustainable because its harsh nature generated pressure for ameliorative countermeasures. Even though the unrepresentative British Parliament had successfully resisted Chartism, it passed the Ten Hours Bill of 1846, which limited the workday; the Public Health Act of 1848, which facilitated the construction of proper sewers and water supplies; and in subsequent decades, legislation that legalized labor unions and regulated gas utilities. None of these measures were planned or coordinated in advance, Polanyi pointed out. They resulted from efforts by a diverse group of reformers and pressure groups—from High Tory paternalists to workers' organizations to Benthamite technocrats—who were responding to the degradations imposed on society by unregulated capitalist development. "While *laissez-faire* economy was the product of deliberate state action, subsequent restrictions on *laissez-faire* started in a spontaneous way," Polanyi wrote. "*Laissez-faire* was planned; planning was not."[37]

Polanyi described the process of marketization imposed from above followed by social reforms instigated from below as the "double movement." Although he focused on the British example, he argued that this pattern applied to any capitalist society where market and the profit motive were given free rein. In the final third of *The Great Transformation*, he moved his narrative to the late nineteenth century and the huge expansion of international trade and commerce that was stimulated by the steamship and other technological innovations. As industrial capitalism developed on a global scale, Polanyi pointed out, it was accompanied by a rise in protectionism, government interventionism, and imperialism. "These conditions themselves were set by the 'double movement,'" he wrote. "The pattern of international trade which was now spreading at an accelerated rate was crossed by the introduction of protectionist institutions designed to check the all-round action of the market."[38] Polanyi also noted how the so-called Long Depression of 1873–86, which affected many industrial countries, accentuated social and political tensions. By the time the slump ended, he wrote, "Germany had surrounded herself with protective tariffs, established a general cartel organization, set up an all-round social insurance system, and was practicing high-pressure colonial policies."[39]

In Polanyi's telling, no industrialized country could escape the currents and countercurrents of the double movement. "Nations and peoples were mere puppets in a show utterly beyond their control. They shielded themselves from unemployment and instability with the help of central banks and customs tariffs, supplemented by migration laws."[40] The rise of European and US imperialism was another characteristic of the double movement. "Trade and the flag were racing in one another's wake," Polanyi wrote. "Imperialism and half-conscious preparation for autarchy were the bent of Powers which found themselves more and more dependent upon an increasingly unreliable system of world economy."[41] By the start of the twentieth century, the double movement was fundamentally changing the nature of that system. "Less and less could markets be described as autonomous and automatic mechanisms of competing atoms."[42] Laissez-faire and the individualist model of society it was associated with were being superseded, and "external wars merely hastened its destruction."[43]

This sweeping narrative set the stage for Polanyi's treatment of the interwar period. He argued that the great folly of policymakers in the leading industrial countries was to try and re-create the free market capitalist model. "Economic liberalism made a supreme bid to restore the self-regulation of the system," he wrote, "by eliminating all interventionist policies which interfered with the freedom of markets for land, labor, and money."[44] On the domestic front, this restoration project involved balancing budgets, paying down debts, bringing down inflation, and allowing wages to find their natural price in the market. At the international level, it entailed stabilizing currencies by restoring the gold standard, a goal to which "questions of social organization had to be wholly subordinated."[45]

Echoing Keynes, Polanyi said these deflationary policies "heaped up the deficits of the various national economies" and "burdened finance with the unbearable strain of massive economic dislocations" to the point where "a disruption of the remnants of international division of labor became inevitable."[46] In the political realm, the policies accentuated tensions between the forces of capital and organized labor. "The captains of industry were subverting the population from allegiance to their own freely elected rulers, while democratic bodies carried on warfare against the industrial system on which everybody's livelihood depended," Polanyi wrote. "Eventually, the moment would come when both the economic and political systems were threatened by complete paralysis. Fear would grip the people, and leadership would be thrust upon those who offered an easy way out at whatever ultimate price. The time was ripe for the fascist solution."[47]

Having written extensively about fascism in the 1930s, Polanyi didn't spend much time in *The Great Transformation* exploring its philosophical underpinnings. He did say that it, "like socialism, was rooted in a market society that refused to function."[48] If the economic conditions were ripe, he warned, authoritarianism could attract widespread support in many different cultural and racial environments, from Catholic Portugal to Protestant Holland, from militaristic Prussia to civilian Austria, from Aryan Belgium to non-Aryan Japan. "In fact," Polanyi insisted, "there was no type of background—of religious, cultural, or national tradition—that made a country immune to fascism, once the conditions for its emergence were given."[49]

This was the nub of Polanyi's argument. Efforts to subjugate society to the dictates of the free market and the profit motive weren't merely destabilizing. Ultimately, they were incompatible with democracy. As a practical matter, Polanyi explained, the fascist solution to the paralysis of capitalist democracy consisted of "a reform of the market economy achieved at the price of the extirpation of all democratic institutions, both in the industrial and in the political realm."[50] In economic terms, the reform program consisted of smashing the independent labor movement and breaking away from the global trading system to create a self-sufficient economy, a capitalist counterpart of Stalin's socialism in one country.

Pointing to the Nazis' economic policies in Germany, which combined a drive toward autarky with public works projects to soak up unemployment and the cartelization of various business sectors, Polanyi argued that they had been widely misunderstood. He noted that many foreign observers, including Montagu Norman, the head of the Bank of England, continued to believe that the Nazi economic policies were a temporary aberration, and that Hjalmar Schacht, the president of the Reichsbank, would eventually "restore orthodox economics in Germany."[51] (In the early 1920s, Schacht had introduced the currency reform that ended hyperinflation.) These illusions "survived in Downing Street up to the time of Munich and after," Polanyi wrote.[52] He also criticized free market liberals for supporting deflationary policies during the 1920s and refusing to support any efforts to tame the market. Trapped in their ideology, these liberal thinkers and policymakers couldn't see that their visions of a self-regulating free market economy were destined to end in tragedy. "Nowhere did the liberals in fact succeed in re-establishing free enterprise, which was doomed to fail for intrinsic reasons," Polanyi remarked. "Yet the victory of fascism was made practically unavoidable by the liberals' obstruction of any reforms involving planning, regulation, or control."[53]

The thesis presented in *The Great Transformation* was a dark one that challenged the basic foundations of capitalist democracy. At the end of the book, however, Polanyi looked to the future and struck a more upbeat note. Throughout it all—the collapse of Red Vienna, the years of struggle in Britain, and his move to the United States—he had retained his belief in democratic socialism as a sane and civilized alternative to fascism. Even events in the Soviet Union hadn't caused him to abandon the faith. Despite the show trials of the 1930s, he continued to defend Stalin's collectivist policies as historically necessary and economically productive.

Since his first visit to the United States, in the mid-1930s, he had found fresh reasons for optimism. He was greatly enamored of the New Deal, its grand public works projects, and its creator, FDR, whom he regarded as a "great leader" who was creating a "great transformation" in the United States.[54] When, after Pearl Harbor, the Roosevelt administration rapidly placed the US economy on war footing, using administrative fiat to convert great swaths of industry into a huge armaments factory, Polanyi was even more impressed. He hailed the rapid economic mobilization to confront the Axis powers as a demonstration of "democracy at its marvellous best."[55] He fervently hoped that the wartime shift to economic planning and interventionism on both sides of the Atlantic marked a historical turning point. In the final chapter of *The Great Transformation*, he wrote:

> The passing of market economy can become the beginning of an era of un-
> precedented freedom. Judicial and actual freedom can be made wider and
> more general than ever before; regulation and control can achieve free-
> dom not only for the few, but for the all. Freedom not as an appurtenance
> of privilege, tainted at the source, but as a prescriptive right extending
> far beyond the narrow confines of the political sphere into the intimate
> organization of society itself. Thus will old freedoms and civic rights be
> added to the fund of new freedom generated by the leisure and security
> that industrial society offers to all. Such a society can afford to be both
> just and free.[56]

These ringing words appeared the same year that Friedrich Hayek, Polanyi's more famous Austrian contemporary, published *The Road to Serfdom*, his jeremiad against socialism, social democracy, and wartime planning. In Vienna during the 1920s, Polanyi had engaged in a debate with Hayek's intellectual mentor, Ludwig von Mises, about the practicality of socialist planning. As a supporter of democracy, he was sensitive to the argument of Mises, Hayek, and their followers that planning led to the abridgment of freedoms and, ultimately, to dictatorship. He argued that in a guild socialist economy of the sort he favored, decision-making could largely remain decentralized, he argued, with conflicts being resolved through negotiations between groups representing all the major economic interests. By the middle of the Second World War, the debates of the 1920s may have seemed somewhat remote to Polanyi. But at the very end of *The Great Transformation*, he returned to the issue of socialist planning and liberty, writing: "As long as [man] is true to his task of creating more abundant freedom for all, he need not fear that either power or planning will turn against him and destroy the freedom he is building by their instrumentality. This is the meaning of freedom in a complex society; it gives us all the certainty that we need."[57]

Unlike *The Road to Serfdom*, *The Great Transformation* didn't cause much of a stir when it was published. Hayek was invited to go on an American book tour, where he spoke to packed halls, and *Reader's Digest* put out a condensed version of his book. Polanyi was left to mull over his academic reviews, some of which were mixed. "Despite the brilliance of *The Great Transformation* the work is marred by serious flaws," a reviewer in *The American Historical Review* said.[58] At least the book got written about in the United States. In Britain, leading academic journals initially ignored it. This may have been partly because their editors still regarded Polanyi as an outsider lacking prestigious affiliations, but there was another factor. Many English historians regarded his account of British history as oversimplified and, in some aspects, plain wrong. In a letter to Polanyi, G. D. H. Cole described his claim that before 1834 the Speenhamland system of outdoor relief had prevented the emergence of a competitive labor market as a "monstrous exaggeration."[59]

Largely lost in these criticisms was a recognition that *The Great Transformation* wasn't really a history book. It was a work of political economy, which presented a stark and stripped-down model of capitalist development. In assessing any such model, the pertinent question isn't whether it is wrong—any such model is contradicted by some particulars—but whether it is useful in organizing disparate facts and explaining overall trends. Hobson's model of imperialism satisfied this requirement. So did Kondratiev's "long wave" model of capitalist development and Keynes's model of an economy trapped in an underemployment equilibrium. Polanyi's "double movement" was another theory that explained a lot with a little. Its emphasis on the role that the state played in creating a market economy, and on the pressures for reform this unregulated economy inevitably generated, was to stand the test of time.

Unfortunately for Polanyi's standing as a public intellectual, at the moment that *The Great Transformation* was published it didn't seem to be particularly relevant. The disastrous experiences of the interwar years had discredited free market capitalism in many people's eyes, and there was no immediate prospect of it being resurrected in its pre–Great Depression form. As Hayek lamented, history appeared to be moving in the opposite direction. During the Second World War, there was broad political consensus in favor of centralized direction of production and other emergency measures, such as taxing high incomes and windfall profits. And after the war ended in 1945, Keynesianism and social democracy, of various stripes, rose to the ascendancy on both sides of the Atlantic.

In this political environment, Polanyi's work received little attention outside the academy. He remained a good deal less celebrated than his brother Michael, who, in 1944, was elected to the Royal Society in recognition of his scientific achievements. At the end of 1944, Polanyi and his wife, Ilona, returned to London, where he again failed to secure a full-time academic post. After a couple of years of part-time teaching, he decided to return to the United States and wrote to Columbia University, in New York, which had a strong tradition in institutional economics. The economics department offered him a visiting professorship for the spring term of 1947, which he gladly accepted. On arriving in Morningside Heights, he impressed his new colleagues. Shortly after his visiting professorship came to an end, Columbia offered him a more permanent teaching post. So did the University of Chicago and the New School for Social Research, in New York. He accepted the offer from Columbia.

Finally, in his early sixties, Polanyi settled into the life of a respected academic. He lived near the Columbia campus, presided over a graduate seminar in economic history, worked on his own research projects, and socialized with other intellectual refugees from central and eastern Europe. The one major complication in his life was that the US government refused to grant a permanent resident visa to Ilona on account of her Communist past. Eventually he persuaded her to move to Toronto, where he visited her on weekends. In 1953 he retired from his teaching duties at Columbia and moved to Canada himself, although he returned to New York regularly to participate in seminars and other events.

During these years, Polanyi's research focused largely on precapitalist societies, but he also toyed with writing a sequel to *The Great Transformation*. He even came up with a provisional title—*Freedom from Economics*. In a letter he wrote to a colleague in January 1952, he said the new work would "theorize the adjustment of the world to a post-market society with the economy 'consciously embedded' in non-economic institutions."[60] Polanyi didn't complete this book, and his optimism about the possibilities of transcending the market faded. He had lost faith in the postwar British Labour government of Clement Attlee for being too moderate after its initial raft of reforms. He loathed the rise of the Cold War and its chilling impact on intellectual freedom. The reality remained, however, that governments on both sides of the Atlantic had largely jettisoned the religion of laissez-faire, accepting the need for a social safety net, financial regulation, and countercyclical macroeconomic policies. If the process of embedding economic activity in nonmarket institutions wasn't proceeding as rapidly as Polanyi had hoped, there *was* a widespread recognition among Western economic policymakers that unleashing capitalism in the raw would risk repeating the catastrophes of the 1930s. Until this consensus shattered and the supporters of laissez-faire regained political power, Polanyi and other critics of the postwar order would remain somewhat peripheral. But that didn't necessarily imply that their arguments didn't have force. Modern history didn't stop in 1945 or 1955. In many parts of the world, it was only beginning.

17

Two Skeptics of Keynesianism:
Paul Sweezy and Michał Kalecki

It's easy to see why the three decades after the Second World War are often referred to as the Golden Age of industrial capitalism. In the United States between 1950 and 1973, inflation-adjusted GDP grew at an annual rate of 4 percent,[1] and the jobless rate averaged about 4.7 percent.[2] In western Europe, the economic performance was even better: inflation-adjusted GDP grew at an annual rate of 4.8 percent,[3] and unemployment averaged just 2.6 percent.[4] In Japan, where the Western allies created a democratic political system after occupying the country in 1945, economic growth was little short of miraculous: more than 9 percent a year between 1950 and 1973,[5] a period in which the unemployment rate averaged just 1.6 percent.[6] Throughout the advanced economies, productivity, wages, and life expectancy all rose steadily. In the United States, for example, inflation-adjusted median family income—the income of the family right in the middle of the income distribution—doubled between 1947 and 1975.[7]

The official statistics don't identify who the median American family was each year, but it was most likely headed by a non-college-educated factory worker or office worker. In the Western core of the global economy, at least, Keynesian managed capitalism was delivering steadily rising living standards to many workers, especially members of labor unions. In two landmark contracts that General Motors reached with the United Auto Workers in 1948 and 1950, the carmaker agreed to give its workers annual pay raises tied to the cost of living and productivity improvements, as well as providing them with pensions and health insurance. In return, the UAW agreed to respect GM's authority to make managerial and investment decisions. These collective bargaining agreements, the latter of which *Fortune* magazine labeled "The Treaty of Detroit," provided a model for other manufacturing firms. The postwar prosperity was far from shared equally. The United States was still riven by regional and racial divides. Discrimination against Blacks in employment, education, housing, and other aspects of daily life remained a blight on US society. But the overall trend was upward, and it was slanted toward the section of society that Americans refer to as the middle class and other countries call the property-owning working class. As wages and living standards rose, income inequality declined. In 1950 the top 1 percent of American households received about 16 percent of pretax income; by 1973, that figure had fallen to about 11 percent.[8]

The statistics for wages and incomes don't fully capture the scale of the postwar transformation, which also involved a big expansion in the role of government. In Britain, the Labour government of 1945–51, led by Clement Attlee, provided universal old-age pensions, child allowances, unemployment benefits, and sickness benefits. The 1944 Education Act, which was passed by Churchill's wartime coalition, had already introduced universal secondary education. And in 1948, the taxpayer-financed National Health Service went into operation, supplying universal healthcare that was free at the point of service. The Attlee government also strengthened workers' negotiating rights, launched a substantial home-building program, and nationalized some major industries, including coal, power generation and transmission, iron and steel, and the railways.

Attlee and his colleagues viewed these policies as the enactment of democratic socialism British style—a "new Jerusalem" that combined Keynesian economics with active social policy; a Fabian belief in the possibility of creating new public institutions, like the National Health Service; and a limited commitment to state ownership and control. The postwar reforms were born of a dual desire to honor the sacrifices the British citizenry had made during the Second World War and create a more stable, inclusive economy that transcended the individualistic model that had failed so disastrously in the 1920s and '30s. The Attlee government's policies went beyond the US New Deal, but they reflected the same communitarian philosophy that FDR had expounded in his 1941 "Four Freedoms" speech, when he added freedom from want and fear to the traditional mantra of freedom of speech and worship. In an address that Attlee gave when he introduced Labour's manifesto for the 1951 election, the transatlantic echoes were evident:

> We want a society of free men and women—free from poverty, free from fear, able to develop to the full their faculties in co-operation with their fellows, everyone giving and having the opportunity to give service to the community, everyone regarding his own private interest in the light of the interest of others, and of the community; a society bound together by rights and obligations, rights bringing obligations, obligations fulfilled bringing rights; a society free from gross inequalities and yet not regimented nor uniform.

Although the break with the prewar era was particularly evident in Britain, state intervention and state spending also ramped up elsewhere. Taking France, Germany, the UK, and Holland together, total government spending as a share of GDP rose from 29.8 percent in 1950 to 42 percent in 1973, an unprecedented jump outside wartime.[9] In the United States, a big rise in federal spending was initially driven largely by the defense budget, but in the 1960s spending on nondefense programs also picked up sharply. Taking account of federal, state, and local expenditures, overall government spending as a share of US GDP rose from 21.4 percent in 1950 to 31.1 percent in 1973.[10] In virtually all the industrial countries, the fastest-growing area of spending was on social security and other social programs, which increased from 7 percent of GDP to 15 percent between 1950 and 1973, on average.[11]

Especially in Britain, there was a widespread recognition that the creation of a comprehensive welfare state and the expansion of government intervention in other areas of the economy were historic developments. Some center-left thinkers hailed them as utterly transformative. In a 1951 essay entitled "The Transition from Capitalism," Anthony Crosland, a Labour MP and author, wrote: "The most characteristic features of capitalism have all disappeared: the absolute rule of private property, the subjection of the whole of economic life to market influences, the domination of the profit motive, the neutrality of government, typical *laissez-faire* division of income, and the ideology of individual rights."[12] That definitive assessment was premature, to say the least. But Crosland was correct when he pointed out that an epochal change was taking place. In Britain, the state had taken on the responsibility to build an adequate social safety net, keep unemployment low, tame the financial sector, bring utilities under public ownership, tax the rich, and rationalize some key industries. This new form of managed capitalism was more than a mirage, and some of the shrewder left-wing critics of capitalism quickly realized that it represented a serious challenge to their doctrines.

In 1942 Paul Sweezy, a young economics lecturer at Harvard, published *The Theory of Capitalist Development*, which to this day is perhaps the clearest introduction to Marxian and post-Marxian economics. As well as expounding Marx's surplus value theory, Sweezy examined various accounts of capitalist breakdown, including the theories of falling profits and underconsumption, and he went on to discuss imperialism and fascism. It was a panoramic survey, and one of the things that distinguished it from earlier treatments was Sweezy's acknowledgment that Keynesian economics represented a big challenge to some classic leftist theories. "By instituting and continuing a sufficient rate of state consumption . . . it would seem that the state is in a position to bring the economy to a level of full employment and hold it there," Sweezy wrote. Once full employment was achieved, the government could, "through altering the pattern and volume of taxation and expenditure, influence total consumption and total accumulation in any desired direction."[13] In this new policy framework, Sweezy went on, the tendency to underconsumption, "instead of translating itself into chronic depression at a certain stage of development, becomes merely a tendency . . . which may be counteracted by new force, the deliberate action of the state.

"If the drift to economic stagnation can be successfully countered, then why must we assume that unemployment, insecurity, sharper class and international conflict are in prospect for capitalism?" Sweezy went on. "Why not, on the contrary, a 'managed' capitalist society, maintaining economic prosperity through government action and perhaps even gradually evolving into a full-fledged socialist order?"[14]

In answering these questions, Sweezy moved beyond the mechanics of Keynesian policies and, reasserting his Marxian perspective, queried their political underpinnings. "The state cannot simply be dragged in as a deus ex machina to solve the demonstrated contradictions of the accumulation process," he wrote. "Its position and function in capitalist society must be examined to see what can and what cannot be expected of it."[15] The vulnerability of the Keynesian approach wasn't to be found in theoretical shortcomings, Sweezy explained further on in the book. "Generally speaking their logical consistency cannot be challenged, either on their own ground or on the basis of the Marxian analysis of the reproduction process."[16] The problem with Keynesian policy prescriptions was "their faulty (usually implicit) assumptions about the relationship, or perhaps one should say lack of relationship, between economics and political action. The Keynesians tear the economic system out of its social context and treat it as though it were a machine to be sent to the repair shop there to be overhauled by an engineer state."[17]

This was an astute observation. To many mainstream economists, one of the main attractions of Keynesian ideas was that they could be readily translated into mathematical and engineering terms. During the Second World War, Lawrence Klein, an economics PhD at MIT, built a statistical model of the US economy that incorporated Keynesian concepts such as the multiplier and the principle of effective demand. Based on the amounts of inputs (labor, capital, and raw materials) that were available, and decisions about monetary and fiscal policy, Klein's model could be used to predict the path of GDP, employment, and inflation. At the London School of Economics in the late 1940s, the New Zealand–born economist Bill Phillips, who had trained as an engineer, built a refrigerator-size analog computer model of the economy that used water tanks, pipes, floats, and hydraulic levers to demonstrate how government spending and changes in taxes (represented by water) circulated through the economy. On both sides of the Atlantic, there was excitement about utilizing the new Keynesian methods in policymaking. In 1948, Klein's doctoral adviser at MIT, Paul Samuelson, published the first edition of his famous undergraduate textbook, which, with the aid of some simple diagrams, illustrated how Keynesian policymakers could manage the level of aggregate demand to ensure full employment.

Ironically, Keynes himself had been skeptical of efforts to turn economics into a mathematical science. He believed there was too much innate uncertainty in the economy, and that psychological factors played too large a role, for economists and policymakers to be able to estimate with any confidence the quantitative relationships between key variables, such as interest rates and the level of capital investment, or government spending and total employment. During the decades immediately following the publication of *The General Theory*, Keynes's strictures had little impact. Armed with new statistical models and new estimates of national income and its components, which were another important product of the 1930s and '40s, the postwar Keynesians were confident in their ability to understand and operate the economic machine. Analyzing its historical and political underpinnings seemed like a secondary concern.

Sweezy had a very different perspective. The son of a New York banker, and a graduate of Phillips Exeter Academy and Harvard, where he edited the college newspaper, the *Crimson*, he had a top-down view of America's class system. As a graduate student in Harvard's economics department during the mid-1930s, he became a teaching assistant for Joseph Schumpeter, the eminent Austrian economist and former finance minister who had moved to the United States in 1932. Although the pair's political views diverged sharply—Schumpeter was a free market liberal; Sweezy was an avowed leftist—they got along. Sweezy later described himself as "perhaps . . . something of an ersatz son" to the aristocratic Austrian.[18]

One thing that Sweezy and Schumpeter shared was a deep interest in Marx's portrait of capitalism as a dynamic system in which capitalists' efforts to save costs and raise profits were constantly replacing outmoded products and production techniques with new ones. "This process of Creative Destruction is the essential fact about capitalism," Schumpeter wrote in his 1942 book *Capitalism, Socialism, and Democracy*.[19] But if Schumpeter agreed with Marx about how capitalism developed, he entirely disagreed with him about its results. Schumpeter viewed capitalistic creative destruction as the engine of economic growth and rising living standards. He downplayed class conflict, arguing that the employees and owners of a capitalist firm usually had a common interest in ensuring its success and profitability. (Not surprisingly, Schumpeter's views would endear him to generations of business innovators.)

Sweezy, in *The Theory of Capitalist Development*, hewed much closer to Marx than to Schumpeter, focusing on the pathologies and contradictions of industrial capitalism: exploitation, monopoly, imperialism, and instability. In discussing the potential for Keynesian demand management to stabilize the capitalist economy, he reurned to another tenet of Marxian analysis: the subjugation of the political system to business interests. Echoing *The Communist Manifesto*, he wrote: "[T]he state in capitalist society had always been first and foremost the guarantor of capitalist property relations. In this capacity it has been unmistakably the instrument of capitalist class rule . . ."[20]

Building on this observation, Sweezy returned to his observation that the fundamental weakness of Keynesianism was its unspoken assumption that a democratic government could rise above class interests to impose order and rationality on the economy. Having laid down this marker, he qualified it, noting that the captive relationship between the state and the capitalist class had evolved in an era when there had been "relatively unlimited opportunities for capital to expand."[21] In an era where investment opportunities were more limited, and capitalists had demonstrated an inability to keep up the level of investment sufficiently to maintain a low level of unemployment, it was at least conceivable that the "norms of state policy" could shift somewhat, Sweezy acknowledged. But he insisted that this shift could proceed only up to the point at which managing the economy in the public interest came into conflict with capitalists' drive to accumulate capital and expand their profits.

Going beyond this point would require a mass workers' party taking power and eliminating capitalists and their representatives from any role in policymaking, Sweezy said. In the short term, this wasn't a realistic prospect, he said: "In the sober world of reality, capital holds the strategic positions. Money, social prestige, the bureaucracy, and the armed forces of the state, the channels of public communication—all these are controlled by capital, and they are being and will continue to be used to the utmost to maintain the position of capital."[22] Given this stranglehold, there was little prospect of lasting changes in policy. Should any serious threat emerge, the capitalists would buy off reformist leaders, and media propaganda would keep the masses in check. "The outcome is not the reform of capitalism, but the bankruptcy of reform," Sweezy concluded. "This is neither an accident nor a sign of the immorality of human nature; it is a law of capitalist politics."[23]

Sweezy wasn't the only left-leaning economist to question the political foundations of Keynesianism. In an October 1943 article in *Political Quarterly*, a British journal, Michał Kalecki, a Polish theorist who had moved to England during the 1930s, put forward an argument that complemented Sweezy's. Kalecki's piece was titled "Political Aspects of Full Employment." It argued that business leaders would eventually turn against a Keynesian policy regime out fear that low unemployment rates would deprive them of the ability to discipline their workers and control wages. "Their class instinct tells them that lasting full employment is unsound from their point of view, and that unemployment is an integral part of the 'normal' capitalist system," Kalecki wrote.[24]

For a long time, the Pole was a neglected figure of twentieth-century economics. He was born into an assimilated Polish Jewish family on June 22, 1899, in the city of Łódź. According to Jan Toporowski, the author of a deeply researched two-volume biography of Kalecki that filled in many gaps about his life, his father, Abram, owned a wool-spinning mill. The family had a handsome house and a housekeeper, but it was far from untroubled. When Kalecki was ten, his mother, Klara, left. And after the 1905 revolution, his father's business ran into financial trouble.[25] In 1917 Kalecki enrolled at Warsaw Polytechnic to study civil engineering. After doing his military service in the army of the newly independent Polish state, he switched to the Polytechnic of Gdánsk. When his father ran into financial difficulties, he left college without completing his degree. Subsequently, he worked as an accountant and an economics writer. A gifted mathematician and a committed socialist (but not a Leninist), he had gotten interested in economic theory after reading the writings of Rosa Luxemburg and Mikhail Tugan-Baranovsky, the Ukrainian economist who had taught the young Kondratiev. Kalecki also studied Marx. In 1929 he took a job at the Institute of Research on Business Cycles and Prices in Warsaw.

For the next several years, Kalecki wrote commentaries on the Great Depression. He also did theoretical work, and in 1933 he published a paper about business cycles that, in the subsequent judgment of the aforementioned Lawrence Klein, the American Keynesian, contained "everything of importance in the Keynesian system."[26] Other economists have disputed this assessment. There's no doubt, though, that Kalecki's paper was highly original. (In 1935, an English version of it appeared in the journal *Econometrica*.)[27] Framed in terms of economy-wide aggregates, it combined distributional concepts that could be traced to Marx with a multiplier mechanism that related the level of production to the amount of capital expenditure by businesses. For theoretical purposes, Kalecki divided the economy into two groups: workers who consume all their wages and have no savings; and capitalists who spend some of their incomes on consumer goods and save the rest. In this setup, capital investment by firms is the driving force of the economy. Using some fairly forbidding mathematics, Kalecki showed how changes in the volume of investment give rise to a series of business cycles, each consisting of a period of prosperity followed by a depression.

Some of Kalecki's analysis certainly anticipated parts of *The General Theory*. This was particularly true of his multiplier mechanism, in which increments to capital investment filtered through the economy generating second-round effects that also raised output. Some admirers of Kalecki's work have argued that his paper was more advanced than Keynes's analysis because it was explicitly dynamic. The equations representing orders for capital equipment, such as factory machinery, and the delivery of this equipment featured time lags, and it was the interaction of these lags that generated economic cycles. By contrast, Keynes largely relied on the Marshallian methodology of comparative statics, which involved comparing different points at which the economy might come to rest without explaining mathematically how it moves from one to another.

It's also true, however, that *The General Theory* was more comprehensive than Kalecki's 1933 paper, which didn't explicitly incorporate the labor market or the government sector. Ultimately, perhaps, comparing the two approaches isn't very fruitful, because Kalecki and Keynes had different goals. Working in the Marxian tradition, Kalecki was trying to demonstrate how a bare-bones capitalist economy driven by capital accumulation would alternate between periods of expansion and contraction. Keynes wanted to show how the economy could get stuck in a slump, with its powers of recuperation failing it, and how the government could revive it by increasing public spending. Both economists succeeded in their goals. But Keynes's *General Theory* had more immediate policy implications than Kalecki's paper, and he was already far more famous when it was published.

When Kalecki read *The General Theory*, he realized that his own theoretical work would likely be overshadowed. It did help him obtain a traveling fellowship from the Rockefeller Foundation, which in 1936 he used to visit Sweden and then Britain. After spending some time at the London School of Economics, he gravitated to Cambridge, where he struck up friendships with some of the younger economists associated with Keynes, including Joan and Austin Robinson, Richard Kahn, and Piero Sraffa. They were a close-knit group, not necessarily welcoming to outsiders. Kalecki's obvious smarts helped him fit in. Joan Robinson would later describe him as a "strange visitor who was not only already familiar with our brand-new theories, but had even invented some of our private jokes."[28] Robinson's husband, Austin, recounted that Kalecki "could talk English of a sort, and he shouted at the top of his voice."[29] Kalecki also met Keynes and submitted articles to *The Economic Journal*, which Keynes edited from upon high. Although the two never became close, Keynes appears to have recognized that Kalecki possessed a penetrating mind and formidable mathematical skills. At one point, according to the English economist Malcolm Sawyer, who wrote a valuable survey of Kalecki's work, Keynes tried to secure a research post for him in Cambridge, but the effort fell through.[30]

In 1940, Kalecki moved to Oxford, where he had been offered a job at the university's Institute of Statistics, which provided regular commentary on the British economy. As a consequence of conscription and heavy spending on armaments, the unemployment rate had fallen to about 3 percent, and Keynes had identified the emergence of an "inflationary gap" between aggregate demand and aggregate supply. To reduce spending power and close this gap, he called on the government to impose income taxes on workers whose wages had previously been excluded from the tax system. Trade unions and Labour MPs depicted Keynes's plan as an effort to finance the war on the back of the working class. Kalecki didn't like it, either. He believed it was inequitable and based on an incorrect view of inflation. Although he acknowledged that an inflationary wage-price spiral could develop as workers sought to catch up with rising prices, he insisted that the main driving force of inflation was businesses raising their prices faster than their costs were rising, to boost their profits.[31] In a June 1941 article in the *Oxford Bulletin of Statistics*, he wrote: "The only fair and efficient way to stop the inflationary tendencies is some type of comprehensive rationing."[32]

In this policy debate, Kalecki eventually emerged as the winner on points. As the war continued and inflationary pressures increased, the government introduced tax increases *and* rationing. To obtain the daily necessities of life, the British population were assigned coupon books. Ordinary workers saw their wages taxed, but the tax rates on the highest earners and business were much higher. The government raised the top rate of income tax to 97.5 percent and brought in an excess profits tax of 60 percent. Keynes accepted these punitive policies as a wartime necessity; Kalecki welcomed them. He was equally enthusiastic about the 1942 Beveridge Report on social insurance, drafted by the liberal economist William Beveridge, which called for the provision of universal benefits, including payments to the sick and unemployed, old-age pensions, and child allowances. In a commentary on the Beveridge plan, Kalecki said these types of programs would serve the dual purpose of raising living standards and boosting aggregate demand to ensure full employment. He dismissed objections that enacting the plan would raise businesses' costs and provide disincentives to work for low-wage workers. If the latter problem emerged, he noted, the solution was simple: raise wages.[33]

Based on his own theorizing and that of other Keynesians, Kalecki believed it was technically feasible for governments of capitalist countries to achieve full employment by altering monetary and fiscal policy. Like Sweezy, his doubts about Keynesianism revolved around its social and political foundations. In a 1942 lecture to the Marshall Society in Cambridge, Kalecki discussed some of these doubts, and the following year he turned his verbal presentation into the article for *Political Quarterly* that was mentioned earlier. It began with a brief synopsis of the Keynesian approach to policymaking: "The effective demand created by the government acts like any other increase in demand. If labour, plants, and foreign raw materials are in ample supply, the increase in demand is met by an increase in production." As long as the effort to reduce unemployment "stops short of increasing effective demand over the full employment mark, there is no need to be afraid of inflation."[34]

The real constraint on pursuing policies aimed at full employment wasn't rising inflation, Kalecki argued. It was resistance on the part of big business. Even during the depths of the Great Depression, he pointed out, major corporations had opposed efforts to counter mass joblessness by raising government spending everywhere except in Germany. And Germany was a special case, Kalecki said, because German big businesses had entered a "partnership" with the Nazi regime, which pursued full employment as a goal but also suppressed labor unions. "One of the important functions of fascism," he wrote, "as typified by the Nazi system, was to remove capitalist objections to full employment."[35] In other countries, he reminded his readers, business leaders had opposed expansionary fiscal policies even though these policies could well have boosted the demand for their firms' products. How could this self-defeating attitude be explained?

Kalecki provided three possible explanations. The first one was that businesses feared that if the government maintained full employment, their political power would be greatly reduced. In an unmanaged capitalist system, the level of employment depends to a great extent on the level of business confidence, Kalecki noted. If this confidence vanishes, firms cut back on capital investment, which can lead to a fall in output and employment:

i.e., a recession. "This gives the capitalists a powerful indirect control over government policy: everything which may shake the state of confidence must be carefully avoided because it would cause an economic crisis."[36] However, Kalecki went on, "once the government learns the trick of increasing employment by its own purchases, this powerful controlling device loses its effectiveness." To avoid this outcome, businesses responded to any effort to raise aggregate demand by stressing and exaggerating the dangers of running a budget deficit. "The social function of the doctrine of 'sound finance' is to make the level of employment dependent on the state of confidence," Kalecki noted caustically.

He also said that capitalists were worried about governments encroaching on areas previously reserved for private enterprise. Even if policymakers initially directed additional public expenditures to things like healthcare, education, and roadbuilding, where municipalities and other nonprofit concerns had long played a prominent role, business leaders wouldn't believe things would stop there. "The scope for public investment of this type is rather narrow," Kalecki wrote, "and there is a danger that the government, in pursuing this policy, may eventually be tempted to nationalize transport or public utilities so as to gain a new sphere for investment."[37]

The third and most important reason that business leaders staunchly oppose full employment policies, Kalecki argued, is because they don't want to lose control of the workplace. In an economy where jobs were plentiful and workers were able to find employment easily, fear of being laid off "would cease to play its role as disciplinary measure," he noted. "The social position of the boss would be undermined, and the self-assurance and class-consciousness of the working class would grow. Strikes for wage increases and improvements in conditions of work would create political tension."[38] At first sight, this passage looked like a straightforward application of Marx's argument that the presence of a reserve army of unemployed workers is essential to discipline workers and maintain businesses' profits; but Kalecki was also making a more subtle point. Under a policy regime of high demand and full employment, profits could actually be higher, on average, than they were under laissez-faire, he noted. But corporate interests would still reject this framework because "'discipline in the factories' and 'political stability' are more appreciated than profits by business leaders."[39]

This argument illustrates how Kalecki, like Keynes, believed that economic reasoning couldn't be entirely reduced to dollars and cents: psychological and political factors were also important. Given all the concerns that business interests had about full employment undermining their economic prerogatives, political power, and control of their factories, Kalecki argued, any effort to maintain it for a lengthy period was sure to run into a backlash. "In the slump, either under the pressure of the masses, or even without it, public investment financed by borrowing will be undertaken to prevent large-scale unemployment," Kalecki wrote.

> But if attempts are made to apply this method in order to maintain the high level of employment reached in the subsequent boom, strong opposition by "business leaders" is likely to be encountered . . . A powerful alliance is likely to be formed between big business and rentier interests, and they would probably find more than one economist to declare that the situation was manifestly unsound. The pressure of all these forces, and in particular of big business . . . would most probably induce the government to return to the orthodox policy of cutting down the budget deficit.[40]

The Keynesian medicine would be abandoned, but things wouldn't end there, Kalecki pointed out. As the government reduced spending, aggregate demand would fall back, firms would start laying off workers, and the economy would plunge into a recession. But then, as the unemployment rate rose, there would be growing public demands for ameliorative action, creating a new political environment "in which government spending policy would again come into its own."[41] Keynesian measures to boost growth and employment would be adopted once more, and the recession would come to an end. But this policy stance wouldn't be permanent, either. At some point, big business's opposition to full employment, and demands for a return to fiscal rectitude, would prompt policymakers to reverse course again and slam on the brakes. In short, the economy would be subject to a "political business cycle." Kalecki said this theory was "not entirely conjectural. Something very similar happened in the United States in 1937–38."[42] Looking forward, he suggested that these sorts of cycles could become commonplace: "The regime of the political business cycle would be an artificial restoration of the position as it existed in nineteenth-century capitalism. Full employment would be reached only at the top of the boom, but slumps would be relatively mild and short-lived."[43]

The *Political Quarterly* article didn't attract very much attention when it was published, but some readers appreciated the arguments it made. "I have just read with much sympathy and interest your article on Political Aspects of Full Employment in PI. Q. An exceedingly good article and very acute," Keynes said in a handwritten note to Kalecki dated December 20, 1943.[44] Doubtless the recipient was grateful for the letter, but he remained frustrated at his inability to get a full-time teaching post in England. In 1945 he resigned from the Oxford Institute of Statistics and moved to Paris, then to Montreal, where he worked for the International Labour Organization. In 1946 he got a more prestigious job, becoming deputy director of a section of the economics division at the newly founded United Nations in New York. For almost a decade, he lived in the United States, worked on the UN's annual World Economic Reports, and continued his own theoretical research.

Sweezy was also a public official for a time. During the Second World War, he was an economic researcher at the Office of Strategic Services (OSS), the forerunner to the CIA, in Washington, DC. When the war ended, he hoped to return to Harvard. After being passed over for a tenured job, he resigned his teaching post and became a full-time writer, journalist, and activist. In 1949 he cofounded *Monthly Review*, an independent socialist magazine published in New York. The first issue contained an article by Albert Einstein entitled "Why Socialism?" and an essay on recent developments in American capitalism by Sweezy, which made two arguments that would feature prominently in leftist critiques of the so-called Golden Age: "(1) that without the support provided by enormous expenditures on imperialist and militaristic ventures, American capitalism would quickly sink into a morass of chronic depression and mass unemployment; and (2) that American capitalism is coming increasingly under the domination of a few giant corporations which in turn are owned and controlled by a handful of extremely rich capitalists."[45]

US defense spending was certainly rising. During the ensuing two decades, as a consequence of the Cold War with the Soviet Union and the hot wars in Korea and Vietnam, it would rise a lot further. As Sweezy pointed out in his ongoing commentaries in *Monthly Review*, military spending boosted aggregate demand in the US economy. So did the construction of interstate highways and other roads, which created a car-based suburban society. In 1945 there were already about 30 million passenger cars and commercial vehicles on America's roads. By 1970, the figure had risen to more than 100 million.[46] As new suburbs proliferated around major US cities, middle-class Americans furnished their new homes with the latest consumer appliances, such as washing machines, air conditioners, and record players. Similar developments took place in Europe, where American multinationals like Ford, General Motors, and General Electric built factories to supply local markets. With household incomes rising and domestic and global markets expanding, the postwar partnership between the public and private sectors appeared to be thriving.

As the postwar expansion continued, it was buttressed by a growing political consensus. In Britain, the Conservative governments that were in power from 1951 to 1964 left in place most of the Attlee government's reforms. Even in the United States, similarly, some conservative politicians recognized that the New Deal policies were too popular to be overturned. In his 1956 reelection campaign, the Republican president Dwight Eisenhower ran on a platform that promised to balance the federal budget but also pointed to his record of expanding Social Security and unemployment insurance, raising the federal minimum wage, encouraging collective bargaining between workers and employers, and creating the Department of Health, Education, and Welfare, the first new federal department in forty years.[47]

Over time, many businesses and business groups also came to accept the postwar settlement. As long as demand for their products remained strong and productivity growth outpaced increases in wages, Keynesianism was consistent with higher corporate earnings. Between 1950 and 1965, US corporate profits doubled in dollar terms,[48] and the share of corporate profits in US gross domestic income rose from 5.7 percent to 7.4 percent.[49] In Britain between 1948 and 1965, annual gross corporate profits rose from £2 billion to £7.6 billion.[50]

On the face of things, these developments seemed to have belied the skepticism of Sweezy and Kalecki. In his 1943 article, Kalecki had written, "If capitalism can adjust itself to full employment, a fundamental reform will have been incorporated in it. If not, it will show itself an outmoded system which must be scrapped."[51] By the end of the 1950s, the adjustment of capitalism seemed to be going relatively smoothly, at least in the Western world. Kalecki was no longer there to witness it personally. In 1954 he resigned from the United Nations and returned to Poland, which was now under Communist rule and part of the Eastern Bloc. He stayed there until his death in 1970.

Sweezy kept up his economic commentaries, and in the 1960s he acknowledged the political impact of two decades of Keynesianism. Attitudes toward taxation and government spending among the "American ruling class, at any rate its leading echelon of managers of giant corporations," had "undergone a fundamental change," Sweezy and his coauthor, Paul Baran, wrote in their 1966 book, *Monopoly Capital*, which became a key text for a generation of leftists. The old hostility to big government hadn't disappeared, they went on, but "the modern Big Businessman, though he sometimes speaks the traditional language, no longer takes it so seriously as his ancestors. To him, government spending means more effective demand, and he senses that he can shift most of the associated taxes forward onto consumers or backwards onto workers."[52]

Whereas in the 1940s, at the dawn of Keynesianism, Sweezy had queried its political foundations, and the ability of the state to stick with it, he and Baran now emphasized the role that government spending, particularly military spending, played in mopping up the huge financial surpluses that corporate giants like General Motors, General Electric, and IBM were generating. These surpluses raised the danger of saving outstripping investment and pushing the economy into a slump, the two authors argued. "On what could the government spend enough to keep the system from sinking into the mire of stagnation? On arms, more arms, and even more arms."[53] They cited figures indicating that between 1929 and 1957, US defense spending had risen from 0.7 percent of GNP to 10.3 percent.[54]

Sweezy and Baran were unabashed Marxists; they dedicated *Monopoly Capital* to Che Guevara. In the economics profession, they were fringe figures. But there were also some prominent Keynesian economists who bemoaned the rise of the Cold War and the emergence of what might be termed Pentagon Keynesianism. One of them had known Keynes and Kalecki personally and discussed their theories extensively with them. She was a major theorist in her own right, and a rare woman in the upper echelons of a male-dominated profession. In fact, she was one of the most notable economists of the twentieth century.

18

Joan Robinson and the "Bastard Keynesians"

Joan Violet Robinson was what the English call a "blue blood." Her father was a senior officer in the British Army who had served in India and South Africa. Her maternal great-great-grandfather was Spencer Perceval, who served as a Tory prime minister from 1809 to 1812 and is the only holder of that office to have been assassinated. (The killer was a disgruntled merchant.) Interestingly, there was also a nonconformist scholar in her lineage. Her paternal great-grandfather, Frederick Denison Maurice, was an eminent Christian Socialist theologian who lost his post at King's College, Cambridge, after saying he didn't believe in eternal damnation. Robinson was born Joan Violet Maurice on October 31, 1903, in Camberley, Surrey, an affluent town thirty miles southwest of London that has long been associated with the nearby Royal Military Academy Sandhurst, where her father taught. She attended the private St. Paul's Girls' School, in West London, which was founded in 1904. There she developed a passion for poetry, particularly the works of Shelley and Byron, but her main subject was history. In 1921 she won a scholarship to Girton College, Cambridge, the first women's Oxbridge college, where she switched to economics. "I did not have much idea of what it was about," she recalled much later in life. "I had some vague hope that it would help me to understand poverty and how it could be cured. And I hoped that it would offer more scope for rational argument than history (my school subject) as it was taught in those days. I was somewhat disappointed on both counts."[1]

As an undergraduate, Robinson ingested Alfred Marshall's *Principles of Economics* and attended lectures by Marshall's chosen successor, Arthur

Cecil Pigou. Like many students before and after her, she found Marshal-lian economics—which represented consumers and businesses as rational automatons who maximize their "utility" and profits in a world of "perfect competition"—abstract and bizarre. In a presentation to the student Mar-shall Society, she and a friend read aloud a spoof essay entitled "Beauty and the Beast" that related the story of a rich merchant who inadvertently traded his favorite daughter to a beast, only for the beast to transform into a hand-some prince. "With this happy union of producer's and consumer's surplus, they then lived happily ever after," the essay concluded, "constantly keeping in mind their higher ideals and maximizing their satisfaction by equalizing the marginal utility of each object of expenditure."[2]

The Cambridge economics course was divided into two parts, a first year of introductory study followed by two years of more intensive material. To her disappointment, Joan didn't obtain top marks in either set of exami-nations, and she was awarded an upper second-class degree. Shortly after graduating, she married Austin Robinson, an economics graduate of Christ's College, and departed for India, where he had been invited to tutor the Ma-harajah of Gwalior, a city in the center of the subcontinent. The newlyweds spent four years there and returned in 1929 to Cambridge, where Austin had obtained a fellowship at Sidney Sussex College. Joan, who took her husband's surname, wasn't offered a formal position. Determined to pursue her ambi-tion to become a professional economist, she tutored some undergraduates on a semi-casual basis and pursued her own research, which focused on the issue of monopoly.

By the 1930s, big corporations like Ford and General Motors in the United States, and Krupp and Siemens in Germany, dominated many indus-tries, controlling the entire production process—from research and design to manufacturing to marketing and distribution. But these industrial giants played only a bit role in orthodox economics textbooks, which still analyzed markets with many competitors, each of them too small for their actions to affect prices or wages. An exception was recognized in the case of firms that were the sole supplier in a given market, such as power utilities. Marshall, in his *Principles*, had devoted a chapter to these monopolies. But economics sorely lacked a theory that applied to industries dominated by a handful of large businesses. This was the void that Robinson and other ambitious young economists were setting out to fill.

In 1926 Piero Sraffa, a twenty-eight-year-old Italian economist, published a paper in *The Economic Journal* that pointed out some of the flaws of orthodox price theory, including the fact that unit costs tended to fall, rather than rise, as the scale of production increased.[3] (The textbooks featured rising cost curves.) In 1927 Sraffa moved to Cambridge at the invitation of Keynes. (As a Jew and a close friend of the imprisoned socialist leader Antonio Gramsci, he was facing great danger in Mussolini's Italy.) Sraffa's work greatly influenced Robinson and her tight-knit circle of economist friends, which included her husband and Richard Kahn, a recent graduate of King's College. But the primary influence on Robinson, at this stage, was Professor Pigou, whose 1920 book, *The Economics of Welfare*, contained an extensive discussion of monopoly. It also analyzed the "exploitation" of labor, which it defined as a situation in which firms forced their workers to "accept in payment for their services less than the value which the marginal net product of their services has to these employers."[4] But Pigou treated this situation as an exceptional case rather than the norm.

Throughout his analysis, Pigou employed the standard Marshallian framework: supply and demand curves, cost curves, "marginal utility," and so on. Like Marshall, he regarded these concepts as scientific tools that could be applied for "the bettering of human life" and the elimination of poverty.[5] Robinson would eventually reject the Marshallian framework on the grounds that it served to cloak rather than reveal the real dynamics of capitalism. At this juncture, however, she embraced orthodox techniques for her research on monopoly power, which she turned into a book, *The Economics of Imperfect Competition*, which came out in 1933. Much as Marx had used a Ricardian framework to undermine Ricardo's defense of laissez-faire, Robinson used Marshall's tools to undermine assertions that the market system produces an efficient allocation of resources and a just distribution of income.

In the standard textbook model of perfect competition, firms can produce and sell as many goods as they want at the market price, and also hire as many workers as they want at the prevailing wage. Robinson took it as her starting point that this was unrealistic and that many businesses were big enough for their actions to affect prices and wages. "The whole theory of value should be treated in terms of monopoly analysis," she wrote.[6] In a market where firms have monopoly power, they can set prices above costs without losing all their market share. If they want to sell more goods, they must lower their prices; in order to hire more workers, they must offer higher wages. These statements may seem obvious to non-economists, but Robinson demonstrated how they upended the standard efficiency arguments for a competitive capitalist economy.

The reason that perfectly competitive markets allocate resources efficiently, in a certain sense, is that they force consumers and firms to equalize marginal benefits and marginal costs. In pricing their goods, firms set the price equal to the incremental cost of producing another item. And since the additional revenue they get from selling this extra item is the market price, the incremental benefit to the firm is the same as the incremental cost. That's efficient. But in a modern industrial economy, most markets don't work like this. If Ford cuts the price of F-150 trucks to sell more of them, it will receive a lower price for all the F-150s it sells, not just the additional sales. Its incremental revenue from a new sale will therefore be less than the purchase price and less than its incremental cost. It may even end up making a loss. Once Ford's managers realize this, they will restrict the firm's output, operate its plants at sub-capacity, and raise prices. Compared to the perfectly competitive outcome, output is lower and prices are higher. That's inefficient.

Robinson presented this argument using some clever new diagrams. With Richard Kahn's help, she also included some algebraic derivations, but it was her graphical analysis that grabbed the attention of the economics profession. The key innovation was the presence of a downward-sloping "marginal revenue curve" that was situated below the market demand curve. The slope and position of this curve determined precisely where the market would settle.[7]

Unknown to Robinson, a young Harvard economist, Edward Chamberlin, had come up with a very similar analysis a few years earlier in his doctoral thesis, which was also published in 1933, under the title *The Theory of Monopolistic Competition*. Despite the formal similarity of the two treatments, their authors regarded them very differently. Chamberlin viewed his analysis as a modification to the competitive model, which didn't undermine its overall legitimacy. Later in life, he would join the Mont Pelerin Society, an international association of free market economists that Friedrich Hayek set up after World War II. Robinson took a different view of the theory of imperfect competition. She believed she had successfully repudiated the ruling orthodoxy, particularly in a part of her treatise where she applied analysis to the labor market and challenged the long-standing claim that workers' wages reflected their productivity.

It was John Bates Clark, Veblen's teacher, who had formalized this argument at the turn of the twentieth century. In a perfectly competitive labor market, Clark showed, workers' wages would settle at a level equal to the value of their "marginal products." If hiring another worker enabled a firm to produce two more items a day, each of which sold for ten dollars, the worker would get paid twenty dollars a day. But the competitive logic assumes that the firm is too small for its hiring and output decisions to affect wages and prices. Robinson analyzed the situation in which firms are big enough for their hiring decisions to influence wages—a situation she called "monopsony." Using another clever diagram, she showed how, in this environment, the key marginal condition for efficiency no longer held.[8] Firms would pay workers less than the value of their marginal products, hire fewer of them than a competitive firm, and reap higher profits. Robinson referred to this behavior as "monopsonistic exploitation of labor" and devoted an entire chapter to it.[9] She also showed how the problem could be partly remedied by imposing a minimum wage, which, by eliminating firms' monopoly power in the labor market, could lead to higher wages *and* higher levels of employment.

Robinson's treatise highlighted other features of a monopolistic economy. Because firms would be making higher profits than they would in a competitive setting, the level of wealth inequality would be higher, it pointed out.[10] To be sure, this conclusion wouldn't have come as news to Henry George, Thorstein Veblen, or Rosa Luxemburg. On both sides of the Atlantic, socialists and left-liberals had long tied the rise of monopolies, trusts, and other big capitalist concerns to intensified exploitation of workers and greater inequality. Robinson's achievement was to demonstrate this linkage using techniques that the economics profession couldn't brush aside. Even in "Pigou's own terms," she subsequently noted, "it is not true that wages are equal to the value of the marginal product of labour."[11] She also acknowledged, however, that large firms may be more efficient than small firms because they can exploit economies of scale and use the latest production techniques. "In order to form a judgment on the present-day movement toward monopoly we must decide whether it is worth while to put power into the hands of large concerns for the sake of the increase in productivity which they promise to bring about," she wrote. "This is a problem which no amount of abstract analysis can help us to solve."[12]

Shortly after *The Economics of Imperfect Competition* was published, Cambridge University offered Robinson a permanent academic post. If she had decided to sit on her laurels, the book would have assured her a prominent position in the history of economic theory. Sitting back wasn't her way. In 1934–35, as Keynes was putting together successive drafts of *The General Theory*, she and Kahn acted as his readers and sounding boards. "With these two [Keynes] could feel complete confidence that they understood what he was driving at," Roy Harrod, the author of the first full-length biography of Keynes, noted.[13] A year after *The General Theory* was published, Robinson wrote a primer for interested parties who might be bewildered by Keynes's esoteric presentation. She also wrote a second book, *Essays in the Theory of Employment*, which addressed various tricky issues arising from Keynes's magnum opus, including whether a sustained period of full employment would lead to rising inflation.

Bringing unemployment down to a very low level, and keeping it there, would increase the bargaining power of workers and the willingness of employers to pay them more, Robinson pointed out. "When labour is scarce," she wrote, "not only are Trade Unions very powerful, but employers themselves throw their weight into the scale of rising wages."[14] As wages rise, she went on, businesses try to pass on some of their additional costs to consumers by raising prices, which in turn prompts labor unions to submit higher wage demands. Although Robinson didn't use the term *wage-price spiral*, which wouldn't come into vogue until the 1970s, she clearly had such an outcome in mind. Noting how inflation can erode purchasing power, she warned: "The point of full employment, so far from being an equilibrium resting place, appears to be a precipice over which, once it has reached the edge, the value of money must plunge into a bottomless abyss."[15]

If prices did start to rise, Robinson went on, much would depend on how policymakers reacted. If they raised interest rates promptly, they could reduce aggregate demand, lower the demand for labor, and choke off the inflation threat. Rentiers and others on fixed incomes would benefit from such a policy, but it would also lead to an increase in joblessness. "We are here presented with a conflict of interests which *a priori* reasoning can do nothing to resolve," Robinson wrote.[16] One conceivable solution would be for the authorities to prevail on labor unions to moderate their wage demands, she added, but achieving such an outcome would be challenging, because "Trade Union policy is only very loosely coordinated, and since the duty of each Union is to regard only the interests of its members, gains and losses are very unevenly distributed between industries."[17] In the depressed era of the 1930s, when deflation was a bigger threat than inflation, the significance of this analysis wasn't immediately obvious.

Unlike some Keynesians, Robinson never regarded demand management policies as a solution to all the contradictions of a capitalist economy. But she did believe that Keynes had liberated the economics profession from the dogma of laissez-faire. "By making it impossible to believe any longer in an automatic reconciliation of conflicting interests into a harmonious whole, the *General Theory* brought out into the open the problem of choice and judgement that the neo-classicals had managed to smother," she wrote later in her life. "The ideology to end ideologies broke down. Economics once more became Political Economy."[18] In taking this approach, Robinson was increasingly influenced by Marxist ideas, which hitherto she had largely ignored. In December 1940, she wrote to Richard Kahn: "My next project is to make a dictionary to Marx so that he can be read by economists. 'Value = man hours. Surplus value = product-real wages etc.'"[19] In another letter to Kahn, she commented: "There is a lot of excellent stuff in Marx, e.g., that the quantity of money is determined by prices, not vice versa. But none of the Marxists seem to understand him."[20]

Robinson's interest in Marx prompted her to write a short book, *An Essay on Marxian Economics*, that was published in 1942 and managed to annoy Marxists and orthodox economists alike. One of the leftist faithful's grouses was that Robinson dismissed the labor theory of value, which Marx had used extensively, saying it "fails to provide a theory of prices"[21]—a point that some of Marx's critics in the late nineteenth century had made. Robinson also criticized Marx's theory that the profit rate tended to fall, describing it as "confused and redundant."[22] But despite tossing these elements of *Capital* onto the scrap heap, she said that modern economists "have much to learn"[23] from its author, including a clear-eyed recognition of the relationship between economics and capitalism:

> The orthodox economists, on the whole, identified themselves with the system and assumed the role of its apologists, while Marx set himself to

understand the working of capitalism in order to hasten its overthrow. Marx was conscious of his purposes. The economists were in general unconscious. They wrote as they did because it seemed to them the only possible way to write, and they believed themselves to be endowed with scientific impartiality.[24]

Robinson also praised Marx for foreshadowing, in his analysis of the centralization of capital, the modern theory of monopolies, and for rejecting Say's Law and pointing to the possibility of deficient demand and involuntary unemployment. After outlining the two-sector model of the economy that Marx developed in volume II of *Capital*, Robinson wrote: "Marx does not develop a full theory of the trade cycle, or of the long-run movement of capitalism, but he points the direction in which a theory can be found. He rejected the crude under-consumption theory current in his day, but his own analysis clearly leads to the view that maldistribution of consuming power is the root of the trouble."[25] Robinson also hailed the breadth of Marx's ambition, comparing his eagerness to confront the big issues of capitalist development with the small-bore research projects that many academics engaged in. "The orthodox economists have been much preoccupied with elegant elaborations of minor problems, which distract the attention of their pupils from the uncongenial realities of the modern world, and the development of abstract argument has run far ahead of any possibility of empirical verification," she wrote. "Marx's intellectual tools are far cruder, but his sense of reality is far stronger, and his argument towers above their intricate constructions in rough and gloomy grandeur."[26]

Robinson was steadily becoming more skeptical of orthodox economic methods and their applicability to modern reality. In an insightful 2022 article on Robinson's 1942 *Essay*, the University College London economist Carolina Alves, who was formerly the Joan Robinson Research Fellow in Heterodox Economics at Cambridge, noted: "Marxian economics gave Robinson the insights and motivation she needed to move away from Marshallian economics and closer to a more classical approach."[27] This shift was evident in other articles that Robinson wrote. In "Control of Monopoly," a 1943 piece, she pointed out how monopolistic businesses were keeping prices too high, restricting their spending on capital investments, and blocking the introduction of new technologies.[28] The same year, she published a pamphlet entitled *Private Enterprise or Public Control*, in which she called for the establishment of a National Investment Board to mobilize capital investment throughout the economy in accordance with a comprehensive national plan.[29] Robinson also called for the public takeover of large firms that didn't have any competition, such as utilities. At one point, she seemed to advocate nationalization of the entire industrial sector, but she didn't adopt this position consistently.[30]

Her central point, which echoed some of the more subversive passages of *The General Theory,* was that leaving the volume and direction of capital accumulation to the private sector was no longer a viable option. The rise of modern science had changed the nature of industrial innovation, she insisted, turning it into a collective endeavor that required state support. "The age of bright ideas is already gone," she wrote. "The modern scientist works as one of a team in an expensively equipped laboratory . . . Under a planned system scientists and technicians, given adequate facilities, would supply a superabundance of new discoveries."[31] In this way, as in others, history was overtaking the free market model of capitalist enterprise, Robinson argued.

In Britain's wartime economy, that certainly seemed to be true, but after the war ended, the switch to comprehensive economic planning and socialization of capital investment that Robinson advocated for didn't happen—or not in the way that she had hoped for. In the United States, government support for scientific research was largely funneled through an expanding defense budget. In Britain, the postwar Labour government, even as it nationalized about a fifth of the industrial sector, left the majority of investment decisions to the private sector. And the capital budgets of the newly nationalized industries were often restricted because of concerns about the public finances.

To Robinson's dismay, Attlee's Labour government also adopted a staunchly anti-Communist policy, supporting the formation of NATO to contain Stalin's Soviet Union, which had occupied parts of eastern Europe, and also, following the US use of atomic bombs against Japan at the end of the Second World War, successfully testing its own nukes. By the early 1950s, Robinson was increasingly disillusioned. In 1951, an undergraduate magazine at Cambridge asked her to contribute an "economist's view" of the international situation. In Korea, which had been divided into Soviet- and US-supported zones, an East-West proxy war had begun, and the United States had sent men and matériel to defend its South Korean ally. Robinson agreed to write an article, which was typically direct and forthright. "The great question which overshadows everything," she wrote, "is whether Russia is planning aggression, for, if not, our whole policy is nonsensical."[32] The commonly drawn analogy between Stalin and Hitler "seems to me to be totally false," she went on. "The Russians have none of the economic motives for aggression that Hitler had. They have any amount of *Lebensraum* and untapped natural resources to develop." What is more, Robinson added, Russia, unlike Germany after World War I, didn't have "a humiliating defeat to live down." Thus, she concluded: "I cannot see any objective reason why the Russians should be aggressive, and the main danger from them, I feel, is that our own sabre rattling (and atom-bomb-rattling) will terrify them into violence."[33]

Echoing Paul Sweezy, Robinson also emphasized the economic consequences of the rising Pentagon budget. Between 1948 and 1951, the US Congress had approved big increases in defense spending to counter the perceived threat from Communism. Subsequently, US growth had accelerated, and the unemployment rate had fallen sharply—to just 3.1 percent in August 1951.[34] "The great boom in America built up on rearmament has gone too far for comfort . . . and yet the prospect of a peaceful *détente* and a sudden cessation of rearmament expenditure is a menace to their economy," Robinson wrote. Her point was that sustained federal spending was necessary to keep the economy growing, and that, given the difficulty in getting political agreement for increases in non-defense spending, the path of least resistance was rising defense budgets and international confrontation: "That is what seems to me the biggest menace in the present situation."[35]

Robinson's book on imperfect competition and her role in the Keynesian revolution had turned her into a widely respected scholar. During the 1950s and '60s, however, she became involved in a bitter transatlantic dispute that brought her into conflict with some of America's leading economists. On one level, "the Cambridge capital controversy," as it came to be known, was a recondite theoretical dispute about the nature of physical capital. To Robinson, however, it was ultimately about the ways in which economic orthodoxy was used to rationalize existing economic arrangements.

The theoretical origins of the set-to can be traced to 1939, when Roy Harrod, the Oxford economist who had first met Keynes seventeen years earlier, published an article in which he sought to extend the analytical framework of *The General Theory* to long-term growth. Using a deceptively simple model, Harrod demonstrated that, based on his assumptions, the economy would be permanently on a knife edge between booms and slumps.[36] This result rested on one of Keynes's key insights: in a capitalist economy, decisions to save money and decisions to invest in capital equipment are made by different people, and there is no compelling reason why their actions should balance. Harrod showed how if they didn't balance, the economy would veer off in one direction or another—into an unsustainable boom or a devastating bust.

In 1948, Harrod published a book extending his analysis. Reviewing the tome, Robinson hailed it as an interesting and important work, albeit one that was "extremely hard to follow." In some parts of Cambridge, Massachusetts, Harrod's model (and a similar one derived by Evsey Domar, a Russian-American economist who taught at Harvard) received a cooler reception. One of the skeptics was Robert Solow, a mathematically adept young MIT professor who was a protégé of Paul Samuelson. To Solow, Harrod's depiction of capitalism as chronically unstable didn't ring true. "An expedition from Mars arriving on Earth having read this literature would have expected to find only the wreckage of a capitalism that had shaken itself to pieces long ago," he later recounted. "Economic history was indeed a record of fluctuations as well as growth, but most business cycles seemed to be self-limiting. Sustained, though disturbed growth was not a rarity."[37]

After studying Harrod's model, Solow concluded that the instability result hinged on an assumption that technology was of a particularly restrictive type, with no possibility of substituting capital for labor—by, for example, employing two machines and ten workers instead of one machine and twenty workers. In a 1956 paper, Solow demonstrated that if technology was more flexible, the knife-edge problem would disappear. To show this, he utilized a "production function"—a mathematical equation summarizing the production possibilities of the economy—that allowed practically unlimited substitution of inputs. By combining this equation with a national income identity and the assumption that markets were competitive, Solow was able to construct a model economy that exhibited steady growth, with output, capital, and labor (measured in efficiency units) all growing at the same rate over the long run. "The system can adjust to any given rate of growth of the labor force," he wrote, "and eventually approach a state of steady proportional expansion."[38]

Today the Solow growth model features prominently in textbooks on macroeconomics. Robinson wasn't having any of it. Even before Solow published his 1956 paper, she had written an article in which she described the very concept of a production function as "a powerful instrument of mis-education."[39] Explaining her point with the aid of some simple algebra, she wrote:

> The student of economic theory is taught to write $O = f(L, C)$ where L is a quantity of labour, C a quantity of capital and O a rate of output of commodities. He is instructed to assume all workers alike and to measure L in man-hours of labour; he is told something about the index-number problem involved in choosing a unit of output; and then he is hurried on to the next question, in the hope that he will forget to ask in what units C is measured. Before ever he does ask, he has become a professor, and so sloppy habits of thought are handed on from one generation to the next.

In 1956 Robinson published her own book on growth, *The Accumulation of Capital*, the title of which she borrowed from Rosa Luxemburg. (In 1951, Robinson had contributed a complimentary introduction to a new edition of Luxemburg's 1913 treatise.)[40] Eschewing the neoclassical methods favored by Solow and his colleagues, Robinson's book developed a theory of economic growth in which the level of capital investment was determined by the profit rate, which in turn depended on the class struggle between capital and labor over wages and profits. (In some ways, this formulation evoked the earlier work of Michał Kalecki.) Unlike the Solow model, the dynamics of Robinson's economy were neither predetermined nor self-stabilizing. The outcome depended on institutional forces, expectations, and history.

The intellectual battle was on. On the British side, Robinson and her colleague Nicholas "Nicky" Kaldor were the commanding generals, aided by a timely intervention from Sraffa, who in 1960 finally unveiled an anti-neoclassical treatise he had been working on for decades: *The Production of Commodities by Means of Other Commodities*. Solow and Samuelson led the Cambridge, Massachusetts, battalion, which recruited some orthodox British economists to its ranks. Roughly speaking, the first half of the conflict was taken up with arguments about the nature of physical capital and whether it was legitimate to aggregate it into a single whole for theoretical and empirical purposes, as Solow and other neoclassical economists did routinely. The second stage of the conflict was even more abstruse: it centered on whether, as the neoclassical model assumed, there is a strict one-way relationship between capital intensity (the amount of capital equipment per worker) and the rate of profit, or interest.

Obscure as the entire dispute may seem, it revolved around some fundamental methodological differences. Solow, Samuelson, and their allies regarded themselves as scientific pragmatists who were using the latest technical tools available, imperfect as they have been, to understand and regulate the economy: they believed they were living up to Keynes's dictum that in the future economists should be like dentists. Robinson, on the other hand, thought the American Keynesians were ignoring the central message of *The General Theory*, which was that the task of directing productive investment couldn't be left to a capitalist casino. She also viewed the use of production functions as an underhanded effort to rehabilitate J. B. Clark's argument that wages and profits reflected the productive contributions of labor and capital, rather than the outcome of a class struggle over the economic surplus that was mediated through specific historical circumstances and institutional structures. Generally speaking, Robinson believed that even though many of her opponents identified as Keynesians, their neoclassical version of the creed served to obfuscate the true nature of capitalism. She was determined to fight them tooth and nail.

Throughout much of the lengthy controversy, Robinson kept up a barbed correspondence with Solow and Samuelson. "I should like to say that I think your comments on my paper are a complete red herring," Solow wrote to Robinson in May 1962.[41] Robinson replied: "Dear Bob, To me you are a fascinating study:—A clever man who cannot see a simple point. I suppose to you I am just a dense woman. But we have made some progress if you now agree that your model requires the wage bargain to be made in real terms. Yours sincerely, Joan."[42] Throughout the 1960s, the back-and-forth continued, often occasioned by the appearance of a new paper or lecture. Eventually both sides lost patience with each other. "I write only out of sheer old-world politeness. Please let us stop this nonsense," Solow wrote in a May 1971 missive.[43] Robinson replied: "I agree that it is hopeless so goodbye. Yours, Joan."[44]

If we look back at the saga, it's evident that the Cambridge, UK, side won some significant theoretical victories, especially after it recruited a cadre of mathematical economists, some of Italian extraction, to play the MIT professors at their own game. Samuelson eventually conceded that the aggregate production function was merely a "parable" and that, in some cases, the one-way relationship between capital intensity and profit rates broke down—the phenomenon known as "reswitching." In practical terms, however, Team Cambridge, USA, emerged triumphant. Robinson and her colleagues failed in their goal to displace the production function, and the theories that relied on it, from their central place in the economics canon. The rival models that she, Kaldor, and others devised lived on mainly in the subfield of "post-Keynesian economics." Orthodox economists relegated them to the status of heterodoxy and largely ignored them.

One reason for this outcome was that Solow's approach to economic growth proved amenable to empirical analysis and yielded interesting results. In a 1957 paper, he fitted his growth equation to aggregate US data for GNP, labor inputs, and a measure of the capital stock for the period from 1909 to 1949, a period in which GNP per hour had more than doubled.[45] His statistical analysis found that growth in capital inputs accounted for only a fraction of this rise—12.5 percent of it, to be precise. Technical progress accounted for the other 87.5 percent.[46] At first glance, these findings seemed to suggest that both capital accumulation and the class struggle between capital and labor were something of a sideshow in economic development: the main driving force was technology.

Over time, Solow's "growth accounting" methodology came to play a central role in empirical and policy debates about economic growth. Attributing Team MIT's victory entirely to its superior empirics may be a mistake, however. In the early 1970s, Anwar Shaikh, a Pakistani American economist who was then a graduate student at Columbia University, showed that Solow's neoclassical production function was essentially an accounting identity—a mathematical relationship that is true by definition—and could be fitted to virtually any set of data points for capital per capita and output per capita, including one that spelled out the world *humbug* when plotted on a graph.[47] Despite this unnerving result, Shaikh's article on "The Humbug Production Function" didn't have much impact on the economics profession—an indication, perhaps, that larger issues than statistical explanatory power were at play during the long-running capital controversy.

Robinson surely believed this. In her mind, the resurgence of neoclassical macroeconomics, including Samuelson's mechanical interpretation of *The General Theory* as well as Solow's growth theory, couldn't be separated from US capitalism's rise to global dominance. From the early 1960s onward, she took to referring to her neoclassical opponents as "bastard Keynesians."[48] According to Marjorie S. Turner, the author of the 1989 book *Joan Robinson and the Americans*, Robinson first used this term in print in a 1962 review of a book by the Canadian economist Harry Johnson on trade and economic growth. Subsequently, Turner noted, "Robinson used the term 'bastard Keynesian' freely, not limiting it to Americans."[49] In fact, she applied it to practically any economist who adopted the neoclassical methodology, or who believed that using the levers of fiscal and monetary policy to prop up demand was sufficient to fix the contradictions in capitalism that Keynes had identified. In a 1976 lecture at Barnard College, she said that Keynes and Kalecki diagnosed "an inherent defect in the *laisser-faire* system but the bastard Keynesians turned the argument back into being a defence of *laisser-faire*, provided that just one blemish was going to be removed."[50] In an article the following year, she complained: "The bastard Keynesian doctrine, evolved in the United States, invaded the economics faculties of the world, floating on the wings of the almighty dollar. (It established itself even amongst intellectuals in the so-called developing countries, who have reason enough to know better.)"[51]

One possible interpretation of the battle between the two Cambridges is that no single theory can explain every aspect of economic development. In examining why countries like Germany and France were able to grow rapidly in the postwar years, or why Japan and South Korea did so well, the Solow model is useful because it shows how countries that have ready access to technology but have fallen behind the countries at the technology frontier can catch up rapidly. The post-Keynesian models, including the Harrod-Domar model and its modern variants, are useful for explaining the economic challenges facing both poor countries, which don't have enough savings to finance large-scale capital investments, and advanced countries operating at the technology frontier, such as the United States.

Robinson didn't see the Cambridge Capital Controversy in these terms. She believed it was ultimately an ideological contest. As it dragged on, she continued to engage in broader debates about the progress of what the French demographer Jean Fourastié would label *Les Trente Glorieuses*. In 1957 Harold Macmillan, the Conservative prime minister, issued his famous remark: "Most of our people have never had it so good." Five years later President John F. Kennedy declared in the 1962 *Economic Report of the President*, "The record of the economy since 1946 is a vast improvement over the prolonged mass unemployment of the 1930's."[52] The report was prepared by the Council of Economic Advisers, whose chairman, Walter Heller, taught at the University of Minnesota. Heller and his colleagues outlined "a three-part program for sustained prosperity" that was avowedly Keynesian. It consisted of temporary income tax reductions, an expansion in federal capital expenditures, and a strengthening of the unemployment insurance system. "These three measures will enable the Government to counter swings in business activity more promptly and more powerfully than ever before," the report confidently asserted.[53]

The postwar economic record also colored Robinson's views, but she interpreted it very differently from Heller and other optimists. In a 1962 article entitled "Latter-Day Capitalism," which appeared in *New Left Review*, a journal published in London, she noted that in 1944, when the Beveridge Report had issued its commitment to full employment, it would have "seemed Utopian" to imagine the unemployment rate averaging 3 percent year to year. In fact, the rate had barely touched 2 percent since the war ended. "Whatever our present discontents, this is by no means to be despised," Robinson wrote. ". . . But however thankful we should be for these blessings, it is too soon to claim that full employment vindicates latter-day capitalism. First of all we must ask how it has been achieved."[54]

Robinson went on to reemphasize the role military expenditures had played in propping up aggregate demand. In the United States, she pointed out, defense spending accounted for nearly 10 percent of GDP and about 60 percent of gross investment. "Whatever might have been, in fact Keynesian prosperity has been a by-product of the Cold War," she wrote.[55] In her 1962 book *Economic Philosophy*, which presented a short, sharp history of economic doctrines, Robinson made a related argument, saying that building weapons systems had turned into a substitute for Keynes's semi-ironic proposal in *The General Theory* for governments to deliberately engage in wasteful spending, as the ancient Egyptians did when they built the pyramids. "Nowadays the paradoxes"—in Keynesianism—"are taken in sober earnest and building weapons that become obsolete faster than they can be constructed has turned out far better than pyramids ever did to keep up profit without adding to wealth," Robinson wrote. "The relapse on Wall Street that follows any symptom of relaxation in the Cold War is a clear demonstration of the correctness of Keynes's theory, but also a demonstration of the falsity of his optimistic view that, when the theory was understood, reason would prevail."[56]

The sustainability of the postwar boom was far from obvious to Robinson. In one of her essays, she brought up Rosa Luxemburg's argument that capitalism could only survive by expanding into new territories. In an age of decolonization, when the rise of state socialism in the Soviet Union and China had closed off a substantial part of the world to capitalist incursions, the system was facing new challenges, Robinson argued in a 1961 essay published in *Monthly Review*. "Nineteenth century capitalism was an expanding system in the literal sense," she wrote. "It did not have to keep itself suspended by the bootstraps of its inner dynamism; it had its feet planted on new lands to be peopled, full of natural wealth to be exploited. There is much force in Rosa Luxemburg's prediction that when capitalism can no longer expand geographically it will not know what to do with itself."[57]

In the United States, Robinson wrote in the same essay, the annual growth rate of inflation-adjusted GDP had already slowed to about 2 percent, well below the potential growth rate that economists estimated on the basis of growth in the labor supply and productivity. "At each recovery from a mild recession, the gap between the best realized performance and the potential grows greater," she noted.[58] In the United Kingdom, she saw a different challenge emerging, one that Kalecki had predicted in the 1940s: a political business cycle, in which interest rates were raised in response to industrialists' claims that, because of full employment, the workers were getting "out of hand."[59] Recently, she noted in her *New Left Review* article, the "*Economist* newspaper, and several professors, have often argued for the greater 'flexibility' that would be introduced into the economy by a *little more* unemployment."[60] The conservative backlash was in train.

All of these concerns related to the question of whether Keynesianism could deliver on its promise to deliver sustained economic growth and banish the mass unemployment of the 1930s. But Robinson insisted there was another issue to be considered, an even deeper one: "Whether capitalism, even when prosperous, can provide us with what we really want."[61] To live a fulfilling life, she pointed out, people needed decent housing, reliable healthcare, and a good education, but "growing wealth always leaves us with a greater deficiency in just those things." This was no accident, she insisted: it came down to economics and profits. "Capitalist industry is dazzlingly efficient at producing goods to be sold in the shops, and, directly or indirectly, profits are derived from selling," she wrote in her *New Left Review* piece. "The services to meet basic human needs do not lend themselves to mass production: they are not an easy field for making profits, especially as, with our egalitarian democratic notions, they have to be offered irrespective of means to pay. Consequently, they must be largely provided through taxation." Given the opposition of businesses and wealthy people to paying higher taxes, this created a serious problem. "To supply goods is a source of profit, but to supply services is a 'burden upon industry.' It is for this reason that when, as a nation, 'we have never had it so good,' we find that we 'cannot afford' just what we most need."[62]

Robinson held her views passionately, sometimes to the point of blindness. Convinced that state-led industrialization was the most viable way for underdeveloped countries to grow and throw off the yoke of colonialism, she "defended Stalin into the 1950s and 1960s," Geoffrey Harcourt and Prue Kerr, two Cambridge-affiliated economists, wrote in a 2009 book about Robinson.[63] After visiting China in 1967, she wrote a sympathetic short book on the first stages of Mao's Cultural Revolution, which she described as "a popular rising" rather than "an inner Party purge."[64] Subsequently, she reluctantly reversed course. "She was always looking for Utopia," Harcourt, who knew Robinson personally, recalled in a 1995 interview. "She didn't find it in Russia, then she didn't find it in Eastern Europe, then eventually she didn't find it in China, and she backed off on China."[65]

If Robinson's ardor sometimes led her astray, many of her strictures about postwar Keynesianism proved prescient. In her 1962 essay "Latter-Day Capitalism," she wrote: "The Keynesian prescription for preventing recessions left an important problem unsolved—inflation."[66] In the same piece, she noted that, as far back as her 1936 book on the Keynesian theory of employment, she had pointed out that combining continuous full employment with an unregulated wage system would likely lead to a "vicious spiral," in which wages and prices chased each other upward. By 1962, this outcome hadn't yet materialized, but the British inflation rate *had* risen to more than 4 percent, generating consternation in official circles.[67] The previous year, the Conservative government had reluctantly introduced a "Pay Pause" to try to limit wage inflation. Robinson noted: "It seems that the authorities . . . preferred to remain in a fog of confusion in order not to have to face an awkward political situation at the practical level, or to admit, at the philosophical level, that the mechanisms of a 'free' capitalist system are inherently incapable of regulating themselves."[68]

Robinson's analysis implied that tackling the emerging problem of accelerating wage and price increases would be far from easy. Repeating a point she had made decades earlier, she said that British labor unions operated in a highly independent fashion, and that getting them to limit their wage claims in a coordinated manner would be "a daunting task."[69] In one of her later essays, Robinson would also point out that Keynes himself hadn't proposed any simple remedies to the inflation dilemma. "It was the bastard Keynesians who concocted bromides from his acid treatment of orthodox nonsense."[70]

As the 1960s and '70s proceeded, and rising inflation gave new life to pre-Keynesian economic doctrines, Robinson became increasingly cast down by the state of her subject and the world. In 1970, she retired from her Cambridge professorship, but she continued to speak out on issues that concerned her. In her 1976 lecture at Barnard College, which she subsequently published as an essay, she reminded the audience of Kalecki's 1943 warning that, in an environment of low unemployment, new institutions would have to be developed to reflect the enhanced power of the working class. "It is precisely because changes in the social and political institutions did not occur that the age of growth has been so uneasy and is now in danger of bringing itself to an end," she said.[71] During the same lecture, Robinson brought up growing concerns about environmental degradation, and economists' failure to address them adequately. "The bastard Keynesian theory never even pretended to discuss the use of resources," she said. "It fell back upon the old defence of *laisser-faire*: what is profitable is right . . . The great corporations must be allowed to go on chewing up the planet, else they will not be able to make profits and provide employment."[72]

By the early 1980s, Robinson was in poor health and depressed about many things, including the election of Margaret Thatcher and Ronald Reagan, and the subsequent intensification of the Cold War. "She saw the arms race going out of control at the beginning of the 1980s," Geoff Harcourt recounted. "I think it was just an accumulation of things which led her to a nihilistic state of mind."[73] Early in 1982, the student economics society at University College, Oxford, invited Robinson to speak. Although she looked frail, her gaze was penetrating and her mind sharp. But her disillusionment was palpable. One student asked what she would do if she had her life to live over. She replied that she would study something more useful, such as biology.[74] Later in 1982, Robinson took up a visiting fellowship at Williams College, in Massachusetts. The economist Juliet Schor, who was teaching at Williams, later recalled how, at one point, she shook the shoulders of a female student and said, "Whatever you do, promise me you won't go into economics."[75] On August 5, 1983, Robinson died at the age of seventy-nine.

19

"Nature . . . faithful and submissive
to those who respect her"

J. C. Kumarappa and the Economics
of Permanence

On May 9, 1929, J. C. Kumarappa, a thirty-seven-year-old accountant and economist who lived in Mumbai (which was then called Bombay), traveled to Ahmedabad, in Gujarat, to meet Mahatma Gandhi, the leader of the pro-independence Indian National Congress. Kumarappa had recently returned to India from New York, where he had obtained a master's degree in public finance at Columbia University. When he arrived at Gandhi's ashram, which was located on the banks of the Sabermati River, he saw a diminutive old man clad in a simple dhoti (loincloth) sitting under a tree spinning cotton.[1] Gandhi, who to hundreds of millions of Indians was a spiritual leader as well as a political one, invited Kumarappa to sit beside him. At the age of fifty-nine, the mahatma was then at the height of his influence. During the previous decade, his strategy of leading peaceful protests against British rule—satyagraha—had turned him into an iconic figure at home and abroad.

The following year, Gandhi would undertake his famous Salt March in the coastal town of Dandi, where he and his followers openly flouted the colonial laws by gathering salt on the salt flats. (Since the Salt Act of 1882, Britain had monopolized production of the mineral and imposed a sales tax on it that hurt the poor.) When Gandhi met Kumarappa, however, his mind was on economics rather than politics. Indian nationalists had long claimed that British colonial policies, particularly the tax system it had imposed, impoverished the majority of the native population. Gandhi was looking for someone to conduct a detailed survey of Matar Taluka, a poor rural area in the Kheda District of Gujarat. His goal, he later explained, was to build an "Indian economics" from the "bottom by the a posteriori method of securing rock bottom facts and drawing therefrom, by the most rigid process of reasoning, conclusions which no amount of jugglery could controvert."[2] In some ways, Gandhi and Kumarappa were very different: Gandhi was a Hindu ascetic from Gujarat; Kumarappa, a Christian businessman from Tamil Nadu, in the south of India. But they hit it off, and Gandhi offered Kumarappa the job of leading the survey.

Enlisting the help of some students from a college that Gandhi had founded, he dispatched them to fifty-four villages, where they used questionnaires to inquire into every aspect of economic life, from crop choices and irrigation methods, to levels of income and indebtedness, to hygiene and health. On the basis of this research, Kumarappa put together a report that described a culture of grinding poverty, in which more than 90 percent of families in Matar Taluka didn't earn enough money to support a basic subsistence budget and the population was steadily declining "due to a higher death rate consequent upon want of vitality and dire poverty."[3] The report described how the local farmers, who tilled modest smallholdings, were obliged to pay land taxes that in some places amounted to between 70 and 215 percent of the value of their annual crop yields: "That is, in simple language, the farmer has to pay to the Government twice what he gets from his fields."[4] Many farmers were forced to take out loans from local moneylenders at high rates of interest, which made their predicament even worse. "In other parts of the world where people labour with such low production the Government support the sufferers with doles to keep them from starvation," the report noted archly. "But in India, the government taxes them more heavily and drives them into the quick-sands of indebtedness."[5]

The report made a series of recommendations for raising living standards in Matar Taluka. They included allowing farmers to pay their taxes in kind as they had done under the Mughals, giving them the freedom to cultivate wastelands, developing local handicrafts, and creating a new organization to "draw surplus capital from the cities and make it available to the farmers" at reasonable rates of interest. The report called on farmers to "improve their methods of cultivation by avoiding all waste,"[6] but it placed the main burden on the authorities, concluding: "The Government, on its part, should cease to attempt to draw blood out of stone and turn its attention to finding ways and means of helping the people out of 'the slough of despond' in which we find them today."[7]

Packed with facts and figures, Kumarappa's report amounted to a searing indictment of British colonial rule. It marked the beginning of a lengthy relationship between him and Gandhi, which would last until the Indian leader was assassinated by a fanatical Hindu nationalist in January 1948, just five months after India became an independent nation. During this long association, Kumarappa worked on many of Gandhi's projects and developed a distinctive approach to economic development, which he called "Gandhian economics." In a series of pamphlets and books, he put forward a vision of an Indian economy based on self-sufficient local communities that would grow their own food and develop their own handicrafts industries. At a time when Jawaharlal Nehru, Gandhi's successor as leader of the Indian nationalist movement, was advocating state-led industrialization to catch up with the West, Kumarappa rejected any economic strategy—be it state socialism or industrial capitalism—aimed at maximizing economic growth and embracing material values. "Modern worldly wiseacres may throw cheap gibes at the other worldliness and religious trends of the orient," he wrote in his book, *Economy of Permanence*, which was published the same year as Gandhi's death. "The enduring qualities of these civilizations are pointers to the great farsighted standards of value our forefathers had made use of, in laying the foundations of a lasting society."[8]

Joseph Chelladurai Cornelius Kumarappa was born on January 4, 1892, in the ancient city of Thanjavur, where there are Hindu temples that date to the eleventh century. He came from an educated family. His grandfather was an Anglican clergyman. (The nineteenth century saw extensive efforts by British missionaries to convert Indians.) His father was an officer in the Indian Civil Service, which the British government slowly opened to talented Indians during the decades after 1858, when it formally assumed sovereignty from the East India Company. Kumarappa attended Doveton College, a Christian school in the city of Chennai (then known as Madras). In 1912, after leaving school, he moved to London, where he went by the name Cornelius, trained to be a chartered accountant, and greatly impressed his employers. "I must pay Mr. Cornelius the compliment that few Britishers have the same clever grasp of detail," one of his bosses wrote.[9]

In 1919, Kumarappa returned to India and started working in Mumbai. Six years later he cofounded his own auditing firm: Cornelius and Davar. He was also active in the local branch of the Young Men's Christian Association. In 1927, for reasons that aren't entirely clear, Kumarappa moved to the United States, where one of his brothers was obtaining a doctorate. After studying business at Syracuse University, he enrolled for a master's degree in public finance at Columbia University in New York. During the program, he did courses in taxation, fiscal policy, money and credit, international economics, and the history of economic thought. His teachers included two eminent American economists: Herbert J. Davenport, a former student of Thorstein Veblen, and Edwin Seligman, an expert on public finance who was also a progressive activist and a former president of the Society for Ethical Culture.

Seligman supervised Kumarappa's master's thesis, which was entitled "The Contribution of Public Finances to the Present Economic State of India." In this, his first lengthy piece of scholarship, Kumarappa pointed out that the subcontinent had a large, industrious population and lots of fertile land. Why, then, was it so backward and poor? Kumarappa blamed British misrule: rather than developing India and its people, the colonists had treated the country as a tributary state—a source of extractable wealth. He pointed out how the East India Company had introduced Western-style property rights and fixed annual taxes, which many peasants struggled to pay. "In the main," he wrote, "the exploitation policy of the East India Company was continued when the British Crown assumed responsibility for India, although it was no longer a barefaced commercial concern but was heralded by high-sounding trumpets of Divine Ordinance."[10]

Kumarappa's indictment of the British was powerful but not entirely original. In 1901 Dadabhai Naoroji, a Gujarati journalist and businessman who had moved to England and, in 1892, become the first Asian to be elected to the House of Commons, as a member of the Liberal Party, published *Poverty and Un-British Rule in India*, in which he claimed that Britain had long been draining wealth from the subcontinent. The following year Romesh Chunder Dutt, a retired Indian civil servant, published the first volume of a pathbreaking two-part economic history of India, in which he argued that the British "had not contributed a shilling" to the administration of its Indian empire.[11] Throughout the centuries-long rule of the East India Company and the British Raj, Dutt pointed out, a steady stream of profits and tax revenues had been transferred to London, which more than covered the cost of building the Indian railroad network that defenders of British rule cited as an example of colonial benevolence. And when the British government took over the East India Company's commercial operations during the nineteenth century, the financial burden of compensating its stockholders was placed on the Indian taxpayer in the form of loans issued by the colonial government. "The empire was thus transferred from the Company to the Crown, but the Indian people paid the purchase-money . . . [and do] to this day . . . in the shape of interest on [the] Debt," Dutt wrote.[12]

In Kumarappa's thesis, he cited Dutt and carried out his own analysis of India's finances. Roughly 95 percent of the national budget, he calculated, went to the Indian Army (which the British used to put down insurrections), other administrative expenditures, and debt service. These outlays left next to nothing for investing in public works and improving the lot of ordinary Indians, Kumarappa noted. He also emphasized how the policy of opening India to international trade and competition from British-made goods, including cottons from Lancashire, had negatively impacted many rural areas: "The old-time skilled craftsmen and artisans have lost their trade, and no industry has replaced them, but these men have been driven to the land to eke out a precarious living . . . Part of the year they work, but when the dry season sets in, they are let idle."[13]

After Kumarappa returned to India in early 1929, Gandhi's *Young India* newspaper published parts of his thesis in a series of articles. This may have been what brought him to the attention of the Congress leader, who had always closely aligned himself with the rural poor. Gandhi's moral creed emphasized *satya* (truth), *ahimsa* (nonviolence), *aparigraha* (renunciation of personal possessions), and *sarvadoya* (the welfare of all). In his autobiography, which was published in installments between 1925 and 1929, he recalled how he had been greatly influenced by *Unto This Last*, a critical collection of essays on political economy and morality by the Victorian social critic John Ruskin. In 1908 Gandhi translated Ruskin's essay into Gujarati, adding some commentary on its implications for Indian self-rule, or *swaraj*, which he invested with moral as well as political connotations. "If Swaraj cannot be attained by the sin of killing Englishmen, it cannot be attained either by the erection of huge factories," he wrote. "Gold and silver may be accumulated but they will not lead to the establishment of Swaraj. Ruskin has proved this to the hilt."[14]

Like Ruskin, Gandhi rejected the idea that the economy existed as a separate realm, with its own laws and morality. He believed that all human interactions, including economic ones, should be judged by the impact they had on other people, particularly weaker ones. In practical terms, he was constantly looking for ways to alleviate rural poverty. In 1918 he started his movement for *khadi*, handspun cloth, and adopted the ancient wooden spinning wheel as a symbol of rural pride and self-sufficiency. According to Percival Spear, an English historian who lived in India during the 1920s and '30s, Gandhi "envisaged a peasant society of self-supporting workers, with simplicity as its ideal and purity as its hallmark: the state would be a loose federation of village republics."[15] But Gandhi's public statements about economics were somewhat inconsistent. He referred to the laws of supply and demand as "laws of the devil." However, he also criticized price controls. And despite his jeremiads against industrialization, he was politically allied with a rising class of Indian industrialists who supported the Congress Party.

Gandhi wasn't an economist: he had trained as a lawyer. He was also deeply religious. In Kumarappa, he found an Indian economist with Western training and firsthand experience of capitalist economies who nonetheless expounded a distinctly Indian, and nonmaterialistic, view of economic development. In 1930, when the British authorities imprisoned Gandhi for inciting the salt protests that spread across the subcontinent, he called on Kumarappa to edit his weekly newspaper, *Young India*. In 1931 the British released Gandhi from prison and invited him to London for talks with the Labour government led by Ramsay MacDonald, which, at least in theory, was sympathetic to Indian demands for self-rule. Gandhi asked Kumarappa to prepare a report for him on the financial relationship between India and Britain, which he did. The talks in London didn't get very far, though. In 1932, following the collapse of the Labour government and its replacement with a more conservative National Government, the British authorities in India introduced another crackdown. Since Kumarappa was now a known associate of Gandhi, they arrested him and jailed him for two years.

In 1934, the year Gandhi turned sixty-five, he announced his retirement from the Congress Party, but that didn't herald his departure from public life. In December 1934 he announced the foundation of an All-India Village Industries Association (AIVIA), which had as its goal "the revival, encouragement and improvement of village industries, and the moral and physical advancement of the villages of India."[16] Emphasizing AIVIA's ties to the countryside, Gandhi located its headquarters in the small town of Wardha, in central India, where the railroad lines from Bombay to Calcutta and Madras to New Delhi crossed. The plan was to establish a campus of workshops and laboratories and classrooms, where hand-based techniques of production could be developed and studied. To run AIVIA, Gandhi appointed Kumarappa, who left his home in Bombay, moved to Wardha, and used his new position to expand upon the ideas about economic development that he had put forward in his graduate thesis and his report on Matar Taluka.

Kumarappa, like Gandhi, viewed the ancient Indian village as the subcontinent's key economic institution. Unlike the socialists in the Congress Party, who wanted to urbanize and industrialize the country as quickly as possible, following the Soviet example, Kumarappa and Gandhi were searching for a way to preserve and lift up the villages and their inhabitants. Making India's countless farms more productive was obviously central to this goal, but Kumarappa also wanted to build up small-scale manufacturing and handicrafts at the local level. One of his main goals at AIVIA was to replace commercially made goods with village-made equivalents, such as the homespun cotton—*khadi*—that Gandhi had long promoted. "Khadi in the place of mill cloth, village earthen pots instead of factory-made china, reed-pen instead of steel pen, hand-made paper . . . leather goods made in villages out of village-flayed cattle instead [of] tanned hide, the ordinary village *gur* instead of factory sugar, hand-pounded whole rice," one of AIVIA's pieces of literature explained.[17] To get this process started, the new organization recruited agents across India to study the economic strengths and weaknesses of local areas and submit a report on how they could be developed. The agent's job went beyond mere reporting. He (the agents were invariably men) should also "induce reliable merchants to store village products for sale, at prices mutually fixed between the merchants and the agent," the AIVIA article explained, and "carry on an intensive propaganda to create a favorable public opinion for the program in his area."[18]

In 1936 Kumarappa expanded his ideas into a book, *Why the Village Movement? A Plea for a Village Centered Economic Order in India*, which was published under the auspices of the AIVIA. It pointed out that in many different handicrafts, India already had a rich tradition of artisanal skills and knowledge: the challenge was to resuscitate and nurture them. To this end,

Kumarappa called on the central government to set up vocational schools in every village, where Indian children ages seven to fourteen would be taught basic literacy and numeracy but also handicrafts, such as spinning, basket weaving, embroidery, pottery, beekeeping, and carpentry. These schools would turn out "men and women with a backbone of character and self-respect who will not purr round the feet of foreign masters for a silken couch to lie on," Kumarappa wrote, "but who will hold their head erect, be independent, and be prepared to share the lowly life of the general rule of the people."[19]

Gandhi, who was a fervent promoter of self-reliance, had spurred some controversy by suggesting that the new village schools should be self-supporting, which was widely taken to mean their budgets would be paid for by selling goods that their students made. Kumarappa insisted that the mahatma had been misunderstood. "This is too narrow a financial viewpoint and it can never be true," he wrote. "What is meant is a much wider value, not in terms of money only, but in terms of future services rendered by the child as a well-trained citizen."[20] For decades, Gandhi had supported the *swadeshi* self-sufficiency movement, which called for the replacement of imported goods with Indian-made ones. Kumarappa portrayed AIVIA's mission of making India's villages and their inhabitants more productive as the heir to this tradition. The "import of finished goods which can be made from raw materials available locally is creating unemployment," he wrote. "This immediately gives us a solution to this problem. The more we use locally made goods the less will the unemployed be."[21]

The vision embodied in AIVIA was based on decentralizing production and devolving administrative authority, but Kumarappa also called on the central government to provide technical and financial support to local producers. As an example, he cited leather tanning, a trade that had long been dominated by members of the lowly Chamars caste. "The carcass has to be flayed and the hide should be salted immediately," Kumarappa noted. "Any delay in salting will allow putrifaction to set in." To address his problem, he called on the government to provide the tanners with duty-free salt and cheap tanning materials, and to "protect the industry from outside competition." If these types of policies were introduced, Kumarappa said, the various elements that go into efficient production could be "coordinated and divided between the State and the people, each functioning in the processes it is best fitted to perform."[22]

Kumarappa also recognized that the central government had an important role to play in larger-scale projects that were beyond the scope of local communities, such as providing transport links, dams, irrigation canals, and energy facilities. He referred to his vision of decentralized production with government support in some areas as "planning." But it wasn't central planning of the Soviet variety, which during the 1930s and '40s gained the support of many members of the Congress, including Nehru, who was president of the party from 1929 onward. Kumarappa remained skeptical of the Soviet experiment. In one of his essays, "Communism and the Common People," which was published in 1935, he lauded the Bolshevik regime for modernizing Russia and providing educational and job opportunities to women, but he warned that "economic militarism . . . is driving away all freedom of thought, speech and action."[23] Kumarappa believed that any system based on maximizing the volume of production was inherently dehumanizing, and in this context, he equated communism with capitalism. "Under mass production, whether under capitalism or communism, every person becomes a 'hand' or a 'mouth,'" he wrote. "We have invented machines that have become masters . . . Inventors should . . . devise tools and machines that can be operated by one or two and which will remain the servant of Man and will enable every owner to earn his own modest livelihood without squeezing out the life blood of his fellow man."[24]

In August 1935, the British Parliament passed a Government of India Act that granted more political autonomy to the Indian states and, at the national level, created an Indian central bank. The law stopped short of granting India dominion status of the sort enjoyed by Australia, Canada, and South Africa, but eventual independence now seemed conceivable. In 1938 Nehru invited Kumarappa to serve on a National Planning Committee, which was tasked with drawing up economic plans for self-rule. Kumarappa accepted the post, but a few months later he resigned. Most of the commission members thought that developing heavy industry was the key to India's future economic success. Kumarappa believed this approach was fundamentally misguided. "We are poor but we have an ocean of labor wealth," he wrote in a 1939 article. "Therefore an intelligent plan will find that the cottage method fits into the scheme for our country."[25] In some ways, Kumarappa was making a similar argument to the one that Kondratiev had made in Russia, where he argued that the country should exploit its huge endowments of land and labor by prioritizing the growth of agriculture rather than heavy industry. Unlike Kondratiev, however, Kumarappa had little interest in integrating India into the global economy. At the local and national level, self-sufficiency was his goal.

The outbreak of World War II interrupted the debate about economic development policy. In September 1939, Viceroy Linlithgow, the top British official on the subcontinent, announced that India and the Indian Army would enter the war against Hitler. Nehru told Linlithgow that the Congress Party would cooperate with this policy only if the British promised India independence at the end of the conflict. Gandhi supported this stance, and for a time, there was an uneasy standoff. In October 1940, however, the Congress Party launched a peaceful disobedience campaign, and in August 1942, at a meeting of its central committee in Bombay, Gandhi demanded that Britain leave India immediately and called on his countrymen to rally behind this demand. "The mantra is 'Do or Die,'" he declared. "We shall either free India or die in the attempt; we shall not live to see the perpetuation of our slavery."[26] After this dramatic address, the central committee passed a resolution formalizing the mahatma's demands. The British government reacted by arresting Gandhi, Nehru, and other Congress leaders, which prompted widespread protests, riots, and further arrests.

Kumarappa participated in the protests. He was arrested and sentenced to seven and a half years of hard labor. At the start of his incarceration in the city of Jabalpur, the only reading material he was allowed was the Bible. Making the best of the circumstances, he wrote a short book titled *Practice and Precepts of Jesus*. He also started work on a second book, which he completed after being released in 1944 on grounds of poor health. (He had high blood pressure.) This book, *The Economy of Permanence*, which originally appeared as an AIVIA pamphlet, was Kumarappa's most ambitious and lasting work. It began with three chapters on "Nature," in which he introduced the concept of economic sustainability without using the actual term. The world, he said, contains two types of natural endowments: raw materials, such as petroleum, coal, and other minerals and ores, which "being available in fixed quantities, may be said to be 'transient'"; and other resources, such as "the current of overflowing water in a river or the constantly growing timber of a forest," which "may be considered 'permanent' as their stock is inexhaustible in the service of man when only the flow or increase is taken advantage of."[27]

The key to creating a lasting and balanced economy was to rely on permanent resources rather than transient ones, Kumarappa said.

In nature, he explained, the term *work* means actions that preserve and reproduce the system: plants taking nourishment from the air and the sunlight; earthworms breaking up soil; bees pollinating flowers; animals devouring each other. All this happens without any external prompting. But what distinguishes human activity from the rest of nature, Kumarappa argued, is the free will that humankind exercises and its ability to upend nature's checks and balances. "By exercising this gift in the proper way he can consciously bring about a much greater co-operation and coordination of nature's units than any other living being," he wrote. "Conversely, by using it wrongly he can create quite a disturbance in the economy of nature and in the end destroy himself."[28] Nature is "faithful and submissive to those who respect her," but to those who "of their own 'Freewill' choose to ignore her requirements, she is sterner than justice and visits such transgressors with unrelenting punishments of violence and death as a reward for their sins."[29]

Writing in the 1940s, Kumarappa couldn't foresee environmental disasters like mass deforestation, ocean pollution, and climate change. But he ran through various ways, from small to large, in which nature punished behavior focused on the short term. Overeating damaged people's health; sexual promiscuity spread disease—on some matters, he was a conservative Christian to the end; bleaching rice and other grains leached out their nutrients, which led to vitamin deficiencies and other ailments. Underlying all these calamities, Kumarappa said, was the substitution of hedonistic and monetary values for eternal human ones. "Our economic system gets a lopsided development," he wrote. "Our lands are being shifted from food cultivation to the production of raw materials for mills. People are starving due to the shortage of rice, while rice lands are made to produce oil for soap-making . . . The existence of such a state of affairs proves that money values are not dependable scales of human need."[30]

"An economy that is based purely on monetary or material standards of value, does not take in a realistic perspective in Time and Space," Kumarappa went on. "This shortcoming leads to a blind alley of violence and destruction from which there is no escape."[31] The embrace of material values and mass production for profit wasn't merely economically harmful, he insisted: it also morally degraded a society and the people who lived in it. Evoking Ruskin and other early critics of industrial capitalism, he wrote: "Moral values are always attached to every article exposed for sale in the market. We cannot ignore such values and say 'business is business.' Goods produced under conditions of slavery or exploited labour, are stained with the guilt of oppression. Those of us who purchase such goods become parties to the existence of the evil conditions under which those goods were made."[32]

During his lifetime, Kumarappa was often accused of being a Luddite, a utopian, or some combination of the two. The criticisms of him emanated from two wings of the Congress Party: the pro-business right, which was heavily invested in industrialization, and the neo-Marxist left, which regarded the vision of a decentralized rural economy as reactionary and utopian. "It is reactionary because it turns back the productive forces of society," Jayaprakash Narayan, a prominent activist and labor leader, commented on one of Kumarappa's essays. "It is illusory because not having a class basis it cannot materialize. Furthermore, it means lower standards of living for the people."[33]

In *Economy of Permanence*, Kumarappa had sought to preempt some of the arguments that were leveled against him. He recognized the productivity benefits of industrial-scale production, and he foresaw a future in which state-run companies would dominate heavy industries, such as mining, energy, and chemical manufacturing. But he envisaged the rest of the economy being organized on a much smaller scale, around largely self-supporting communities. Local regions would trade with each other, exchanging items that they had in surplus for things they needed. But this process would take place through organized barter rather than anonymous monetary transactions.

Kumarappa also argued that a shift to mass production and global integration wouldn't necessarily translate into an increase in human welfare. In a chapter devoted to "Standards of Living," he compared the lifestyles of a senior Indian government official—a Dewan—and an English gardener or American factory worker. The Dewan resides in a small house with little furniture, goes barefoot at home, and buys mainly products that are locally made, such as sleeping mats made out of reeds, he noted. The English gardener sleeps on a metal-spring mattress. And the American resides in an apartment equipped with comfortable furniture and the latest labor-saving devices. But the latter's ability to keep up his level of consumption depends on his keeping his job, Kumarappa pointed out. "Thus are his freedom of movement and bargaining power curbed and the worker is glued down to his work bench."[34] Strictly in monetary terms, the Dewan may have a lower standard of living, Kumarappa said, but he lives a freer and more fulfilling life. Moreover, the modest sums he spends on his sleeping mats "go directly to support and maintain the artisans and their families and so forms a complete cycle with the locally available reeds which constitute the raw materials."[35]

Echoing Thorstein Veblen, Kumarappa also argued that in modern societies a great deal of consumption was driven by fashion and social pressures rather than genuine need. "For a while the fashion will be to eat soup out of a soup plate with a rim round the bowl, with a large elliptical spoon," he wrote. "A few years later the fashion will change. A soup bowl without a rim will now be used and a spoon more or less circular in shape will be the proper style. These frequent changes are productive of snobbery and are good for business."[36] Although this type of spending was usually associated with countries like Britain and France, it was spreading to India, Kumarappa complained. In Bombay, "one will soon get to know what to expect in every other house," he wrote. "The same modern laminated wood furniture with glass tops to tables . . . There is no variety, no imagination, no original ideas . . . These homes are more dead than graves. Everything is done for the consumer by the manufacturer under the pretext of making life comfortable and easy; such ease leads to the benumbing of the higher faculties which spells death to progress and development. If life is to be creative, such deadening standardization must go."[37]

Writing in the aftermath of the second disastrous world war in thirty years, Kumarappa also argued that a decentralized, locally based economy would be innately more peaceful than a globally integrated mass-production economy, which he equated with imperialism and international conflict. Returning to his example of the Indian official supporting local producers with his purchases, he wrote: "Such an economy does not require the Army, the Navy and the Air Force to secure their raw materials, find or make the markets and to keep the ocean lanes open and safe. Hence, they have no need of violence, as would be the case if the Dewan patronized spring mattresses made in Britain and included them in his 'Standard of Living.'"[38]

Like Smith, Marx, and Veblen, Kumarappa framed his economic analysis in historical terms. Looking back over human evolution, he identified five different types of social organization: the "parasitic economy"; the "predatory economy"; the "economy of enterprise"; the "economy of gregation"; and the "economy of service."[39] The Greek and Roman empires, which were both based on slave labor, were parasitic economies, he said. As examples of predatory economies, he cited the British opium trade in Asia and King Leopold's plunder of the Congo. But he also classed as predators New York financiers who loaned money to South American republics and shareholders in modern corporations, both of whom reaped their rewards without "contributing any personal effort in production."[40] Similarly, "the great cartels, trusts and combines, which through monopolistic control, get a greater share of benefit in proportion to their contribution, are largely predatory." Moving on to enterprise societies, Kumarappa pointed to the ancient civilizations of India and China, which were "supported largely by artisans pursuing their vocations peacefully for profit."[41] He defined an economy of "gregation" as one in which individuals subjugated their own interests to the collective body. As an example, he cited the activities of a village cooperative.

Kumarappa made clear that an "economy of service," the fifth and final form of social organization, was his ideal because it involved all the people working disinterestedly and peacefully for the good of the community. So far, he conceded, no human society had progressed to this stage, which he also referred to as the "Advanced or Spiritual State." But referencing the AIVIA and the All-India Spinners' Association, which the mahatma had set up in 1925, he described attaining this state as the "goal that Gandhi is pressing forward to with all his might." If it were achieved, Kumarappa concluded, "a nonviolent Economy of Permanence would have been established ushering in a civilization of lasting peace or Ram Raj or Kingdom of God on earth."[42]

When *Economy of Permanence* was published, the ideas it contained were distinctly out of favor. When India became independent in August 1947, Nehru became the country's first prime minister. According to sources cited by the historian Mark Lindley, whose admirable 2007 book on Kumarappa I have relied on heavily for biographical details, Gandhi wanted Kumarappa to be appointed finance minister. This didn't happen, and Gandhi's assassination robbed Kumarappa of his main political sponsor. The new government did appoint him to an economic planning committee, which put forward radical proposals for rural reforms, including redistributing some land from large estates to village communities and making taxes on farmers more progressive. But nothing much came of these suggestions. The primary focus of Nehru's government was resolving chronic food shortages and preparing the ground for rapid industrialization. In 1950 it created a Planning Commission, which helped to formulate an initial Five-Year Plan that called for 35 billion rupees of capital investment, with most of the money to be allocated to basic infrastructure: irrigation, energy, and transport. The Second Five-Year Plan (1956–61) raised the capital investment target to 62 billion rupees, with an emphasis on heavy industry, particularly steel. Nehru said the Congress Party's goal was to achieve socialism, and his government did nationalize some parts of the economy—the railroads in 1951, Air India in 1953, and the Imperial Bank of India in 1955. However, these policies stopped far short of Soviet-style command and control. Much of the Indian economy, including countless small farms, remained under private ownership. Newly independent India became a bureaucratic state rather than a communistic one.

Kumarappa supported some of the infrastructure investments that Nehru's government made, but he wanted more emphasis on rural development programs of the sort that he and Gandhi had long promoted. In 1949 the Congress Party appointed him head of another committee, this one tasked with making recommendations for further agrarian reforms. The committee's report echoed Kumarappa's previous calls for the central government to provide cheap credit to farmers, reduce rural indebtedness, and promote modern agricultural practices. It also recommended that any land seized by the government should be used to set up local farming cooperatives rather than be transferred directly to peasant farmers. Despite the committee's report, however, Nehru's government failed to pursue radical land reforms, and Kumarappa gradually became disillusioned with the new regime.

With Gandhi gone, his political influence, which had never been enormous, was rapidly declining. He was approaching sixty, and his health was not good. In 1954 he retired to his native south, where he lived in a modest house surrounded by his books. Before departing the political scene, however, he put together another book, *Gandhian Economic Thought*, which was published in 1951, the same year that the Congress government's First Five-Year Plan went into effect. In this short work, Kumarappa reiterated his critique of mass production societies and made some provocative statements. "Large scale industries will politically lead to dictatorship," he wrote. "Even the so-called democratic countries like America, Russia etc., became actual dictators under the stress of war . . . There is hardly any difference between Stalin, Roosevelt, Churchill, Hitler or Mussolini. One is as good, or as bad, as the other."[43] Equating the wartime heroes of Britain and the United States with fascist and Communist dictators wasn't designed to win Kumarappa friends in the West. But it reflected his belief that economic rivalry between the great economic powers had caused two world wars. He was convinced that any economic system based on large-scale production and unrestricted growth would eventually extinguish peace and democracy. By contrast, "village industries provide the conditions for the development of democracy," he wrote. "To make use of village industries is not really going back to savagery unless democracy is savagery, but leads to civilization and culture, bringing out man's dignity and his independence and taking him out of the slavery of his own fellow men."[44]

Kumarappa also provided more details of how his model rural communities would operate. Each one would assess its needs for food, shelter, and consumer goods, then plan its production accordingly. "Supposing we want to have a balanced diet for 6000 persons," Kumarappa wrote. "We have the menu; we would require 36000 lbs. of wheat if we allow 6 ounces a person. Similarly we calculate all other requirements. Having taken the total requirements we plan the amount of acreage that should be placed under wheat, etc."[45] As this passage indicates, Kumarappa didn't equate decentralization with maximizing production for the sake of it. To the contrary, he argued that production should be carefully modulated to preserve an ecological balance and prevent wastage. Each community would organize its activities through a local cooperative, which would control some key resources, such as irrigation tanks and fuel oil. Larger infrastructure projects, such as power plants, energy grids, and transport networks, would be organized at the regional or national level. These industries would be regarded as "necessary evils," Kumarappa said. They "must be under state control and not under private ownership and run not for profit but only run on a service basis."[46] Some manufacturers would also be allowed to operate nationally, but they would be prevented from "flooding the country with unnecessary things."[47] Kumarappa also laid out a political structure for his new society. The smallest administrative unit—the panchayat—would include twenty or thirty villages. There would be larger administrative bodies at the district and provincial levels, all staffed by trained civil servants.

In discussing these practical details, Kumarappa sounded rather like William Thompson or Charles Fourier, more than a century earlier, explaining how their new communities would function. The early socialist intellectuals didn't live to see their ambitious visions become a reality, and neither did he. He died in 1960 in Madurai, a city in his native state of Tamil Nadu. He was sixty-eight. The Congress Party was still in power, and it was still pursuing a strategy of state-led growth, although the outcomes were deteriorating. (During the Second Five-Year Plan, annualized GDP growth was more than 4 percent; during the Third Five-Year Plan, which was in operation from 1961 to 1966, growth slowed to below 3 percent.) At the end of the twentieth century, after the Soviet Union collapsed, India would do an about-face and embrace deregulation and market forces, but the underlying policy goal remained the same: maximizing economic growth and making the country richer, or at least less poor.

Over time, this goal was accomplished. According to figures from the World Bank, India's GDP per capita in inflation-adjusted terms rose from just $305.80 in 1960 to $2,239 in 2023, with most of the gains coming in the era of liberalization.)[48] The social and environmental consequences of this transformation were also dramatic, however. Income inequality rose, and there were a series of environmental calamities, including the infamous Bhopal disaster of 1984, when a highly toxic gas leaked from a Union Carbide chemical plant, killing nearly four thousand people in the immediate aftermath. "Whether under state planning in the past or under the business-friendly regime now in place, India's economic and technological policies have taken little (often no) account of the country's resource endowments or of broader questions of environmental sustainability," the historian Ramachandra Guha wrote in his authoritative 2018 biography of Gandhi. Consequently, Guha went on, modern India is "an ecological disaster zone, marked by deforestation, species loss, chemical contamination of the soil, declining soil fertility, depleting groundwater aquifers, and massively high rates of atmospheric and river pollution."[49]

This outcome wouldn't have surprised Kumarappa. Despite his close ties to Gandhi, his economic ideas didn't have a great deal of impact during his lifetime or in the decades after his death. As a new millennium dawned, however, a new generation of environmental activists and progressives hailed him as a prophet of sustainability and degrowth, a status he certainly earned. "This is not an impossible 'heaven on earth' that we are seeking," he wrote at the end of *Gandhian Economic Thought*. "Humanity is being driven by force of circumstances towards self-sufficiency in food and primary needs. If this tendency is resisted persistently the other alternative is the wiping out of the human race by competitive armament and progressive destruction and annihilation of one nation by another. Will man have the foresight to choose the right path?"[50]

20

"Vast sugar factories owned by a camarilla of absentee capitalist magnates and worked by a mass of alien proletarians"

Eric Williams on Slavery and Capitalism

In the summer of 1935, as Keynes was revising the final manuscript of *The General Theory* in Cambridge, a twenty-three-year-old Trinidadian named Eric Williams sat for his final examinations in modern history at England's other ancient university, Oxford. Three years earlier Williams had received Trinidad's Island Scholarship, the highest academic honor that a high school student could attain on the small British colony located in the southern Caribbean, close to Venezuela. Despite the social, racial, and geographic gulfs that separated Oxford from Trinidad, Williams had settled in, doing well academically and playing cricket for the university. His tutor at St. Catherine's College, R. Trevor Davies, a Welsh clergyman who was an expert on Imperial Spain, served as his mentor and friend. Still, taking finals in Oxford is a grueling challenge for anyone, and Williams's ordeal was extended when, after completing his written papers, he was summoned to an additional verbal examination, known as a "viva voce." When he arrived to meet the examiners he got a pleasant surprise. Rather than grilling him on his written answers, the chief examiner informed him that he had achieved a distinguished first-class degree and inquired about his interest in colonial history, which he had chosen as his elective. "Well, I am a colonial," Williams replied. The examiner asked if he meant that there was a connection between a scholar's own environment and their studies, to which Williams replied that he didn't see the value of study unless such a connection existed. The examiner "then congratulated me on my excellent performance in the examination," Williams recounted later in his life, "commented on the regularity of my handwriting and the speed with which I could obviously write, and wished me success in my future career."[1]

He had already come a long way. The eldest of twelve children, one of whom died in infancy, Williams was born in Port of Spain, Trinidad's capital, in 1911. His father, Thomas, was a postal clerk whose lack of "social qualifications" had frustrated his own hopes for career advancement. "The necessary social qualifications were color, money, and education, in that order of importance," Williams recounted in his autobiography. "My father lacked all three."[2] His mother, Eliza, was a homemaker who supplemented her husband's modest income by baking and selling bread and cakes. Perennially struggling to make ends meet, the family moved from rental to rental, "and in one bad case the bailiff arrived," Williams recalled.[3] These sorts of privations were far from atypical on an island that had long been organized to benefit its colonial rulers. (Before Britain claimed sovereignty in 1802, Trinidad had been a possession of Spain.) Its biggest industries were exporting cocoa, sugar, and oil, and the companies that dominated these industries were largely British owned.

The island's heterogenous makeup also reflected its colonial history. Its residents included African descendants of slaves who had been transported in the triangular trade; Indians (and some Chinese) who had been imported as indentured workers following the abolition of slavery; white colonial administrators and property owners; and many people of mixed race. The Williams family had African and French heritage, and, despite their financial challenges, they considered themselves middle class. Beneath them on the social totem pole were manual workers and, at the very bottom, indentured Indian workers, who lived in poverty and squalor.

At the age of eleven, Williams won a scholarship to the top high school on the island, Queen's Royal College, where students wore uniforms, played competitive sports, and studied a rigorous curriculum modeled on what was taught at private schools in England. Williams racked up an impressive academic record, particularly in Latin. One of his history teachers was the Trinidadian author C. L. R. James, who was a graduate of the college and just ten years older than Williams. Outside of the classroom, James was a budding writer and anti-colonialist activist. He and Williams shared a love of cricket, but Williams, in his autobiography, said that another teacher, W. D. Inniss, had had more influence on him.[4]

Having received an outstanding degree, Williams, on the advice of his Oxford tutors, decided to stay in England and pursue further studies. He applied for a prestigious prize fellowship at the graduate-only All Souls College, but the application process, which included attending a formal dinner at high table, didn't go well—a failure he attributed to racism. "It was not that I felt that I had won the fellowship," he recalled years later. "I knew I had not. But I knew that I could never win one. This is one of these difficulties that whites can never understand. Only Negroes and other racial groups exposed to racial prejudice can."[5] Despite his disappointment, Williams stayed in Oxford and began working on a doctoral thesis. The government of Trinidad agreed to fund him for another year. As his research topic, he chose the British abolition of slavery, which, according to the standard accounts, had come about after William Wilberforce and his colleagues in the early nineteenth-century abolitionist movement persuaded the House of Commons that the institution was a moral abomination. Williams regarded this story as self-serving and inaccurate because it omitted the role played by economic factors, particularly the declining profitability of Britain's Caribbean slave plantations during the post-Napoleonic era. After delving into the imperial archives in Oxford and London, he wrote a thesis entitled *The Economic Aspect of the Abolition of the West Indian Slave Trade and Slavery*. The work took longer to complete than Williams had hoped, and he was short of money. But finally, in December 1938, he obtained his doctorate.

In August of the following year, the month before Hitler's forces invaded Poland, he sailed for the United States, where he had been offered a teaching post in the political science department at Howard University in Washington, DC. Howard was the most prestigious Black college in the country. During the nine years he was there, Williams taught a freshman survey course on the history of civilization and published two books. The first one, *The Negro in the Caribbean*, was an introduction to colonialism and slavery in the islands. It came out in 1942 and was praised for filling a big gap in the literature. This success set the stage for Williams's second book, a broader look at the economics of slavery, which expanded his doctoral thesis to include the relationship between the triangular trade and the industrial revolution. After completing a manuscript in early 1943, he submitted it to the University of North Carolina Press, along with a one-page prospectus that said it "attempts to place in historical perspective the relation between early capitalism in Europe, as exemplified by Great Britain, and the Negro slave trade and Negro slavery in the West Indies."[6] After receiving positive comments on the manuscript from several more established academics, the university press agreed to publish it on the proviso that Williams pay $700—a considerable sum in those days—to help cover the cost. The press could hope for sales of just four hundred or five hundred copies, its director explained. Eager to see his work published and hopeful that he could somehow raise the money, Williams agreed to the terms, and, after some more haggling, the publisher accepted the title he suggested: *Capitalism and Slavery*. The book was published in November 1944. Although some of its claims are still disputed, it is today widely regarded as a classic text.

In addressing the economics of British colonialism, Williams entered a debate that can be dated back at least to 1776, as discussed earlier, when Adam Smith, in *The Wealth of Nations*, described the colonial system, including the slave labor and mercantilist policies that featured prominently in it, as hindrances rather than fillips to economic development.[7] In volume I of *Capital*, Marx took a very different view, emphasizing how colonialist plunder and slavery helped to generate the seed capital of industrial capitalism, a process he termed "primitive accumulation."[8] Subsequently most British economic historians followed Smith, downplaying any linkages between slavery and the industrial revolution. In explaining the genesis of industrialization, they emphasized internal factors, such as technological advances, population growth, the ready availability of energy from coal, and a culture of entrepreneurialism. Although Williams wasn't a Marxist, his approach to this question was more in the Marxian tradition. He placed Britain's industrialization in the context of its role in an international economic system characterized by colonialism and slavery.

Williams wasn't the only Black scholar who was reassessing slavery and its aftermath. In the decade from 1935 to 1945, three remarkable books appeared: *Black Reconstruction in America*, by W. E. B. Du Bois, the African American sociologist, historian, and civil rights activist; *The Black Jacobins*, a history of the Haitian Revolution, by C. L. R. James, Williams's former high school teacher; and *Capitalism and Slavery*. Each of these books presented a distinctive thesis, but they all emphasized the economic importance of slave labor and challenged existing interpretations. Du Bois wrote about the failure of Reconstruction in the face of determined (and often violent) resistance on the part of the Southern whites. James told the epic tale of Toussaint L'Ouverture, the Haitian general whose army of former slaves routed the French colonialists from Saint-Domingue, which he described as "an integral part of the economic life of the age, the greatest colony in the world, the pride of France, and the envy of every other imperialist nation."[9]

It is surely no accident that these three seminal works appeared within ten years of each other. Du Bois, James, and Williams were all supporters of a decolonization movement that had grown in strength since the First World War, during which the imperial powers had enlisted in their armed forces large numbers of colonial citizens from Asia, Africa, and the Americas. The anti-colonial struggle was primarily concerned with ending imperial rule, but it also involved a reassessment of colonial history, a conscious effort to supplant the narratives and interpretations established by white historians, and a more critical assessment of the ties between capitalism and racial exploitation. The cataclysms that befell the international system between 1914 and 1945 gave further impetus to the anti-colonial movement. In 1900, the European empires had seemed indestructible. By the 1930s and '40s, the earth was shaking beneath the imperial core, raising new possibilities for its colonial subjects, who, partly through the works of writers like Williams, James, and Du Bois, were finding a public voice that had long been denied them.

Du Bois grew up in Great Barrington, Massachusetts, and was a generation older than the other two. A founding member of the National Association for the Advancement of Colored People, he was also a major figure in the Pan-African movement, which promoted independence for African nations and unity among Black people everywhere. During the early 1930s, James left Trinidad for England, where he earned a living as a cricket journalist. He also worked on his own writing, joined a Trotskyite group, and edited a newsletter for a Pan-African group. Williams, in his formative decades, didn't express strong political views, but, as he indicated to the Oxford examiner during his viva voce, his entire outlook had been shaped by his upbringing in a British colony. The Californian scholar Cedric Robinson, in his 1983 book *Black Marxism*, which introduced the term *racial capitalism* to intellectual discourse, discussed at length the contributions of Du Bois, James, and Williams, whom he described as part of a group of highly educated "black radicals." Citing the Black novelist and poet Richard Wright, Robinson argued that the critique of capitalism developed by these thinkers was "grounded from below in the historical consciousness of black masses."[10] Whether this reading is accepted or not, *Black Reconstruction in America*, *Black Jacobins*, and *Capitalism and Slavery* were undoubtedly products of their moment—a time when global capitalism was convulsed with the dual crises of depression and fascism, decolonization was becoming a more realistic prospect, and fresh thinking was demanded.

Du Bois, in the decades since the publication of his classic work *The Souls of Black Folk* in 1903, had become increasingly influenced by the class-based economic analysis of Marx and other socialist thinkers. In 1926, he had visited the Soviet Union, where he was impressed by the efforts to build a classless society. In writing *Black Reconstruction*, he adopted a broadly materialist approach, emphasizing the role that economic factors played in creating and sustaining the racist ideology of Southern whites before and after the Civil War. "The espousal of the doctrine of Negro inferiority by the South was primarily because of economic motives and the inter-connected political urge necessary to support slave industry," he wrote.[11] After the Emancipation Proclamation, he pointed out, the Southern planters were desperate to find cheap labor, and working-class whites feared that free Blacks would undercut their wages and take their jobs: "It must be remembered and never forgotten that the civil war in the South which overthrew Reconstruction was a determined effort to reduce black labor as nearly as possible to a condition of unlimited exploitation and build a new class of capitalists on its foundation."[12]

But even as Du Bois adopted a class framework, he also emphasized that the history of the South couldn't be understood without introducing racism, not merely as a consequence of capitalism, but as an independent factor that undercut the binary Marxian taxonomy of capitalists and proletariat. In the Southern states, he pointed out, there were two separate proletariats—a Black one and a white one. This fracturing had prevented the emergence of a working-class movement unified by a class consciousness and opposition to capitalist exploitation, which is the principal agent of history in the Marxist model. "Most persons do not realize how far this failed to work in the South,"

Du Bois wrote, "and it failed to work because the theory of race was supplemented by a carefully planned and slowly evolved effort, which drove such a wedge between the white and black workers that there are probably not today in the world two groups of workers with practically identical interests who hate and fear each other so deeply and who are kept so far apart that neither sees anything of common interest."[13]

These racial antagonisms were a key factor in the perpetuation of white rule through the passage of Jim Crow laws and the effective disenfranchisement of many Blacks, Du Bois pointed out. He also noted that the principal beneficiaries of this reconstituted system of racial domination were former planters and Northern capitalist "carpet baggers" who moved to the South in search of easy profit. Working-class whites also supported and benefited from the system, Du Bois said, because "while they received a low wage, [they] were compensated in part by a sort of public and psychological wage. They were given public deference and titles of courtesy because they were white. They were admitted freely with all classes of white people to public functions, public parks and the best schools." On the other side of the color line, the Black Southerner was "subject to public insult; was afraid of mobs; was liable to the jibes of white children and the unreasoning fears of white women; and was compelled almost continuously to submit to various badges of inferiority."[14]

In emphasizing racial divisions within the working class and invoking the concept of a "psychological wage" that white workers derived from structures of racial oppression, Du Bois went well beyond the traditional Marxist framework. His analysis can be seen as a way of answering a question about capitalism that had long perplexed leftist thinkers: How could such an exploitative system prove so difficult to dislodge? The answer Du Bois gave was that, at least in the case of the American South, any coherent account of capitalism's endurance has to consider race and racism alongside class. It has to examine how racial cleavages and racial discrimination map onto the basic economic division between propertyless workers and owners of capital.

This approach clearly had implications for interpreting other multiracial societies, and the global capitalist system, in which the division of labor was partly, or even largely, arranged along racial lines. It's easy to see why Cedric Robinson and others viewed Du Bois as a progenitor of the theory of racial capitalism, which emphasizes that capitalist elites exploit racism to entrench their power, and that capitalism and racism have been associated since the rise of capitalism. Du Bois was ahead of his time, though it should also be noted that, at this stage of his life, he regarded the racial lens as an essential companion to class analysis rather than an alternative to it. The result of racial divisions in the South, he wrote in *Black Reconstruction*, "was that the wages of both classes"—working-class Blacks and working-class whites—"could be kept low, the whites fearing to be supplanted by Negro labor, the Negroes being threatened by the substitution of white labor."[15]

Williams, during his years as a scholar, was less overtly political than Du Bois and James, but he was equally intent on forging new narratives that reflected new realities. "Every age rewrites history, but particularly ours, which has been forced by events to re-evaluate our conceptions of history and economic and political development," he said in the preface to *Capitalism and Slavery*.[16] In the book's first chapter, "The Origin of Negro Slavery," he discussed the economic roots of the transatlantic slave trade, pointing out that European plantation owners in the Americas turned to Africa as a source for labor after initially relying on Indigenous slaves and white indentured workers. "Slavery in the Caribbean has been too narrowly identified with the negro," Williams wrote. "A racial twist has thereby been given to what is basically an economic phenomenon. Slavery was not born of racism: rather, racism was the consequence of slavery. Unfree labor in the New World was brown, white, black, and yellow; Catholic, Protestant and pagan."[17] Williams described how indentured whites, some of whom were convicts or Irish rebels, were "packed like herrings" into disease-plagued ships for the journey across the Atlantic, to work in British colonies in the Caribbean and on the mainland of North America.[18] The main reason that the plantation owners switched to African slave labor, he explained, was that it was more economical: "The money which procured a white man's services for ten years could buy a Negro for life. As the governor of Barbados stated, the Barbadian planters found by experience that 'three blacks work better and cheaper than one white man.'"[19]

Williams didn't have access to modern databases that have documented in detail the enormous size of the transatlantic slave trade. Citing the evidence that was available to him, he said that in 1760 alone, 146 slave ships, with a capacity for 36,000 slaves, left British ports for Africa, and by 1771, "the number of ships had increased to 190 and the number of slaves to 47,000." He continued: "The importation into Jamaica from 1700 to 1786 was 610,000 and it has been estimated that the total import of slaves into all the British colonies between 1680 and 1786 was over two million."[20]

Williams's account of the triangular trade was unsparing. "The purchase of slaves called for a business sense and shrewd discrimination," he wrote. "An Angolan Negro was a proverb for worthlessness; Coromantines (Ashantis), from the Gold Coast, were good workers but too rebellious; Mandingoes (Senegal) were too prone to theft; the Eboes (Nigeria) were timid and despondent; the Pawpaws or Whydahs (Dahomey) were the most docile and best-disposed."[21] On arriving in the Caribbean, the African captives who had survived the often deadly Middle Passage were sold at auction to owners of plantations, particularly sugar plantations, some of which had hundreds of enslaved workers. Williams described how, on some of the islands, the rise of the plantations squeezed out colonialist farmers who operated on a smaller scale and caused the white population to decline. "King Sugar had begun his depredations," Williams wrote, "changing flourishing commonwealths of small farmers into vast sugar factories owned by a camarilla of absentee capitalist magnates and worked by a mass of alien proletarians."[22]

Describing enslaved workers as proletarians captured the key point that, from an economic point of view, slavery and factory labor were alternative ways of obtaining large quantities of labor power. Adam Smith had argued that wage labor was the cheaper and more efficient option, but his argument begged the question of whether it was ever a feasible one for plantations in the Americas, where labor had to be imported from afar. It also downplayed the reality that, for a long time, slave-based plantation capitalism generated large profits. Williams described how in Barbados, one of the larger British colonies, the price of land skyrocketed with the development of the sugar industry, and enormous fortunes were made. The plantation owners dominated the island economies, and in their homeland they constituted a nouveau riche elite who flouted their wealth by building grand country houses such as Fonthill Mansion in Wilshire,[23] which was owned by the Beckford family, and Bromley Hill Place in Kent, a property of the Longs.[24]

In describing the economic workings of the slave trade, Williams didn't dwell on the boundless human misery and cruelty that underpinned it. But he also didn't gloss over the deep-rooted racism of the slave traders and plantation owners that inured them to the terrible reality of their business. "The slave traders were among the leading humanitarians of their age," he noted ironically. "John Cary, advocate of the slave trade, was conspicuous for his integrity and humanity and was the founder of a society known as the 'In-corporation of the poor.' . . . Brian Blundell of Liverpool . . . engaged in both the slave and West Indian trades, was for many years trustee, treasurer, chief patron and most active supporter of a charity school."[25] In another passage, Williams pointed out how "the blood of the Negro slaves reddened the Atlantic and both of its shores."[26] He went on to note archly: "Strange that an article like sugar, so sweet and necessary to human existence, should have occasioned such crimes and bloodshed!"

Other scholars, including the English historians Herman Merivale and V. T. Harlow and the Americans Charles McLean Andrews and Lowell J. Ragatz, had already written authoritatively about slavery and the Caribbean plantations. Williams referred to some of their works; indeed, he dedicated his book to Ragatz, a professor at George Washington University, noting his "monumental labors in this field."[27] But Williams went beyond earlier historians in addressing the economic impact of slavery and plantation capitalism on overall British economic development. Enslaved labor didn't merely create great riches for individual colonialists, he argued; it played a key role in fostering the rise of industrial capitalism. This argument subsequently became known as the Williams Thesis.

Williams didn't claim that colonialism and slavery were the only factors that propelled the British economy forward: "But it must not be inferred that the triangular trade was solely and entirely responsible for the economic development," he wrote. "The growth of the internal market in England, the ploughing-in of the profits from industry to generate still further capital and achieve still greater expansion, played a large part."[28] But Williams did hold that the triangular trade was a major accelerant of British economic growth, and he presented his argument in parts. He examined the triangular trade and sought to demonstrate how it boosted specific manufacturing industries in Britain, particularly the vital Lancashire cotton industry. Then he described how the profits generated by slavery and plantation capitalism filtered through the rest of the British economy and "fertilized" its development.

The argument began with the basics. "The slave ship sailed from the home country with a cargo of manufactured goods," Williams wrote. "These were exchanged at a profit on the coast of Africa for Negroes, who were traded on the plantations, at another profit, in exchange for a cargo of colonial produce to be taken back to the home country. As the volume of the trade increased, the triangular trade was supplemented, but never supplanted, by a direct trade between home country and the West Indies."[29] Drawing on a pioneering survey of Britain's trade balance carried out in 1776 by Sir Charles Whitworth, an English government official, he estimated that during the period from 1714 to 1773, the Caribbean accounted for about 20 percent of Britain's imports and 12 percent of its overall foreign commerce.[30] The American mainland, which included the slave colonies of the South, accounted for another 10 percent of foreign commerce. Britain's trade relationship with India was probably bigger than the transatlantic trade, Williams conceded. "It is even probable that the profits from the slave trade were smaller than those made by the British East India Company," he added. And yet he insisted, "these trades were far less important than the slave trade."[31]

How so? The business model of the East India Company, Williams pointed out, consisted of using British gold and silver to buy Indian products—such as spices, silk, and cotton—which it then shipped to Britain and sold at a large markup. From "the mercantilist standpoint the India trade was a bad trade," Williams wrote. "It drained Britain of bullion to buy unnecessary wares."[32] The triangular trade, on the other hand, created new markets for British manufactured goods and supplied Britain with important industrial raw materials, particularly cotton. To illustrate his argument, Williams described the cargo on one British slave ship that was bound for Africa in the year 1787:

> Cotton and linen goods, silk handkerchiefs, coarse blue and red woolen cloths, scarlet cloth in grain, course and fine hats, worsted caps, guns, powder, shot, sabers, lead bars, iron bars, pewter basons, copper kettles and pans, iron pots, hardware of various kinds, earthen and glass ware, hair and gilt leather trunks, beads of various kinds, silver and gold rings and ornaments, paper, coarse and fine checks, linen ruffled shirts and caps, British and foreign spirits and tobacco.
>
> This sundry assortment was typical of the slave trader's cargo. Finery for Africans, household utensils, cloths of all kinds, iron and other metals, together with guns, handcuffs and fetters: the production of these stimulated capitalism, provided employment for British labor, and brought great profits to England.[33]

Among the direct beneficiaries of the triangular trade were the British port cities that served it, including Bristol, Glasgow, and Liverpool. Between 1700 and 1773, the population of Liverpool rose from 5,000 to 34,000.[34] The city's first slave ship departed for West Africa in 1709. By 1730, there were fifteen slavers, and by 1771 more than a hundred, Williams pointed out.[35] He also identified some of the local beneficiaries from the triangular trade. Among them was John Gladstone, the chairman of Liverpool's West India Association, a trade group for planters and merchants involved in the triangular trade, whose son, William Ewart Gladstone, would serve as Britain's prime minister on four different occasions in the late nineteenth century. After starting out as a merchant, the elder Gladstone "through foreclosures, acquired large plantations in British Guiana and Jamaica," Williams wrote. "The sugar and other produce which he sold on the Liverpool Exchange were grown on his own plantations and imported on his own ships. The fortune amassed by this means permitted him to open up trade connections with Russia, India and China and to make large and fortunate investments in land and property in Liverpool."[36]

Aside from the merchants and shipbuilders of the port cities, there were many other interests and regions in Britain that benefited from the triangular trade, Williams emphasized. In Bristol in 1799, he noted, there were twenty sugar refineries, and in London there were eighty.[37] In the inland city of Birmingham and its surrounding areas, metals manufacturers exported a wide range of products to Africa, including cutlery, brass pans and kettles, iron bars (which the slave traders used to make chains and padlocks and branding irons), and guns. "The Birmingham guns of the eighteenth century were exchanged for men," Williams wrote, "and it was a common saying that the price of a Negro was one Birmingham gun."[38] Some local businesses made specialized goods for the African market. Williams singled out the Cheadle Company, which manufactured the brass *manelloes* (rings) that were often used as currency to purchase slaves. Between 1734 and 1780, the firm's "capital increased eleven times," he pointed out.[39]

Building on these examples, Williams argued that the triangular trade had a pervasive impact on the British economy. "By 1750," he wrote, "there was hardly a trading or a manufacturing town in England which was not in some way connected with the triangular or direct colonial trade."[40] These links weren't confined to manufacturing and shipping. Williams also identified banks and other financial institutions that helped finance various aspects of the slave trade, including Lloyd's of London, the famous insurance market. Williams described how in the market's early existence, when it was little more than a coffeehouse in London's Financial District frequented by merchants and shipowners, "many advertisements in the London Gazette about runaway slaves listed Lloyd's as the place where they should be returned."[41] Later, as Lloyd's established a virtual monopoly on marine insurance, it "insured slaves and slave ships, and became vitally interested in legal decisions as to what constituted 'natural death' and 'perils of the sea,'" Williams noted.

Williams wasn't the first writer to point out that the slave trade and plantation capitalism enriched the colonizing countries and boosted their economies. In *Black Jacobins*, which was published six years before *Capitalism and Slavery*, James cited the growth of Nantes, France's primary port serving the slave trade; Marseilles, which did a lot of trade with its Caribbean territories; and Bordeaux, which supplied brandy and wine to the colonies. "Nantes, Bordeaux and Marseilles were the chief centers of the maritime bourgeoisie, but Orleans, Dieppe, Berey-Paris, a dozen great towns, refined raw sugar and shared in the subsidiary industries," James wrote. "A large part of the hides worked in France came from San Domingo. The flourishing cotton industry of Normandy drew its raw cotton in part from the West Indies, and in all its ramifications the cotton trade occupied the population of more than a hundred French towns."[42]

Williams's argument about the commercial impact of slavery echoed James's analysis. His signature contribution was to expand it and apply it to the emergence of the world's first industrial capitalist economy. The great engine of the British industrial revolution, of course, was the Lancashire cotton industry, and Williams insisted that slavery and the triangular trade played a significant role in its development. His argument had three components, and the first two were based on the elementary economic concepts of demand and supply.

In the slave-trading ports on the west coast of Africa, Williams noted, cottons and linens were among the goods most in demand, and Lancashire's cotton manufacturers were more than happy to supply this market, where their wares competed with cheap cottons made on the Indian subcontinent. Lancashire cottons were also shipped to British colonies in the Caribbean and the Americas, where they were used to clothe the enslaved workers and for other purposes. Some of these items were transported on slave ships, via Africa. Others went directly across the Atlantic. "What the building of ships for the transport of slaves did for eighteenth century Liverpool, the manufacture of cotton goods for the purchases of slaves did for eighteenth century Manchester," Williams wrote. "The first stimulus to the growth of Cottonopolis came from the African and West Indian markets."[43] In the forty years from 1739 to 1779, he pointed out, Manchester's exports increased from £14,000 to £303,000. "Up to 1770 one-third of this export went to the slave coast, one-half to the American and West Indian colonies," he added. "It was this tremendous dependence on the triangular trade that made Manchester."[44]

Having dealt with demand, Williams moved on to supply factors. To make cotton linens in large quantities, the cotton mills needed a large and reliable supply of raw cotton. They largely sourced this essential raw material from slave plantations in the Caribbean and the Americas. During the early eighteenth century, Williams pointed out, the West Indies supplied up to three-quarters of all the cotton imported to Britain, and in 1780 the share was still two-thirds.[45] During the ensuing decades, he noted, the sourcing of cotton gradually shifted from the Caribbean to the American mainland.

In Lancashire, the application of water and then steam power to cotton spinning greatly increased the industry's productive capacity and raised its demand for raw cotton. In the United States, in 1794, the Massachusetts inventor Eli Whitney received a patent for his cotton gin, a mechanized device that enabled the rapid harvesting and cleaning of short staple cotton, which was much easier to grow than the traditional long staple variety grown in the Caribbean. Whitney's invention enabled cotton plantations in the American South to undercut the prices of West Indian producers and produce in greater volume. The gradual eclipse of the Caribbean cotton producers by competitors on the American mainland would have major historical consequences for both regions. From the perspective of the Lancashire cotton industry, Williams emphasized, it simply represented a shift to a lower-cost foreign supplier. "When the cotton gin permitted the cultivation of the short-staple cotton by facilitating the task of cleaning, the center of gravity shifted from the islands to the mainland to meet the enormous demands of the new machinery in England," he wrote.[46]

In 1807, under pressure from abolitionists led by the Yorkshire evangelical William Wilberforce, Parliament prohibited the slave trade inside the British Empire. But the new law didn't free the enslaved or proscribe buying the goods they produced. Between 1784 and 1832, British imports of raw cotton rose from £11 million to £283 million.[47] And by the end of that period, American cotton plantations were supplying three-quarters of the raw cotton that the Lancashire mills relied on. "The Manchester capitalist from his mountain, like Moses on Pisgah, beheld the promised land," Williams wrote. "The New World, thanks to Eli Whitney, had come, not for the last time, to the rescue of the Old."[48]

The third element of the Williams Thesis as it related to cotton manufacturing was to become a subject of enduring controversy. He claimed that the slave trade, directly and indirectly, also supplied much of the capital that financed the rise of British industry, particularly in Lancashire. Noting the proximity of Liverpool to Manchester—the two cities are only about thirty-five miles apart—he wrote:

> It was only the capital accumulation of Liverpool which called the population of Lancashire into existence and stimulated the manufactures of Manchester. That capital accumulation came from the slave trade, whose importance was appreciated more by contemporaries than by later historians.[49]

After making this claim, Williams immediately qualified it, writing: "Between the cotton manufacturers of Manchester and the slave traders there were not the close connections that have already been noticed in the case of the shipbuilders of Liverpool."[50] But "two exceptional instances of such connections exist," he went on: Sir William Fazackerly and Samuel Touchet, a pair of Manchester businessmen who "were both members of the Company of Merchants trading to Africa."[51] Williams noted that Touchet had a partnership, with his brothers, "in about twenty ships in the West Indian trade," and the Hibberts, a family of Manchester merchants, "owned sugar plantations in Jamaica, and at one time supplied [cottons] to the African Company for the slave trade."[52]

Extending his argument beyond Lancashire, Williams cited a number of other British industrialists who gained access to capital generated in the triangular trade. The most famous of them was the Scottish inventor James Watt, whose steam engines were one of the key innovations of the industrial revolution. "It was the capital accumulated from the West Indian trade that financed James Watt and the steam engine," Williams wrote.[53] Watt and

Matthew Boulton, his partner in the famous engine maker Boulton and Watt, "received advances" from the finance house Lowe, Vere, Williams, and Jennings, which also provided credit to ships that plied the Caribbean trade, he explained.[54] Williams also brought up the ironmonger Anthony Bacon, who cofounded a large ironworks at Merthyr Tydfil in South Wales. Bacon's partner was a West Indian planter, and he himself had been involved in lucrative African ventures, "first victualling troops on the coast and then supplying seasoned and able Negroes for government contracts in the West Indies."[55] Summarizing his argument, Williams wrote: "The triangular trade made an enormous contribution to Britain's industrial development. The profits from this trade fertilized the entire productive system of the country."[56]

The initial notices for *Capitalism and Slavery* were generally positive. A reviewer in *The Times Literary Supplement* called it an "admirably written, argued and original piece of work." In the *New York Herald Tribune*, the American historian Henry Steele Commager said it was "the most penetrating and the most original monograph that has appeared in this field of history." *The Barbados Advocate* hailed it as "nothing short of a masterpiece."[57] Williams was invited to speak at conferences in New York, Boston, Chicago, and other cities. The magazine *Foreign Affairs* asked him to contribute an article on Puerto Rico and the US Virgin Islands.

In some economics and economic history departments, the reaction to *Capitalism and Slavery* was more skeptical. In 1948 T. S. Ashton of the University of Manchester published a widely read account of the British industrial revolution that emphasized the role of technological advances, rapid population growth, and cultural changes: it didn't mention slavery at all. During the 1970s, a new generation of quantitatively minded economic historians queried some of Williams's arguments, particularly his claim that profits from the slave trade helped to finance the development of the Lancashire mills. These scholars pointed out that many of the key technical innovations in the cotton industry—including Richard Arkwright's water frame, James Hargreaves's spinning jenny, Samuel Crompton's spinning mule, and Edmund Cartwright's power loom—were the creations of mechanical tinkerers who had little, if any, outside funding. Furthermore, the early Lancashire cotton mills, where the new inventions were put to use, were small by modern standards, and they didn't need much, if any, external financing, because they generated large profits. "Ploughback of the high profits to be earned in the new sectors enabled successful firms to expand their physical scale of production as rapidly as they wished without recourse to sources of finance outside their immediate circle of family, friends and close business colleagues," Larry Neal, of the University of Illinois at Urbana-Champaign, wrote in a 1994 survey of business finance during the industrial revolution.[58]

Other economic historians challenged Williams's broader claim that profits from the triangular trade "fertilized" the entire British economy. In a 1972 paper, Stanley Engerman of the University of Rochester estimated that in 1770 the entire profits of the British slave trade amounted to just 0.54 percent of British national income and less than 10 percent of industrial capital investment. "Even under some implausible assumptions, the aggregate contribution of slave trade profits to the financing of British capital formation in the eighteenth century could not be so large as to bear weight as *the*, or *a*, major contributing factor," Engerman wrote. "Its role was positive in that there were some profits, and these might have led to some new investment in industrial activities, but relative to total capital formation, this was of a relatively minor magnitude."[59] Patrick O'Brien, an economic historian who was then at Oxford University, expanded the critique beyond slavery to all aspects of European colonialism, challenging the notion that it played a major role in the overall pattern of European growth. This pattern could be explained "mainly by reference to endogenous forces," such as technology, native resources, and intra-European trade, O'Brien wrote in a 1982 article in *The Economic History Review*. O'Brien concluded that "the periphery was peripheral."[60]

Coincidentally or not, these dismissals of the Williams Thesis came during a period in which neoclassical economics was extending its intellectual hegemony throughout many fields of economics, including economic history. More recently, there has been a radical reappraisal of the role of colonialism and slavery in Western economic development. It began, funnily enough, with a paper by Engerman and O'Brien, published at the start of the 1990s, that pointed out that between 1700 and 1773, colonial markets accounted for about 95 percent of the growth in British goods exports.[61] The two scholars emphasized that the slave trade itself accounted for only a small portion of all Britain's colonial trade, but their findings appeared to call into question O'Brien's prior claim that the periphery was unimportant. Subsequent research further undermined it. In a 2015 paper, the American economist Ronald Findlay and the Irish economic historian Kevin H. O'Rourke found that during the eighteenth century, Britain's long-distance trade was growing twice as fast as national income. The two scholars concluded: "The colonial trade was undoubtedly a major driving force of Britain's overall economic growth."[62]

In their 2007 book *Power and Plenty*, a magisterial account of trade and the world economy during the entire second millennium, Findlay and O'Rourke had already emphasized the importance of colonialism to British growth, writing: "The remarkable innovations of the Industrial Revolution would not have had the deep and sustained consequences that they did if British industry had not operated within the global framework of sources of raw materials and markets for finished products that had been developed during the heyday of mercantilism."[63] While this revisionism didn't support Williams's claim that the profits of the triangular trade played a key role in financing the industrial revolution, it supported the broader argument that colonialism played an essential role in creating the conditions in which industrial capitalism was incubated and emerged. Another prominent economic historian also emphasized this point. In a short but insightful introduction to global economic history published in 2011, Robert C. Allen emphasized the changes that took place between 1500 and 1750, noting that, as Britain and Holland developed far-flung commercial empires, "trade with their colonies drove their economies forward. Cities and export-oriented manufacturing grew. The occupational structure changed accordingly," Allen went on. By the eve of the industrial revolution, "there had been far reaching changes. England was the most transformed country . . . England was the most rapidly urbanizing country in Europe."[64]

Some scholars also challenged the presumption, implicit in many of the critiques of the Williams Thesis, that colonialism and slavery had nothing to do with the technical innovations that propelled the industrial revolution. In his 2002 book, *Africans and the Industrial Revolution in England*, Joseph E. Inikori, an economic historian at the University of Rochester, pointed out that competition from cheap Indian cottons in the African market prompted British manufacturers to search for cost-saving innovations, and that growing demand from colonial markets "stimulated the development and diffusion of the new technologies."[65] Giorgio Riello, a historian at Warwick University, wrote in a 2013 book: "Cotton did not become a global commodity because its production was mechanised and industrialised; on the contrary, it became mechanised and industrialised thanks to the fact that it was a global commodity."[66] In a 2014 paper, the Cardiff University historian Pat Hudson highlighted yet another way slavery propelled the British economy forward: by stimulating financial innovations. She pointed out that merchants and shippers in the triangular trade relied heavily for financing on promissory notes known as "bills of exchange" that were privately issued and often backed by finance houses. Growing familiarity with these instruments helped to integrate money markets in London and other British cities, creating a national network of credit providers on which the industrial revolution, Hudson wrote, was "entirely dependent."[67]

In a 2020 review article, the Stanford economic historian Gavin Wright noted that the transformation of expert opinion on the Williams Thesis "seemed all but complete."[68] Striking a definitive tone, Wright wrote: "The slave trade and slave-based commerce were core contributors to British economic development during the eighteenth century." However, Wright also argued that during the nineteenth century, when new markets and new sources of raw materials became available, "slavery was far less valuable for the British economy."[69] This assertion wasn't inconsistent with the Williams Thesis, Wright pointed out. Indeed, it provided support for another controversial argument that the Trinidadian had made in his doctoral thesis, and that he repeated in *Capitalism and Slavery*: economic factors rather than moral outrage were largely responsible for the abolition of slavery. "The commercial capitalism of the eighteenth century developed the wealth of Europe by means of slavery and monopoly," Williams wrote in his concluding chapter. "But in so doing it helped to create the industrial capitalism of the nineteenth century, which turned around and destroyed the power of commercial capitalism, slavery, and all its works. Without a grasp of these economic changes the history of the period is meaningless."[70]

Like Marx, Luxemburg, and indeed Keynes, Williams recognized that capitalism was a global system and could only be understood as such. When he was writing *Capitalism and Slavery*, this system had been upended pending the defeat of the Axis powers. Old power structures were being questioned and new possibilities discussed. This was as true in the developing world as it was in London and Washington, DC. Near the end of his book, Williams noted that writing history couldn't resolve present-day problems, but he also expanded on something else he had said to his examiner in Oxford years earlier. "The historians neither make nor guide history," he wrote. "Their share in such is usually so small as to be almost negligible. But if they do not learn something from history, their activities would then be cultural decoration, or a pleasant pastime, equally useless in these troubled times."[71]

Williams was determined that his own work wouldn't become a mere decoration. In his 1942 book *The Negro in the Caribbean*, he had emphasized the common heritage of the region and advocated a pan-Caribbean federation as a long-term solution to its economic and political challenges. Williams was under no illusion that a small island like Trinidad could prosper on its own even if it eventually gained independence. In 1943 he organized a conference on the economic future of the Caribbean at Howard University, where he pointed out that, in economic terms, the islands of the West Indies were wholly dependent on Britain. "Though not yet articulating it in terms of neocolonialism, Williams argued that a transfer of power to nationalists that left these economic structures intact would allow metropolitan powers to manipulate the policies of the island states," Adom Getachew, a University of Chicago political scientist, wrote in her 2019 book, *Worldmaking After Empire: The Rise and Fall of Self-Determination.*[72]

In regional cooperation, Williams hoped to find a way of breaking the ties of colonial dependency. He got involved with the Anglo-American Caribbean Commission, an international agency that the United States and Britain created in 1942 to promote regional development. After the war ended, Williams traveled broadly and met other future political leaders from the region, including Michael Manley, the leader of the Jamaican nationalist movement, and Luis Muñoz Marín, the Puerto Rican writer and activist. In 1948 he moved back to Trinidad, where he took a full-time post as deputy chairman of the Caribbean Research Council, a branch of the Caribbean Commission.

The council was meant to provide economic advice to the West Indian islands (plus British Guiana, French Guiana, and Suriname on the American mainland). At times, Williams got frustrated by his colonial bosses, who were resisting calls for a more rapid shift to self-rule. In Trinidad, the British had introduced universal suffrage and limited self-government in 1946, but there was still no proper party system, and the governor-general retained ultimate power. In 1954 and 1955 Williams gave a series of lectures on the history and politics of the West Indies at the Trinidad Public Library, which further raised his profile. "The task of building a West Indian nation is the decisive task of the present and future," he declared.[73] He called for schools on the islands to be placed under local control and demanded that they emphasize West Indian history, which hitherto they had largely ignored.

In June 1955 the Caribbean Commission fired Williams, a move he expected. He had decided to enter politics. In January 1956, at a mass meeting in Port of Spain's Woodford Square, he launched a new political party, the People's National Movement (PNM), which was modeled on Manley's People's National Party in Jamaica. It had a long list of demands: full self-rule for Trinidad and its sister island of Tobago; a democratically elected legislature; a national economic plan; a commitment to affordable housing, better schooling, and national health insurance; the establishment of a Caribbean Federation. Williams wrote many of the party's programs and edited its newspaper. His erudite public lectures set him apart from other politicians on the island. In a general election held in September 1956, PNM won a majority in the Legislative Council, and Williams became the chief minister. He also appointed himself economy minister and minister for Tobago affairs.

Under Williams's leadership, the PNM won a series of general elections, and he headed the government until his death in 1981. In 1962, under his leadership, Trinidad and Tobago became politically independent from Britain. (Fourteen years later it renounced its remaining ties to the British Crown and became a republic.) Like many charismatic independence leaders, Williams stayed in power for too long, and some of his critics accused him of harboring dictatorial ambitions. In 1962, C. L. R. James, who had known Williams since his childhood and been a close political ally during the PNM's formative years, but had now soured on his leadership, wrote: "Ultimately Trinidad and Tobago may become a state like Singapore."[74] Williams's government later subjected James to house arrest for a time.

Despite criticisms from the left, Williams remained popular with many ordinary residents of Trinidad and Tobago. "He sent all these white people back and gave our black people, our black professionals, the jobs," Erica James, C.L.R.'s niece, recalled in a 2012 interview. "Like the government railway had always been run by whites, by Englishmen, and when Eric Williams took power, it was over . . . This is why people loved Eric Williams so much."[75] But even as Williams led Trinidad and Tobago peacefully to independence, his governments faced major economic challenges. In the immediate postwar era, GDP growth had risen rapidly as oil production shot up. But during the

1960s, growth slowed sharply. As the population increased rapidly, creating enough jobs was a constant problem.[76] In many parts of the country, poverty was still endemic.

Lining up with dependency theorists throughout the developing world, Williams attributed many of the problems Trinidad had encountered since independence to the legacy of colonialism. "Independence did not bring us a clean slate," he wrote in a 1968 memoir. "Our economy was essentially in foreign hands, the capital coming from outside, the profits being repatriated outside."[77] The island still had poor housing, an inadequate education system, and divisions of race and color that Williams said the colonialists had instigated. "The essence of the colonial system was internal disunity," he remarked.[78] In 1958 a group of Caribbean islands, including Barbados, Jamaica, and Trinidad, did create a West Indies Federation, raising the possibility of the new grouping eventually becoming a single independent state. But the new organization didn't have much power, and after only three years the Jamaican public voted, in a referendum, to leave it, thereby dooming the entire effort. Subsequently, many of the islands became independent on their own, leaving them in a situation where, as Williams had predicted, they too faced major economic challenges.

Williams and his government soldiered on, introducing initiatives to build up Trinidad's infrastructure, grow local businesses, modernize agriculture, extend secondary schooling, and expand exports. But all these things required money, which was in short supply. With Britain having offered only token financial aid, the newly independent nation had little choice but to apply for additional funding from the World Bank and the Inter-American Development Bank, a multilateral lender that had been founded in 1959. Both of these institutions were based in Washington, DC, and were largely beholden to the United States government. To receive financial backing from them, Trinidad would have to agree to a policy regime partly dictated by its external creditors.

After hundreds of years of subjugation, the Caribbean island and its neighbors now ruled themselves, but everywhere they still faced constraints and challenges. "This is the Reality of our Independence," Williams wrote.[79]

21

The Rise and Fall of Dependency Theory in Latin America

Like the Caribbean, Latin America has a history of colonial plunder, resource extraction, and slavery. By 1945, however, many Latin countries had been self-ruling for more than a hundred years. Colombia and Chile became independent in 1810, Venezuela in 1811, Argentina in 1816, Mexico and Peru in 1821, Brazil in 1822, and Uruguay in 1825. Independence had proved a mixed blessing. Throughout the region, landowning elites with historic ties to the colonizers continued to exercise a great deal of political power, and economies remained heavily dependent on agriculture and the export of basic commodities, such as cacao, sugar, and nitrates. Under the international division of labor that had developed in the nineteenth century, primary production was the role allotted to developing countries. With the notable exception of Argentina, which enjoyed rapid export-led growth during the period before the First World War, it had left much of Latin America mired in poverty and underdevelopment. During the Great Depression, a collapse in commodity prices accentuated the region's problems and highlighted its enduring dependency on conditions in the industrialized countries. Economic crisis created new political currents. In Brazil, the government of Getúlio Vargas, before and after the *autogolpe* of 1937 that turned Vargas into a virtual dictator, encouraged the growth of domestic industry using import quotas, tariffs, and credits from the state-owned Banco do Brasil.[1] In Mexico, the populist government of Lázaro Cárdenas nationalized the country's oil industry, expropriating the foreign companies that operated there.[2]

When, in 1948, the newly founded United Nations created an Economic Commission for Latin America, known as ECLA (CEPAL in Spanish), the debate about what economic strategy the region should pursue was a live one. On the left, echoing the theories of imperialism that Luxemburg and Lenin had put forward, many critics argued that underdevelopment was the inevitable product of an exploitative global system. Some orthodox economists, echoing the arguments of David Ricardo and Nikolai Kondratiev, believed it made sense for underdeveloped countries with large endowments of land and labor to concentrate on agriculture and other forms of primary production. The new commission, which was based in Santiago, scheduled a conference for Havana in 1949, and in advance of this meeting it commissioned an expert report on Latin America's economic prospects. To produce the report, it hired Raúl Prebisch, a prominent Argentinian economist and former central banker, who had recently published an introduction to Keynesian economics.

Prebisch hailed from a conservative background. He was born in 1901 in the northern city of Tucumán. His father was a German immigrant who established a printing business, and his mother came from a family that could trace its roots back to the conquistadors. After graduating from the University of Buenos Aires with a degree in economics, Prebisch briefly worked as research director for the Sociedad Rural Argentina, which was closely associated with Argentina's landed oligarchy. From 1927 to 1930, he worked at the Banco de la Nación Argentina, the country's biggest commercial bank. In 1930 he was appointed as Under Secretary of Finance. From 1935 until 1943, he served as the general manager of Argentina's new central bank under a series of military-backed governments.[3]

Until the Great Depression, Prebisch was, in his own words, "a firm believer in neoclassical theories."[4] He supported free trade, the gold standard, and the Ricardian argument that the competitive advantage of developing countries lay in exporting agricultural products. From an Argentinian perspective, there was historical evidence to support this claim. In the decades before the First World War, the development of steamships and refrigeration had enabled Argentina to greatly expand its exports of beef, wheat, and other agricultural products. An influx of foreign capital, especially from Britain, financed an extensive railroad network. Immigrants flocked to the country. Buoyed by these developments, Argentina became the richest nation in

Latin America. In 1913, according to estimates from the economic data expert Angus Maddison, it was more than four times as rich as its neighbor Brazil on a GDP per capita basis.[5] Indeed, Maddison's figures suggest that Argentina was as rich as some European countries and not very far behind Britain. To be sure, many of the gains from this rapid economic growth had accrued to the landed oligarchy, but overall wages and living standards had also risen appreciably. However, the Great Depression and the accompanying collapse in commodity prices caused a sharp deterioration in Argentina's "terms of trade"—the prices of its exports relative to the prices of its imports. To purchase the same quantity of goods that it had been importing before the Depression, the country would have to increase its exports by almost three-quarters, Prebisch noted in a 1934 paper.[6] During a global slump, this was obviously impossible. The system of international capitalism that had enriched Argentina was now punishing it for being a primary producer.

Prebisch stayed at the central bank until 1943, when a coup brought to power a government led by the fascist-leaning General Pedro Martínez, which fired him. He returned to the University of Buenos Aires, where he taught courses and worked on a book proposal about monetary policy and Argentina's economic predicament. At a 1946 conference of central bankers and academics, he identified the United States as the "cyclical center" of the global economy and Latin America as "the periphery of the economic system."[7] The taxonomy of center and periphery wasn't new: the German economist Werner Sombart had used it in his multivolume history of capitalism. But it was Prebisch who introduced it to economic policymakers and central bankers. He argued that the United States, as the core country of the international monetary system and the issuer of its reserve currency, could adjust interest rates at will to maintain full employment, but countries at the periphery had no such freedom. Upswings and downswings in their economies were determined by the US economic cycle and US policies, Prebisch said. They were hostage to external developments.

In his report for ECLA, which ran to almost sixty pages, Prebisch mentioned this monetary dependency, but mainly he focused on international trade and global patterns of production. "In Latin America, reality is undermining the out-dated schema of the international division of labour, which achieved great importance in the nineteenth century," the report began. This schema had "no place within it for industrialization of the new countries. It is nevertheless being forced upon them by events."[8] Citing figures prepared by a German-born British economist, Hans Singer, who was working at the United Nations headquarters in New York, Prebisch pointed out that between 1870 and 1939—i.e., over a period of nearly seventy years—the prices of primary products had fallen considerably faster than prices of manufactured goods, with the cumulative difference totaling more than 30 percent. These figures showed that although industrial and agricultural producers were both making productivity gains, the international trading system wasn't sharing out these gains equally, Prebisch insisted. Countries at the periphery were passing along the benefits of rising agricultural productivity to consumers in the developed world by cutting the prices of their products. But in industrial countries, much of the rise in productivity was being passed on to domestic workers in the form of higher wages, which meant that prices of industrial goods exported to developing regions didn't fall as quickly. "In other words," Prebisch wrote, "while the centres kept the whole benefit of the technical development of their industries, the peripheral countries transferred to them a share of the fruits of their own technical progress."[9]

Prebisch couched his argument in dry economic prose, but the import of it was clear. Rather than benefiting all countries, as the economic textbooks said, the global trading system was transferring economic value from the poor periphery to the rich center. Through the terms of trade effect, it was acting as a reverse Robin Hood. When the top officials at ECLA received Prebisch's report, they decided it was too controversial to put out as an official publication representing the views of the new organization. Rather than publishing it as an ECLA report, they submitted it to the UN secretary-general as a research essay under Prebisch's name with the title: *The Economic Development of Latin America and Its Principal Problems*. In a foreword, the commission said it hoped the essay would "arouse further interest in economic investigations in the Latin-American countries."[10]

Prebisch's report certainly attracted interest. It was quickly hailed as a manifesto for Latin American countries to challenge the center-periphery economic model by protecting and building up their own industries. In 1950 Prebisch became the executive secretary of ECLA, where he gathered around him a talented team of economists from across the region. The "Cepalistas," as they came to be known, advocated tariffs on imported consumer goods and government support for domestic industries—a policy that came to be known as "import substituting industrialization," or ISI. The Cepalistas' goal wasn't state socialism or autarky: they believed that countries in the periphery should continue to engage with global capitalism. But they wanted to reshape this engagement to the benefit of developing countries. Prebisch, echoing Eric Williams, also advocated regional cooperation as a way of leveling the playing field with advanced countries. He and his colleagues called for the establishment of a regional free trade area with external trade barriers—a Latin counterpart to the European Economic Community, which was created in 1957. "Preferential treatment is needed inside the area to promote specialization in industrial products and primary commodities," Prebisch wrote in a 1959 article. "Latin America needs preferences to develop new forms of reciprocal trade, mainly in industrial products, that practically did not exist before."[11]

Although some of ECLA's critics portrayed it as radical, it was in large part advocating the same development strategy that the United States and Germany had successfully adopted in the nineteenth century, when they created unified domestic markets surrounded by tariff walls. By the 1950s, though, the United States, as the world's most productive economy, was filling the role previously occupied by Britain and promoting free trade. In this environment, Prebisch stood out as a dissenting voice. Shortly after he took over ECLA, the United States sought to merge the commission with the Organization of American States, a multilateral entity that it dominated. With the support of Latin American governments, Prebisch managed to head off the merger proposal. US efforts to undermine ECLA continued through the activities of the International Monetary Fund, which was strongly opposed to tariffs and government interventionism. Prebisch later recalled a former managing director of the IMF, the French businessman Pierre-Paul Schweitzer, saying to him: "You know Raúl, when I joined the Fund you were presented to me as the Devil."[12]

Despite US protestations, ECLA's arguments proved popular across Latin America. Nationalist sentiment fused with the self-interest of native capitalists to create a strong coalition of support for government-led ISI. By the 1960s, Mexico was imposing tariffs of 74 percent on imported manufactured goods; in Argentina, the tariffs were 84 percent; in Brazil, they were 184 percent.[13] To support domestic manufacturing, Latin governments also provided subsidized loans and kept their exchange rates high, which made it cheaper to import machinery and other capital goods. These protectionist policies had a big impact. By the early 1960s, according to one account, plants located in Brazil "were supplying 99 percent of the country's consumer goods, 91 percent of its intermediate inputs (such as steel and chemicals), and 87 percent of its capital goods (machinery and equipment)."[14] Many Latin American countries also followed the example of Cárdenas's Mexico by nationalizing key utilities, including electricity grids, railroads, ports, and telecommunications. Some governments also established or took over industrial concerns that were considered strategic, including energy producers, chemicals manufacturers, and steel mills. In Brazil, for example, Vargas's wartime regime established a national steel company, and during his second stint as president, in the 1950s, the government created Petrobras, the national oil company, and granted it a monopoly on production.

In terms of GDP growth, the results of ISI were pretty impressive. Between 1950 and 1973, according to Angus Maddison's estimates, GDP per capita across Latin America rose at an annual rate of 2.5 percent.[15] While this performance didn't match the quantum leap in Japan and western Europe, it was a big step up compared to the prior half-century, and it came at a time when Latin America's population was growing rapidly. (Between 1950 and 1973, it rose from 165.8 million to 308.4 million.)[16] Economic growth was particularly rapid in Brazil and Mexico, where GDP per capita more than doubled during the period.[17] Mexico's growth spurt became known as the Mexican Miracle.

The fruits of more rapid growth were spread very unevenly, however. Economic development was concentrated in the cities, where industry was located, and many rural areas remained chronically poor. Even in the cities, income gains tended to be concentrated in a few capital-intensive industries that had relatively highly paid workers. Outside this sector, masses of poor people lived at or below subsistence levels. At the top of the heap, meanwhile, the new industrialists joined the old agricultural oligarchy in a closeted property-owning elite. In short, ISI didn't resolve Latin America's most acute problem: its entrenched inequality and rigid class divisions, many of which had a racial component. Between 1950 and 1970, according to estimates from the Chilean economist André Hofman, the average Gini coefficient (a widely used measure of income inequality) for six big Latin countries, including Argentina, Brazil, and Mexico, rose slightly.[18]

ISI brought with it other challenges, including high prices and rising joblessness. Since Latin American manufacturers were protected from foreign competition, they could charge high prices for goods that weren't necessarily of high quality. Over time continually rising prices—inflation—also became a problem. Furthermore, although the industrial sector was growing rapidly in countries pursuing ISI, it still wasn't creating enough jobs to keep up with population growth. Between 1945 and 1960, according to one estimate, industrial employment across the region rose by 2.8 percent each year, whereas the urban population grew at a rate of 4.3 percent.[19] In many Latin American cities, urban poverty became increasingly acute. Yet another endemic issue with ISI was rising trade imbalances. The expanding industrial sector imported raw materials, fuels, and industrial components, but it didn't export many of its products. This left countries vulnerable to currency crises when they couldn't generate sufficient foreign exchange reserves to pay for essential imports. "It is thus ironic that the net result of ISI has been to place Latin American countries in a new and more dangerous dependency relationship with the more advanced industrial countries than ever before," Werner Baer, an economist who was then at Vanderbilt University, wrote in a 1972 article about the unsteady progress of Prebisch's agenda.[20]

Prebisch himself came to agree with some of the criticisms of the ISI strategy. Until the early 1960s, he recounted years later, he "had not paid sufficient attention to the problem of income disparities, except in the case of the outdated land tenure system. Nor had I paid enough attention in the early CEPAL years to the fact that growth had not benefited large masses of the low-income population, while at the other extreme of the social structure high incomes flourished."[21] On the left, critics had focused heavily on these phenomena, which they attributed to the fact that ISI hadn't gone nearly far enough in breaking Latin America's ties with an international capitalist system that ensured its dependent status. This critique became known as dependency theory. Broadly speaking, its exponents came in two varieties: structuralist and neo-Marxist.[22] Close up, the boundaries between the two groups blurred. The fundamental divide between them was over whether it was possible for peripheral economies to make significant economic progress within the existing global system. The structuralists believed in the possibility of reform and progress. The neo-Marxists didn't.

The structuralist strain of dependency theory can be traced to Celso Furtado, a Brazilian economic historian who headed ECLA's development division from 1950 to 1957 but eventually broke with Prebisch. Furtado hailed from the poverty-stricken state of Paraíba in northeastern Brazil. As an undergraduate at the Federal University of Rio de Janeiro, he studied law, then he served in World War II with the Brazilian Expeditionary Force, which fought on the side of the Allies. When Hitler had been defeated, he enrolled in a doctoral program in economics at the Sorbonne, in Paris. In 1949, after completing a thesis on Brazil's economy during the colonial period, he joined ECLA and rose to head its economic development division. Under Furtado's leadership, the division emphasized how high levels of inequality and social exclusion were holding back economic development throughout Latin America. Across the continent, it pointed out, many people lived outside the formal economy; wages were too low to support aggregate demand; and rich people spent their wealth on conspicuous consumption rather than on productive capital investments. To remedy these failures, Furtado's team called for extensive government interventions, including income subsidies for the poor and detailed economic planning. It also queried the usefulness of orthodox economic theory in dealing with complicated development issues rooted in history and class conflict. Inside ECLA, Furtado's department became known as the Red Division.[23]

In the mid-1950s, relations between Furtado and Prebisch deteriorated. One source of tension inside ECLA was Prebisch's willingness to act as economic adviser to the military junta that deposed Juan Perón, the populist Argentine leader, in 1955. Claiming that Argentina was "in the worst economic crisis of its history,"[24] the regime issued a draconian economic austerity plan in Prebisch's name. Even setting aside the issue of Prebisch lending his intellectual authority to a nondemocratic government, there were serious questions about the regime's economic prognosis. "The cafés of Buenos Aires flourished as usual," Edgar J. Dosman, Prebisch's biographer, noted dryly. "Argentina's per capita wealth was higher than that of Brazil, Mexico, or Chile, or for that matter of Japan, France, or Italy."[25] Furtado disagreed with the proposed spending cuts, and he later suggested that Prebisch might have been "too involved with his old group of friends in Argentina."[26] But the decisive break between the two came over an in-depth report on the Mexican economy that Furtado and his team produced, which argued that the country's pursuit of ISI had accentuated inequality and monopolization. The Mexican government objected to publication of the report. After much back-and-forth, Prebisch agreed to suppress it, and Furtado resigned.

He moved to Cambridge, England, for the academic year 1957–58, where, building on his doctoral thesis, he wrote an economic history of Brazil from colonial times onward. In 1959, Furtado returned home at the invitation of the reformist President Juscelino Kubitschek, who appointed him to head a new development agency for his native northeastern region, which had heinously high rates of poverty and infant mortality. Furtado produced an ambitious five-year development plan that encompassed agriculture and industry, with the financing to come from the Brazilian government and overseas aid agencies. The blueprint earned him an invitation to Washington from the Kennedy administration, but it was never put into effect. In 1961 Furtado became minister of planning in the left-leaning government of João Goulart. Three years later, when Brazilian military leaders staged a coup with Washington's support, he was forced into exile.

Throughout his work, Furtado emphasized the enduring legacy of colonialism. In *Development and Underdevelopment*, a book published in English in 1964, he contrasted the process of industrialization in advanced countries, which he referred to as "autonomous," with the industrialization efforts taking place in "dependent economies" in poorer regions, including Latin America.[27] In western Europe, Furtado pointed out, the industrial revolution had developed organically in an environment where a shortage of labor and high wages gave capitalists an incentive to develop labor-saving technologies. With high levels of capital accumulation and rapid technical progress, rising productivity and wages eventually became self-reinforcing. Contemporary Latin American countries faced a very different set of circumstances, Furtado emphasized. They weren't *un*developed areas, he said, but "underdeveloped" parts of a global system (colonialism) that had allotted them a subsidiary role as suppliers of primary products. "The study of underdevelopment must start with the identification of the structures created in the periphery of the capitalist economy by this system of international division of labour," Furtado wrote in a different article. "To isolate an underdeveloped economy from the general context of the expanding capitalist system is to dismiss from the beginning the fundamental problem . . . of such an economy, namely the fact of its global dependence."[28]

This argument was similar to the one that Eric Williams had made in his articles and books on the Caribbean, and it also echoed Rosa Luxemburg's point that colonial capitalism had been organized to benefit the colonialists, not the Indigenous peoples. Furtado identified one key colonial legacy as a rigid class system featuring a landed oligarchy, a small native bourgeoisie, and a sea of impoverished workers, rural and urban. Enduring tensions among these groups had hampered efforts to form governments that could promote broad-based development, he argued. Another colonial legacy that he pointed to was a lack of manufacturing expertise and technology, which meant that Latin countries had to import machinery and production techniques that weren't necessarily suited to local circumstances. Echoing J. C. Kumarappa's critique of the Congress Party's economic policies in newly independent India, Furtado criticized Latin countries for focusing on building up capital-intensive industries, such as steel and autos, rather than labor-intensive industries, such as textiles, which would have provided more employment to the masses.

He also highlighted the paradox that ISI tended to concentrate capital and production in the hands of large foreign-owned firms, such as Ford and General Motors, which established local subsidiaries to work around the region's protectionist policies. These multinationals maintained strict ownership of their technology and repatriated much of the profit that they generated, Furtado pointed out. They also extracted financial concessions from host governments, including favorable tax treatment and exemptions from import controls. Furtado regarded these developments as examples of US capitalism steadily exerting its hegemony throughout the developing world. By establishing foreign subsidiaries or taking over local firms, the big US multinationals could expand even in adverse economic conditions. "Thus the economic stagnation of Latin America has coincided with a great expansion of American firms which operate in that region," Furtado wrote in a 1968 essay.[29]

To promote more inclusive growth, Furtado called for restrictions on the activities of multinationals and measures that he had advocated for during his time at ECLA, including development programs for backward areas and economic planning at the national level. Some Latin countries sympathized with Furtado's ideas, particularly the smaller ones, which couldn't ignore their weakness in the face of international capital. The high point of the structuralist approach to development came in 1969, when five Latin countries—Bolivia, Chile, Colombia, Ecuador, and Peru—established the Andean Community, or Grupo Andino, an ambitious effort to promote intraregional trade and coordinate the growth of domestic industries, such as metalworking, autos, paper and pulp, and chemicals and fertilizers, behind a common tariff wall. In August 1972, Grupo Andino released its first industrial development plan, which was very detailed: for example, it assigned seventy-two product lines in the metalworking sector to different countries.[30] To help finance public and private sector investment projects, the member countries also established a regional development bank, the Andean Development Corporation.

The avowedly Marxist wing of the dependency movement was skeptical of any efforts to develop Latin American economies within the confines of the global capitalist system. Inspired by the 1959 revolution in Cuba, in which Fidel Castro and his band of guerrillas overthrew the corrupt US-backed dictatorship of Fulgencio Batista, Latin leftists hailed Castro's regime as a beachhead of socialism in the Americas. When the Kennedy administration sought to overthrow Castro in the abortive Bay of Pigs invasion of April 1961, the US intervention confirmed to many of them that global capitalism was irredeemable. (Even before the Cuban Revolution, the CIA had covertly engineered the ouster of a democratically elected government in Guatemala, which had moved to expropriate large unused tracts of land, including some owned by the United Fruit Company, a US multinational corporation.)

One of those inspired by Castro's Cuba was Andre Gunder Frank, a German-born economist who received an orthodox training in the United States before settling in Chile in 1964. In a letter he wrote in the summer of that year to his friends and former colleagues in the United States, Frank said he was reading some classic Marxist texts and had been told that he now reasoned like a Marxist dialectician. "Be that Marxism or not," Frank wrote, "I myself recognize that both as a person and a scientist I view and analyze the social, economic, and political reality around me so differently from my liberal friends and erstwhile colleagues that we hardy seem to be living in the same world."[31] He added that he supported "the present Chinese position on major world problems and . . . the most militant black nationalists such as Malcolm X and Robert Williams on American domestic ones." His goal, he said, was to develop the "science, policy, and politics" necessary for the liberation of the underdeveloped world: "This may involve, of course, fighting with more than a pen."[32]

Frank was born in 1929 in Berlin. His father, Leonhard Frank, was a pacifist writer who left Germany after Hitler took power and ended up living in the United States, where, among other things, he worked on Hollywood movies. The younger Frank attended high school in Ann Arbor, Michigan, and then attended Swarthmore College. Interested in economics, he enrolled in the University of Chicago's graduate program, where he took classes with Milton Friedman, who wasn't nearly as famous then as he was to become. Frank's doctoral thesis was a critical examination of Stalin's collectivization of agriculture in Ukraine. After completing it, he got a job as an assistant professor at Michigan State University. In 1959 he spent some time at MIT's Center for International Studies, where he met Walt Rostow, the economic historian and staunch Cold Warrior, who was working on his book *Stages of Economic Growth: A Non-Communist Manifesto*. Frank would later recall Rostow saying his life's work was providing the world with a better alternative to Karl Marx.[33] Frank was already starting to move in the opposite direction.

Radicalized by the Cold War and the baleful effect it was having on the social sciences in the United States, he resigned his job at Michigan State and went traveling. In 1962 he journeyed through Mexico, Guatemala, Venezuela, Peru, and Chile. He wanted to move to Cuba and see the aftermath of the revolution, but that didn't work out. In Santiago, he met a Chilean woman named Martha Fuentes, and the two quickly got married. At the start of 1963, they moved to Brazil, where Frank taught a class at the new University of Brasília. Latin America fascinated Frank. In a 1963 book review for *Monthly Review*, the New York–based journal coedited by Paul Sweezy, he took issue with the novelist Carlos Fuentes's description of the region as a "decrepit feudal castle with a cardboard capitalist facade." Latin America could "better be called a decrepit capitalist castle with a feudal-seeming façade," Frank wrote.[34] "Latin American societies resulted from the worldwide expansion of 'Western' mercantilism, capitalism, and imperialism," he went on, and the only way to understand them was as products of "the dialectic development of a single capitalist system."[35]

As Frank moved on to expand this argument in other articles and individual country studies, he would freely acknowledge the influence of a fellow American leftist, Stanford's Paul Baran, who in a 1957 book, *The Political Economy of Growth*, had argued that rich capitalist countries contrived, through a variety of methods, to prevent the independent development of poor countries. Baran had a cosmopolitan background. Born in 1909 in the Ukrainian city of Mykolaiv, which was then part of the Russian Empire, he received his PhD from the University of Berlin in 1933, shortly after Hitler took power. To escape the Nazis, he moved to France, Lithuania, and Russia, before immigrating to the United States at the start of World War II. After enrolling in the graduate economics program at Harvard, he befriended Sweezy, who was then working on his 1942 book, *The Theory of Capitalist Development*. When the United States entered the war, Baran worked at the Office of Price Administration and the Office of Strategic Services, the forerunner of the CIA, which employed many European intellectuals. Once the war was over, he got a job at the Federal Reserve Bank of New York. But he wanted to be an academic, and in 1949, Stanford hired him.

In 1952, Baron published an article in a British economics journal, *The Manchester School*, which examined why so many colonies and former colonies remained poor despite being integrated into the capitalist system. In his articles on India, Marx had described colonialism as a battering ram that would break down feudal traditions and stimulate economic development. The reality, Baran argued, was that the "superimposition of business mores over ancient oppression by landed gentries resulted in compounded exploitation, more outrageous corruption, and more glaring injustice."[36] The key to this development, Baran said, was that in many developing countries the members of the middle class, small business owners and professionals, had joined "into an alliance with the aristocratic and monopolistic reaction"—big landowners and big business—and set up governments that existed primarily to "safeguard and to abet the existing property rights and privileges." In this manner, the native bourgeoisie in the periphery had failed to carry out the historic task that Marx and Engels had allotted to it: maximizing the pace of capitalist development. The only way to promote genuine social and economic development in these places, Baran argued, was to rupture the "alliance between feudal landlords, industrial royalists, and the capitalist middle classes." If the bourgeoisie failed to "rise to its responsibilities," he remarked, then the "backward countries of the world will inevitably turn to economic planning and social collectivism."[37]

Baran expanded these arguments in *The Political Economy of Growth*. He also introduced a new economic concept, the "potential economic surplus," which he defined as the difference between an economy's maximum level of output, given its technology and natural resources, and the minimum level of consumption its citizens needed to survive and reproduce. The essence of colonialism, Baran argued, was extracting some of this surplus from poor countries and transferring it to the capitalist core.

As an example of extractive colonialism, Baran pointed to the British in

India. Citing authorities as varied as Thomas Macaulay and the Indian historian Romesh Dutt, he said that British rule under the East India Company had "systematically destroyed all the fibres and foundations of Indian society," including its village economies and its artisan cotton spinners, while "creating new classes and vested interests who were tied up with that rule and whose privileges depended on its continuance," such as client princes, landowners, and tax collectors.[38] Baran contrasted India with Japan, where the Meiji Restoration "succeeded in creating the political and economic framework indispensable for capitalist development," including a centralized state that protected property rights, invested in public infrastructure, and provided credit and contracts to Indigenous capitalists.[39] The modernization of Japan was a complex process, Baran conceded, but it was also "simple" because "reduced to its core, it comes down to the fact that Japan is the only country in Asia (and in Africa and in Latin America) that escaped being turned into a colony or dependency of Western European or American capitalism, that had a chance of independent national development."[40]

Frank adopted an analytical framework similar to Baran's, and he used it to analyze the history of individual Latin countries. In a 1966 essay, "The Development of Underdevelopment," which appeared in *Monthly Review*, he explained how in Brazil the Portuguese colonists initially developed certain parts of the country—including the northeast and the center-south—turning them into export economies, only to largely abandon them as the markets that they served waned. "Underdevelopment is not due to the survival of archaic institutions and the existence of capital shortage in regions that have remained isolated from the stream of world history," Frank wrote. "On the contrary, underdevelopment was and still is generated by the very same historical process which also generated economic development: the development of capitalism itself."[41]

By this stage, Frank was a committed to expanding the Cuban Revolution throughout Latin America, and he brooked no dissent from his radical approach. In a paper prepared for a conference in Havana in January 1968, he described the structuralists associated with ECLA, including Prebisch and Furtado, as "ideologists for the national bourgeoisie." He also claimed—without foundation in the case of Furtado—that they failed to analyze the internal class structure of Latin America and said their intellectual approach was "superficially not fundamentally different from the imperialist model."[42] Frank even criticized some "Marxists" (his quotation marks) for unwarranted revisionism.[43] The reality, he insisted, was that there were only two policy alternatives, which were expressed in the title of his paper: "Capitalist Underdevelopment or Socialist Revolution."

In Europe and the United States, the student and antiwar protests of 1968 marked a high mark of leftist activism. The protests spread to Latin American countries, including Mexico and Brazil, where they led to heightened interest in dependency theory and other currents of anti-colonialism. The movement "seemed to offer an alternative response to the orthodox received-wisdom of 'modernizers' like Rostow who wanted to bomb Vietnam back into the Stone Age and others who argued that 'we have to destroy it to save it,'" Frank subsequently recalled.[44] The year before the student protests erupted, he became a fellow at the University of Chile's Center of Socioeconomic Studies (CESO) in Santiago, where a number of neo-Marxist dependency theorists were already in residence. One of them was Theotônio Dos Santos, a Brazilian sociologist whom Frank had taught briefly during a spell at the University of Brasília. Dos Santos hailed from Carangola in the state of Minas Gerais. As a student, he helped to found a radical left-wing party, but he subsequently broke with its members over their conviction that a small vanguard of armed rebels could bring about a socialist revolution.

At CESO, Dos Santos led a research project that examined dependency from a regional rather than a national perspective. He developed a theory of "dependent capitalism" that also harked back to Baran's approach, but provided a new explanation for how the core countries were able to extract surpluses from the periphery. Whereas many of the early dependency arguments had largely revolved around foreign trade, Dos Santos centered his analysis on production in developing countries and the class struggle there between capitalists and workers. In January 1970 he delivered a lecture at the annual meeting of the American Economic Association, which took place that year in New York City. (Paul Sweezy, who still had some links to the US economics establishment, engineered his invitation to speak.)

In his presentation, which was subsequently reprinted in *The American Economic Review*, Dos Santos argued that over the course of Latin American history, three distinct types of dependence had developed: colonial dependence, financial-industrial dependence, and technological-industrial dependence. Even though these phenomena were distinct, they shared a key attribute, Dos Santos insisted: the center "carries off part of the surplus generated domestically and leads to a loss of control over their productive resources."[45] Under colonial dependence, Dos Santos said, the process of extracting the surplus was plain to see. The colonist established a monopoly on international trade, which was complemented by "a colonial monopoly of land, mines, and manpower (serf or slave)." Financial-industrial dependence consolidated itself at the end of the nineteenth century, Dos Santos argued, when, with the aid of foreign capital, the now-independent Latin American countries organized their economies around exports of primary products. The key to surplus extraction in this version of dependence was that wages in the export sector were kept artificially low. This "superexploitation" generated large surpluses for domestic and foreign capital, while also limiting the growth of domestic incomes and restricting economic development.[46] Dos Santos's final category of dependence, technological-industrial dependence, he defined as a largely post–Second World War phenomenon, and he associated it with the ISI approach that ECLA had promoted.

Here was a direct attack on Prebisch's policy legacy, and one that went beyond Furtado's earlier critique. Dos Santos emphasized the fact that ISI required the import of complex machinery and other modern technologies, which were very costly. Theoretically, the surplus generated in the primary goods sector could have been used to finance these imports. But since much of this surplus was siphoned off by foreign owners, there was a "foreign financing" gap that had to be filled by overseas capital in the form of investments by multinational corporations or foreign aid, Dos Santos said.[47] He argued that both of these sources of financing fostered new forms of exploitation and dependency. The multinationals generated large profits, most of which were repatriated. Citing data from the US Department of Commerce, Dos Santos said that between 1946 and 1967, US direct investments of capital into Latin America totaled about $5.4 billion, while the transfer of profits from Latin America to the United States totaled about $14.8 billion. "The ratio of remitted capital to new flow is around 2.7 for the period 1946–67; that is, for each dollar that enters $2.70 leaves," he noted.[48] Foreign aid also came with drawbacks, Dos Santos said, including pressure to open up markets and balance budgets, as well as requirements that some of the money be used to import technology from donor countries. And aid wasn't a gift. It was provided in the form of loans, which eventually had to be repaid. "The hard truth is," Dos Santos wrote, "that underdeveloped countries have to pay for all of the 'aid' they receive."[49]

Based on this analysis, the Brazilian concluded that the policy proposals put forward by agencies like ECLA and the Inter-American Development Bank "do not appear to permit destruction of these terrible chains imposed by dependent development." Far from bringing an end to backwardness, misery, and social marginalization, the "dependent capitalism" that they fostered reproduced these historical phenomena. "Everything now indicates that what can be expected is a long process of sharp political and military confrontations and of profound social radicalization which will lead these countries to a dilemma: governments of force, which open the way to fascism, or popular revolutionary governments, which open the way to socialism," Dos Santos concluded. "Intermediate solutions have proved to be, in such a contradictory reality, empty and utopian."[50]

Dependency theory emerged from a set of historic conditions specific to Latin America. Clearly, though, it had implications for other parts of the developing world, particularly newly independent countries in Africa and Asia. In 1972, Walter Rodney, a young Guyanese historian and political activist, published *How Europe Underdeveloped Africa*, in which he explored the history and impact of colonialism, including the slave trade and the nineteenth-century land grabs, on the continent. Echoing the Latin dependency theorists, Rodney argued that the oppressive structures and extractive nature of colonial exploitation were directly responsible for the low levels of economic development throughout Africa. "All of the countries named as 'underdeveloped' in the world are exploited by others; and the underdevelopment with which the world is now preoccupied is a product of capitalist, imperialist, and colonialist exploitation," he wrote. "African and Asian societies were developing independently until they were taken over directly or indirectly by the capitalist powers. When that happened, exploitation increased and the export of surplus ensued, depriving the societies of the benefit of their natural resources and labor. That is an integral part of underdevelopment in the contemporary sense."[51]

Rodney had done his doctoral dissertation at SOAS University of London; its subject was the slave trade on the upper Guinea coast. While he was in England, he joined a study group that C. L. R. James, the Trinidadian author of *Black Jacobins*, had established. Subsequently, he taught at the University of Dar es Salaam in Tanzania and at the University of the West Indies in Jamaica. In *How Europe Underdeveloped Africa*, which he wrote while he was in Dar es Salaam, he said that much of the economic literature on development and underdevelopment "seeks to justify capitalism." On a more positive note, he referenced the works of James, Eric Williams, W. E. B. Du Bois, Frank, and Furtado. He also emphasized that colonial activities like mining and cash-crop farming did little to develop the rest of the economy in African countries, and in many cases, the arrival of the colonists led to a decline of native industries, such as handicrafts and small-scale farming. Rodney also criticized the first generation of postcolonial African political leaders, lamenting that too many of them "were frankly capitalists and shared fully the ideology of their bourgeois masters."[52] In political terms, Rodney was a revolutionary socialist and a Pan-Africanist. He insisted that only a united African working class could overthrow the existing system and generate widely shared economic progress. In advance of the Sixth Pan-African Congress, which was held in Tanzania in 1975, he called on the Congress to recognize that "the principal enemies of the African people are the capitalist class in the U.S.A., Western Europe and Japan," and that "African liberation and unity will be realized only through struggle against the African allies of international capital."[53] (Rodney would be killed in a 1980 car explosion in Georgetown, Guyana, which the country's national assembly ultimately deemed a "State organized assassination.")[54]

On September 4, 1970, Chile, the home of dependency theory, held a general election. Salvador Allende, the socialist leader of a left-wing coalition, Popular Unity, received 36.6 percent of the vote, placing him slightly ahead of a center-right candidate. After more than a month of negotiations, vacillations, and the assassination of a top military leader who had rebuffed right-wing entreaties to prevent Allende from becoming president, the Chilean Congress confirmed him to the office. The sixty-two-year-old former physician vowed to enact the program he had campaigned on, La vía chilena al socialismo (The Chilean Path to Socialism).[55] Among its contents were pledges to nationalize the country's copper mines and big banks; expand educational access to the poor; raise wages; build affordable homes; redistribute land to small farmers; and provide jobs for all.

Allende's economics minister was Pedro Vuskovic, an economist who had spent many years at ECLA. As a Keynesian and a structuralist, Vuskovic wanted to raise government spending and workers' wages, which he believed would increase economic welfare and boost demand. Inflation and the trade balance would be secondary concerns. During Allende's first few months in office, the new government established a minimum wage, cut taxes for the low-paid and small businesses, provided free milk and lunches for school-children, fixed the price of bread, provided educational grants to Indigenous children, and announced a big homebuilding program. This was just the be-ginning. In the ensuing couple of years, the government expanded enroll-ment in primary and secondary schools, made university tuition free, sharply increased social security payments and family allowances, and doubled the length of maternity leave. It also nationalized copper mines, a key sector of the Chilean economy, and seized landed estates, which it proceeded to break up, much to the outrage of the landowners. In an effort to facilitate the management of state-run enterprises, it launched a novel information management system, Project Cybersyn, in which telex machines were used to forward details about production inputs and outputs to a central main-frame computer, which in turn generated automatic alerts to factories and their managers.

For a time, this leap toward democratic socialism seemed to pay off. Allende's spending programs raised living standards and produced a surge in industrial output and GDP. Between 1970 and 1971, GDP per capita rose by about 8 percent after adjusting for inflation.[56] Then things went awry. In 1972 the rate of inflation shot up to more than 150 percent on a yearly basis, swallowing workers' wage gains and creating economic hardship. The gov-ernment responded by expanding price controls, but this led to shortages of basic foodstuffs and the emergence of black markets. Adding to the problems, the price of copper, which made up about half of Chile's exports, plummeted on world markets. That put pressure on the currency, the escudo, and the government was forced to devalue it by 50 percent—a move that raised the cost of imports and added to inflation pressures.

Another country caught in this situation would have been a candidate for an IMF bailout. But the Nixon administration, outraged at the prospect of Fidel Castro gaining an ally on the South American mainland, ordered a covert economic war on Chile. The US government leaned on the World Bank and other lending agencies to curtail the flow of credit to Santiago. In June 1972, Allende replaced Vuskovic with a new economics minister, but the problems continued. In the second half of 1972, a wave of protests and strikes led by trucking companies, small businesses, and professional organizations paralyzed the country. (It was later revealed that the CIA helped to finance the trucking strike.) In early 1973, inflation rose further—it would eventually reach 500 percent[57]—and there was another strike. As political tensions rose, the center-right Christian Democratic Party joined the right-wing National Party in accusing Allende of trying to establish one-party rule. In mid-August the national Congress passed a resolution accusing the government of seeking absolute power and conducting Marxist indoctrination. The resolution called on Chile's armed forces to direct their efforts "toward the full restoration of constitutional rule."

Allende offered to hold a referendum on the future of the country. But with two of the three biggest political parties having effectively called for a military coup, events were moving to a grim conclusion. On the morning of September 11, a group of military officers led by General Augusto Pinochet, the head of the army, ordered their forces to occupy key sites in the capital, disable local television stations, and surround the presidential palace. When Allende refused to leave, Pinochet ordered an attack. The presidential bodyguards fought bravely, but they were overrun. Allende refused to be taken alive and shot himself.[58]

A military junta took power, with Pinochet at its head and the CIA actively supporting it.[59] As the new regime tracked down its political opponents, real and imagined, Santiago was no longer safe for left-wing intellectuals. Dos Santos, fearing he was on the wanted list, took refuge in the Panamanian embassy and eventually made his way to Mexico. When the airports reopened, Frank and his family flew to Germany. He was convinced that the dependency movement had come to an end. "General Pinochet decapitated it with his sword on September 11, 1973," he later wrote. "Then he instituted an ultra-right counter-revolution and counter-reform."[60]

22

"Shock treatment"

Milton Friedman and the Rise of Neoliberalism

On April 23, 1964, Karl Polanyi died in Toronto. He was anything but a household name. *The New York Times* published a single-column obituary that described him as a "former Hungarian political leader" who taught at Columbia University.[1] Polanyi's death came at a moment when history appeared to have moved on from the free market version of industrial capitalism he had warned about in his 1944 book *The Great Transformation*. Despite some incipient signs of inflation in Britain and a few other parts of the West, the Keynesian model of managed capitalism was still ascendant in Western countries. Since the end of the Second World War, it had delivered rapid economic growth, rising living standards for the majority, and declining levels of income inequality.

With moderate Keynesian economists—Joan Robinson's "bastard Keynesians"—holding sway from the White House to Harvard Yard and beyond, supporters of the old laissez-faire religion were reduced to issuing jeremiads and supporting Senator Barry Goldwater's quixotic 1964 presidential campaign. The most notable of these rightist dissidents was the University of Chicago economist Milton Friedman, who in 1962 had published *Capitalism and Freedom*, a ringing defense of free markets and small government. Ever since attending high school in blue-collar Rahway, New Jersey, Friedman had been precocious and opinionated. After completing his undergraduate degree at Rutgers in 1932, he did graduate work at the University of Chicago and Columbia, but he initially struggled to get an academic post, a difficulty he later attributed partly to antisemitism. (His mother and father were Jewish immigrants from eastern Austria-Hungary.) Eventually he landed a job in Washington at the National Resources Committee, a New Deal agency, and during the Second World War, he worked at the Treasury Department. Friedman's stint in the nation's capital didn't enamor him of the federal government. After the war ended, he spent a year at the University of Minnesota, then moved back to the economics department at the University of Chicago, which had held out against the Keynesian tide.

In *Capitalism and Freedom*, Friedman described the concentration of government power as "the great threat to freedom,"[2] but his libertarian animus toward federal spending and regulation went far beyond concerns about totalitarianism. He questioned the government's role in highway building, public education, social security, public housing, banking regulation, and even national parks, such as Yellowstone and the Grand Canyon. "If the public wants this kind of activity enough to pay for it, private enterprise will have every incentive to provide such parks," he wrote.[3] Friedman's odes to the free market were out of tune with the times, though. *Capitalism and Freedom* didn't get reviewed in *The New York Times*, *Newsweek*, or *Time*. Even the *Chicago Tribune*, his local broadsheet, ignored it. "Those of us who were deeply concerned about the danger to freedom and prosperity from the growth of government, from the triumph of welfare-state and Keynesian ideas, were a small beleaguered minority regarded as eccentrics by the great majority of our fellow intellectuals," he recalled in the preface to a later edition of his book.[4]

But Friedman wouldn't remain an outsider for very long. During the two decades after he penned his free market manifesto, he would become one of the most famous and controversial economists in the world, and a policy adviser to conservative political leaders on three continents, including President Ronald Reagan.

Friedman's rise to intellectual celebrity status didn't come out of nowhere. It was part of a conservative backlash against Keynesianism at the domestic and international levels. This counterrevolution was to prove so successful politically that, by the 1980s, when the cult of Friedman was at its height, some observers with a more critical opinion of unmanaged capitalism were digging up the works of Polanyi, his warnings about the destructive impact of an unfettered market economy, and its association with authoritarianism. Finally, forty years after *The Great Transformation* was published, it would find a wide audience because, indeed, a great transformation was taking place.

A number of factors created the conditions for this metamorphosis. The most important was a steady rise in inflation that undermined the political foundations and intellectual hegemony of Keynesianism. In 1965 the US inflation rate was 1.6 percent; by 1970 it had reached 5.8 percent.[5] One driver of this rise was a surge in government spending. Lyndon Johnson's administration fought an expensive war in Vietnam and simultaneously enacted costly domestic programs. Federal outlays as a percentage of GDP rose from 15.9 percent in 1965 to 18.2 percent in 1970.[6] Strong aggregate demand drove the unemployment rate down to 3.5 percent in 1969.[7] As wage bills and input prices increased, businesses passed along their rising costs in higher prices for the goods and services they produced.

From late 1967 onward, the Federal Reserve raised interest rates to slow the economy and bring down inflation. The rising cost of borrowing eventually brought on a recession. In early 1971 Richard Nixon, the Republican president who had succeeded Johnson, proposed an expansionary budget to get the economy going again, telling some television journalists in an off-camera comment that he was "now a Keynesian in economics."[8] Months later Nixon introduced emergency controls on wages and prices to tackle the stubbornly high inflation rate, which, among other things, was putting more pressure on the dollar in foreign exchange markets. Officials at the Treasury Department and the White House believed a currency devaluation was necessary to relieve the pressure on the dollar and boost the competitiveness of US exports—a weaker dollar makes American goods cheaper overseas—but that would involve breaking the long-standing gold parity. On Sunday, August 15, after spending a couple of days with his economic advisers at Camp David, Nixon announced that his administration was closing the gold window, which meant international investors could no longer swap their dollars for gold. The postwar era of fixed exchange rates was at an end. A few days later, at the headquarters of the IMF, someone circulated a note that said: "R.I.P. We regretfully announce the not unexpected passing away after a long illness of Bretton Woods at 9 P.M. last Sunday. Bretton was born in New Hampshire in 1944 and died a few days after his 27th birthday."[9]

For a time, Nixon's expansionary policies seemed to work. In the presidential election of 1972, he trounced Senator George McGovern, his Democratic opponent. By January 1973, when Nixon reentered the White House, the economy was growing again, and the jobless rate was back below 5 percent. The inflation rate was only 3.6 percent. But then came the Yom Kippur War of October 1973, which prompted Arab oil producers to introduce an embargo of Western nations that supported Israel. In a matter of months, the price of crude oil more than tripled, plunging the gas-guzzling American economy into the deepest recession since the 1930s. Unlike in previous slumps, inflation and unemployment spiked simultaneously. By the start of 1975, the inflation rate was around 12 percent and the unemployment rate stood at 8.1 percent. Speaking to the British House of Commons a decade earlier, the Conservative politician Iain Macleod had referred to a combination of high inflation and stagnant economic growth as "stagflation." The oil price shock created an acute version of stagflation and presented a major challenge to Keynesian doctrines.

According to the Phillips Curve, a version of which Bill Phillips, of the London School of Economics, had formulated in the late 1950s, unemployment and inflation were supposed to be inversely related: if the jobless rate went down, the rate of inflation would go up, and vice versa. This trade-off seemed to offer policymakers the option of choosing a low jobless rate at the cost of somewhat higher inflation. But now the two variables were going up together. How could this be explained? The answer wasn't immediately obvious, but one person who had an explanation was Friedman. In a December 1967 presidential address to the American Economic Association, he had argued that there was a "natural rate of unemployment," and that if policymakers tried to keep the jobless rate below this figure inflation would accelerate.[10] Another way of expressing Friedman's argument was to say that the long-run Phillips Curve was vertical, so policymakers couldn't maintain low unemployment by accepting higher inflation. "There is always a temporary trade-off between inflation and unemployment," Friedman said. "There is no permanent trade-off."[11] Given this reality, Friedman argued, Keynesian efforts to keep unemployment low by using fiscal and monetary policy to manipulate aggregate demand were doomed to failure. The best thing policymakers could do was ensure slow but steady growth in the money supply, which would keep inflation anchored. This was the policy doctrine that became known as "monetarism."

It wasn't immediately clear to some people at the time, but Friedman was resurrecting two highly problematic pre-Keynesian economic theories. One of them was the claim that the economy automatically gravitates to a position of balance: in his model, this resting spot was at the natural rate of unemployment. Friedman didn't really explain what determined this rate. He merely said it was the result of "the Walrasian system of general-equilibrium relations," which was a jargon-ridden way of saying it depended on many other things in the economy. Friedman also revived the ancient quantity theory of money, which, in its simplest form, says that the price level is proportional to the money supply. One appeal of this theory is that it suggests that policymakers can control inflation simply by restricting the money supply, but in reality things aren't so straightforward. In modern economies, the size of the money supply is largely determined by the banking system rather than by policymakers. Bank deposits make up the biggest component of the supply, and the relationship between the overall quantity of money and inflation is tenuous, at best. But despite its theoretical and empirical shortcomings, Friedman's revival of pre-Keynesian economics had one great strength: it seemed to fit the moment.

During the late 1960s and early '70s, US policymakers had tried to keep the jobless rate at a low level, and price rises had accelerated, just as Friedman's "natural rate" model predicted. Then unemployment and inflation had risen simultaneously, which further discredited the downward-sloping Phillips Curve and the simplistic forms of Keynesianism that relied on it. In view of this record, many economists and policymakers were willing to gloss over the details of Friedman's theoretical framework. In the United States, the natural rate of unemployment and the vertical long-run Phillips Curve quickly became fixtures of mainstream economics textbooks. Elsewhere, textbook writers didn't take long to adopt the same theory.

At the policy level, the onset of stagflation seemed to have left the Keynesians stymied, and by the mid-1970s, even some center-left policymakers had lost faith in their prescriptions. In 1976 James Callaghan, the new prime minister of Britain, said at the annual conference of his ruling Labour Party: "We used to think that you could spend your way out of a recession and increase employment by cutting taxes and boosting Government spending. I tell you in all candour that that option no longer exists and that insofar as it ever did exist, it only worked on each occasion since the war by injecting a bigger dose of inflation into the economy, followed by a higher level of unemployment as the next step."[12] If the 1962 *Economic Report of the President* represented the high point of postwar Keynesianism, Callaghan's speech marked its existential crisis. A day after he delivered it, his government took the humiliating step of asking the IMF for an emergency loan, which the British Treasury deemed necessary because of a large budget deficit and downward pressure on the pound sterling. Looking on from Cambridge, Joan Robinson lamented these developments. "The hopes which accompanied the Keynesian revolution, of reforming capitalism so as to ensure continuous prosperity with full employment, are now all but extinguished," she commented in a 1977 article that she cowrote with a colleague. "The slide into crisis in the capitalist world has re-established the pre-Keynesian orthodoxy as the conventional wisdom in economic policymaking at both the national and international levels. The inevitable consequence of this is a much higher general level of unemployment and recurrent crises, involving a massive waste of resources and considerable human misery."[13]

Rising inflation was the cudgel that conservative economists and politicians wielded to bash Keynesianism, but it can't fully explain the demise of the postwar policy consensus. Ultimately, sustained inflation is the product of a distributional struggle over who gets what in the economy. As costs rise, workers try to protect their living standards by demanding higher wages, and companies try to protect their profit margins by raising prices. Friedman's solution to this dilemma was to raise the unemployment rate to a level at which labor unions and workers didn't have sufficient bargaining power to push through higher wage demands. He called this level of joblessness the "natural rate," but there was nothing natural about it. He was essentially calling on policymakers to restore Marx's "reserve army" of the unemployed to a level at which it could exercise its traditional role of disciplining labor and ensuring that businesses could maintain control of the workplace.

Even before inflation emerged as a serious problem, there were other indications that the long period of low unemployment had shifted the industrial power balance toward workers, including a reduction in corporate profit margins. Among the first observers to highlight this issue were two English economists of a left-wing bent, Andrew Glyn and Bob Sutcliffe. "As foreign trade gathered pace and labour markets grew tighter in the late fifties and early sixties, the tendency for the profit share to be squeezed between the pressure of wages and international competition emerged as a clearly observable trend in more and more countries," Glyn and Sutcliffe wrote in a 1972 book, *Capitalism in Crisis*.[14] The extent of the profit squeeze varied across countries, they noted. It was most notable in Great Britain, but especially from the second half of the 1960s it was also visible elsewhere. Britain, as the oldest capitalist economy, was providing "an example of the path which other capitalist economies might quite rapidly follow," the two economists suggested. They included a chart showing that between 1950 and 1970, the share of wages and salaries in total income—the obverse of the profit share—had risen in the United States, Germany, France, Italy, the Netherlands, and Japan as well as Britain.[15] During the earlier part of this period, the two economists noted, rapid productivity growth had alleviated the pressures on profitability and allowed businesses to maintain high levels of capital investment, which in turn sustained high rates of growth in output-per-worker and GDP. But now a decline in productivity growth and profitability was making it difficult to maintain a high level of capital accumulation, and "the foundations of the long post-war expansion have been undermined."[16]

Leftist economists weren't the only ones raising concerns about a profits squeeze. In 1970 Arthur Okun, a Yale economist who had just completed a two-year stint as chairman of the White House Council of Economic Advisers in the Nixon administration, coauthored an article that highlighted how the US profit share had fallen from 11 percent of gross national product in 1966 to 8 percent four years later. Okun and George L. Perry, of the Brookings Institution, attributed this development to a decline in productivity growth, which meant that wages were rising faster than output and crimping their profit margins. The two economists expressed the hope that these trends were "attributable to transitory factors," particularly a slowdown in GDP growth.[17] When growth picked up, productivity growth and profits should rebound sharply, they said. But this prognosis turned out to be overly optimistic. After reviving in 1971–73, the share of corporate profits in US GDP turned down again in 1974.

Undoubtedly, some special factors made the 1970s especially challenging for Western capitalism, including the OPEC oil price shock. But the decline in profit rates went further back, and Glyn and Sutcliffe were surely right to argue that it reflected some deep underlying trends. Back in the late 1930s and early '40s, at the start of the Keynesian era, Sweezy and Kalecki had warned that a long period of low unemployment could turn business interests and their political representatives against the Keynesian policy regime. Robinson had raised the specter of rising inflation. Experience confirmed the prescience of these warnings.

In theory, there was a cooperative way to relieve distributional conflicts and prevent a wage-price spiral. If workers agreed to moderate their wage demands, if firms agreed to keep price rises modest, and if the government kept up the level of overall demand, inflation could be brought down without a recession. But how could workers be persuaded to hold back without the threat of higher unemployment? At the end of 1970, the Organisation for Economic Co-operation and Development (OECD), an intergovernmental research organization based in Paris, issued a report on inflation that addressed this issue. "Circumstances vary considerably from country to country, but the fundamental problem is how to get people to exercise the moderation that they would do if they believed that a major recession was possible, without actually having to administer the lesson," the report said.[18]

One possible solution was an economy-wide "incomes policy," in which the government, after consulting with representatives of labor and capital, would suggest (or dictate) an annual level of wage and price increases that was consistent with productivity growth. From a societal perspective, the logic of tying increases in wages to productivity growth was clear. But for an individual union or the employees at a given plant, obtaining a bigger wage increase is always a plus, so they are unlikely to exercise restraint. The same goes for price-setting by individual businesses. In terms of game theory, the players face a Prisoner's Dilemma, and the dominant strategy is to defect from the cooperative solution. Or, as the OECD report put it: "It is thus all too easy for leaders on both sides to be persuaded into accepting over-ambitious commitments on behalf of their members."[19] Income policies would be hard to sustain.

The other potential solution to the inflation problem was the confrontational one that Friedman and other conservative economists recommended: dismantle the power of organized labor by raising the level of unemployment, weakening labor laws, and removing other restrictions on businesses. As efforts to introduce price controls and income policies foundered, this was the option that a number of Western countries would gravitate toward. By the mid-1970s, one high-inflation nation outside of the Western core had already adopted such a strategy, with Friedman's explicit approval: General Pinochet's Chile.

After deposing Salvador Allende, the country's first socialist president, in September 1973, the Pinochet regime rounded up many of Allende's supporters and killed a large number of them. It banned the leftist political parties that had made up his coalition and suppressed labor unions. The new economics minister was a general, Rodolfo González, but the key development was the appointment, as a senior adviser to González, of Sergio de Castro, a free market economist. De Castro was one of "the Chicago Boys," a group of young Chileans who had studied economics at the University of Chicago under an arrangement with the Catholic University of Chile. (De Castro had obtained a doctorate.) Pinochet and other members of the new junta in Santiago didn't know much about economic theory, but with the unemployment rate in the double digits and inflation running at about 700 percent, they were keen to get the Chilean economy going again. De Castro and some of his fellow Chicago Boys had developed a lengthy economic plan, which became known as *El Ladrillo* (in English, *The Brick*).

In his 2023 history, *The Chile Project: The Story of the Chicago Boys and the Downfall of Neoliberalism*, Sebastian Edwards, a Chilean-born economist at the University of California, Los Angeles, recounted how *The Brick* was commissioned before the coup by a former naval commander and active admiral who were considering toppling Allende.[20] Edwards said it's still not clear how many of the eleven economists who wrote the report—nine of whom had attended the University of Chicago—knew about its origins in military plotting. In any case, the report was completed before Allende was overthrown. By today's standards, Edwards writes, its policy recommendations "look mild and quite run-of-the-mill."[21] But that wasn't how they appeared to the report's authors, or to some of Pinochet's generals, who were suspicious of the free market economists.

The Brick called for rolling back some of Allende's income-support measures and focusing anti-poverty programs on the extremely poor. More broadly, it demanded a historic break with the import-substitution and state-led economic development policies that Chilean governments had followed during the postwar decades. Rather than relying on state planning, the country should allow market forces to allocate resources. It should eliminate government controls, privatize state-owned businesses, replace the state pension scheme with a system of individual savings accounts, free up the financial sector, and, except in the case of monopolies, eliminate price controls, which were practically universal. To promote competition and trade, the blanket quotas that restricted imports and protected Chilean producers should be replaced with a uniform tariff of 30 percent.

The generals weren't the only influential Chileans who were initially lukewarm about the Chicago Boys' proposals. Many business leaders, who were used to operating in protected markets under government direction, were initially resistant to making a radical shift, and it wasn't clear if Pinochet and his colleagues would go down that route. In March 1975, Milton Friedman visited Santiago for six days with one of his colleagues from the University of Chicago economics department, Arnold "Al" Harberger, who spoke Spanish, was married to a Chilean woman, and had written a journal article on inflation in Chile. The inflation rate was still running at nearly 350 percent, and unemployment had risen sharply since the coup.[22] Friedman and Harberger met for about three-quarters of an hour with Pinochet, and Friedman advised the Chilean leader to introduce a program of "shock treatment," consisting of deep spending cuts and measures designed to liberalize the economy. Pinochet "was sympathetically attracted to the idea of a shock treatment but was clearly distressed at the possible temporary unemployment that might be caused," Friedman later recalled in a memoir.[23]

After Friedman returned home, he wrote the Chilean leader a lengthy letter that began "Dear Mr. President" and advised him to adopt an eight-point program that could "end inflation in months, and would set the state for the solution of your second major problem—promoting an effective social market economy."[24] Friedman's proposals included cutting government spending across the board by 25 percent within six months, pledging to stop printing money to finance government spending, and removing "as many obstacles as possible that now hinder the private market." He also advised the dictator to continue with efforts to liberalize trade and assured him, "If Chile now takes the right track, I believe it can achieve another economic miracle."

Friedman subsequently claimed that, even before he arrived in Santiago, the Chicago Boys had decided on a program of shock treatment, and the role that he and Harberger played was merely to give this program a "stamp of approval, and help to sell it to the public and the military junta."[25] The sales effort seems to have worked. The month after Friedman left, Pinochet's regime adopted a Plan for Economic Recovery and appointed Sergio de Castro as minister of economics.[26] The new plan, which Pinochet enacted by presidential fiat, included a pledge to slash government spending by 15 percent—not quite the 25 percent that Friedman had recommended, but still a huge cut. It also called for the elimination of price and import controls, the privatization of publicly owned firms and the public pension system, and deregulation of the financial sector. Shock treatment it was.

From some perspectives, the combination of deep austerity and radical liberalization worked as planned. In the late 1970s, Chile's inflation rate fell sharply: by 1981, it was under 10 percent.[27] Business investment revived, exports rose, and in the four years from 1977 to 1980, inflation-adjusted GDP grew at an annual rate of 8.5 percent.[28] However, the shock treatment also exacted heavy social and economic costs. Among Chile's poor, the cuts to government programs caused a great deal of hardship. By 1978, inflation-adjusted wages had fallen by nearly a quarter, and close to 20 percent of the workforce was unemployed or on emergency government programs that paid minimal wages.[29]

Moreover, the strong GDP growth didn't last. In late 1981 Chile experienced a foreign debt crisis. During the years of growth, it had built up big external debts. But now its currency fell sharply, and the government was forced to take over a number of large banks, which were teetering on the edge of collapse, prompting some wags to point to "the Chicago road to socialism."[30] The economy entered a deep recession, in which the jobless rate rose to more than 25 percent and inflation started rising again.[31]

Defenders of the Chicago Boys and Friedman point out that between 1973 and 1990, when Chile returned to democracy, its GDP per capita rose by about a third, which was a strong performance compared to the country's history.[32] The supporters of the shock therapy don't tend to dwell on the fact that it had been made possible only by the elimination of Pinochet's political critics, the suppression of the labor movement, and the brutal exercise of absolute power. (During the seventeen years of military dictatorship, according to a subsequent report by the Chilean National Commission on Truth and Reconciliation, 2,279 people were killed for political reasons. Tens of thousands more were tortured.)[33] One of Pinochet's former ministers did subsequently acknowledge the political reality that underpinned the free market shock treatment, noting that the Chilean experiment "could be so revolutionary because we had a very authoritarian regime."[34]

None of this would have come as a surprise to Karl Polanyi, of course. In *The Great Transformation*, he had emphasized that, historically, it had taken strong states to create the conditions in which free market capitalism could consolidate itself and thrive: a Smithian economy didn't emerge naturally.

In the big Western democracies, the shift to the right in economic policymaking was more gradual but increasingly visible. During the 1976 US presidential campaign, Jimmy Carter, running as a moderate Democratic outsider, criticized President Gerald Ford, Nixon's Republican successor, for running big budget deficits and allowing inflation to rise. After Carter won the election and entered the White House, he focused on restraining spending and bringing down the deficit: during his four-year term, the deficit as a share of GDP declined from 4 percent to 2.6 percent.[35] Carter's embrace of fiscal rectitude didn't buy him lasting relief from price pressures, though. During his first two years in office, the inflation rate averaged about 7 percent, and the unemployment rate barely dropped below 6 percent. And in 1979, after the Iranian Revolution sent the price of crude oil and gasoline soaring again, the inflation rate rose to double digits.[36] On July 15, 1979, with the public mood souring, Carter delivered a prime-time address in which he said, "The erosion of our confidence in the future is threatening to destroy the social and the political fabric of America."[37] Carter also vowed to make the United States energy independent, but that wasn't what the address was remembered for. Although he didn't use the term *malaise*, it subsequently became known as the "malaise speech."

In this environment, Friedman's policy prescriptions attracted increasing support, particularly from business interests. Some of his followers claimed that bringing down inflation by restricting the growth of the money supply would be relatively painless. Once workers and firms realized that the central bank was determined to hold the line, their expectations of future inflation would diminish, and this would translate into smaller wage claims and price increases. Under the guise of the theory of "rational expectations," which swept through American economics departments like a virus during the mid-1970s, some conservative economists (but not Friedman) took this argument to its logical extreme and claimed that, if commitment to eliminating inflation was credible enough, inflation would fall sharply pretty much immediately. Once the central bank announced that it was restricting the growth of the money supply to, say, 3 percent, wage negotiators would adopt that figure as their estimate of expected inflation and adjust their wage claims accordingly. Inflation would drop with no increase in unemployment.

Many policymakers were skeptical of the theory of rational expectations, but the idea that a credible central bank could bring down inflation relatively easily appealed to elected politicians who didn't like being held responsible for the rising cost of living. In 1977, the US Congress, with support from both parties, directed the Federal Reserve to set targets for the growth rate of the money supply and report back to it on whether they were being met. Monetarist dogma also provided a convenient cover for old-school inflation hawks who were determined to break the wage-price spiral whatever the cost. The key figure in this camp was Paul Volcker, a six-foot-seven New Jerseyite whom Carter appointed as chairman of the Federal Reserve in 1979. In September 1979, Volcker formally committed the Fed to monetarism, although many observers, Friedman included, believed this was just a feint to distract from the central bank's determination to push up interest rates. Between September 1979 and March 1980, the Fed raised its discount rate from 10.7 percent to 13 percent.[38] At the start of 1980, a recession began.[39]

Friedman's hostility toward organized labor and government regulation also appealed to many politicians and business groups. Since the original publication of *Capitalism and Freedom*, the Republican Nixon administration had created two large new regulatory agencies, the Environmental Protection Agency (EPA) and the Occupational Safety and Health Administration (OSHA), which were given extensive powers to enforce new and preexisting regulations. In response to these developments, American corporations and wealthy interests looked for ways to bolster their political influence. In 1972, a number of CEOs from major corporations established the Business Roundtable as a lobbying group. The United States Chamber of Commerce and the National Association of Manufacturers, which already existed, increased their political budgets and expanded their presence in Washington, DC. So did individual corporations. Under the Federal Election Campaign Act of 1971, corporations and labor unions were allowed to set up and fund political action committees (PACs) that could support political candidates. By 1976, there were more than one hundred corporate PACs in existence.[40] Simultaneously, a number of very rich right-wing individuals provided funding for new conservative publications and think tanks. In 1973, the conservative Colorado beer magnate Joseph Coors helped to finance the establishment of the Heritage Foundation, which quickly started churning out articles critical of regulation, welfare, and Keynesianism.

The embrace of deregulation wasn't confined to the Republican Party. In 1974, Senator Ted Kennedy, the "liberal lion" of Massachusetts, became chairman of a new Senate subcommittee on "administrative practice and procedure," which organized public hearings on the airline industry, where the Civil Aeronautics Board (CAB) had long controlled prices and allocated routes between airlines. As chief counsel of the subcommittee, Kennedy hired Stephen Breyer, a Harvard law professor whom Bill Clinton would eventually nominate to the Supreme Court. Like Kennedy, Breyer was a Democrat, but he believed, with some justification, that airline regulation operated against the interest of consumers, who were paying high fares on planes flown by a cozy cartel of major carriers. "The CAB was supposed to be protecting the public, but regulation was leading to higher prices," he would later recall. "It spent 95 percent of its time keeping prices from being too low instead of pushing to get them lowered."[41]

In 1977, Carter appointed another Democratic critic of regulation, the Cornell University economist Alfred Kahn, to run the CAB. Kahn was an independent-minded academic who had no time for special pleading from the big carriers. In 1978, he helped shepherd through Congress the Airline Deregulation Act, which eliminated the federal government's authority to set fares and made it easier for new entrants to fly routes dominated by the big carriers. These reforms revolutionized the airline industry, opening the way to an era of cheaper fares, discount airlines, crowded planes, and wage cuts for workers at legacy carriers. The philosophy behind airline deregulation was encapsulated in a remark of Breyer's: "Why regulate something if it can be done better by the market?"[42] After this market-friendly philosophy was applied to the airline industry, administrations of both parties would gradually extend it to many other industries, including telecommunications, power generation, and finance—all of which had been heavily regulated during the postwar decades. The era of deregulation had begun.

In 1980, Friedman and his wife, Rose, created a ten-part PBS television series, *Free to Choose*, that, according to the journalist Thomas Edsall, was partly funded by a $650,000 grant from the Scaife Foundation.[43] A book that Friedman and Rose wrote to accompany the television series sold four hundred thousand copies in hardcover and was translated into seventeen languages. In it, the Friedmans expounded many of Milton's old themes, including the claim that government regulation was almost always harmful and unnecessary. Among the federal agencies they criticized were the EPA, the Consumer Product Safety Commission, the Securities and Exchange Commission, and the Food and Drug Administration, which they claimed had "done more harm by retarding progress in the production and distribution of valuable drugs than it has done good by preventing the distribution of harmful or ineffective drugs."[44] The Friedmans cleverly presented their radical free market agenda as an effort to restore traditional American values. "We have been forgetting the basic truth that the greatest threat to human freedom is the concentration of power, whether in the hands of government or anyone else," they wrote. "Fortunately, we are waking up."[45]

It was this sort of language that had drawn Ronald Reagan to Friedman. Their relationship was a long-standing one. Friedman first met the former screen actor when he was serving as governor of California from 1967 to 1975. He met with Reagan during his failed 1976 presidential campaign and advised him in his successful 1980 bid. After Reagan entered the White House, he appointed Friedman to a panel of outside economic advisers who met with him occasionally. Friedman wasn't involved with day-to-day policymaking, but he didn't need to be physically present to exert his influence. The administration's policy platform was the same as his: cut taxes, deregulate, weaken labor laws, and wherever possible, downsize the federal government. (The Pentagon budget was a glaring exception, of course.) In short, undo the postwar political settlement and promote free market capitalism. And Reagan retained warm feelings toward Friedman. His domestic policy adviser Martin Anderson later recalled: "He could just not resist Friedman's infectious enthusiasm and Reagan's eyes sparkled with delight every time he engaged in a dialogue with him."[46]

As conservative economics and the deregulation movement were sweeping through the American political arena, a number of more skeptical economists were registering serious concerns. One of them was Hyman Minsky, of Washington University in St. Louis, who was an expert on money and banking. As a left-liberal whose immigrant parents were active in the labor union movement, Minsky disliked Friedman's conservative policy recommendations for political reasons, but he also believed they were grounded in outdated economics. He was particularly critical of Friedman's assumption that a capitalist economy, if left to its own devices, will gravitate toward a position of balance, or "equilibrium."

Minsky believed that in a modern financialized economy such as that of the United States, businesses and financial institutions were incentivized to take on too much risk and too much debt, and this made the financial system very fragile. If it was given too much leeway—and the proponents of deregulation wanted to give it as much as possible—it was apt to blow up and plunge the economy into a deep recession, or even a depression. "This implies that policies to control and guide the evolution of finance are necessary," Minsky wrote in a 1978 paper.[47] His language was understated, but the argument was potentially devastating to the policy of deregulating the financial system, which had begun even before Reagan came to power, with the passage of the 1980 Depository Institutions Deregulation and Monetary Control Act. (The legislation removed long-standing caps on the interest rates that banks could pay on their customer accounts.)

Minsky, who died in 1996, sometimes described himself as a "financial Keynesian." It would be equally accurate to call him an institutional economist, because he believed that economic theory was useful only if it could be applied to the actual institutions of a capitalist economy rather than the textbook versions. Rare among academics, he had firsthand experience of the banking system. After doing his undergraduate degree at the University of Chicago and completing his doctorate in 1954 at Harvard, where his first supervisor was Joseph Schumpeter, he taught at Brown and Berkeley. In 1965 he moved to St. Louis, where, in addition to teaching at Washington University, he began a long-standing association with the local Mark Twain Bank, eventually serving as a director. Throughout the 1970s, Minsky published various versions of his theory, which he termed "the Financial Instability Hypothesis," before summarizing and restating it in his 1978 paper, which described it as "an alternative to the neo-classical synthesis, i.e., to today's standard economic theory. It is designed to explain instability as a result of the normal functioning of a capitalist economy."[48]

Minsky said his theory was in the spirit of Keynes, who also had firsthand knowledge of the financial industry. In a modern economy, he emphasized, there were two parallel structures: the business sector, which invested in buildings and capital equipment to produce things, and the banking sector, which lends money to business based on their expected cash flows. Standard economics textbooks concentrated on the production side of the economy. Minsky emphasized the availability of credit and how it changes over time. In the early stages of a business cycle, he pointed out, financial institutions tend to lend only to business projects whose cash flows are expected to comfortably exceed their financial commitments, including interest costs. Minsky referred to this safety-first setup as "hedge finance." Unfortunately, it doesn't last.

As the cycle proceeds and the prices of assets, such as stocks and real estate, rise sharply, Minsky explained, banks and other lenders lower their credit standards and start lending to ventures that generate enough cash to meet their interest payments but not their other financial commitments. These types of businesses need to roll over their debts on a regular basis to keep operating, Minsky pointed out. He called this type of arrangement "speculative finance." It is obviously riskier than hedge finance, but it isn't the final word in financial recklessness. Minsky said that variant arrives, typically late in the cycle, in the form of "Ponzi finance."

At this stage, lending standards have deteriorated so much that banks extend credit to ventures that don't generate enough cash even to pay their interest bills. This is lending on the basis of a wish and a prayer. As the ratio of speculative and Ponzi finance to hedge finance increases, the fragility of the financial system becomes increasingly evident, Minsky noted. If for any reason the supply of new credit dries up, perhaps because of a rise in interest rates or a fall in profits, the Ponzi businesses are forced to sell assets to raise cash, "only to discover that their assets cannot be sold at a price that comes even close to covering debts."[49] Selling begets more selling, asset prices collapse, and borrowers face even greater difficulties servicing their debts. "What has been sketched out is the route to a financial crisis," Minsky noted dryly.[50]

When he wrote these words, he wasn't well-known, and they didn't have much impact. Unlike Friedman, Minsky wasn't invited to the White House or featured in a PBS television series. But as the great experiment in deregulation unfolded and the financial sector was unleashed, his instability hypothesis would eventually be rediscovered.

23

"Any use of the natural resources for the satisfaction of non-vital needs means a smaller quantity of life in the future"

Nicholas Georgescu-Roegen and the Limits to Growth

During the postwar decades, all the major economic systems—Western capitalism, Soviet and Chinese Communism, and the hybrid model of state-led industrialization that many former colonies pursued—prioritized a high rate of economic growth and judged themselves by how effectively they achieved it. Any signs of faltering GDP growth were regarded as cause for alarm. "We have not in recent years maintained the 4 to 4½ percent growth rate which characterized the early postwar period," the White House Council of Economic Advisers lamented in the aforementioned 1962 *Economic Report of the President*. "We should not settle for less than the achievement of a long-term growth rate matching the early postwar record."[1]

The economists who wrote these words were Keynesians of the Harvard/MIT school, but the goal of maximizing GDP growth was shared by socialist planners, nationalist postcolonialists, and free market conservatives. The economic advisers at the Kremlin and the Lok Kalyan Marg in New Delhi believed just as fervently in eternal economic expansion as the Keynesians in the White House; so did the members of the University of Chicago's economics department. "Economic growth is the grand objective," the English economist Roy Harrod wrote in 1965. "It is the aim of economic policy as a whole."[2] Economists from many different schools shared a belief that the easiest and most effective way to increase human welfare and raise the poor out of poverty was to grow the economic pie. Socialists and liberals believed in sharing it out more equally; conservatives and supporters of the free market tended to be less concerned about distributive shares. Few economic policymakers anywhere queried the need to expand the size of the pie.

In this ecumenical church of growth, the faithful viewed the GDP hockey stick as a settled feature of the modern world. The big debate among them was how to make it rise more steeply. It was generally agreed that poorer countries, if they mobilized unused labor and imported technology, could grow even faster than advanced countries for a time—a phenomenon known as the "catch-up" effect. The rate of expansion in rich countries was believed to be largely determined by the pace of technological progress. When economists looked at the seemingly endless stream of innovations that scientists had developed since World War II—space rockets, mainframe computers, fertilizers, miracle drugs and vaccines, to name but a few—most of them assumed that growth could continue indefinitely, especially if policies were put in place that encouraged scientific research and innovation.

Environmental concerns weren't entirely absent from this consensus. There was a growing recognition that unrestricted economic development could have harmful side effects, such as ground and air pollution. In 1948 the US Congress had passed the Federal Water Pollution Control Act, and in 1955 it had enacted the Air Pollution Control Act. In 1963 the state of California had introduced its first emissions standards for automobiles. Thanks to the efforts of some pioneering writers, public opinion was shifting. In 1962 Rachel Carson published *Silent Spring*, which documented the harmful effects of toxic pesticides, such as DDT, that the chemical industry had claimed were safe. A year later Stewart Udall, the secretary of the interior in the Kennedy administration, published *The Quiet Crisis*, in which he declared: "America today stands poised on a pinnacle of wealth and power, yet we live in a land of vanishing beauty, of increasing ugliness, of shrinking open space, and of an overall environment that is diminished daily by pollution and noise and blight."[3]

In issuing these warnings, Carson and Udall could draw on a long tradition of American naturism and civic activism. A young Benjamin Franklin had campaigned for the removal of tanneries from Philadelphia because of the toxic wastes that seeped into local streams and rivers. In 1864, George

Perkins Marsh, a diplomat and philologist, published *Man and Nature*, a landmark work in which he cataloged how human activity had transformed parts of the natural environment, often with disastrous results. "Man has too long forgotten that the earth was given to him for usufruct alone, not for consumption, still less for profligate waste," Marsh wrote.[4] Among other things, he claimed that forest clearing and soil degradation had contributed to the decline of ancient Mediterranean civilizations. His widely read book helped create the modern conservation movement, which by the end of the nineteenth century had scored some significant victories, including the creation of Adirondack Park in upstate New York and the establishment of other national forest reserves in many parts of the country.

In Britain, too, going back to the nineteenth-century writers William Morris and John Ruskin, critics had pointed out the harmful side effects of capitalist development. Even inside the field of economics, some of these evils had long been acknowledged. In his 1848 textbook *Principles of Political Economy*, John Stuart Mill, a keen botanist, had referred to virgin land as "the original inheritance of the whole species" and lamented the prospect of it being appropriated as private property and filled with human development.[5] In the 1920s Arthur Cecil Pigou, Alfred Marshall's successor at Cambridge, had developed Marshall's concept of externalities, or negative spillovers, to describe how some economic activities, such as smoke pollution, had harmful effects that weren't fully accounted for in the price system. Pigou's solution to this problem, which economists now refer to as "market failures," was to tax polluters and disincentivize their harmful behavior. Other economists favored direct regulation.

During the postwar period, economists developed some new tools to deal with complex environment issues, such as cost-benefit analysis, which they used to evaluate the economic gains and losses, including the environmental impact, attached to any given development project, such as a new airport. Where economists and policymakers had come up short, or so their critics claimed, was in integrating these *micro*economic techniques with their *macro*economic analysis, which largely proceeded as if environmental concerns didn't matter, or, at least, as if they could be dealt with adequately through taxes and regulation. In the sixth edition of Paul Samuelson's textbook on economics, which was published in 1964, the terms *environment* and *pollution* didn't appear in the index.[6] Neglect of environmental issues wasn't restricted to the capitalist world. The Soviet Union was a major polluter. Per unit of GDP, according to a 1994 study, it generated 1.5 times as much pollution as the United States did.[7] Russia's post-Communist government acknowledged that roughly 40 percent of the country was under moderately high or high ecological stress.[8]

While East and West pursued the grail of growth, it was largely left to noneconomists to query its physical and theoretical underpinnings. One of the few heretics inside the economics profession was Nicholas Georgescu-Roegen, a strong-minded Romanian who had done his graduate work at Harvard under Joseph Schumpeter in the 1930s and subsequently taught at Vanderbilt University. In 1971, Georgescu-Roegen published *The Entropy Law and the Economic Process*, a sprawling tome that identified the rapid depletion of the earth's stock of natural resources as a limiting factor in growth. It said: "The almost fabulous comfort . . . attained by many past and present societies had caused us to forget, however, the most elementary fact of economic life, namely, that of all the necessaries for life, only the purely biological ones are absolutely indispensable for our survival."[9] Although *The Entropy Law and the Economic Process* didn't have much immediate impact on policy debates, it is now widely recognized as a founding text of ecological economics.

Georgescu-Roegen had a hardscrabble upbringing. He was born in 1906 in Constanţa, an ancient town located on the Black Sea, about 140 miles east of Bucharest. "It was then an ethnic mosaic of Romanians, Greeks . . . Germans, Jews, Armenians, Turks, Tartars, and a few Bulgarians," he recalled in his old age. "Because the environment of my childhood was truly cosmopolitan, my ethos has remained so ever since."[10] Romania was an underdeveloped country full of impoverished peasants. Georgescu-Roegen's family was a bit further up the social ladder: his father was a retired army captain; his mother taught needlework. Georgescu-Roegen obtained a scholarship to a military high school, where he rose to the top of his class and won a succession of national student prizes in mathematics. He went on to study mathematics at Bucharest University, where he again excelled. After graduating in 1926, he was awarded a graduate scholarship to the Sorbonne, in Paris.

There Georgescu-Roegen attended lectures by eminent French mathematicians, including Émile Borel, Henri Lebesgue, and Édouard Goursat. He specialized in the rapidly developing field of mathematical statistics. In his doctoral thesis, he came up with a new technique to isolate cyclical movements in a time series, such as annual births, daily rainfall, or quarterly retail sales. (The actual time series Georgescu-Roegen used was for rainfall in Paris.) After obtaining his doctorate, he moved to University College, London, where he collaborated with Karl Pearson, a leading figure in mathematical statistics. Georgescu-Roegen wasn't intending to become an economist, but his work on time series attracted attention. A representative of the Rockefeller Foundation asked if he would be interested in applying for a fellowship to the United States, where the Harvard University Economics Barometer had begun using new statistical methods to analyze economic cycles.

Georgescu-Roegen applied for the fellowship and got it. In 1934 he and his wife, Otilia, a fellow mathematician whom he had met when they were both undergraduates, arrived in Cambridge, Massachusetts, only to discover that the Harvard University Economics Barometer had closed up shop after failing to predict the Great Depression. At a loss about what to do, Georgescu-Roegen approached Joseph Schumpeter, Harvard's renowned Austrian economist, who was teaching a course on business cycles. Schumpeter expressed interest in Georgescu-Roegen's research and introduced him to Wassily Leontief, a Russian mathematical economist who had arrived at Harvard a couple of years earlier. With Leontief's encouragement, Georgescu-Roegen delved into the mathematical theory of consumer choice. Despite having no formal background in economics, he quickly wrote a series of papers that cemented his reputation as a wunderkind. Schumpeter was so impressed that he asked Georgescu-Roegen to join the Harvard faculty. Feeling obliged to return to Romania, the young scholar turned down the offer, a decision he came to regret.

He stayed in Romania for more than a decade, teaching at the University of Bucharest and advising the country's central statistical agency. During World War II, Romania fought on the side of the Nazis under General Ion Antonescu, whose fascist regime participated in the Holocaust. After the war ended and Antonescu was overthrown, a new democratic government appointed Georgescu-Roegen as general secretary of an armistice commission. But with the Red Army occupying much of the country, Romania was falling under the control of the Soviet Union. In 1948, shortly after the establishment of a one-party Marxist-Leninist state, Georgescu-Roegen and his wife fled to Turkey aboard a freight ship. After making their way across Europe, they sailed from Cherbourg to the United States. When they got to

Cambridge, the Harvard economics community welcomed them back and gave Georgescu-Roegen a temporary teaching post, but Schumpeter's offer of a permanent position had long since lapsed. In 1949 Georgescu-Roegen accepted an invitation to join the economics faculty at Vanderbilt University in Nashville, where he would remain for the rest of his life.

As a mature scholar, Georgescu-Roegen concentrated mainly on practical questions of economic development and growth. He had grown skeptical about the usefulness of orthodox economic theories, many of which were largely built on axioms of individual choice and the notion of equalizing marginal benefits and costs. In poor societies like the Romania he grew up in, Georgescu-Roegen once pointed out, many people worked as long as they could, regardless of any such calculations. "In the lands of scarcity, income distribution is made not according to marginal pricing, but according to some institutional rules (as within most families, yours too, I think)," he remarked.[11]

A second problem with economic orthodoxy that Georgescu-Roegen identified was that it largely neglected natural resources and the dangers of degrading or depleting them. In a 1965 paper, "Process in Farming Versus Process in Manufacturing," he distinguished between two types of inputs to production: "flows" and "funds."[12] The flows were inputs that got used up or transformed into outputs and waste (or pollution) during the production process: things like coal, iron ore, and industrial components, such as screws and rivets. The funds were the "agents of production," such as labor and physical capital, that helped transform the other inputs into outputs but didn't get used up themselves. In differentiating between inputs in this way, Georgescu-Roegen was essentially agreeing with Joan Robinson and her colleagues in Cambridge, England, that the neoclassical "production function," which featured just labor and capital as inputs, was oversimplified and not generally applicable. But it wasn't until he wrote *The Entropy Law and the Economic Process* that he turned this critique into a broader critique of perpetual growth as an economic goal.

The 1971 book is an intellectual tour de force, which ranges across economics, physics, biology, mathematics, and the philosophy of science virtually at will. Sections on statistical mechanics and the arithmetical continuum lap up against accounts of Marx's two-sector model of economic growth and Georgescu-Roegen's answer to his own question: "Why Is Economics Not a Theoretical Science?"[13] (Its "laws" aren't truly general, he said. They apply to specific institutional settings, such as a capitalist economy with wage labor and private ownership of capital. In other settings, such as a peasant economy, they break down.) Between these intellectual perambulations, Georgescu-Roegen laid out the essence of his argument, which was that all forms of economic production—capitalist, socialist, and preindustrial—are physical activities, and therefore they are subject to the laws of nature.

More particularly, they must respect the Second Law of Thermodynamics— the law of degradation or entropy—which states that all energy transfers result in the loss of some usable energy, so that over time the amount of usable energy in the system declines, and the amount of unusable energy, or waste, increases. To illustrate his point, Georgescu-Roegen cited the operation of a railroad steam engine that pulls carriages along a track and turns its fuel, coal, into useless ashes. He argued that economists, in representing the economy as a closed system wherein money flows from households to businesses and back again in an endless loop, had made a major error: "Even if only the physical facet of the economic process is taken into consideration, this process is not circular, but *unidirectional*," he wrote. "As far as this facet alone is concerned, the economic process consists of a continuous transformation of low entropy into high entropy, that is, into *irrevocable waste*, or, with a topical term, into pollution."[14]

One interpretation of Georgescu-Roegen's invocation of the entropy law is that, since any economic system relies on energy, and many energy sources are in limited supply, the degradation law places an upper limit on economic production, which eventually will be reached, with potentially catastrophic consequences for humanity. This is the lesson that many commentators have taken from Georgescu-Roegen's magnum opus, and it is certainly something that he wanted to get across. Noting that the path of economic development had produced an ever-increasing reliance on fossil fuels, he wrote, "every Cadillac produced at any time means fewer lives in the future."[15] Emphasizing the pressure of rising populations, he added: "Population pressure and technological progress bring *ceteris paribus* the career of the human species nearer to its end only because both factors cause a speedier decumulation of its dowry."

But Georgescu-Roegen didn't confine his argument about rising entropy to energy resources. He applied it to the economy as a whole, arguing that the entire production process involved converting "low entropy" commodities, such as cotton, lumber, and metal ores, into "high entropy" goods, such as steel frames, automobiles, and domestic appliances. After the book was published, some physicists pointed out that, strictly speaking, this was a misuse of the degradation law, which didn't apply to such objects. But Georgescu-Roegen's slipup about the scope of the entropy law didn't negate his larger argument that economic development was subject to physical constraints and the threat of exhausting natural resources. His essential claim, he would subsequently make clear, was that these resources couldn't be re-created or recycled indefinitely—a point on which he was scientifically correct. "It can be shown that even by recycling (for instance, glass bottles), we cannot go back to the original situation without lowering the quality of the natural resources that we can consume," the Danish scientist John Schmitz, the author of a book about the Second Law of Thermodynamics, wrote in a 2007 article about Georgescu-Roegen.[16]

In *The Entropy Law and the Economic Process*, Georgescu-Roegen didn't say when resource depletion would reach a crisis point, but his language suggested that the moment of reckoning wasn't too far off. The intensification and mechanization of agriculture could "enable mankind to feed a population even greater than seven billions by 2000 A.D," he wrote, but this would be possible only by "eating more quickly into the 'capital' of low entropy with which our planet is endowed."[17] In the two centuries since the start of the industrial revolution, Georgescu-Roegen said, humanity had placed itself "in the position of a fantastic spendthrift," and the running down of key resources had raised the question of how much would be left for future generations to exploit. "There can be no doubt about it," he wrote. "Any use of the natural resources for the satisfaction of non-vital needs means a smaller quantity of life in the future. If we understand well the problem, the best use of our iron resources is to produce plows or harrows as they are needed, not Rolls Royces, not even agricultural tractors."[18]

Georgescu-Roegen was essentially arguing that most members of his own profession were very poor guides to existential questions of resource depletion. He said that they had gone astray by representing industrial production as a process that "neither induces any qualitative change nor is affected by the qualitative change of the environment into which it is anchored."[19] Occasionally economists did discuss natural resources, he acknowledged, "yet the fact remains that, search as one may, in none of the numerous economic models in existence is there a variable standing for nature's perennial contribution."

The book appeared at a moment when, outside the economics profession at least, concerns about population growth, resource depletion, and environmental degradation were rising. On April 22, 1970, millions of Americans attended rallies and other events to observe the first Earth Day, which was organized by Senator Gaylord Nelson, a Wisconsin Democrat, and Denis Hayes, a Harvard graduate student. In 1972 a group of environmentalists and systems analysts connected to MIT, led by the wife-and-husband team of Donella and Dennis Meadows, published a lengthy report titled *The Limits to Growth*. Citing extensive computer simulations, the report warned: "If the present growth trends in world population, industrialization, pollution, food production, and resource depletion continue unchanged, the limits to growth on this planet will be reached sometime within the next one hundred years."[20] To prevent such a disastrous blowup, the authors called on humanity to prepare for "a period of great transition—the transition from growth to global equilibrium."[21]

The Limits to Growth wasn't merely an academic jeremiad. It was commissioned by an international group of politicians and business leaders known as the Club of Rome. Bearing this semiofficial imprimatur, the report attracted a great deal of media attention—and a lot of hostile fire from economists, who questioned everything about it: its methodological basis, its simulations, and its purported neglect of basic economics. The report's "imposing apparatus of computer technology and systems jargon conceals a kind of intellectual Rube Goldberg device—one which takes arbitrary assumptions, shakes them up and comes out with arbitrary conclusions that have the ring of science," Peter Passell, Marc Roberts, and Leonard Ross wrote in *The New York Times Book Review*.[22] In the journal *Challenge*, under the ironic headline "Is the End of the World at Hand?," MIT's own Robert Solow—the same Solow who had spent a decade and a half tussling with Joan Robinson—said "the Doomsday Models are bad science and therefore bad guides to public policy."[23] The most serious problem with their simulations was that they ignored the market price system and technical progress, Solow argued. As essential resources like oil and iron ore got scarcer, he said, their prices would rise sharply, which would give countries a strong incentive to use them more efficiently and develop substitutes for them. In fact, this was already happening, Solow claimed. He provided figures to show that, relative to each dollar of GNP that the US economy produced, the inputs of iron ore and copper it used had fallen significantly during the previous two decades. "I am no believer that the market is always right, and I am certainly no advocate of *laissez-faire* where the environment is concerned," Solow wrote. "But the price system is, after all, the main social institution evolved by capitalist economies (and, to an increasing extent, socialist economies too) for registering and reacting to relative scarcity."[24]

The economists who criticized *The Limits to Growth*, and there were many of them, didn't confine their arguments to querying its computer simulations and economic logic. They also questioned its call for a new "global equilibrium." The report's simulations showed that, in order to attain this state, the global population and global capital stock would eventually have to be held constant.[25] Clearly, this would involve reducing the rate of births and holding the rate of capital accumulation to the same rate at which capital depreciated. After two centuries of capital-driven industrial expansion, net capital accumulation would cease. So, for all intents and purposes, would exponential economic growth—although the authors of *The Limits to Growth* argued that technological progress would continue to raise living standards. Many economists were aghast. Restating a basic precept of postwar Keynesianism, Wilfred Beckerman, an economist at Oxford University, emphasized the role that economic growth and rising prosperity had played in alleviating social divisions and fending off political extremism. "If growth were to be abandoned as an objective of policy, democracy too would have to be abandoned," Beckerman wrote in his 1974 book *In Defence of Economic Growth*. "The costs of deliberate non-growth, in terms of the political and social transformation that would be required in society, are astronomical."[26]

In the short term, the economists largely prevailed in the argument over resource constraints. In October 1973, OPEC introduced its oil embargo on Western countries, and crude oil prices tripled. High energy prices led to significant conservation efforts in advanced countries, including the development of more fuel-efficient motor vehicles and the allocation of more research dollars to renewable energy. On this point, at least, Robert Solow had been proved right: the price system and the profit motive did lead to changes in technology and behavior. Homeowners and businesses started to insulate their buildings, and the rising cost of gasoline prompted the Detroit carmakers to retire their most egregious gas guzzlers, at least temporarily. (Decades later, when gas prices were low again, they would bring them back in the form of SUVs.) According to the organization Our World in Data, per capita carbon dioxide emissions in the United States and the United Kingdom peaked in the early 1970s and have been generally declining ever since.[27] With the American population still growing, however, overall US emissions continued to climb until the new millennium, when they started to fall back.[28] And on a global basis, CO_2 emissions continued to rise, with impacts on the climate that were increasingly difficult to dismiss.

Amidst all the criticism of the *Limits to Growth* report, there was one member of the economics profession who was willing to defend it: Georgescu-Roegen. As a skeptic of formal models, he didn't find convincing the timeline it presented, with an ecological disaster occurring within a hundred years, but its overall argument was clearly in the same spirit as his thesis in *The Entropy Law and the Economic Process*. In November 1972 he wrote to Dennis Meadows and asked him to send all the critical comments about the report by economists, so he could write a rebuttal. In his response, Meadows said: "Your analysis of the entropic nature of resources has had a substantial influence on the thinking of the members of my group."[29] Georgescu-Rogen's rebuttal eventually appeared in *Southern Economic Journal* in 1975, and it singled out Solow's arguments for inspection. Even if the resource intensity of some production processes was declining, he pointed out, the rapid growth of GDP meant that the overall consumption of natural resources was still increasing sharply: in a single decade, US steel consumption had risen by almost 50 percent. Addressing Solow's claim that higher prices would prompt countries to economize on their use of scarce resources and switch to more plentiful ones, Georgescu-Roegen referred to it as "the fallacy of endless substitution."[30] He conceded that it was sometimes possible to switch one input for another (for example, by using aluminum instead of copper in making kitchenware and electrical power lines), but he pointed out that the substitute resources (bauxite, in this case) were also in limited supply and would eventually run out, too. To overlook this basic fact of nature was "to ignore the difference between the actual world and the Garden of Eden."[31]

In his article, which was titled "Energy and Economic Myths," Georgescu-Roegen also addressed the possibility of creating alternative sources of energy. He said that the only limitless, or virtually limitless, energy source was sunlight, but in the 1970s efforts to capture solar energy hadn't progressed very far. For the foreseeable future, therefore, humanity would have to rely on carbon fuels and other scarce resources. The issues raised by *The Limits of Growth* couldn't be wished away by economists "who have always suffered from growthmania," Georgescu-Roegen wrote.[32] Even if there was no scientific basis for the Club of Rome report's claim that a continuation of current growth trends would generate a terminal crisis within a century, "it would be madness to ignore the study's general warnings about population growth, pollution, and resource depletion."[33]

By the mid-1970s, the environmental movement was emerging as a major presence on the international stage. In 1972 the United Nations held its first Conference on the Human Environment. Three years later the US Congress passed the Energy Policy and Conservation Act, which created new energy conservation standards for appliances and fuel-efficiency requirements for cars. The rising concern with ecological issues prompted a critical reexamination of industrial capitalism from a number of different perspectives. In 1973 E. F. Schumacher, a German-born British economist, published *Small Is Beautiful: Economics as If People Mattered*, which advocated a shift away from the factory system and mass production to smaller-scale, less energy-intensive production methods. Channeling Carlyle, Marx, and many other critics, Schumacher started from the premise that the modern industrial economy was not merely environmentally unsustainable but also dehumanizing and psychologically unsatisfying: "Wisdom demands a new orientation of science and technology toward the organic, the gentle, the non-violent, the elegant and beautiful."[34] Like J. C. Kumarappa, Schumacher had studied village-based economies in India. He quoted from one of Kumarappa's books with approval, and his overall philosophy of rejecting materialism and encouraging the growth of small-scale production shared a good deal with the approach that Gandhi's economist had espoused. Indeed, Schumacher even used some of the same terminology as Kumarappa: "From an economic point of view, the central concept of wisdom is permanence . . . ," he wrote. "Nothing makes economic sense unless its continuance for a long time can be projected without running into absurdities."[35]

In environmentalist circles, there was a lot of discussion about how much growth, if any, could be countenanced going forward. Schumacher said: "There can be 'growth' towards a limited objective, but there cannot be unlimited, generalised growth."[36] The *Limits to Growth* report had outlined a scenario in which net capital accumulation would cease. But some members of the Club of Rome argued that a lower level of GDP growth would be consistent with ecological balance if strenuous efforts were taken to conserve energy, reduce emissions, and develop clean power sources, such as solar and hydroelectric. This idea became known as "sustainable development," and it would go on to gain widespread support.

Georgescu-Roegen and his followers rejected it out of hand. In his 1977 book, *Steady-State Economics*, Herman E. Daly, an American World Bank economist who had been a student of the Romanian at Vanderbilt, advocated a future in which the population remains constant and economic growth virtually ceases. The concept of a steady-state economy wasn't new. But when John Stuart Mill and other classical economists wrote about it during the nineteenth century, they conceived of it as arriving of its own accord, after all productive investment opportunities were exhausted. Daly presented the steady-state economy as an essential goal, an alternative to "money fetishism and growthmania" that would preserve the Earth's resources and prevent an ecological disaster.[37] To help make it a reality, he called for birth quotas to curtail population growth and strict limits on the use of depletable resources.

Georgescu-Roegen himself staked out an absolutist position. For a time, he joined the Club of Rome, but he quickly fell out with its leadership over its endorsement of limited growth. He even rejected the idea of a steady state economy. In his article "Energy and Economic Myths," he referred to it as a "topical mirage" and added: "The crucial error consists in not seeing that not only growth, but also a zero-growth state . . . cannot exist forever in a finite environment."[38] Two years later he expanded this argument in a more technical paper, which appeared in the journal *BioScience*.[39] Maintaining the global economy at its current scale would require perpetually exploiting carbon fuels and minerals, which would eventually run out, the article pointed out. To illustrate the point, Georgescu-Roegen included a drawing of the universe as an hourglass, with its trove of resources running down.

Going beyond the steady-state advocates, Georgescu-Roegen advocated a drastic new approach to preserving ecological balance that he called bioeconomics. "The term is intended to make us bear in mind continuously the biological origin of the economic process and thus spotlight the problem of mankind's existence with a limited store of *accessible* resources, unevenly located and unequally appropriated," he wrote in a 1977 journal article.[40] In practical terms, Georgescu-Roegen advocated concerted efforts to develop solar energy, "the only clean and essentially unlimited source,"[41] and he put forward a "minimal bioeconomic program"[42] that was designed to curb the use of depletable resources. This program included gradually reducing the global population to a level "that could be adequately fed only by organic agriculture";[43] strictly regulating energy usage; ending the production of "instruments of war"[44] and devoting the resources that were used on armaments to underdeveloped countries; ending the "morbid craving for extravagant gadgetry";[45] and substituting leisure for worktime. "We must come to realize," he wrote, "that an important prerequisite for a good life is a substantial amount of leisure spent in an intelligent manner."[46]

If Georgescu-Roegen's final recommendation had echoes of Keynes's famous essay "Economic Possibilities for Our Grandchildren," the rest of his program went far beyond what most economists were willing to contemplate. He insisted that orthodox approaches to resource depletion, which relied on market prices and market forces, "cannot even dream of handling this problem," because they ignored the interests of countless generations of people who will live in the distant future, "say, those of A.D. 3000, let alone those that might exist a hundred thousand years from now."[47] The rapid and accelerating depletion of natural resources amounted to a dictatorship of the present over the future, he remarked, as "future generations are not, simply because they cannot be, present on today's market."

In 1976 Georgescu-Roegen retired from Vanderbilt. As he aged, he had become increasingly estranged from his colleagues in the economics department. According to one account, none of them attended his leaving party. In retirement, he continued to write but largely kept to himself and his family. To those who knew him, his disappointment and rancor were evident. "Along with others of his friends I was saddened that his latter years were so marked by bitterness and withdrawal, brought on in part by the failure of the profession to give his work the recognition that it truly merited, and in part by his own irascible and generally demanding personality," Herman Daly wrote in an essay about Georgescu-Roegen that was published a year after his death, which came in 1994, at the age of eighty-eight.[48]

But if many of his colleagues in the economics profession had failed to appreciate Georgescu-Roegen's intellectual contribution, by the time he died his reputation was rising in other quarters as concerns about environmental degradation and climate change intensifed. In 1979, Jacques Grinevald, a

French writer and environmentalist, translated *The Entropy Law and the Economic Process* into French. Grinevald used as his title *La décroissance: Entropie-Écologie-Économie*. The term *décroissance*, which in English means "reduction" or "decline," struck a chord. In 2001, in the city of Lyon, a group of environmental and political activists started a Decroissance movement, demanding, among other things, car-free cities, the establishment of food cooperatives, and an end to corporate advertising. Four years later the anti-growth journal *La Décroissance* was founded.[49] Outside of France, similar developments were afoot. In many countries, calls to curb the pace of economic development and make the economy less resource intensive were garnering support from environmentalists and young people. The "degrowth" movement was taking off.

Georgescu-Roegen would surely have welcomed these developments: in many ways, he was the intellectual godfather of degrowth. But he wouldn't necessarily have been reassured. Perhaps because of his experience of Nazism as a young man, he didn't hold high hopes for human redemption. "Will mankind listen to any program that implies a constriction of its addiction to exosomatic comfort?" he wrote in 1975. "Perhaps, the destiny of man is to have a short, but fiery, exciting and extravagant life rather than a long, uneventful and vegetative existence. Let other species—the amoebas, for example—which have no spiritual ambitions inherit an earth still bathed in plenty of sunshine."[50]

24

Silvia Federici and Wages for Housework

In November 1975 a group of women opened a storefront at 288B Eighth Street, off Fifth Avenue in Park Slope, Brooklyn, not far from the famous Park Slope Food Coop, which had been established a couple of years earlier. The members of the New York Wages for Housework Committee, a grassroots organization that was demanding payment from the government for domestic labor, were keen to establish a permanent base where they could hold meetings, distribute their posters and literature, and welcome members of the local community. To mark the opening, they strung up banners across Fifth Avenue and held a street party, with refreshments and music.[1] One of the founding members of the Committee, Silvia Federici, a young feminist activist who was Italian by birth, delivered a speech in which she expressed distrust of politicians and journalists who celebrated motherhood and ignored the harsh economic realities that many mothers faced, relying on their spouses or welfare for money to raise their families. "It seems to us that if instead of praising our sacrifices they sent us a check at the end of the month, then we would have something to celebrate," Federici declared. She also emphasized the essential role that housework and childrearing played in supporting and re-creating the workforce in the paid economy. "If we were not at home doing housework, none of their factories, mines, schools and hospitals, could run, none of their profits could flow," she said. "With our work we make it possible for other people to go to work; we slave, so our husbands and children can slave. No wonder they say the family is the pillar of society."[2]

As well as running the storefront and leafleting women on the streets, Federici and her colleagues put a lot of effort into creating posters that couched their message in everyday terms. One featured a drawing of Lady Liberty clutching a household broom in one hand and a fistful of dollars in the other, with three needy children clutching at her dress. "THE WOMEN OF THE WORLD ARE SERVING NOTICE!" the poster declared. "WE WANT WAGES FOR EVERY DIRTY TOILET, EVERY INDECENT ASSAULT, EVERY PAINFUL CHILD-BIRTH, EVERY CUP OF COFFEE, AND EVERY SMILE. AND IF WE DON'T GET WHAT WE WANT WE WILL SIMPLY REFUSE TO WORK ANY LONGER!"[3] Another poster showed a steaming iron sitting on an ironing board atop a pair of trousers that was waiting to be ironed. The poster read: "STRIKE! WHILE THE IRON IS HOT! WAGES FOR HOUSEWORK."[4]

Although the Wages for Housework movement was small, it was also international, with branches in Italy, where the movement originated, Canada, and the United Kingdom. In the United States, there were groups in a number of cities outside New York, including Boston, Philadelphia, and Cleveland. Most of the members of these groups were educated white women. From 1976 onward, there were also Black Women for Wages for Housework groups in a number of places. Wilmette Brown, an African American activist who was originally from New Jersey, and Margaret Prescod, a Barbadian-American teacher at Queens College in New York, founded the first group in New York, which eventually spawned offshoots in other cities.[5] In 1975, a Wages Due Lesbians movement emerged from the international Wages for Housework campaign and eventually organized in various cities, including London, Philadelphia, and San Francisco.[6]

Wages for Housework wasn't part of the mainstream women's movement, which had made great strides in the United States and other countries since the emergence of Second Wave feminism in the 1960s. Indeed, the relationship between the two was an uneasy one. Groups like the National Organization for Women (NOW), which the writer Betty Friedan and other American feminists had founded in 1966, campaigned for reproductive rights and sexual equality in the workplace. Wages for Housework supported reproductive rights and higher wages for women, but the movement focused primarily on housework, and the economic plight of domestic workers of all ages and races. "Like other feminists, we were convinced that housework was the root of our oppression as women," Federici wrote in a 2018 book about the New York Committee. "Unlike them, we believed that, for this very reason, it should be our main ground of struggle, and that the most effective way to free ourselves from it should be to refuse to do it for free."[7]

Another distinguishing characteristic of Wages for Housework was its historical lineage. Whereas Second Wave feminism emerged alongside the civil rights movement in the United States during the early 1960s, Wages for Housework grew out of the student and worker protests of the late 1960s, and it had an explicitly leftist perspective. As a student in Italy in the mid-1960s, Federici viewed unpaid domestic labor as a key cog of global capitalism, and her efforts to abolish it as part of a larger endeavor. "We must admit that capital has been very successful in hiding our work. It has created a true masterpiece at the expense of women," she wrote in a 1974 pamphlet, *Wages Against Housework*. "First of all, it has got a hell of a lot of work almost for free, and it has made sure that women, far from struggling against it, would seek that work as the best thing in life (the magic words: 'Yes, darling, you are a real woman'). At the same time, it has disciplined the male worker also, by making *his* woman dependent on *his* work and *his* wage, and trapped him in this discipline by giving him a servant after he himself has done so much serving at the factory or the office."[8]

Intellectually, the tying of female exploitation in the home to capitalist exploitation in the workplace was arguably the most important feature of the Wages for Housework movement. In Second Wave feminism, capitalism was seen as a potentially liberating force: if sexual equality could be introduced into the workplace, women could escape their historical position of subjugation. The tension between these views dated back to the early days of industrial capitalism, when many young women left their homes to work in textile factories, and many male artisans, such as weavers, lost their livelihoods. In *The Condition of the Working Class in England*, Engels had described how in 1840s Manchester it was common to see families in which the woman and children were the main breadwinners.[9] But as heavy industries, such as steel, engineering, and chemicals, came to dominate industrial economies, their workforces became overwhelmingly male. A new gendered division of labor arose, with women tending to leave the labor force once they had children. By 1911, only 10 percent of married British women were in the workforce, although more than 70 percent of single women were.[10] The trends in the United States were similar. A Census Bureau survey from 1900 classified just

20.6 percent of all American women over the age of sixteen as "breadwinners," and just 16 percent of those were married.[11] Most married women became full-time mothers and housewives, engaging in domestic labor and relying on their husbands for their livelihood.

In her 1892 book, *Women and Economics*, Charlotte Perkins Gilman, the American feminist writer and social reformer, noted two basic facts about the subservient role assigned to women. First, economic progress and rising productivity were largely a masculine affair because "such economic processes as women have been allowed to exercise are of the earliest and most primitive kind."[12] Second, "whatever the economic value of the domestic industry of women is, they do not get it. The women who do the most work get the least money, and the women who have the most money do the least work . . . It is held to be their duty as women to do this work; and their economic status bears no relation to their domestic labors, unless an inverse one."[13] Perkins didn't call for government payment for domestic labor, but she argued that society should be rearranged to make it less burdensome. She suggested setting up common kitchens in apartment buildings, an idea she may have picked up from the early socialist communitarians. She also called for men and women to share housework, and she encouraged women to go out to work wherever possible.

During an era when American women couldn't even vote, nothing came of these suggestions. In 1920, the year that saw the ratification of the Nineteenth Amendment, which introduced female suffrage, the women's rights campaigner Crystal Eastman proposed more direct help for female domestic laborers. In an essay titled "Now We Can Begin," Eastman called for a "motherhood endowment"—a financial payment from the government that would make women and children less dependent on a male breadwinner. "What is the problem of women's freedom?" Eastman asked.

> It seems to me to be this: how to arrange the world so that women can be human beings, with a chance to exercise their infinitely varied gifts in infinitely varied ways, instead of being destined by the accident of their sex to one field of activity—housework and child-raising. And second, if and when they choose housework and child-raising, to have that occupation recognized by the world as work, requiring a definite economic reward and not merely entitling the performer to be dependent on some man.[14]

These early feminists fully recognized the economic value of domestic labor, and how heavily industrial capitalist societies depended on it. In her 1939 essay collection, *In Woman's Defense*, the Kentucky-born author and activist Mary Inman explained that the home was critical to the economic system because "the most valuable of all commodities is still produced there: Labor Power."[15] To illustrate her point, Inman cited the domestic work carried out by the wives of male workers at a Firestone tire factory in California. This "labor is as inseparably knit into those tires," she wrote, "as is the labor of their husbands."[16] In Britain, meanwhile, Eleanor Rathbone, a women's rights campaigner and social worker, who in 1929 was elected an independent member of the British Parliament, was tirelessly campaigning for the government to send mothers a monthly payment that they would receive independently of their husbands. Only such a system could recompense women for their housework and guarantee the financial independence of women, Rathbone argued. She advocated for the idea for years, including in a 1924 book, *The Disinherited Family*. Some labor unions opposed it on the grounds that it would prompt employers to reduce the wages they paid to male breadwinners. But during the Second World War, the Liberal peer William Beveridge proposed a limited version of it in his famous report on social insurance, and in the Family Allowances Act of 1945 it was passed into law.

During the postwar decades, scientific and social developments gradually transformed the economic role of women. The contraceptive pill became widely available, fertility rates declined, and more and more women went out to work. Between December 1948 and December 1970, the share of adult American females who were active in the labor force rose from 33 percent to 43.4 percent.[17] (By 1997, it would reach 60 percent.) Even as women flooded into the workplace, however, they earned much lower wages than their male counterparts, and corporate executive suites remained a male preserve. Slowly, the political system started to come to terms with these developments. In June 1963, President John F. Kennedy signed into law an Equal Pay Act, which outlawed pay discrimination on the basis of sex. The following year the Civil Rights Act outlawed discrimination in many other areas on the basis of race, color, religion, sex, or national origin. In 1965, in *Griswold v. Connecticut*, the Supreme Court asserted a "right to marital privacy" that prohibited the government from restricting the use of contraceptives. One immediate question was whether these new civil rights laws would be effectively enforced. In creating NOW, Friedan and other feminists were motivated in large part by the desire to make sure that they were.

The Second Wave feminist movement had some major successes. In 1973 the Supreme Court issued its ruling in the *Roe v. Wade* case, which greatly expanded access to abortion. A year later Congress passed the Women's Educational Equity Act, which was designed to remove barriers facing women at all levels of education. Under pressure from NOW and other women's groups, many states passed laws enacting no-fault divorce, which made it possible for women to leave marriages of their own accord. The issue of unpaid domestic labor received far less attention, however. Some feminists were suspicious of any policies that would keep women tied to the hearth. In her 1963 book *The Feminine Mystique*, Friedan argued that women who went out to work and had a career were happier and more fulfilled than women who were full-time homemakers. But where did this leave the countless women, particularly working-class women, who were stuck in the unpaid role of raising children and doing housework?

Federici was born in 1942 in the northern Italian city of Parma. Her father was a professor of philosophy at the local university. After finishing high school, she attended the University of Bologna, where she studied literature and philosophy and became involved in leftist politics. In the mid-1960s the Italian Communist Party, which was committed to Marxist-Leninism, still dominated the left in Italy, but there were signs of change, including the emergence of Potere Operaio (Workers' Power), a competing far-left group that set out to organize workers directly in their factories. After getting her bachelor's degree, Federici started graduate work, but she had to live at home because of a lack of money. In 1967 she obtained a Fulbright Fellowship to do graduate work in political philosophy at the State University of New York at Buffalo, which had some noted Marxist scholars on its faculty. "When in 1967 I came to the US I was already a natural rebel," she recounted in a 2022 interview.[18]

One of Federici's roommates in Buffalo organized feminist meetings on the campus. Federici was sympathetic to the cause. Growing up in Italy, she had witnessed firsthand how a traditional patriarchal society worked and, as she and many other female activists learned, how leftist men were far from immune to sexism. Initially, however, she struggled to reconcile

American-style feminism with the leftist perspective she had embraced in Bologna, which emphasized that the fundamental economic divide in society was between labor and capital. Federici would later recount how her attitude to feminism changed during a train ride from Boston to New York in early 1972, when she read an essay by another young Italian leftist, Mariarosa Dalla Costa, who taught political science at the University of Padua. The article was titled "The Power of Women and the Subversion of the Community," and it set out to analyze what Dalla Costa termed the "Woman Question" through the framework of the capitalist division of labor. "The oppression of women, after all, did not begin with capitalism," Dalla Costa wrote. "What began with capitalism was the more intense exploitation of women *as* women and the possibility at last of their liberation."[19] Federici didn't know Dalla Costa personally, but she found the essay captivating. "By the time I read the last page," she subsequently wrote, "I knew that I had found my home, my tribe and my own self, as a woman and a feminist."[20]

Dalla Costa, who was born in 1943 in the northern Italian city of Treviso, had been a member of the "workerist" movement in Padua. Before teaching her classes, she got up early to leaflet workers outside factory gates in the nearby industrial zone of Porto Margherita. Almost all these workers were male. In the essay that Federici read on the train journey to New York, she noted how the rise of modern capitalism had left many women isolated in their homes, where they were cut off from industrial production but still an integral part of the economic system because of their role in feeding and looking after existing workers and raising new ones. Following the lead of earlier leftists, including Mary Inman, Dalla Costa called this domestic labor "social production" and insisted that it created a great deal of economic value. She referred to the nuclear family as the "social factory," where female domestic workers endured a parallel existence to industrial workers, being exploited and dehumanized. "In the same way as women are robbed of the possibility of developing their creative capacity, they are robbed of their sexual life which has been transformed into a function for reproducing labour power," Dalla Costa wrote. "Either the vagina is primarily the passage to the reproduction of labor power sold as a commodity, the capitalist function of the uterus, or it is part of our natural powers, our social equipment."[21] By ignoring or downplaying these realities, leftist thinkers, including Marx, hadn't merely made an analytical error, Dalla Costa argued. They had robbed their cause of a potent weapon: the prospect of women withdrawing their domestic labor and upending the traditional family unit, which served as "the very pillar of the capitalist organization of work." "Let us sum up," Dalla Costa concluded. "The role of housewife, behind whose isolation is hidden social labor, must be destroyed."[22]

This was the critical theoretical framework that Federici had been searching for: one that combined an indictment of the patriarchy with a leftist economic analysis. At the time she read "The Power of Women and the Subversion of Society," she was living in Brooklyn and trying to finish her doctoral dissertation. She wrote a note to Dalla Costa, and the two started to correspond. In July 1972, Federici went back to Italy to see her family. While she was there, she traveled to Padua. The previous year Dalla Costa and some fellow activists in the Italian city had created a new feminist group, Lotta Femminista (Feminist Struggle). While Federici was in Padua, she attended a two-day meeting with Dalla Costa and other members of the group, as well as some feminist activists who were visiting from different countries, including Selma James, a member of the Notting Hill Women's Liberation Workshop in London, who had helped Dalla Costa to write and edit the published version of her essay. At the end of the Padua meeting, the participants, who numbered about twenty, constituted themselves as the International Feminist Collective and issued a declaration, which said: "We identify ourselves as Marxist feminists and take this to mean a new definition of class . . . based on the subordination of the wageless worker to the wage worker behind which is hidden the productivity, i.e. the exploitation, of the labour of women in the home."[23] The members of the collective vowed to launch wages for housework campaigns in their own countries. They knew they would face many challenges, including skepticism from the mainstream women's movement and male leftists. "Despite the anticipated difficulties, by the time I left Italy I had embraced the project," Federici recalled later in her life.[24]

Shortly after Federici returned to the United States, she and some colleagues founded the New York Wages for Housework Committee. On Mother's Day, they went to Prospect Park and handed out a flyer that said: "Let us call mothers, wives, singles, grandmothers, daughters, sisters by their true name: HOUSEWORKERS."[25] Many of the women they approached talked about their own struggles raising children and doing housework and the lack of appreciation that they felt. "We were all, at the time, in our late twenties or thirties, white, with jobs, though often precarious, and none of us for a while fit the classic image of the housewife," Federici wrote in her history of the New York Committee. "Few of us were married, and even fewer had children. Yet, we were not embarrassed to admit that we had not escaped domestic work, nor the social expectations deriving from its naturalization as 'women's' work."[26] Although the New York Committee was still small, it sought to establish connections to other left-wing activists, such as union organizers and tenants' rights campaigners. While Federici was dedicated to Wages for Housework and saw it as an organization with great potential, she always viewed it as part of a broader movement to empower working-class women and men.

As well as being a tireless organizer, Federici was a gifted writer, who could express in graphic terms the moral and economic arguments that underpinned the movement. In *Wages Against Housework*, her 1974 pamphlet, she explained that female houseworkers were, in some ways, even more subjugated than wage workers, who could at least switch jobs. "The difference lies in the fact that not only has housework been imposed on women, but it has been transformed into a natural attribute of our female physique and personality, an internal need, an aspiration, supposedly coming from the depth of our female character," she wrote. "In its turn, the unwaged condition of housework has been the most powerful weapon in reinforcing the common assumption that *housework is not work*, thus preventing women from struggling against it, except in the privatized kitchen-bedroom quarrel that all society agrees to ridicule, thereby further reducing the protagonist of a struggle. We are seen as nagging bitches, not workers in struggle."[27] Turning to the movement's practical demands, Federici emphasized that demanding payments for housework was "only the beginning."[28] Although the money would be extremely useful to many women, particularly working-class women, the larger goal was to demystify and undermine the economic system that had kept female domestic workers in a state of unpaid subjugation. "To say that we want wages for housework is to expose the fact that housework is already money for capital, that capital has made and makes money out of our cooking, smiling, fucking," Federici wrote. "At the same time, it shows that we have cooked, smiled, fucked throughout the years not because it was easier for us than for anybody else, but because we did not have any other choice."[29]

In the fall of 1974, the Wages for Housework movement held its first international conference, in Brooklyn, with attendees coming from Canada,

England, and Italy, as well as other US cities. They put together a lengthy statement, "Theses on Wages for Housework," which emphasized the role unpaid domestic labor played in propping up the capitalist system. "Our wageless condition is the material basis of our dependence on men within the family and in society," the statement said. "The family is a colony where power is delegated to men to supervise our work. The power they have over us is the power of the wage. But their power over us is ultimately their weakness with respect to capital, for our dependence on them is a discipline on their labor. It is the chain that ties them to their jobs."[30]

One of the key figures in the international expansion of Wages for Housework was Selma James, who had a long history of campaigning against capitalism and colonialism. She was born Selma Deitch in 1930 in the Ocean Hill–Brownsville section of Brooklyn. Her father was a Polish Jewish immigrant truck driver, who taught himself to read English and became an organizer with the Teamsters Union. After leaving school at fifteen, Selma moved to Los Angeles, where she worked in a factory, got married, had a son, and eventually became a writer. In 1952 she wrote an article, "A Woman's Place," that was based on her own experience and on interviews with female neighbors and coworkers about their domestic labor. Emphasizing the powerlessness and frustration that many of them felt, the piece said: "The way that the house is set up, neither the husband nor the children have any idea how much effort and real hard work and time have gone into cleaning the house . . . You have no control over the hours of work, the kind of work you will have to do, and how much work you do. These are what women want to control."[31]

Before leaving Brooklyn, Deitch met C. L. R. James, the Jamaican writer and historian: they were both members of a small Trotskyite group, the Johnson-Forest Tendency. After separating from her first husband and becoming a writer, she reconnected with James, who was by then a well-known writer and anti-colonialist activist. In 1955, Deitch and James moved to London. The following year they got married, and Selma took James's surname. On many issues, they were like-minded, but Selma James was very much her own thinker and writer. In early 1972, she wrote a paper titled "Women, the Unions and Work, or . . . What Is Not to Be Done," which she presented at the National Conference of Women, in Manchester. The paper argued that Britain's powerful labor unions were ignoring the interests of women and outlined six demands to remedy this situation. The first two were: WE DEMAND THE RIGHT TO WORK LESS, and WE DEMAND A GUARANTEED INCOME FOR

WOMEN AND FOR MEN WORKING OR NOT WORKING, MARRIED OR NOT. The ruling class had glorified motherhood only when it involved unpaid labor, James went on. "Let them pay us, or else we can go to the factories and offices and put our children in their father's laps. Let's see if they can make Ford cars and change nappies at the same time. WE DEMAND WAGES FOR HOUSE-WORK."[32] Initially, James's agenda didn't gain much traction in the British women's movement. Some feminists feared that paying for domestic labor would institutionalize women remaining in the home. Others saw going out to work as the road to liberation. James wasn't put off. A dedicated activist, she regarded the Wages for Housework movement as an essential extension of feminism and the anti-capitalist movement.

As the New York Committee geared up its activism, the media started paying attention to it. In January 1976, *The New York Times* published a news story headlined "Brooklyn Women Seek Wages for Housework," which quoted Federici saying: "No one works as hard as women do for nothing . . . If we stopped, the economy would be paralyzed." Asked about the specifics of the organization's demands and how its wage program would operate, Federici replied: "It's unwise to work out too many details until we have a mass movement."[33] Other publications, including the New York *Daily News*, the *Los Angeles Times*, and England's *Western Daily Press*, also printed articles about Wages for Housework. In April 1976, *Life* magazine published a picture of Federici and a dozen of her colleagues standing in the kitchen of her Brooklyn apartment behind a table stacked with pots and pans.[34]

The opening of the storefront on Eighth Street marked another significant development for the New York Committee. "We got a miserable little room, but it was great," Federici recounted decades later. "A storefront with a big window onto the street. It's a New York thing. So the room was small, but we filled it with all our posters. Whenever possible, the door was open so women could walk in, pick up a flyer and then periodically, we had meetings and we posted about it in the community. That was a way of getting the information out."[35] Despite garnering media attention and establishing a physical base, however, Wages for Housework never attracted an enduring mass following. To some extent, this failure reflected its radicalism. Although its demand for housework to be paid had great popular appeal, its broader goal of subverting the very nature of work in a capitalist system wasn't one that necessarily spoke to hard-pressed working-class women, to whom revolutionary politics seemed like a distant concern.

At the national and international level, meanwhile, Wages for Housework operated in the shadow of the broader women's movement, whose demands for equal pay and conditions in the paid workplace were being embraced by major political parties and international organizations. In 1975 the United Nations held a World Conference on Women in Mexico City, at which it called on member governments to guarantee sexual equality and ensure the full integration of women in the economy. Federici was skeptical of these developments. She viewed the UN and other international organizations, such as the International Monetary Fund and the World Bank, as props for global capitalism. She believed that what she termed "liberal feminism" ultimately fulfilled a similar role, because it lacked a proper critical perspective and allowed itself to be co-opted. "With the intervention of the United Nations in feminist politics," she later commented, "we have seen an attempt to institutionalize the movement in order to defuse and neutralize its struggles and its subversive potential."[36]

Another challenge that the New York Committee encountered was the economic crisis of the mid-1970s, which placed enormous pressures on all workers' and leftist movements. Following the OPEC oil price shock of 1973, when the price of crude tripled, the US economy fell into a recession, and New York City experienced a fiscal crisis that saw it move to the brink of defaulting on some of its municipal bonds. In September 1975, the New York State legislature created an Emergency Financial Control Board that took over the city's finances. To balance the budget, the control board slashed spending on many programs, including welfare programs that benefited working-class women and children. The control board also laid off some city workers and imposed wage freezes and cuts in employee benefits on many others. Federici would compare this austerity package to the structural adjustment programs that the IMF and World Bank imposed on developing countries that had run into financial problems. As the city's labor unions fought in vain to resist these measures, she and her colleagues, some of whom were also active in union organizing and other leftist causes, got swept up in this political struggle. Recalling a failed effort by the progressive Local 1199 to organize thousands of care workers, Federici wrote: "The defeat was palpable, as in everyone's bones there was the sense that this was the beginning of an era in which only roll backs would be possible. Soon, moreover, it became clear that the disciplining of the New York workforce was part of a restructuring of the world economy that was to institute an austerity regime for years to come."[37]

As the fiscal and political crisis intensified, the New York Committee continued its activities. In April 1976 it organized a conference on welfare, which was attended by dozens of women from Wages for Housework groups across the United States and allied organizations. At the time, conservative politicians were vilifying women on welfare, particularly Black women, as "welfare queens," in an effort to win votes and undermine the Great Society programs that had provided financial support to poor families. Federici regarded the response of the broader women's movement to these attacks as woefully inadequate. But despite the activism of the New York Committee and protests by other groups, Federici and her colleagues were powerless to prevent the cuts to spending and welfare benefits. Moreover, the economic crisis and its aftermath heightened differences on strategy and tactics that had emerged inside the Wages for Housework movement, including tensions between the New York Committee and some members of the recently formed Black Women for Wages for Housework. At a 2021 event in Toronto, one of the founders of that group, Margaret Prescod, said that when she and her colleagues were campaigning at Queens College for the right of students who were mothers on welfare to keep their student grants and their welfare payments, some white members of the New York Committee didn't support them. "They didn't consider that wages for housework, but we did," Prescod recounted.[38] Other schisms also emerged, and in 1977 the New York Committee dissolved itself.

In later years, Federici was reluctant to discuss the circumstances surrounding this dissolution. After it happened, she quickly went on to other projects, including the creation of a new political journal, *Tap Dance*. She also did historical research on the origins of the gendered division of labor, which turned into an influential 1984 book *The Great Caliban: History of the Rebel Body in the First Phase of Capitalism*, cowritten with Leopoldina Fortunati, an Italian feminist theorist. In 1978, Dalla Costa's Padua branch of Wages for Housework also shut down. Other parts of the movement carried on, including the International Wages for Housework Campaign and Black Women for Wages for Housework. But the shuttering of the New York

Committee and the Wages for Housework branch in the Italian city where the movement had been founded marked an ending of a sort.

Like many radical movements, Wages for Housework didn't achieve its primary goals and ended up splintering. That doesn't mean it failed. Initially, the idea that domestic labor was productive in an economic sense because it helped to maintain and reproduce the capitalist workforce ran into resistance from some leftist intellectuals. "Workerist theoreticians insisted that what we called production—that is production, and reproduction of labor power—belonged rather to the sphere of circulation, as Marx described in *Das Kapital*," Dalla Costa recalled in an interview with Louise Toupin, a Canadian political scientist who wrote an illuminating history of the international Wages for Housework movement that was published in 2018.[39] Over time, however, the importance of "social reproduction," as domestic labor came to be known, became widely accepted on the left. "I think there is now a sense that what we call domestic work is the production of the workforce," Federici said in an interview in 2022 with *The White Review*, a London-based magazine. "And it gave a material basis to a radical feminist analysis of sexual and personal relations, the idea that the personal is political, because what happens in the home is connected to the broader organisation of work. The privatisation of the home actually hides the exploitation."[40]

It wasn't only intellectuals on the left who came to recognize the economic importance of domestic labor. In the world of economics and policymaking, the rise of Wages for Housework helped spark a debate about how economic statistics should treat domestic labor. Since housework and childrearing weren't paid and monetized, they weren't counted in the gross domestic product—an omission that led to some absurdities, one of which became notorious. If a man hired a female housekeeper to clean his house and do his washing, the money he paid her was included in GDP. If the man married the housekeeper, and she carried on doing the same work on an unpaid basis, GDP would fall even though the women's economic contribution remained the same. Clearly, the official statistics were failing to count some crucial economic contributions. In 1975, researchers at the US Social Security Administration took a step toward addressing this omission by trying to place a dollar value on housework. They estimated how much it would cost in the marketplace to purchase the services that a typical housewife provided, such as cooking and cleaning. The researchers concluded that housewives between the ages of twenty-five and twenty-nine who had children did work that was worth, on average, $6,417 a year, not far off the $7,495 earned on average outside the home by female workers of the same age.[41]

Another significant step came in 1980, when delegates at a UN conference in Copenhagen put forward a motion demanding the recognition of unpaid domestic work—a proposal that ran into opposition from India, the USSR, and the Vatican.[42] One of the conference attendees who supported the motion was a young politician from New Zealand named Marilyn Waring who, at twenty-three years old, had become the youngest member of the parliament in Wellington. Waring was a member of the center-right National Party, but she held liberal views on many issues, including women's rights and the environment. After she got back from Copenhagen, she started working on a research paper about national income accounting, the data-collation process that generates GDP statistics. Her research formed the basis of a 1988 book that is now widely acknowledged as an intellectual landmark: *If Women Counted: A New Feminist Economics.*

In her prologue, Waring brought up Wages for Housework, saying she shared Mariarosa Dalla Costa's "original intention of providing a tool for raising consciousness and for mobilizing women everywhere."[43] She also hailed Ester Boserup, a Danish economist whose 1970 book, *Woman's Role in Economic Development*, had emphasized the positive economic contributions that women in developing countries made through their paid and unpaid labor inside and outside the home. Noting that she was writing in the same tradition as these and other feminist pioneers, Waring said her goal was to demystify the UN System of National Accounts, the set of accounting conventions that most countries used to calculate GDP. She wrote: "It is my confirmed belief that this system acts to sustain, in the ideology of patriarchy, the universal enslavement of women and Mother Earth in their productive and reproductive activities."[44]

Waring traced the origins of national income accounting back to Sir William Petty, a seventeenth-century English polymath who in 1665 produced some rough estimates of his country's overall riches, distinguishing between stocks (wealth) and flows (income). Waring also described how, during the 1930s and '40s, when American and British economists generated the first detailed estimates of national income for the United States and the United Kingdom, they excluded unpaid work, including women's domestic labor. This decision was partly driven by practical considerations rather than conscious sexism, Waring explained. Governments wanted to track their economies so they could estimate how much money they could raise in taxes, but unpaid labor couldn't be taxed, and it was therefore left out. In 1953 the United Nations issued an international set of guidelines for national accounting that was based on the British and US model. It recommended the creation of a "production boundary" between the "producing and consuming entities" in the economy, which placed domestic workers in the nonproductive sector.[45] During the decades since 1953, Waring noted, some minor changes had been made to the UN accounting guidelines, particularly those concerning household production in developing countries. But cleaning, cooking, and childcare—the basic forms of domestic labor—were still classed as nonproductive activities. The "reasons given by men for their failure to account for women's work are 1) conceptual problems and 2) the practical difficulties of collecting data," Waring wrote. "It does not seem to occur to them that if you have a conceptual problem about the activity of half the human species, you then have a conceptual problem about the whole."[46]

Waring coupled her criticisms of GDP figures, and governments that compiled them, for ignoring domestic labor with a call for the statisticians to also recognize the enormous flows of value created by natural resources, such as fresh air, clean water, and sites of natural beauty. Like the economic benefits of housework, these flows had remained hidden for far too long, she argued. In her final chapter, she called for a global campaign of consciousness raising around these issues, and she commended the activism of Dalla Costa and Wages for Housework for having "helped to have feminist issues understood by 12 million Italian housewives—which is no mean feat."[47]

Replicating this success on a global scale represented a mighty challenge, she conceded. But she pointed to some signs of progress, including a wave of strikes and walkouts that had taken place in more than twenty countries in October 1985 to demand that unwaged work be recognized in GDP. "We women are visible and valuable to each other, and we must, now in our billions, proclaim that visibility and that worth," Waring wrote. "And if there is still confusion about who will achieve that, then we must each of us walk to a clear pool of water. Look *at* the water. It has value. Now look *into* the water. The woman we see there counts for something. She can help to change the world."[48]

25

Theorists of Thatcherism:
Stuart Hall vs. Friedrich Hayek

On February 11, 1975, the British Conservative Party, having lost two elections in a row, selected the forty-nine-year-old Margaret Thatcher as its first female leader. Some time after Thatcher's elevation, she visited the Institute for Economic Affairs (IEA), a conservative think tank based in a Georgian terrace house on Lord North Street, Westminster. The IEA's director, Lord Ralph Harris, introduced her to Friedrich Hayek, the Austrian British economist, who in 1974 had been awarded a share of the Nobel Memorial Prize for Economic Sciences. Since publishing his wartime jeremiad against social democracy, *The Road to Serfdom*, the seventy-five-year-old Hayek had expounded his free market views from academic perches at the London School of Economics, the University of Chicago, and since 1962, the University of Freiburg in West Germany. He had also organized the Mont Pelerin Society, an international organization committed to "private property and the competitive market" that counted Milton Friedman and other conservative luminaries among its members. During the prosperous postwar decades, however, Hayek had fallen out of fashion. As the economic philosophy of his old intellectual foes Keynes and William Beveridge held sway on both sides of the Atlantic, he had retreated into obscurity.

The Nobel award, which came as a surprise to many economists, brought Hayek back into the public eye, and in Thatcher he found an eager pupil. "Although she is known as being a rather overpowering lady, she sat down like a meek schoolgirl and listened," Harris later recalled of the meeting at the IEA.[1] Hayek was smitten with the new Conservative leader. "She's so beautiful," he said after she left.[2] During a stint as minister of education in Edward Heath's 1970–74 government, Thatcher wasn't regarded as a right-wing ideologue, but the industrial relations environment of the 1970s had radicalized her. In early 1972, miners in Britain's publicly owned coal industry went on strike, demanding higher pay to catch up with rising inflation. As coal stocks ran down, there were extensive power outages. After seven weeks, the dispute ended in a victory for the miners: the National Coal Board awarded them a pay increase of more than 20 percent. In 1973, emboldened by this success, the National Union of Mineworkers (NUM) issued fresh wage demands, and its members refused to work overtime. Fearing a complete shutdown, Heath's government ordered many businesses to work a three-day week to conserve energy. In February 1974 the miners voted to strike again. Heath called a snap general election, framing it as a choice between order and union-induced chaos: one of the Conservative Party's campaign slogans was "Who Governs Britain?" The voters decided it would no longer be the Conservatives: on election day, the party lost its overall majority in the House of Commons. The Labour Party formed a minority government and quickly settled the dispute with the NUM, agreeing to give the miners another big pay raise.

Thatcher watched all this with dismay. The Oxford-educated daughter of a grocery store proprietor in the Lincolnshire market town of Grantham, she had many of the characteristic beliefs and prejudices of the petit bourgeoisie. She distrusted labor unions, big government, and even big businesses, especially the big publicly owned industries, such as coal and steel, that the postwar Labour government had nationalized. "She did not need to read books by Milton Friedman or Friedrich von Hayek to learn the importance of sound money or that the power of the State was the enemy of freedom," the English political journalist Peter Jenkins wrote. "She had learnt these self-evident truths at her father's knee."[3] Hayek and Friedman did provide Thatcher with the economic arguments she could use to back up her instincts and confront the Keynesian orthodoxy. From Hayek, she got the message that the main source of Britain's economic problems was its powerful labor unions. In an August 1977 letter to the *Times* of London, he wrote: "The trade unions, being politically sacrosanct, have been allowed to destroy the British economy . . . It is high time that somebody had the courage to eradicate that cancer of the British economy."[4]

Hayek certainly wasn't the first economist to argue that the country's fractious industrial relations system was holding back capital investment, innovation, and productivity growth. Relative to Germany and the United States, output-per-person was much lower in Britain, particularly in manufacturing. Repeated efforts to address this problem had foundered on the refusal of local union branches to abide by agreements reached at the national level that tied wage rises to productivity growth. In Germany, labor unions were powerful, but they were organized on national lines. They had representatives on the boards of major companies, and when they reached an agreement with management, their members usually honored it. In Britain, the situation was different. Unions were organized at the factory level, and local union officials, known as shop stewards, reveled in their independence and militancy. One of them, the car worker Derek Robinson—dubbed "Red Robbo" by the Fleet Street newspapers—led 523 walkouts at a Birmingham plant during a period of thirty months.[5]

Well before Thatcher became prime minister, there had been political efforts to address these problems, but they hadn't worked. In 1969 Harold Wilson's Labour government published a consultative document, *In Place of Strife*, that recommended reducing the autonomy of plant-level unions and establishing a national Industrial Board with statutory powers to enforce pay settlements that companies and union leaders had reached. Faced with strong opposition from the Trades Union Congress, the Wilson government eventually dropped these proposals. In 1971 Heath's Conservative government passed an Industrial Relations Act that, in theory, weakened "closed shop" agreements that obliged workers to join a union, limited wildcat strikes, and made labor agreements legally enforceable. Opposition to the legislation was so intense that it was never fully enforced. When the Labour Party returned to power in 1974, it was repealed.

What made Hayek's views distinct was less his description of the British trades unions as a cancer on the economy—many Conservative MPs and Fleet Street editorial writers agreed with him—than his calls for an all-out effort to destroy their power. After watching the unions defeat Heath, most Conservatives believed the country could be ruled only with their consent. Hayek, however, was on a mission. He had long depicted organized labor not merely as a brake on economic efficiency but as threat to political freedom. In his book *The Constitution of Liberty*, which was published in 1960, he wrote, "The whole basis of our free society is gravely threatened by the powers arrogated by the unions."[6] He went on to call for the prohibition of mass picketing, in which striking workers sought to blockade their factories or plants, and "closed shops."[7] In the United States, the Taft-Hartley Act of 1947 had proscribed closed shops, but in Britain they were legal.

Hayek's politics were diametrically opposed to those of his fellow Vienna product Karl Polanyi, but both of them recognized the importance of rising labor power and other efforts to embed the free market in an institutional framework that would constrain its operations. To Polanyi, these developments were part of a "double movement" that was both inevitable and necessary to contain the destructive power of the market. To Hayek, they represented a disease that would prove fatal to the system and to democracy itself. Thatcher shared many of Hayek's instincts and welcomed his bold declamations. According to one frequently recounted story, she was once sitting through a presentation by a member of the Conservative Party's research department when she cut short the presenter, slammed a copy of Hayek's *The Constitution of Liberty* down on the table, and declared: "*This* is what we believe." The website of the Margaret Thatcher Foundation, which contains a trove of correspondence between Hayek, Thatcher, and her associates, says this account is "perhaps a little too perfect to be actually true."[8] But the foundation's website also acknowledges that Thatcher "absorbed deeply" Hayek's "idea that you cannot compromise with socialism, even in mild social democratic forms, because by degrees socialism tends always to totalitarian outcomes, regardless of the intentions, professed or real, of its proponents."[9]

Throughout the mid- and late 1970s, Britain's economic problems continued, and the Labour government of James Callaghan struggled to contain them. In an effort to relieve inflation pressures, it reached a "social contract" with the Trades Union Congress, in which wage rises were limited to agreed levels. This pact helped to bring inflation down below 10 percent, but price rises were still running ahead of wage gains, and in 1978 many unions demanded catch-up pay agreements. At the end of the year, truck drivers went on strike, which led to the closure of gas stations, factories, and other businesses. In the first months of 1979, many public sector workers, including train drivers, nurses, and ambulance drivers, staged walkouts. In some cities, they were joined by garbage collectors, gravediggers, and crematorium workers.

The Conservatives and their supporters on Fleet Street seized upon these events, which became known as the Winter of Discontent. Accusing the unions of holding the country to ransom, Thatcher called on Callaghan to declare a state of emergency. She also proposed a series of labor reforms, many of which could be traced right back to *The Constitution of Liberty*. They included a ban on secondary picketing, the prohibition of closed shops, mandatory secret ballots before strikes could be called, and a no-strike clause in the work agreements of some public sector workers. After a decade of industrial disputes, Thatcher's hard line struck a chord with many British voters, particularly after the industrial disputes that disrupted the country at the end of 1978 and start of 1979.

In late October, a Gallup poll showed Labour with a lead of 5.5 points over the Conservatives.[10] By the middle of February 1979, after all the strikes, a survey by the same polling organization showed the Conservatives leading by 20 points.[11] During a general election campaign that began in early April, polls showed the gap between the parties narrowing somewhat. But when the vote was held on May 3, the Conservatives defeated Labour by 7 points and won a majority of forty-four seats in the House of Commons.

After Thatcher entered 10 Downing Street, she kept in touch with Hayek on an intermittent basis. In an August 1979 letter to her, he suggested holding a referendum on reforming the trade unions.[12] Although Thatcher agreed with his sentiments, she had a more immediate priority: bringing down the inflation rate, which was in double digits when she entered office.[13] At this stage, Milton Friedman's monetarism had more impact on her policies than Hayek's demands for institutional reforms. In early 1980, the government adopted a Medium Term Financial Strategy in which it pledged to restrain the growth of the money supply and cut the budget deficit. The immediate results of this strategy were disastrous. As monetary policy was tightened, interest rates shot up, the value of the pound sterling rose sharply on the foreign exchanges, and the international competitiveness of British industry was decimated. The economy fell into the deepest recession since the 1930s. Between January 1980 and January 1982, the unemployment rate rose from 5.8 percent to 10.4 percent.[14] The number of people out of work rose to 3 million.[15]

By the fall of 1981, polls indicated that Thatcher had the lowest approval rating of any prime minister since the Second World War.[16] Rather than reverse course, she purged her cabinet of her internal critics—the "wets"—and plowed ahead. In the Employment Act of 1980, which banned the picketing of businesses not directly involved in a labor dispute, she had made a start on Hayek's anti-union agenda, but she wasn't ready yet for a full-scale assault. In 1981 the government-run National Coal Board (NCB), which had been steadily running down the number of mines on the grounds that the older ones couldn't produce coal cheaply enough to be economic, announced plans to shutter another twenty-three pits. The NUM threatened a strike. Thatcher and her colleagues knew that the key to withstanding a lengthy miners' walk-out was to keep the country's coal-fired power stations going, but they had only six weeks of coal stocks. The NCB and the government backed down from the threatened pit closures.

Watching from Germany, Hayek was frustrated with the slow pace of reform. Through the letters page of the *Times*, he continued to make his views known, and when he visited London, he occasionally saw Thatcher. In early 1982 he spoke at a private dinner arranged by an investment banker, which the prime minister also attended. At this event, Hayek pointed to the economic program of Pinochet's Chile as a model for the United Kingdom. In a letter dated February 17, 1982, Thatcher wrote to Hayek, saying that she had enjoyed his presentation and agreed with him that the "progression from Allende's Socialism to the free enterprise capitalist economy of the 1980s is a striking example of economic reform from which we can learn many lessons." "However," she went on, "I am sure you will agree that, in Britain with our democratic institutions and the need for a high degree of consent, some of the measures adopted in Chile are quite unacceptable. Our reform must be in line with our traditions and our Constitution."[17] Thatcher knew the political constraints she was operating under. The Britain of the 1980s wasn't the Britain of the early nineteenth century, where an oligarchic Parliament could push through aggressive measures oblivious to the public reaction. "At times the [reform] process may seem painfully slow," she went on in her letter to Hayek. "But I am certain we shall achieve our reforms in our own way and in our own time. Then they will endure."

That time wasn't long coming. A year after emerging emboldened from the 1982 Falklands War, in which a British naval task force routed thousands of Argentine soldiers who had occupied two British dependent territories in the South Atlantic, Thatcher appointed Ian McGregor, a flinty, Scottish-born American industrialist to head the National Coal Board. In McGregor's previous job at British Steel, he had halved the workforce. His appointment to the coal board signaled that more job cuts were ahead for miners, too. Arthur Scargill, a leftist firebrand from Yorkshire who had been elected president of the National Union of Mineworkers in 1981, claimed the government's goal was "to destroy the coal industry and the NUM."[18] The second half of Scargill's quote was certainly true. Going back to the General Strike of 1926, the NUM had represented the vanguard of the British labor movement. Thatcher knew that if she could defeat the union as she had defeated the Argentine military junta, the victory would have implications far beyond the coal industry.

Other Thatcherite MPs thought the same way. Even before Thatcher took power, one of them, Nicholas Ridley, had drawn up a secret plan for defeating a national miners' strike. The plan consisted of building up coal stocks, using nonunion truck drivers to transport coal to power stations, and training and equipping the British police to confront and disperse large numbers of picketers.[19] Thatcher quietly established a ministerial committee that dusted off the Ridley Plan. The government also ordered power stations to build up at least six months' supply of coal stocks. Working with police chiefs across the country, it created large, mobile units equipped with riot gear, which could be used to assist local forces at flash points during a strike. Some of Thatcher's aides even prepared plans for using the British Army to make sure coal could be moved to power stations.[20]

In March 1984 the National Coal Board announced the imminent closure of twenty mines, with the loss of about twenty thousand jobs. Scargill walked into Thatcher's trap. Claiming the government had secret plans to close more than seventy pits, he called a national strike without holding a national ballot of his members. In Yorkshire and South Wales, miners walked off the job en masse. But in some coal areas, particularly Derbyshire and Nottinghamshire, many miners rejected Scargill's strike call and kept working. As the striking workers set up picket lines to prevent stockpiled coal from reaching power plants, the government deployed thousands of police, in full riot gear, to disperse them. There were numerous violent clashes, including a particularly brutal one at a coking plant in South Yorkshire, where the police charged into strikers wielding shields and batons, causing many injuries.

The employment of state violence on a scale that evoked the government crackdowns on protesters after the Napoleonic Wars caused an uproar. In Parliament and the media, questions were raised about the police tactics. Thatcher was utterly unapologetic. At the height of the dispute, in a speech to Tory MPs, she compared the striking miners to General Galtieri's dictatorship in Argentina, labeling them "the enemy within." Targeting this alleged internal threat, MI5, Britain's domestic security service, tapped the phones of union leaders, including Scargill.

The miners kept their strike going for almost a year. In many mining communities, there were impressive displays of solidarity, which included thousands of miners' wives creating soup kitchens and standing on the picket line with their husbands. But confronted by the full might of the state, including the courts, which ruled the strike illegal, the miners were outmatched. By early 1985, the NUM's strike funds were exhausted. Many of the union members were virtually penniless, and some of them reluctantly returned to work.

In March 1985, NUM delegates finally called off the strike. With the union vanquished, the management and the government had free rein to rationalize the coal industry. Scargill turned out to be right about the prospect of mass pit closures. In the decade from 1984 to 1994, the number of people working in the British coal industry fell from 139,000 to 7,000 a decline of more than 90 percent.[21] In 1987 the government transformed the NCB into the British Coal Corporation. Seven years later this entity sold its English pits to a private mining company.

Thatcher's victory over the miners marked the decisive moment in the transition from postwar-era British social democracy to the neoliberal era that succeeded it. It had ramifications well beyond the United Kingdom. After all, Britain was the original industrial nation. Labor unions originated there, and they had been legalized at the height of the Victorian era. During the twentieth century, the labor movement had been a central player in British politics and capitalism. Although the unions' plant-based structure and internal divisions prevented them from following the German model of centralized corporatism, their mass membership and militancy limited the freedom of maneuver of politicians and business leaders alike.

In breaking the NUM, Thatcher signaled that this consensual model of capitalism was at an end, at least in Britain. She asserted the primacy of the market, stigmatized the union movement, and jettisoned the last vestiges of Tory paternalism, which could be dated back to early nineteenth-century social reformers like Michael Thomas Sadler and Lord Ashley. In November 1984 one of the few surviving representatives of this tradition, the ninety-year-old Harold Macmillan, who served as Britain's Conservative prime minister from 1957 to 1963, arose in the House of Lords and said: "It breaks my heart to see—and I cannot interfere—what is happening in our country today. This terrible strike, by the best men in the world, who beat the Kaiser's and Hitler's armies and never gave in."[22] Although Macmillan didn't directly criticize Thatcher or the heavy-handed tactics of the police, he lamented growing regional divides, dismissed monetarism as an American invention, and called for a moral and spiritual revolution.

Macmillan's speech didn't have any impact on policy. In the months and years after the miners' strike ended, the Thatcher government broadened its attack on the labor movement, stripping unions of many of their legal immunities, eliminating their capacity to conduct mass pickets, and abolishing their closed shops. Labor organizers were forced onto the defensive. Between 1979, when Thatcher was elected, and 2000, the number of union members in Britain fell from about 13.2 million to 7.8 million, a decline of about 40 percent.[23] In historical terms, the crushing of the miners' strike was a twentieth-century version of the 1834 passage of the Poor Law Amendment Act: a signal that a new regime was being established, in which labor would be treated as a commodity, market forces would be unleashed, and the state would use its power to enforce the harsh new rules of the game.

The weakening of the labor movement enabled Thatcher to proceed with other parts of her Conservative counterrevolution. A priority was to slash taxes on high earners. In the 1970s, the highest rate of income tax on earned income was 83 percent; by 1990, it had been reduced to 40 percent.[24] At the other end of the income scale, the government cut unemployment benefits and restricted access to them. It also deregulated the financial sector, replaced local property taxes with a uniform national poll tax, and gave millions of people living in public housing the right to buy their homes at a discount to their market value. This latter policy proved popular with former tenants who were able to buy their homes on the cheap, but it contributed to a shortage of affordable social housing.

Following advice that Milton Friedman had offered during the 1970s, and during a visit to England in 1980, Thatcher's government sold off dozens of publicly owned companies, including British Aerospace, British Airways, British Gas, British Steel, and Rolls-Royce.[25] British Leyland, the nationalized car company that had been home to "Red Robbo," was dismantled and sold to other car companies in bits. Despite public opposition, the government even sold off the country's regional water and sewage companies and listed them on the stock exchange. The justification Thatcher offered for these "privatizations"—a term chosen by David Howell, one of her ministers—was straight out of one of Friedman's free market tomes: market forces worked better than regulations, and business executives could do a better job of managing companies than government bureaucrats.

But there was also a long-term political agenda in play: Thatcher was determined to expand the ranks of Tory-voting property owners. As the privatizations proceeded, her government launched large-scale marketing campaigns to introduce nonwealthy Britons to the idea of investing in stocks. In 1984, more than 2 million Britons, many of them first-time investors, bought shares in British Telecom, the national phone provider, which were deliberately priced at a discount from the company's true value.[26] Two years later, about 1.5 million people bought stock in British Gas, the national gas utility.[27] Thatcher would later claim that the sale of British Telecom, which established the privatization model, "did more than anything else to lay the basis for a share-owning popular capitalism in Britain."[28]

Just as striking as Thatcher's actual reforms was the impact her long premiership had on attitudes toward the economy and economic policymaking. By the time the Labour Party finally made it back to Downing Street in 1997, it had rebranded itself as New Labour, abandoned its (largely symbolic) commitment to common ownership of the means of production, and openly embraced market forces, including welfare-to-work policies. Center-left parties in other countries, including the US Democrats, had moved in a similar direction. "Bill Clinton and Tony Blair have so much in common that they've adopted all the stories, all the thoughts, the policies, originally that go back to Keith Joseph and to Margaret Thatcher, and that's been the big change," another of Thatcher's ministers, Lord Young, said in an interview for the PBS documentary series *The Commanding Heights*.[29] Young's statement was an exaggeration. Blair's New Labour was committed to making major public investments in schools, hospitals, and other social infrastructure. It called for a minimum wage, which Britain lacked; the establishment of regional development agencies; a larger foreign aid budget; and windfall taxes on the profits of the utilities that Thatcher had privatized.

Still, Thatcher and Thatcherism undoubtedly shifted economic policy debates in Britain significantly to the right. During the 1997 election campaign, Blair promised to leave in place the key labor reforms that Thatcher had introduced, keep individual tax rates low and cut the business tax rate,

restrict the growth of overall government spending, and encourage entrepreneurship. In 1999, when Blair had been in 10 Downing Street for two
years, he told an interviewer from *The New Yorker* that old-style socialism
was dead.[30]

When Thatcher took office in 1979, few observers thought that such a transformation was possible, let alone likely. In academic circles during the 1970s,
it was fashionable to say that Britain was becoming ungovernable, and that
no prime minister could make much of a difference to policy outcomes.
Inside the Conservative Party, many old-school Tories regarded Thatcher's
right-wing policies as an aberration and predicted that the party would eventually return to the pragmatic, one-nation approach of Macmillan. In the
Labour Party, many people recognized that Thatcher's emergence reflected
the party's failure to deal with stagflation and industrial unrest, but they
consoled themselves that she didn't have a viable solution, either. Across the
political spectrum, many observers underestimated the lasting importance
of Thatcherism.

One observer who didn't make this mistake was Stuart Hall, a Jamaican-
born scholar who had long been associated with the Centre for Contemporary
Cultural Studies at Birmingham University. Hall wasn't a member of any political party. But in January 1979, four months before Thatcher was elected, he
published in *Marxism Today*, the magazine of the Communist Party of Great
Britain, an essay titled "The Great Moving Right Show" in which he analyzed
the rise of "Thatcherism," a term that wasn't yet in popular use. Hall started
out saying that the swing to the right in British politics "no longer looks like
a temporary swing in the political fortunes, a short-term shift in the balance
of forces."[31] It had been developing since the late 1960s, "and, though it has
developed through a series of different stages, its dynamic and momentum
appears to be sustained." The core feature of Thatcherism, Hall said, was its
challenge to the labor movement, which had played a central role in that
postwar model of British capitalism. In "deploying the discourses of 'nation'
and 'people' against 'class' and 'unions,'" Thatcher was conducting "an assault, not on this or that piece of 'irresponsible bargaining' by a particular
union, but on the very foundation and *raison d'être* of organized labour."[32]
Hall also emphasized how successful Thatcher had already been in rallying
support in elite circles for a sharp break with the past. To have discredited

Keynesianism "in some of the most powerful and influential apparatuses of government, research and the universities," he wrote, "and restored in its place Friedman and von Hayeck is, in itself, a remarkable reversal."[33]

Like C.L.R. James and Eric Williams, Hall hailed from a middle-class Caribbean background. Whereas they were from Trinidad, he was from Kingston, Jamaica. His family had African, English, and Indian ancestry, and his father worked as an accountant for the United Fruit Company.[34] As a schoolboy, Hall attended the elite Jamaica College. In 1951, at the age of nineteen, he was awarded a Rhodes Scholarship to Oxford, where he studied English at Merton College. After graduating, Hall stayed in England to continue his studies, and by the 1970s he had become an influential cultural theorist. His account of how political messages and narratives could be encoded in popular culture, such as film, and then decoded by different audiences, was widely used by other scholars. He was a prominent figure in the British New Left that emerged during the 1960s and was one of the founders of the movement's house journal, *New Left Review.*

Like many 1960s leftists, Hall was heavily influenced by the writings of Antonio Gramsci, the Italian Marxist philosopher whom Mussolini's fascist regime imprisoned for more than a decade until his death in 1937. In the notebooks that he wrote in prison, Gramsci emphasized the role that cultural values and cultural institutions played in maintaining capitalist rule. By inculcating the masses with the belief that the status quo, and their subordinated position within it, represented the natural order of things, the bourgeoisie established a cultural hegemony that reinforced their political and economic power. Gramsci also said that crises of capitalism could last for decades and didn't necessarily lead to a collapse of the system, as the early Marxists had predicted. Rather, they created a fluid environment in which capitalist elites would try to put together a new "historical bloc" of political forces, and a new ideological narrative, to secure their power. The ultimate outcome of the crises was uncertain.

In "The Great Moving Right Show," Hall referred to some of Gramsci's writings on capitalist crises, and he interpreted Thatcherism, through a Gramscian prism, as an effort to construct a new hegemony. "To sustain its possible credibility as a party of government in a crisis of capital," he wrote, "'Thatcherism' retains some lingering and ambivalent connections to . . . centre territory." But the movement's real goal was the "construction of a national consensus of its own."[35] Within this overall framework, Hall also emphasized two factors that made the late 1970s unique: an unprecedented crisis of the core institutions of social democracy, particularly the Labour Party; and an aggressive effort by the right to change the entire terms of political and economic debate, transcending traditional class alignments. In seeking to mediate distributional arguments between capital and labor, the Labour governments of Harold Wilson and Jim Callaghan had strayed from the party's historical role as the political representative of Britain's workers, Hall wrote, and this shift had "had profound effects in disorganizing and fragmenting working class responses to the crisis itself." In this unsettled environment, he went on, elements of the right had sought to win over some traditional Labour voters by exploiting cultural issues like immigration, law and order, an alleged breakdown of social discipline, and "the dilution of British stock by alien Black elements."[36]

This shift to the right had been developing since the late 1960s, Hall reminded his readers. He pointed to the emergence of far-right groups, including the National Front (NF), a whites-only, anti-immigrant political party whose supporters staged provocative marches through many British cities during the 1970s. The NF was a fringe organization. It never won a parliamentary seat, and in the October 1974 general election, its ninety candidates received about twelve hundred votes each. But despite its small size, the NF couldn't be easily dismissed. With its racist ideology, hypernationalism, and thuggish street tactics, it hailed back to Oswald Mosley's fascist movement of the 1930s. Moreover, it wasn't entirely cut off from mainstream politics. Some members of the Conservative Party, most famously Enoch Powell, an MP and former minister, had adopted elements of the far-right message, particularly its racial stigmatization of recent immigrants to Britain, many of whom hailed from South Asia and the Caribbean, and its calls for a drastic reduction in immigration.

Twinned with the attack on immigrants, Hall noted, were media stories that fanned fear of crime and portrayed Black youths in the inner cities as potential muggers. In 1978, the year before "The Great Moving Right Show" was published, Hall had coauthored a book, *Policing the Crisis: Mugging, the State, and Law and Order*, which highlighted these developments and the aggressive police responses they engendered. These included police officers using authorities established under the Vagrancy Act to stop, search, and potentially arrest people (particularly young Black men) simply on the suspicion that they might be intent on committing crimes. Hall and his four coauthors tied concerns about crime and race, and their amplification by the media, to Britain's broader problems and the "crisis of hegemony" that the established order was facing, not just in economic terms, but also in cultural terms with the emergence of a counterculture that encompassed feminism, student unrest, environmentalism, and the permissive society. Race, the authors wrote, came "to provide the objective correlative of crisis—the arena in which complex fears, tensions and anxieties, generated by the impact of the totality of the crisis . . . can be most conveniently and explicitly projected."[37]

In "The Great Moving Right Show," Hall emphasized that many of the cultural themes that Thatcher and her colleagues voiced—law and order, the need for social discipline, fear of being "swamped" by non-white immigrants—had been articulated well before the economic crisis of the mid- and late 1970s.[38] (Powell gave his incendiary "Rivers of Blood" speech in April 1968.) It was therefore a grave error to regard the rise of Thatcherism as just a symptom of economic distress and lack of trust in the Labour government. "What we have to explain," Hall wrote, "is a move toward 'authoritarian populism'—an exceptional form of the capitalist state—which, unlike classical fascism, has retained most (though not all) of the formal representative institution in place, and which at the same time has been able to construct around itself an active popular consent. This undoubtedly represents a decisive shift in the balance of hegemony."[39] A key element in the right's success, Hall went on, was its use of cultural messaging to generate popular support for a radical shift in economic policy. "Neither Keynesianism nor Monetarism win votes in the electoral marketplace," he wrote.

> But in the doctrines and discourses of "social market values"—the resto-
> ration of competition and personal responsibility for effort and reward,
> the image of the over-taxed individual, enervated by welfare coddling,
> his initiative sapped by handouts by the state—"Thatcherism" has found a
> powerful means of popularizing the principles of a Monetarist philosophy:
> and in the image of the welfare "scavenger" a well-designed folk devil.[40]

After "The Great Moving Right Show" appeared, some leftists criticized Hall for deemphasizing economics and class and overemphasizing culture, but that wasn't really a fair criticism. He didn't argue that Thatcherism's popular appeal was based solely on cultural factors, or that culture trumped economics in determining history. Following Gramsci (and indeed Marx), he argued that, while cultural and political struggles developed their own momentum and had no preset outcomes, the framework in which they played out was largely determined by economics and class. "Gramsci always insisted that hegemony is *not* exclusively an ideological phenomenon. There can be no hegemony without the decisive nucleus of the economic," Hall wrote in his essay "Gramsci and Us," which *Marxism Today* published in June 1987 as Thatcher won her third election victory.[41]

In the case of British Keynesianism, the economic nucleus had been split apart by the economic crisis of the 1970s, which hit ordinary people hard and undermined their faith in the system to deliver prosperity and stability. At the end of "The Great Moving Right Show," Hall stressed this point in a discussion of why right-wing populism of the sort that Thatcher espoused was proving popular. "This is no rhetorical device or trick, for this populism is operating on genuine contradictions, and it has a rational and material core," he wrote. "Its success and effectivity does not lie in its capacity to dupe unsuspecting folk but in the way it addresses real problems, real and lived experiences, real contradictions—and yet is able to represent them within a logic of discourse which pulls them systematically into line with policies and class strategies of the Right."[42]

This argument shouldn't be taken too far. Although Thatcher became the first British prime minister in the age of universal suffrage to win three elections in a row, she remained an extremely divisive figure. In many parts of Britain, she was reviled throughout her premiership, and her governments never gained majority support. In the three elections that she won, the Conservative Party received between 42 percent and 44 percent of the vote. Britain's first-past-the-post electoral system translated an electoral plurality into large majorities in the House of Commons.

Still, despite these qualifications, Thatcher's strident nationalism together with her get-tough message on violent crime and welfare recipients appealed to certain elements of the British working class. So did her "popular capitalism" agenda, such as giving public housing tenants the right to buy their homes and selling cheap shares in companies like British Telecom and British Gas. "Council house buyers, privatized share purchasers, and employed union leavers had distinctive attitudes toward nationalization and redistribution," the political scientist Geoffrey Garrett wrote in a 1992 study of survey data from the 1980s. "In all instances, those directly affected by the

Conservatives' reforms supported the 'free market' positions of more privatization and less redistribution of societal wealth. In fact, their attitudes more closely resembled those of traditional Conservative voters."[43]

Hall recognized these types of developments. In "Gramsci and Us," he argued that a good deal of confusion of the left about the impact of Thatcherism could be attributed to the fact it was "simultaneously, regressive and progressive." In seeking to re-create a nineteenth-century political economy beloved of Hayek and Friedman, it was taking the country backward. "But don't misunderstand it," Hall went on. "It's also a project of 'modernisation.' It is a form of *regressive modernisation*."[44] Echoing Hayek and other critics of postwar managed capitalism, Hall said the Thatcher project involved stripping British capitalism of ties to the past that were holding it back. Thatcherism "had its beady eye fixed on one of the most profound historical facts about the British social formation: that it never ever properly entered the era of modern bourgeois civilisation," Hall wrote. "It never made that transfer to modernity. It never institutionalised, in a proper sense, the civilisation and structures of advanced capitalism—what Gramsci called 'Fordism.'"[45] Hall was arguing that Britain had failed to embrace capitalist mass production in the same way as the United States, Germany, and Japan. Thatcher was deeply aware of this failure, he added, and so, deep down, were many of her fellow Britons. "Mrs. Thatcher knows that there is no serious political project in Britain today which is not also about constructing a politics and an image of what *modernity* would be like for our people. And Thatcherism, in its regressive way, drawing on the past, looking backwards to former glories rather than forwards to a new epoch, has inaugurated the project of reactionary modernisation."[46]

Hall was a cultural theorist rather than an economist, but when he remarked that British capitalism had struggled to develop the appropriate "structures" of advanced capitalism, he was onto something very important. The issue wasn't as simple as failing to adopt mass production. For many decades, multinational companies like Ford and General Motors had been operating large factories in the United Kingdom. So had British firms like British Leyland and British Steel. The problem, as Hall indicated, was an institutional one: the relationship, or lack of a relationship, between workers and management. Ford and GM factories in Britain were dogged with the same types of labor disputes that afflicted car factories operated by British

Leyland. Between Ford plants in Essex and Detroit, which used similar machinery, there was a significant gap in productivity. In some deep way, British capitalism was lagging behind its major competitors.

How can this failure be explained? The most convincing answer is that the postwar British economy, partly because of the country's early lead in industrialization and partly because of its imperial heritage, inherited a set of institutions that were ill-adapted to an era in which international competition was increasing and commercial success depended on constant innovation and productivity growth. One of the institutions that weighed on British economic development was the City of London, many denizens of which tended to have a transactional view of finance and a short time horizon. These two attributes made them shy away from the sort of semipermanent investments that many German banks, for example, held in large German industrial companies. In British industry, lack of access to long-term capital was a common complaint.

Another handicap that Britain inherited was a fragmented system of industrial relations. In many global industries, regular investments to modernize plants and equipment are required to remain competitive. Given the power and independence of Britain's plant-level labor unions, however, it was very difficult for firms (or entire industries) to get lasting agreements that reduced staffing levels in return for higher levels of capital investment and higher wages. "This was not an economy with a higher degree of patience either among investors or workers," Nicholas Crafts, one of Britain's leading economic historians, wrote in a 2018 history of British economic growth since the industrial revolution. "Either the absence of unions or strong corporatist trade unionism would have been preferable to the idiosyncratic British industrial relations system."[47]

In game theoretical terms, British industry was stuck in a low-trust, low-productivity equilibrium. Thatcherism can be seen as a brutal effort to change the rules of the game by kneecapping one of the players: organized labor. Once the unions had been sufficiently weakened, managers would have the power to close less productive plants, eliminate restrictive practices, and invest in more labor-saving machinery. The result would be a decline in manufacturing employment but a pickup in productivity growth, which over the long term would lead to rising prosperity. That was the theory, anyway.

During the 1980s, productivity growth did pick up somewhat, prompting Crafts to argue in a 2011 article that Thatcherism made the British economy more adaptable and innovative. "As the age of information technology and communications technology came along, Britain was able to embrace the opportunities associated with rapid diffusion of the new technologies, which required big changes in working practices and management hierarchies, better than its continental-European peer group," Crafts wrote. "This would not have happened with 1970s-style industrial relations and a heavily-regulated service sector."[48]

That, in a nutshell, is the case for Thatcherism: it modernized Britain. The case against it is that it created tremendous social costs and didn't resolve some of British capitalism's underlying economic problems, such as chronic underinvestment in physical and human capital and in research and development. The most obvious cost was high unemployment. Between 1960 and 1979, the UK jobless rate averaged 3.7 percent. Between 1980 and 1999, it averaged 9.1 percent.[49] These jobless figures don't account for millions of British workers who dropped out of the labor force and went on disability benefits. Thanks to the high value of the pound and aggressive downsizing, some parts of Britain, particularly in northern England and South Wales, were turned into rust belts, with emptied-out factories and decaying towns. The poverty rate rose from 13.4 percent of households in 1979 to 22.2 percent in 1990, the year that Thatcher's fellow Conservative MPs voted her out of office.[50] Wealth and income inequality also shot up. Between 1980 and 1990, the share of after-tax income received by the top 1 percent of British adults rose from 6 percent to 10 percent.[51]

This was what Hall's "reactionary modernization" looked like in practice. Market forces were unleashed, and British capitalism was transformed. The result was an economy that was more flexible and open to innovation, yet still plagued by many of the problems that Keynesian managed capitalism had sought to eliminate: economic insecurity, high rates of unemployment and poverty, widening inequality, and financially driven instability. Hall detested the society that Thatcherism created. But he was also critical of his fellow leftists for having failed to create a rival version of modernity that went beyond the traditional framework of class and recognized the heterogeneity and fragmentation of contemporary societies. The organized left "doesn't see that it is in the very nature of modern capitalist civilisation to proliferate the centres of power, and thus to draw more and more areas of life into social antagonism," he wrote in "Gramsci and Us." "It does not recognise that the identities which people carry in their heads—their subjectivities, their cultural life, their sexual life, their family life, their ethnic identities, their health—have become massively *politicised*."[52]

Passages like this illustrate why Hall is often portrayed as one of the founders of multiculturalism and identity politics. Given the emphasis that he placed on race and culture, he certainly earned this designation, but it needs to be applied carefully. Also in "Gramsci and Us," he wrote: "The nature of power in the modern world is that it is also constructed in relation to political, moral, intellectual, cultural, ideological, sexual questions."[53] Notice the word *also*. Unlike some of his followers, Hall didn't overlook economic factors. He believed that economic and cultural factors were *both* important drivers of history. Indeed, his critique of the Labour Party and some of his fellow leftists was that they had failed to comprehend how changes to the economy, driven by technical progress and globalization, were undermining traditional social structures and cultural values and creating a society of kaleidoscopic complexity and variety.

In this new world, Hall argued, it was essential to rethink and renew "the whole socialist project in the context of modern social and cultural life." Explaining his pessimism about the Labour Party's political prospects, he said he suspected that it "does secretly still believe that there's a little bit of lee-way left in the old, economic-corporate, incremental, Keynesian game." He went on: "I honestly believe that that option is now closed. It's exhausted. Nobody believes in it any more. Its material conditions have disappeared. The ordinary British people won't vote for it because they know in their bones life is not like that anymore."[54]

26

Parsing Globalization: Samir Amin, Dani Rodrik, and Joseph Stiglitz

In July 1993 a new open-air museum opened on the southern outskirts of Budapest. Memento Park featured dozens of Communist-era monuments that had been put in storage a few years earlier when Hungary ended decades of one-party rule. Among them were a bronze statue of Vladimir Lenin, which had long stood in the city center, and granite statues of Karl Marx and Friedrich Engels, which had loomed over the entrance to the Hungarian Communist Party's headquarters. In creating what was effectively a Communist theme park, Budapest's city council wasn't honoring the patron saints of Marxist-Leninism: it was trying to stimulate the local economy. "It is more interesting for tourists than for Hungarians," Mayor Gábor Demszky explained. "We want it to become an international attraction."[1]

Hungary had established a multiparty democracy in October 1989, the month before the Berlin Wall came down. During the following two years, the Soviet Union unraveled, and the Cold War came to an end. By 1993 Mayor Demszky wasn't the only one eager to move on from forty years of ideological struggle, which had climaxed, during the 1980s, with the dramatic sight of Margaret Thatcher and Ronald Reagan, after both championing huge arms buildups, engaging with a reformist Soviet leader, Mikhail Gorbachev. In early 1992 the Chinese leader Deng Xiaoping restarted the economic reform program that he and his Communist Party colleagues had halted after crushing the Tiananmen Square protests in 1989. During a visit to Shenzhen, a Special Economic Zone in southern China that had been established to attract foreign investment, Deng said: "Development is the only hard truth. It doesn't matter if policies are labeled socialist or capitalist, so long as they foster development."[2] India, too, was taking steps to reinvigorate its moribund economy. Under the guidance of finance minister Manmohan Singh, an Oxbridge-educated economist, the Congress Party government liberalized trade, removed restrictions on foreign investment, and chopped back the "License Raj," a bureaucratic quagmire that required businesses to obtain approval from many different government agencies before they could enter a new market or open a new factory.

The embrace of global capitalism also extended to Latin America. In Brazil in 1995, a center-left government led by Fernando Henrique Cardoso, a former Marxist sociology professor, took office. Back in the late 1960s, Cardoso had coauthored a book, *Dependency and Development in Latin America*, which had become an important text in the dependency movement. Now he championed market-led growth. His government sold off publicly owned industries, cut tariffs, tried to attract foreign investments, and introduced a monthly cash grant for poor families. Like his British counterpart Tony Blair, Cardoso insisted that market-friendly policies and moderate redistribution represented the future of progressive politics. "We must continue to be, in this sense, socialists, concerned about the social," he said in 1997. "But this cannot be done in the old fashioned way, as if it were possible, by an act of political will, to push a button and make things happen."[3]

As center-left politicians tried to come to terms with globalization, multinational corporations were leaping on the double opportunity it presented to them: new markets and cheap labor. From Shanghai to Mumbai to Moscow, foreign companies and bankers rushed in to explore investment opportunities. A century and a half after the publication of *The Communist Manifesto*, the representatives of international capital really were nestling everywhere and remaking the world in their likeness. The process of global integration appeared to be unstoppable. Between 1985 and 1995, the overall volume of international trade nearly doubled,[4] and the daily value of foreign exchange transactions rose more than eightfold.[5] The financial markets were the beating heart of global capitalism, and they operated virtually around the clock. The trading day started in Asia. When the markets closed in Hong Kong and Singapore, traders at international banks handed off their positions to their colleagues in London and Frankfurt, who in turn passed the buck to New York and Chicago, before the action flipped back across the Pacific. Globalization, an overused term, wasn't fully adequate to describe these developments. Capitalism wasn't merely expanding across the globe. It was deepening, shape-shifting, transforming itself into a ubiquitous hypercapitalism.

There was much more to this transformation than the implosion of the Soviet Union and the discrediting of state socialism. Indeed, those developments were arguably as much a reflection of the broader phenomenon as a cause of it. The underlying causes were political and technological. After the inflation and profits crisis that convulsed Western capitalism in the 1970s, many big businesses and conservative political parties were eager to break out of managed capitalism. In countries like China and India, policymakers were having similar thoughts about state-led economic development. Free market economists like Hayek and Friedman provided a policy map for the metamorphosis, but it was a series of technological developments that made it practically feasible. One key development was shipping containerization, which had massively reduced the cost of transporting raw materials, finished products, and industrial components around the world. A second vital factor was the rise of information technology, particularly telecommunications technology, which enabled the rapid transfer of business information, such as component orders, production plans, and internal corporate messages. By the mid-1990s, most multinational companies were leasing international communications networks. All these things made it easier for companies to unbundle their supply chains and spread them out around the world: distance was shrinking.

Considered separately, the neoliberal pivot in the West, the embrace of market forces by underdeveloped countries, and the rise of information technology and global supply chains all had huge ramifications. (The opening up of China and India alone potentially expanded the global capitalist workforce by more than a billion people.) Taken together, these three developments amounted to a new industrial revolution, and in Kondratiev's terms, they created the basis for a new long wave of global economic development. Initially, many economists struggled to grasp the full implications of this transformation, partly because they tended to interpret it from within their own silos. Trade economists, thinking in terms that David Ricardo would have recognized, emphasized the economic gains generated by the expansion of global commerce and a more finely developed global division of labor. Labor economists focused on wage stagnation in the United States and other industrialized countries, but they tended to blame "skill-biased technical change" rather than globalization. Macroeconomists welcomed an era of price stability, which they attributed to Western governments handing over the task of inflation-fighting to independent central banks.

These explanations weren't so much wrong as incomplete. Changing patterns of trade and production generated unprecedented income gains in China and India, as well as lower prices for consumers in Western countries. In many developing nations, they also produced sweatshops and working conditions redolent of early nineteenth-century Britain. Skill-biased technical progress was a genuine phenomenon, but so was corporate offshoring, which undermined workers' bargaining power and held down wages. Inflation-targeting central banks weren't operating in a vacuum. It was much easier for them to hit their inflation targets when anti-union legislation and the threat of automation and offshoring had left workers in such a weak position.

As the world market that Marx and Engels had prophesied was becoming a reality and workers' wages in some developed countries were diverting from productivity growth in a manner similar to what had happened in Britain during the first industrial revolution, it perhaps shouldn't have been surprising that some of the earliest commentary to grasp the magnitude of globalization came from the far left, where a global perspective had long been part of the analytical toolkit. One theorist who was associated with both the center-periphery dependency model and the "world systems theory" that the American sociologist Immanuel Wallerstein developed in the 1970s was Samir Amin, a Franco-Egyptian economist who, from 1970 to 1980, had been the director of the UN's African Institute for Development and Planning (IDEP), which is headquartered in Dakar, Senegal. A revolutionary communist since high school, Amin interpreted globalization in terms of Marx's concept of surplus value, which he extended to the global level. "A new contradiction now characterizes world capitalism," he wrote in his 1997 book, *Capitalism in the Age of Globalization*. "On the one hand, the centres of gravity of the economic forces commanding accumulation have shifted outside the frontiers of individual states; on the other hand, there is no political, social, ideological and cultural framework at world level that can give coherence to the overall management of the system."[6] Ostensibly, the multilateral institutions created at Bretton Woods—the IMF and the

World Bank—and the World Trade Organization, which was created in 1995, managed globalization in the interests of everybody. In reality, Amin said, these institutions were "merely the instruments of capital's management of the market."[7] In lumping together all international institutions, Amin was arguably oversimplifying things and overlooking the World Bank's efforts to reduce poverty in poor countries. But in pointing out the lack of an effective governing framework for globalization, he identified a problem that would become increasingly hard to ignore even for its defenders.

He was born in Cairo in 1931, nine years after Egypt gained its independence from Britain, to an educated family with Coptic Christian and French heritage. Both his parents were doctors, and his father managed the government health system in Port Said, a city at the northern end of the Suez Canal. In 1947 Amin sailed to France, where he enrolled at the elite Lycée Henry IV in Paris. After finishing high school, he enrolled at the Paris Institute of Political Studies, widely known as Sciences Po, where he was an active member of the French Communist Party's student section. "We used to spend a lot of time in the *Sciences Po* entrance hall, discussing everything under the sun, organizing petitions, trying to get students to come on demonstrations," he recalled in a 2006 memoir.[8] After getting a law degree, Amin switched to economics for graduate work and studied Marx, but also Smith, Ricardo, Keynes, and a lot of history. "What this also meant, however," he recounted, "was that I wasted little time on mainstream economic literature, the compulsory reading of which nowadays has an effect that I would almost describe as mind-numbing."[9] His doctoral thesis, "The Structural Effects of the International Integration of Precapitalist Economies,"[10] was essentially an early exposition of dependency theory: it described how the peripheral role allotted to poor countries stunted their development. (A "break with the world market is the primary condition for development," he wrote in a subsequent book that elaborated upon his thesis. "Any development strategy that accepts the framework of integration into this market must fail.")[11] After completing his doctorate, Amin spent a few years back in Egypt, moved to Mali, and then to Senegal, where he had been offered a fellowship at IDEP, which the United Nations had recently created to support the economic development efforts of newly independent African countries.

During the 1970s, these efforts focused on an initiative to create a New International Economic Order (NIEO), which in retrospect looks like a bold, though doomed, attempt to create an alternative model of globalization that empowered the Global South.[12] The movement's aspirations were summarized in a May 1974 resolution of the UN General Assembly, which called for sovereign equality of all states, including absolute sovereignty over their natural resources; regulation and supervision of multinational corporations; preferential treatment for developing countries in the international trading system; and expanded development assistance from rich countries.[13] At a conference in Algiers, seventy-seven nonaligned nations issued an "action plan" to make the NIEO a reality and raise their share of global GDP from under 10 percent to a quarter.[14]

Amin had mixed feelings about the NIEO. In a 1982 article, he said its economic demands constituted "a coherent programme" given "the contradictory nature of the accumulation of capital on a world scale."[15] From the beginning of the NIEO project, however, he believed that it didn't represent a decisive enough break with international capitalism, and he was convinced that politically it was a nonstarter because Western countries would reject it wholesale. "The fact is that the themes of the new order involve the aspiration to control natural resources and to strengthen national states, which imperialism does not accept," he wrote in a 1977 article.[16] This skepticism about the prospects for the NIEO proved well-founded. The nonaligned nations were divided on its ultimate goals, conservatives in the Global North attacked it, and by the end of the 1970s, it was effectively a dead letter.

The failure confirmed Amin in his belief that the gaining of independence by former colonies hadn't marked the end of imperialism but merely its reconstitution in new forms. In some parts of the world, particularly apartheid South Africa, a racial capitalism had been created, in which large parts of the native Black population had been turned into proletarians who were "obliged to sell their labour power in the European mine, factory, or plantation," he argued.[17] Throughout the developing world, he said, the core capitalist countries retained a series of monopolies over technology, finance capital, media and communications, natural resources, and weapons of mass destruction. "These five monopolies, taken as whole, define the framework within which the law of globalized value operates," he wrote in *Capitalism in the Age of Globalization*. "What results is a new hierarchy, more unequal than ever before, in the distribution of income on a world scale, subordinating the industries of the peripheries and reducing them to the role of subcontracting."[18]

Amin's commitment to international socialist revolution led him to take some very extreme positions. In his 2006 memoir, he said he stayed faithful to the positions of the Chinese Communist Party until after 1980, that is until well after the truth about the Cultural Revolution had been revealed.[19] In 1981 he published an article in which he said the genocidal Khmer Rouge regime in Cambodia had led a "popular, anti-imperialist revolution, opening up the road to socialism."[20] Amin loathed global capitalism and believed the system was plagued by contradictions. However, he was under no illusion that it was about to collapse. "Capitalism and crisis are not incompatible: far from it, because the logic of capital necessarily generates crisis," he wrote in *Capitalism in the Age of Globalization*. "Left to itself, capitalism can manage the crisis but cannot resolve it."[21] He portrayed globalization as a way for multinational corporations to access cheap labor, and for capitalism, at large, to manage the contradiction that John Hobson and Rosa Luxemburg had identified: the tendency for capitalist production to outrun demand, generating an ever-pressing need for new markets and new outlets for surplus capital.

Amin regarded Luxemburg's argument that capitalism expands by destroying noncapitalist societies as fundamental. Although industrialization was proceeding rapidly in parts of the developing world, he insisted that the West's monopolies over things like technology and finance would perpetuate the North-South divide. However, he was forced to acknowledge that the Asian Economic Miracle—which by the 1990s encompassed former colonies like Indonesia, Malaysia, Singapore, and South Korea—was hard to reconcile with traditional dependency theory. The East Asian countries, beginning with Japan, had not "followed the policy prescriptions of liberalism," he wrote. "They have, in fact, done the opposite."[22] That was only partially correct. The Asian Tiger model featured extensive government interventionism and support for new manufacturing industries. But the entire development strategy was also based on export-led growth, which hinged on integrating these industries successfully into the capitalist world market—the option Amin had earlier dismissed as nonviable. In his 1997 book, he didn't dispute the obvious success of this strategy, but he questioned its long-term sustainability in a world where the rise of China in particular represented a potential threat to US hegemony. "It goes almost without saying that the future development of China threatens all global equilibria," he wrote. "And that is why the United States will feel threatened by her development. In my opinion the United States and China will be *the* major antagonists in any future global conflict."[23]

In Western corridors of power, it was rare to hear any notes of caution expressed during the years after the Berlin Wall came down. The ruling narrative was that capitalism, market forces, and liberal democracy had triumphed forever. The American political scientist Francis Fukuyama, who was then the deputy director of policy planning staff at the State Department, encapsulated this moment in his famous essay suggesting that the end of the Cold War marked "the end of history as such: that is, the endpoint of mankind's ideological evolution."[24] As Ivy League economists jetted off to Moscow and other eastern European capitals to dispense policy advice on how to create a market economy, it was easy for them to view the collapse of state socialism and the rise of globalization as a new dawn for humanity.

One of the first US-based economists to query this consensus was Dani Rodrik, who taught at Harvard's Kennedy School of Government. In 1997 Rodrik published a short book, *Has Globalization Gone Too Far?*, that emphasized the rising social costs of "hyperglobalization." Pointing to labor strikes in France and Korea, political battles over pension cuts in Germany, and Pat Buchanan's protectionist run for the US presidency in 1996, Rodrik wrote: "The international integration of markets for goods, services, and capital is pressuring societies to alter their traditional practices, and in return broad segments of these societies are putting up a fight."[25] Rodrik also highlighted the offshoring of jobs from Western countries, including the United States, to places like China and Thailand, where wages were lower and labor regulations were weak or nonexistent: "The fact that 'workers' can be more easily substituted for each other across national boundaries undermines what many conceive to be a post-war social bargain between workers and employers, under which the former would receive a steady increase in wages and benefits in return for labor peace."[26]

Rodrik was born into a prosperous family in Istanbul in 1957. His father ran a business that manufactured ballpoint pens. After attending an elite private school, he moved to the United States to attend Harvard, where he majored in government. During the early 1980s, he did a PhD in economics at Princeton, specializing in international trade, a field dominated, then as now, by supporters of free trade. Rodrik was skeptical of what he learned in the classroom. "I knew from my own experience that without a certain amount of trade protection in Turkey, a lot of the middle class, or the upper-middle class to which I belonged, wouldn't have existed," he recounted in a 2019 interview. "That was, in many ways, the beginning of my unorthodox views on economic development."[27] After finishing his doctorate in 1985, Rodrik moved back to Harvard, where he worked on a range of issues, including the impact of trade liberalization on developing economies.

It was the era of "the Washington Consensus," a phrase originally coined in 1989 by John Williamson, a senior fellow at the Institute for International Economics in Washington, to describe a set of pro-market policies that the IMF and other international institutions prescribed for highly indebted countries in Latin America and elsewhere.[28] By the mid-1990s, the term was used to apply to a broader policy framework that the IMF and the US government urged on all developing countries, including the transition countries in eastern Europe. These policies included cutting government spending and balancing the budget; reducing marginal tax rates; eliminating tariffs and other barriers to trade; privatizing publicly owned companies; encouraging foreign companies to make direct investments; and liberalizing flows of financial capital. In some respects, the Washington Consensus policy regimen resembled the free market "shock treatment" that Milton Friedman had urged on General Pinochet during the mid-1970s. Its stated goal was to stabilize troubled economies and create a basis for sustainable market-driven growth. Critics claimed it led to deeper slumps, more hardship, and more financial instability.

Rodrik believed that the free market fundamentalism embodied in the Washington Consensus ignored the vital role that government directives and financial support had played in the rapid development of Japan, South Korea, and other East Asian economies. He also questioned the conviction among American economists that international trade had played little role in creating the wage stagnation that had emerged in the United States during the early 1970s and persisted for more than twenty years. In a 1995 article, the economist Paul Krugman, who was then at MIT, pointed out that economists' skepticism about the impact of trade on wages rested largely on the fact that the volume of international trade, "despite its growth . . . is still quite small compared with the economies of advanced nations. Imports of manufactured goods from developing countries were only about 2 percent of the combined GDP of the OECD countries, Krugman pointed out.[29] Rodrik argued that the volume of trade didn't necessarily tell the full story.

Referring to the work of the British economist Adrian Wood, the author of a 1994 book on trade, employment, and inequality, Rodrik noted that the constant threat of low-wage competition from abroad could prompt American manufacturers to introduce labor-saving technology. If this phenomenon was widespread, Wood had pointed out, the "skill-biased technical change" that many economists identified as the cause of wage stagnation could actually be a product of globalization.[30] Rodrik also cited research showing how firms' ability to move production offshore had weakened the bargaining power of their workers and made it easier for them to demand wage cuts.[31] He also explained how globalization was undermining the tax base in many countries. As capital became more mobile, it was becoming harder for governments to tax their corporations and rich citizens effectively. Multinationals could shift their operations, or at least their accounting profits, to low-tax countries like Ireland and Singapore. Wealthy individuals could hide assets abroad.

Rodrik pointed out that this undermining of the tax base was occurring at the same time that intensified international competition was undermining job security and creating a need for bigger social safety nets. Challenging the common perception that trade and openness were associated with laissez-faire and small government, he pointed out that it was "in the most open countries, such as Sweden, Denmark, and Netherlands, that spending on income transfers has expanded the most."[32] But now even the Scandinavian countries were facing competitive pressures to rein in their welfare states. If these trends continued, Rodrik said, support for open markets was likely to diminish "to the point where a generalized resurgence of protectionism becomes a serious possibility."[33] To survive in a democratic age, any economic system must maintain a basic level of political legitimacy. Citing Karl Polanyi's *The Great Transformation*, Rodrik argued that this represented a particular challenge for a globalized system, because "the international market is the only market that is not regulated by an overarching political authority. Consequently, transactions undertaken in the international marketplace carry the least inherent legitimacy."[34] If globalization were to lose its legitimacy entirely, nobody, not even the wealthiest citizens who were its biggest winners, would be spared the consequences, Rodrik warned. "Social disintegration is not a spectator sport," he wrote. "Ultimately, the deepening of social fissures can harm all."[35]

The Clinton administration was a big supporter of globalization. In December 1993, Bill Clinton signed into law the North American Free Trade Agreement (NAFTA), which eliminated virtually all tariffs between the United States, Canada, and Mexico. "NAFTA means jobs: American jobs, and good-paying American jobs," Clinton said at a signing ceremony.[36] Subsequently, his administration helped push through a major agreement on global trade, the so-called Uruguay Round, which was completed in 1994. This accord created the World Trade Organization, headquartered in Geneva, which was tasked with promoting and umpiring global trade. It also eliminated restrictions on trade in services and created new intellectual property protections for major multinational corporations. The completion of the Uruguay Round was widely hailed as the most important expansion of world trade since the General Agreement on Tariffs and Trade in 1947.

The were some free trade skeptics. During the 1992 presidential campaign, Ross Perot, a Texas businessman who ran as a third-party candidate, had warned that the completion of NAFTA would lead to a "giant sucking sound," as companies and jobs moved to Mexico. Many labor groups also opposed NAFTA, the results of which were less dramatic than Perot had predicted. Some US companies, particularly auto companies, did shift production and well-paying jobs south of the border, but manufacturing employment as a whole remained stable during the eight years that Clinton was in office,[37] and total nonfarm employment rose by about 23 million.[38] Workers' wages continued to stagnate, though, and inside the administration there were some debates about whether globalization was playing a role.

One official who raised this question was Joseph Stiglitz, a Princeton economics professor who joined the White House Council of Economic Advisers in 1995 and subsequently served as its chair. In the economics world, Stiglitz was known as a brilliant theorist who had written influential papers on subjects ranging from finance to public economics to labor economics. A member of the "new-Keynesian" school, whose members sought to provide a rigorous microeconomic foundation for Keynesian macroeconomics, he was most renowned for his work on information asymmetries, in which one party to an economic transaction has certain information that another party lacks. (A classic example is that someone looking to buy auto insurance knows more about how likely they are to drive recklessly than the insurance company does.) Stiglitz viewed himself as a centrist, but he had a progressive streak. As an undergraduate at Amherst in the early 1960s, he had participated in the March on Washington. And while growing up in Gary, Indiana, a steel town, he had seen how cheap foreign competition could hollow out once-thriving communities.[39]

In principle, Stiglitz supported expanding trade based on arguments that went back to Smith and Ricardo: by expanding markets and encouraging international specialization, trade raised efficiency and expanded overall welfare. But Stiglitz was also sensitive to the fact that trade created losers as well as winners, and that the losers were likely to include many US workers who made things that competed with products made in China and other low-wage countries. "Wages of unskilled workers would fall and employment would increase," Stiglitz later recounted. "But when I put this observation before my colleagues in the Clinton administration, they shrugged their shoulders."[40] In early 1994, the White House did propose a federal retraining program for workers who had lost their jobs because of trade deals or corporate downsizing. But the proposal never got anywhere on Capitol Hill.

Another issue that concerned Stiglitz was the Treasury Department's support for financial liberalization, both at home and in developing countries. In his 2003 book, *The Roaring Nineties*, Stiglitz recounted how in 1993, before he joined the administration, the White House Council of Economic Advisers had opposed Treasury's efforts to force South Korea to liberalize rapidly. At the time the Treasury secretary was Robert Rubin, a former co-chairman of Goldman Sachs. Stiglitz thought he detected the influence of the Wall Street lobby. "Why push Korea to move faster?" he wrote. "What would Americans gain by having Korea liberalize a few years earlier than it otherwise would have done? American workers would gain nothing, but Wall Street firms were worried: gradual liberalization might allow others to enter as well, or even enable Korean firms to compete on an equal footing."[41] The White House economists lost the debate, and the Treasury Department's view prevailed, Stiglitz recalled.

In 1997 Stiglitz left the White House and joined the World Bank. What he found most troubling as he made the job switch, he would later recount, was that the Treasury Department and the IMF were busy promoting policies abroad that clashed with the Clinton administration's domestic positions. "We fought against privatization of Social Security at home, while we pushed it abroad," he wrote. "At home, we fought against the balanced-budget amendment, which would have constrained our ability to use expansionary fiscal policy in the event of a downturn; but abroad, we imposed contractionary fiscal policies on countries going into recessions . . . We pushed market fundamentalism on the rest of the world, both directly and through the IMF. I could have understood Ronald Reagan or Margaret Thatcher doing this. I could not understand Bill Clinton doing this."[42]

Stiglitz wasn't the only prominent economist in the Clinton administration. In 1993 Harvard's Lawrence Summers was appointed under secretary for international affairs at the Treasury Department; in 1995, he was promoted to deputy secretary; from July 1999 to January 2001, he served as Treasury secretary. Like Stiglitz, Summers was an Ivy League Keynesian with some liberal credentials. In the 1980s, he had coauthored a paper that argued that hostile takeovers, rather than creating real economic value, merely shifted "rents" from a firm's workers and suppliers to its stockholders.[43] By the mid- to late 1990s, however, Summers's economic views had shifted. He now referred to himself as a "market-orientated progressive"[44] and publicly extolled the virtues of free market capitalism. "What's the single most important thing to learn from an economics course today?" he said to Daniel Yergin and Joseph Stanislaw, the authors of the 1998 book *Commanding Heights*. "What I tried to leave my students with is the view that the invisible hand is more powerful than the hidden hand. Things will happen in well-organized efforts without direction, controls, plans. That's the consensus among economists. That's the Hayek legacy."[45]

As under secretary for international affairs and then as deputy secretary of the Treasury, Summers was the Treasury's point man on globalization, which meant dealing with the IMF and other international agencies. In his public appearances, he acknowledged some of the challenges that greater international integration posed, such as threats to labor standards and impingements on national sovereignty. But he also defended free trade and economic openness, arguing in a 1999 speech that their benefits "show up in the form of higher living standards resulting from higher wages and higher returns to capital and quite likely in the form of higher rates of growth."[46] In the same speech, Summers challenged the argument that globalization led to job losses in rich countries and emphasized the rapid economic growth that some developing nations, especially China and India, were experiencing. "More than a quarter of humanity is enjoying growth at rates where living standards quadruple within a generation," he said, adding that this was "unprecedented in economic history."

Official figures suggested this was true. But while Summers was at Treasury the era of hyperglobalization experienced its first major blowup. In the summer of 1997 a financial crisis erupted in Thailand and quickly spread to South Korea, Indonesia, Malaysia, and Singapore. Currencies plunged, stock markets crashed, economies fell into recession, and some of the afflicted countries were forced to ask the IMF for emergency loans. During the previous two decades, these East Asian countries had been among the most economically successful in the world: poster boys for globalization. Nonetheless, the IMF, backed by the US Treasury Department, followed its usual crisis playbook and demanded that they raise interest rates, cut their budget deficits, and restructure their financial sectors. These austerity policies deepened the economic slump. In 1998, inflation-adjusted GDP plunged by 6.7 percent in South Korea, 7.4 percent in Malaysia, and 13.1 percent in Indonesia.[47] Bankruptcies and joblessness soared.

Throughout Asia, this experience generated a backlash against the IMF and the Washington Consensus. In September 1998, the Malaysian government of Mahathir Mohamad targeted international speculators by introducing controls on the movement of financial capital and fixing the country's exchange rate against the dollar. Rather than causing the earth to cave in, these two violations of IMF orthodoxy bought Malaysia some respite from relentless market pressures, and other Asian countries noticed this success. They didn't follow Malaysia's example directly. But many of them started to build up vast reserves of foreign currencies, which they hoped would make them less vulnerable to a future crisis and less likely to have to deal with the IMF.

In the years preceding the blowup, East Asia had seen big influxes of financial capital and run up large debts. Even among supporters of globalization, the ensuing crash raised doubts about the wisdom of liberalizing capital flows. In a 1998 article, "The Capital Myth," Jagdish Bhagwati, a Columbia professor who was a prominent supporter of trade liberalization, argued that Washington policymakers had made a big error by treating money as just another commodity and letting it flow across borders at will. Unlike trade in tangible items like clothes and computers, international flows of money are sometimes driven by speculative manias, which often end in a bust. In foisting financial liberalization on the rest of the world, Bhagwati said, the "Wall Street–Treasury complex" had been "unable to look much beyond the interest of Wall Street."[48]

After Stiglitz left the World Bank in 2000 and moved to Columbia University, he publicly criticized the US government and the IMF for the policies they had imposed on Asian countries. In a 2002 book, *Globalization and Its Discontents*, he argued that the primary cause of the crisis had been "excessively rapid financial and capital market liberalization," and he added that the IMF's draconian demands made a bad situation worse.[49] Broadening his criticisms, he said the lending agency routinely made decisions "on the basis of what seemed a curious blend of ideology and bad economics, dogma that sometimes seemed to be thinly veiling special interests." Rather than considering each country on its merits, the fund followed a "standard" template that it was loath to alter.[50] "Alternative opinions were not sought," Stiglitz wrote. "Open, frank discussion was discouraged—there was no room for it . . . These attitudes made me cringe."[51]

In Stiglitz's account of globalization, the IMF was the arch-villain, and its commitment to market fundamentalism was part of a larger problem, the same one Amin had pointed to: the lack of a coherent and politically accountable framework to oversee and manage international integration. "Instead, we have a system that might be called *global governance without global government*," Stiglitz wrote, "one in which a few institutions—the World Bank, the IMF, the WTO—and a few players—the finance, commerce, and trade ministries, closely linked to certain financial and commercial interests—dominate the scene, but in which many of those affected by their decisions are left almost voiceless."[52] To remedy this situation, Stiglitz called for reform of the Bretton Woods institutions, including changes to their voting structures. He insisted that globalization as currently constituted wasn't working for many of the world's poor, for the environment, or for the stability of the global economy. Capitalism was at a crossroads, just as it had been during the Great Depression, when Keynes saved the system by laying out a new policy framework that created jobs and stabilized the world economy. "Now," Stiglitz concluded, "millions of people around the world are waiting to see whether globalization can be reformed so that its benefits can be more widely shared."[53]

The publication of *Globalization and Its Discontents* wasn't universally welcomed. The Harvard economist Kenneth Rogoff, who was the IMF's chief economist at the time, dismissed the book's policy recommendations as "at best highly controversial, at worst, snake oil."[54] Stiglitz's focus on the crisis programs of the IMF did present a somewhat narrow view of globalization, but his basic argument that market fundamentalism had led to big problems was hard to dispute. The failure could be seen in the diverging fates of post-Communist Russia and post-Maoist China as they transitioned toward capitalism. Russia, following the advice of market-friendly Western economists, liberalized prices, jettisoned state planning directives, and privatized state-owned firms; China adopted a more gradual and nuanced approach, maintaining a large state-owned sector and allowing private, market-driven enterprises to emerge alongside it. During much of the 1990s, China's GDP grew at double-digit rates. In Russia, GDP collapsed, poverty soared, and life expectancy plummeted. "The contrast between what happened in China and what has happened in countries like Russia, which bowed to IMF ideology, could not be starker," Stiglitz noted.[55]

By the start of the new millennium, Stiglitz and Asian policymakers weren't the only ones who were having second thoughts about globalization. In many countries, there was widespread concern about Western firms outsourcing production to countries where sweatshops, child labor, and dangerous working conditions were common. In May 1993 a fire at a toy factory on the outskirts of Bangkok killed at least 188 people and likely many more. (Some of the factory's workers were never accounted for.) "All but fourteen of the dead were women, most of them young, some as young as thirteen years old," the American journalist William Greider recounted in his 1997 book *One World, Ready or Not*. "Hundreds of the workers had been trapped on upper floors of the burning building, forced to jump from third- or fourth-floor windows, since the main exit doors were kept locked by the managers, and the narrow stairways became clotted with trampled bodies or collapsed."[56]

Greider had traveled to Thailand, where he toured textile factories, spoke to workers, and visited some of the rural villages from which many of them hailed. Unburdened by an economics PhD, the veteran journalist had a firm grasp on the realities of the new global economic order. Kader Industrial Toy Company of Thailand, the business that owned the burned-out Bangkok facility, manufactured items for Toys "R" Us, Fisher-Price, Hasbro, and JCPenney, he pointed out. Among the items found in the wreckage of its factory were dolls depicting the Muppets, Bugs Bunny, and Big Bird. Although the Thai company bore primary responsibility for the unsafe working conditions, the factory fire "was ordained and organized by the free market itself," Greider wrote. "The toy industry—much like textiles and garments, shoes, electronics assembly, and other low-wage sectors—existed (and thrived) by exploiting a crude ladder of desperate competition among the poorest nations. Its factories regularly hopped to new locations where wages were even lower, where the governments would be even more tolerant of abusive practices."[57] The Kader Industrial Toy Company had recently opened two factories in China, a country where many young women worked fourteen hours a day. Greider posed the question: "Why should a company worry about sprinkler systems or fire escapes for a dusty factory in Bangkok when it could hire brand-new workers in China for only $20 a month, one fifth of the labor cost in Thailand?"[58]

Why indeed? In the United States and Europe, concerns about sweatshop labor, corporate greed, and climate change fed the growth of an anti-globalization movement that included labor union members, environmentalists, human rights and peace activists, and anarchists committed to overthrowing capitalism. The new World Trade Organization (WTO) was the focus of many of these groups' anger. At the end of November 1999, tens of thousands of protesters converged on Seattle, Washington, where the WTO was holding a four-day ministerial meeting that President Clinton was scheduled to attend. On the first morning, the demonstrators blocked intersections and resisted police efforts to disperse them, which included the use of tear gas. Most of the demonstrators were peaceful, but hundreds of anarchists smashed shop windows, sprayed graffiti, and set bonfires.[59] The opening ceremony had to be canceled, and the mayor of Seattle declared a state of emergency.[60] Protests, arrests, and sporadic violence continued throughout the meeting and generated media coverage around the world.

In a 2000 article motivated by the Seattle protests, Dani Rodrik noted that globalization was facing "a deep crisis of legitimacy that threatens to overwhelm the world's trading regime."[61] Far from reversing course, Western governments had expanded their commitment to bringing down trade barriers by agreeing to admit China to the WTO despite complaints about its human rights record and weak labor laws. China formally joined the organization in December 2001. During the ensuing years its commodity exports to the

United States and other Western countries rose at astronomical rates: between 2001 and 2008, their value went from $19.8 billion to $115.5 billion.[62] This unprecedented surge coincided with a sharp drop in US manufacturing employment, from 17.1 million in January 2001 to 13.7 million in January 2008.[63]

These developments intensified the debate about the consequences of globalization, and even some skeptical economists started to take seriously the idea that trade was harming workers in the developed world. The strongest counterargument that globalization's advocates put forward was the one Summers had made: it was helping to lift hundreds of millions of people in poor countries out of acute poverty. In his 2004 book, *In Defense of Globalization*, Jagdish Bhagwati cited figures from the Asian Development Bank that showed that between 1978 and 1998, the poverty rate in China had fallen from 28 percent to 9 percent, and in India from 51 percent to 26 percent.[64] "With the usual caveat that in the social sciences one can rarely establish the degree of credibility for one's argument that one can aspire to in the physical sciences," Bhagwati wrote, "one can conclude that freer trade is associated with higher growth and that higher growth is associated with reduced poverty."[65]

That wasn't the entire story, however. The most widely used international poverty threshold, which researchers at the World Bank had created, was extremely low. It was originally set at an income of $1 a day, adjusted for different prices across countries. Following criticisms, the bank raised the threshold to $1.25, and in a paper first published in 2008, two of its economists, Shaohua Chen and Martin Ravallion, provided revised poverty estimates. The good news was that they still showed a big drop. Between 1981 and 2005, the number of people in the developing world who were living under the $1.25-a-day poverty line declined from about 1.9 billion to about 1.4 billion people. Taking into account population growth, this translated into a shift from about half the population to about a quarter of the population.[66] Obviously, this was a very welcome development, but the regional breakdowns in the Chen and Ravallion paper showed that it needed to be interpreted carefully. The decline in acute poverty was heavily concentrated in China. Between 1981 and 2005, the number of Chinese living on less than $1.25 a day fell from 835.1 million to 207.7 million—a drop of 627.4 million.[67] Excluding China from the global figures, the number of people living under the $1.25-a-day threshold slightly increased over the period, from about 1.1 billion to about 1.2 billion.[68] In India, the acute poverty rate fell from 59.8 percent to 41.6 percent,[69] but because of very rapid population growth, this decline translated into a slight rise in the absolute numbers.[70]

Taken overall, these figures confirmed that the developing countries that had engaged most strenuously with globalization—China and India—experienced rapid economic growth and historic drops in rates of acute poverty. It's hard to overstate the significance of these developments. Two centuries after industrial capitalism emerged in Britain, some developing countries were finally beginning to close the huge income gap with the West that had opened in the nineteenth century and continued to widen during the twentieth. On a worldwide basis, the income distribution was finally getting a bit more compressed. One commonly used measure of inequality is the Gini coefficient, which is named after the Italian statistician and demographer Corrado Gini. Beginning around the year 2000, the Gini coefficient for global income started to fall.[71]

On the other side of the ledger, globalization appeared to be generating higher levels of income inequality *within* individual countries, including the United States and China. Moreover, the gap between the richest and poorest nations was still a gaping one. In 2005, according to the World Bank, US GDP per capita was $44,123, compared to $417 in Malawi and $334 in Tajikistan.[72] In some parts of the developing world, the absolute number of people in acute poverty was rising sharply. In Sub-Saharan Africa and South Asia, Chen and Ravaillon reported, the figure had risen from 762 million people in 1981 to 986 million in 2005, an increase of nearly 30 percent.[73] Globalized capitalism was lifting some boats, but certainly not all of them.

The Asian Financial Crisis and the failure of shock therapy in Russia dented the Washington Consensus, but the biggest blow to market fundamentalism came in 2007, with the onset of the Global Financial Crisis. The drama began with the bursting of a US real estate bubble, which had been pumped up by low interest rates, lax lending standards, and property speculators.[74] As home prices fell, many homeowners who had taken out "subprime" mortgages that they couldn't really afford defaulted on their loans. This wave of defaults, in turn, caused a collapse in the price of subprime mortgage securities, which Wall Street investment banks had cobbled together from baskets of high-risk home loans, falsely claiming they were safe. The next daisies in the chain were the Wall Street firms themselves, in particular Bear Stearns and Lehman Brothers. As Bear tottered on the brink in March 2008, the US Treasury and the Federal Reserve orchestrated a rescue, in which the Fed provided an emergency loan and JPMorgan Chase bought the firm's operations for a song. Six months later, when Lehman found itself in a similar pickle, the Treasury and the Federal Reserve refused to bail it out. On Monday, September 15, 2008, Lehman filed for bankruptcy.

The subprime blowup provided confirmation for Hyman Minsky's Financial Instability Hypothesis, which he had expounded in the 1970s. As the great real estate boom proceeded, the level of risk-taking by homeowners, mortgage providers, and Wall Street issuers of mortgage securities gradually ramped up. By the later stages, mortgage providers were issuing home loans to buyers who, based on their incomes, couldn't hope to meet the true financing costs, and often didn't even understand the nature of the commitments they were taking on. In many cases, their loans came with low "teaser" rates that lasted for only a year or two before resetting to much higher rates. The idea was that the buyers would refinance before the reset date, using the capital gains they made from further increases in house prices. Of course, this scheme only worked as long as prices kept rising. In Minsky's terminology, it was "Ponzi finance." When home prices plunged, the Ponzi scheme collapsed, almost bringing down the entire financial system with it.

After Lehman Brothers went bust, financial markets around the world plummeted, and concerns rose about the health of many other financial institutions. In Britain, savers lined up to withdraw their deposits from Northern Rock, an inaptly named bank whose finances were already shaky. Facing the first bank run that the country had seen in more than a century, the British government guaranteed all deposits at Northern Rock, which would eventually be nationalized. Despite this move, and pledges from central banks to flood the financial system with money, the panic continued, prompting more government action. Within a week, the Republican administration of George W. Bush had proposed a $700 billion taxpayer bailout for major US banks. Mindful of a voter backlash, the Republican-controlled House of Representatives voted against the bailout. The markets promptly had another conniption, which caused some of the refusenik lawmakers to change their minds. On October 3 the Emergency Economic Stabilization Act of 2008 was passed into law.

A combination of bailouts, ultraloose monetary policy, and emergency lending programs from the Fed and other central banks eventually stabilized the global financial system. But the panic brought on the deepest global slump since the Great Depression. After this experience, it was hard for promoters of deregulation to argue that unfettered financial capitalism represented a viable economic model for the world, although that didn't stop some of them from trying. On the center left and far left, meanwhile, a small army of economists, journalists, and commentators wrote books that sought to draw lessons from the crisis. Among the authors were Amin, Stiglitz, and Rodrik.

Amin provided the most expansive analysis. In his 2013 book, *The Implosion of Contemporary Capitalism*, he attributed the blowup to the financialization of the Western economies, which he portrayed as a response to monopoly capitalism's chronic tendency to generate huge surpluses that couldn't find a profitable outlet. As the global surplus rose, owners of capital, rather than investing in physical assets, such as factories and offices, diverted their money to bonds, stocks, and other financial products, which proliferated "at dizzying speeds, not commensurate with growth in GDP . . . or with investment in real production."[75] This process fueled economic growth, rising asset prices, and rising inequality, but it was inherently unstable and couldn't go on indefinitely, Amin argued. "It is this system—commonly called 'neoliberal,' the system of generalized monopoly capitalism . . . that is imploding before our eyes," he wrote. "This system, apparently unable to overcome its growing internal contradictions, is doomed to continue its wild ride."[76]

Stiglitz, in his 2010 book *Freefall*, placed the primary blame for the financial crisis on the Federal Reserve, for allowing a real estate bubble to develop, and a series of administrations, including the Clinton administration, for embracing financial deregulation. He singled out two episodes: the 1999 repeal of the Depression-era Glass-Steagall Act, which had separated commercial banks from investment banks; and the Treasury Department's torpedoing of an effort to regulate derivative securities, such as credit default swaps, which ended up playing an important role in the subprime blowup. "The head of the Commodity Futures Trade Commission, Brooksley Born, had called for such regulation," Stiglitz recalled. "But Secretary of Treasury Robert Rubin, his deputy, Larry Summers, and [Fed chairman] Alan Greenspan were adamant—and successful—in their opposition."[77]

Rodrik took a somewhat different tack. "Financial globalization lay at the core of the crisis," he wrote in his 2011 book *The Globalization Paradox*, which was a follow-up to *Has Globalization Gone Too Far?*[78] During the years leading up to 2007, Rodrik pointed out, China and the Gulf Oil states had parked much of their vast savings in US Treasury bonds. This helped to keep US interest rates, including mortgage rates, low, fueling the real estate bubble. Rodrik recounted how, after the bubble popped, it emerged that a number of foreign banks, particularly in Germany, had invested in American subprime securities and incurred significant losses. "Financial globalization ended up promulgating instability rather than higher investment and more rapid growth," he wrote.[79] This was surely true. The panic selling in the markets plunged countries as far afield as Ireland, Hungary, and Jamaica into crisis. The Wall Street crash of 1929 reverberated around the world, but this was contagion on an unprecedented scale, and it was practically instant.

Between the publication of *Has Globalization Gone Too Far?* and the outbreak of the Global Financial Crisis, a decade had passed. Rodrik placed the financial blowup in the context of other developments since 1997, including the Asian Financial Crisis, the violent demonstrations in Seattle, and anti-austerity riots in Argentina. Going beyond the doubts that he had raised previously, he said the entire globalization project needed rethinking before it led to further disasters. Rodrik didn't mention Polanyi by name this time, but when he described the folly of efforts to build a single world market, with no allowance for inherited customs or national peculiarities, there were echoes of the Austrian's account of interwar attempts to re-create the nineteenth-century laissez-faire model. "We cannot simultaneously pursue democracy, national determination, and economic globalization," Rodrik wrote. "If we want to push globalization further, we have to give up either the nation state or democratic politics."[80]

As a fervent supporter of democracy and a skeptic about the prospects of global governance, Rodrik called for the abandonment of hyperglobalization and its replacement with "A Sane Globalization."[81] In his estimation, sanity would include allowing countries to opt out of trade rules that violated their labor standards or environmental laws; placing limitations on movements of financial capital; expanding temporary work visas for migrants from poor countries; and reforming the Bretton Woods institutions, particularly the IMF, to make them more accountable and give a bigger voice to developing nations. On the latter point, Rodrik, Stiglitz, and Amin were all agreed, but their strictures, and those of other would-be reformers, had little impact. Even though the shock of the Global Financial Crisis had discredited free market fundamentalism, the subsequent stabilization of the financial markets and the unwillingness of the United States and other powerful countries to countenance major changes ensured that Amin's "wild ride" of globalization would continue. And so would the political reaction against it.

27

Thomas Piketty and Rising Inequality

"With all due respect to the 'dismal science,' this doesn't happen often," the *Guardian* journalist Stuart Jeffries wrote in a piece published on June 17, 2014. "Hundreds of people are queueing round the block for an economics lecture on a lovely summer's evening in London. And those are the people who have successfully booked seats. There's another queue of shifty-looking people hoping for return tickets and steeling themselves for disappointment."[1] The speaker at the Peacock Theater, just off the Aldwych, was Thomas Piketty, a forty-three-year-old professor at the Paris School of Economics who had recently published a seven-hundred-page book, *Capital in the Twenty-First Century*, in which he traced the long-term dynamics of inequality and warned that the prospect of recent trends continuing was "potentially terrifying."[2]

Piketty's book met the moment. The Global Financial Crisis and Occupy Wall Street's denunciations of "the 1 percent" were still on people's minds. Although the protest encampment at Zuccotti Park in lower Manhattan only remained in place for about two months in the fall of 2011, it came to symbolize widespread outrage about rising inequality and the privileges accorded to the financial sector and the uberwealthy. Occupy movements sprang up in other cities and countries, and even mainstream politicians responded to the concerns that the protesters raised. In a December 2013 speech, President Barack Obama described "dangerous and growing inequality and lack of upward mobility" as "the defining challenge of our time."[3] After an obscure German publisher put out Marx's *Capital* in 1867, it was largely ignored for years. *Capital in the Twenty-First Century* rapidly became an international bestseller. It was published in French in 2013. In April 2014 Harvard University Press rushed out an English version, which quickly sold out on Amazon .com. Shortly before Piketty arrived in London, the book reached number one on the *New York Times* Best Seller list for hardcover nonfiction.[4] By January 2015, it had reportedly sold more than 1.5 million copies worldwide.

Piketty was born in 1971 in a northern suburb of Paris. His parents were left-wing activists who, for a time, operated a goat farm in the French countryside. After high school, Piketty secured a place at the École Normale Supérieure, one of France's leading universities, where he did a degree in mathematics and economics. Graduate work followed at the London School of Economics and the École des Hautes Études en Sciences Sociales. He wrote a doctoral dissertation on the theory of taxation. In 1993, when he was just twenty-two, he moved to MIT as an assistant professor. Piketty seemed to be on the path to becoming an economic theorist at a top US university, a well-trodden path for mathematically adept French economists. But he decided to avoid that route. "I did not find the work of US economists entirely convincing," he recalled in the introduction to *Capital in the Twenty-First Century*. "To be sure, they were all very intelligent, and I still have many friends from that period of my life. But something strange happened: I was only too aware of the fact that I knew nothing at all about the world's economic problems."[5] Piketty decided to return to France and follow the example of his early intellectual inspirations, the French historians of the Annales School, such as Lucien Febvre and Fernand Braudel, who provided detailed chronologies of daily life over the centuries, creating a new kind of bottom-up history. After joining the French National Center for Scientific Research, he delved into historical data about income and wealth distribution, an area that many members of the economics profession had neglected.

In mainstream economics, the modern study of inequality dates to 1953, when Simon Kuznets, a Russian émigré who taught at Harvard, published a pioneering study of income trends in the United States. Kuznets's paper showed that between 1913 and 1948 the percentage share of total income received by the richest 1 percent of taxpayers had fallen from 14 percent to 9.5 percent.[6] In a December 1954 lecture to the American Economic Association, Kuznets hypothesized that inequality increases during the early stages of capitalist development, as rural workers move to higher-paying industrial jobs in the cities, then gradually falls back once a majority of the workforce is employed in the high-paying sector.[7] Over time, then, inequality follows an inverted U-shape, which became known as the Kuznets Curve. This reassuring pattern seemed to fit the United States in the period from 1870 to 1950, and the Kuznets Curve became widely accepted. However, even before Piketty started to study inequality, recent income data from the US Census Bureau was contradicting the Kuznets theory. Instead of continuing to decline, at least some measures of inequality—including the commonly used Gini coefficient—had started to rise again. "From 1966 (when the Gini coefficient reaches its lowest value of 0.405) to 1993, there is a clear upward trend in inequality," Edward N. Wolff, an economist at New York University, wrote in his 1997 textbook, *Economics of Poverty, Inequality, and Discrimination*, which was ahead of its time.[8] Over the same period, Wolff noted, the share of income received by the top 5 percent of households had risen from 15.2 percent to 18.6 percent.[9]

After examining tax data on income, wages, and inheritances, Piketty wrote a paper on how income shares had evolved in France over the twentieth century. His main finding was that from 1914 to 1945 inequality had fallen considerably, but it had subsequently remained pretty stable—a trend that didn't fit the Kuznets Curve.[10] A 2003 paper that Piketty wrote with Emmanuel Saez, a young French economist who had done a PhD at MIT, looked at the American experience and confirmed it didn't match Kuznets's pattern, either. "Top wage shares were flat before World War II, dropped precipitously during the war, and did not start to recover before the late 1960s but are now higher than before World War II," the Piketty-Saez paper said.[11]

How general were these findings? Since inequality statistics weren't entirely consistent across countries, it was hard to say. To address this problem, Piketty and Anthony Atkinson, an economist at Oxford, launched an international research project that generated consistent case studies of ten Western countries: Australia, Canada, France, Germany, Ireland, the Netherlands, New Zealand, Switzerland, the United Kingdom, and the United States. The studies, which were published in a 2007 volume, showed that during the first half of the twentieth century, inequality had declined across virtually all these countries, but more recently there had been a significant divergence. Since the 1970s, all six Anglo-Saxon countries had experienced a rise in top income shares, with the most dramatic shift coming in the United States.

In 2011, Piketty and his colleagues created a World Top Incomes Database, which is now called the World Inequality Database and covers dozens of countries. Two years later, Piketty, Atkinson, Saez, and another economist, Facundo Alvaredo, published an article in the *Journal of Economic Perspectives* that distilled their findings. It featured a chart showing the top 1 percent's income share from 1910 to 2010 in four English-speaking countries: the United States, the United Kingdom, Australia, and Canada.[12] Rather than resembling an inverted U—a Kuznets Curve—the lines on the chart looked more like a right-way-up U, with the bottom of the curves situated about 1980, when the Thatcher-Reagan revolution began. In 1910 the top 1 percent in the US had received about 18 percent of pretax income, the chart indicated. By 1979, this share had fallen to about 9 percent, but by 2010 it had rebounded to about 20 percent.

Although Piketty and his coauthors didn't provide a definitive explanation for the 1 percent's share doubling in just three decades, they suggested it was tied to the big reductions in the top rate of income tax that Reagan and Thatcher had pioneered. "When top marginal tax rates were very high, the net reward to a highly paid executive for bargaining for more compensation was modest," the economists wrote. "When top marginal tax rates fell, high earners started bargaining more aggressively to increase their compensation. In this scenario, cuts in top tax rates can increase top income shares, but the increases in top 1 percent incomes now come at the expense of the remaining 99 percent."[13] The language was calm, but the inference was clear: since the onset of the neoliberal era, the corporate plutocracy had been successfully waging a class war in reverse.

In *Capital in the Twenty-First Century*, Piketty laid out this message for a more general audience. The book featured a number of U-shaped income share curves, as well as data on inheritances, profit rates, income tax rates, and much else. "I will show that this spectacular increase in inequality largely reflects an unprecedented explosion of very elevated incomes from labor, a veritable separation of the top managers of large firms from the rest of the population," Piketty wrote in the introduction.[14] Of the top 0.1 percent of earners in the United States—the richest 10 percent of the 1 percent—he noted further on in the book, six or seven in ten were senior corporate executives or "supermanagers." "In all the English-speaking countries," he went on, "the primary reason for increased income inequality in recent decades is the rise of the supermanager in both the financial and non-financial sectors."[15]

Piketty wasn't the first observer to highlight the skyrocketing pay of CEOs, of course. After decades of financialization in the United States and other Anglo-Saxon economies, the path to megariches that Disney's Michael Eisner, General Electric's Jack Welch, and others had established in the 1990s was by now a well-trodden one. In 2011, Tim Cook, Apple's CEO, received salary, stock options, and other benefits worth $378 million:[16] 6,258 times the annual wages of an average Apple employee.[17] Such gargantuan payouts were justified on the grounds that the CEO's job was to create "shareholder value," which Apple had certainly done. (Between December 2001 and December 2014, its stock price had risen nearly a hundredfold.)

The triumph of the shareholder value movement was by this stage so complete that few people pointed out that its origins were relatively recent, or that one of its original promoters, the economist Michael Jensen, had expressed misgivings about some of its consequences. After a series of big accounting scandals in the early 2000s, including a huge one at the energy trading firm Enron, Jensen told an interviewer: "I was a defender of the move toward stock options and more liberal rewards for C.E.O.s. But I'm now a critic of where we got to."[18]

Piketty didn't address the shareholder value movement directly, but he dismissed the argument sometimes put forward by defenders of CEOs that their productivity had increased sharply, and their compensation had simply risen to match it. A more plausible explanation, he argued, was "that these top managers by and large have the power to set their own remuneration, in some cases without limit and in many cases without any clear relation to their individual productivity."[19] At most major corporations, pay for top executives was set by remuneration committees led by supposedly independent outside directors. But these directors tended to be senior executives, or former senior executives, at other major companies, and in many cases they rubber-stamped the huge "incentive" packages demanded by CEOs. "It is only reasonable to assume that people in a position to set their own salaries have a natural incentive to treat themselves generously, or, at the very least, to be rather optimistic in gauging their marginal productivity," Piketty noted wryly.[20]

His description of a self-enriching corporate elite harked back to Veblen's description of the "captains of industry" of his day. Piketty didn't make the connection, but citing estimates from *Forbes* magazine, he noted that the number of billionaires on the planet had risen from around 140 in 1987 to more than 1,400 in 2013.[21] Relying on various other sources, he estimated that the richest 0.1 percent of individuals in the world owned nearly 20 percent of all global wealth; the top 1 percent owned about 50 percent; and the top 10 percent owned somewhere between 80 and 90 percent.[22] Rampant wealth inequality was a global phenomenon.

Arguably, the charts and data that Piketty compiled in *Capital in the Twenty-First Century* were his biggest contributions to the public discourse. You didn't need a degree in economics, or an understanding of the Gini coefficient, to grasp the meaning of a line showing the income share of the 1 percent rising toward the sky. This empirical work helped shape the political debate about inequality in many countries, including the United States. However, Piketty—like Marx—wasn't content to describe how capitalism worked: he also wanted to explain its laws of motion. Much of *Capital in the Twenty-First Century* was taken up with discussions of the underlying economic forces that were driving up income and wealth inequality. In another evocation of Marx, Piketty developed a pair of simple mathematical equations that he said represented "The First Fundamental Law of Capitalism" and "The Second Fundamental Law of Capitalism."

Some of Piketty's exposition of these "laws" wasn't readily comprehensible to anybody who hadn't studied economic theory. But his basic ideas were straightforward enough. In a capitalist economy at any time, he explained, there are "forces of convergence" tending to lower inequality and "forces of divergence" tending to generate more inequality.[23] Among the benign forces that Piketty identified were rising education levels, which make workers more productive and raise their wages; higher taxes on the rich; and the diffusion of scientific knowledge, which gives people in poor countries access to technological advances. The forces of divergence included underinvestment in education, tax cuts for the rich, and the avarice of top executives. But Piketty argued that the most important factor was the tendency for the rate of return on capital—the annual income it generates in profits, interest, and dividends divided by its market value—to exceed the economy's growth rate.

At first glance, this observation, which can be expressed in mathematical terms as $r > g$, appears to be a trivial one, but it isn't. Over the long term, Piketty explained, the rate at which the economy expands sets an upper limit on the growth rate of wages and incomes. So if r is greater than g, the income (and wealth) of capitalists (including CEOs with large stock grants) tends to grow faster than workers' pay, and inequality increases. Piketty referred to the relationship $r > g$ as the "fundamental force for divergence" and, in another place, as "the central contradiction of capitalism."[24]

During much of the twentieth century, he pointed out, this contradiction had been held in abeyance because r had been less than g: Western economies had grown faster than the rate of return on capital, which he estimated at 4 to 5 percent a year in inflation-adjusted terms. As a result, inequality had fallen. But much of this rapid economic growth, Piketty argued, represented unrepeatable "catch-up" growth from the devastation of two world wars and the Great Depression. Going forward, he said, there was "ample reason to believe that the growth rate will not exceed 1–1.5 percent in the long run, no matter what economic policies are adopted."[25] It was likely, therefore, that "$r > g$ will again become the norm in the twenty-first century, as it had been throughout history until the eve of World War I."[26]

It was this dynamic that Piketty referred to as "potentially terrifying." In the first half of the twentieth century, he said, it had taken two world wars, which destroyed a great deal of capital and prompted governments to tax the rich at punitive rates, to produce a historic reduction in inequality. Then during the postwar decades, a combination of rebuilding, full employment, a new social contract between capital and labor, and the retention of high taxes on the wealthy had kept inequality in check for a further period. "A concatenation of circumstances . . . created a historically unprecedented situation, which lasted for nearly a century," Piketty wrote. "All signs are, however, that it is about to end."[27] With executive pay skyrocketing and globalization and political capture undermining the ability of individual governments to raise taxes on the rich, the forces of divergence appeared to be in ascendancy again, particularly in America. "The risk of a drift toward oligarchy is real and gives little reason for optimism about where the United States is headed," Piketty concluded.[28]

To counter these tendencies, he called for "a progressive annual tax on global wealth."[29] If democracy was to regain control over globalized capitalism, it needed to invent new tools, he said. His proposed levy would apply to all forms of wealth, including financial assets, real estate, and business assets, with "no exceptions." In the current political constellation, Piketty readily conceded, a global wealth tax was a "utopian idea." But he argued that the proposal was a useful "reference point" that, at least in theory, "would provide a way to avoid an endless inegalitarian spiral." Fortunes of less than a million euros would be exempted from the new tax. People with fortunes of one to 5 million euros would pay an annual levy of 1 percent, and people with more than 5 million euros would pay a 2 percent levy. Piketty also suggested that "one might prefer a much more steeply progressive tax on the largest fortunes (for example a rate of 5 or 10 percent on assets above 1 billion Euros)."

Despite all the hoopla that surrounded Piketty after *Capital in the Twenty-First Century* was published, the book got a mixed reception from his fellow economists. Writing in *The New York Review of Books*, Paul Krugman, who had highlighted the economic and political repercussions of soaring inequality in his own writings, called it "magnificent" and said it would "change both the way we think about society and the way we do economics."[30] In *The New Republic*, Robert Solow, the grand old man of American Keynesianism, hailed Piketty's $r > g$ formulation, labeling it the "rich-get-richer dynamic."[31] Elsewhere, however, Piketty encountered criticism from several different quarters, some of it well founded. Writing in *Dissent* magazine, James K. Galbraith, a Keynesian of the older school, pointed out that in commingling physical capital used in production (factories, machinery, and so on) with financial capital and real estate, Piketty had ignored the thorny question of how aggregate capital should be defined and counted, which Joan Robinson and her colleagues had raised in the 1950s. "This, I fear, is a source of terrible confusion," Galbraith wrote.[32]

Some Marxists criticized Piketty for dealing in theoretical abstractions that obfuscated the exploitation and class conflict at the heart of the capitalist system. On the right, reviewers suggested Piketty was propagating a "new Marxism." Amidst all these competing interpretations, Piketty didn't help matters by telling an interviewer that, despite the title of his book, he had barely read the original *Capital* and didn't consider Marx an important influence on him.[33] Inadvertently backing up these claims, Piketty also claimed that Marx's books didn't contain any data. Evidently, he hadn't made it as far as the famous chapter twenty-five of *Capital*, "The General Law of Capitalist Accumulation," in which Marx included a lengthy section on income trends in Victorian England that prefigured, in some ways, the sort of analysis that Piketty himself presented a century and a half later.

Politically, Piketty was a supporter of the progressive left rather than the revolutionary left. Intellectually, he regarded Marx's economics as overly simplistic. But in the introduction to his book, he had also acknowledged that "the principle of infinite accumulation that Marx proposed contains a key insight": if the growth rates of productivity and population are low, "then accumulated wealth naturally takes on considerable importance, especially if it grows to extreme proportions and becomes socially destabilizing."[34] As John Judis, an American author and journalist, pointed out in an article about Piketty and Marx, they both viewed capitalism as a historical process beset by internal contradictions, one of which was a tendency for inequality to increase.[35]

Although Piketty was using different intellectual tools, he was plowing in the same furrow as Marx. Indeed, the entire Piketty phenomenon was testimony to the reemergence, on a global scale, of the extremely top-heavy capitalism that the German revolutionary had made his subject. During much of the twentieth century, the forces of convergence—wars, tax policies, progressive social norms, public education, the enhancement of worker skills, labor unions—had held in check some of the system's darker tendencies. But by the new millennium the combination of neoliberal policies, globalization, labor-saving technological progress, and a shareholder value movement that glorified wealth creation had shifted the balance of power (and material rewards) back in favor of capital.

Despite the positive reviews from Krugman and Solow, some mainstream economists took Piketty to task for getting his neoclassical economics mixed up. They brought up something called the "elasticity of substitution," which is a measure of how easy it is to substitute capital for labor, or vice versa, in production. Piketty had assumed this elasticity was greater than one, which implies that the rate of return, r, doesn't decline much as capital expands, and so the share of income accruing to capital increases. In a 2014 article, Harvard's Lawrence Summers said the empirical evidence strongly suggested that the elasticity was less than one and concluded that "it is not at all clear that there is any kind of iron law of capitalism that leads to rising wealth and income inequality."[36] Another criticism came from the economist Matthew Rognlie, who was then a graduate student at MIT. After looking at the sectoral data on profits and income, Rognlie pointed out that in the United States, at least, much of the increase in the share of income going to owners of capital could be accounted for by the rising price of housing, which Piketty counted as part of the capital stock. Outside the housing sector, Rognlie said, the capital share hadn't increased much.[37]

Interesting as these critiques were to economists, they didn't take much away from Piketty's essential points that income and wealth inequality had risen sharply, and that so long as *r* remained disproportionately high, the "rich-get-richer dynamic" would likely continue to operate. The most serious and sustained challenge to Piketty's narrative came from Gerald Auten, an economist at the Treasury Department, and David Splinter, an economist at the Joint Committee on Taxation of the US Congress, who contested the basic claim that income inequality in the United States had skyrocketed. In a 2018 draft of a paper that was based on anonymized data from individual tax returns, Auten and Splinter said that if you looked at income after tax and transfer payments rather than at pretax income, which is what Piketty and Saez had done, and if you made some different adjustments for under-reported income, the picture was very different. Between 1979 and 2015 the share received by the top 1 percent went from 8.2 percent to 8.8 percent—an increase, but a very modest one compared to the doubling that Piketty and Saez identified.[38] In this revisionist version of recent American economic history, a progressive tax and benefits system had done much to mitigate diverging pretax incomes.

The paper by Auten and Splinter led to an extended back-and-forth with Piketty and his associates. In a 2018 article, Piketty, Saez, and Gabriel Zucman of Berkeley used a new methodology to estimate trends in US pretax *and* post-tax income. They conceded that "posttax national income is more equally distributed than pretax income: the tax and transfer system is progressive overall."[39] But their results still showed the 1 percent's share of post-tax income rising from 9.1 percent in 1979 to 15.7 percent in 2014, a very large increase.[40] Auten and Splinter contested this finding. In a 2023 paper, they updated their data to 2019 and concluded: "For after-tax income, which includes transfers, our analysis shows that the top one per cent share increased only 1.4 percentage points."[41]

The papers by Auten and Splinter received a good deal of media attention, and some commentators claimed they had discredited Piketty's thesis. Even on the basis of the authors' own figures, that was an exaggeration. In their 2023 paper, Auten and Splinter reported that between 1979 and 2019 the share of *pretax income* received by the 0.1 percent rose from 3.2 percent to 5.4 percent, a striking jump in proportional terms, and that the share of *post-tax income* increased from 2.1 percent to 3.0 percent, which was also a big increase.[42] So if you looked at the very, very rich, as opposed to the merely very rich, then, based on Austen and Splinter's own findings, income inequality had risen sharply. The two researchers also calculated Gini coefficients, which provide the broadest measure of inequality, for pre-tax and post-tax income. In both cases, the Ginis indicated a significant rise in inequality between 1980 and 2019.[43]

These findings jibed with other data. In 1982, when *Forbes* magazine published its first ranking of the wealthiest people in America, the shipping tycoon Daniel Ludwig topped the list with a net worth of $2 billion (about $6.5 billion in 2024 dollars).[44] In the 2023 *Forbes* list, Elon Musk was in first place, with a net worth of $251 billion, and there were eight other individuals worth more than $100 billion.[45] Merely to get on the *Forbes* list, you had to be worth nearly $3 billion. At the start of 1990, according to the Federal Reserve, the top 0.1 percent owned 8.6 percent of total US wealth; by the end of 2023, their share had risen to 13.5 percent.[46] An academic paper published in 2023 in the *Quarterly Journal of Economics* went further back in time and found an even bigger jump. Between 1978 and 2016, the article said, the top 0.1 percent's share of total wealth more than doubled—from 7.1 percent to 15.7 percent.[47]

Efforts to refute the basic picture that Piketty described were ultimately unconvincing. A more valid criticism of *Capital in the Twenty-First Century* was that it didn't fully explain where these huge new agglomerations of wealth at the very top were coming from. The proximate answer was clear: they were based on the remarkable growth of the tech sector, captive corporation remuneration boards, and stratospheric stock market valuations, which, in turn, reflected soaring profits and a high rate of return on capital. But what was it about twenty-first-century capitalism that was keeping profits so high that r remained above g year after year?

In a 2015 interview, Joseph Stiglitz emphasized the rise of monopolies and rent-seeking behavior, developments he had discussed in his 2012 book, *The Price of Inequality*. "So when you look at the top, it's monopoly power," Stiglitz said.[48] In an illuminating 2017 volume of essays titled *After Piketty*, Suresh Naidu, an economist at Columbia, argued that technological and political developments had combined to make it a lot easier for businesses and financial interests to extract monopoly rents from consumers and workers. The technology part of Naidu's thesis, which he labeled "wild Piketty," was that in the high-tech sector, firms' unit costs tend to decline as their output (or the number of people on their platform) increases: in economics jargon, these are "increasing returns" industries. "In a world of generic increasing returns, high fixed costs, and low marginal costs, monopolies will be pervasive," Naidu wrote.[49] In other words, the high-tech sector simply doesn't conform to the textbook picture of a competitive market. It is another beast entirely.

But rising monopoly power wasn't confined to high-tech, Naidu emphasized. In many other industries—airlines, banking, energy, pharmaceuticals, media—regulators had nodded through waves of consolidation that had reduced competition and left a few giants controlling the entire sector. "Generalized retrustification of the U.S. economy should make us dust off the old copies of Hilferding, Hobson, and Lenin," Naidu remarked.[50] During the same period, conservative legislation had weakened labor unions; conservative courts had strengthened property rights, such as patents, which he identified as a key component of capital; and investors had cheered these developments by revaluing corporate assets in the stock market. Put all this together, and widening inequality wasn't just a tech story. Ultimately, it was rooted in the conservative political backlash and financialization of the economy that began in the 1970s and continued unabated for decades.

On one level, this explanation was consistent with Piketty's argument that the Reagan-Thatcher tax cuts encouraged CEOs to grab more of the pie for themselves. But Naidu's narrative was a broader one, about how the owners of capital were able to mobilize the entire political system to protect their interests. "There is little in *Capital in the Twenty-First Century* about how inequality changes the political system," he noted. "This is a gaping missing chapter."[51] In trying to fill the hole, Naidu highlighted some new and old tools that the ultrarich could use to influence policies. Among the former were large campaign contributions, which the US Supreme Court had enabled in its landmark 2010 *Citizens United* ruling. Naidu pointed to research suggesting that roughly a quarter of traceable individual contributions came from members of the 0.1 percent. "When . . . the means to contest elections are allocated via the cash nexus, it is a short step to policy being set by the media dollar," he noted.

Turning to older tools that owners of capital had at their disposal, Naidu brought up the possibility of a "capital strike," in which businesses refuse to invest large amounts of capital in a political environment that they don't like, and the threat of capital flight to foreign countries with lower taxes and less regulation. Piketty himself had cited France during the Socialist administration of François Mitterand, in the 1980s, as an example where owners of capital effectively went on strike against policies they opposed, including a reduction in the workweek, the nationalization of some large companies, and the "solidarity tax on wealth." The examples of governments shaping their tax policies to satisfy the demands of the financial markets and multinational corporations were too numerous to need listing individually.

This discussion harked back to the doubts about Keynesianism that Michał Kalecki and Paul Sweezy had raised in the 1940s. It also went back to the three earlier thinkers whom Naidu mentioned—Hobson, Hilferding, and Lenin and indeed, all the way back to the *Communist Manifesto*'s description of the modern state as "a committee for organizing the common affairs of the whole bourgeoisie."[52] Naidu didn't go that far. He did say that anyone interested in reducing wealth inequality and containing the forces of divergence that Piketty identified needed to concentrate on "lowering the share of income paid out to property titles" and "regulating the financial markets that price those titles."[53]

Another issue with *Capital in the Twenty-First Century* was that it largely focused on trends in Western countries, where data was more readily available. (To their great credit, Piketty and his colleagues at the World Inequality Database subsequently expanded their coverage to the entire world, including developing countries.) In an era of hyperglobalization, this obviously raised the question of what was happening to inequality at the global level. One economist who set out to answer this question was Branko Milanović, an expert on inequality at the World Bank who subsequently moved to CUNY Graduate Center in New York. In his work at the Bank, Milanović and a colleague, Christoph Lakner, sought to reconcile the evidence that wages were stagnating in Western countries with the rapid income growth in places like China and India, which had been heavily exposed to globalization. In a 2013 paper, Milanović and Lakner encapsulated these global trends in a memorable chart that became known as the Elephant Curve because it looked like an elephant with its trunk in the air (see the figure on the next page).[54]

On the horizontal axis, the chart showed the entire world population divided into percentiles of after-tax income, and on the vertical axis, it showed

THE "ELEPHANT CURVE" (CHANGE IN REAL INCOME FROM 1998 TO 2008)

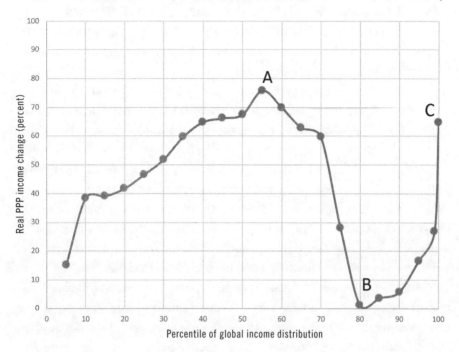

cumulative income growth (inflation adjusted) from 1988 to 2008. Reflecting the gaping divergence in incomes across countries, the incomes on the horizontal axis went from under $450 on the extreme left of the chart to about $1,400 in the middle to $71,000 on the extreme right. Most people in poor countries resided in the left third, near the elephant's tail, and most residents of advanced countries resided somewhere in the right third, near the elephant's trunk. The middle third consisted of three groups: residents of middle-income countries, the richest people in poor countries, and the very poorest folk in rich countries. By capturing everybody on the planet on one graph, Milanović and Lakner were able to display very clearly who the winners and losers from globalization had been.

The graph indicated that during the era of globalization, the biggest gainers were the people in the middle third, on the elephant's back, who saw their incomes rise by more than 60 percent over the twenty-year period. In his 2016 book, *Global Inequality: A New Approach for the Age of Globalization*, which expanded on his earlier article, Milanović explained that nine out of ten of these folks lived in a handful of Asian countries, which included China, India, Indonesia, Thailand, and Vietnam. The other people who had done very well out of globalization were those at the tip of the elephant's trunk on the far right of the chart, whom Milanović referred to as "global plutocrats."[55]

Conversely, two sets of people had made up the least ground. The world's poorest people, those residing on the elephant's tail, saw their paltry incomes rise by about 15 percent. The other laggards were located between the seventieth and ninetieth income percentiles, in the middle of the elephant's trunk. Most of them lived in advanced countries, Milanović explained. They were well off by global standards but not rich by the standards of their own societies. "In short: the great winners have been the Asian poor and middle classes; the great losers, the lower middle classes of the rich world," he wrote. "Such a bald statement may not surprise many people today, but it would certainly have been surprising to many if it had been made in the late 1980s."[56]

Milanović's last point was well taken. Rapid income growth in countries that not so long ago had been very poor, particularly China and India, defied widespread pessimism about the economic prospects of the developing world. Similarly, the income stagnation experienced by many workers in developed nations seemed to contradict the optimistic claims made by promoters of globalization in those countries. "Politicians in the West who pushed for greater reliance on markets in their own economies and the world after the Reagan-Thatcher revolution could hardly have expected that the much vaunted globalization would fail to deliver palpable benefits to the majority of their citizens," Milanović wrote.[57] The key takeaway from his fascinating book was that how you judged globalization depended very much on where you stood. For hundreds of millions of people in China and India, it had provided an escape route from the most acute poverty. But for residents of textile towns in the Carolinas or parts of the industrial American Midwest, globalization represented an existential threat. "It is this fundamentally ambivalent nature of globalization that I hope to bring out," Milanović wrote. "The reader needs to be constantly aware that globalization is a force both for good and bad."[58]

By the time Milanović's book appeared, an overdue reassessment of the impact of trade, particularly trade with China, on US jobs was taking place. In a 2012 paper for the National Bureau of Economic Research, three US economists—David H. Autor of MIT, David Dorn of the University of Zurich, and Gordon H. Hanson of the University of California at San Diego—pointed out that between 1991 and 2007 China's exports to the United States had increased by more than 1100 percent.[59] During roughly the same time period, China's share of global manufacturing had increased from about 1 percent to about 20 percent. "That's a massive, massive change," Autor pointed out in a 2017 interview. "We never see things like this occur in modern history."[60]

To isolate its impact on US manufacturing, Autor, Dorn, and Hanson divided the United States into more than seven hundred commuter zones. Previous studies had looked at the country as a whole and found the effects from rising trade to be small or nonexistent. Using their more geographically focused approach, Autor, Dorn, and Hanson found that areas with a lot of businesses that had been exposed to competition from China experienced several ill effects. "Rising exposure increases unemployment, lowers labor force participation, and reduces wages in local labor markets," the economists wrote. "Conservatively, it explains one-quarter of the contemporaneous aggregate decline in U.S. manufacturing employment."[61]

The economic fallout from the "China shock" helped to produce a political backlash against globalization that Donald Trump and other protectionists eagerly exploited. During his 2016 presidential campaign, Trump labeled NAFTA and the WTO "a disaster" and pledged to withdraw the United States from the Trans-Pacific Partnership, a trade deal that the Obama administration had negotiated with eleven Pacific Rim countries.[62]

In a paper published after the 2016 election, Autor, Dorn, Hanson, and a fourth author, Kaveh Majlesi, said they had identified a link at the county level between trade shocks and voting patterns in the election. "We find a robust positive effect of rising import competition on Republican vote share gains," they wrote.[63] The suggestion that trade and globalization could have cost the Democrats the 2016 election was hotly disputed. Other studies of voting patterns found that race, religion, and other cultural factors played a bigger role than economics in Trump's victory over Hillary Clinton.[64] But it was surely no coincidence that in 2021, when another Democrat, Joe Biden, returned to the White House, he adopted a much more skeptical approach to globalization than his Democratic predecessors. Biden left some of Trump's tariffs in place and introduced an ambitious industrial policy, which was designed to boost US manufacturing and "onshore" production that had moved abroad.[65]

As these debates about globalization and inequality were raging, Piketty largely kept a low profile. In June 2015, he had lunch with a journalist from the *Financial Times* at a deli not far from his office at the Paris School of Economics. A year had passed since his appearance at London's Peacock Theater. "I have had phases of promotion and conferences, which I enjoy very much, but I need to get back to normal life," he told the journalist.[66] Like it or not, though, Piketty had turned into a public intellectual in the grand French tradition. At the start of 2015, the Socialist government of François Hollande awarded him the Légion d'honneur: previous recipients included the existentialist philosophers Jean-Paul Sartre and Albert Camus, as well as the film actor Brigitte Bardot. Piketty refused to accept the prestigious prize, telling a reporter: "I don't think it's up to a government to say who is honorable. They would do better to focus on reviving growth in France and Europe."[67]

Piketty's decision to turn down the Légion d'honneur reflected his disillusionment with Hollande, whose government was following centrist policies and presiding over slow growth and high unemployment. In the 2017 Socialist presidential primary, Piketty supported Benoît Hamon, a former minister of education who campaigned on an ambitious program that included the introduction of a universal basic income, a shorter workweek, and big investments in green energy. The economist Julia Cagé, Piketty's wife, became Hamon's chief economic adviser, and Piketty himself wrote articles in *Le Monde* defending his proposals. At the end of January 2017, Hamon secured the Socialist Party nomination, defeating Manuel Valls, the former prime minister. But in the general election, which took place on April 23, he received just 6.4 percent of the vote, less than a third of the share garnered by Jean-Luc Mélenchon, the candidate of the far left.[68]

Piketty wasn't responsible for this crushing defeat, of course. It reflected a broader crisis of western Europe's center-left parties, which extended to Germany, Greece, Italy, Spain, and the United Kingdom. When these parties did achieve power, as the French Socialists did in 2012, they felt obliged to follow fiscally "responsible" policies, which, as Piketty intimated, checked economic growth and prevented them from expanding programs designed to raise living standards. Inside the eurozone, the adoption of fiscal auster-ity policies had been enshrined in the 1992 Maastricht Treaty, which was a triumph of neoliberal economics. A quarter of a century later, the policy straitjacket was still in place. Meanwhile, globalization and automation con-tinued to diminish the ranks of the industrial working class, which had been the traditional base of the center left.

Further heightening the difficulties facing the center-left, many working-class and lower-middle-class voters were shifting to the right, supporting anti-immigrant rabble-rousers like Le Pen and Trump, who stoked the same nativist and pro-authoritarian sentiments that Stuart Hall had remarked on in early Thatcherite Britain. In theory, these voters were the ones who would have benefited most from the redistributive tax-and-spending policies pro-posed by Hamon and Jeremy Corbyn, the leftist leader of Britain's Labour Party, who appointed Piketty to an advisory panel. Yet, these voters were increasingly supporting right-wing parties whose economic populism was strictly for show. Younger and more educated voters were trending left, but many of them were attracted to anti-establishment parties, like Podemos in Spain and the Five Star Movement in Italy. The crisis of "labourism," which Hall had identified three decades earlier, appeared to be turning into an exis-tential one—and one that certainly wasn't resolved by the resounding victory of the British Labour Party in the July 2024 general election, or the last-ditch victory days later of a broad-left coalition in the second round of French parliamentary elections.

Piketty, for his part, had become convinced that the economic splin-tering that was driving political polarization couldn't be reduced entirely to mechanistic economic trends of the sort encaspulated in the "laws" that he'd explored in *Capital in the Twenty-First Century*. In fact, he had come to believe that the persistence of chronic inequality in a democratic society could ultimately be explained only in the realm of ideas. "Every human soci-ety must justify its inequalities," he wrote in the opening passage of *Capital and Ideology*, a follow-up book that came out in 2019. "Unless reasons for them are found, the whole political and social edifice stands in danger of collapse."[69] The new book was even more massive than its predecessor, and it traced the history of dogmas that had been used to justify unequal outcomes. In premodern societies, Piketty argued, the notion of society as an organic whole served as the rationalization for rigid caste systems. Following the Brit-ish, French, and American revolutions, "ownership societies" arose, in which the "sacralization" of private property served as the basis of inequality.[70] In the twentieth century, more egalitarian and less market-friendly ideas gained ground, including those associated with social democracy and communism, only for them to be subjected to a successful counterattack, which ushered in an age of "hypercapitalism" and rising inequality. "Inequality is neither economic nor technological; it is ideological," Piketty wrote. "This is no doubt the most surprising conclusion to emerge from the historical approach I take in this book."[71]

It certainly surprised some readers of *Capital in the Twenty-First Century*, who had been led to believe that the economic formula $r > g$ was the "fundamental force for divergence." Now the famous formula had "all but disappeared," the writer Idrees Kahloon commented in *The New Yorker*.[72] Piketty appeared to have adopted Keynes's dictum that "the power of vested interests is vastly exaggerated compared with the gradual encroachment of ideas."[73] At first glance, his stated interest in the construction of "dominant narratives" that underpinned "the existing inequality regime"[74] also seemed to have echoes of Gramsci. But while the Italian Marxist had worked within a framework of class rule, he regarded intellectuals as the "deputies" of the dominant "historical bloc."[75] Piketty explicitly disavowed this approach, writing, "I insist that the realm of ideas, the political-ideological sphere, is truly autonomous."[76]

Piketty's intellectual evolution made for some interesting reviews, but in practical terms he ended up in the same place he had been in *Capital in the Twenty-First Century*: arguing for radical policies to reverse rising inequality. "The inequalities and institutions that exist today are not the only ones possible, whatever the conservatives may say," he wrote.[77] Incorporating his previous call for a global wealth tax, he laid out a reform agenda that included three key elements: power sharing within large firms, with workers' representatives getting half the voting rights on corporate boards; punitive tax rates on very high incomes and large fortunes to "make ownership of capital temporary";[78] and the introduction of a "universal capital endowment" along with a universal basic income. Taken together, Piketty wrote, these reforms would create the foundations for "a participatory socialism for the twenty-first century" that would "transcend today's capitalist system."[79]

If fully enacted, Piketty's policy agenda would surely have transcended the plutocracy. Keynes had raised the possibility of low interest rates euthanizing the rentier. Piketty was now proposing expropriation through the tax system.

Under his proposals, governments would introduce a "triptych" of progressive taxes on income, property, and inheritances, with marginal rates as high as 90 percent on the largest fortunes and incomes. Based on simple arithmetic, it seemed likely that Piketty's levies would hit the likes of Elon Musk, Bernard Arnault, and Jeff Bezos with tax bills of tens of billions of dollars. Piketty compared their putative impact to the breaking up of great landed estates in France during the French Revolution and, later, in Ireland, Spain, and Mexico. Once his ultraprogressive tax system was in place, he said, there would be sufficient revenues to fund all existing government programs, a new universal basic income, and a new universal capital endowment, which would provide every citizen with a lump sum payment of about 120,000 euros at the age of twenty-five, which would "open up new possibilities such as purchasing a house or starting a business."[80] The ultimate policy goal, Piketty said, was a "just society that allows all of its members access to the widest possible range of fundamental goods," with the latter term defined to include a proper education, decent healthcare, the right to vote, and the ability to participate as fully as possible in social and civic life.[81]

When *Capital and Ideology* was published, Trump was in the White House, Emmanuel Macron was in the Élysée Palace, and Angela Merkel was in the German Chancellery. Not surprisingly, some reviewers dismissed Piketty's tax and spending proposals as pie in the sky. In an immediate sense, this criticism was justified, but Piketty was drawing on the large canvas of history rather than setting out a program to win the next election. "The balance of power at any moment," he wrote in his conclusion, "depends on the interaction of the short-term logic of events with long-term intellectual evolutions from which come a wide range of ideas that can be drawn on in moments of crisis."[82] During the 2020 Democratic primary, the Democratic senators Elizabeth Warren and Bernie Sanders both proposed new wealth taxes. Two of Piketty's research associates, Emmanuel Saez and Gabriel Zucman, helped to design Warren's version, which would have imposed an annual tax of 2 percent on fortunes worth between $50 million and $1 billion, and 3 percent on fortunes above $1 billion.

In the big picture, the "long-term intellectual evolution" that Piketty was trying to bring about was a reformulation of the postwar social bargain to meet the changed circumstances of the twenty-first century. In September 2023, he gave a talk via video to a conference in New York organized by Columbia University's Center on Capitalism and Society. After reviewing some recent economic history and talking about some of the policies he proposed in *Capital and Ideology*, he stepped back from the experience of the past few decades and defended the social democratic experiment in managed capitalism that had preceded it. If we take a longer-term perspective, going back to the nineteenth century, the movement to reduce inequality and broaden prosperity had proved very successful, particularly in Europe, he insisted. "But there is still a long way to go," he added. "Social democracy is not a finished product."[83] Nobody in Piketty's audience, or outside it, could argue with that conclusion.

28

The End of Capitalism, or the Beginning?

On September 19, 2023, António Guterres, the secretary-general of the United Nations, addressed the seventy-eighth General Assembly in apocalyptic terms. "Our world is becoming unhinged," he declared. "Geopolitical tensions are rising. Global challenges are mounting. And we seem incapable of coming together to respond." Guterres, a former prime minister of Portugal, mentioned the war in Ukraine and military coups in the Sahel, but the core challenges he highlighted were more systemic: inequality, rising debt levels, authoritarianism, a "dysfunctional, outdated, and unjust" financial architecture, and "the most immediate threat to our future: our overheating planet." If the world didn't tackle these issues quickly, Guterres warned, it faced the prospect of "a Great Fracture in economic systems and financial systems and trade relations."[1]

The secretary-general wasn't the only one issuing dire warnings. Earlier in the year, a report from the World Economic Forum (WEF), which hosts an annual conference of political and business bigwigs in Davos, Switzerland, said, "We have seen a return of 'older' risks—inflation, cost-of-living crises, trade wars, capital outflows from emerging markets, widespread social unrest, geopolitical confrontation and the spectre of nuclear warfare—which few of this generation's business leaders and public policy-makers have experienced." And these risks were being "amplified by comparatively new developments . . . including accelerating climate change, unsustainable levels of debt, a new era of low growth, [and] low global investment and de-globalization."[2] In a survey of its network of "thought leaders" in business, government, academia, and civil society, the WEF listed five statements about the coming decade and asked the respondents to pick the one that most closely resembled their views. The most commonly selected statement was "consistently volatile across economies and industries with multiple shocks accentuating divergent trajectories."[3]

Declarations that global capitalism was in crisis were nothing new, of course: ever since the ringing declarations of *The Communist Manifesto*, critics had been predicting the demise of the system. In the 1940s, even two of capitalism's biggest champions—Schumpeter and Hayek—argued that it was doomed. (To them, the fatal threats were bureaucracy and socialism.) But had global capitalism ever faced so many serious challenges simultaneously? Writing in the *Financial Times* in October 2022, Adam Tooze, an economic historian at Columbia University, described the current conjuncture as a "polycrisis," noting: "In the polycrisis the shocks are disparate, but they interact so that the whole is even more overwhelming than the sum of the parts."[4] In a demonstration of just how fraught and contested the times were, some leftist commentators even criticized the term *polycrisis*, claiming that it obfuscated the fact that there was only one underlying crisis: capitalism itself. "Pandemics, climate breakdown, wars and global deflationary pressures are not mere externalities of the capitalist system but intrinsic to its operations— long predicted by a diverse group of thinkers," Farwa Sial, a research fellow at the University of Manchester, wrote on the *Developing Economics* blog.[5]

Throughout the history of capitalism, critics had argued that it was amoral, inequitable, and destructive, but rarely had the criticisms come together in such dramatic fashion. "The climate emergency, rising inequality, and pandemic diffusion have raised the question: for what purpose is capitalism fit?" the economists Wendy Carlin and Samuel Bowles, two cofounders of the CORE Econ project, which provides open-access teaching materials for economics students, wrote in a 2021 article about constructing a new political economy paradigm.[6] A 2023 opinion poll by the Harris Poll and *Forbes* found that "almost half of Americans, regardless of generation and race, say that capitalism is headed on the wrong path."[7]

In short, global capitalism was facing a crisis of legitimacy of a sort it hadn't experienced since the 1930s—one that extended to the right as well as to the left. During the Biden administration, two new conservative research institutes in Washington, DC, put out stinging critiques of globalization and market fundamentalism. "What has happened to capitalism in America?" one of the reports, from American Compass, began. "Businesses still pursue profit, yes, but not in ways that advance the public interest . . . Globalization crushed domestic industry and employment, leaving collapsed communities in its wake. Financialization shifted the economy's center of gravity from Main Street to Wall Street, fueling an explosion in corporate profits along-side stagnating wages and declining investment."[8] The other report, from the Edmund Burke Foundation's National Conservatism project, commented that "trans-national corporations showing little loyalty to any nation damage public life by censoring political speech, flooding the country with danger-ous and addictive substances and pornography, and promoting obsessive, destructive personal habits."[9]

In some ways, these criticisms echoed what leftists had been saying for generations. In others, they evoked the writings of the nineteenth-century arch-conservative Thomas Carlyle. Certain free market conservatives had constructed a moral defense of capitalism by adopting the sociologist Max Weber's argument that it was based on the Protestant values of hard work, thrift, sobriety, and self-reliance. The emergence of a new plutocracy, whose conspicuous consumption evoked the Gilded Age "captains of industry" that Veblen wrote about, made a mockery of this claim. In 2023 Amazon's Jeff Bezos took possession of a custom-built 417-foot-long superyacht that came with a helipad-equipped support vessel and was rumored to cost $500 million.[10] Meta's Mark Zuckerberg was building a fourteen-hundred-acre compound in Hawaii that reportedly included a blast-proof underground bunker.[11] "Nobody believes any more in a moral revival of capitalism," the sociologist Wolfgang Streeck, the longtime director of the Max Planck Insti-tute for the Study of Societies in Cologne, wrote. "The Weberian attempt to prevent it from being confounded with greed has finally failed, as it has more than ever become synonymous with corruption." Streeck made this com-ment in 2014. The subsequent decade only confirmed his point.[12]

So, what was the prognosis for capitalism, two and a half centuries af-ter Richard Arkwright opened Cromford Mill? One scenario was that the polycrisis would continue, intensify, and possibly even prove fatal—an out-come that Streeck predicted. Citing the examples of Polanyi, Marx, Keynes, Schumpeter, and others, the German scholar readily acknowledged that many of capitalism's most illustrious theorists had mistakenly predicted its demise. "I believe that this time is different," he added.[13] The list of systemic ills that Streeck identified was similar to the ones that Guterres and the WEF would produce years later: it included slow growth in output and productivity, "oligarchic redistribution," rising political extremism, and a lack of effective global leadership. The future, Streeck wrote, would bring a series of cascading crises in which "predictability and governability will decline further (as they have for decades now)." At some point, "the myriad provisional fixes devised for short-term crisis management will collapse under the weight of the daily disasters produced by a social order in profound, anomic disarray."[14]

Streeck didn't provide a timetable for the coming collapse, which was a shrewd omission on his part. Any prediction of capitalism's demise needs to take account of its powers of rejuvenation, which Marx himself pointed to, and the ability of governments to manage it through sticky patches. Although Keynesian policies are out of fashion today, they invariably reappear whenever capitalism is under serious threat. In 2020, as many countries shuttered large parts of their economies to control the coronavirus pandemic, global GDP fell by 2.7 percent, according to the IMF. This was first worldwide recession since 2009 and the deepest since World War II. But in 2021, after many Western governments introduced large stimulus packages and scientists discovered vaccines for Covid-19, global GDP rebounded strongly, rising 6.5 percent. In 2022 and 2023, it grew by 3.5 and 3.2 percent, respectively, confirming the recovery from the pandemic.[15]

For the second time in a decade and a half, governments had stepped in to save global capitalism. The Global Financial Crisis and the pandemic were obviously two very different phenomena, but both of them highlighted the dangers of unleashing the market and relying on the profit motive to allocate resources and capital. In advance of the 2008 blowup, deregulation led to excessive risk-taking by large financial institutions. During the pandemic, the global supply chain froze up, leaving many Western countries short of essential items like respiratory masks, diagnostic testing kits, computer chips, and baby formula. "The industries at the center of the supply chain—from shipping and rail to meat processing—had liberated themselves from rules imposed to limit their dominance," the journalist Peter S. Goodman wrote in his illuminating 2024 book, *How the World Ran Out of Everything*. "They had reprised the era of the Robber Barons in achieving monopoly status. This had delivered stupendous profits to shareholders while yielding danger and dysfunction for society at large."[16]

Still, global capitalism did survive the pandemic and it started to adapt to a new reality. The US government offered companies financial incentives to manufacture masks and computer chips on the US mainland. Major US companies, adopting the mantra of "resiliency," looked to source some of their most vital inputs from closer to home. This was another demonstration of capitalism's ability to shape-shift in response to new circumstances and policy regimes. From the nineteenth-century ideal of free trade and small government that was pioneered by Britain; to the Keynesian managed capitalism of the postwar era; to the globalized hypercapitalism of the late twentieth century; to the Chinese state capitalism that some observers see as the winning model for the twenty-first century—there have been many varieties of capitalism. In the decade and a half after the Global Financial Crisis, economists and commentators across the ideological spectrum were busy proposing new economic models—or old ones in new guises. The options being touted included a technology-driven revival in productivity and income growth that would give free market capitalism another lease on life; a drastic shift away from materialism and economic growth in the name of sustainability; a retreat into protectionism and economic nationalism; and the creation of a new managed capitalism for a postindustrial age of algorithms and platform monopolies.

Hovering over many of these discussions was the emergence of potentially transformative digital technologies, such as self-driving vehicles, drones, 3D printing, robotics, and, most ominously, large language artificial intelligence models. In their 2014 book *The Second Machine Age*, Erik Brynjolfsson and Andrew McAfee, two economists at MIT, wrote: "The key building blocks are already in place for digital technologies to be as important and transformational to society and the economy as the steam engine."[17] Modern economists refer to a technology that impacts the entire economy over extended periods as a "general purpose technology." (The idea goes back at least as far as Kondratiev, although he rarely gets the credit.) Brynjolfsson and McAfee argued that AI could turn out to be the most powerful general purpose technology of all. In response to the question "Is growth over?" they wrote, "Not a chance. It's just being held back by our inability to process all the new ideas fast enough."[18]

In 2020, Nicholas Crafts, the late English economic historian known for his foundational research on the British industrial revolution and his quantification of the productivity gains from Thatcherism, gave a presentation to the Bank of England about "AI as a General Purpose Technology."[19] Industrial revolutions are often associated with particular inventions, such as steam engines and electricity, but they really center on inventing new methods of invention, Crafts said in his talk, which he subsequently turned into a paper. During the first industrial revolution, he explained, the new methodology involved "systematic empiricism and experimentation," relying on basic mechanical principles.[20] In the second industrial revolution, during the late nineteenth century, many firms created product development laboratories that applied scientific research to the creation of marketable items. This was a more effective method of invention, Crafts said, and he identified another one associated with the spread of computers from the 1960s to the 2000s, which greatly reduced the cost of accessing knowledge and led to a third industrial revolution. The diffusion of AI, with its incredible capacity for scouring data and recognizing patterns, may amount to another new method of invention, Crafts argued, in which case it could be "the basis for a Fourth Industrial Revolution." As examples of AI's potential to facilitate the creation of new things, he cited halicin, the antibiotic discovered by MIT scientists in February 2020, and the solution of the "protein-folding problem" by Google's DeepMind model in November 2020.[21]

In November 2022, OpenAI, a Silicon Valley company that started out as a not-for-profit research laboratory, startled the world with its release of ChatGPT, a chatbot that could write essays, jokes (not necessarily funny ones), and computer code. Essentially a statistical prediction model that had been trained on massive amounts of data scraped from the internet, the chatbot had an astonishing ability to understand and generate natural language. Within two months of ChatGPT's launch, 100 million people were using it, making it the fastest-growing computer application ever, according to analysts at the Swiss bank UBS.[22]

By the fall of 2024, OpenAI was generating more than a billion dollars in revenue, according to media reports, and in the private markets, where venture capitalists and other investors buy securities that aren't publicly traded, it achieved a valuation of $157 billion.[23] Many prominent pioneers of AI had expressed concerns about the rapid commercialization of a potentially dangerous technology, but the profit motive had won out. Microsoft had invested $13 billion for a stake in OpenAI. Google had started including AI summaries in its search results. Meta and Amazon had released their own AI tools, as had the Chinese internet companies Baidu, SenseTime, and Alibaba. On Wall Street, the mania for AI-related stocks, particularly the semiconductor manufacturer Nvidia, had generated comparisons to the dot-com bubble of the late 1990s.

Amidst all this activity, it was hard to distinguish hype from reality, but the capabilities of chatbots impressed many of their users, Brynjolfsson included. "On a recent Friday morning, one of us sat down in his favorite coffee shop to work on a new research paper regarding how AI will affect the labor market," he and two colleagues, Martin Baily and Anton Korinek, wrote in a May 2023 article. "After entering a few plain-English prompts, the system was able to provide a suitable economic model, draft code to run the model, and produce potential titles for the work. By the end of the morning, he had achieved a week's worth of progress on his research." Raising the productivity of economists wouldn't necessarily do much for the economy. But what about researchers in mechanical engineering, materials sciences, chemistry, robotics? "If cognitive workers are more efficient, they will accelerate technical progress and thereby boost the rate of productivity growth—in perpetuity," the three economists wrote, echoing the argument of the economic historian Crafts. Their article included a chart showing how, in an optimistic scenario, the diffusion and further development of AI could lead to GDP and productivity nearly doubling in twenty years.[24]

In this scenario, Western capitalism would be resurgent, and the pessimists would be routed. Or would they? Toward the end of their article, Baily, Brynjolfsson, and Korinek acknowledged that a "bigger pie does not automatically mean everyone benefits evenly, or at all." They pointed to studies indicating that up to half of all US workers could eventually see many of their job tasks performed by AI. Many of these people could suffer wage cuts or lose their jobs entirely, Brynjolfsson, Baily, and Korinek conceded. But they also argued that history suggested the job losers would find new employment, writing: "Job destruction has always been offset by job creation."[25]

History does show that fears of the "end of work" have turned out to be exaggerated. It also demonstrates that the deployment of new technologies can have a devastating impact on the wages and livelihoods of certain groups of workers, handloom weavers in Lancashire and India being two famous examples. Given the speed at which digital technologies can be disseminated, it seems perfectly possible that the AI revolution will be even more disruptive than previous ones. After James Watt developed his steam engine in 1776, it took half a century for it to be widely deployed in factories across Britain. The spread of chatbots took a matter of months, and it was only one of the emerging technologies that could have a big impact on work patterns.

In a separate piece for *Daedalus*, a journal published by the American Academy of Arts and Sciences, Brynjolfsson acknowledged that managing the transition to AI represented a great challenge. The essential task, he said, was to persuade technology companies to turn away from developing products that replace human workers, and toward developing products that augment human skills and make workers more productive. "When AI augments human capabilities, enabling people to do things they never could before, then humans and machines are complements," Brynjolfsson wrote. "Complementarity implies that people remain indispensable for value creation and retain bargaining power in labor markets and in political decision-making."[26] Under these circumstances, human labor still has a productive and well-compensated role. But "when AI replicates and automates existing human capabilities," Brynjolfsson went on, "machines become better substitutes for human labor, workers lose economic and political bargaining power and become increasingly dependent on those who control the technology."[27] In more emotive language, a capitalist technological dystopia emerges.

Worries about the impact of AI merged with other concerns about the direction capitalism was taking, including its role in promoting climate change. "We are in the beginning of a mass extinction, and all you can talk about is money and fairy tales of eternal economic growth. How dare you!" Greta Thunberg, the young Swedish activist, said at a UN climate change summit in 2019.[28] For years a figurehead of the environmental movement, Thunberg was now associating herself with "degrowth," the idea that had its origins in turn-of-the-millennium France and the works of Nicholas Georgescu-Roegen.

The degrowth movement encompassed a number of different viewpoints, but they all shared the rejection of maximizing GDP growth as the primary goal of economic policy. "The faster we produce and consume goods, the more we damage the environment," Giorgos Kallis, an ecological economist at the Autonomous University of Barcelona, wrote in his 2018 book *Degrowth*.[29] "If humanity is not to destroy the planet's life support systems, the global economy should slow down." In a widely read manifesto, *Prosperity Without Growth*, that was originally published in 2009 and republished in 2017, Tim Jackson, a professor of sustainable development at the University of Surrey in England, wrote: "The myth of growth has failed us. It has failed the 1 billion people who still attempt to live on half the price of a cup of coffee each day. It has failed the fragile ecological systems on which we depend for survival. It has failed, spectacularly, in its own terms, to provide economic stability and secure people's livelihoods."[30]

As the debate about economic growth and sustainability intensified, one strand of discussion took up where the *Limits to Growth* debate of the 1970s left off, addressing the question of what rate of economic growth, if any, is consistent with very low, or even zero, carbon emissions. At the encouragement of member governments, the World Bank, the OECD, and the UN Development Program had endorsed "green growth," in which the rapid development of renewable energy sources and the spread of electronic vehicles, heat pumps, and other clean technologies would allow rising GDP to "decouple" from higher emissions. "This approach can deliver growth that is strong, sustainable, balanced, and inclusive," the Global Commission on the Economy and Climate, an international group of economists, former government officials, and business leaders, declared in a 2018 report.[31] Supporters of green growth pointed to the United Kingdom, which cut its carbon emissions in half between 1990 and 2022,[32] even as its inflation-adjusted GDP rose by about 80 percent.[33] This decoupling was achieved largely by eliminating coal-fired power stations and replacing them with a combination of renewable energy sources and natural gas. In April 2024, 59 percent of Britain's electricity came from renewables.[34]

Skeptics of green growth pointed out that most rich countries hadn't matched the UK's performance and that the developed world, taken as a whole, had failed to meet the commitments it made in the 2015 Paris Accords, which was designed to limit the global temperature increase to 1.5°C above preindustrial levels. "At the achieved rates, these countries would on average take more than 220 years to reduce their emissions by 95%, emitting 27 times their remaining 1.5C fair-shares in the process," Jason Hickel, an anthropologist at the Autonomous University of Barcelona, and Jefim Vogel, a PhD student at the University of Leeds, wrote in a study published in *The Lancet Planetary Health* in 2023. If the rich countries were to meet their Paris targets, Hickel and Vogel concluded, they "will need to pursue post-growth demand-reduction strategies, reorienting the economy toward sufficiency, equity, and human wellbeing, while also accelerating technological change and efficiency improvements."[35]

The emphasis on well-being and equity has long been a part of the degrowth movement. Although it is closely associated with the environmental movement, its intellectual roots also go back to the skepticism about capitalism and mass production that was voiced by thinkers like Carlyle, Ruskin, Veblen, J. C. Kumarappa, and E. F. Schumacher. Echoing some of these heretics, Jackson, in *Prosperity Without Growth*, called on advanced countries to shift their economies to the provision of local services, such as nursing and teaching, and to the development of more rewarding and less resource-intensive professions like handicrafts. "People can flourish without endlessly accumulating more stuff," he wrote. "Another world is possible."[36]

That may well be true. But abandoning economic growth as an objective rather than reformulating it as "green growth" would create huge challenges. As the Oxford economist Wilfred Beckerman pointed out in the 1970s, the strong growth of the postwar era helped keep distributional conflicts in check. The subsequent slowdown in growth coincided with rising political polarization and extremism. Another vital issue is whether shifting to degrowth would impose intolerable burdens on the world's poorest countries, many of which would dearly like to follow the growth path that China and India have trodden in recent decades. Even in low- to middle-income countries, the pursuit of GDP growth is widely seen as an imperative, and that's hardly surprising. On a global basis, according to the World Bank, the median household income in 2022 was just $7.75 a day.[37]

Can degrowth policies be reconciled with allowing poor countries to raise the living standards of their populations toward Western levels? In a 2021 blog post, Branko Milanović, the CUNY economist and expert on global inequality, explored two possible options for keeping global GDP constant, which is the most literal definition of degrowth. The first one involved freezing the world income distribution, so that everybody kept their current incomes. Under this option, Milanović pointed out, half of the world's population would have to live permanently on seven dollars a day or less, which surely wouldn't be acceptable to developing countries or proponents of degrowth. The second option involved reducing the living standards of people with incomes above the global average and raising the living standards of those below the average. According to Milanović's calculations, anybody living on more than sixteen dollars a day, which in Western countries is about 86 percent of the population, would be affected. The degrowthers "cannot condemn to perpetual poverty people in developing countries who are just seeing the glimpses of a better life, nor can they reasonably argue that incomes of 9 out of 10 Westerners ought to be reduced," he wrote. "The way out of the impasse is to engage in semi-magical and then outright magical thinking."[38]

In a blog post responding to Milanović, Jason Hickel, the author of the 2020 book *Less Is More: How Degrowth Will Save the World*, argued that in rich countries zero growth in GDP, or even declines, would be consistent with increases in human well-being if these countries reorganized their economies to eliminate wasteful consumption and meet genuine needs, such as healthcare, education, and a clean environment. "When it comes to human well-being, counting GDP is irrelevant," Hickel said. The real issue was that "capitalism is highly inefficient when it comes to meeting human needs; it produces so much, and yet leaves 60% of the human population without access to even the most basic goods."[39] What was ultimately needed, he insisted in *Less Is More*, was an "alternative, post-capitalist economy."[40]

The backlash against globalization that Dani Rodrik predicted during the 1990s didn't end with Brexit and the 2016 election of Donald Trump; neither did the rise of right-wing populism and the attacks on liberal democracy associated with it. "Half of democratic governments around the world are in decline, undermined by problems ranging from restrictions on freedom of expression to distrust in the legitimacy of elections," the Stockholm-based International Institute for Democracy and Electoral Assistance said on the occasion of releasing its annual review for 2022.[41] In the 2024 elections for the European Parliament, populist right-wing parties made big gains in many countries. And, of course, later in the year Trump won reelection. To be sure, many noneconomic factors contributed to the rise of the right; anti-immigrant sentiment, opposition to liberal cultural values, outright racism, and the propagation of conspiracy theories over social media all played a role. But demagogues like Trump, Viktor Orbán in Hungary, and Marine Le Pen in France were certainly exploiting a widespread feeling that globalization wasn't delivering the rewards its proponents had promised.

In response to the rightward shift, many centrist politicians, including President Joe Biden, reexamined their parties' commitment to free trade and ever-closer international integration. The Biden administration kept some of Trump's tariffs in place. It also embarked on an ambitious industrial policy, which provided generous subsidies for makers of semiconductors, solar panels, and electric vehicles that located production plants in the United States. In the first half of 2024, the administration raised import levies on steel and a range of Chinese goods, including semiconductors and electric vehicles. Although White House officials described these measures as limited and targeted, they provided a stark demonstration of how attitudes toward trade and globalization had shifted in the quarter of a century since the US government had championed China's entry to the World Trade Organization.[42]

In this changed environment, some economists argued that globalization was in wholesale retreat; others said the reversal had been exaggerated. Despite Brexit, the rising popularity of protectionist measures, and the coronavirus shutdowns in many countries, the volume of world trade and international capital flows, two standard metrics of globalization, had continued to rise. In 2022, according to the World Trade Organization, the overall value of merchandise trade (imports and exports of all goods) reached a new record of $25.3 trillion,[43] before falling back slightly in 2023 as the global rebound from the pandemic slowed.[44] Data on capital flows is incomplete, but cross-border lending by banks and other financial intermediaries had also continued to expand. In the first quarter of 2023, according to the Bank for International Settlements, banks' total cross-border claims reached $37 trillion.[45]

But proponents of the "deglobalization" thesis could also point to figures that supported their case. If you looked at the volume of trade in goods relative to the size of the world economy as a whole, rather than in dollar terms, it peaked in 2008, at about 50 percent, then fell back to about 42 percent in 2020.[46] According to the OECD, the level of foreign direct investment—cross-border purchases of ownership stakes in companies or projects—relative to world GDP was lower in 2023 than it was in 2013.[47] During the same period, rising threats of protectionism and the coronavirus pandemic's exposure of the fragility of international supply chains had led to a wave of "onshoring," in which multinational companies moved production or input sourcing closer to home. According to Barclays investment bank, the number of companies mentioning onshoring in their communications quadrupled between 2020 and 2022.[48]

The political pressures that were driving this turnaround showed no signs of relenting. In a November 2023 survey that the pollster YouGov carried out for the conservative think tank American Compass, 47 percent of respondents said the United States had suffered from globalization, compared to 33 percent who said it had benefited.[49] Attitudes were split along class and regional lines. Just 26 percent of "working class" respondents said the United States had benefited, whereas 44 of "upper class" respondents gave this answer. A similar division was evident between residents of US coastal cities and Americans living inland. As Rodrik predicted, the winners and losers from globalization had sorted themselves into rival camps.

This process wasn't necessarily complete. The trade theorist Richard Baldwin of the IMD Business School in Lausanne predicted that the next wave of offshoring would come in "intermediate services," such as running the numbers for accounting firms, analyzing medical data for insurance companies, and drawing up plans for architecture firms. Developing countries, Baldwin pointed out, still had a huge supply of workers who could do these jobs at lower cost than their equivalents in developed countries, especially if they utilized new AI tools. "What we will see therefore in the emerging markets is hundreds of millions of people getting richer," he wrote. "And in developed countries, your virtual offices will be filled with 'telemigrants.' The bad news, of course, is that this will likely foster a backlash against globalization in high-wage nations."[50] That backlash was already well advanced. The question was how far AI would accentuate it.

When Antonio Gramsci was languishing in Mussolini's prisons during the 1920s and '30s, he had all too much time to think about the relationship between economic forces and economic ideologies. One of the key insights in the notebooks he kept was that in certain circumstances, the two came together in a "historical bloc" that could exercise political power through consent rather than force, a phenomenon he referred to as "hegemony." Much ink has been spilled on the relative importance that Gramsci attributed to the forces and the ideologies, but he stated clearly that it was the combination that mattered. He distinguished between "willed" ideologies, which were arbitrary and rationalistic human creations, and "historically organic ideologies," which arose from definite material circumstances and were "necessary to a given structure." The former had little practical influence, Gramsci argued, but the latter could move mountains.[51]

The managed capitalism of the postwar era was based on a hegemonic bloc consisting of manual workers, educated liberals, domestically focused businesses, long-term capital, the continued exclusion of many parts of the world, and Keynesian/social democratic policy ideas. The globalized hypercapitalism that followed the end of the Cold War was based on a bloc consisting of educated workers, internationally minded businesses, short-term capital, the entry of previously excluded parts of the world, and free market policy ideas. The question, going into the second quarter of the twenty-first century, was what sort of historical bloc, if any, could exercise power in a world shrunken by digital technology but also increasingly splintered.

Chinese state capitalism arguably represented a potentially hegemonic force. But its undemocratic nature blunted its appeal in other countries, and so did the dramatic slowdown in the Chinese economy after Xi Jinping took over as China's leader in 2012. In many countries, including the United States and Germany, right-wing parties supported by disgruntled and nativist voters were still making progress. Trump's return to the White House on a platform of tariffs and mass deportation of undocumented immigrants was the most dramatic manifestation of this trend. The presence in his circle of Elon Musk and various Wall Street tycoons who had benefitted enormously from globalization and financialization highlighted some of the glaring inconsistencies in the right-wing populist movement, but that didn't trouble Trump or his vice president, J. D. Vance, who had once worked for a venture capital firm and defended globalization, but now positioned himself as an ersatz philosopher of the new right. At the 2024 Republican National Convention, Vance stated blithely, "We're done . . . catering to Wall Street. We'll commit to the working man."[52]

On the far left, replacing capitalism remained the ultimate goal. But with what? In some places, such as East Germany, there was still some nostalgia for the old communist model of state ownership and central planning. Elsewhere, though, many people on the left were more enthusiastic about creating new institutions and spaces that operated independently of the state and of the monolithic capitalist economy: protest encampments, worker cooperatives, bartering and recycling networks, communal farms, and small-scale artisanal enterprises.

Even though names like Owen and Thompson and Fourier no longer figured prominently on the left, the goal of creating institutions, communities, and entire subeconomies that operate beyond the cash nexus and the profit motive was one that went back to the early nineteenth century. Two centuries on, its modern proponents hadn't really demonstrated how they would overcome the practical problems that plagued their predecessors, especially if their ideas were to be applied at the national or global level. But the lure of what Silvia Federici, in her 2019 book, *Re-enchanting the World*, described as a "new commons" is a timeless one. "For what the commons in essence stands for," Federici wrote, "is the recognition that life in a Hobbesian world, where one competes against all and prosperity is gained at the expense of others, is not worth living and is a sure recipe for defeat."[53]

On the center left, where the intellectual blueprint for the postwar version of managed capitalism had originated, the search for a new form of the genus that could transcend social, racial, and geographic divides was particularly urgent. There was no shortage of proposals to address specific problems. In a 2019 essay, "Economics After Neoliberalism," Dani Rodrik, Columbia's Suresh Naidu, and Berkeley's Gabriel Zucman presented a long list of policy ideas from a new group they had created, Economists for Inclusive Prosperity. The proposals included establishing wage boards in low-wage industries to rein in employers' monopsony power, which Joan Robinson highlighted in her early work; expanding early childhood education programs as a means of raising the lifetime incomes of children from poor families; taxing multinational corporations where they make their sales to reduce tax avoidance; reforming the patent system to reduce monopoly power; beefing up international financial regulation; and including labor standards in trade agreements. The thinking behind this expansive agenda was that there was no quick fix for twenty-first-century capitalism: the entire system needed a makeover. "These proposals take Polanyi's words to heart," Rodrik, Naidu, and Zucman wrote: "To work well, crucial markets (including markets for labor, land, and capital) must be embedded in nonmarket institutions, and the 'rules of the game' must be supplied by government."[54]

The mention of Polanyi was a reminder of the stakes in these policy debates. In containing capitalism within a set of rules and social norms, postwar Keynesian social democracy had seemingly refuted Polanyi's argument that socialism or fascism was the logical end point of the system. But when neoliberalism supplanted Keynesianism, it enabled capitalism, once again, to break free of its bounds. In their 2021 paper where they raised the question of what purpose capitalism served, Samuel Bowles and Wendy Carlin argued that efforts to build a new economic paradigm should be organized around reversing this process and "shrinking capitalism" to a "diminished space," where its strengths, such as the capacity of competition to spur innovation, would serve the community.

Political and economic forces were aligning with this new paradigm, Bowles and Carlin argued. Intensifying concerns about climate change, inequality, and wage stagnation were undermining support for capitalism in general terms, while the rise of AI and robotics represented a threat to the traditional hierarchical capitalist firm, in which workers carried out routine, preassigned tasks for a set wage or salary. As technology eliminated these positions, the jobs that survived would involve more nuanced and complex tasks, which were far more difficult for employers to monitor effectively. One potential solution to this problem, Bowles and Carlin said, was to switch to teamwork and reputation-based rewards, of the sort common in open-source and open-science settings. A more draconian option was to introduce Amazon-style surveillance of employees. A third option was to abandon the traditional corporate structure and hire gig workers who get paid on a piecework basis. "By reducing the share of economic activity over which capitalist firms have a comparative advantage, the first and the third solution—team-based open source and the gig economy—shrink capitalism," Bowles and Carlin wrote. "The second—Amazon-type monitoring—has convinced many that capitalism should be shrunk."[55]

Bowles and Carlin weren't endorsing the pernicious practices of platform companies like Uber and Lyft. They were pointing out that doing gig work is different from being employed on a full-time basis—they compared it to the preindustrial "putting out" system—and pointing out that technology-driven capitalism was, to some extent, eating itself. They also argued that this cannibalization was creating space for new economic ideas and alternative economic forms, such as not-for-profits, worker-owned cooperatives, and community-organized public commons, which had broad appeal across the entire left and possibly beyond it. "This is a confluence that could propel a new paradigm in political economy to dominance," the article concluded.[56]

The idea of shrinking capitalism seemed like one a broad range of thinkers could unite around, from Bowles and Carlin to Silvia Federici to Joseph Stiglitz. In his 2024 book *The Road to Freedom: Economics and the Good Society*, Stiglitz called for a "decentralized economy with a rich ecology of institutions." Noting the many encroachments that capitalism had made in recent decades, he wrote, "There must be large parts of the economy that are not and cannot be driven by profits. These include much of the health, education, and care sectors, in which the narrow pursuit of profits often leads to perverse results."[57] Stiglitz also called for restrictions on the activities of platform monopolies, particularly social media companies, arguing that their algorithms had "enabled the incitement of violence and the spread of hate speech and induced anti-social behavior."[58]

That some of Stiglitz's criticisms jibed with those of Federici and others with the National Conservatism project was perhaps an indication of the scope for creating a broad-ranging coalition to rein in hypercapitalism. Already, however, efforts to create a new economic paradigm were running into pushback from free market conservatives. In July 2023, dozens of them, including Jeb Bush, Karl Rove, and representatives of the Mont Pelerin Society, the American Enterprise Institute, and the Capitalist League, issued a statement of principles proclaiming, "The free enterprise system is the foundation of prosperity."[59] During the 1930s American conservatives had issued similar arguments when they opposed FDR's New Deal. In the early 1940s, Hayek issued his famous warning that the shift toward collectivism could lead to serfdom. More recently, some conservatives had argued that the government response to the coronavirus pandemic, which included large stimulus programs, had been overweening. It wasn't perfect, but it had succeeded in heading off a lengthy economic slump, and, in some of its particulars, it was highly illuminating. The American Rescue Act converted an existing program of tax credits for low-paid workers with children into a monthly universal cash benefit of $300 per child. In 2021, after this policy was introduced, the rate of child poverty, as measured by the Census Bureau's Supplemental Policy Measure, fell from 9.7 percent to 5.2 percent in one year. In 2022, after the expanded tax credits were eliminated, the child poverty rate shot up to 12.4 percent—the biggest one-year increase on record.[60]

The lesson of this brief policy experiment was clear: where the political intent is present, it is perfectly possible to reduce child poverty, just as it was possible, in the twentieth century, to reduce the prevalence of poverty in old age by introducing state pensions.

The system can be reformed: the challenge is to summon the will and the means to do it. With the rise of right-wing populism, profit-driven AI, and a tech and finance oligarchy that was increasingly uninhibited about exerting its political influence, the task, going into the second quarter of the twenty-first century, seemed more formidable than ever. But for more than two hundred years, capitalism has evolved in waves and counterwaves, some of which are driven by its inner conflicts, as identified by Marx and his followers; some by technological developments, as in the Kondratiev "long wave" model; and others by political pressures, as in Polanyi's "double movement." At any given moment, it's difficult (if not impossible) to tell how long the current configuration will survive, or what will succeed it. But the system cannot rest. This has been true throughout its history. It will remain true until Wolfgang Streeck or one of his descendants is eventually proved right.

Notes

Introduction

1. Jeff Stein, "Here's the Full Text of Bernie Sanders's Iowa Speech," *Vox*, February 2, 2016, https://www.vox.com/2016/2/2/10892752/bernie-sanders-iowa-speech.
2. Frank Newport, "Democrats More Positive About Socialism Than Capitalism," Gallup, August 13, 2018, https://news.gallup.com/poll/240725/democrats-positive-socialism-capitalism.aspx.
3. "Public Opinion in the Post-Brexit Era," Legatum Institute, October 2017, 13, https://lif.blob.core.windows.net/lif/docs/default-source/default-library/1710-public-opinion-in-the-post-brexit-era-final.pdf.
4. William Haller, "Southey's Later Radicalism," *PMLA* 37, no. 2 (June 1922), 286, https://www.jstor.org/stable/pdf/457385.pdf.
5. G.D.H. Cole, *Socialist Thought: The Forerunners 1789–1850* (London: Macmillan, 1953).
6. John Ruskin to Lily Armstrong, November 19, 1866, in *The Letters of John Ruskin, Volume 1: 1827–1869* (London: George Allen, 1909), 520.
7. "Capitalism: What Is It?," *Throughline*, NPR, June 24, 2021, https://www.npr.org/transcripts/1008906741.
8. Karl Marx and Frederick Engels, *The Communist Manifesto: A Modern Edition* (London: Verso Books, 1998), chapter 3.
9. Johnny Fuller, "Panic of 1857," *The Economic Historian*, January 6, 2022, https://economic-historian.com/2020/07/panic-of-1857.
10. Karl Marx and Frederick Engels, *Collected Works, Volume 40: Letters 1856–59* (London: Lawrence and Wishart, 2010), 191.
11. Marx and Engels, *Collected Works, Volume 40*, 197.
12. Jürgen Kocka, *Capitalism: A Short History* (Princeton, NJ: Princeton University Press, 2016), 3.
13. *Encyclopaedia Britannica*, 1922; Kocka, *Capitalism*, 5.
14. Kocka, *Capitalism*, viii.

1. William Bolts and the East India Company

1. R. S. Fitton, *The Arkwrights: Spinners of Fortune* (Manchester: Manchester University Press, 1989), 28.
2. Derwent Valley Mills World Heritage Site, "Key Sites—Cromford Mill Complex," n.d., https://

www.derwentvalleymills.org/discover/derwent-valley-mills-history/derwent-valley-mills
-key-sites/cromford-mill-complex.

3. E. J. Hobsbawm, *The Age of Revolution: 1789–1848* (London: Weidenfeld and Nicolson, 1962), 29.

4. Nicholas Crafts, *Forging Ahead, Falling Behind and Fighting Back: British Economic Growth from the Industrial Revolution to the Financial Crisis* (Cambridge: Cambridge University Press, 2018), 2, table 1.

5. "Global GDP over the Long Run," Our World in Data, May 16, 2024, https://ourworldindata.org/grapher/world-gdp-over-the-last-two-millennia.

6. US Census, "Historical Estimates of World Population: 1750, UN Estimate," December 5, 2022, https://www.census.gov/data/tables/time-series/demo/international-programs/historical-est-worldpop.html; 2023 estimate: Worldometer, "Current World Population," https://www.worldometers.info/world-population.

7. Nick Robins, *The Corporation That Changed the World* (London: Pluto Press, 2012); William Dalrymple, *The Anarchy* (New York: Bloomsbury, 2019).

8. William Bolts, *Considerations on India Affairs; Particularly Respecting the Present State of Bengal and Its Dependencies to Which Is Prefixed, a Map of Those Countries, Chiefly from Actual Surveys*, 2nd ed. (London, 1772), 12, https://archive.org/details/in.ernet.dli.2015.195631.

9. Robins, *Corporation That Changed the World*; Dalrymple, *Anarchy*; N. L. Hallward, *William Bolts: A Dutch Adventurer Under John Company* (Cambridge: Cambridge University Press, 1920), https://archive.org/details/williamboltsdutc00hallrich.

10. Robins, *Corporation That Changed the World*, 66.

11. Robins, *Corporation That Changed the World*, chapters 3 and 4.

12. Robins, *Corporation That Changed the World*, chapter 4; Dalrymple, *Anarchy*, chapters 3–5.

13. Robins, *Corporation That Changed the World*, 77.

14. Robins, *Corporation That Changed the World*, 29.

15. Nicholas B. Dirks, *The Scandal of Empire: India and the Creation of Imperial Britain* (Cambridge, MA: Belknap Press of Harvard University Press, 2006), 250–58.

16. Dalrymple, *Anarchy*, 168.

17. Sir John Malcolm, *The Life of Robert, Lord Clive*, vol. 2 (London: John Murray, 1836), chapter 14, https://www.gutenberg.org/files/54633/54633-h/54633-h.htm#f271.

18. Robins, *Corporation That Changed the World*, 97. These estimates are derived from P. J. Marshall, *East Indian Fortunes: The British in Bengal in the Eighteenth Century* (Oxford: Clarendon Press, 1976), table VI, 232; table VII, 241; table VIII, 250.

19. Robins, *Corporation That Changed the World*, 89; Dirks, *Scandal of Empire*, 53.

20. Hallward, *William Bolts*, 89; Bolts, *Considerations on India Affairs*, 123–24.

21. Hallward, *William Bolts*, 115–31.

22. Robins, *Corporation That Changed the World*, 84–101.

23. Robins, *Corporation That Changed the World*, 95.

24. Robins, *Corporation That Changed the World*, 94.

25. Dalrymple, *Anarchy*, 220.

26. Dalrymple, *Anarchy*, 219.

27. Bolts, *Considerations on India Affairs*, 191; Dalrymple, *Anarchy*, 226–28.

28. Bolts, *Considerations on India Affairs*, 193.

29. Bolts, *Considerations on India Affairs*, 190.

30. Bolts, *Considerations on India Affairs*, ix.

31. Bolts, *Considerations on India Affairs*, 192.

32. Bolts, *Considerations on India Affairs*, 219–20. Also quoted in James M. Vaughn, *The Politics of Empire at the Accession of George III* (New Haven, CT: Yale University Press, 2019), 199.

33. Dirks, *Scandal of Empire*, 254.

34. Robins, *Corporation That Changed the World*, 81. See also Romesh Dutt, *The Economic History of India Under Early British Rule* (1906); and Sanjeev Sabhlok, "William Bolts's 1772 Book, 'Considerations on India Affairs,'" August 18, 2018, https://www.sabhlokcity.com/2018/08/william-bolts-1772-book-considerations-on-india-affairs.

35. "Lord Clive's Speech in the House of Commons," March 30, 1772, famineanddearth.exeter.ac.uk.

36. Robins, *Corporation That Changed the World*, 80.
37. For details of bailout and subsequent legislation, see Robins, *Corporation That Changed the World*, 111–12; and Dalrymple, *Anarchy*, 228–31.
38. Hallward, *William Bolts*, 203.

2. Adam Smith on Colonial Capitalism and Slavery

1. Ian Simpson Ross, *The Life of Adam Smith* (New York: Oxford University Press, 1995), 241; Adam Smith, *The Correspondence of Adam Smith*, ed. Ernest Campbell Mossner and Ian Simpson Ross (Indianapolis: Liberty Classics, 1987), 162.
2. Ross, *Life of Adam Smith*, 241.
3. Adam Smith, *An Inquiry into the Nature and Causes of the Wealth of Nations*, Books I–III (London: Penguin Classics, 1986), Book I, 109–10.
4. Smith, *Wealth of Nations*, Book I (1986), 115.
5. Adam Smith, *An Inquiry into the Nature and Causes of the Wealth of Nations*, Books IV–V (London: Penguin Classics, 1999), 214.
6. Smith, *Wealth of Nations*, Book IV (1999), 32.
7. Dugald Stewart, "Account of the Life and Writings of Adam Smith, LL.D.," *Transactions of the Royal Society of Edinburgh* (1793), 322, https://delong.typepad.com/files/stewart.pdf.
8. Branko Milanović, *Visions of Inequality* (Cambridge, MA: Belknap Press of Harvard University Press, 2023), 62.
9. Smith, *Wealth of Nations*, Book I (1986), 232.
10. Smith, *Wealth of Nations*, Books IV–V (1999), xxxi.
11. Smith, *Wealth of Nations*, Books IV–V (1999), 153.
12. Smith, *Wealth of Nations*, Books IV–V (1999), 162.
13. Smith, *Wealth of Nations*, Books IV–V (1999), 212.
14. Smith, *Wealth of Nations*, Books IV–V (1999), 217.
15. Smith, *Wealth of Nations*, Books IV–V (1999), 215.
16. Smith, *Wealth of Nations*, Books IV–V (1999), 221.
17. Smith, *Wealth of Nations*, Books IV–V (1999), 220–21.
18. Smith, *Wealth of Nations*, Books IV–V (1999), 224.
19. Ross, *Life of Adam Smith*, 253.
20. Smith, *Wealth of Nations*, Books IV–V (1999), 223.
21. Smith, *Wealth of Nations*, Books IV–V (1999), 225.
22. Smith, *Wealth of Nations*, Books IV–V (1999), 226.
23. Smith, *Wealth of Nations*, Books IV–V (1999), 187.
24. Smith, *Wealth of Nations*, Books IV–V (1999), 165.
25. Smith, *Wealth of Nations*, Books IV–V (1999), 72.
26. Smith, *Wealth of Nations*, Books IV–V (1999), 209.
27. Trans-Atlantic Slave Trade Database, 2021, Slavevoyages,org, https://www.slavevoyages.org/assessment/estimates.
28. Trans-Atlantic Slave Trade Database.
29. Trans-Atlantic Slave Trade Database.
30. The National Archives, "Slavery and the British Transatlantic Slave Trade," https://www.nationalarchives.gov.uk/help-with-your-research/research-guides/british-transatlantic-slave-trade-records.
31. Richard B. Sheridan, "The Formation of Caribbean Plantation Society, 1689–1748," in *The Oxford History of the British Empire, Volume II: The Eighteenth Century* (New York: Oxford University Press, 1998), table 18.2, 401.
32. Joyce Appleby, *The Relentless Revolution: A History of Capitalism* (New York: W. W. Norton, 2010), 63.
33. Richard B. Sheridan, *Sugar and Slavery: An Economic History of the British West Indies, 1623–1775* (Baltimore: Johns Hopkins University Press, 1974), 306.
34. J. R. Ward, "The Profitability of Sugar Planting in the British West Indies, 1650–1834," *The Economic History Review* 31, no. 2 (May 1978), table 9, 207.
35. Sheridan, "Formation of Caribbean Plantation Society," 412.
36. Sanchez Manning, "Britain's Colonial Shame: Slave-owners Given Huge Payouts After Abo-

lition," *Independent* (US ed.), February 24, 2013, https://www.independent.co.uk/news/uk/home-news/britain-s-colonial-shame-slaveowners-given-huge-payouts-after-abolition-8508358.html.

37. Smith, *Wealth of Nations*, Book III (1986), 488–89.
38. Trans-Atlantic Slave Trade Database.
39. Anthony Tibbles, "TextPorts Conference, April 2000," Liverpoolmuseums.org.uk /ports-of-transatlantic-slave-trade.
40. Malachy Postlethwayt, *The African Trade, the Great Pillar and Support of the British Plantation Trade in North America* (London, 1745), 4.
41. Postlethwayt, *African Trade*, 34.
42. James Steuart, *An Inquiry into the Principles of Political Economy*, Book II: *Of Trade and Industry* (1767), https://www.marxists.org/reference/subject/economics/steuart/book2.htm.
43. Smith, *Wealth of Nations*, Books IV–V (1999), 178–79.
44. Smith, *Wealth of Nations*, Books IV–V (1999), 187.
45. Robert C. Allen, *Global Economic History: A Very Short Introduction* (New York: Oxford University Press, 2011), 23.
46. Allen, *Global Economic History*, 21–25; "GDP per Capita in England," Our World in Data, https://ourworldindata.org/grapher/gdp-per-capita-in-the-uk-since-1270.
47. John Brewer, *The Sinews of Power: War, Money, and the English State, 1688–1783* (Cambridge, MA: Harvard University Press, 1990), xvii.
48. Nick Robins, *The Corporation That Changed the World* (London: Pluto Press, 2012), 118; Ross, *Life of Adam Smith*, 353, 360.
49. Smith, *Wealth of Nations*, Books IV–V (1999), 343.
50. Smith, *Wealth of Nations*, Books IV–V (1999), 341.
51. Smith, *Wealth of Nations*, Books IV–V (1999), 330–31.
52. Sven Beckert, *Empire of Cotton: A Global History* (New York: Knopf, 2014), 76.

3. The Logic of the Luddites

1. Brian Bailey, *The Luddite Rebellion* (New York: NYU Press, 1998), 30.
2. Bailey, *Luddite Rebellion*, 53–57.
3. Bailey, *Luddite Rebellion*, 41–43.
4. Bailey, *Luddite Rebellion*, 94–108.
5. Bailey, *Luddite Rebellion*, 103.
6. Bailey, *Luddite Rebellion*, x–xi.
7. Bailey, *Luddite Rebellion*, 63.
8. Kirkpatrick Sale, *Rebels Against the Future* (Reading, MA: Addison-Wesley, 1996), 70; see also J. L. Hammond and Barbara Hammond, *The Town Labourer, 1760–1832* (London: Longmans, 1966).
9. Michael E. Rose, Keith Falconer, and Julian Holder, *Ancoats: Cradle of Industrialisation* (Swindon: English Heritage, 2011), https://historicengland.org.uk/images-books/publications/ancoats/ancoats.
10. Sven Beckert, *Empire of Cotton: A Global History* (New York: Knopf, 2014), 74.
11. H. Heaton, "Benjamin Gott and the Industrial Revolution in Yorkshire," *The Economic History Review* 3, no. 1 (January 1931), 52–53, https://www.jstor.org/stable/2590622.
12. Heaton, "Gott and the Industrial Revolution," 54.
13. Heaton, "Gott and the Industrial Revolution," 46.
14. Jean-Baptiste Say, *England and the English People*, 2nd ed., trans. John Richter (London, 1816), 5–6, https://books.google.com/books?id=AAF8dRnRfdoC&printsec=frontcover&source=gbs_atb#v=onepage&q&f=false.
15. Say, *England and the English People*, 38.
16. E. P. Thompson, *The Making of the English Working Class* (New York: Vintage, 1966), 531–33.
17. Frank Darvall, *Popular Disturbances and Public Order in Regency England* (London: Oxford University Press, 1934), 33, 44; see also Thompson, *Making of the English Working Class*, 533.
18. Thompson, *Making of the English Working Class*, 535.
19. Bailey, *Luddite Rebellion*, 19–20.
20. Bailey, *Luddite Rebellion*, 22.

21. Thompson, *Making of the English Working Class*, 523.
22. Thompson, *Making of the English Working Class*, 524–25.
23. Thompson, *Making of the English Working Class*, 529.
24. Sale, *Rebels Against the Future*, 117.
25. Bailey, *Luddite Rebellion*, 70.
26. Robert Allen, "The Hand-Loom Weaver and the Power Loom: A Schumpeterian Perspective" (Abu Dhabi: NYU Working Paper, 2017), table 1, 15.
27. Thompson, *Making of the English Working Class*, 276.
28. Allen, "Hand-Loom Weaver," figure 1; see also George Henry Wood, "The Statistics of Wages in the Nineteenth Century, Part XIX," *Journal of the Royal Statistical Society* 73, part 6 (June 1910), https://www.jstor.org/stable/2339904?read-now=1&seq=14#page_scan_tab_contents.
29. Bailey, *Luddite Rebellion*, 50.
30. Archibald Prentice, *Historical Sketches and Personal Recollections of Manchester* (London: C. Gilpin, 1851), 53.
31. Thompson, *Making of the English Working Class*, 568.
32. Kevin Binfield, ed., *Writings of the Luddites* (Baltimore: Johns Hopkins University Press, 2004), 172.
33. Binfield, *Writings of the Luddites*, 174–75.
34. Allen, "Hand-Loom Weaver," figure 1.
35. Thompson, *Making of the English Working Class*, 286.
36. Allen, "Hand-Loom Weaver," table 1.
37. Thompson, *Making of the English Working Class*, 549.
38. "Lord Byron's Maiden Speech in the House of Lords, February 27, 1812," reproduced in Bailey, *Luddite Rebellion*, 160.
39. "Lord Byron's Maiden Speech," 160.
40. "Lord Byron's Maiden Speech," 163.
41. "Lord Byron's Maiden Speech," 163–64.
42. Lord Byron, "Song for the Luddites," 1816, PoetryVerse, https://www.poetryverse.com/lord-byron-poems/song-for-the-luddites.

4. William Thompson's Utilitarian Socialism

1. "Letter from a Journeyman Cotton Spinner," *Black Dwarf*, 1818, quoted in E. P. Thompson, *Making of the English Working Class* (New York: Vintage, 1966), 200–201.
2. "Letter from a Journeyman Cotton Spinner," 199–201.
3. Richard Pankhurst, *William Thompson (1775–1833): Pioneer Socialist* (London: Pluto Press, 1991); Fintan Lane, "William Thompson, Bankruptcy, and the West Cork Estate," *Irish Historical Studies* 39, no. 153 (May 2014), 24–39.
4. Lane, "Thompson, Bankruptcy, and the West Cork Estate"; Fintan Lane, "William Thompson, Class and His Irish Context," in Fintan Lane, ed., *Politics, Society and the Middle Class in Modern Ireland* (Basingstoke: Palgrave Macmillan, 2010), 21–47.
5. Pankhurst, *William Thompson*, 6.
6. William Thompson, "Practical Education for the South of Ireland," in Pankhurst, *William Thompson*, 7; Dolores Dooley, "William Thompson (1775–1833)," Humanist Heritage, https://heritage.humanists.uk/william-thompson-1775-1833.
7. Jeremy Bentham, "Preface," in *A Fragment on Government* (Cambridge, UK: Cambridge University Press, 1988), 3.
8. Pankhurst, *William Thompson*, chapter 2.
9. William Thompson, *An Inquiry into the Principles of the Distribution of Wealth Most Conducive to Human Happiness* (Elibron Classics, 2005), xxxi.
10. Pankhurst, *William Thompson*, 13.
11. Pankhurst, *William Thompson*, 12.
12. See Nick Robins, *The Corporation That Changed the World* (London: Pluto Press, 2012), 8–9.
13. Pankhurst, *William Thompson*, 38; for the thought of Saint-Simon and Sismondi, see G. D. H. Cole, *Socialist Thought: The Forerunners, 1789–1850* (London: Macmillan, 1953).
14. Mike Donaldson, "The Working Class," 2006, https://ro.uow.edu.au/cgi/viewcontent.cgi

?article=1147&context=artspapers; M.-L. Tuan, *Simonde de Sismondi as an Economist* (New York: Columbia University Press, 2019), https://doi.org/10.7312/tuan92810.

15. Simonde de Sismondi, *New Principles of Political Economy* (1819), 19–21, referenced at https://glencoe.mheducation.com/sites/0217511447/student_view0/chapter26/origin_of_the_idea.html.

16. Thompson, *Inquiry into the Principles of the Distribution of Wealth* (2005), xxviii.

17. Thompson, *Inquiry into the Principles of the Distribution of Wealth* (2005), xxix.

18. Thompson, *Inquiry into the Principles of the Distribution of Wealth* (2005), 2–3.

19. Thompson, *Inquiry into the Principles of the Distribution of Wealth* (2005), 57–59.

20. Thompson, *Inquiry into the Principles of the Distribution of Wealth* (2005), 133.

21. Thompson, *Inquiry into the Principles of the Distribution of Wealth* (2005), 128.

22. Thompson, *Inquiry into the Principles of the Distribution of Wealth* (2005), 128.

23. Thompson, *Inquiry into the Principles of the Distribution of Wealth* (2005), 129.

24. Thompson, *Inquiry into the Principles of the Distribution of Wealth* (2005), 131.

25. Thompson, *Inquiry into the Principles of the Distribution of Wealth* (2005), 164.

26. Thompson, *Inquiry into the Principles of the Distribution of Wealth* (2005), 132.

27. Thompson, *Inquiry into the Principles of the Distribution of Wealth* (2005), 138.

28. Thompson, *Inquiry into the Principles of the Distribution of Wealth* (2005), 132.

29. See the Fourier chapter in Cole, *Socialist Thought*; and Gareth Stedman Jones and Ian Patterson, eds., *Fourier: The Theory of the Four Movements* (Cambridge: Cambridge University Press, 1996).

30. Cole, *Socialist Thought*, 86–94; and Robert L. Heilbroner, *The Worldly Philosophers*, 4th ed. (New York: Simon and Schuster, 1972), 109–16.

31. Robert Owen, *The Life of Robert Owen* (New York: Knopf, 1920); see also Cole, *Socialist Thought*, 86–94; and Heilbroner, *Worldly Philosophers*, 109–16.

32. Robert Owen, *Report to the County of Lanark of a Plan for Relieving Public Distress, and Removing Discontent* (Glasgow: Wardlaw and Cunninghame, 1821).

33. Frank Podmore, "Robert Owen and Cooperation," *The Economic Journal* 15, no. 58 (June 1905), 257–65, https://www.jstor.org/stable/pdf/2221015.pdf?refreqid=fastly-default%3A8c6 28a585821f31b314a0fbdc465d5b2&ab_segments=&origin=&initiator=&acceptTC=1.

34. Thompson, *Inquiry into the Principles of the Distribution of Wealth* (2005), 272.

35. Thompson, *Inquiry into the Principles of the Distribution of Wealth* (2005), 135; Pankhurst, *William Thompson*, 30.

36. Thompson, *Inquiry into the Principles of the Distribution of Wealth* (2005), 75.

37. Thompson, *Inquiry into the Principles of the Distribution of Wealth* (2005), 138–39.

38. Thompson, *Inquiry into the Principles of the Distribution of Wealth* (2005), 142.

39. Thompson, *Inquiry into the Principles of the Distribution of Wealth* (2005), 107.

40. Thompson, *Inquiry into the Principles of the Distribution of Wealth* (2005), 133.

41. Thompson, *Inquiry into the Principles of the Distribution of Wealth* (2005), 274.

42. Thompson, *Inquiry into the Principles of the Distribution of Wealth* (2005), 394.

43. Thompson, *Inquiry into the Principles of the Distribution of Wealth* (2005), 276.

44. Thompson, *Inquiry into the Principles of the Distribution of Wealth* (2005), 392.

45. Thompson, *Inquiry into the Principles of the Distribution of Wealth* (2005), 276.

46. Thompson, *Inquiry into the Principles of the Distribution of Wealth* (2005), 278.

47. Thompson, *Inquiry into the Principles of the Distribution of Wealth* (2005), 431.

48. John Stuart Mill, *Autobiography of John Stuart Mill* (New York: Columbia University Press, 1924), 86–87; see also Pankhurst, *William Thompson*, 70–71, and this reference to William Lovett's account of the debate: Paul Bowman, "The Continuing Appeal of William Thompson," August 8, 2021, https://eidgenossen.mcdium.com/the-continuing-appeal-of-william-thompson-1ba8f8608dbe.

49. Thomas Hodgskin, "Labour Defended Against the Claims of Capital," Lillian Goldman Law Library, 1825, https://avalon.law.yale.edu/19th_century/labdef.asp.

50. [William Thompson], *Labor Rewarded: The Claims of Labor and Capital Conciliated* (London, 1827).

51. Cole, *Socialist Thought*, 100.

52. Pankhurst, *William Thompson*, 95–96.

53. Pankhurst, *William Thompson*, 101.

54. William Thompson, *Practical Directions for the Speedy and Economical Establishment of Communities* (London, 1830), ii.
55. Thompson, *Practical Directions*, ii.
56. Pankhurst, *William Thompson*, 110–11, 121.
57. Pankhurst, *William Thompson*, 111.
58. Pankhurst, *William Thompson*, 124.
59. Pankhurst, *William Thompson*, 125–28.

5. Anna Wheeler and the Forgotten Half of Humanity

1. William Thompson, *Appeal of One Half the Human Race, Women, Against the Pretensions of the Other Half, Men, to Retain Them in Political, and Thence in Civil and Domestic, Slavery* (London, 1825).
2. William Thompson, "Introductory Letter to Mrs. Wheeler," in Thompson, *Appeal of One Half the Human Race*, xiv.
3. Thompson, "Introductory Letter," v.
4. Dolores Dooley, *Equality in Community: Sexual Equality in the Writings of William Thompson and Anna Doyle Wheeler* (Cork, Ireland: Cork University Press, 1996), 58–63; Pankhurst, *William Thompson*, 50–52.
5. Dooley, *Equality in Community*, 58–59.
6. Dooley, *Equality in Community*, 58–63; Pankhurst, *William Thompson*, 50–52.
7. Pankhurst, *William Thompson*, 51.
8. Dooley, *Equality in Community*, 59.
9. Dooley, *Equality in Community*, 60.
10. Dooley, *Equality in Community*, 62.
11. Thompson, "Introductory Letter," ix–x.
12. Thompson, "Introductory Letter," vi–vii.
13. Pankhurst, *William Thompson*, 57–59.
14. Thompson, *Appeal of One Half the Human Race*, 31.
15. Thompson, *Appeal of One Half the Human Race*, 148.
16. Thompson, *Appeal of One Half the Human Race*, 63.
17. Thompson, *Appeal of One Half the Human Race*, 40.
18. Thompson, *Appeal of One Half the Human Race*, 55.
19. Thompson, *Appeal of One Half the Human Race*, 57.
20. Thompson, *Appeal of One Half the Human Race*, 79.
21. Thompson, *Inquiry into the Principles of the Distribution of Wealth* (2005), 300.
22. Thompson, *Appeal of One Half the Human Race*, vi.
23. Thompson, *Appeal of One Half the Human Race*, xii.
24. Thompson, *Appeal of One Half the Human Race*, 125–26.
25. Joyce Burnette, "Women Workers in the British Industrial Revolution," table 2, EH.Net Encyclopedia, ed. Robert Whaples, March 26, 2008, https://eh.net/encyclopedia/women-workers-in-the-british-industrial-revolution.
26. "The Mill Girls of Lowell," NPS.gov, April 8, 2024, https://www.nps.gov/lowe/learn/historyculture/the-mill-girls-of-lowell.htm.
27. Joyce Burnette, "An Investigation of the Female-Male Wage Gap During the Industrial Revolution in Britain," *The Economic History Review* 50, no. 2 (May 1997), 257–81, https://www.jstor.org/stable/pdf/2599060.pdf.
28. Mariana Valverde, "'Giving the Female a Domestic Turn': The Legal, Social and Moral Regulation of Women's Work in British Cotton Mills, 1820–1850," *Journal of Social History* 21, no. 4 (Summer 1998), 622.
29. Jane Humphries, *Childhood and Child Labour in the British Industrial Revolution* (Cambridge: Cambridge University Press, 2010).
30. Jane Humphries, *"Because They Are Too Menny . . .": Children, Mothers, and Fertility Decline*, University of Oxford Discussion Papers Economic and Social History, no. 64, September 2006, 25, https://www.nuff.ox.ac.uk/economics/history/paper64/64humphries.pdf.
31. Thompson, *Appeal of One Half the Human Race*, xiii–xiv.
32. Thompson, *Appeal of One Half the Human Race*, xiv.

33. Pankhurst, *William Thompson*, 51–52.
34. Dooley, *Equality in Community*, 74–75.
35. Dooley, *Equality in Community*, 75.
36. Pankhurst, *William Thompson*, 53.
37. Anna Wheeler, "The Rights of Women," in Dooley, *Equality in Community*, 89–92; Anna Wheeler, "Rights of Women," 1829, https://speakingwhilefemale.co/womens-lives -wheeler; Margaret McFadden, "Anna Doyle Wheeler (1785–1848): Philosopher, Socialist, Feminist," *Hypatia* 4, no. 1 (Spring 1989), 91–101, https://www.jstor.org/stable/pdf/3809936 .pdf.
38. Dooley, *Equality in Community*, 101–102.
39. Dooley, *Equality in Community*, 82.
40. Dooley, *Equality in Community*, 82.
41. Pankhurst, *William Thompson*, 130.
42. Pankhurst, *William Thompson*, 130.
43. Dooley, *Equality in Community*, 103.
44. Dooley, *Equality in Community*, 77.
45. Flora Tristan, *The London Journal of Flora Tristan, 1842, or, The Aristocracy and the Working Class of England*, trans. Jean Hawkes (London: Virago, 1982), 208; see also Dooley, *Equality in Community*, 98.
46. Dooley, *Equality in Community*, 103.

6. Flora Tristan and the Universal Workers' Union

1. Flora Tristan, *The London Journal of Flora Tristan, 1842, or, The Aristocracy and the Working Class of England*, trans. Jean Hawkes (London: Virago, 1982), 211.
2. Tristan, *London Journal*, 212.
3. Tristan, *London Journal*, 213.
4. For details of Tristan's biography, I relied on Dominique Desanti, *A Woman in Revolt: A Biography of Flora Tristan* (New York: Crown, 1976); Doris Beik and Paul Beik, "Introduction," in *Flora Tristan: Utopian Feminist: Her Travel Diaries and Personal Crusade* (Bloomington: Indiana University Press, 1993); Jean Hawkes, "Introduction," in Tristan, *London Journal*; and Magda Portal, *Flora Tristan: A Forerunner Woman* (Trafford, 2012).
5. Desanti, *Woman in Revolt*, 23; Beik and Beik, "Introduction," xi.
6. Desanti, *Woman in Revolt*, chapter 4.
7. Desanti, *Woman in Revolt*, 28–30.
8. Desanti, *Woman in Revolt*, 41–45.
9. Desanti, *Woman in Revolt*, 63; Beik and Beik, "Introduction," xii, xiv.
10. Desanti, *Woman in Revolt*, 63–109.
11. Beik and Beik, *Flora Tristan*, 10.
12. Beik and Beik, *Flora Tristan*, 10.
13. Beik and Beik, *Flora Tristan*, 15.
14. Daron Acemoglu, Simon Johnson, and James A. Robinson, "The Colonial Origins of Comparative Development: An Empirical Investigation," *American Economic Review* 91, no. 5 (December 2001), 1369–401.
15. Beik and Beik, *Flora Tristan*, 24.
16. Beik and Beik, *Flora Tristan*, 26.
17. Beik and Beik, *Flora Tristan*, 25.
18. Beik and Beik, *Flora Tristan*, 30.
19. Beik and Beik, *Flora Tristan*, 31–32.
20. Desanti, *Woman in Revolt*, 131–32.
21. Desanti, *Woman in Revolt*, 116–18.
22. Desanti, *Woman in Revolt*, 119.
23. Desanti, *Woman in Revolt*, 131–32.
24. Elizabeth Mirella Solórzano Giraldo, "Flora Tristán and Transnational Feminism" (master's thesis, University of Lisbon, 2022), 68, https://repositorio.ul.pt/bitstream/10451/56547/1 /ulflemsgiraldo_tm.pdf; Desanti, *Woman in Revolt*, 132.
25. Desanti, *Woman in Revolt*, 133–35.

26. Flora Tristan, *Flora Tristan's London Journal, 1840*, trans. Dennis Palmer and Giselle Pincetl (Boston: Charles River Books, 1980), 224.
27. Desanti, *Woman in Revolt*, 145–46.
28. Desanti, *Woman in Revolt*, 136–38.
29. Desanti, *Woman in Revolt*, 150–61.
30. Tristan, *London Journal*, 16.
31. Tristan, *London Journal*, 57–65.
32. Tristan, *London Journal*, 178–87.
33. Tristan, *London Journal*, 84–87.
34. Tristan, *London Journal*, 86–87.
35. Tristan, *London Journal*, 157.
36. Tristan, *London Journal*, 72–76.
37. Tristan, *London Journal*, 68.
38. Tristan, *London Journal*, 68–69.
39. Tristan, *London Journal*, 69.
40. Tristan, *London Journal*, 69–70.
41. Tristan, *London Journal*, 71.
42. Tristan, *London Journal*, 71–72.
43. Mitchell Abidor, trans., "Manifesto of Equals," in *History of the French Revolution: Gracchus Babeuf and the Conspiracy of the Equals* (1796), https://www.marxists.org/history/france /revolution/conspiracy-equals/1796/manifesto.htm.
44. Tristan, *London Journal*, 48.
45. Desanti, *Woman in Revolt*, 202–22.
46. Desanti, *Woman in Revolt*, 216–18; Beik and Beik, *Flora Tristan*, xix.
47. Flora Tristan, *The Workers' Union*, reprinted in Beik and Beik, *Flora Tristan*, 104. Also a freestanding reprint from the University of Illinois Press, 1983, 37.
48. Beik and Beik, *Flora Tristan*, 104.
49. Beik and Beik, *Flora Tristan*, 104–105.
50. Beik and Beik, *Flora Tristan*, 105.
51. Beik and Beik, *Flora Tristan*, 109.
52. Beik and Beik, *Flora Tristan*, 109.
53. Beik and Beik, *Flora Tristan*, 110.
54. Beik and Beik, *Flora Tristan*, 123.
55. Beik and Beik, *Flora Tristan*, 112.
56. Beik and Beik, *Flora Tristan*, 115–16.
57. Beik and Beik, *Flora Tristan*, 119.
58. Beik and Beik, *Flora Tristan*, 120.
59. Beik and Beik, *Flora Tristan*, 116.
60. Beik and Beik, *Flora Tristan*, 116.
61. Beik and Beik, *Flora Tristan*, 121.
62. Beik and Beik, *Flora Tristan*, 122.
63. Desanti, *Woman in Revolt*, 215.
64. Desanti, *Woman in Revolt*, 225.
65. Desanti, *Woman in Revolt*, 224–25.
66. Desanti, *Woman in Revolt*, 214.
67. Desanti, *Woman in Revolt*, 231.
68. Desanti, *Woman in Revolt*, 231.
69. Beik and Beik, *Flora Tristan*, 106.
70. Beik and Beik, "Introduction," xix–xx; Desanti, *Woman in Revolt*, 238–61.
71. Beik and Beik, *Flora Tristan*, 171.
72. Desanti, *Woman in Revolt*, 262–66.

7. Thomas Carlyle on Mammon and the Cash Nexus

1. For Carlyle's biography, see Fred Kaplan, *Thomas Carlyle: A Biography* (Ithaca, NY: Cornell University Press, 1983); "Thomas Carlyle: A Brief Biography," The Victorian Web, https:// victorianweb.org/authors/carlyle/carlyle4.html; also a good introduction at Henry David

Gray, ed., *Thomas Carlyle's On Heroes, Hero-Worship, and the Heroic in History* (New York: Longmans, Green, 1906), https://ia801608.us.archive.org/28/items/thomascarlyleson00carl/thomascarlyleson00carl.pdf.

2. Thomas Carlyle, "Signs of the Times," 1829, The Victorian Web, https://www.victorianweb.org/authors/carlyle/signs1.html.
3. Carlyle, "Signs of the Times."
4. Carlyle, "Signs of the Times."
5. Carlyle, "Signs of the Times."
6. Carlyle, "Signs of the Times."
7. Kaplan, *Thomas Carlyle*, 154.
8. Kaplan, *Thomas Carlyle*, 202.
9. Ralph Waldo Emerson, entry for March 5, 1838, in Bliss Perry, ed., *The Heart of Emerson's Journals* (New York: Dover, 2014), 124.
10. Thomas Carlyle, *Chartism* (London: James Fraser, 1840), 9.
11. "The Newport Rising and Chartism in Wales," BBC Wales, September 22, 2020, https://www.bbc.co.uk/programmes/articles/zGNhgXwFT8TmZDhhnpnwP8/the-newport-rising-and-chartism-in-wales; and Kathryn Rix, "Parliament Versus the People: The Newport Rising of 1839," The History of Parliament, November 4, 2019, https://thehistoryofparliament.wordpress.com/2019/11/04/parliament-versus-the-people-the-newport-rising-of-1839.
12. Carlyle, *Chartism*, 2.
13. Carlyle, *Chartism*, 12.
14. Carlyle, *Chartism*, 13.
15. Carlyle, *Chartism*, 15.
16. Carlyle, *Chartism*, 58.
17. Carlyle, *Chartism*, 61.
18. Carlyle, *Chartism*, 66.
19. Carlyle, *Chartism*, 51.
20. Carlyle, *Chartism*, 53.
21. Carlyle, *Chartism*, 54.
22. Carlyle, *Chartism*, 60.
23. Carlyle, *Chartism*, 28.
24. Thomas Carlyle, *Past and Present* (London: Chapman and Hall, 1843), 74, https://www.gutenberg.org/ebooks/13534.
25. Kaplan, *Thomas Carlyle*, 526–27.
26. "Social Unrest and Income Tax," National Museums Liverpool, https://www.liverpoolmuseums.org.uk/plug-riots#; and "General Strike 1842," Chartist Ancestors, https://www.chartistancestors.co.uk/general-strike-1842.
27. Gray, *Thomas Carlyle's On Heroes*, 21.
28. Carlyle to Edwin Chadwick, August 1, 1842, in *Carlyle Letters Online*, https://carlyleletters.dukeupress.edu/volume/15/lt-18420801-TC-ECH-01; Kaplan, *Thomas Carlyle*, 290, 579n50.
29. Carlyle, *Past and Present*, 4.
30. Carlyle, *Past and Present*, 36.
31. Carlyle, *Past and Present*, 36.
32. Carlyle, *Past and Present*, 229.
33. Carlyle, *Past and Present*, 183.
34. Carlyle, *Past and Present*, 209.
35. Carlyle, *Past and Present*, 350.
36. Carlyle, *Past and Present*, 337.
37. Carlyle, *Past and Present*, 365.
38. Carlyle, *Past and Present*, 367.
39. Paul E. Kerry, Albert D. Pionke, and Megan Dent, eds., *Thomas Carlyle and the Idea of Influence* (Vancouver: Fairleigh Dickinson University Press, 2018), 282.
40. John Stuart Mill, "The Claims of Labour," in *Collected Works of John Stuart Mill*, vol. 4, *Essays on Economics and Society* (Toronto: University of Toronto Press, 1967), 370.
41. Charles H. Kegel, "Carlyle and Ruskin: An Influential Friendship," *BYU Studies Quarterly* 5, no. 3 (1964), 225, https://scholarsarchive.byu.edu/cgi/viewcontent.cgi?article=1152&context=byusq.
42. John Ruskin, "Nature of Wealth: Variations of Value, the National Store, Nature of Labor,

Value and Price, the Currency," footnote 2. (Originally published in "Essays on Political Economy," *Fraser's Magazine*, 1862–63.)

43. Richard J. Dunn, "Dickens, Carlyle, and the 'Hard Times' Dedication," *Dickens Studies Newsletter* 2, no. 3 (September 1971), 90.

44. Ralph Waldo Emerson, "Past and Present," *The Dial* 4, no. 1 (July 1843), https://www.google.com/books/edition/The_Dial/VnsAAAAAYAAJ?hl=en&gbpv=1.

45. Emerson, "Past and Present."

46. Emerson, "Past and Present."

47. Henry David Thoreau, "Thomas Carlyle and His Works," 1847, https://theanarchistlibrary.org/library/henry-david-thoreau-thomas-carlyle-and-his-works.

48. Gerald M. Straka, "The Spirit of Carlyle in the Old South," *The Historian* 20, no. 1 (November 1957), 39.

49. [Thomas Carlyle], "Occasional Discourse on the Negro Question," *Fraser's Magazine for Town and Country*, December 1849, 672–73, https://babel.hathitrust.org/cgi/pt?id=inu.30000080778727&view=1up&seq=690.

50. Carlyle, "Occasional Discourse," 671.

51. Carlyle, "Occasional Discourse," 675.

52. Carlyle, "Occasional Discourse," 673.

53. Carlyle, "Occasional Discourse," 676–77.

54. [John Stuart Mill], "The Negro Question," *Fraser's Magazine for Town and Country* 41 (January–June 1850), 25.

55. "Carlyle on West India Emancipation," *DeBow's Review and Industrial Resources, Statistics, etc.* 8, no. 6 (June 1850), 527.

56. Rachel Cohen, "Can You Forgive Him?," *The New Yorker*, October 31, 2004, https://www.newyorker.com/magazine/2004/11/08/can-you-forgive-him-3.

57. Frederick Engels, "A Review of *Past and Present*, by Thomas Carlyle, London, 1843," *Deutsch-Französische Jarbücher* (1844), https://www.marxists.org/archive/marx/works/1844/df-jahrbucher/carlyle.htm.

8. Friedrich Engels and *The Communist Manifesto*

1. Edwin Canaan, "The Growth of Manchester and Liverpool, 1801–1891," *The Economic Journal* 4, no. 13 (March 1894), 111–14.

2. Chelsea Follett, "Centers of Progress, Pt. 22: Manchester (Industrialization)," Human Progress, February 18, 2021, https://humanprogress.org/centers-of-progress-pt-22-manchester-industrialization/#:~:text=By%20the%20end%20of%20the,that%20nation%27s%20 "second%20city."; Michael E. Rose, Keith Falconer, and Julian Holder, *Ancoats: Cradle of Industrialisation*, Historic England, September 15, 2011, https://historicengland.org.uk/images-books/publications/ancoats; and Richard J. Williams, "Manchester After Engels," *Places Journal*, June 2020, https://placesjournal.org/article/manchester-after-engels/?cn-reloaded=1.

3. This and other details of Engels's life are taken from the biography by Tristram Hunt, *Marx's General* (New York: Holt, 2009), 11–13, 75–112.

4. Hunt, *Marx's General*, 36.

5. David McLellan, *The Young Hegelians and Karl Marx* (New York: F. A. Praeger, 1969), 74, https://ia902606.us.archive.org/6/items/237410/The%20young%20Hegelians%20and%20Karl%20Marx.pdf; Hunt, *Marx's General*, 45–55.

6. "Engels to Franz Mehring, end of April 1895," in Marx and Engels, *Collected Works, Volume 50: Letters 1892–95* (London: Lawrence and Wishart, 2010), 503, https://www.hekmatist.com/Marx%20Engles/Marx%20&%20Engels%20Collected%20Works%20Volume%2050_%20Ka%20-%20Karl%20Marx.pdf; see also Hunt, *Marx's General*, 63.

7. Friedrich Engels, *The Condition of the Working Class in England* (Oxford: Oxford University Press, 1999), xiv.

8. Hunt, *Marx's General*, 89.

9. Frederick Engels, "A Review of *Past and Present*, by Thomas Carlyle, London, 1843," *Deutsch-Französische Jarbücher* (1844), https://www.marxists.org/archive/marx/works/1844/df-jahrbucher/carlyle.htm; see also Hunt, *Marx's General*, 93.

10. Sarah Irving, "Frederick Engels and Mary and Lizzy Burns," *Manchester's Radical History*, March 15, 2010, https://radicalmanchester.wordpress.com/2010/03/15/frederick-engels-and -mary-and-lizzy-burns; Hunt, *Marx's General*, 94–95.

11. Engels, *Condition of the Working Class*, 61.

12. Engels, *Condition of the Working Class*, 61.

13. Engels, *Condition of the Working Class*, 62.

14. Engels, *Condition of the Working Class*, 63.

15. Engels, *Condition of the Working Class*, 69.

16. Frederick Engels, "The Condition of the Working Class in England," in Marx and Engels, *Collected Works, Volume 2: Frederick Engels 1838–42* (London: Lawrence and Wishart, 2010), 378.

17. Engels to Marx, November 19, 1844, in Marx and Engels, *Collected Works, Volume 38: Letters 1844–51* (London: Lawrence and Wishart, 2010), 10.

18. Engels, *Condition of the Working Class*, 58.

19. Engels, *Condition of the Working Class*, 109.

20. Engels, *Condition of the Working Class*, 152.

21. Engels, *Condition of the Working Class*, 161–75.

22. Engels, *Condition of the Working Class*, 282.

23. David McLellan, "Introduction," in Engels, *Condition of the Working Class*, xii.

24. Engels, *Condition of the Working Class*, 28.

25. Engels, *Condition of the Working Class*, 21.

26. Engels, *Condition of the Working Class*, 15.

27. Engels, *Condition of the Working Class*, 88.

28. Engels, *Condition of the Working Class*, 91.

29. Engels, *Condition of the Working Class*, 88.

30. Hunt, *Marx's General*, 99.

31. Engels, *Condition of the Working Class*, 87.

32. Engels, *Condition of the Working Class*, 96.

33. Engels, *Condition of the Working Class*, 93.

34. Engels, *Condition of the Working Class*, 95.

35. Engels, *Condition of the Working Class*, 95.

36. Engels, *Condition of the Working Class*, 96.

37. Engels, *Condition of the Working Class*, 96.

38. Engels, *Condition of the Working Class*, 299–300.

39. Engels, *Condition of the Working Class*, 300.

40. Engels, *Condition of the Working Class*, 300.

41. Hunt, *Marx's General*, 112.

42. Frederick Engels, "Outlines of a Critique of Political Economy," *Deutsch-Französische Jarbücher* (1844), https://www.marxists.org/archive/marx/works/1844/df-jahrbucher/outlines.htm.

43. Engels, "Outlines of a Critique."

44. Karl Marx, "Preface," in *A Contribution to the Critique of Political Economy* (1859), https://www.marxists.org/archive/marx/works/1859/critique-pol-economy/preface.htm.

45. David McLellan, *Marx: A Biography* (London: Macmillan Press, 1973), 109; Karl Marx, *Economic and Philosophic Manuscripts of 1844*, https://www.marxists.org/archive/marx/works /1844/manuscripts/preface.htm.

46. Marx, *Economic and Philosophic Manuscripts*.

47. Marx, *Economic and Philosophic Manuscripts*.

48. McLellan, *Marx*, 104.

49. McLellan, *Marx*, 117–18.

50. Frederick Engels, "On the History of the Communist League," *Sozialdemokrat*, November 12–26, 1885, https://www.marxists.org/archive/marx/works/1847/communist-league /1885hist.htm.

51. Hunt, *Marx's General*, 123.

52. McLellan, *Marx*, 135–36.

53. Hunt, *Marx's General*, 125.

54. Hunt, *Marx's General*, 124, 130, 141–44.

55. Frederick Engels, "The Principles of Communism, 1847," https://www.marxists.org/archive/marx/works/1847/11/prin-com.htm.
56. Engels, "Principles of Communism."
57. Engels, "Principles of Communism."
58. Karl Marx and Frederick Engels, *The Communist Manifesto: A Modern Edition* (London: Verso Books, 1998), 33.
59. Marx and Engels, *Communist Manifesto*, 34.
60. Marx and Engels, *Communist Manifesto*, 36.
61. Marx and Engels, *Communist Manifesto*, 36.
62. Marx and Engels, *Communist Manifesto*, 37–38.
63. Marx and Engels, *Communist Manifesto*, 38–39.
64. Marx and Engels, *Communist Manifesto*, 38.
65. Marx and Engels, *Communist Manifesto*, 40–41.
66. Marx and Engels, *Communist Manifesto*, 39.
67. Marx and Engels, *Communist Manifesto*, 39.
68. Marx and Engels, *Communist Manifesto*, 39–40.
69. Marx and Engels, *Communist Manifesto*, 41.
70. Marx and Engels, *Communist Manifesto*, 41–42.
71. Marx and Engels, *Communist Manifesto*, 42.
72. Marx and Engels, *Communist Manifesto*, 42.
73. Marx and Engels, *Communist Manifesto*, 44–45.
74. Marx and Engels, *Communist Manifesto*, 49–50.
75. Marx and Engels, *Communist Manifesto*, 50.
76. Eric Hobsbawm, "Introduction," in Marx and Engels, *Communist Manifesto*, 16.
77. "Nominal Wages, Consumer Prices and Real Wages, United Kingdom, 1750 to 2015," Our World in Data, https://ourworldindata.org/grapher/nominal-wages-consumer-prices-and-real-wages-in-the-uk-since-1750.
78. Pim de Zwart, Bas van Leeuwen, and Jieli Li, "Real Wages Since 1820," in Jan Luiten van Zanden, Joerg Baten, Marco Mira d'Ercole, et al., eds., *How Was Life? Global Well-Being Since 1820* (Paris: OECD, 2014), https://pure.knaw.nl/ws/files/1067837/3014041ec008_1_.pdf and https://www.oecd-ilibrary.org/economics/how-was-life_9789264214262-en.
79. Charles Feinstein, "Pessimism Perpetuated: Real Wages and the Standard of Living in Britain During and After the Industrial Revolution," *The Journal of Economic History* 58, no. 3 (September 1998), appendix table 1, 653.
80. Robert C. Allen, "Engels' Pause: Technical Change, Capital Accumulation, and Inequality in the British Industrial Revolution," *Explorations in Economic History* 46, no. 4 (October 2009), 418–35, https://www.nuff.ox.ac.uk/Users/Allen/engelspause.pdf.
81. Allen, "Engels' Pause," 419.
82. Allen, "Engels' Pause," 419.
83. Sylvia Nasar, *Grand Pursuit: The Story of Economic Genius* (New York: Simon and Schuster, 2011), 83–84.
84. Hunt, *Marx's General*, 159.
85. "News from Paris," *Neue Rheinische Zeitung—Politisch-ökonomische Revue*, no. 27 (June 27, 1848), reprinted in Marx and Engels, *Collected Works, Volume 7: Marx and Engels 1848* (London: Lawrence and Wishart, 2010), 128, https://www.koorosh-modaresi.com/MarxEngels/V7.pdf.
86. For details of the 1848 revolution in France, see Alfred Cobban, *A History of Modern France, Volume 2: From the First Empire to the Second Empire, 1799–1871*, 2nd ed., 131–44.

9. Karl Marx's Capitalist Laws of Motion

1. David McLellan, *Karl Marx: His Life and Thought*, 2nd ed. (London: Papermac, 1995), 226; Gareth Stedman Jones, *Karl Marx: Greatness and Illusion* (Cambridge, MA: Belknap Press of Harvard University Press, 2016); and Tristram Hunt, *Marx's General* (New York: Holt, 2009).
2. Stedman Jones, *Karl Marx*, 317–18.
3. Stedman Jones, *Karl Marx*, 325.

4. Karl Marx, "The Class Struggles in France, 1848 to 1850, Part I: The Defeat of June, 1848," https://www.marxists.org/archive/marx/works/1850/class-struggles-france/ch01.htm.

5. Karl Marx and Frederick Engels, "Review: January–February 1850," *Neue Rheinische Zeitung—Politisch-ökonomische Revue*, https://www.marxists.org/archive/marx/works/1850 /01/31.htm.

6. *The Railway Record, Mining Register, and Joint Stock Companies' Reporter, for 1851. January to December (Inclusive)* (London: Railway Record Office, 1851); Leigh Shaw-Taylor and Xuesheng You, "The Development of the Railway Network in Britain 1825–1911," in Leigh Shaw-Taylor, Dan Bogart, and Max Satchell, eds., *The Online Historical Atlas of Transport, Urbanization and Economic Development in England and Wales c.1680–1911*, https://www .campop.geog.cam.ac.uk/research/projects/transport/onlineatlas/railways.pdf; and "Victorian Railways: Did They Create More Crime?," National Archives, nationalarchives.gov.uk /education/resources/victorian-railways.

7. Asa Briggs, *The Age of Improvement, 1783–1867* (London: Longman, 1979), 395.

8. Eric Hobsbawm, *The Age of Capital, 1848–1875* (New York: Vintage Books, 1996), 39.

9. Karl Marx and Frederick Engels, "Review: May–October 1850," *Neue Rheinische Zeitung—Politisch-ökonomische Revue*, https://www.marxists.org/archive/marx/works/1850/11/01.htm.

10. McLellan, *Karl Marx*, 241.

11. Marx and Engels, "Review: May–October 1850."

12. For details of journalism for *New-York Daily Tribune*, see McLellan, *Karl Marx*, 284–89.

13. McLellan, *Karl Marx*, 284.

14. Karl Marx, "The Future Results of British Rule in India," *New-York Daily Tribune*, August 8, 1853.

15. Karl Marx, "The Government of India," *New-York Daily Tribune*, July 20, 1853.

16. Marx, "Future Results of British Rule in India."

17. Stedman Jones, *Karl Marx*, 357.

18. Marx, "The British Rule in India," *New-York Herald Tribune*, June 25, 1853.

19. Marx, "Future Results of British Rule in India."

20. Marx, "Future Results of British Rule in India."

21. Karl Marx, *Grundrisse: Foundations of the Critique of Political Economy* (Rough Draft) (New York: Penguin, 1997), https://www.marxists.org/archive/marx/works/1857/Grundrisse.

22. McLellan, *Karl Marx*, 298; see also Stedman Jones, *Karl Marx*, 375–400.

23. McLellan, *Karl Marx*, 299–302.

24. Karl Marx to Frederick Engels, January 16, 1858, in *Marx and Engels Collected Works, Volume 40: Letters 1856–59* (London: Lawrence and Wishart, 2010), 248, https://www.hekma tist.com/Marx%20Engles /Marx%20 &%20Engels%20Collected%20Works%20Volume%20 40_%20Ka%20 -%20Karl%20Marx .pdf.

25. Karl Marx, "Preface," in *A Contribution to the Critique of Political Economy*, 1859, https:// www.marxists.org/archive/marx/works/1859/critique-pol-economy/preface.htm.

26. Marx, "Preface"; see also McLellan, *Karl Marx*, 308–10.

27. McLellan, *Karl Marx*, 310.

28. McLellan, *Karl Marx*, 310–24.

29. Hunt, *Marx's General*, 190–92.

30. Karl Marx to Frederick Engels, January 20, 1857, in Marx and Engels, *Collected Works, Volume 40*, 93.

31. McLellan, *Karl Marx*, 337.

32. Karl Marx to Frederick Engels, June 22, 1867, in Marx and Engels, *Collected Works, Volume 42: Letters 1864–68* (London: Lawrence and Wishart, 2010), 383.

33. McLellan, *Karl Marx*, 338.

34. Karl Marx to Frederick Engels, February 13, 1866, in Marx and Engels, *Collected Works, Volume 42*, 227.

35. McLellan, *Karl Marx*, 338.

36. Karl Marx, *Capital: A Critique of Political Economy, Volume I* (London: Penguin Classics, 1990), 92.

37. Marx, *Capital: Volume I*, 90.

38. Marx, *Capital: Volume I*, 91.

39. Karl Marx, *Capital: A Critique of Political Economy, Volume 1* (Moscow: Progress Publishers, 1971), 116. (In the Penguin edition, "Moneybags" is translated as "the money-owner.")
40. Marx, *Capital: Volume I*, 274.
41. Marx, *Capital: Volume I*, 300–302.
42. Marx, *Capital: Volume I*, 301. (In my example, I simplified Marx's arithmetic.)
43. Marx, *Capital: Volume I*, 302.
44. Marx, *Capital: Volume I*, 320–29.
45. Shigeto Tsuru, "On Reproduction Schemes," appendix A in Paul M. Sweezy, *The Theory of Capitalist Development* (New York: Oxford University Press, 1942).
46. Marx, *Capital: Volume I*, 742.
47. Marx, *Capital: Volume I*, 763.
48. Marx, *Capital: Volume I*, 769.
49. Marx, *Capital: Volume I*, 769–70.
50. Marx, *Capital: Volume I*, 770.
51. Marx, *Capital: Volume I*, 798.
52. Marx, *Capital: Volume I*, 792.
53. Friedrich Engels, *The Condition of the Working Class in England* (Oxford: Oxford University Press, 1999), 145.
54. Marx, *Capital: Volume I*, 793.
55. Marx, *Capital: Volume I*, 554.
56. Marx, *Capital: Volume I*, 557.
57. Marx, *Capital: Volume I*, 554.
58. Marx, *Capital: Volume I*, 763.
59. Marx, *Capital: Volume I*, 769.
60. Marx, *Capital: Volume I*, 799.
61. Marx, *Capital: Volume I*, 799.
62. Marx, *Capital: Volume I*, 799.
63. James Skipper and George P. Landow, "Wages and Cost of Living in the Victorian Era," The Victorian Web, https://www.victorianweb.org/economics/wages2.html.
64. Marx, *Capital: Volume I*, 804.
65. Marx, *Capital: Volume I*, 806.
66. Marx, *Capital: Volume I*, 777.
67. Marx, *Capital: Volume I*, 778.
68. Marx, *Capital: Volume I*, 779.
69. Marx, *Capital: Volume I*, 929.
70. Marx, *Capital: Volume I*, 929.
71. Meghnad Desai, *Marx's Revenge: The Resurgence of Capitalism and the Death of Statist Socialism* (London: Verso, 2004), 60.
72. McLellan, *Marx*, 422.
73. Karl Marx, Part III. The Law of the Tendency of the Rate of Profit to Fall, *Capital: Volume III: The Process of Capitalist Production as a Whole* (New York: International Publishers, 1967), 153–86.
74. Karl Marx, *Capital: A Critique of Political Economy, Volume III: The Process of Capitalist Production as a Whole* (London: Penguin Classics, 1993), 320, http://digamo.free.fr/penguin3.pdf.
75. Marx, *Capital: Volume III*, 329.
76. Marx, *Capital: Volume III*, 326.
77. Karl Marx, "The Chapter on Capital, Notebook VII, Third Section: Capital as Fructiferous: Transformation of Surplus Value into Profit," *Grundrisse*, 745–893, https://www.marxists.org/archive/marx/works/1857/grundrisse/ch15.htm.
78. Marx, *Capital: Volume III*, 358.
79. McLellan, *Marx*, 434.
80. Hunt, *Marx's General*, 290.
81. Hunt, *Marx's General*, 294.
82. John Maynard Keynes, "A Short View of Russia," *Essays in Persuasion* (London: Macmillan, 1931), https://www.economicsnetwork.ac.uk/archive/keynes_persuasion/A_Short_View_of_Russia.htm.

83. Anwar Shaikh, "The Transformation from Marx to Sraffa," in Ernest Mandel and Alan Free-man, eds., *Ricardo, Marx, Sraffa, The Langston Memorial Volume* (London: Verso, 1984), http://gesd.free.fr/shaikh84.pdf.

84. Güney Işıkara and Patrick Mokre, "Price-Value Deviations and the Labour Theory of Value: Evidence from 42 Countries, 2000–2017," *Review of Political Economy* 34, no. 1 (January 2022), 165–80.

85. S. Broadberry, B. M. Campbell, A. Klein, M. Overton, and B. Van Leeuwen, "Nominal Wages, Consumer Prices and Real Wages, United Kingdom, 1750–2015," Our World in Data, https://ourworldindata.org/grapher/nominal-wages-consumer-prices-and-real-wages -in-the-uk-since-1750.

86. Fixed capital stock figures are from Charles Feinstein, "National Income, Output and Ex-penditure of the United Kingdom 1855–1965" (1972), https://www.escoe.ac.uk/research /historical-data/capital-and-productivity.

87. Michael Heinrich, *An Introduction to the Three Volumes of Karl Marx's Capital* (New York: Monthly Review Press, 2004), 53.

88. Michael Roberts, *Marx 200: A Review of Marx's Economics 200 Years After His Birth* (Lulu, 2018), 42.

89. Esteban Ezequiel Maito, "The Historical Transience of Capital: The Downward Trend in the Rate of Profit Since XIX Century," MPRA Paper 55894, Munich Personal RePEc Archive, May 11, 2014, https://mpra.ub.uni-muenchen.de/55894/1.

90. Ivan Trofimov, "Profit Rates in Developed Capitalist Countries: A Time Series Investiga-tion," *PSL Quarterly Review* 70, no. 281 (June 2017), 85–128.

91. Deepankar Basu, Julio Huato, Jesus Lara Jauregui, and Evan Wasner, "World Profit Rates, 1960–2019," Working Paper No. 2022–02, University of Massachusetts, Amherst, Econom-ics Department Working Paper Series, 318.

10. Henry George's Moral Crusade

1. Kate Chesley, "First Transcontinental Railroad and Stanford University," May 8, 2019, *Stan-ford Report*, https://news.stanford.edu/2019/05/08/first-transcontinental-railroad-stanford -forever-linked.

2. Karl Marx, *Capital: A Critique of Political Economy, Volume I* (London: Penguin Classics, 1990), 414.

3. Marx, *Capital: Volume I*, 414.

4. Marx, *Capital: Volume I*, 940.

5. Caitlin Rosenthal, *Accounting for Slavery: Masters and Management* (Cambridge, MA: Har-vard University Press, 2018).

6. For mortgages secured by slaves, see Brook Endale, "How Banks Played a Role in Uphold-ing Slavery," *GW Today*, October 17, 2023, https://gwtoday.gwu.edu/how-banks-played-role -upholding-slavery-during-19th-century; for insurance policies, see Michael Ralph, "Value of Life: Insurance, Slavery, and Enterprise," in Sven Beckert and Christine Desan, eds., *American Capitalism: New Histories* (New York: Columbia University Press, 2018).

7. Charles A. Beard and Mary R. Beard, *The Rise of American Civilization, Volume 2: The In-dustrial Era* (New York: Macmillan, 1927), 136–37.

8. Aaron O'Neill, "Population of the United States from 1610 to 2020," Statista, August 2019, https://www.statista.com/statistics/1067138/population-united-states-historical.

9. Joseph H. Davis, "U.S. Industrial Production Index (1790–1915)," National Bureau of Economic Research, Technical Data Appendix, https://www.nber.org/research/data/us -industrial-production-index-1790–1915.

10. Alan Greenspan and Adrian Wooldridge, *Capitalism in America: A History* (New York: Penguin, 2018), 101.

11. Nicholas Crafts, *Forging Ahead, Falling Behind and Fighting Back: British Economic Growth from the Industrial Revolution to the Financial Crisis* (Cambridge: Cambridge University Press, 2018), 14, table 2.2.

12. Karen Braun, "How the 19th Century Boosted America to the Top of the World Corn Mar-ket: A History of U.S. Grain Trade," June 12, 2020, https://www.linkedin.com/pulse/how -19th-century-boosted-america-top-world-corn-market-karen-braun.

13. Aaron O'Neill, "Cotton Output and the Production Area in the United States from 1790 to 1988," Statista, February 2, 2024, https://www.statista.com/statistics/1070570/us-cotton-output-area-historical. On cotton production post–Civil War, see also Alan L. Olmstead and Paul W. Rhode, "Cotton, Slavery, and the New History of Capitalism," *Explorations in Economic History* 67 (January 2018), 1–17.

14. Alba M. Edwards, "Part II: Comparative Occupation Statistics for the United States, 1870–1930," *Sixteenth Census of the United States: 1940: Population* (Washington, DC: US Government Printing Office, 1943), https://usa.ipums.org/usa/resources/voliii/pubdocs/1940/Population/00312147ch2.pdf.

15. "US Business Cycle Expansions and Contractions," National Bureau of Economic Research, March 14, 2023, https://www.nber.org/research/data/us-business-cycle-expansions-and-contractions.

16. Arthur Latham Perry, *Elements of Political Economy* (New York: Scribner, Armstrong, 1877), 161.

17. Perry, *Elements of Political Economy*, 162.

18. Perry, *Elements of Political Economy*, 171.

19. For George's biographical details, see Charles Albro Barker, *Henry George* (Oxford: Oxford University Press, 1955); Edward T. O'Donnell, *Henry George and the Crisis of Inequality* (New York: Columbia University Press, 2015); Henry George Jr., *The Life of Henry George* (New York: Doubleday and McClure, 1900), https://archive.org/details/lifehenrygeorge01georgoog/page/n7/mode/2up.

20. Barker, *Henry George*, 69.

21. O'Donnell, *George and Crisis of Inequality*, 20; Barker, *Henry George*, 102.

22. Henry George, "What the Railroad Will Bring Us," *The Overland Monthly* 1, no. 4 (October 1868), 302.

23. George Jr., *Life of Henry George*, 210.

24. Henry George, *Our Land and Land Policy* (1871), reprinted in *The Complete Works of Henry George: Our Land and Land Policy: Speeches, Lectures and Miscellaneous Writings* (Garden City, NY: Doubleday, Page, 1911), http://livinghistoryofillinois.com/download/Our_Land_and_Land_Policy_The_Complete_Works_of_Henry_George.pdf.

25. George, *Our Land and Land Policy*.

26. George, *Our Land and Land Policy*.

27. Barker, *Henry George*, 122–23; O'Donnell, *George and Crisis of Inequality*, 124–25; John H. Beck, "Henry George and Immigration," *The American Journal of Economics and Sociology* 71, no. 4 (October 2012), 966–87.

28. Barker, *Henry George*, 133–34.

29. O'Donnell, *George and Crisis of Inequality*, 28–34.

30. O'Donnell, *George and Crisis of Inequality*, 42, 63–66; Barker, *Henry George*, 232, 252–53.

31. Barker, *Henry George*, 314.

32. O'Donnell, *George and Crisis of Inequality*, 63–65; Cliff Cobb, "Publisher's Foreword," in Henry George, *Progress and Poverty*, ed. Bob Drake (Princeton, NJ: Robert Schalkenbach Foundation, 2006), https://www.henrygeorge.org/pintro.htm.

33. Henry George, *Progress and Poverty*, popular ed. (New York: D. Appleton, 1881), 3.

34. George, *Progress and Poverty*, 6.

35. George, *Progress and Poverty*, 7.

36. George, *Progress and Poverty*, 9.

37. George, *Progress and Poverty*, 11.

38. George, *Progress and Poverty*, 137.

39. George, *Progress and Poverty*, 126.

40. George, *Progress and Poverty*, 205.

41. George, *Progress and Poverty*, 146.

42. George, *Progress and Poverty*, 200.

43. George, *Progress and Poverty*, 153.

44. George, *Progress and Poverty*, 153–54.

45. George, *Progress and Poverty*, 154.

46. Richard Reeves, *John Stuart Mill: Victorian Firebrand* (London: Atlantic Books, 2007), 459–62.

47. George, *Progress and Poverty*, 295.

48. George, *Progress and Poverty,* 363.
49. George, *Progress and Poverty,* 364.
50. George, *Progress and Poverty,* 389.
51. George, *Progress and Poverty,* 389–90.
52. George, *Progress and Poverty,* 397.
53. George, *Progress and Poverty,* 407.
54. George, *Progress and Poverty,* 410.
55. George, *Progress and Poverty,* 410.
56. Barker, *Henry George,* 332; William B. Weeden and Willard Brown, "Progress and Poverty," *The Atlantic Monthly,* December 1880, 846–54, https://www.theatlantic.com/magazine/archive/1880/12/progress-and-poverty/633110.
57. Barker, *Henry George,* 347.
58. Barker, *Henry George,* 357.
59. Karl Marx to Friedrich Adolph Sorge, June 20, 1881, https://www.marxists.org/archive/marx/works/1881/letters/81_06_20.htm.
60. Marx to Sorge, June 20, 1881.
61. O'Donnell, *George and Crisis of Inequality,* 120.
62. "The Anarchists and the Haymarket Square Incident, May 4, 1886," PBS, https://www.pbs.org/wgbh/americanexperience/features/chicago-anarchists-and-haymarket-square-incident.
63. O'Donnell, *George and Crisis of Inequality,* 173–82.
64. O'Donnell, *George and Crisis of Inequality,* 201–203.
65. O'Donnell, *George and Crisis of Inequality,* 204; Barker, *Henry George,* 464.
66. O'Donnell, *George and Crisis of Inequality,* 219.
67. O'Donnell, *George and Crisis of Inequality,* 232.
68. O'Donnell, *George and Crisis of Inequality,* 233–35.
69. O'Donnell, *George and Crisis of Inequality,* 162.
70. O'Donnell, *George and Crisis of Inequality,* 162.
71. Henry George, interview in *North American Review,* July 1885, cited in Martin Adams, "Henry George in Favor of a Basic Income," Progress.org, November 28, 2015, https://www.progress.org/articles/henry-george-in-favor-of-a-basic-income.
72. Christopher Chantrill, USGovernmentSpending.com, https://www.usgovernmentspending.com/downchart_gs.php?year=1800_1899&view=1&expand=&units=p&fy=fy10&chart=F0-total&bar=0&stack=1&size=m&title=Total%20Spending&state=US&col=c.
73. Federal Reserve Bank of St. Louis, "Rental Income of Persons with Capital Consumption Adjustment (CCAdj)," FRED Economic Data, May 30, 2024, https://fred.stlouisfed.org/series/RENTIN#0.
74. Andrew Mazzone, "Discussion of Revised 2016 GDP Accounts," in Edward Nell, *Progress and Poverty in Economics: Henry George and How Growth in Real Estate Contributes to Inequality and Financial Instability* (London: Palgrave Macmillan, 2019), 63.
75. White House Council of Economic Advisers, "Benefits of Competition and Indicators of Market Power," May 2016, https://obamawhitehouse.archives.gov/sites/default/files/page/files/20160502_competition_issue_brief_updated_cea.pdf.
76. Nell, *Progress and Poverty in Economics,* 13.
77. George, *Progress and Poverty,* 480–81.
78. George, *Progress and Poverty,* 495.
79. George, *Progress and Poverty,* 473.
80. George, *Progress and Poverty,* 495.

11. Thorstein Veblen and the Captains of Industry

1. Mark Twain and Charles Dudley Warner, *The Gilded Age: A Tale of Today* (Hartford, CT: American Publishing, 1873), https://www.gutenberg.org/files/3178/3178-h/3178-h.htm.
2. Matthew Josephson, *The Robber Barons* (New York: Harcourt, Brace and World, 1962).
3. Alfred D. Chandler, *The Visible Hand* (Cambridge, MA: Belknap Press of Harvard University Press, 1977), 339.

4. J. Bradford DeLong, *Slouching Towards Utopia* (New York: Basic Books, 2022), 62.

5. "Sherman Anti-Trust Act (1890)," Milestone Documents, Archives.gov, https://www
.archives.gov/milestone-documents/sherman-anti-trust-act.

6. Thomas K. McCraw and Forest Reinhardt, "Losing to Win: U.S. Steel's Pricing, Investment Decisions, and Market Share, 1901–1938," *The Journal of Economic History* 49, no. 3 (September 1989), 593.

7. Susannah Broyles, "Vanderbilt Ball: How a Costume Ball Changed New York Elite Society," Museum of the City of New York, August 6, 2013, https://www.mcny.org/story/vanderbilt-ball.

8. Sidney Fine, "Richard T. Ely, Forerunner of Progressivism, 1880–1901," *The Mississippi Valley History Review* 37, no. 4 (March 1951), 599–624.

9. For Veblen's life, see Joseph Dorfman, *Thorstein Veblen and His America* (New York: Viking Press, 1934); and Charles Camic, *Veblen* (Cambridge, MA: Harvard University Press, 2020).

10. Dorfman, *Veblen and His America*, 56.

11. Dorfman, *Veblen and His America*, 31.

12. Dorfman, *Veblen and His America*, 86–87.

13. T. B. Veblen, "Some Neglected Points in the Theory of Socialism," *The Annals of the American Academy of Political and Social Science* 2, no. 3 (November 1891), 57–84.

14. Dorfman, *Veblen and His America*, 90–104; Camic, *Veblen*, 236.

15. Dorfman, *Veblen and His America*, 90–104; Camic, *Veblen*, 257–59.

16. John Caldbick, "Panic of 1893 and Its Aftermath," HistoryLink.org, Essay 20874, October 1, 2019, https://www.historylink.org/file/20874.

17. Dorfman, *Veblen and His America*, 105–107.

18. T. B. Veblen, "The Army of the Commonweal," *Journal of Political Economy* 2, no. 3 (June 1894), 456–61.

19. Camic, *Veblen*, 180–81.

20. Richard T. Ely, "Thoughts on Immigration," no. 2, *The Congregationalist*, July 5, 1894; see Clifford F. Thies and Ryan Daza, "Richard T. Ely: The Confederate Flag of the AEA?," *Econ Journal Watch* 8, no. 2 (May 2011), 147–56, https://econjwatch.org/File+download/488 /ThiesDazaMay2011.pdf?mimetype=pdf.

21. Edward A. Ross, "The Causes of Race Superiority," *The Annals of the American Academy of Political and Social Science* 18 (July 1901), 67–89.

22. Thorstein Veblen, "Review of *Misère de la Philosophie* by Karl Marx, and of *Socialisme et Science Positive* by Enrico Ferri," *Journal of Political Economy* 5, no. 1 (December 1896), 100, https://www.jstor.org/stable/1817518?seq=4, reprinted in Charles Camic and Geoffrey M. Hodgson, eds., *The Essential Writings of Thorstein Veblen* (New York: Routledge, 2011); see also Emilie J. Raymer, "A Man of His Time: Thorstein Veblen and the University of Chicago Darwinists," *Journal of the History of Biology* 46 (2013), 669–98.

23. Veblen, "Review of *Misère de la Philosophie*," 97–103.

24. Camic, *Veblen*, 261–63.

25. Camic, *Veblen*, 295–96.

26. Dorfman, *Veblen and His America*, 132.

27. "1897 Sears, Roebuck and Incorporated Consumers Guide," no. 104, https://www.google
.com/books/edition/1897_Sears_Roebuck_Co_Catalogue/_gdrCgAAQBAJ?hl=en&gbpv=1
&pg=PA1&printsec=frontcover.

28. Thorstein Veblen, "The Economic Theory of Woman's Dress," *The Popular Science Monthly*, no. 46 (1894), 198–205, http://www.modetheorie.de/fileadmin/Texte/v/Veblen-The_Economic
_Theory_of_Fashion_1894.pdf.

29. Thorstein B. Veblen, "The Socialist Economics of Karl Marx and His Followers II: The Later Marxism," *The Quarterly Journal of Economics* 21, no. 1 (February 1907), 299–322, 304; see also Camic, *Veblen*, 319.

30. Thorstein Veblen, "Why Is Economics Not an Evolutionary Science?," *The Quarterly Journal of Economics* 12, no. 4 (July 1898), 373–97.

31. Camic, *Veblen*, 274.

32. Camic, *Veblen*, 274.

33. Camic, *Veblen*, 298.

34. Thorstein Veblen, *The Theory of the Leisure Class* (New York: Oxford University Press, 2007), 10.

35. Veblen, *Theory of the Leisure Class*, 21.

36. Veblen, *Theory of the Leisure Class*, 24.

37. Veblen, *Theory of the Leisure Class*, 26.

38. Veblen, *Theory of the Leisure Class*, 26.

39. Veblen, *Theory of the Leisure Class*, 29.

40. Veblen, *Theory of the Leisure Class*, 29.

41. Veblen, *Theory of the Leisure Class*, 60.

42. Veblen, *Theory of the Leisure Class*, 52.

43. Veblen, *Theory of the Leisure Class*, 53.

44. Veblen, *Theory of the Leisure Class*, 59.

45. Veblen, *Theory of the Leisure Class*, 59.

46. Veblen, *Theory of the Leisure Class*, 59.

47. Veblen, *Theory of the Leisure Class*, 138.

48. Veblen, *Theory of the Leisure Class*, 139.

49. Veblen, *Theory of the Leisure Class*, 149.

50. Veblen, *Theory of the Leisure Class*, 150.

51. Veblen, *Theory of the Leisure Class*, 160.

52. Veblen, *Theory of the Leisure Class*, 151.

53. Veblen, *Theory of the Leisure Class*, 157.

54. Veblen, *Theory of the Leisure Class*, 158.

55. Veblen, *Theory of the Leisure Class*, 157.

56. Veblen, *Theory of the Leisure Class*, 156.

57. William Dean Howells, "An Opportunity for American Fiction," *Literature: An International Gazette of Criticism*, no. 16 (April 28, 1899), 361–62, and no. 17 (May 5, 1899), http://www.geocities.ws/veblenite/txt/rv_tlcho.txt.

58. John Cummings, "The Theory of the Leisure Class," *The Journal of Political Economy* 7, no. 4 (September 1899), 425–55, https://www.jstor.org/stable/1817954.

59. Cummings, "Theory of the Leisure Class," 432.

60. Cummings, "Theory of the Leisure Class," 441, 443.

61. Camic, *Veblen*, 10–11.

62. Cummings, "Theory of the Leisure Class," 443–44.

63. Thorstein Veblen, "Mr. Cummings's Strictures on 'The Theory of the Leisure Class,'" *The Journal of Political Economy* 8, no. 1 (December 1899), 106–17.

64. Camic, *Veblen*, 321–22.

65. Thorstein Veblen, *The Theory of Business Enterprise* (New York: C. Scribner's Sons, 1904; 2016 reprint), 18.

66. Veblen, *Theory of Business Enterprise*, 18–19.

67. Veblen, *Theory of Business Enterprise*, 28–29.

68. Veblen, *Theory of Business Enterprise*, 27.

69. Veblen, *Theory of Business Enterprise*, 35.

70. "Supreme Court Upholds Antitrust Act in *Northern Securities Co. v. United States*," *Constitutional Law Reporter*, https://constitutionallawreporter.com/2016/02/09/supreme-court-uphold-antitrust-act-in-northern-securities-co-v-united-states.

71. Veblen, *Theory of Business Enterprise*, 35.

72. Veblen, *Theory of Business Enterprise*, 38.

73. Veblen, *Theory of Business Enterprise*, 41.

74. Veblen, *Theory of Business Enterprise*, 102.

75. Veblen, *Theory of Business Enterprise*, 99.

76. Veblen, *Theory of Business Enterprise*, 92.

77. Veblen, *Theory of Business Enterprise*, 24.

78. Veblen, *Theory of Business Enterprise*, 21.

79. Veblen, *Theory of Business Enterprise*, 104.

80. Veblen, *Theory of Business Enterprise*, 226.

81. Veblen, *Theory of Business Enterprise*, 227.

82. Veblen, *Theory of Business Enterprise*, 227–28.

83. Veblen, *Theory of Business Enterprise*, 230.
84. Veblen, *Theory of Business Enterprise*, 231.

12. John Hobson's Theory of Imperialism

1. P. J. Cain, "J. A. Hobson, Cobdenism, and the Radical Theory of Economic Imperialism, 1898–1914," *The Economic History Review* 31, no. 4 (November 1978), 565–84, https://www .jstor.org/stable/2595749?read-now=1&seq=1#page_scan_tab_contents.
2. M. E. Chamberlain, "Imperialism and Social Reform," chapter 7 in C. C. Eldridge, ed., *British Imperialism in the Nineteenth Century* (London: Palgrave, 1984), https://link.springer .com/chapter/10.1007/978-1-349-17655-7_8.
3. See Cain, "J. A. Hobson, Cobdenism," note 1, 571.
4. J. A. Hobson, *Confessions of an Economic Heretic* (London: George Allen and Unwin, 1938), 61.
5. Niall Ferguson, *Empire* (New York: Basic Books, 2003), 190.
6. Hobson, *Confessions of an Economic Heretic*, 61.
7. Hobson, *Confessions of an Economic Heretic*, 62.
8. Hobson, *Confessions of an Economic Heretic*, 61.
9. Hobson, *Confessions of an Economic Heretic*, 61.
10. Hobson, *Confessions of an Economic Heretic*, 62.
11. Ferguson, *Empire*, 191.
12. Cecil Rhodes, "Confession of Faith" (1877), quoted in John E. Flint, *Cecil Rhodes* (Boston: Little, Brown, 1974), 248–52, https://sites.pitt.edu/~syd/rhod.html.
13. Hobson, *Confessions of an Economic Heretic*, 15.
14. Hobson, *Confessions of an Economic Heretic*, 25–26.
15. Hobson, *Confessions of an Economic Heretic*, 30.
16. Hobson, *Confessions of an Economic Heretic*, 28.
17. Hobson, *Confessions of an Economic Heretic*, 30.
18. A. F. Mummery and J. A. Hobson, *The Physiology of Industry* (London: John Murray, 1889), v.
19. Mummery and Hobson, *Physiology of Industry*, iv.
20. John Maynard Keynes, *A Treatise on Money, Volume II: The Applied Theory of Money* (London: Macmillan, 1930), 148–62, https://archive.org/details/bmshri.treatiseonmoneyv0000johnvol -II/page/148/mode/2up?q=mere+.
21. Mummery and Hobson, *Physiology of Industry*, vi.
22. Hobson, *Confessions of an Economic Heretic*, 30.
23. John A. Hobson, *The Evolution of Modern Capitalism: A Study of Machine Production* (London: Walter Scott, 1894), 380, http://tankona.free.fr/hobson1894b.pdf.
24. Hobson, *Confessions of an Economic Heretic*, 28–39.
25. Hobson, *Confessions of an Economic Heretic*, 35–36.
26. Hobson, *Confessions of an Economic Heretic*, 21–28.
27. J. A. Hobson, *Imperialism: A Study of the History, Politics and Economics of the Colonial Powers in Europe and America* (London: James Nisbet, 1902), iv.
28. Hobson, *Imperialism: A Study*, 42.
29. Hobson, *Imperialism: A Study*, 51.
30. Hobson, *Imperialism: A Study*, 51.
31. Hobson, *Imperialism: A Study*, 54.
32. Hobson, *Imperialism: A Study*, 54.
33. Hobson, *Imperialism: A Study*, 56–57.
34. Hobson, *Imperialism: A Study*, 58.
35. Hobson, *Imperialism: A Study*, 57.
36. Hobson, *Imperialism: A Study*, 60.
37. Hobson, *Imperialism: A Study*, 60–61.
38. Hobson, *Imperialism: A Study*, 82–83, 85.
39. Hobson, *Imperialism: A Study*, 86.
40. Hobson, *Imperialism: A Study*, 86.
41. Hobson, *Imperialism: A Study*, 88.
42. Hobson, *Imperialism: A Study*, 92.

43. Hobson, *Imperialism: A Study*, 92.
44. Hobson, *Imperialism: A Study*, 90–91.
45. Hobson, *Imperialism: A Study*, 91.
46. Hobson, *Imperialism: A Study*, 95.
47. Hobson, *Imperialism: A Study*, 95.
48. Hobson, *Imperialism: A Study*, 95.
49. J. A. Hobson, *Imperialism: A Study* (London: James Nisbet, 1902), 45.
50. J. A. Hobson, *The War in South Africa: Its Causes and Effects* (London: James Nisbet, 1900), 226.
51. Hobson, *Imperialism: A Study*, 64.
52. Hobson, *Imperialism: A Study*, 96.
53. Hobson, *Imperialism: A Study*, 149.
54. Bruce Murray, "The 'People's Budget' a Century On," *Journal of Liberal History* 64 (Autumn 2009), http://www.liberalhistory.org.uk/wp-content/uploads/2014/10/64_Murray_Peoples _Budget.pdf.
55. J. A. Hobson, *The Crisis of Liberalism: New Issues of Democracy* (London: P. S. King and Son, 1909), 3.
56. Angus Maddison, *The World Economy*, 2 vols. (Paris: OECD, 2006), 426–27; and Ferguson, *Empire*, 240.
57. Hobson, *Confessions of an Economic Heretic*, 94.

13. Rosa Luxemburg on Capitalism, Colonialism, and War

1. Paul Frölich, *Rosa Luxemburg* (1940; reprinted by Haymarket Books, 2010), 2–4.
2. J. P. Nettl, *Rosa Luxemburg*, 2 vols. (London: Verso, 2019), 56.
3. Frölich, *Rosa Luxemburg*, 6.
4. Frölich, *Rosa Luxemburg*, 9.
5. Julius Wolf, *Autobiography of Julius Wolf* (Leipzig, 1924), 12; quoted in Nettl, *Rosa Luxemburg*, 64.
6. Rosa Luxemburg, *The Industrial Development of Poland*, sec. 1.3, https://www.marxists.org /archive/luxemburg/1898/industrial-poland/ch03.htm.
7. Luxemburg, *Industrial Development*.
8. Frölich, *Rosa Luxemburg*, 12.
9. Frölich, *Rosa Luxemburg*, 14.
10. Nettl, *Rosa Luxemburg*, 72–73.
11. Nettl, *Rosa Luxemburg*, 34.
12. Nettl, *Rosa Luxemburg*, 131.
13. Frölich, *Rosa Luxemburg*, 47–51.
14. Edward Bernstein, *Evolutionary Socialism*, Edith C. Harvey, trans. (New York: B. W. Huebsch, 1909), xi.
15. Bernstein, *Evolutionary Socialism*, xi.
16. Bernstein, *Evolutionary Socialism*, xiv.
17. Peter Gay, *The Dilemma of Democratic Socialism* (New York: Columbia University Press, 1952), 67.
18. Nettl, *Rosa Luxemburg*, 138.
19. Rosa Luxemburg, *Reform or Revolution?* (Paris: Foreign Languages Press, 2020), 54.
20. Luxemburg, *Reform or Revolution?*, 18.
21. Luxemburg, *Reform or Revolution?*, 34.
22. Luxemburg, *Reform or Revolution?*, 1.
23. Luxemburg, *Reform or Revolution*, 2.
24. Frölich, *Rosa Luxemburg*, 73–74.
25. Frölich, *Rosa Luxemburg*, 99.
26. Nettl, *Rosa Luxemburg*, 346.
27. Nettl, *Rosa Luxemburg*, 348–50.
28. Nettl, *Rosa Luxemburg*, 351–57.
29. Nettl, *Rosa Luxemburg*, 359–60.
30. Nettl, *Rosa Luxemburg*, 378–82.
31. Nettl, *Rosa Luxemburg*, 390.

32. Rosa Luxemburg to Leo Jogiches, January 9, 1899, in Peter Hudis and Kevin B. Anderson, eds., *The Rosa Luxemburg Reader* (New York: Monthly Review Press, 2004), 380–81.
33. Nettl, *Rosa Luxemburg*, 399.
34. Rosa Luxemburg to Konstantin Zetkin, November 1911, in Georg Adler, Peter Hudis, and Annelies Laschitza, eds., *The Letters of Rosa Luxemburg* (London: Verso, 2011), quoted in Nettl, *Rosa Luxemburg*, 530.
35. Rosa Luxemburg to Hans Diefenbach, May 12, 1917, quoted in Frölich, *Rosa Luxemburg*, 159.
36. Rosa Luxemburg, *The Accumulation of Capital: A Contribution to the Economic Theory of Imperialism* (1913), in Peter Hudis and Paul Le Black, eds., *The Complete Works of Rosa Luxemburg*, vol. 2 (London: Verso, 2016), 6.
37. Luxemburg, *Accumulation of Capital*, 7.
38. Luxemburg, *Accumulation of Capital*, 240.
39. Luxemburg, *Accumulation of Capital*, 249.
40. Luxemburg, *Accumulation of Capital*, 302.
41. Luxemburg, *Accumulation of Capital*, 303.
42. Karl Marx and Frederick Engels, *Manifesto of the Communist Party*, https://www.marxists.org/archive/marx/works/1848/communist-manifesto/ch01.htm.
43. Karl Marx, *Capital, Volume 1*, chapter 31, 915, 917.
44. Luxemburg, *Accumulation of Capital*, 262.
45. Luxemburg, *Accumulation of Capital*, 263.
46. Luxemburg, *Accumulation of Capital*, 267.
47. Luxemburg, *Accumulation of Capital*, 292.
48. Luxemburg, *Accumulation of Capital*, 285.
49. Luxemburg, *Accumulation of Capital*, 270.
50. Luxemburg, *Accumulation of Capital*, 270.
51. Luxemburg, *Accumulation of Capital*, 274.
52. Luxemburg, *Accumulation of Capital*, 325.
53. Luxemburg, *Accumulation of Capital*, 341.
54. Nettl, *Rosa Luxemburg*, 532.
55. Nettl, *Rosa Luxemburg*, 533.
56. Paul M. Sweezy, *The Theory of Capitalist Development* (New York: Monthly Review Press, 1942), 204.
57. Joan Robinson, "Introduction," in Rosa Luxemburg, *The Accumulation of Capital* (New Haven, CT: Yale University Press, 1951), 28.
58. Robinson, "Introduction," 28.
59. Nettl, *Rosa Luxemburg*, 621.
60. Rosa Luxemburg, *The Crisis in the German Social-Democracy: The "Junius" Pamphlet* (New York: Socialist Publication Society, 1919), 8.
61. Luxemburg, *Crisis in the German Social-Democracy*, 97.
62. Luxemburg, *Crisis in the German Social-Democracy*, 127.
63. Luxemburg, *Crisis in the German Social-Democracy*, 128.
64. Rudolf Hilferding, *Finance Capital* (London: Routledge and Kegan Paul, 1981), 367.
65. Karl Kautsky, "Ultra-imperialism," *Die Neue Zeit*, September 11, 1914, https://www.marxists.org/archive/kautsky/1914/09/ultra-imp.htm.
66. V. I. Lenin, *Imperialism, the Highest Stage of Capitalism: A Popular Outline* (Moscow: Foreign Languages Publishing House, 1951), 18.
67. Lenin, *Imperialism*, 151.
68. Lenin, *Imperialism*, 37.
69. Lenin, *Imperialism*, 140.
70. Lenin, *Imperialism*, 141.
71. Lenin, *Imperialism*, 104.
72. Lenin, *Imperialism*, 87.
73. Lenin, *Imperialism*, 98.
74. Lenin, *Imperialism*, 183.
75. Lenin, *Imperialism*, 211.
76. Lenin, *Imperialism*, 196.

77. Rosa Luxemburg, *The Russian Revolution*, extracts reprinted in Peter Hudis and Kevin B. Anderson, eds., *The Rosa Luxemburg Reader* (New York: Monthly Review Press, 2004), 290.
78. Luxemburg, *Russian Revolution*, 307.
79. Frölich, *Rosa Luxemburg*, 265.
80. Frölich, *Rosa Luxemburg*, 283.
81. Nettl, *Rosa Luxemburg*, 772.
82. Nettl, *Rosa Luxemburg*, 772–75.
83. Nettl, *Rosa Luxemburg*, 780.

14. Nikolai Kondratiev and the Dynamics of Capitalist Development

1. Vincent Barnett, *Kondratiev and the Dynamics of Economic Development* (New York: St. Martin's, 1998), 27.
2. Barnett, *Kondratiev*, 32.
3. Barnett, *Kondratiev*, 28–30.
4. Barnett, *Kondratiev*, 11.
5. V. I. Lenin, *The State and Revolution*, in *Collected Works, Volume 25*, 70, https://www.marxists.org/ebooks/lenin/state-and-revolution.pdf.
6. Edward Hallett Carr, *The Russian Revolution: From Lenin to Stalin (1917–1929)* (London: Macmillan Press, 1979), 24.
7. Alec Nove, *An Economic History of the USSR* (New York: Penguin Books, 1978), 94.
8. Nove, *Economic History of the USSR*, 86.
9. H. G. Wells, *Russia in the Shadows* (New York: George H. Doran, 1921), https://www.bradford-delong.com/2010/08/h-g-wells-liveblogs-the-consolidation-of-the-bolshevik-regime.html.
10. Nikolai Kondratiev, *The Year of Revolution from the Economic Point of View* (1918), quoted in Barnett, *Kondratiev*, 38.
11. Nove, *Economic History of the USSR*, 94.
12. Barnett, *Kondratiev*, 143–46.
13. Barnett, *Kondratiev*, 146–51.
14. Barnett, *Kondratiev*, 65.
15. Barnett, *Kondratiev*, 98.
16. Barnett, *Kondratiev*, 71.
17. Carr, *Russian Revolution*, 78.
18. Carr, *Russian Revolution*, 78.
19. Nikolai Kondratiev, *The World Economy and Its Conjuncture During and After the War* (Moscow, 1922).
20. Barnett, *Kondratiev*, 25.
21. Barnett, *Kondratiev*, 107.
22. Leon Trotsky, "The Curve of Capitalist Development"; originally published in *Vestnik Sotsialisticheskoi Akademii*, April 1923, https://www.marxists.org/archive/trotsky/1923/04/capdevel.htm.
23. Trotsky, "Curve of Capitalist Development."
24. Trotsky, "Curve of Capitalist Development."
25. Trotsky, "Curve of Capitalist Development."
26. Barnett, *Kondratiev*, 118.
27. Barnett, *Kondratiev*, 112–15.
28. N. D. Kondratieff, "The Long Waves in Economic Life," W. F. Stolper, trans., *The Review of Economic Statistics* 17, no. 6 (November 1935), 105–15, https://www.jstor.org/stable/1928486?seq=7; George Garvy, "Kondratieff's Theory of Long Cycles," *The Review of Economic Statistics* (November 1943), 203–20, https://www.jstor.org/stable/1927337.
29. Garvy, "Kondratieff's Theory of Long Cycles," 208.
30. Garvy, "Kondratieff's Theory of Long Cycles," 208.
31. Kondratieff, "Long Waves in Economic Life," 112.
32. Kondratieff, "Long Waves in Economic Life," 113.
33. Kondratieff, "Long Waves in Economic Life," 112.
34. Kondratieff, "Long Waves in Economic Life," 112.

35. Kondratieff, "Long Waves in Economic Life," 112.
36. Paul Mason, *Postcapitalism: A Guide to Our Future* (New York: Farrar, Straus and Giroux, 2015), 40.
37. Garvy, "Kondratieff's Theory of Long Cycles," 210.
38. Mason, *Postcapitalism*, 41.
39. Mason, *Postcapitalism*, 41.
40. Barnett, *Kondratiev*, 112.
41. Joseph Stalin, "Political Report of the Central Committee," *The Fourteenth Congress of the C.P.S.U.(B.)*, December 18–31, 1925.
42. Carr, *Russian Revolution*, 110.
43. Vincent Barnett, "At the Margins of the Market: Conceptions of the Market and Market Economics in Soviet Economic Theory During the New Economic Policy, 1921–1929" (doctoral thesis, Glasgow University, 1992), 214, https://core.ac.uk/download/pdf/293039513.pdf.
44. Barnett, *Kondratiev*, 158.
45. Nove, *Economic History of the USSR*, 144.
46. Nove, *Economic History of the USSR*, 145.
47. Barnett, *Kondratiev*, 121.
48. Barnett, *Kondratiev*, 189.
49. Garvy, "Kondratieff's Theory of Long Cycles," 204.
50. Barnett, *Kondratiev*, 192.
51. R. W. Davies, "Peaches from Our Tree," *London Review of Books* 17, no. 17 (September 7, 1995), https://www.lrb.co.uk/the-paper/v17/n17/r.w.-davies/peaches-from-our-tree.
52. Davies, "Peaches from Our Tree."
53. Barnett, *Kondratiev*, 196.
54. Yuri Yakovets, "The Heritage of Nikolai Kondratieff: A View from the 21st Century," *Comparative Civilizations Review*, 2007, 6.
55. Yakovets, "Heritage of Nikolai Kondratieff," 7.
56. Orlando Figes, "Section 10: Revolution from Above: Economic Growth and Living Standards During the 1930s," OrlandoFiges.info, http://www.orlandofiges.info/section10_RevolutionfromAbove/EconomicGrowthandLivingStandardsDuringthe1930s.php.
57. Ian Kershaw, *To Hell and Back* (New York: Allen Lane, 2015), 165.
58. Robert Allen, "A Reassessment of the Soviet Industrial Revolution," *Comparative Economic Studies* 47, no. 2 (June 2005), 315–32, 315.
59. Scott Gehlbach, "What Did Stalinist Industrialization Accomplish?," Broadstreet, March 22, 2021, https://broadstreet.blog/2021/03/22/what-did-stalinist-industrialization-accomplish.
60. Joseph A. Schumpeter, *Business Cycles: A Theoretical, Historical, and Statistical Analysis of the Capitalist Process* (New York: McGraw Hill, 1939), 11.
61. Garvy, "Kondratieff's Theory of Long Cycles," 218.
62. Eirini Ozouni, Constantinos Katrakylidis, and Grigoris Zarotiadis, "Technology Evolution and Long Waves: Investigating Their Relation with Spectral and Cross-Spectral Analysis," *Journal of Applied Economics* 21, no. 1 (December 2018), 160–74.

15. John Maynard Keynes's Blueprint for Managed Capitalism

1. Roy Harrod, *The Life of John Maynard Keynes* (London: St. Martin's Press, 1963), 318.
2. John Maynard Keynes, *The Economic Consequences of the Peace* (London: Macmillan, 1920), 251.
3. Jeffry A. Frieden, *Global Capitalism: Its Rise and Fall in the Twentieth Century* (New York: W. W. Norton, 2007), 130, 132.
4. Frieden, *Global Capitalism*, 132.
5. Minutes of the Second Congress of the Second International, Seventh Session, July 30, 1920, https://www.marxists.org/history/international/comintern/2nd-congress/ch07.htm.
6. B. BlackPast, "(1921) Marcus Garvey, 'Address to the Second UNIA Convention,'" BlackPast.org, September 29, 2011, https://www.blackpast.org/african-american-history/1921-marcus-garvey-address-second-unia-convention.
7. Robert Skidelsky, *John Maynard Keynes, Volume 1: Hopes Betrayed, 1883–1920* (New York: Viking, 1986), 176.

8. Leon Edel, *Bloomsbury: A House of Lions* (Philadelphia: Lippincott, 1979), 245.
9. John Maynard Keynes, "Am I a Liberal?," *The Nation and Athenaeum*, August 8 and 15, 1925, https://www.hetwebsite.net/het/texts/keynes/keynes1925liberal.htm.
10. John Maynard Keynes, "Economic Possibilities for Our Grandchildren," 1930; reprinted in John Maynard Keynes, *Essays in Persuasion* (London: Macmillan, 1931).
11. Keynes, "Economic Possibilities for Our Grandchildren."
12. John Maynard Keynes, *A Tract on Monetary Reform* (London: Macmillan, 1923), 172, https://www.gutenberg.org/cache/epub/65278/pg65278-images.html.
13. Keynes, *Tract on Monetary Reform*, 175.
14. Keynes, *Tract on Monetary Reform*, 67.
15. Robert Skidelsky, *John Maynard Keynes, Volume 2: The Economist as Savior, 1920–1937* (London: Macmillan, 1992), 152.
16. Skidelsky, *John Maynard Keynes, Volume 2*, 152; David Jacks, "The First Great Trade Collapse: The Effects of World War I on International Trade in the Short and Long Run," in Stephen Broadberry and Mark Harrison, eds., *The Economics of the Great War: A Centennial Perspective* (London: CEPR Press, 2018). (There are various estimates.)
17. John Maynard Keynes, "Does Unemployment Need a Drastic Remedy?," *The Nation and Athenaeum*, May 24, 1924.
18. Keynes, "Does Unemployment Need a Drastic Remedy?"
19. John Maynard Keynes, "Does Unemployment Need a Drastic Remedy?: A Reply to the Critics," *The Nation and Athenaeum*, June 7, 1924.
20. John Maynard Keynes, *The End of Laissez-Faire* (London: Hogarth Press, 1926), https://www.panarchy.org/keynes/laissezfaire.1926.html.
21. Keynes, *End of Laissez-Faire*.
22. Skidelsky, *John Maynard Keynes, Volume 2*, 340.
23. Frieden, *Global Capitalism*, 175.
24. Harrod, *Life of John Maynard Keynes*, 398.
25. Frieden, *Global Capitalism*, 175.
26. Gary Richardson, "Banking Panics of 1930–31," Federal Reserve History, November 22, 2013, https://www.federalreservehistory.org/essays/banking-panics-1930–31.
27. Harrod, *Life of John Maynard Keynes*, 407.
28. Donald Moggridge, *Maynard Keynes: An Economist's Biography* (London: Routledge, 1992), 523.
29. Moggridge, *Maynard Keynes*, 528.
30. Skidelsky, *John Maynard Keynes, Volume 2*, 481.
31. Skidelsky, *John Maynard Keynes, Volume 2*, 506.
32. Linda Levine, *Job Creation Programs of the Great Depression: The WPA and the CCC*, Congressional Research Service, January 14, 2010, https://www2.law.umaryland.edu/marshall/crsreports/crsdocuments/R41017_01142010.pdf.
33. Mark Blyth, *Great Transformations: Economic Ideas and Institutional Change in the Twentieth Century* (Cambridge: Cambridge University Press, 2002), 108–10.
34. Walter Galenson and Arnold Zellner, "International Comparison of Unemployment Rates," *The Measurement and Behavior of Unemployment* (National Bureau of Research, 1957), appendix 1, 548, https://www.nber.org/system/files/chapters/c2649/c2649.pdf.
35. Skidelsky, *John Maynard Keynes, Volume 2*, 520.
36. John Maynard Keynes, *The General Theory of Employment, Interest, and Money* (San Diego: Harvest/Harcourt, Brace, Jovanovich, 1964), 25.
37. Keynes, *General Theory*, 28.
38. Keynes, *General Theory*, 127–28.
39. Keynes, *General Theory*, 129.
40. Keynes, *General Theory*, 375–76.
41. Keynes, *General Theory*, 376.
42. Keynes, *General Theory*, 378.
43. Keynes, *General Theory*, 378.
44. Keynes, *General Theory*, 377.
45. Keynes, *General Theory*, 380.
46. Keynes, *General Theory*, 381.

47. John Maynard Keynes, "The Great Slump of 1930," reprinted in John Maynard Keynes, *Essays in Persuasion* (London: Macmillan, 1931), http://www.gutenberg.ca/ebooks/keynes -slump/keynes-slump-00-h.html.

48. Keynes, *General Theory*, 383.

49. US Office of Management and Budget and Federal Reserve Bank of St. Louis, "Federal Surplus or Deficit [-] as Percent of Gross Domestic Product," Federal Reserve Bank of St. Louis, FRED Economic Data, March 28, 2024, https://fred.stlouisfed.org/series/FYFSGDA188S.

50. House of Lords, *Employment Policy* (London: His Majesty's Stationery Office, 1944), 3, https://hansard.parliament.uk/Lords/1944–07–05/debates/9a840ad0–58c5–48bc-b5e7–99b159 289d27/EmploymentPolicy.

51. Alan Brinkley, *The End of Reform* (New York: Vintage, 1996), 233.

52. Brinkley, *End of Reform*, 263.

53. Frieden, *Global Capitalism*, 258.

16. Karl Polanyi's Warnings About Capitalism and Democracy

1. Lee Congdon, "Karl Polanyi in Hungary, 1900–19," *Journal of Contemporary History* 11, no. 1 (January 1976), 167–83, 171, https://www.jstor.org/stable/260008.

2. Gareth Dale, *Karl Polanyi: A Life on the Left* (New York: Columbia University Press, 2016), 48.

3. Dale, *Karl Polanyi*, 59.

4. Dale, *Karl Polanyi*, 67.

5. Dale, *Karl Polanyi*, 69.

6. Dale, *Karl Polanyi*, 71.

7. Dale, *Karl Polanyi*, 70.

8. Karl Polanyi, *The Great Transformation: The Political and Economic Origins of Our Time* (Boston: Beacon Press, 1957), 288.

9. Tim Rogan, *The Moral Economists: R. H. Tawney, Karl Polanyi, E. P. Thompson, and the Critique of Capitalism* (Princeton, NJ: Princeton University Press, 2017), 60.

10. Dale, *Karl Polanyi*, 86; see also 311n117.

11. Dale, *Karl Polanyi*, 88.

12. Dale, *Karl Polanyi*, 81.

13. Karl Polanyi, "The Essence of Fascism," in John Lewis, Karl Polanyi, and Donald K. Kitchin, eds., *Christianity and the Social Revolution* (London: Victor Gollancz, 1935), 359, http://kpolanyi.scoolaid.net:8080/xmlui/handle/10694/565.

14. Polanyi, "Essence of Fascism," 367.

15. Polanyi, "Essence of Fascism," 367.

16. Polanyi, "Essence of Fascism," 391.

17. Polanyi, "Essence of Fascism," 391.

18. Karl Polanyi, "Marxism Re-stated," *New Britain* 3, no. 59 (1934); quoted in Dale, *Karl Polanyi*, 126.

19. Polanyi, "Essence of Fascism," 392.

20. Polanyi, "Essence of Fascism," 392.

21. Polanyi, "Essence of Fascism," 391.

22. Karl Polanyi, "The Fascist Virus," first and second drafts, http://kpolanyi.scoolaid.net:8080/xmlui/handle/10694/658.

23. Dale, *Karl Polanyi*, 176.

24. Dale, *Karl Polanyi*, 169.

25. Dale, *Karl Polanyi*, 178.

26. Polanyi, *Great Transformation*, 3.

27. Polanyi, *Great Transformation*, 3.

28. Polanyi, *Great Transformation*, 3–4.

29. Polanyi, *Great Transformation*, 139.

30. Polanyi, *Great Transformation*, 140.

31. Polanyi, *Great Transformation*, 216.

32. Polanyi, *Great Transformation*, 102.

33. Polanyi, *Great Transformation*, 137.

34. Polanyi, *Great Transformation*, 226.
35. Polanyi, *Great Transformation*, 225.
36. Polanyi, *Great Transformation*, 226.
37. Polanyi, *Great Transformation*, 141.
38. Polanyi, *Great Transformation*, 214.
39. Polanyi, *Great Transformation*, 216.
40. Polanyi, *Great Transformation*, 217.
41. Polanyi, *Great Transformation*, 217.
42. Polanyi, *Great Transformation*, 218.
43. Polanyi, *Great Transformation*, 249.
44. Polanyi, *Great Transformation*, 231.
45. Polanyi, *Great Transformation*, 233.
46. Polanyi, *Great Transformation*, 233.
47. Polanyi, *Great Transformation*, 236.
48. Polanyi, *Great Transformation*, 239.
49. Polanyi, *Great Transformation*, 238.
50. Polanyi, *Great Transformation*, 237.
51. Polanyi, *Great Transformation*, 245.
52. Polanyi, *Great Transformation*, 245.
53. Polanyi, *Great Transformation*, 257.
54. Dale, *Karl Polanyi*, 146.
55. Dale, *Karl Polanyi*, 147.
56. Polanyi, *Great Transformation*, 256.
57. Polanyi, *Great Transformation*, 258.
58. J. H. Hexter, "The Great Transformation. By Karl Polanyi," book review, *The American Historical Review* 50, no. 3 (April 1945), 502.
59. Rogan, *Moral Economists*, 80.
60. Dale, *Karl Polanyi*, 220; see also 349*n149*.

17. Two Skeptics of Keynesianism: Paul Sweezy and Michał Kalecki

1. Samuel H. Williamson, "Annualized Growth Rate of Various Historical Economic Series," MeasuringWorth.com, 2024, https://www.measuringworth.com/calculators/growth.
2. US Bureau of Labor Statistics, "Unemployment Rate [UNRATE]," Federal Reserve Bank of St. Louis, FRED Economic Data, June 7, 2024, https://fred.stlouisfed.org/series/UNRATE.
3. Angus Maddison, *The World Economy: A Millennial Perspective* (Paris: OECD, 2001), 131.
4. Maddison, *World Economy*, 134.
5. Maddison, *World Economy*, 126.
6. Maddison, *World Economy*, 134.
7. Russell Sage Foundation, "Real Mean and Median Income, Families and Individuals, 1947–2012, and Households, 1967–2012," *Chartbook of Social Inequality*, https://www.russellsage.org/sites/all/files/chartbook/Income%20and%20Earnings.pdf.
8. Thomas Piketty, Emmanuel Saez, and Gabriel Zucman, "Distributional National Accounts: Methods and Estimates for the United States," National Bureau of Economic Research Working Paper 22945, December 2016, 43, figure 2.
9. Maddison, *World Economy*, 135.
10. Maddison, *World Economy*, 135.
11. Jeffry A. Frieden, *Global Capitalism: Its Rise and Fall in the Twentieth Century* (New York: W. W. Norton, 2007), 297.
12. C.A.R. Crosland, "The Transition from Capitalism," in R.H.S. Crossman, ed., *New Fabian Essays* (New York: Praeger, 1952), 33–68.
13. Paul M. Sweezy, *The Theory of Capitalist Development* (New York: Modern Reader Paperbacks, 1968), 235.
14. Sweezy, *Theory of Capitalist Development*, 236.
15. Sweezy, *Theory of Capitalist Development*, 236.
16. Sweezy, *Theory of Capitalist Development*, 348.
17. Sweezy, *Theory of Capitalist Development*, 348–49.

18. John Bellamy Foster, "On the Laws of Capitalism: 1. Insights from the Sweezy-Schumpeter Debate," *Monthly Review*, May 1, 2011, https://monthlyreview.org/2011/05/01/on-the-laws -of-capitalism.

19. Joseph A. Schumpeter, *Capitalism, Socialism, and Democracy*, 3rd ed. (New York: Harper Brothers, 1950), 83.

20. Sweezy, *Theory of Capitalist Development*, 349.

21. Sweezy, *Theory of Capitalist Development*, 349.

22. Sweezy, *Theory of Capitalist Development*, 351–52.

23. Sweezy, *Theory of Capitalist Development*, 352.

24. Michał Kalecki, "Political Aspects of Full Employment," *Political Quarterly* 14, no. 4 (October 1943), https://delong.typepad.com/kalecki43.pdf.

25. Jan Toporowski, *Michał Kalecki: An Intellectual Biography, Volume I: Rendezvous in Cambridge, 1899–1939* (New York: Palgrave Macmillan, 2013).

26. L. R. Klein, "The Life of John Maynard Keynes," book review, *Journal of Political Economy* 59, no. 5 (October 1951), 447, https://www.jstor.org/stable/1825258?seq=5.

27. M. Kalecki, "A Macrodynamic Theory of Business Cycles," *Econometrica* 3, no. 3 (July 1935), https://archive.org/details/Kalecki1935.AMacrodynamicTheoryOfBusinessCycles/page/n1 /mode/2up?view=theater.

28. Marjorie S. Turner, *Joan Robinson and the Americans* (Armonk, NY: M. E. Sharpe, 1989), 63.

29. Turner, *Joan Robinson*, 63.

30. Malcolm C. Sawyer, *The Economics of Michał Kalecki* (New York: M. E. Sharpe, 1985), 6.

31. See Ivan Figura, "Michal Kalecki," *BIATEC* 13, no. 10 (2005), https://www.nbs.sk/_img /documents/biatec/bia10_05/21_25.pdf.

32. M. Kalecki, "What Is Inflation?," *Bulletin of the Oxford University Institute of Economics and Statistics* 3, no. 8 (June 1941).

33. M. Kalecki, "Economic Implications of the Beveridge Plan," *Bulletin of the Oxford University Institute of Economics and Statistics* 5, suppl. 4 (February 20, 1943); Sawyer, *Economics of Michał Kalecki*, 131–32.

34. M. Kalecki, "Political Aspects of Full Employment," section I, *The Political Quarterly* 14, no. 4 (October 1943).

35. M. Kalecki, "Political Aspects of Full Employment," section III, *The Political Quarterly* 14, no. 4 (October 1943).

36. M. Kalecki, "Political Aspects of Full Employment," section II, *The Political Quarterly* 14, no. 4 (October 1943).

37. Kalecki, "Political Aspects of Full Employment," section II.

38. Kalecki, "Political Aspects of Full Employment," section II.

39. Kalecki, "Political Aspects of Full Employment," section II.

40. Michal Kalecki, "Political Aspects of Full Employment," section IV, *The Political Quarterly* 14, no. 4 (October 1943).

41. Kalecki, "Political Aspects of Full Employment," section IV.

42. Kalecki, "Political Aspects of Full Employment," section IV.

43. Kalecki, "Political Aspects of Full Employment," section IV.

44. Kalecki, "Political Aspects of Full Employment," section IV, footnote 1.

45. Paul M. Sweezy, "Recent Developments in American Capitalism," *Monthly Review* 1, no. 1 (May 1949), 16–21.

46. Statista Research Department, "Number of Passenger Cars and Commercial Motor Vehicles in Use in the United States from 1900 to 1988," Statista, December 31, 1993, https:// www.statista.com/statistics/1246890/vehicles-use-united-states-historical.

47. Gerhard Peters and John T. Woolley, "Republican Party Platform of 1956," The American Presidency Project, August 20, 1956, https://www.presidency.ucsb.edu/documents/republican -party-platform-1956.

48. US Bureau of Economic Analysis, "Corporate Profits After Tax (Without IVA and CCAdj) (CP)," Federal Reserve Bank of St. Louis, https://fred.stlouisfed.org/series/CP.

49. US Bureau of Economic Analysis, "Shares of Gross Domestic Income: Corporate Profits with Inventory Valuation and Capital Consumption Adjustments, [W273RE1A156NBEA]," Federal Reserve Bank of St. Louis, June 28, 2024, https://fred.stlouisfed.org/series /W273RE1A156NBEA.

50. "Income Based: Gross Operating Surplus of Corporations: Total: CP SA £m," Census 2021, https://www.ons.gov.uk/economy/grossdomesticproductgdp/timeseries/cgbz/pn2.
51. Michal Kalecki, "Political Aspects of Full Employment," section V, *The Political Quarterly* 14, no. 4 (October 1943).
52. Paul A. Baran and Paul M. Sweezy, *Monopoly Capital: An Essay on the American Economic and Social Order* (New York: Monthly Review Press, 1966), 148.
53. Baran and Sweezy, *Monopoly Capital*, 213.
54. Baran and Sweezy, *Monopoly Capital*, 152, table 5.

18. Joan Robinson and the "Bastard Keynesians"

1. Joan Robinson, "Reminiscences," in Joan Robinson, *Contributions to Modern Economics* (Oxford: Basil Blackwell, 1978), ix.
2. Joan Robinson, "Beauty and the Beast," in Robinson, *Contributions to Modern Economics*, 274.
3. Pierro Sraffa, "The Law of Returns Under Competitive Conditions," *The Economic Journal* 36, no. 144 (December 1926), 535–50.
4. A. C. Pigou, *The Economics of Welfare* (London: Macmillan, 1920), 512.
5. Pigou, *Economics of Welfare*, vii.
6. Joan Robinson, "Foreword," in *The Economics of Imperfect Competition* (London: Macmillan, 1933), vii.
7. Robinson, *Economics of Imperfect Competition*, 52, figure 17.
8. Robinson, *Economics of Imperfect Competition*, 294, figure 78.
9. Robinson, *Economics of Imperfect Competition*, 52, figure 17.
10. Robinson, *Economics of Imperfect Competition*, 320.
11. Robinson, *Contributions to Modern Economics*, x.
12. Robinson, *Economics of Imperfect Competition*, 324.
13. Roy Harrod, *The Life of John Maynard Keynes* (London: St. Martin's Press, 1963), 451.
14. Joan Robinson, *Essays in the Theory of Employment*, 2nd ed. (Oxford: Basil Blackwell, 1947), 10.
15. Robinson, *Essays in the Theory of Employment*, 17.
16. Robinson, *Essays in the Theory of Employment*, 25.
17. Robinson, *Essays in the Theory of Employment*, 28.
18. Joan Robinson, *Economic Philosophy* (New York: Pelican Books, 1983), 73.
19. Geoffrey Harcourt and Prue Kerr, *Joan Robinson* (Houndmills, Basingstoke, Hampshire: Palgrave Macmillan, 2009), 35.
20. Harcourt and Kerr, *Joan Robinson*, 35.
21. Joan Robinson, *An Essay on Marxian Economics* (London: Macmillan, 1942), 17.
22. Robinson, *Essay on Marxian Economics*, 6.
23. Robinson, *Essay on Marxian Economics*, v.
24. Robinson, *Essay on Marxian Economics*, 2.
25. Robinson, *Essay on Marxian Economics*, 56–57.
26. Robinson, *Essay on Marxian Economics*, 3.
27. Carolina Alves, "Joan Robinson on Karl Marx: 'His Sense of Reality Is Far Stronger,'" *Journal of Economic Perspectives* 36, no. 2 (Spring 2022), 258.
28. Harcourt and Kerr, *Joan Robinson*, 62.
29. Harcourt and Kerr, *Joan Robinson*, 63.
30. Harcourt and Kerr, *Joan Robinson*, 66.
31. Harcourt and Kerr, *Joan Robinson*, 63.
32. Joan Robinson, "Preparation for War," *Monthly Review* 3, no. 6 (October 1951), 194; see also Marjorie S. Turner, *Joan Robinson and the Americans* (Armonk, NY: M. E. Sharpe, 1989), 87.
33. Robinson, "Preparation for War," 195.
34. US Bureau of Labor Statistics, "Unemployment Rate [UNRATE]," Federal Reserve Bank of St. Louis, June 27, 2024, https://fred.stlouisfed.org/series/UNRATE.
35. Robinson, "Preparation for War," 195.
36. R. F. Harrod, "An Essay in Dynamic Theory," *The Economic Journal* 49, no. 193 (March 1939), 14–33.
37. Robert M. Solow, "Growth Theory and After," Nobel Prize Lecture, December 8, 1987, https://www.nobelprize.org/prizes/economic-sciences/1987/solow/lecture.

38. Robert M. Solow, "A Contribution to the Theory of Economic Growth," *The Quarterly Journal of Economics* 70, no. 1 (February 1956), 73.
39. Joan Robinson, "The Production Function and the Theory of Capital," *The Review of Economic Studies* 21, no. 2 (1953–54), 81.
40. Joan Robinson, "Introduction," in Rosa Luxemburg, *The Accumulation of Capital*, Agnes Schwarzschild, trans. (New Haven, CT: Yale University Press, 1951), 13.
41. Turner, *Joan Robinson and the Americans*, 115.
42. Turner, *Joan Robinson and the Americans*, 116.
43. Turner, *Joan Robinson and the Americans*, 122.
44. Turner, *Joan Robinson and the Americans*, 122.
45. Robert M. Solow, "Technical Change and the Aggregate Production Function," *The Review of Economics and Statistics* 39, no. 3 (August 1957), 315, table 1.
46. Solow, "Technical Change and the Aggregate Production Function," 320.
47. Anwar Shaikh, "Laws of Production and Laws of Algebra: The Humbug Production Function," *The Review of Economics and Statistics* 56, no. 1 (February 1974), 118.
48. Turner, *Joan Robinson and the Americans*, 110.
49. Turner, *Joan Robinson and the Americans*, 111.
50. Joan Robinson, "The Age of Growth," Gildersleeve Lecture, 1976, in Joan Robinson, *Further Contributions to Modern Economics* (Oxford: Basil Blackwell, 1980), 34.
51. Joan Robinson and Frank Wilkinson, "What Has Become of Employment Policy?," *Cambridge Journal of Economics* 1, no. 1 (March 1977), in Joan Robinson, *Contributions to Modern Economics* (Oxford: Basil Blackwell), 256.
52. *Economic Report of the President*, January 1962, 3, https://www.presidency.ucsb.edu/sites/default/files/books/presidential-documents-archive-guidebook/the-economic-report-of-the-president-truman-1947-obama-2017/1962.pdf.
53. *Economic Report of the President*, 4.
54. Joan Robinson, "Latter-Day Capitalism," *New Left Review* 1, no. 16 (July–August 1962), in Robinson, *Contributions to Modern Economics*, 229.
55. Robinson, "Latter-Day Capitalism," 231.
56. Robinson, *Economic Philosophy*, 92.
57. Joan Robinson, "Has Capitalism Changed?," *Monthly Review* 13, no. 6 (October 1961), in Robinson, *Contributions to Modern Economics*, 226.
58. Robinson, "Latter-Day Capitalism," 233.
59. Robinson, "Latter-Day Capitalism," 231.
60. Robinson, "Latter-Day Capitalism," 232.
61. Robinson, "Latter-Day Capitalism," 239.
62. Robinson, "Latter-Day Capitalism," 239.
63. Geoffrey Harcourt and Prue Kerr, *Joan Robinson* (New York: Palgrave Macmillan, 2009), 66.
64. Joan Robinson, *The Cultural Revolution in China* (London: Pelican Books, 1969), 24.
65. Geoff Harcourt and John King, "Talking About Joan Robinson: Geoff Harcourt in Conversation with John King," *Review of Social Economy* 53, no. 1 (Spring 1995), 56.
66. Robinson, "Latter-Day Capitalism," 234.
67. World Bank Group, "Inflation, Consumer Prices (Annual %)—United Kingdom," https://data.worldbank.org/indicator/FP.CPI.TOTL.ZG?locations=GB.
68. Robinson, "Latter-Day Capitalism," 234.
69. Robinson, "Latter-Day Capitalism," 235.
70. Robinson, "Age of Growth," 38.
71. Robinson, "Age of Growth," 39.
72. Robinson, "Age of Growth," 42.
73. Harcourt and King, "Talking About Joan Robinson," 56.
74. Author's recollection.
75. Turner, *Joan Robinson and the Americans*, 206.

19. J. C. Kumarappa and the Economics of Permanence

1. Mark Lindley, *J. C. Kumarappa: Mahatma Gandhi's Economist* (Mumbai: Popular Prakashan, 2007); and Venu Madhav Govindu and Deepak Malghan, *The Web of Freedom:*

J. C. Kumarappa and Gandhi's Struggle for Economic Justice (New Delhi: Oxford University Press, 2016).

2. Venu Madhav Govindu and Deepak Malghan, "Building a Creative Freedom: J. C. Kumarappa and His Economic Philosophy," *Economic and Political Weekly* 40, no. 52 (December 24–30, 2005), 2.

3. J. C. Kumarappa, *An Economic Survey of Matar Taluka (Kheda District)* (Ahmedabad: Gujarat Vidyapith, 1952), 3.

4. Kumarappa, *Economic Survey of Matar Taluka*, 71.

5. Kumarappa, *Economic Survey of Matar Taluka*, 115.

6. Kumarappa, *Economic Survey of Matar Taluka*, 86, 117.

7. Kumarappa, *Economic Survey of Matar Taluka*, 118.

8. J. C. Kumarappa, *The Economy of Permanence* (Varanasi, India: Sarva Seva Sangh Prakashan, 1957), 41.

9. Lindley, *J. C. Kumarappa*, 4.

10. Lindley, *J. C. Kumarappa*, 22.

11. Lindley, *J. C. Kumarappa*, 65–66.

12. Lindley, *J. C. Kumarappa*, 66.

13. J. C. Kumarappa, *Public Finance and Our Poverty: The Contribution of Public Finance to the Present Economic State of India* (Ahmedabad: Navajivan Publishing House, 1948), 13.

14. M. K. Gandhi, *Unto This Last: A Paraphrase* (1908); reprinted by the Navajivan Trust, 1956, https://www.jmu.edu/gandhicenter/_files/gandhiana-ruskin.pdf.

15. Percival Spear, *India: A Modern History* (London: Penguin, 1966), 199.

16. Ramachandra Guha, *Gandhi: The Years That Changed the World, 1914–1948* (London: Penguin, 2019), 493.

17. Lindley, *J. C. Kumarappa*, 31.

18. Lindley, *J. C. Kumarappa*, 31.

19. J. C. Kumarappa, *Why the Village Movement? A Plea for a Village Centered Economic Order in India* (Wardha, India: All India Village Industries Association, 1936), 145, https://archive.org/details/in.ernet.dli.2015.118819.

20. Kumarappa, *Why the Village Movement?*, 141.

21. Kumarappa, *Why the Village Movement?*, 120–21.

22. Kumarappa, *Why the Village Movement?*, 104–105.

23. Lindley, *J. C. Kumarappa*, 34.

24. Lindley, *J. C. Kumarappa*, 34.

25. Lindley, *J. C. Kumarappa*, 119.

26. Larraine Boissoneault, "The Speech That Brought India to the Brink of Independence," *Smithsonian Magazine*, August 8, 2017, https://www.smithsonianmag.com/history/speech-brought-india-brink-independence-180964366.

27. Kumarappa, *Economy of Permanence*, 9.

28. Kumarappa, *Economy of Permanence*, 17.

29. Kumarappa, *Economy of Permanence*, 18.

30. Kumarappa, *Economy of Permanence*, 37.

31. Kumarappa, *Economy of Permanence*, 37.

32. Kumarappa, *Economy of Permanence*, 38.

33. Lindley, *J. C. Kumarappa*, 33.

34. Kumarappa, *Economy of Permanence*, 76.

35. Kumarappa, *Economy of Permanence*, 78.

36. Kumarappa, *Economy of Permanence*, 57.

37. Kumarappa, *Economy of Permanence*, 57–58.

38. Kumarappa, *Economy of Permanence*, 78–79.

39. Kumarappa, *Economy of Permanence*, 12–13.

40. Kumarappa, *Economy of Permanence*, 31.

41. Kumarappa, *Economy of Permanence*, 31.

42. Kumarappa, *Economy of Permanence*, 32.

43. J. C. Kumarappa, *Gandhian Economic Thought* (Bombay: Vora, 1951; reprinted by Varanasi, India: Sarva Seva Sangh Prakashan, 2010), 33, https://www.mkgandhi.org/ebks/Gandhian-Economic-Thought.pdf.

44. Kumarappa, *Gandhian Economic Thought*, 33.
45. Kumarappa, *Gandhian Economic Thought*, 53.
46. Kumarappa, *Gandhian Economic Thought*, 48.
47. Kumarappa, *Gandhian Economic Thought*, 48.
48. World Bank estimates of GDP per capita in constant (inflation adjusted) dollars are from World Bank, "GDP per Capita, PPP (constant 2021 international $)—India," World Development Indicators Database, n.d., https://data.worldbank.org/indicator/NY.GDP.PCAP.PP .KD?locations=IN.
49. Guha, *Gandhi*, 927.
50. Kumarappa, *Gandhian Economic Thought*, 57.

20. Eric Williams on Slavery and Capitalism

1. Eric Williams, *Inward Hunger: The Education of a Prime Minister* (Princeton, NJ: Markus Wiener, 2006), 43.
2. Williams, *Inward Hunger*, 26.
3. Williams, *Inward Hunger*, 27.
4. Williams, *Inward Hunger*, 36.
5. Williams, *Inward Hunger*, 46.
6. Colin A. Palmer, "Introduction," in Eric Williams: *Capitalism and Slavery* (Chapel Hill: University of North Carolina Press, 1994), xii.
7. Adam Smith, *An Inquiry into the Nature and Causes of the Wealth of Nations*, Books IV–V (New York: Penguin Books, 1999), 212.
8. Karl Marx, *Capital: A Critique of Political Economy, Volume I* (London: Penguin Classics, 1990), 873–76.
9. C. L. R. James, *The Black Jacobins: Toussaint L'Ouverture and the San Domingo Revolution* (New York: Vintage Books, 1989), ix.
10. Cedric Robinson, *Black Marxism* (Chapel Hill: University of North Carolina Press, 2000), 316.
11. W. E. B. Du Bois, *Black Reconstruction* (New York: Harcourt Brace, 1935), 39.
12. Du Bois, *Black Reconstruction*, 670.
13. Du Bois, *Black Reconstruction*, 700.
14. Du Bois, *Black Reconstruction*, 700.
15. Du Bois, *Black Reconstruction*, 701.
16. Williams, *Capitalism and Slavery*, ix.
17. Williams, *Capitalism and Slavery*, 7.
18. Williams, *Capitalism and Slavery*, 13.
19. Williams, *Capitalism and Slavery*, 19.
20. Williams, *Capitalism and Slavery*, 32–33.
21. Williams, *Capitalism and Slavery*, 37.
22. Williams, *Capitalism and Slavery*, 24.
23. Williams, *Capitalism and Slavery*, 87.
24. Williams, *Capitalism and Slavery*, 89.
25. Williams, *Capitalism and Slavery*, 47.
26. Williams, *Capitalism and Slavery*, 27.
27. Williams, *Capitalism and Slavery*, v.
28. Williams, *Capitalism and Slavery*, 105–106.
29. Williams, *Capitalism and Slavery*, 51–52.
30. Williams, *Capitalism and Slavery*, 53–54.
31. Williams, *Capitalism and Slavery*, 37.
32. Williams, *Capitalism and Slavery*, 37.
33. Williams, *Capitalism and Slavery*, 65.
34. Williams, *Capitalism and Slavery*, 63.
35. Williams, *Capitalism and Slavery*, 34.
36. Williams, *Capitalism and Slavery*, 89.
37. Williams, *Capitalism and Slavery*, 74–75.
38. Williams, *Capitalism and Slavery*, 82.

39. Williams, *Capitalism and Slavery*, 83.
40. Williams, *Capitalism and Slavery*, 52.
41. Williams, *Capitalism and Slavery*, 104.
42. James, *Black Jacobins*, 49.
43. Williams, *Capitalism and Slavery*, 68.
44. Williams, *Capitalism and Slavery*, 68.
45. Williams, *Capitalism and Slavery*, 72.
46. Williams, *Capitalism and Slavery*, 72.
47. Williams, *Capitalism and Slavery*, 128.
48. Williams, *Capitalism and Slavery*, 128.
49. Williams, *Capitalism and Slavery*, 63.
50. Williams, *Capitalism and Slavery*, 70.
51. Williams, *Capitalism and Slavery*, 70.
52. Williams, *Capitalism and Slavery*, 70.
53. Williams, *Capitalism and Slavery*, 102.
54. Williams, *Capitalism and Slavery*, 102.
55. Williams, *Capitalism and Slavery*, 103.
56. Williams, *Capitalism and Slavery*, 105.
57. Williams, *Inward Hunger*, 71.
58. Larry Neal, "The Finance of Business During the Industrial Revolution," in Roderick Floud and D. N. McCloskey, eds., *The Economic History of Britain Since 1700, Volume I: 1700–1860* (Cambridge: Cambridge University Press, 1994), 152.
59. Stanley L. Engerman, "The Slave Trade and British Capital Formation in the Eighteenth Century: A Comment on the Williams Thesis," *The Business History Review* 46, no. 4 (Winter 1972), 441.
60. Patrick K. O'Brien, "European Economic Development: The Contribution of the Periphery," *The Economic History Review* 35, no. 1 (February 1982), 18.
61. P. K. O'Brien and S. L. Engerman, "Exports and the Growth of the British Economy from the Glorious Revolution to the Peace of Amiens," in Barbara L. Solow, ed., *Slavery and the Rise of the Atlantic System* (Cambridge: Cambridge University Press, 1991), 177–209.
62. Ronald Findlay and Kevin Hjortshøj O'Rourke, "The Triangular Trade from a Global Perspective," in Colin A. Palmer, ed., *The Legacy of Eric Williams: Caribbean Scholar and Statesman* (Kingston, Jamaica: University of the West Indies Press, 2015), 165–89.
63. Ronald Findlay and Kevin H. O'Rourke, *Power and Plenty: Trade, War, and the World Economy in the Second Millennium* (Princeton, NJ: Princeton University Press, 2007), 339.
64. Robert C. Allen, *Global Economic History: A Very Short Introduction* (Oxford: Oxford University Press, 2011), 20–23.
65. Joseph E. Inikori, *Africans and the Industrial Revolution in England: A Study in International Trade and Development* (New York: Cambridge University Press, 2002), xviii.
66. Giorgio Riello, "The Globalization of Cotton Textiles: Indian Cottons, Europe, and the Atlantic World, 1600-1850," in Giorgio Riello and Prasannan Parthasarathi, eds., *The Spinning World: A Global History of Cotton Textiles, 1200–1850* (Oxford: Oxford University Press, 2009), 282.
67. Pat Hudson, "Slavery, the Slave Trade, and Economic Growth: A Contribution to the Debate," in Catherine Hall, Nicholas Draper, and Keith McClelland, eds., *Emancipation and the Remaking of the British Imperial World* (Manchester: Manchester University Press, 2014), 36–59.
68. Gavin Wright, "Slavery and Anglo-American Capitalism Revisited," *The Economic History Review* 73, no. 2 (May 2020), 358, https://economics.stanford.edu/sites/economics/files/ehr12962.pdf.
69. Wright, "Slavery and Anglo-American Capitalism Revisited," 378.
70. Williams, *Capitalism and Slavery*, 210.
71. Williams, *Capitalism and Slavery*, 212.
72. Adom Getachew, ed., *Worldmaking After Empire: The Rise and Fall of Self-Determination* (Princeton, NJ: Princeton University Press, 2019), 111.
73. Williams, *Inward Hunger*, 116.
74. C. L. R. James, *Party Politics in the West Indies* (Port of Spain, 1962), 45.

75. Minkha Makalani, "'A Very Unusual People': An Interview with Erica James and Henry James, Niece and Nephew of C.L.R. James," sx salon, July 2014, http://smallaxe.net/sxsalon/interviews/very-unusual-people.
76. "Trinidad and Tobago Economy—Patterns of Development," Theodora.com, November 1987, https://photius.com/countries/trinidad_and_tobago/economy/development.html.
77. Williams, *Inward Hunger*, 338.
78. Williams, *Inward Hunger*, 339.
79. Williams, *Inward Hunger*, 342.

21. The Rise and Fall of Dependency Theory in Latin America

1. Stanley E. Hilton, "Vargas and Brazilian Economic Development, 1930–1945," *The Journal of Economic History* 35, no. 4 (December 1975), 754–78.
2. Office of the Historian, US Department of State, "Mexican Expropriation of Foreign Oil, 1938," *Milestones in the History of U.S. Foreign Relations*, https://history.state.gov/milestones/1937–1945/mexican-oil.
3. For details on Prebisch's life, see Edgar J. Dosman, *The Life and Times of Raúl Prebisch, 1901–1986* (Montreal: McGill-Queen's University Press, 2010).
4. Raúl Prebisch, "Five Stages in My Thinking on Development," in Gerald M. Meier and Dudley Seers, eds., *Pioneers in Development* (New York: Oxford University Press, 1984), 175.
5. Angus Maddison, *The World Economy: A Millennial Perspective* (Paris: OECD, 2006), 195, table A2-c.
6. Joseph L. Love, "Raúl Prebisch and the Origins of the Doctrine of Unequal Exchange," *Latin American Research Review* 15, no. 3 (1980), 50.
7. Love, "Raúl Prebisch and the Origins of the Doctrine of Unequal Exchange," 54.
8. Raúl Prebisch and United Nations Economic Commission for Latin America and the Caribbean, *The Economic Development of Latin America and Its Principal Problems* (New York: United Nations, Department of Economic Affairs, 1949), 1.
9. Prebisch and UN Economic Commission, *Economic Development of Latin America*, 10.
10. Prebisch and UN Economic Commission, *Economic Development of Latin America*, v.
11. Raúl Prebisch, "Commercial Policy in the Underdeveloped Countries," *The American Economic Review*, Papers and Proceedings of the Seventy-first Annual Meeting of the American Economic Association, 49, no. 2 (May 1959), 251–73.
12. David Pollock, Daniel Kerner, and Joseph L. Love, "Raúl Prebisch on ECLAC's Achievements and Deficiencies: An Unpublished Interview," *CEPAL Review*, no. 75 (December 2001), 19.
13. Jeffry A. Frieden, *Global Capitalism: Its Rise and Fall in the Twentieth Century* (New York: W. W. Norton, 2007), 304.
14. Frieden, *Global Capitalism*, 305.
15. Maddison, *World Economy*, 126, table 3–1a.
16. Maddison, *World Economy*, 192, table A–g.
17. Maddison, *World Economy*, 195, table A2–c.
18. André Hofman, *The Economic Development of Latin America in the Twentieth Century* (Cheltenham, UK: Edward Elgar, 2000), table 2.2, 16.
19. Geoffrey Kay, *Development and Underdevelopment: A Marxist Analysis* (London: Macmillan Press, 1975), 127–28.
20. Werner Baer, "Import Substitution and Industrialization in Latin America: Experiences and Interpretations," *Latin American Research Review* 7, no. 1 (Spring 1972), 106.
21. Prebisch, "Five Stages in My Thinking on Development," 181.
22. In using this taxonomy, I am following the Bucknell economist Matias Vernengo's very useful survey article, "Technology, Finance, and Dependency: Latin American Radical Political Economy in Retrospect," *Review of Radical Political Economics* 38, no. 4 (Fall 2006), 551–68.
23. Dosman, *Life and Times of Raúl Prebisch*, 267.
24. Dosman, *Life and Times of Raúl Prebisch*, 303.
25. Dosman, *Life and Times of Raúl Prebisch*, 304.
26. Pedro Cezar Dutra Fonseca and Ivan Colangelo Salomão, "Furtado vs. Prebisch: A Latin American Controversy," *Investigación Económica* 77, no. 306 (2018), 74–93.

27. Celso Furtado, *Development and Underdevelopment*, Ricardo W. de Aguiar and Eric Charles Drysdale, trans. (Berkeley: University of California Press, 1964).
28. Celso Furtado, "The Brazilian 'Model,'" *Social and Economic Studies* 22, no. 1 (March 1973), 122–31.
29. Werner Baer, "Furtado on Development: A Review Essay," *The Journal of Developing Areas* 3, no. 2 (January 1969), 270–80.
30. See Reynold E. Carson, "The Andean Common Market: An Experiment in Regional Cooperation," Issues in International Education Report No. 2, Institute of International Education, 1975, 8, https://files.eric.ed.gov/fulltext/ED125443.pdf.
31. Andre Gunder Frank, Letter, Santiago, Chile, July 1, 1964, https://rrojasdatabank.info /agfrank/carta00.pdf.
32. Frank, Letter, July 1, 1964.
33. Andre Gunder Frank, "The Cold War and Me," *Bulletin of Concerned Asian Scholars* 29, no. 3 (1997), 80.
34. Andre Gunder Frank, "Not Feudalism—Capitalism," *Monthly Review* 15, no. 8 (December 1963), 468.
35. Frank, "Not Feudalism—Capitalism," 470.
36. Paul A. Baran, "On the Political Economy of Backwardness," *The Manchester School* 20, no. 1 (January 1952), 67.
37. Baran, "On the Political Economy of Backwardness," 84.
38. Paul A. Baran, *The Political Economy of Growth* (New York: Penguin Books, 1973), 282–83, http://digamo.free.fr/baran57.pdf.
39. Baran, *Political Economy of Growth*, 289.
40. Baran, *Political Economy of Growth*, 294.
41. Andre Gunder Frank, "The Development of Underdevelopment," *Monthly Review* 18, no. 4 (September 1966), 23.
42. Andre Gunder Frank, "Capitalist Underdevelopment or Socialist Revolution," in *Latin America: Underdevelopment or Revolution* (New York: Monthly Review Press, 1969), 406.
43. Frank, "Capitalist Underdevelopment or Socialist Revolution," 407.
44. Frank, "Cold War and Me," 82.
45. Theotônio dos Santos, "The Structure of Dependence," *The American Economic Review*, Papers and Proceedings of the Eighty-second Annual Meeting of the American Economic Association, 60, no. 2 (May 1970), 231.
46. Dos Santos, "Structure of Dependence," 232.
47. Dos Santos, "Structure of Dependence," 233.
48. Dos Santos, "Structure of Dependence," 234.
49. Dos Santos, "Structure of Dependence," 233.
50. Dos Santos, "Structure of Dependence," 236.
51. Walter Rodney, *How Europe Underdeveloped Africa* (Brooklyn, NY: Verso Press, 2018), 16.
52. Walter Rodney, "Aspects of the International Class Struggle in Africa, the Caribbean and America," in Horace Campbell, ed., *Pan-Africanism: Struggle Against Neo-Colonialism and Imperialism, Documents of the Sixth Pan-African Congress* (Toronto: Afro-Carib Publications, 1975), 18–41.
53. Rodney, *How Europe Underdeveloped Africa*, 344.
54. National Security Archive, "The Walter Rodney Murder Mystery in Guyana 40 Years Later," February 3, 2022, https://nsarchive.gwu.edu/briefing-book/human-rights/2020–06–13/the -walter-rodney-murder-mystery-in-guyana-40-years-later.
55. Salvador Allende, "Our Road to Socialism," First Speech to the Chilean Parliament After His Election, 1970, https://www.marxists.org/archive/allende/1970/september/20.htm#Our _road_to_Socialism.
56. "Chile—GDP per Capita," Index Mundi, https://www.indexmundi.com/facts/chile/gdp-per -capita.
57. "Macrotrends: Chile Inflation Rate, 1971–2024," https://www.macrotrends.net/global-metrics /countries/chl/chile/inflation-rate-cpi.
58. "Chile Inquiry Confirms President Allende Killed Himself," *BBC News*, July 19, 2011, https:// www.bbc.com/news/world-latin-america-14210729.

59. Central Intelligence Agency, "CIA Activities in Chile," September 19, 2000, https://nsarchive2.gwu.edu/news/20000919/01-02.htm.

60. Andre Gunder Frank, "The Underdevelopment of Development," in Sing C. Chew and Robert A. Denemark, eds., *The Underdevelopment of Development: Essays in Honor of Andre Gunder Frank* (Thousand Oaks, CA: Sage Publications, 1996), https://rrojasdatabank.info/agfrank/underdev.html.

22. Milton Friedman and the Rise of Neoliberalism

1. "Dr. Karl Polanyi, Economist, 77, Dies," *The New York Times*, April 25, 1964, 29, https://timesmachine.nytimes.com/timesmachine/1964/04/25/issue.html.

2. Milton Friedman, *Capitalism and Freedom* (Chicago: University of Chicago Press, 1962); reissued 1982, 2.

3. Friedman, *Capitalism and Freedom*, 31.

4. Friedman, *Capitalism and Freedom*, vi.

5. World Bank Group, "Inflation, Consumer Prices (Annual %)—United States," https://data.worldbank.org/indicator/FP.CPI.TOTL.ZG?locations=US.

6. US Office of Management and Budget and Federal Reserve Bank of St. Louis, "Federal Net Outlays as Percent of Gross Domestic Product (FYONGDA 188S)," Federal Reserve Bank of St. Louis, FRED Economic Data, March 28, 2024, https://fred.stlouisfed.org/series/FYONGDA188S.

7. US Bureau of Labor Statistics, "Unemployment Rate [UNRATE]," Federal Reserve Bank of St. Louis, FRED Economic Data, June 7, 2024, https://fred.stlouisfed.org/series/UNRATE.

8. "Nixon Reportedly Says He Is Now a Keynesian," *The New York Times*, January 7, 1971, https://www.nytimes.com/1971/01/07/archives/nixon-reportedly-says-he-is-now-a-keynesian.html.

9. Jeffry A. Frieden, *Global Capitalism: Its Rise and Fall in the Twentieth Century* (New York: W. W. Norton, 2007), 342.

10. Milton Friedman, "The Role of Monetary Policy," Presidential Address Delivered to the Eightieth Annual Meeting of the American Economic Association, December 29, 1967; reprinted in *The American Economic Review* 58, no. 1 (March 1968), 8.

11. Friedman, "Role of Monetary Policy," 11.

12. James Callaghan (Labour), "Leader's Speech, Blackpool 1976," British Political Speech, http://www.britishpoliticalspeech.org/speech-archive.htm?speech=174.

13. Joan Robinson and Frank Wilkinson, "What Has Become of Employment Policy?," *Cambridge Journal of Economics* 1, no. 1 (March 1977); reprinted in Joan Robinson, *Contributions to Modern Economics* (Oxford: Basil Blackwell, 1978), 263–64.

14. Andrew Glyn and Bob Sutcliffe, *Capitalism in Crisis* (New York: Pantheon Books, 1972), 73.

15. Glyn and Sutcliffe, *Capitalism in Crisis*, 76.

16. Glyn and Sutcliffe, *Capitalism in Crisis*, 102.

17. Arthur M. Okun and George L. Perry, "Notes and Numbers on the Profits Squeeze," *Brookings Papers in Economic Activity*, no. 3 (1970).

18. Organisation for Economic Co-operation and Development, "A New Approach to Fighting Inflation," *The O.E.C.D. Observer*, no. 49 (December 1970), 29, https://www.oecd-ilibrary.org/economics/oecd-observer/volume-1970/issue-6_observer-v1970-6-en.

19. OECD, "New Approach to Fighting Inflation," 30.

20. Sebastian Edwards, *The Chile Project: The Story of the Chicago Boys and the Downfall of Neoliberalism* (Princeton, NJ: Princeton University Press, 2023), 75–78.

21. Edwards, *Chile Project*, 80.

22. Edwards, *Chile Project*, 93.

23. Milton Friedman and Rose D. Friedman, *Two Lucky People: Memoirs* (Chicago: University of Chicago Press, 1998), 399.

24. Friedman and Friedman, *Two Lucky People*, 591–94.

25. Friedman and Friedman, *Two Lucky People*, 400.

26. Edwards, *Chile Project*, 98.

27. Sebastian Edwards, "Economic Policy and the Record of Economic Growth in Chile in the 1970's and 1980's," UCLA Working Papers, no. 283 (November 1982), 1, http://www.econ .ucla.edu/workingpapers/wp283.pdf.
28. Edwards, "Economic Policy and the Record of Economic Growth," 2.
29. Edwards, *Chile Project*, 104.
30. Daniel Yergin and Joseph Stanislaw, *The Commanding Heights: The Battle Between Government and the Marketplace That Is Remaking the Modern World* (New York: Simon and Schuster, 1998), 239.
31. Edwards, "Economic Policy and the Record of Economic Growth," 23.
32. David R. Henderson, "A Fascinating History of Chile's Economic Reforms and Reversals," review of Sebastian Edwards, *The Chile Project*, *Financial and Economic Review* 22, no. 3 (September 2023), 178.
33. "Report of the Chilean National Commission on Truth and Reconciliation," United States Institute of Peace, 1993, appendix II: Statistics, 1122.
34. Patrick Iber, "When Milton Friedman Met Pinochet," newrepublic.com, May 15, 2023.
35. US Office of Management and Budget and Federal Reserve Bank of St. Louis, "Federal Surplus or Deficit [-] as Percent of Gross Domestic Product (FYFSGDA188S)," Federal Reserve Bank of St. Louis, FRED Economic Data, March 28, 2024, https://fred.stlouisfed.org/series /FYFSGDA188S.
36. "U.S. Inflation Rate 1960–2024," Macrotrends, https://www.macrotrends.net/global-metrics /countries/USA/united-states/inflation-rate-cpi.
37. Jimmy Carter, "A Crisis of Confidence," Address to the Nation, July 15, 1979, Great Speeches Collection, The History Place, https://www.historyplace.com/speeches/carter-confidence.htm.
38. International Monetary Fund, "Interest Rates, Discount Rate for United States [INTD-SRUSM193N]," Federal Reserve Bank of St. Louis, FRED Economic Data, October 4, 2021, https://fred.stlouisfed.org/series/INTDSRUSM193N.
39. National Bureau of Economic Research, "US Business Cycle Expansions and Contractions," https://www.nber.org/research/data/us-business-cycle-expansions-and-contractions.
40. Federal Election Commission, "PAC's Increase in Number," January 14, 1983, https://www .fec.gov/resources/news_releases/1983/19830114_PACcount.pdf.
41. Yergin and Stanislaw, *Commanding Heights*, 343.
42. Yergin and Stanislaw, *Commanding Heights*, 342.
43. Thomas Byrne Edsall, *The New Politics of Inequality* (New York: W. W. Norton, 1984), 120.
44. Milton Friedman and Rose Friedman, *Free to Choose: A Personal Statement* (New York: Avon Books, 1981), 195.
45. Friedman and Friedman, *Free to Choose*, 297.
46. Martin Anderson, *Revolution* (San Diego: Harcourt Brace Jovanovich, 1988), 172.
47. Hyman P. Minsky, "The Financial Instability Hypothesis: A Restatement," Thames Papers in Political Economy (Autumn 1978), 3.
48. Minsky, "Financial Instability Hypothesis: A Restatement," 2.
49. Minsky, "Financial Instability Hypothesis: A Restatement," 17.
50. Minsky, "Financial Instability Hypothesis: A Restatement," 17.

23. Nicholas Georgescu-Roegen and the Limits to Growth

1. *Economic Report of the President: Transmitted to the Congress, January 1962, Together with the Annual Report of the Council of Economic Advisers* (Washington, DC: US Government Printing Office, 1962), 9, https://www.presidency.ucsb.edu/sites/default/files/books /presidential-documents-archive-guidebook/the-economic-report-of-the-president-truman -1947-obama-2017/1962.pdf.
2. Roy Harrod, *Reforming the World's Money* (London: Macmillan, 1965), 77.
3. Stewart L. Udall, *The Quiet Crisis* (New York: Avon Books, 1963), viii.
4. George P. Marsh, *Man and Nature; or, Physical Geography as Modified by Human Action* (New York: Charles Scribner, 1867), 36, https://www.gutenberg.org/files/37957/37957-h /37957-h.htm.
5. John Stuart Mill, *Principles of Political Economy*, abridged version (New York: D. Appleton, 1884), 173.

6. Paul A. Samuelson, *Economics: An Introductory Analysis*, 6th ed. (New York: McGraw-Hill, 1964), 811–38, https://archive.org/details/economicssixthed0000unse/page/n5/mode/2up.

7. Maria Shahgedanova and Timothy P. Burt, "New Data on Air Pollution in the Former Soviet Union," *Global Environmental Change* 4, no. 3 (September 1994), 201–27.

8. Glenn E. Curtis, ed., *Russia: A Country Study* (Washington, DC: Federal Research Division, Library of Congress, 1996), https://countrystudies.us/russia/25.htm.

9. Nicholas Georgescu-Roegen, *The Entropy Law and the Economic Process* (Cambridge, MA: Harvard University Press, 1971), 277.

10. Nicholas Georgescu-Roegen, "An Emigrant from a Developing Country: Autobiographical Notes I," in J. A. Kregel, ed., *Recollections of Eminent Economists* (Rome: Banca Nationale del Lavoro, 1989), 99, https://rosa.uniroma1.it/rosa04/psl_quarterly_review/article/view/11104/10978.

11. Nicholas Georgescu-Roegen, "Nicholas Georgescu-Roegen About Himself," in Michael Szenberg, ed., *Eminent Economists: Their Life Philosophies* (Cambridge: Cambridge University Press, 1992), 133.

12. Nicholas Georgescu-Roegen, "Process in Farming Versus Process in Manufacturing: A Problem of Balanced Development," in Ugo Papi and Charles Nunn, eds., *Economic Problems of Agriculture in Industrial Societies* (London: Palgrave Macmillan, 1969).

13. Georgescu-Roegen, *Entropy Law and the Economic Process*, 322–30.

14. Georgescu-Roegen, *Entropy Law and the Economic Process*, 281.

15. Georgescu-Roegen, *Entropy Law and the Economic Process*, 304.

16. John Schmitz, "Nicholas Georgescu-Roegen," Secondlawoflife.wordpress.com, April 28, 2007.

17. Georgescu-Roegen, *Entropy Law and the Economic Process*, 303.

18. Georgescu-Roegen, *Entropy Law and the Economic Process*, 21.

19. Georgescu-Roegen, *Entropy Law and the Economic Process*, 2.

20. Donella H. Meadows, Dennis L. Meadows, Jørgen Randers, and William W. Behrens III, *The Limits to Growth* (New York: Universe Books, 1972), 29.

21. Meadows et al., *Limits to Growth*, 29.

22. Peter Passell, Marc Roberts, and Leonard Ross, "The Limits to Growth," *The New York Times Book Review*, April 2, 1972, 1, https://www.nytimes.com/1972/04/02/archives/the-limits-to-growth-a-report-for-the-club-of-romes-project-on-the.html.

23. Robert M. Solow, "Is the End of the World at Hand?," *Challenge* 16, no. 1 (March/April 1973), 43.

24. Solow, "Is the End of the World at Hand?," 46.

25. Passell, Roberts, and Ross, "The Limits to Growth," 173.

26. Wilfred Beckerman, *In Defence of Economic Growth* (London: Jonathan Cape, 1974).

27. Hannah Ritchie, Pablo Rosado, and Max Roser, "CO_2 and Greenhouse Gas Emissions," Our World in Data, https://ourworldindata.org/co2-and-greenhouse-gas-emissions.

28. Ritchie, Rosado, and Roser, "CO_2 and Greenhouse Gas Emissions."

29. Clement Levallois, "Can De-Growth Be Considered a Policy Option?," *Ecological Economics* 69, no. 11 (June 2010), 19, https://www.researchgate.net/publication/222832017.

30. Nicholas Georgescu-Roegen, "Energy and Economic Myths," *Southern Economic Journal* 41, no. 3 (January 1975), 347–81, https://www.uvm.edu/~jfarley/EEseminar/readings/energy%20myths.pdf.

31. Georgescu-Roegen, "Energy and Economic Myths," 361.

32. Georgescu-Roegen, "Energy and Economic Myths," 365.

33. Georgescu-Roegen, "Energy and Economic Myths," 366.

34. E. F. Schumacher, *Small Is Beautiful: Economics as If People Mattered* (London: Blond and Briggs, 1973), 20.

35. Schumacher, *Small Is Beautiful*, 19.

36. Schumacher, *Small Is Beautiful*, 19.

37. Herman E. Daly, *Steady-State Economics*, 2nd ed. (Washington, DC: Island Press, 1991), 186.

38. Georgescu-Roegen, "Energy and Economic Myths," 367.

39. Nicholas Georgescu-Roegen, "The Steady State and Ecological Salvation: A Thermodynamic Analysis," *BioScience* 27, no. 4 (April 1977), 266–70.

40. Nicholas Georgescu Roegen, "Inequality, Limits, and Growth from a Bioeconomic View-point," *Review of Social Economy* 35, no. 3 (December 1977), 361–75.
41. Georgescu-Roegen, "Energy and Economic Myths," 377.
42. Georgescu-Roegen, "Energy and Economic Myths," 374.
43. Georgescu-Roegen, "Energy and Economic Myths," 378.
44. Georgescu-Roegen, "Energy and Economic Myths," 377.
45. Georgescu-Roegen, "Energy and Economic Myths," 377.
46. Georgescu-Roegen, "Energy and Economic Myths," 378.
47. Georgescu-Roegen, "Energy and Economic Myths," 374.
48. Herman E. Daly, "On Nicholas Georgescu-Roegen's Contributions to Economics: An Obitu-ary Essay," *Ecological Economics* 13, no. 3 (June 1995), 149–54.
49. See Federico Demaria, Filka Sekulova, Joan Martinez-Alier, and Francois Schneider, "What Is Degrowth? From an Activist Slogan to a Social Movement," *Environmental Values* 22, no. 2 (April 2013), 191–215.
50. Georgescu-Roegen, "Energy and Economic Myths," 379.

24. Silvia Federici and Wages for Housework

1. Silvia Federici and Arlen Austin, eds., *Wages for Housework: The New York Committee 1972–1977: History, Theory, Documents* (Brooklyn, NY: Autonomedia, 2018), 87–89.
2. Federici and Austin, *Wages for Housework*, 91.
3. Federici and Austin, *Wages for Housework*, 41.
4. Betsy Warrior, *Strike! While the Iron Is Hot! Wages for Housework*, poster, 48.2 × 35.5 cm, Yanker Poster Collection, Library of Congress, https://www.loc.gov/item/2015649375.
5. Federici and Austin, *Wages for Housework*, 121–22.
6. See, e.g., "The International Wages for Housework Campaign" (newsletter), https://freedom archives.org/Documents/Finder/DOC500_scans/500.020.Wages.for.Housework.pdf; and "International Lesbian Conference," *Power of Women: Magazine of the International Wages for Housework Campaign*, no. 5 (1975), https://bcrw.barnard.edu/archive/lesbian/Power_of _Women.pdf.
7. Federici and Austin, *Wages for Housework*, 17.
8. Silvia Federici, *Wages Against Housework* (Bristol: Falling Wall Press, 1975), 3.
9. Friedrich Engels, *The Condition of the Working Class in England* (Oxford: Oxford University Press, 2009), 152.
10. Kathleen E. Gales and P. H. Marks, "Twentieth Century Trends in the Work of Women in England and Wales," *Journal of the Royal Statistical Society* 137, no. 1 (1974), 60–74, table 2, https://www.jstor.org/stable/2345145.
11. US Census Bureau, "1900 Census Special Reports: Statistics of Women at Work Based on Unpublished Information Derived from the Schedules of the Twelfth Census," 1907, table 21, https://www.census.gov/library/publications/1907/dec/women-at-work.html.
12. Charlotte Perkins Stetson, *Women and Economics: A Study of the Economic Relation Between Men and Women as a Factor in Social Evolution* (Boston: Small, Maynard, 1900), 8.
13. Stetson, *Women and Economics*, 14–15.
14. Crystal Eastman, "Now We Can Begin," *Liberator*, December 1920, https://www.american yawp.com/reader/22-the-new-era/crystal-eastman-now-we-can-begin-1920.
15. Mary Inman, *In Woman's Defense* (Los Angeles: The Committee to Organize the Advance-ment of Women, 1940), 149.
16. Inman, *In Woman's Defense*, 142.
17. Federal Reserve Bank of St. Louis, "Labor Force Participation Rate—Women (LNS11300002)," FRED Economic Data, June 7, 2024, https://fred.stlouisfed.org/series/LNS11300002.
18. Rachel Andrews, "Interview with Silvia Federici," *The White Review* (January 2022), https:// www.thewhitereview.org/feature/interview-with-silvia-federici.
19. Mariarosa Dalla Costa and Selma James, *The Power of Women and the Subversion of the Community* (Bristol: Falling Wall Press, 1972), 23, https://anarch.cc/uploads/mariosa-dalla -costa/the-power-of-women-and-the-subversion-of-community.pdf.
20. Silvia Federici, *Revolution at Point Zero: Housework, Reproduction, and Feminist Struggle*, 2nd ed. (Oakland, CA: PM Press, 2020), 50.

21. Dalla Costa and James, *Power of Women*, 43.
22. Dalla Costa and James, *Power of Women*, 49.
23. Federici and Austin, *Wages for Housework*, 30.
24. Federici and Austin, *Wages for Housework*, 18.
25. Federici and Austin, *Wages for Housework*, 46.
26. Federici and Austin, *Wages for Housework*, 20.
27. Federici, *Wages Against Housework*, 2–3.
28. Federici, *Wages Against Housework*, 6.
29. Federici, *Wages Against Housework*, 5.
30. "Theses on Wages for Housework," in Federici, *Wages Against Housework*, 32.
31. Selma James, "A Woman's Place," February 1953; originally published in the workers' news-paper *Correspondence*, https://anth1001.wordpress.com/wp-content/uploads/2012/11/james_a-womans-place.pdf.
32. Selma James, "Women, the Unions and Work, or . . . What Is Not to Be Done," *Radical America* 7, no. 4–5 (1973), 67, https://caringlabor.wordpress.com/wp-content/uploads/2010/08/selmajamesra.pdf.
33. Wendy Schuman, "Brooklyn Women Seek Wages for Housework," *The New York Times*, January 11, 1976; reprinted in Federici and Austin, *Wages for Housework*, 172.
34. "Wages for Housework," *Life* (April 1976), https://maydayrooms.org/wp-content/uploads/2014/06/WfHw_SF_LifeMagazine1976.jpg.
35. Andrews, "Interview with Silvia Federici."
36. Louise Toupin, *Wages for Housework: A History of an International Feminist Movement, 1972–1977* (London: Pluto Press, 2018), 246.
37. Federici and Austin, *Wages for Housework*, 24.
38. "Feminist Generations: A Conversation with Selma James, Margaret Prescod and Chanda Prescod-Weinstein," Women and Gender Studies Institute Research Seminar, January 19, 2022, https://wgsi.utoronto.ca/wp-content/uploads/2022/01/feminist-generations-closed-captions-converted.pdf.
39. Toupin, *Wages for Housework*, 22.
40. Andrews, "Interview with Silvia Federici."
41. Keith Love, "How Do You Put a Price Tag on a Housewife's Work?," *The New York Times*, January 13, 1976; reprinted in Federici and Austin, *Wages for Housework*, 192–93.
42. Marilyn Waring, *If Women Counted: A New Feminist Economics* (New York: HarperCollins, 1990), 4.
43. Waring, *If Women Counted*, 7.
44. Waring, *If Women Counted*, 44.
45. Waring, *If Women Counted*, 74–75.
46. Waring, *If Women Counted*, 80.
47. Waring, *If Women Counted*, 323.
48. Waring, *If Women Counted*, 326.

25. Theorists of Thatcherism: Stuart Hall vs. Friedrich Hayek

1. Ralph Harris, Arthur Seldon, and Stephen Erickson, *A Conversation with Harris and Seldon*, Occasional Papers 116, Institute of Economic Affairs, 2001, 53.
2. Alan Ebenstein, *Friedrich Hayek* (New York: Palgrave, 2001), 291.
3. Peter Jenkins, *Mrs. Thatcher's Revolution: The Ending of the Socialist Era* (Cambridge, MA: Harvard University Press, 1988), 81.
4. Friedrich A. Hayek, "Trade Union Privileges," *The Times* (London), August 2, 1977, https://www.margaretthatcher.org/document/114631.
5. Riyah Collins, "Red Robbo: The Man Behind 523 Car Factory Strikes," *BBC News*, November 3, 2017, https://www.bbc.com/news/uk-england-birmingham-41834559.
6. Friedrich Hayek, *The Constitution of Liberty* (Chicago: University of Chicago Press, 1960, reprinted 2011), 386, https://ia800702.us.archive.org/26/items/TheConstitutionOfLiberty/The%20Constitution%20of%20Liberty.pdf.
7. Hayek, *Constitution of Liberty*, 397.
8. "Thatcher, Hayek, and Friedman," Margaret Thatcher Foundation, https://www.margaretthatcher.org/archive/Hayek.

9. "Thatcher, Hayek, and Friedman."
10. Anthony Wells, "Voting Intention 1974–1979," UK Polling Report, https://pollingreport.uk/articles/voting-intention-1974-1979.
11. Wells, "Voting Intention 1974–1979."
12. Ebenstein, *Friedrich Hayek*, 292.
13. "Inflation Great Britain 1979," Inflation.eu, https://www.inflation.eu/en/inflation-rates/great-britain/historic-inflation/cpi-inflation-great-britain-1979.aspx.
14. Office for National Statistics, "Unemployment Rate (Aged 16 and Over, Seasonally Adjusted): %," Census 2021, https://www.ons.gov.uk/employmentandlabourmarket/peoplenotinwork/unemployment/timeseries/mgsx/lms.
15. "1982: UK Unemployment Tops Three Million," On This Day, *BBC News*, http://news.bbc.co.uk/onthisday/hi/dates/stories/january/26/newsid_2506000/2506335.stm.
16. Jenkins, *Mrs. Thatcher's Revolution*, 97.
17. Margaret Thatcher, Letter to Friedrich Hayek, February 17, 1982, https://c59574e9047e61130f13-3f71d0fe2b653c4f00f32175760e96e7.ssl.cf1.rackcdn.com/3D5798D9C38443C6BD10B1AB166D3CBF.pdf.
18. "1983: Macgregor Named as Coal Boss," On This Day, *BBC News*, http://news.bbc.co.uk/onthisday/hi/dates/stories/march/28/newsid_2531000/2531033.stm.
19. Economic Reconstruction Group, "Final Report of the Nationalised Industries Policy Group," July 8, 1977, https://c59574e9047e61130f13-3f71d0fe2b653c4f00f32175760e96e7.ssl.cf1.rackcdn.com/FABEA1F4BFA64CB398DFA20D8B8B6C98.pdf.
20. Alan Travis, "Thatcher Had Secret Plan to Use Army at Height of Miners' Strike," *The Guardian*, January 3, 2014, https://www.theguardian.com/politics/2014/jan/03/margaret-thatcher-secret-plan-army-miners-strike.
21. Our World in Data, "Employment in the Coal Industry in the United Kingdom," August 17, 2020, https://ourworldindata.org/grapher/employment-in-the-coal-industry-in-the-united-kingdom.
22. R. W. Apple Jr., "Macmillan, at 90, Rouses the Lords," *The New York Times*, November 14, 1984.
23. Simon Lewis, "How Union Membership Has Grown—and Shrunk," *The Guardian*, April 30, 2010, https://www.theguardian.com/news/datablog/2010/apr/30/union-membership-data.
24. William Keegan, "This Is Not the 1970s. Tory Pledges to Cut Taxes Are Absurd," *The Guardian*, August 21, 2022, https://www.theguardian.com/business/2022/aug/21/this-is-not-the-1970s-tory-pledges-to-cut-taxes-are-absurd.
25. Edward Nelson, "Reaffirming the Influence of Milton Friedman on U.K. Economic Policy," Finance and Economics Discussion Series 2017–096, Board of Governors of the Federal Reserve System, 2017, https://www.federalreserve.gov/econres/feds/files/2017096pap.pdf.
26. "The Privatisation of British Telecom (1984)," https://www.instituteforgovernment.org.uk/sites/default/files/british_telecom_privatisation.pdf.
27. Andrew Oxlade, "British Gas Shares Have Increased 12 Times in Value in the 25 Years Since Privatisation," ThisIsMoney.co.uk, November 14, 2011, https://www.thisismoney.co.uk/money/investing/article-2061085/How-privatisation-shares-like-British-Gas-paid-handsomely.html.
28. Margaret Thatcher, *The Downing Street Years* (New York: HarperCollins, 1993), 89.
29. Lord Norman Tebbit, Lord John Wakeham, Lord Cecil Parkinson, and Lord David Young, "Up for Debate: Privatization and the Thatcher Legacy," *Commanding Heights*, PBS, https://www.pbs.org/wgbh/commandingheights/shared/minitext/ufd_privatizethatcher_full.html#.
30. John Cassidy, "The Blair Project," *The New Yorker*, November 28, 1999, https://www.newyorker.com/magazine/1999/12/06/the-blair-project.
31. Stuart Hall, "The Great Moving Right Show," *Marxism Today* 23, no. 1 (January 1979), 14.
32. Hall, "Great Moving Right Show," 17.
33. Hall, "Great Moving Right Show," 17.
34. Lovia Gyarkye, "Permission to Imagine," *Dissent*, Fall 2021, https://www.dissentmagazine.org/article/permission-to-imagine.
35. Hall, "Great Moving Right Show," 16.
36. Hall, "Great Moving Right Show," 16.
37. Stuart Hall, Charles Critcher, Tony Jefferson, et al., *Policing the Crisis: Mugging, the State, and Law and Order* (London: Palgrave Macmillan, 1978), 333.
38. Evan Smith, "'Rather Swamped': Thatcher, Moral Panics and Racist Rhetoric," New Histori-

cal Express, November 1, 2022, https://hatfulofhistory.wordpress.com/2022/11/01/rather-swamped-thatcher-moral-panics-and-racist-rhetoric.

39. Hall, "Great Moving Right Show," 15.
40. Hall, "Great Moving Right Show," 17.
41. Stuart Hall, "Gramsci and Us," *Marxism Today*, June 1987. Reprinted in Stuart Hall, *The Hard Road to Renewal* (London: Verso Books, 1988).
42. Hall, "Great Moving Right Show," 20.
43. Geoffrey Garrett, "The Political Consequences of Thatcherism," *Political Behavior* 14, no. 4 (December 1992), 361–82.
44. Hall, "Gramsci and Us."
45. Hall, "Gramsci and Us."
46. Hall, "Gramsci and Us."
47. Nicholas Crafts, *Forging Ahead, Falling Behind and Fighting Back* (Cambridge: Cambridge University Press, 2018), 87.
48. Nicholas Crafts, "Competition Cured the 'British Disease,'" *VoxEU*, June 5, 2011, https://cepr.org/voxeu/columns/competition-cured-british-disease.
49. Author's calculations from "A Millennium of Macroeconomic Data," Bank of England, https://www.bankofengland.co.uk/statistics/research-datasets.
50. John Cassidy, "The Economic Case for and Against Thatcherism," *The New Yorker*, April 9, 2013, https://www.newyorker.com/news/john-cassidy/the-economic-case-for-and-against-thatcherism.
51. Cassidy, "Economic Case for and Against Thatcherism."
52. Isaac Delestre, Wojciech Kopczuk, Helen Miller, and Kate Smith, "Top Income Inequality and Tax Policy," Institute of Fiscal Studies, April 7, 2022, https://ifs.org.uk/books/top-income-inequality-and-tax-policy.
53. Hall, "Gramsci and Us."
54. Hall, "Gramsci and Us."

26. Parsing Globalization: Samir Amin, Dani Rodrik, and Joseph Stiglitz

1. Peter Maas, "Lenin Returns—To Eastern Europe's First Communist Theme Park," *The Washington Post*, July 9, 1993.
2. Barry Naughton, *The Chinese Economy: Transitions and Growth* (Cambridge, MA: MIT Press, 2007), 99.
3. Ted George Goertzel, *Fernando Henrique Cardoso: Reinventing Democracy in Brazil* (Boulder, CO: Lynn Rienner, 1999), 160.
4. World Trade Organization, "Evolution of Trade Under the WTO: Handy Statistics," https://www.wto.org/english/res_e/statis_e/trade_evolution_e/evolution_trade_wto_e.htm.
5. Foreign exchange figures are from the Bank for International Settlements, "Turnover of OTC Foreign Exchange Instruments, by Country," https://www.bis.org/statistics/d11_2.pdf.
6. Samir Amin, *Capitalism in the Age of Globalization* (London: Zed Books, 1997), xi.
7. Amin, *Capitalism in the Age of Globalization*, 33.
8. Samir Amin, *A Life Looking Forward: Memoirs of an Independent Marxist* (London: Zed Books, 2006), 56.
9. Amin, *Life Looking Forward*, 65.
10. Samir Amin, "Les effets structurels de l'intégration international des économies précapitalistes: une étude théorique de mécanisme qui a engendré," PhD dissertation, Université de Paris, 1957, https://search.worldcat.org/title/31362974.
11. Samir Amin, *Accumulation on a World Scale: A Critique of the Theory of Underdevelopment* (New York: Monthly Review Press, 1974), 32.
12. For a succinct history of the NIEO see Nils Gilman, "The New International Economic Order: A Reintroduction," *Humanity*, Spring 2015, https://humanityjournal.org/issue6–1/the-new-international-economic-order-a-reintroduction.
13. United Nations General Assembly, Resolution A/RES/S-6/3201, Declaration on the Establishment of a New International Economic Order (May 1, 1974), http://www.un-documents.net/s6r3201.htm.
14. United Nations General Assembly, "Economic Declaration: Fourth Conference of Heads of

State or Government of Non-Aligned Countries," Algiers, September 5–9, 1973, 57–74, http://cns.miis.edu/nam/documents/Official_Document/4th_Summit_FD_Algiers_Declaration_1973_Whole.pdf.

15. Samir Amin, "After the New International Economic Order: The Future of International Economic Relations," *Journal of Contemporary Asia* 12, no. 4 (1982), http://patrimoinenumeriqueafricain.com:8080/jspui/bitstream/123456789/2847/1/After%20the%20New%20International.pdf.

16. Samir Amin, "Self-Reliance and the New International Economic Order," *Monthly Review* 29, no. 3 (July–August 1977), 20.

17. Amin, *Accumulation on a World Scale*, 135, quoted in Patrick Bond, "Samir Amin's Diagnosis of Worst-Case Racial Capitalism," Committee for the Abolition of Illegitimate Debt, November 11, 2023, https://www.cadtm.org/Samir-Amin-s-diagnosis-of-worst-case-racial-capitalism.

18. Amin, *Capitalism in the Age of Globalization*, 3–5.

19. Amin, *Life Looking Forward*, 170.

20. Samir Amin "The Struggle for National Independence and Socialism in Kampuchea," October 1981, South African History Online, June 26, 2019, https://www.sahistory.org.za/sites/default/files/archive-files/the_struggle_for_national_independence_and_socialism_in_kampuchea_by_sAmin_amin.pdf.

21. Amin, *Capitalism in the Age of Globalization*, 96.

22. Amin, *Capitalism in the Age of Globalization*, 99–100.

23. Amin, *Capitalism in the Age of Globalization*, 10.

24. Francis Fukuyama, *The End of History and the Last Man* (New York: Free Press, 1992).

25. Dani Rodrik, *Has Globalization Gone Too Far?* (Washington, DC: Institute for International Economics, 1997), 1.

26. Rodrik, *Has Globalization Gone Too Far?*, 4.

27. Marina N. Bolotnikova, "The Trilemma," *Harvard Magazine*, July–August 2019, https://www.harvardmagazine.com/2019/06/rodrik-trilemma-trade-globalization.

28. John Williamson, "The Washington Consensus as a Policy Prescription for Development," Peterson Institute for International Economics, January 13, 2004, https://www.piie.com/commentary/speeches-papers/washington-consensus-policy-prescription-development.

29. Paul Krugman, "Technology, Trade, and Factor Prices," National Bureau of Economic Research Working Paper 5355, November 1995, https://www.nber.org/papers/w5355.

30. Rodrik, *Has Globalization Gone Too Far?*, 15.

31. Rodrik, *Has Globalization Gone Too Far?*, 23–25.

32. Rodrik, *Has Globalization Gone Too Far?*, 6.

33. Rodrik, *Has Globalization Gone Too Far?*, 6.

34. Rodrik, *Has Globalization Gone Too Far?*, 71.

35. Rodrik, *Has Globalization Gone Too Far?*, 71.

36. "Remarks by President Clinton, President Bush, President Carter, President Ford, and Vice President Gore in Signing of NAFTA Side Agreements," History Central, https://historycentral.com/documents/Clinton/SigningNaFTA.html#google_vignette; John M. Broder and Jim Mann: "Clinton Reverses His Policy, Renews China's Trade Status," *Los Angeles Times*, May 27, 1994, https://www.latimes.com/archives/la-xpm-1994–05–27-mn-62877-story.html.

37. Federal Reserve Bank of St. Louis, "All Employees, Manufacturing (MANEMP)," FRED Economic Data, July 5, 2024, https://fred.stlouisfed.org/series/MANEMP.

38. Federal Reserve Bank of St. Louis, "All Employees, Total Nonfarm (PAYEMS)," FRED Economic Data, July 5, 2024, https://fred.stlouisfed.org/series/PAYEMS.

39. Joseph Stiglitz, interview with the author, April 2024.

40. Joseph Stiglitz, *The Road to Freedom: Economics and the Good Society* (New York: W. W. Norton, 2024), 250–51.

41. Joseph E. Stiglitz, *The Roaring Nineties: A New History of the World's Most Prosperous Decade* (New York: W. W. Norton, 2003).

42. Stiglitz, *Road to Freedom*, 229.

43. Lawrence H. Summers, "Does the Stock Market Rationally Reflect Fundamental Values?," *The Journal of Finance* 41, no. 3 (July 1986); and Andrei Shleifer and Lawrence H. Summers, "Breach of Trust in Hostile Takeovers," in *Corporate Takeovers: Causes and Consequences*, Alan J. Auerbach, ed. (Chicago: University of Chicago Press, 1988).

44. John Cassidy, "The Triumphalist," *The New Yorker*, June 28, 1998.

45. Daniel Yergin and Joseph Stanislaw, *The Commanding Heights* (New York: Simon and Schuster, 1998), 150–51.

46. Lawrence H. Summers, "Reflections on Managing Global Integration," Speech to the Annual Meeting of the Association of Government Economists, January 4, 1999.

47. Asian Development Bank, *Key Indicators 2001*, "Growth Rates of Real GDP and Major Sectors," August 2001, https://www.adb.org/publications/key-indicators-2001.

48. Jagdish N. Bhagwati, "The Capital Myth," *Foreign Affairs*, May/June 1998.

49. Joseph E. Stiglitz, *Globalization and Its Discontents* (New York: W. W. Norton, 2002), xiii.

50. Stiglitz, *Globalization and Its Discontents*, 64.

51. Stiglitz, *Globalization and Its Discontents*, xiv.

52. Stiglitz, *Globalization and Its Discontents*, 21–22.

53. Stiglitz, *Globalization and Its Discontents*, 250.

54. Kenneth Rogoff, "An Open Letter to Joseph Stiglitz," International Monetary Fund, July 2, 2002, https://www.imf.org/external/np/vc/2002/070202.HTM?.

55. Stiglitz, *Globalization and Its Discontents*, 185.

56. William Greider, *One World, Ready or Not* (New York: Simon and Schuster, 1997), 337.

57. Greider, *One World, Ready or Not*, 344.

58. Greider, *One World, Ready or Not*, 345.

59. WTO History Project, "Day Two, November 30, 1999," Harry Bridges Center for Labor Studies and University of Washington Libraries, http://depts.washington.edu/wtohist/day2.htm.

60. Paul Schell, "Local Proclamation of Emergency Order City of Seattle," November 30, 1999, https://archives.seattle.gov/digital-collections/media/collectiveaccess/images/1/7/3/5/30075_ca_object_representations_media_173588_original.pdf.

61. Dani Rodrik, "Seattle . . . and After: Five Simple Principles for World Trade," *The American Prospect*, December 19, 2001.

62. Federal Reserve Bank of St. Louis, "International Merchandise Trade Statistics: Exports: Commodities for China," FRED Economic Data, June 17, 2024, https://fred.stlouisfed.org/series/XTEXVA01CNM667S.

63. Federal Reserve Bank of St. Louis, "All Employees, Manufacturing."

64. Jagdish Bhagwati, *In Defense of Globalization* (New York: Oxford University Press, 2004), 65.

65. Bhagwati, *In Defense of Globalization*, 64.

66. Shaohua Chen and Martin Ravallion, "The Developing World Is Poorer Than We Thought, but No Less Successful in the Fight Against Poverty," World Bank Policy Research Working Paper WPS4703, August 1, 2008, 41, table 5.

67. Chen and Ravallion, "Developing World," 41, table 5.

68. Chen and Ravallion, "Developing World," 41, table 5.

69. Chen and Ravallion, "Developing World," 42, table 6.

70. Chen and Ravallion, "Developing World," 44, table 7.

71. Lucas Chancel, Thomas Piketty, Emmanuel Saez, and Gabriel Zucman, *World Inequality Report 2022*, World Inequality Lab; 2021, 56, figure 2.3, https://wir2022.wid.world/www-site/uploads/2023/03/D_FINAL_WIL_RIM_RAPPORT_2303.pdf.

72. These are current dollar figures from the World Bank, "GDP per Capita (Current US$)," https://data.worldbank.org/indicator/NY.GDP.PCAP.CD.

73. Chen and Ravallion, "Developing World," 44, table 7.

74. For a hopefully accessible account of the Global Financial Crisis, see Part Three, "The Great Crunch," in my 2009 book, *How Markets Fail: The Logic of Economic Calamities* (New York: Farrar, Straus and Giroux, 2009).

75. Samir Amin, *The Implosion of Contemporary Capitalism* (New York: Monthly Review Press, 2013), 16; see also Samir Amin, "The Implosion of the Contemporary Capitalist System," abridged version for the Second South South Forum, https://commons.ln.edu.hk/cgi/viewcontent.cgi?article=1001&context=southsouthforum.

76. Amin, *Implosion of Contemporary Capitalism*, 17.

77. Joseph E. Stiglitz, *Freefall: America, Free Markets, and the Sinking of the World Economy* (New York: W. W. Norton, 2010), 163.

78. Dani Rodrik, *The Globalization Paradox* (New York: W. W. Norton, 2011), xi.

79. Rodrik, *Globalization Paradox*, xvii.

80. Rodrik, *Globalization Paradox*, xviii.
81. Rodrik, *Globalization Paradox*, 251.

27. Thomas Piketty and Rising Inequality

1. Stuart Jeffries, "Piketty Mania: How an Economics Lecture Became the Hottest Gig in Town," *The Guardian*, June 17, 2014, https://www.theguardian.com/books/2014/jun/17/thomas-piketty-lse-capitalism-talk.
2. Thomas Piketty, *Capital in the Twenty-First Century*, Arthur Goldhammer, trans. (Cambridge, MA: The Belknap Press of Harvard University Press, 2014), 571.
3. Barack Obama, "Remarks by the President on Economic Mobility," December 4, 2013, https://obamawhitehouse.archives.gov/the-press-office/2013/12/04/remarks-president-economic-mobility.
4. "Best Sellers: Hardcover Nonfiction," *The New York Times Book Review*, May 18, 2014, https://www.nytimes.com/books/best-sellers/2014/05/18/hardcover-nonfiction.
5. Piketty, *Capital in the Twenty-First Century*, 31.
6. Simon Kuznets and Elizabeth Jenks, "Shares of Upper Income Groups in Savings," in Simon Kuznets and Elizabeth Jenks, *Shares of Upper Income Groups in Income and Savings* (New York: National Bureau of Economic Research, 1953), https://www.nber.org/system/files/chapters/c3060/c3060.pdf.
7. Simon Kuznets, "Economic Growth and Income Inequality," *The American Economic Review* 45, no. 1 (March 1955), https://assets.aeaweb.org/asset-server/files/9438.pdf.
8. Edward N. Wolff, *Economics of Poverty, Inequality, and Discrimination* (Cincinnati: South-Western College Publishing, 1997), 73–74.
9. Wolff, *Economics of Poverty, Inequality, and Discrimination*, 74, table 3.5.
10. Thomas Piketty, "Income Inequality in France, 1901–1998," *Journal of Political Economy* 111, no. 5 (October 2003), 1004–42, http://piketty.pse.ens.fr/fichiers/public/Piketty2003b.pdf.
11. Thomas Piketty and Emmanuel Saez, "Income Inequality in the United States, 1913–1998," *The Quarterly Journal of Economics* 118, no. 1 (February 2003), 1, https://eml.berkeley.edu/~saez/pikettyqje.pdf.
12. Facundo Alvaredo, Anthony B. Atkinson, Thomas Piketty, and Emmanuel Saez, "The Top 1 Percent in International and Historical Perspective," *Journal of Economic Perspectives* 27, no. 3 (Summer 2013), 6, figure 2, https://pubs.aeaweb.org/doi/pdfplus/10.1257/jep.27.3.3.
13. Alvaredo, Atkinson, Piketty, and Saez, "Top 1 Percent," 10.
14. Piketty, *Capital in the Twenty-First Century*, 24.
15. Piketty, *Capital in the Twenty-First Century*, 316.
16. United States Securities and Exchange Commission, Schedule 14A, Apple Inc. Proxy Statement, January 9, 2012, Summary Compensation Table—2011, 2010, and 2009, 30, https://www.sec.gov/Archives/edgar/data/320193/000119312512006704/d275281ddef14a.htm.
17. "Fortune 50 CEO Pay vs. Our Salaries," Fortune 500 2012, CNN Money, https://money.cnn.com/magazines/fortune/fortune500/2012/ceo-pay-ratios/.
18. John Cassidy, "The Greed Cycle," *The New Yorker*, September 15, 2002, 75.
19. Piketty, *Capital in the Twenty-First Century*, 24.
20. Piketty, *Capital in the Twenty-First Century*, 332.
21. Piketty, *Capital in the Twenty-First Century*, 433.
22. Piketty, *Capital in the Twenty-First Century*, 438.
23. Piketty, *Capital in the Twenty-First Century*, 22–23.
24. Piketty, *Capital in the Twenty-First Century*, 57.
25. Piketty, *Capital in the Twenty-First Century*, 572.
26. Piketty, *Capital in the Twenty-First Century*, 572.
27. Piketty, *Capital in the Twenty-First Century*, 356.
28. Piketty, *Capital in the Twenty-First Century*, 514.
29. Piketty, *Capital in the Twenty-First Century*, 515–18.
30. Paul Krugman, "Why We're in a New Gilded Age," *The New York Review of Books*, May 8, 2014.
31. Robert M. Solow, "Thomas Piketty Is Right," *The New Republic*, April 22, 2014.
32. James K. Galbraith, "*Kapital* for the Twenty-First Century?" *Dissent* (Spring 2014).

33. Isaac Chotiner, "Thomas Piketty: I Don't Care for Marx," newrepublic.com, May 5, 2014.
34. Piketty, *Capital in the Twenty-First Century*, 10.
35. John B. Judis, "Thomas Piketty Is Pulling Your Leg," newrepublic.com, May 6, 2014.
36. Lawrence H. Summers, "The Inequality Puzzle," *Democracy*, no. 33 (Summer 2014), https://democracyjournal.org/magazine/33/the-inequality-puzzle.
37. Matthew Rognlie, "Deciphering the Fall and Rise in the Net Capital Share: Accumulation or Scarcity?," Brookings Papers on Economic Activity, Spring 2015, https://www.brookings.edu/wp-content/uploads/2015/03/1_2015a_rognlie.pdf.
38. Gerald Auten and David Splinter, "Income Inequality in the United States: Using Tax Data to Measure Long-Term Trends," August 23, 2018, 29, table 3, https://davidsplinter.com/AutenSplinter-Tax_Data_and_Inequality_2018.pdf.
39. Thomas Piketty, Emmanuel Saez, and Gabriel Zucman, "Distributional National Accounts: Methods and Estimates for the United States," *The Quarterly Journal of Economics* 133, no. 2 (May 2018), 576, https://gabriel-zucman.eu/files/PSZ2018QJE.pdf.
40. Piketty, Saez, and Zucman, "Distributional National Accounts," online appendix, Main Data, "Top 1% Income Share: Pre-Tax vs. Post-Tax," http://gabriel-zucman.eu/usdina.
41. Gerald Auten and David Splinter, "Income Inequality in the United States: Using Tax Data to Measure Long-Term Trends," September 29, 2023, 3, https://www.davidsplinter.com/AutenSplinter-Tax_Data_and_Inequality.pdf.
42. Auten and Splinter, "Income Inequality in the United States," 3.
43. Auten and Splinter, "Income Inequality in the United States," 3.
44. Sarah Thomas-Oxtoby, "Billionaire Streakers," *Forbes*, September 28, 2022, https://www.forbes.com/sites/sarahthomasoxtoby/2022/09/28/forbes-400-billionaire-streakers-people-on-1982-and-2022-lists/?sh=95c6688f88ba.
45. Rob LaFranco and Chase Peterson-Withorn, eds., "The Forbes 400: The Definitive Ranking of the Wealthiest Americans in 2023," *Forbes*, https://www.forbes.com/forbes-400.
46. Board of Governors of the Federal Reserve System, "DFA: Distributional Financial Accounts: Distribution of Household Wealth in the U.S. Since 1989," June 14, 2024, https://www.federalreserve.gov/releases/z1/dataviz/dfa/distribute/chart/#range:1989.4,2023.4;quarter:137;series:Net%20worth;demographic:networth;population:1,3,5,7,9;units:shares.
47. Matthew Smith, Owen Zidar, and Eric Zwick, "Top Wealth in America: New Estimates Under Heterogeneous Returns," *The Quarterly Journal of Economics* 138, no. 1 (February 2023), 557, https://zidar.princeton.edu/sites/g/files/toruqf3371/files/documents/wealth2023.pdf.
48. Lynn Stuart Parramore, "Joseph Stiglitz: Thomas Piketty Gets Income Inequality Wrong," *Salon*, January 2, 2015.
49. Suresh Naidu, "A Political Economy Take on W/Y," in Heather Boushey, J. Bradford DeLong, and Marshall Steinbaum, eds., *After Piketty: The Agenda for Economics and Inequality* (Cambridge, MA: Harvard University Press, 2017), 109.
50. Naidu, "Political Economy Take on W/Y," 111.
51. Naidu, "Political Economy Take on W/Y," 118.
52. Karl Marx and Frederick Engels, *The Communist Manifesto: A Modern Edition* (London: Verso Books, 1998), 37.
53. Naidu, "Political Economy Take on W/Y," 109; and Naidu, "Political Economy Take on W/Y," 116.
54. Christoph Lakner and Branko Milanović, "Global Income Distribution: From the Fall of the Berlin Wall to the Great Recession," World Bank Policy Research Working Paper WPS6719, December 1, 2013, 31, figure 1(a), https://documents1.worldbank.org/curated/en/914431468162277879/pdf/WPS6719.pdf.
55. Branko Milanović, *Global Inequality: A New Approach for the Age of Globalization* (Cambridge, MA: The Belknap Press of Harvard University Press, 2016), 22.
56. Milanović, *Global Inequality*, 20.
57. Milanović, *Global Inequality*, 20.
58. Milanović, *Global Inequality*, 30.
59. David H. Autor, David Dorn, and Gordon H. Hanson, "The China Syndrome: Local Labor Markets Effects of Import Competition in the United States," National Bureau of Economic Research Working Paper 18054, May 2012, 11, table 1.

60. Zeeshan Aleem, "Another Kick in the Teeth: A Top Economist on How Trade with China Helped Elect Trump," *Vox*, March 29, 2017, https://www.vox.com/new-money/2017/3/29/15035498/autor-trump-china-trade-election.

61. Autor, Dorn, and Hanson, "China Syndrome," 11, table 1.

62. "Donald Trump Presidential Campaign, 2016/International Trade," Ballotpedia, https://ballotpedia.org/Donald_Trump_presidential_campaign,_2016/International_trade.

63. David Autor, David Dorn, Gordon Hanson, and Kaveh Majlesi, "A Note on the Effect of Rising Trade Exposure on the 2016 Presidential Election," November 16, 2016.

64. See John Sides, Michael Tesler, and Lynn Vavreck, *Identity Crisis: The 2016 Presidential Campaign and the Battle for the Meaning of America* (Princeton, NJ: Princeton University Press, 2018).

65. John Cassidy, "Joe Biden's Innovative Attempt to Reshape the American Economy," new yorker.com, February 7, 2023.

66. Anne-Sylvaine Chassany, "Lunch with the FT: Thomas Piketty," *Financial Times*, June 26, 2015.

67. "Economist Thomas Piketty Refuses French Legion d'Honneur," *The Irish Times*, January 1, 2015, https://www.irishtimes.com/business/economy/economist-thomas-piketty-refuses-french-legion-d-honneur-1.2052228.

68. "Historic Election 'Drubbing' for French Socialists," France 24, April 24, 2017, https://www.france24.com/en/20170424-historic-french-presidential-election-drubbing-socialists-hamon.

69. Thomas Piketty, *Capital and Ideology*, Arthur Goldhammer, trans. (Cambridge, MA: Harvard University Press, 2020), 1.

70. Piketty, *Capital and Ideology*, 99.

71. Piketty, *Capital and Ideology*, 7.

72. Idrees Kahloon, "Thomas Piketty Goes Global," *The New Yorker*, March 9, 2020, 76.

73. John Maynard Keynes, *The General Theory of Employment, Interest, and Money* (San Diego: Harvest/Harcourt, Brace, Jovanovich, 1964), 383.

74. Piketty, *Capital and Ideology*, 1.

75. Antonio Gramsci, *Selections from the Prison Notebooks of Antonio Gramsci*, Quintin Hoare and Geoffrey Nowell Smith, ed. and trans. (New York: International Publishers, 1972), 12.

76. Piketty, *Capital and Ideology*, 7.

77. Piketty, *Capital and Ideology*, 7.

78. Piketty, *Capital and Ideology*, 972.

79. Piketty, *Capital and Ideology*, 967.

80. Piketty, *Capital and Ideology*, 983.

81. Piketty, *Capital and Ideology*, 967.

82. Piketty, *Capital and Ideology*, 1037.

83. Center on Capitalism and Society, "Thomas Picketty: Speaker: 20th Annual Conference of the Center on Capitalism and Society," Columbia University, https://capitalism.columbia.edu/content/thomas-picketty.

28. The End of Capitalism, or the Beginning?

1. António Guterres, "Secretary-General's Address to the General Assembly," United Nations, September 19, 2023, https://www.un.org/sg/en/content/sg/speeches/2023-09-19/secretary-generals-address-the-general-assembly.

2. World Economic Forum, *The Global Risks Report 2023*, 18th ed. (Geneva: World Economic Forum, 2023), 6, https://www3.weforum.org/docs/WEF_Global_Risks_Report_2023.pdf.

3. World Economic Forum, *Global Risks Report 2023*, 9, figure B, https://www3.weforum.org/docs/WEF_Global_Risks_Report_2023.pdf.

4. Adam Tooze, "Welcome to the World of the Polycrisis," *Financial Times*, October 28, 2022, https://www.ft.com/content/498398e7-11b1-494b-9cd3-6d669dc3de33.

5. Farwa Sial, "Whose Polycrisis?," *Developing Economics* (blog), January 27, 2023, https://developingeconomics.org/2023/01/27/whose-polycrisis.

6. Samuel Bowles and Wendy Carlin, "Shrinking Capitalism: Components of a New Political Economy Paradigm," *Oxford Review of Economic Policy* 37, no. 4 (Winter 2021), 794, https://academic.oup.com/oxrep/article/37/4/794/6423495.

7. "Most Americans Agree That Capitalism Needs to Evolve, the Harris Poll and Forbes Find," Newswire, May 16, 2023, https://www.newswire.com/news/most-americans-agree-that -capitalism-needs-to-evolve-the-harris-poll-22038868.

8. Oren Cass, "Foreword: What Happened to Capitalism?," *Rebuilding American Capitalism,* American Compass, June 2023, https://americancompass.org/rebuilding-american -capitalism/foreword.

9. Will Chamberlain, Christopher DeMuth, Rod Dreher, et al., "National Conservativism: A Statement of Principles," Edmund Burke Foundation, 2022, https://nationalconservatism .org/national-conservatism-a-statement-of-principles.

10. Joshua Rhett Miller, "Jeff Bezos' $500M Yacht Has a 246-foot Support Ship, Lauren Sanchez Figurehead," *New York Post,* May 20, 2023, https://nypost.com/2023/05/20/meet-jeff-bezos -fleet-and-its-lauren-sanchez-figurehead.

11. Guthrie Scrimgeour, "Inside Mark Zuckerberg's Top-Secret Hawaii Compound," *Wired,* December 14, 2023, https://www.wired.com/story/mark-zuckerberg-inside-hawaii-compound.

12. Wolfgang Streeck, "How Will Capitalism End?," *New Left Review,* no. 87 (May/June 2014), https://newleftreview.org/issues/ii87/articles/wolfgang-streeck-how-will-capitalism-end.

13. Streeck, "How Will Capitalism End?"

14. Streeck, "How Will Capitalism End?"

15. International Monetary Fund, *World Economic Outlook,* April 2024, 138, table A1, "Summary of World Output," https://www.imf.org/en/Publications/WEO/Issues/2024/04/16 /world-economic-outlook-april-2024#statistical.

16. Peter S. Goodman, *How the World Ran Out of Everything: Inside the Global Supply Chain* (New York: Mariner Books, 2024), 346.

17. Erik Brynjolfsson and Andrew McAfee, *The Second Machine Age* (New York: W. W. Norton, 2014), 9.

18. Brynjolfsson and McAfee, *Second Machine Age,* 82.

19. Nicholas Crafts, "AI as a GPT: An Historical Perspective," March 25, 2020, https://warwick .ac.uk/fac/soc/economics/staff/nfrcrafts/ai_as_a_gpt.ppt.pdf.

20. Nicholas Crafts, "Artificial Intelligence as a General-Purpose Technology: An Historical Perspective," *Oxford Review of Economic Policy* 37, no. 3 (Autumn 2021), 521–36, https:// academic.oup.com/oxrep/article/37/3/521/6374675.

21. Crafts, "Artificial Intelligence as a General-Purpose Technology," 521–36.

22. Krystal Hu, "ChatGPT Sets Record for Fastest Growing User Base—Analyst Note," Reuters, February 2, 2023, https://www.reuters.com/technology/chatgpt-sets-record-fastest-growing -user-base-analyst-note-2023-02-01.

23. "OpenAI Raises $6.6 Billion in Funds at $157 Billion Value," Bloomberg, October 2, 2024.

24. Martin Neil Bailey, Erik Brynjolfsson, and Anton Korinek, "Machines of Mind: The Case for an AI-Powered Productivity Boom," Brookings Institution, May 10, 2023, figure 2, https:// www.brookings.edu/articles/machines-of-mind-the-case-for-an-ai-powered-productivity -boom.

25. Bailey, Brynjolfsson, and Korinek, "Machines of Mind."

26. Erik Brynjolfsson, "The Turing Trap: The Promise and Peril of Human-Like Artificial Intelligence," *Daedalus* 151, no. 2 (Spring 2022), 273.

27. Brynjolfsson, "Turing Trap," 272–73.

28. Greta Thunberg, "Transcript: Greta Thunberg's Speech at the U.N. Climate Action Summit," NPR, September 23, 2019, https://www.npr.org/2019/09/23/763452863/transcript-greta -thunbergs-speech-at-the-u-n-climate-action-summit.

29. Giorgos Kallis, *Degrowth* (New York: Agenda Publishing, Columbia University Press, 2018), 1.

30. Tim Jackson, *Prosperity Without Growth: Economics for a Finite Planet* (London: Earthscan, 2009), 15.

31. Global Commission on the Economy and Climate, "Key Findings and Executive Summary," *Unlocking the Inclusive Growth Story of the 21st Century: Accelerating Climate Action in Urgent Times,* New Climate Economy, 2018, https://newclimateeconomy.net/content /unlocking-inclusive-growth-story-21st-century.

32. U.K. Department for Energy Security and Net Zero and Claire Coutinho, "UK First Major Economy to Halve Emissions," February 26, 2024, https://www.gov.uk/government/news/uk -first-major-economy-to-halve-emissions.

33. Federal Reserve Bank of St. Louis, "Real Gross Domestic Product for Great Britain (NG-DPRSAXDCGBQ)," FRED Economic Data, June 17, 2024, https://fred.stlouisfed.org/series/NGDPRSAXDCGBQ.

34. Craig Dyke, "Great Britain's Monthly Electricity Stats," National Grid ESO, May 2024, https://www.nationalgrideso.com/electricity-explained/electricity-and-me/great-britains-monthly-electricity-stats.

35. Jefim Vogel and Jason Hickel, "Is Green Growth Happening? An Empirical Analysis of Achieved Versus Paris-Compliant CO2-GDP Decoupling in High-Income Countries," *The Lancet Planetary Health* 7, no. 9 (September 2023), E759–69, https://www.thelancet.com/pdfs/journals/lanplh/PIIS2542–5196(23)00174–2.pdf.

36. Tim Jackson, *Prosperity Without Growth*, 2nd ed. (London: Routledge, 2017).

37. "Median Income or Consumption per Day, 1963–2023," Our World in Data, March 27, 2024, https://ourworldindata.org/grapher/daily-median-income?tab=table.

38. Branko Milanović, "Degrowth: Solving the Impasse by Magical Thinking," *Global Inequality and More 3.0* (blog), June 27, 2021, https://branko2f7.substack.com/p/degrowth-solving-the-impasse-by-magical.

39. Jason Hickel, "Degrowth: A Response to Branko Milanovic," October 27, 2020, https://www.jasonhickel.org/blog/2017/11/19/why-branko-milanovic-is-wrong-about-de-growth.

40. Jason Hickel, *Less Is More: How Degrowth Will Save the World* (London: William Heinemann, 2020), https://blackbooksdotpub.wordpress.com/wp-content/uploads/2021/08/jason-hickel-less-is-more-random-house-2020.pdf.

41. J. D. Tuccille, "The World Is Still Getting Less Free. A Distressing Number of People Think That's Fine," *Reason*, December 14, 2022, https://reason.com/2022/12/14/the-world-is-still-getting-less-free-a-distressing-number-of-people-think-thats-fine.

42. The White House, "Fact Sheet: President Biden Takes Action to Protect American Workers and Businesses from China's Unfair Trade Practices," May 14, 2024, https://www.whitehouse.gov/briefing-room/statements-releases/2024/05/14/fact-sheet-president-biden-takes-action-to-protect-american-workers-and-businesses-from-chinas-unfair-trade-practices.

43. World Trade Organization, *Global Trade Outlook and Statistics* (Geneva: World Trade Organization, April 2023), 2.

44. World Trade Organization, *Global Trade Outlook and Statistics* (Geneva: World Trade Organization, April 2024), 2.

45. Bank for International Settlements, *Statistical Release: BIS International Banking Statistics and Global Liquidity Indicators at End-March 2023*, July 27, 2023, https://www.bis.org/statistics/rppb2307.htm#:~:text=The%20BIS%20locational%20banking%20statistics,1.

46. Richard Baldwin, "The Peak Globalization Myth: Part 1," *VoxEU*, August 31, 2022, figure 1, https://cepr.org/voxeu/columns/peak-globalisation-myth-part-1.

47. Organisation for Economic Co-operation and Development, "FDI in Figures: Global FDI Flows Continued to Decline in 2023," April 2024, 2, figure 1, https://www.oecd.org/content/dam/oecd/en/topics/policy-sub-issues/fdi/FDI-in-Figures-April-2024.pdf.

48. Christian Keller and Renate Marold, "Deglobalization: What You Need to Know," World Economic Forum, January 17, 2023, https://www.weforum.org/agenda/2023/01/deglobalisation-what-you-need-to-know-wef23.

49. American Compass, *The American Rejection of Globalization*, January 11, 2024, https://americancompass.org/the-american-rejection-of-globalization.

50. Richard Baldwin, "Globalization Isn't Dead, It's Transforming—and That Will Change How We Do Business," International Institute for Management Development, June 26, 2023, https://www.imd.org/ibyimd/videos/globalization-isnt-dead-its-transforming-and-that-will-change-how-we-do-business.

51. Antonio Gramsci, *Selections from the Prison Notebooks of Antonio Gramsci*, Quintin Hoare and Geoffrey Nowell Smith, ed. and trans. (New York: International Publishers, 1971, 376–77, https://archive.org/details/AntonioGramsciSelectionsFromThePrisonNotebooks/page/n469/mode/2up.

52. "'We're Done Catering to Wall Street': Trump's VP Vance Pledges 'New Path' at Republican Convention," *Le Monde*, July 18, 2024.

53. Silvia Federici, *Re-enchanting the World: Feminism and the Politics of the Commons* (Oakland, CA: PM Press, 2019), 1.

54. Dani Rodrik, Suresh Naidu, and Gabriel Zucman, "Economics After Neoliberalism," *Boston Review*, February 27, 2019, https://www.bostonreview.net/forum/suresh-naidu-dani-rodrik -gabriel-zucman-economics-after-neoliberalism.

55. Samuel Bowles and Wendy Carlin, "Shrinking Capitalism: Components of a New Political Economy Paradigm," *Oxford Review of Economic Policy* 37, no. 4 (Winter 2021), 798, https:// academic.oup.com/oxrep/article/37/4/794/6423495.

56. Bowles and Carlin, "Shrinking Capitalism," 15.

57. Joseph Stiglitz, *The Road to Freedom: Economics and the Good Society* (New York: W. W. Norton, 2024), 268.

58. Stiglitz, *Road to Freedom*, 180.

59. "Freedom Conservatism: A Statement of Principles," July 2023, https://www.freedomconser vatism.org/p/freedom-conservatism-a-statement.

60. John Cassidy, "Lessons in Conquering Child Poverty," newyorker.com, September 15, 2023.

Acknowledgments

I couldn't have written this book without the help of many people. Eric Chinski, my editor at Farrar, Straus and Giroux, greeted the original proposal enthusiastically, and countless times thereafter provided insightful feedback and much-needed encouragement. His editorial eye and voluminous knowledge of intellectual currents along many dimensions were both invaluable. I am also very grateful to Ian Van Wye, who shepherded the final manuscript through the closing process; Eliza Rudalevige, who expertly assisted with logistics; Janet Biehl, who copyedited; Tanya Heinrich and Vivian Kirklin, who read the proofs; and Nancy Elgin, who oversaw the production of the book, cleaned up the endnotes, and collated too many last-minute changes and additions; Scott Auerbach and Debra Helfand, who kept the process on track; and Tara Sharma, who provided helpful suggestions on a nearly final draft. Without the diligence and forbearance of the FSG editorial and production teams, the book wouldn't have been published on schedule.

The same thing goes for the contributions of Jackson Vail, a colleague at *The New Yorker*, who took on the onerous tasks of checking facts and arguments that ranged across hundreds of years and compiling endnotes from a vast assortment of sources. Operating under a tight deadline, Jackson did yeoman's work and corrected many of my errors. For any that escaped his attention, I apologize.

Researching and writing the book was a lengthy process. For granting me leave from my day job to work on the task and complete it, I want to thank David Remnick, the editor of *The New Yorker*; Michael Luo, the executive editor; Deirdre Foley-Mendelssohn, the deputy editor; and David Rohde, who is now at NBC News. Thanks also to my other *New Yorker* editors, including Cressida Leyshon, Henry Finder, and the late John Bennet, who first encouraged me to explore some of the themes and subjects that reappear here. I am also grateful to my literary agent, Andrew Wylie, and his colleagues at the Wylie Agency, who represented this project with their customary professionalism. And to Stuart Proffitt, my editor at Penguin Press UK, who patiently supported the project throughout, and provided helpful suggestions on a near-final manuscript.

For helpful conversations (and pointers) on various topics related to this book, I would like to thank many people, including Sophia Rosenfeld, Eva Rosenfeld, Jerrold Seigel, Anwar Shaikh, Suresh Naidu, and Scott Moyers. Thanks also to Our World in Data and Branko Milanović for permission to use the charts on pages 15 and 493.

Finally, I am forever indebted to my immediate family for their love and support. As well as putting up with my absence during the countless hours when I was pinned to my computer screen trying to create some intellectual value, if not surplus value, they helped bring the book into the world. My wife, Lucinda Rosenfeld, read many chapter drafts, highlighting ambiguous passages and excising some of my egregious lapses into economic jargon. Our daughter Cornelia helped transfer some late changes onto the manuscript. Her sister Beatrice also helped me across the finish line and promised to promote *Capitalism and Its Critics* on TikTok as a summer beach read. I dedicate it to the three of them.

Index

A Note About the Author

John Cassidy is a staff writer at *The New Yorker* and the author of *Dot.con: The Greatest Story Ever Sold* and *How Markets Fail*, which was a finalist for the Pulitzer Prize in Nonfiction. He lives in New York City.